THE COLLECTED WORKS OF
ANNA LETITIA BARBAULD

VOLUME II

THE COLLECTED WORKS OF
ANNA LETITIA BARBAULD

William McCarthy, General Editor

Volume I
The Poems, Revised
Edited by William McCarthy

Volume II
Writings for Children and Young People
Edited by Paula R. Feldman and Lisa Vargo

Volume III
Literary Criticism
Edited by Elizabeth Kraft

Volume IV
Essays and Discourses
Edited by Scott Krawczyk, William McCarthy,
and Lisa Vargo

Wedgwood medallion of Barbauld, later impression; originally struck between January and July 1775 from a wax profile by Joachim Smith. (Private collection; information from NPG; photograph by John Kotz.)

THE COLLECTED WORKS OF
Anna Letitia Barbauld

VOLUME II

Writings for Children and Young People

EDITED BY

PAULA R. FELDMAN AND LISA VARGO

OXFORD
UNIVERSITY PRESS

Great Clarendon Street, Oxford, OX2 6DP,
United Kingdom

Oxford University Press is a department of the University of Oxford.
It furthers the University's objective of excellence in research, scholarship,
and education by publishing worldwide. Oxford is a registered trade mark of
Oxford University Press in the UK and in certain other countries

Introduction and Editorial Matter © Paula R. Feldman and Lisa Vargo 2024

The moral rights of the authors have been asserted

All rights reserved. No part of this publication may be reproduced, stored in
a retrieval system, or transmitted, in any form or by any means, without the
prior permission in writing of Oxford University Press, or as expressly permitted
by law, by licence or under terms agreed with the appropriate reprographics
rights organization. Enquiries concerning reproduction outside the scope of the
above should be sent to the Rights Department, Oxford University Press, at the
address above

You must not circulate this work in any other form
and you must impose this same condition on any acquirer

Published in the United States of America by Oxford University Press
198 Madison Avenue, New York, NY 10016, United States of America

British Library Cataloguing in Publication Data
Data available

Library of Congress Control Number: 2023939884

ISBN 978–0–19–871919–9

Printed and bound in the UK by
Clays Ltd, Elcograf S.p.A.

Links to third party websites are provided by Oxford in good faith and
for information only. Oxford disclaims any responsibility for the materials
contained in any third party website referenced in this work.

CONTENTS

Illustrations	xi
Acknowledgements	xiii
General Introduction	xv
Anna Letitia Barbauld: A Chronology	xxix
Abbreviations	xxxiii
Volume Introduction	xxxv

LESSONS FOR CHILDREN

Introduction	1
Textual Matters	6
Lessons for Children, from Two to Three Years Old (London, 1778)	13
1808 Additions	37
Lessons for Children, of Three Years Old (London, 1778)	41
1808 Additions	78
Lessons for Children, of Three Years Old, Part Two (London, 1781)	83
1808 additions	125
Lessons for Children, from Three to Four Years Old (London, 1779)	133
1808 Additions	179

HYMNS IN PROSE FOR CHILDREN

Introduction	186
Textual Matters	188
Hymns in Prose for Children	191
1814 Additions	212

PALGRAVE SCHOOL

Introduction — 217

Description of a Curious Animal Lately Found in the Wilds of Derbyshire — 220

Science Lectures — 221
- Earth — 222
- On Plants — 223

Fables — 225
- The Pine and the Olive: A Fable — 226
- The River and the Brook: A Fable — 227
- The Wasp and Bee: A Fable — 227
- The Goose and Horse: A Fable — 228
- The Flying Fish — 228
- The Phenix and Dove — 229
- Confidence and Modesty: A Fable — 230

Dramatics — 231
- Canute's Reproof to his Courtiers — 232
- Alfred, a Drama — 233

FROM *EVENINGS AT HOME*

Introduction — 239

The Young Mouse. A Fable — 241

The Masque of Nature — 242

Things by their Right Names — 243

On Manufactures — 244

The Manufacture of Paper — 251

A Lesson in the Art of Distinguishing — 254

The Four Sisters — 259

WORKS OF IMAGINATION AND INSTRUCTION

Introduction — 263

Description of Two Sisters — 264

Allegory on Sleep — 265

Zephyrus and Flora. Letter to Mrs. W——	268
On the Classics	270
Atalanta	275
Arion	276
Venus and Adonis	277
The King in his Castle	278
Live Dolls	280
The Rich and the Poor: A Dialogue	284
Epitaph on a Goldfinch	289
The Misses (Addressed to a Careless Girl)	290

TEACHING LETTERS TO LYDIA RICKARDS

[Dressing Table Ornaments]	296
A Letter from Miss Susan Slipslop to Miss Fanny Flippant	296
[Dated 6 June 1798]	297
Letters on Grammar, History, and Homer	299
[On Grammar]	300
On the Uses of History [Letter I]	302
On the Uses of History [Letter II]	306
[Geography, Letter III]	310
[Chronology] Letter IV	313
[On Homer]	319
[A Letter Recommending French Books]	322

FROM *A LEGACY FOR YOUNG LADIES*

Pic-nic	327
Letter from Grimalkin to Selima	329
True Magicians	332
On Female Studies	338
Letter I	338
Letter II	340

On Expense: A Dialogue	343
On Riddles	348
I	351
II	351
III	351
IV	352
Letter of a Young King	353
Knowledge and Her Daughter: A Fable	356
A Lecture on the Use of Words	357
The Morning Repast	359
On Friendship	359
The Death-Bed	363
A Dialogue of the Dead, between Helen, and Madame Maintenon	364

FROM *THE FEMALE SPEAKER*

Introduction	369
Preface of the Editor	370

REVIEWS OF EDUCATIONAL BOOKS

Introduction	373
Reviews in the *Annual Review*	376
Reviews in the *Monthly Review*	393
Explanatory Notes	429
Appendix: 'Letter to Recommend French Authors'	475
Principal Sources of the Texts	477
General Bibliography	481
Index of Titles, Authors, and Proper Names	491

ILLUSTRATIONS

Frontispiece: Wedgwood Portrait of Barbauld (private collection). iv

1. A pages from *Lessons for Children, of Three Years Old*, London, 1778 (Glasgow RB4587) alongside the corresponding page, London 1812 (private collection). 8
2. A pages from *Lessons for Children, of Three Years Old*, London, 1778 (Glasgow RB4587) alongside the corresponding page, London 1812 (private collection). 9
3. *Lessons for Children, from Two to Three Years Old*. Title-page, London 1778, first edition (Glasgow University Library). 12
4. *Lessons for Children, of Three Years Old*. Title-page, London 1778, first edition (Glasgow University Library). 40
5. *Lessons for Children, of Three Years Old*. Title-page, Part II, London 1781, presumed second edition (private collection). 82
6. *Lessons for Children, of Three Years Old*. Title-page, London 1806, with facing advertisements (private collection) along with *Lessons for Children, of Three Years Old*, Title-page, London 1812, with facing advertisements (private collection). 124
7. *Lessons for Children, from Three to Four Years Old*. Title-page, London 1779, first edition (Glasgow University Library). 132
8. *Leçons pour les enfans*. Paris 1830. Title-page with frontispiece (private collection). 178
9. Title-page to the first edition of *Hymns in Prose for Children* (British Library). 185
10. Playbill for Palgrave School productions of *Caractacus* by William Mason and *Taste* by Samuel Foote, 27 May 1782 (MS MC 257/63/1/3, Norfolk RO). Courtesy of the Norfolk Record Office. 219
11. *Evenings at Home*. Title-page of Volume 1. British Library, first edition. © The British Library Board (Shelfmark 0 1031.d.15). 240
12. First page of Barbauld's Letter to Lydia Rickards on Homer. New York Public Library MS 4347. 320
13. Frontispiece to *A Legacy for Young Ladies*, to illustrate 'True Magicians' and title-page (private collection). 335
14. Title-page of *The Female Speaker*, first edition (private collection). 368

ACKNOWLEDGEMENTS

Several of the pieces in this volume, specifically *Hymns in Prose for Children*, 'Fashion, a Vision', 'The Young Mouse, A Fable', 'Things by their Right Names', 'The Four Sisters', 'Letter from Grimalkin to Selima', and 'On Female Studies', previously appeared in *Anna Letitia Barbauld: Selected Poetry & Prose*, edited jointly by William McCarthy and Elizabeth Kraft (Broadview Press, 2002). We are grateful to the editors, not only for the original research, writing, and editing that went into preparing these texts for that earlier edition, but for permission to draw from their work for this current volume. We also thank Broadview Press for permission to quote from that book. Moreover, we would like to acknowledge the scholarship of William McCarthy for the initial stages of this volume. He contributed transcriptions of texts and drafts of introductory material, as well as many footnotes and headnotes. We are deeply grateful to him for this considerable work, based upon years of Barbauld research.

We thank the New York Public Library, Astor, Lenox, and Tilden Foundations, for permission to publish for the first time seven letters by Barbauld addressed to her student, Lydia Rickards, and to reproduce an image of one of the manuscripts. We are grateful, as well, to Elizabeth C. Denlinger, Curator for the Pforzheimer Collection, and Charles Carter, Assistant Curator, for providing us with high-definition scans of these letters.

After she located first editions of three out of the four volumes of *Lessons for Children* at the University of Glasgow Library, volumes so rare that they were previously thought not to have survived, Paula R. Feldman funded the extensive conservation work necessary to preserve these fragile books and to scan their pages for research purposes. The texts of these volumes are published here for the first time, along with several images, with permission from the University of Glasgow, and the volumes themselves are now available to scholars. We are grateful, too, to Julie Gardham, Senior Librarian in Special Collections, University of Glasgow, for assisting us in the effort to preserve these rare volumes.[1] Only one copy of the important 1808 London edition of *Lessons for Children* is recorded. Rebecca Nesvet kindly proofed our text against that copy at the British Library.

---

[1] See her blog post on the discovery and conservation efforts: https://universityofglasgowlibrary.wordpress.com/2017/01/09/learning-to-read-with-mrs-barbauld/.

Thomas R. Coughlin expertly compiled the index and proofread a set of page proofs. Andrea Immel, Curator of the Cotsen Children's Library, Princeton University, kindly advised us about early children's books and helped with our *Evenings at Home* research. We thank the Norfolk Record Office, which supplied the image of the *Caractacus* playbill for the Palgrave School productions of *Caractacus* by William Mason and *Taste* by Samuel Foote, 27 May 1782, and gave us permission to publish it; the Liverpool Record Office for allowing us to consult Lucy Aikin's letter to William Roscoe of 29 June 1825; to the Charity of Dr. Daniel Williams, commonly known as Dr. Williams's Trust, for permission to quote from Joshua Thompson's manuscript collection of papers; and to the Vassar College Library for allowing us to consult Barbauld's manuscript letter to Miss Harris [April 1812?]; to Molly Haigh of UCLA Special Collections, for supplying scans of early copies of *Evenings at Home*; and to the helpful staff of the Osborne Collection of Early Children's Books, Toronto Public Library. The title page of *Evenings at Home* is reproduced by permission of the British Library Board.

A Book Manuscript Finalization Award from the Office of the Dean of Arts and Sciences at the University of South Carolina funded assistance with proofreading and indexing the volume. We are grateful to Catriona Brodribb and Simon Martyn, current holders of Barbauld copyrights, for permission to print all hitherto-unpublished materials in this volume, including material from Lucy Aikin's manuscript 'Family History'.

GENERAL INTRODUCTION

We have had to brush aside ranks of cobwebs in order to see Anna Letitia Barbauld the way her contemporaries saw her, and to see her clearly for ourselves: a poet who achieved instant fame with her first book and kept her place among the foremost English poets for 40 years, admired and resented by Wordsworth and Coleridge; a teacher whose *Lessons for Children* and *Hymns in Prose* made it habitual to associate children with Nature and made writing for children and young people a genuine field of literature; a liberal polemicist who dared to advocate political reform at a time when advocating reform was dangerous for men; an incisive essayist, proposing in 'What Is Education?' and 'On Prejudice' views that would come to be known, in the works of male writers, as Existentialist; a 'woman of letters' recognized in her time as the successor to Samuel Johnson and employed, as Johnson had been, to preside over a canon of British writers.

The story of her posthumous reception was not pretty. Revered sentimentally by Victorians as 'good Mrs. Barbauld', a pious hymnist and Christian writer for the young, she became a stuffed owl after Victorian sentimentalism became an object of ridicule. When, in the 1970s, feminist critics came to look at her, she disappointed their need for outspokenly feminist role models. In her lifetime she 'had never', she once told her niece and first biographer, Lucy Aikin, 'been placed in a situation which suited her';[1] and perceptions of her have been dogged by category conflicts. A Protestant Dissenter by family history and upbringing, as an intellectual woman she could have joined the Bluestocking Circle, that group of intellectual women who were arch-Establishment in their religion and politics; and, after 'Bluestocking' came to mean simply 'intellectual woman', Barbauld was assimilated to the historical Bluestockings although in life she kept to the margin of that group. A political reformer in the early 1790s, regarded as a flaming radical by her Tory and Church of England contemporaries, she saw herself charged in print by Mary Wollstonecraft with belittling women in one of her poems. The situations which Barbauld felt never suited her can be seen retrospectively as conflicts about who or what she was: Bluestocking or Dissenter? Feminist or anti-feminist? Pious conformist, or political radical?

---

[1] Le Breton, *Memoir*, 26.

A major reason for misperception was that until now Barbauld's works have never been presented complete, all together in one place. For that, Barbauld herself was partly to blame. She often thought of collecting and reprinting the portion of her work she seems to have valued most, her poems: indeed, in 1803 and 1810 she went so far towards reprinting them that she allowed new editions to be advertised. She was still thinking of reprinting as late as 1822, when her eyesight was weakening and she was depressed; 'but many are the things I think of & never accomplish'.[2] Thus it was left to her brother's daughter, Lucy Aikin, to collect not only Barbauld's poems but her prose works as well: essays from *Miscellaneous Pieces in Prose*, the political pamphlets, a few pieces from the *Monthly Magazine*, a selection of her letters carefully abridged. Aikin did not reprint the books for children or the literary work Barbauld had done for Cadell & Davies, Richard Phillips, and Longmans, or any of her reviews (the principal contents of Volume III in the present edition). In what amounted to a supplementary volume Aikin did gather 35 pieces in verse and prose she had found among Barbauld's papers. Aikin's collections—*The Works of Anna Laetitia Barbauld. With a Memoir* in two volumes, and *A Legacy for Young Ladies* in one, all published in 1825—became the de facto Barbauld canon.

De facto and defective. Not only did the Aikin volumes omit much of Barbauld's identified work, but they omitted also pieces acknowledged by Barbauld but apparently not known to Lucy, such as the essays in John Aikin's short-lived *Athenaeum* (among them 'Thoughts on the Inequality of Conditions', one of Barbauld's most interesting essays). Further, they omitted pieces known to Barbauld's family but not (so far as we know today) published, among them a piece mentioned in a letter by Barbauld's nephew and adopted son, Charles: 'a view of the female part of the creation a century hence on a g[eneral] revolution of manners which is to take place when Mrs Woolstonecraft has been su[...]'.[3] Again, Lucy Aikin omitted pieces Barbauld had published anonymously or pseudonymously but which might have been identifiable from copies or notes among Barbauld's papers, had Lucy examined the papers attentively. She did not take time to do that. Barbauld died on 9 March; the *Morning Post* for 28 April announced that Barbauld's works, with a memoir, would be published on 27 June. Aikin was as good as her word: she sent a set of *Works* to family friend William Roscoe on 29 June.[4] Although it is conceivable that

---

[2] ALB, Letter to Joanna Baillie, 20 Mar. [1822].
[3] CRA, Letter to ALB, 6 Dec. 1792 (quoted in *ALBVE*, 352).
[4] LA, Letter to William Roscoe, 29 June 1825.

Works consists of an organized body of writings left by Barbauld to be sent directly to the family printer, Richard Taylor, that notion is belied by Lucy Aikin's frazzled complaint to Roscoe about the state in which Barbauld left her papers; sifting through them had been 'much more laborious... than you would suppose from the small bulk of the published matter', and the number of what Aikin took to be 'fragments'—unfinished pieces—was, in her word, 'deplorable'. When she followed *Works* at the end of the year with *A Legacy for Young Ladies*, Aikin threw together under that title pieces that don't belong under it, such as a jeu d'esprit about a new arrival at all-boys Palgrave School ('Description of a Curious Animal lately found in the Wilds of Derbyshire') and a poem sent to Mr and Mrs Joseph Priestley, not young ladies, on the birth of their first son. Between omission of many works and jumbling together of others, Lucy Aikin's volumes poorly represent a major writer.

The present edition is the first that has tried to gather all of Barbauld's work in all genres, so that the full range of her literary performance can finally be grasped. That additional poems, essays, or fancy pieces remain to be found in collections of family papers in Great Britain or even the United States is likely, for Barbauld's acquaintance was wide and she was widely admired. For that reason any such discoveries will probably be copies by unknown hands, at some remove from their Barbauld originals. Although Barbauld lived into the age of steam printing, her shorter writings continued to circulate through manuscript networks well into the nineteenth century.

Writer, Teacher, Dissenter, Feminist

Even the slight sketch of Barbauld's writing career given at the opening of this Introduction displays one of its leading features: she was an uncommonly versatile writer. Very few writers of stature can have addressed readers from age two through highly intellectual adulthood, and in language perfectly suited to each audience. To mark two extremes of Barbauld's literary range, Isobel Grundy has quoted two passages from her work: 'Still the loud death drum, thundering from afar' from *Eighteen Hundred and Eleven*, and 'Good morrow, little boy! how do you do?' from *Lessons for Children, of Three Years Old*. Barbauld's literary voices, Grundy has written,

> are richly various... embracing public oratory and domestic chat, intense seriousness and sly humour, the self-deprecating, the professionally confident, and the overtly ambitious. Her voices cannot be separated into male and female, high and

low, public and domestic, even though these dichotomies underlie the huge variety of genres and occasions that shape her styles.⁵

And in thus marking Barbauld's range of styles and genres, Grundy goes far towards explaining why Barbauld the literary figure has been hard to grasp. She is not conveniently univocal. She is a shape-shifter.

Anna Letitia Aikin Barbauld was destined for a career in literature, for she grew up, much as Samuel Johnson did, surrounded by books. Although slow to publish, she won instant and lasting fame with her first book, *Poems* (1773); throughout Great Britain she was celebrated as 'Miss Aikin'. She was also destined to teach. Her father, the Reverend John Aikin, kept a school in the family home in Kibworth, Leicestershire, where Anna Letitia was born; when she was 15 the Aikin family removed to Warrington in Lancashire, where he taught Belles Lettres and Divinity at Warrington Academy. Thus she grew up environed by formal learning. If being surrounded by books destined her to write, being environed by formal learning destined her to teach. With her husband, Rochemont Barbauld, she was to keep a school at Palgrave in Suffolk for 11 years. There she instituted the programme of study and the educational goal, the formation of 'the intelligent and useful citizen', advocated by her father's younger colleague at Warrington and her early friend, Joseph Priestley. At Palgrave School she taught boys from age three to around age 18, boys who would grow up to take positions in business or government and who, as male members of the middle and upper-middle classes, could be expected to share responsibility for the conduct of the nation.⁶ Thus, reflexively if not directly, teaching boys would become for Barbauld the vehicle of a 'large ambitious wish to save [her] country' (her line about Pascal Paoli, the leader of Corsica's insurgency against France). By pedagogy she would form a new and higher kind of citizen: a citizen who would appreciate the natural world (an appreciation encouraged by her lectures 'On Plants' and 'Earth'), who would be aware of the histories and customs of other peoples (her verses on Canada, India, Constantinople, and Lapland for them to recite, her lectures on other nations), who would take a properly sceptical attitude towards kingship (her playlets 'Canute's Reproof to his Courtiers' and 'Alfred, a Drama'), and who would learn to prefer peace to war ('Things by their Right Names').

---

⁵ Grundy, 23–4.
⁶ McCarthy, '"Celebrated Academy"', and *ALBVE*, ch. 8, describe Palgrave School in detail. Surviving texts from the school are printed in this volume of the present edition; the verses on Canada and other regions appear in Volume I.

That was direct, in-person pedagogy, and Barbauld's former pupils testified to its importance in their lives. One pupil, Thomas Denman, who attributed his elocutionary skill (essential for public speaking) to Barbauld's teaching, and whose sister credited Barbauld for Denman's 'steady and decided Liberal tendencies', rose to be Attorney-General of England and drafted the Reform Bill of 1832. William Taylor, one of Barbauld's favourite pupils, who became the leading early proponent of German literature in England, honoured her as 'the mother of [his] mind'.[7] Those of Barbauld's contemporaries who did not experience her teaching in person received instruction from her published writings. 'This lady has been recognised for many years by the public, with grateful complacency, as one of its best benefactors, for contributing her share very liberally both to instruct and reform the community': thus the *Lady's Monthly Museum* in 1798, in a potted but admiring memoir of her.[8] At Palgrave, feeling baulked in what had been a career of literary stardom, Barbauld swerved into what was then a byroad of literature, writing for children. With *Lessons for Children* and *Hymns in Prose for Children* she revived and even increased her literary fame: *Hymns in Prose* especially achieved international circulation and carried Barbauld's name across the next century. Both works inculcated ideas of harmony between humans and the natural world: the four volumes of *Lessons* nest Charles in a natural-and-also-human village setting, imagining the Suffolk village of Palgrave as a social and natural community; *Hymns in Prose* sets that little world under Divine guidance. Together the two works lead the child character Charles, and the child reader, through an ever-expanding horizon of words, things, and creatures, to the universe. (*Lessons for Children* and *Hymns in Prose* appear in this volume of the present edition.) There were also Barbauld's works of adult education, such as the *Civic Sermons* in which she undertook to explain to ordinary people (Edmund Burke's 'swinish multitude') that they had the competence and the right to learn politics, and *Sins of Government, Sins of the Nation*, in which she undertook to instruct her fellow-subjects in the meaning and duties of citizenship. (*Civic Sermons* and *Sins of Government* will appear in Volume IV of the present edition.) Her great *Epistle to William Wilberforce, Esq. on the Rejection of the Bill for Abolishing the Slave Trade* undertook to teach the morally untutored MPs who had just voted to continue the slave trade the *human* meaning of what

---

[7] On Denman and Taylor, see McCarthy, '"Celebrated Academy,"' 316–19, 351–2, and 365, and *ALBVE*, 184 and 185. On Taylor, see further David Chandler, 'The Foundation of "Philosophical Criticism": William Taylor's Connection with the *Monthly Review*, 1792–93', *Studies in Bibliography*, 50 (1997): 359–71.

[8] 'Mrs. Anna-Laetitia Barbauld', 170.

they had done: in recoiling emotionally from their act, it performs what might be called 'shock pedagogy'.

These were Reformist positions, and Barbauld took them because she also grew up a third-generation Protestant Dissenter. Her outlook, moral and intellectual, was formed by the traditions and concerns of Protestant Dissent in England; and Dissent's concerns were formed by its history of legislated subordination to an Established Church. The Church of England enjoyed official government support. Dissenters from the Church, whether Protestant or Catholic, were protected after 1690 by the Toleration Act (that is, their worship and doctrines were permitted within limits), but they were made ineligible, unless they foreswore their Dissent, to hold a large number of public offices. Thus they were made second-class citizens and, as such, were alive to questions of political and personal rights. In 1772 a spokesman delivered a classic statement of their position: 'We dissent because we deny the right of any body of men, whether civil or ecclesiastical, to impose human tests, creeds, or articles; and because we think it our duty, not to submit to any such authority, but to protest against it, as a violation of our essential liberty, to judge and act for ourselves in matters of religion.' To an intellectual, Dissent was a mandate of rational enquiry: 'religious Liberty is a Liberty to be religious, and to be religious is not to take the Sacrament & subscribe Systems [i.e. to swear belief in a creed], but to read, to reason, to conclude & to act.'[9]

As a Dissenter, Barbauld grew up in a world saturated with intellectual enquiry, consciousness of political rights, and a propensity to resistance. Her three major poems, 'Corsica', *An Epistle to William Wilberforce*, and *Eighteen Hundred and Eleven*, all originated in political contestations and take political positions. Her longest pamphlet, *Remarks on Public Worship*, treats an issue in religious conduct—whether worship should be conducted privately and in solitude, or in public assemblies (congregations)—as an issue in political conduct also. It asserts that public worship, in gathering people of different classes together, reminds them of their human equality: public worship is virtually, she asserts, a 'declaration of the rights of man'.[10] Edmund Burke, from 1790 until his death a strenuous defender of the Establishment, accused leading Dissenter Richard Price of mixing theology and politics, and Burke's accusation gave rise to the hostile epithet 'politico-theological'. Mixing religion with politics appeared to Burke and

---

[9] Andrew Kippis, quoted in *M Rev*, 47 (1772): 103–4; Josiah Thompson, 1:9–10.

[10] ALB, *Remarks on Public Worship*, 46. *Remarks* appears in Volume IV of the present edition. 'The rights of man' is the title both of successive French Revolutionary constitutions and Tom Paine's rebuttal to Burke's *Reflections on the Revolution*; to the British Establishment Barbauld's quoting it would have been a red rag.

to the Establishment unholy and dangerous.[11] But Burke was right. British Dissent was inevitably 'politico-theological', a politicized category; as a Dissenter, Barbauld wrote with political awareness whatever her subject.

Her consciousness of religious and political rights explains much of Barbauld's appeal in the early United States. The President of Harvard College, Joseph Willard, expressed solidarity with British Dissenters when he wrote to the Rev. Richard Price: 'I look upon them [Dissenters] to be very great supporters of the civil liberties of your nation.'[12] From 1788, if not earlier, Barbauld's writings were reprinted in newspapers and printing houses across New England and in the mid-Atlantic states, and eminent New England Unitarians such as William Ellery Channing admired her without reserve. She was read by Bronson Alcott and Ralph Waldo Emerson. One of Barbauld's surviving letters is a reply to fan mail from an American girl.[13] Several of her poems first saw print in the United States; her last separate publication, the poem *Eighteen Hundred and Eleven*, was published in Boston and Philadelphia in the year of its first appearance in London. In her later years Barbauld reciprocated, taking friendly interest in the intellectual and artistic progress of the new nation. Her expressions of admiration for George Washington seem, today, a bit excessive, but what she admired him for was real enough: his refusal to accept offers of kingship, his rejection of what came to be called 'Bonapartism'.

Barbauld also, of course, grew up female, and thus became a dissenter, so to speak, within Dissent. Apart from her mother and the maids, she was the only female person in a house full of male persons, her father's pupils. How did she manage? An anecdote from one of her father's pupils suggests how. At age 5, Anna Letitia intervened in a discussion between him and the pupil to correct him: 'I think you are mistaken, papa.'[14] She thus demonstrated that she could join the debate, that she could be one of his pupils too, an honorary 'boy', would he but admit her to the school. He did not, but he did consent to help her learn the Latin that all the boys were taught as a matter of course. In her youth also she achieved the influence over her younger brother, John, which she would retain throughout their

---

[11] Burke stigmatized Price, a leading spokesman for Dissent, as 'a man much connected with... political theologians, and theological politicians' (Burke, *Reflections*, 10). When Barbauld published *Sins of Government* in 1793 the *British Critic* dubbed her a 'politico-theological lady' (quoted in *ALBVE*, 340). *Sins* appears in Volume IV of the present edition.

[12] Price, *Correspondence*, 3:188.

[13] ALB, Letter to a Miss Harris, n.d. (MS, Vassar College Library). Bronson Alcott included *Hymns in Prose* among texts he taught in a class on religion in 1830s Boston; Emerson at age 47 recalled *Hymns* in a notebook entry (McCarthy, 'How Dissent Made Anna Letitia Barbauld', 52–3).

[14] Quoted in *ALBVE*, 32. The pupil was Newcome Cappe.

lives. She and John Aikin became literary partners: John encouraged her to publish her poems and thus to launch her literary career, they published a collection of their essays, *Miscellaneous Pieces in Prose*, jointly, she contributed to his literary projects, and they coordinated their political interventions in the early 1790s.

The literary partnership of Anna Letitia and John Aikin was the first and most equal of those literary family partnerships that came to flourish in the early nineteenth century.[15] Its effect on Barbauld's sense of herself as a writer would be hard to overestimate. Shy and socially uncomfortable, but also assertive by temperament, she enjoyed her brother's unqualified support throughout her writing career. Thus her feminism took the form of assuming and expecting intellectual equality with men in the public realms of politics and literature. She was well aware that the laws governing women were oppressive. Greeting the French Revolution in *An Address to the Opposers*, she exhorted France to abolish the 'domestic tyranny' of husbands; to her admirer Henry Crabb Robinson in 1806 'she argued warmly against the present laws as they affect Women' (to our loss, Robinson did not report her actual words).[16] Knowing this, she acted *as if* women and men were equals in the intellectual domains of writing and politics, much as, in *Sins of Government*, she wrote *as if* Parliamentary reform had actually occurred and it was meaningful to address Britons on their citizenly responsibilities.[17] Of course, arguments she urged in asserting equal rights for religious Dissent could serve also to assert equal rights for other groups. Especially striking is her structural understanding of discrimination as a dialectic set in motion by a ruling group's hostile insistence on another group's difference: 'if we are a party, remember it is you who force us to be so'. Polemical moves made in literature demanding equal rights after 1790 can be found in Barbauld's *Address to the Opposers of the Repeal of the Corporation and Test Acts*.

One reason for the misperception that Barbauld was not a feminist goes back to Lucy Aikin's representation of her in 1825, a time of political reaction when the name 'Wollstonecraft' all but signified 'she-devil'. Aikin was

---

[15] See Krawczyk, *Romantic Literary Families*, and Michelle Levy, *Family Authorship and Romantic Print Culture* (New York: Palgrave Macmillan, 2008).

[16] ALB, *Address to the Opposers of the Corporation and Test Acts*, 2nd edn, 38; HCR, quoted in *ALBVE*, 355. The *Address* appears in Volume 4 of this edition.

[17] Barbauld's preference for regarding men and women as intellectual equals underlay her rejection of a scheme proposed by Maria and Richard Lovell Edgeworth for a 'ladies' paper'—an essay series (perhaps for John Aikin's *Monthly Magazine*) whose contributors would be women only. She replied that the 'joint interest of their sex' did not necessarily lead women to political agreement, and that one ought rather to publish people of similar politics, regardless of their gender. See Le Breton, *Memoir*, 85–91, and *ALBVE*, 360–1.

painfully conscious of the illiberal political climate of the 1820s: '[T]hink of the age we live in!—think of the Quarterly Review, the Saints, the clergy, the tories & the canters.'[18] Fearing for her aunt's—and, probably, her entire family's—good name, she represented Barbauld as properly 'womanly', which to those parties meant being retiring and 'delicate', and she took care to soften Barbauld's image even as she (courageously) reprinted Barbauld's political pamphlets. Another reason why Barbauld was perceived by 'Second-Wave' feminists as not feminist was that feminism itself had changed since Barbauld's time. Barbauld and Wollstonecraft in fact agreed on what they both took to be women's place in society: that women, as rational beings, ought to take responsibility for themselves, that their principal social role was to bring up children, and that in so doing they would exert themselves as social agents. Wollstonecraft proposed, too, that women might 'study politics', something Barbauld was doing as Wollstonecraft wrote.[19] True, unlike Wollstonecraft, Barbauld did not publish a polemic explicitly in support of women's rights; true, also, her one explicit statement of what a woman needed to learn and how she should act ('On Female Studies'), published by Lucy Aikin after Barbauld's death, urged caution and reserve.[20]

Although it was conceptually at one with Wollstonecraft's, Barbauld's feminism was inflected towards accommodation by an intense need to reconcile within herself her allegiance to Dissent with her attraction to many features of the Establishment—and to many Establishment individuals. In marrying Rochemont she had married into an Establishment, indeed a Court, family, even though Rochemont himself became an enthusiastic convert to Dissent. Although she kept to the margin of the Bluestocking 'Society', Barbauld admired one of its most Establishment members, Elizabeth Carter; Carter's translation of Epictetus was an early and strong influence on her thinking. An equally early and strong influence was her friend Joseph Priestley, soon to become a political firebrand whose Unitarian polemics would enrage the Establishment and would have been repudiated by Carter. Like other intellectuals whose social milieus were

---

[18] LA to William Roscoe, 20 Jan. 1823 (quoted in *ALBVE*, xv).

[19] Wollstonecraft, 286. Relations between Barbauld's and Wollstonecraft's views are explored in *ALBVE*, 350–5.

[20] 'On Female Studies' appears in this volume of the present edition. It consists of two letters Barbauld wrote to a prospective pupil she had not yet met; whether she herself would have published it is not known, but Lucy Aikin probably thought it useful for her aim of making Barbauld appear conservative to 1825 reviewers.

deeply at odds with each other, Barbauld strove to transcend their enmities, to make of her life and her work a more inclusive unity.[21]

A Note on the Distribution of Contents in this Edition

Had Barbauld herself gathered her work we would have the benefit at least of knowing what she thought should go where. The editors of Barbauld's *Collected Works* have not felt obliged to take the contents of the Lucy Aikin volumes as directives for our arrangement. The four volumes of the present edition are constituted partly according to form (verse or prose) and partly according to audience (e.g. children and young persons). None of them except Volume I adheres strictly to its category: verse appears in two volumes, reviews of books in three—and, in view of Barbauld's 'politico-theological' consciousness, political writing in all four. Thus we regard our arrangement as little more than a convenience. A reader who thinks to find all Barbauld had to say on education in Volume II will miss the great essays on Education and Prejudice in Volume IV—there by virtue of their appearance in the form of essays in her brother's periodical, the *Monthly Magazine*. To get the full range of Barbauld's efforts and views in any one direction, the reader is advised to open all four of these volumes.

Within each volume, contents are organized according to chronology of composition or publication, albeit not always in the same way from volume to volume. Volume I (*The Poems, Revised*) adheres to chronology of composition as far as that can be determined, taking date of publication in Barbauld's lifetime as the fallback. The present volume (*Writings for Children and Young People*) opens with Barbauld's first published forays into writing for children, the works that brought her to public notice as a writer for the young; but because most of Barbauld's writings for young people were first published after her death, the prevailing chronology is that of composition, and is often conjectural. We have found the most intelligible arrangement for that volume to be an overarching chronology, within which texts are presented according to genre (such as reviews) and institutional use (such as at Palgrave School). Volume III (*Literary Criticism*) will be composed mostly of work Barbauld did for hire (the aspect in which she can be compared to Samuel Johnson), beginning in 1794; its contents, therefore, appear in order of publication. Volume IV (*Essays and Discourses*), like Volume II, will open with Barbauld's first published outings in a form, the essay, and proceed by order of

---

[21] I have treated this theme in more detail, and with a slightly different slant, in 'Anna Letitia Barbauld, Alienated Intellectual', *Enlightenment and Dissent*, 26 (2010): 113–35.

publication except when date of composition differs widely from that and is known.

The Text of the Present Edition

Despite what has been said of them in this Introduction, the Lucy Aikin volumes remain indispensable witnesses to Barbauld's texts because in September 1940 an unknown but large number of Aikin-Barbauld papers perished in the bombing of London. Many records of Barbauld's printers and publishers—William Eyres, Joseph Johnson, Richard Phillips, and the House of Longman—also perished at other times. As a result of those losses there is much about Barbauld's writing and publishing practices, and about her self-conception as a writer, that is not known today. Joseph Johnson's entries of copyright in the Stationers' Register perhaps testify to which of her works Barbauld valued most: she kept the rights to *Poems*, *Miscellaneous Pieces in Prose* (but she shared those with her brother, who might have been the mover there), and *Remarks on Public Worship*. She sold Johnson the rights to her works for children and even her *Epistle to William Wilberforce*.[22] Other works, including the major poem *Eighteen Hundred and Eleven*, do not appear in the Stationers' Register. In her practical literary commentary Barbauld worked for hire: on contract, twice, for Cadell & Davies, then for Richard Phillips, then for the Longman consortium, then as paid reviewer for the *Annual* and *Monthly* reviews. A note from her to Johnson returning proofs for her Addison–Steele anthology witnesses her care in checking proofs: 'To prove that my looking over them is not quite useless please to observe that I have marked eleven faults in this corrected proof.'[23] The manuscripts of Samuel Richardson's correspondence marked by her in 1804 also survive, and on the whole they testify to her good conduct as an editor.[24] Surviving holographs of her original writings vary in their attention to punctuation and capitalization ('accidentals'). Those of her poems—mainly the Rodgers holographs—are

---

[22] *Records of the Worshipful Company of Stationers*, entries for *Poems* (19 Dec. 1772), *Miscellaneous Pieces in Prose* (4 Aug. 1773), *Lessons for Children, from Two to Three Years Old* (4 May 1778), *Lessons for Children of Three Years Old* (12 June 1778), *Lessons for Children, from Three to Four Years Old* (7 Apr. 1779), *Hymns in Prose for Children* (22 Aug. 1781), *Epistle to William Wilberforce* (17 June 1791), *Remarks on... Public or Social Worship* (10 May 1792). Barbauld's later works are unlisted, only because, perhaps, booksellers grew indifferent to entering copyrights.

[23] ALB, Letter to JJ, n.d. (quoted in *ALBVE*, 421). It was customary for printers to correct proofs in the printing house and send them to the author for review. A few pages of proof from the Addison edition survive in St Bride's Printing Library, but they bear no marks by any hand.

[24] See McCarthy, 'What Did Anna Barbauld Do to Samuel Richardson's Correspondence?'

carefully, if at times eccentrically, punctuated; those of her letters are much less so, except for commas. Only one fragmentary holograph of a published prose work is known today, and it suggests that, like most authors, Barbauld expected printers to 'perfect' her texts, that is, to standardize accidentals.[25] As her crisp remark to Johnson quoted above indicates, she paid attention to the work they did.

In her 'Memoir' Lucy Aikin depicts Barbauld as hesitant to publish, even timidly perfectionist. True, there is little doubt that Barbauld did publish selectively and, considering how long she lived, infrequently. She blamed herself for 'indolence'. Probably, however, the major reason for Barbauld's relatively small publication record was her husband's behaviour. Rochemont Barbauld suffered, it is almost certain, from mania. A *Monthly Magazine* piece, 'Character of a Wife', signed 'Humphrey Placid' and attributed to Anna Letitia Barbauld by the General Editor of the present edition, describes behaviour so erratic that 'rest is unknown in our house': the 'wife' remodels and rebuilds constantly, so that the house is in perpetual disorder.[26] If this or something like it were Rochemont's way, regular writing would have been extremely difficult. In his last years Rochemont grew dangerously unstable and abusive; we now know that he would lock his wife in a room and berate her there for hours on end, and in his final psychotic 'break' he physically assaulted her.[27] That she could go on after such treatment to write her most imposing and important poem testifies to uncommon strength of character.

Lucy Aikin's representation of her aunt took care to conceal Rochemont's violence (Lucy was well aware of it, for she lived across the road from the Barbaulds) and to present Barbauld as 'womanly' by the standards of 1825 Toryism; in its euphemizing, her 'Memoir' reads like a Victorian family biography.[28] Her texts of the Barbauld works she prints, however, are not

---

[25] James Thorpe, *Principles of Textual Criticism* (San Marino, CA: Huntington Library, 1972), ch. 5, 'The Treatment of Accidentals'. The fragmentary holograph is a page from a 'discourse' (MS Corbett II.7, Univ. of Birmingham Library).

[26] *MM*, 3 (Mar. 1797): 182–5; item A7 in McCarthy, 'Uncollected Periodical Prose by Anna Letitia Barbauld'. It appears in Volume IV of the present edition. On Rochemont Barbauld's mental disorder, see *ALBVE*, Appendix B. The Barbaulds also socialized intensely during their years in Hampstead and Stoke Newington, and this too may have been an effect of Rochemont's disorder.

[27] Rochemont 'was in the habit of insisting in the most peremptory manner on inexhaustible patience in her to listen for hours together to his fancied complaints & even went so far as frequently to use the most insulting & unhandsome language & to lock the door to prevent her from escaping from his violence. The distress & anxiety which such treatment produced on her feeling heart you will readily conceive' (CRA, Letter to Lydia Rickards, 4 Feb. 1808). Hitherto only an abridged text of this letter was known, from Rickards, 'Mrs. Barbauld and Her Pupil'. On the assault, see *ALBVE*, 436–7.

[28] On Lucy Aikin as a 'sanitizing' family biographer see James.

apparently mishandled. She made mistakes, reprinting, for example, the first edition of *An Address to the Opposers* rather than its revised second edition, and attributing to Barbauld a poem that is not by her; and she misdated a few poems, such as Barbauld's 'Stanzas in the Manner of Spenser', perhaps from assumptions about their meaning in Barbauld's life. Her most significant, and ultimately damaging, misrepresentation concerned Anna Letitia's letter to Rochemont declining a proposal that she manage a school for young 'ladies'. Apart, however, from omitting passages that would identify the addressee as Rochemont Barbauld, Lucy's text of that letter agrees with the text of a copy among the Althorp Papers in the British Library.[29] Discreet concealment and vague implication rather than retouching of texts appear to have been Lucy's method. Indeed, she expressly disclaimed retouching: 'Had [Barbauld] herself presented these pieces to the public, it is probable that she would in some instances have extended them by additions which, from her own pen, would have enhanced their value, but which it would have been presumption in any other to attempt.'[30] And some of what I have suggested were misrepresentations could have been honest errors resulting from Aikin's not knowing details of Barbauld's life.

William McCarthy, 2019

Editorial Principles

In cases where a Barbauld holograph exists, we adopt it as the copy text, in preference to any later published version. In the absence of a holograph manuscript, we accept the earliest published text, if that survives, or, if not, the earliest known printed text. Where no printed text has been found, we adopt as copy text the only text known today, in one case a copy in an unidentified hand of a lost holograph.

With several exceptions outlined below, we have retained Barbauld's own spelling and punctuation but have modernized the long s, and we silently correct obvious printers' errors. Except in *Lessons for Children*, a special case, we have not attempted to reproduce formatting, including spacing, page breaks, line-end hyphens, or pagination. Words written in all caps at the beginning of sentences have been printed with only the initial letter capitalized; those within sentences have been printed with the initial letter capitalized and all others in small caps. Periods at the end of titles, dates,

---

[29] See the text in McCarthy, 'Why Anna Letitia Barbauld Refused to Head a Women's College: New Facts, New Story', *Nineteenth-Century Contexts*, 23.3 (2001): 349–79.
[30] *LYL*, v.

after roman numerals, or beneath superscripts have been silently deleted. Running open quotation marks at the beginning of each line of poetry or quotation have been omitted. In cases of an obvious typographical error that affects the sense, we have corrected the error and recorded the change in a note. We have used square brackets to enclose editorial comments [*italicized type*] and to supply missing text [Roman type]. Markers for Barbauld's or Aikin's own footnotes, such as daggers, crosses, asterisks, and so forth, have been deleted, although these notes have been preserved and the author identified. Long quotations in Barbauld's reviews have been indented. Textual matters of particular significance and editorial emendations are discussed in the notes. We do not choose to include substantive variants for most of the texts in this volume for several reasons. In the case of *Lessons for Children*, early editions are today so rare that it has not been possible to track down and examine each of them for textual variants. In any case, we know that Barbauld closely monitored the printing of the first edition (our copy text for three of the four volumes) but her involvement in the printing of later editions is unclear. More likely than not, any changes in later editions, with the exception of the 1808 edition in which she made extensive additions, were those of the printer or publisher. In the absence of a first edition of the second volume of *Lessons for Children of Three Years Old*, we feel confident that the apparent second edition, published in London shortly afterwards, replicates fairly closely the first and have, out of necessity, adopted it as our copy text. For all volumes of *Lessons*, we include, after the text of the first edition, the text which Barbauld added in 1808. *Hymns in Prose for Children* similarly takes the first edition as its copy text and includes, following the first-edition text, additions made in 1814.

In transcribing manuscripts, we italicize editorial comments and enclose them within square brackets [*thus*]. Reconstructions of missing text are in Roman type and enclosed within square brackets [thus]. Deletions are enclosed within angle brackets <thus> and insertions are enclosed within carets ^thus^.

We identify the copy text chosen for each piece either in a note to the title or at the end of the headnote. 'Principal Sources of the Texts' provides full title-page information for all of Barbauld's book publications and periodical contributions. We also identify manuscript collections from which we have drawn our copy texts.

ANNA LETITIA BARBAULD: A CHRONOLOGY

Dates of publication are the dates of first announcements in newspapers, when known.

1743   Born 20 June (O.S. or N.S. not known) at Kibworth Harcourt, Leics., first child of the Rev. John Aikin (1713–80), Master of Kibworth School, and Jane (born Jennings, 1714–85), both Presbyterian Dissenters.

1747   Birth (15 January) of her brother, John. Her early education is 'entirely domestic, and principally conducted by' her mother (LA, 'Memoir', vi). Later she persuades her father to help her learn Latin, and she reads widely in his library.

1758   John Aikin accepts the post of tutor in languages and belles-lettres at the newly opened Dissenting academy at Warrington, Lancs. The Aikins move to Warrington (July).

1761   Aikin becomes tutor in divinity. His successor in languages and belles-lettres, Joseph Priestley, arrives at Warrington in September. ALA's brother leaves Warrington to begin apprenticeship in Rutland. ALA becomes close friends with Mr and Mrs Priestley.

1763? ALA and her brother exchange verse 'songs' by mail.

1764   Brother leaves for Edinburgh to study medicine (31 October); ALA writes her first datable poem on his departure.

1767   Priestley resigns his Warrington post and moves to Leeds (June). ALA writes 'On Mrs. Priestley's Leaving Warrington', her first surviving poem of known date. Rochemont Barbauld (b. 1749) admitted to Warrington to study divinity (September). While there he converts from the Church of England to Dissent.

1769   Prompted by appeals for support of Corsican independence, ALA writes 'Corsica' (circulating privately by June). She visits the Priestleys in Leeds and writes several poems that will be published in her first volume and become famous.

1771   John Aikin (brother) returns to Warrington (late in the year) and engages ALA in his first literary project, *Essays on Song-Writing*.

1772   Songs I–VI published anonymously in Aikin's *Essays on Song-Writing* (March); Hymns I–V published anonymously in William Enfield's *Hymns for Public Worship* (Summer?); *Poems* published (29 December).

1773 Second and third editions of *Poems* published (May and September); *Miscellaneous Pieces in Prose* published (19 October). Arthur Aikin, ALA's eldest nephew, born (d. 1854).

1774 Corresponds with Elizabeth Montagu (February). Marries Rochemont Barbauld (26 May). Fourth edition of *Poems* published. The Barbaulds settle in Palgrave, Suffolk, and open Palgrave School (25 July).

1775 Beginning of war with American colonies (April). Publishes *Devotional Pieces* (10 October; Dedication dated 10 July); visits Warrington (July?). Charles Rochemont Aikin born (25 August; d. 1847).

1777 Meets Judith Dixon (b. 1762), perhaps her first female pupil (March). Adopts Charles (June), and begins to write lessons for him (between August and year's end).

1778 *Lessons for Children, from Two to Three Years Old* published (28 May). *Lessons for Children, of Three Years Old* (one volume only) entered in Stationers' Register (12 June); reviewed in July. *Three Years Old* in two volumes announced (17 November).

1779 *Lessons for Children, from Three to Four Years Old* entered in Stationers' Register, 7 April; reviewed in June.

1780 *Lessons for Children*, collected in four parts, published (11 May). Father dies (14 December).

1781 *Hymns in Prose for Children* entered in Stationers' Register, 22 August. Published in September (?), but not advertised till 15 February 1782. Lucy Aikin born (6 November; d. 1864). Cornwallis surrenders at Yorktown (October), effectively ending the American war.

1784 John Aikin, having taken a medical degree in Holland (July), relocates to Yarmouth in Norfolk (December).

1785 Mother dies (31 January). The Barbaulds resign from Palgrave School (July) and depart for a tour of France (September).

1786 The Barbaulds arrive in Paris (end of March) for a stay of two and a half months. ALB perhaps meets Jean-Paul Rabaut-St. Étienne (1743–93), spokesman for Protestant toleration and afterwards member of the Girondin party. She forms a literary friendship with Alexandre-César-Annibal Frémin, baron de Stonne (1745–1821). Returning to England (June), the Barbaulds take lodgings in London.

1787 The Barbaulds settle in Hampstead (early in the year). Rochemont ministers to Rosslyn Hill congregation; ALB studies Italian and takes pupils. In subsequent years they visit friends in Norwich (the Taylor and Martineau families) and Bristol (the family of John Estlin, a Warrington Academy graduate).

1789 Capture and demolition of the Bastille by the people of Paris (14 July).

1790 Aroused by the failure of Parliament to repeal the Corporation and Test Acts and by Edmund Burke's speeches against the French Revolution, ALB publishes *An Address to the Opposers of the Repeal of the Corporation and Test Acts* (25 March).

1791 Responding to Parliament's refusal to abolish the slave trade, ALB publishes *An Epistle to William Wilberforce* (11 June). Her translation of Rabaut's *Adresse aux Anglois* is published (26 July). In Birmingham the houses of Dissenters, notably Joseph Priestley's, are sacked by a 'Church and King' mob (14–17 July).

1792 Joining a controversy started by political radical Gilbert Wakefield, ALB publishes *Remarks on Mr. Gilbert Wakefield's 'Enquiry into the Expediency and Propriety of Public or Social Worship'* (printed by mid-May, announced 16 June). Fleeing persecution in Yarmouth, John Aikin settles in London (spring). Royal Proclamation against Seditious Writings and Publications (21 May). ALB publishes *Civic Sermons I* and *II* (anonymously, June and August) and new editions of *Poems* and *Miscellaneous Pieces in Prose* (16 June). Louis XIV is deposed, and a French Republic proclaimed (10 August). Massacre of prisoners in Paris (2–3 September).

1793 John Aikin publishes *Evenings at Home*, Vols 1–2 (January); it contains thirteen pieces by ALB. The French Republic declares war on Britain (1 February); for a government-proclaimed national Fast, ALB publishes *Sins of Government, Sins of the Nation* (28 May).

1794 To escape political persecution, Joseph Priestley emigrates to America (April). ALB visits Scotland (September–October) and electrifies Edinburgh literary society by her reading of William Taylor's translation of Bürger's 'Lenore'.

1795 Cadell & Davies publish an edition of Mark Akenside's *Pleasures of Imagination* with an introduction by ALB (February).

1796 Commencement of the *Monthly Magazine*, Richard Phillips, proprietor (1 March); edited by John Aikin (to 1806). During his editorship ALB contributes poems and essays, usually unsigned.

1797 Cadell & Davies publish an edition of William Collins's poems with an Introduction by ALB (November). Meets Samuel Taylor Coleridge (August).

1798 Perhaps writes for Joseph Johnson's *Analytical Review* (June). John Aikin, seriously ill, moves to Dorking in Surrey; ALB accompanies him (April?). After recovery he settles in Stoke Newington, north of London (October).

1799 Meets Maria and Richard Lovell Edgeworth (May). Visits them at Bristol, where she tries nitrous oxide at Dr Beddoes's Pneumatic Institute (July).

1801 Peace of Amiens closes war with France (October).

1802 Barbaulds remove to Stoke Newington (March).

1803 Britain declares war on France (May). Commencement of the *Annual Review* (to 1809), edited by Arthur Aikin. ALB contributes 'the leading articles in poetry and belles letters' in more than one volume; all are unsigned.

1804 Employed by Richard Phillips to edit correspondence of Samuel Richardson (February); *The Correspondence of Samuel Richardson*, with her biography, published in six volumes (23 July).

1805 *Selections from the Spectator, Tatler, Guardian, and Freeholder, with a Preliminary Essay* published (7 February).

1806 John Aikin resigns from the *Monthly Magazine* (May), lays plans to start *Athenaeum*.

1807 *Athenaeum* commences (January, to mid-1809). ALB contributes essays, begins contributing to the *Monthly Repository* (June), and engages with Longmans to write prefaces for a collection of British novels (March?).

1808 Rochemont Barbauld succumbs to a mental disorder that takes the form of violent assault on ALB (January). The Barbaulds are obliged to separate (March). Rochemont dies by drowning (11 November).

1809 Begins to write for the *Monthly Review* (July, through at least October 1815).

1810 *The British Novelists* (fifty vols) published (25 August).

1811 Compiles *The Female Speaker* (published 15 February). Writes *Eighteen Hundred and Eleven* (completed by 30 November).

1812 Publishes *Eighteen Hundred and Eleven* (12 February), to almost uniformly hostile reviews by journals committed to the war.

1813 Unacknowledged break with Edgeworths over *Eighteen Hundred and Eleven*.

1815 At the Battle of Waterloo Napoleon is defeated; the war ends.

1816 Resumes relations with Edgeworths (August).

1819 Death of Elizabeth Belsham Kenrick, ALB's second cousin and oldest friend (January).

1822 Eyesight deteriorates. Death of John Aikin (7 December).

1823 Last known publications (poems in *Monthly Repository* and Joanna Baillie's *Collection of Poems*).

1825 Dies at Stoke Newington (9 March). *Works* and *A Legacy for Young Ladies*, both edited by Lucy Aikin, published (June and December, respectively).

ABBREVIATIONS

ALB	Anna Letitia Barbauld
ALBVE	William McCarthy, *Anna Letitia Barbauld, Voice of the Enlightenment*
A Rev	*The Annual Review; and History of Literature*
Beinecke	Beinecke Rare Book and Manuscript Library, Yale University
BL	British Library, London
C Rev	*The Critical Review* (London)
Chr Ref	*The Christian Reformer* (London)
CRA	Charles Rochemont Aikin
ESTC	English Short-Title Catalogue
FMG	Hunter, *Familiae Minorum Gentium*
Folger	The Folger Shakespeare Library, Washington, DC
GC	Betsy Rodgers, *Georgian Chronicle: Mrs Barbauld and her Family*
GM	*The Gentleman's Magazine*
HCR	Henry Crabb Robinson
HMCL	Library of Harris Manchester College, Oxford University
Hornel	The Hornel Library, The National Trust for Scotland, Broughton House, Kirkcudbright
JA	John Aikin, MD
JJ	Joseph Johnson
JP	Joseph Priestley
JRL	The John Rylands Library of Manchester University
LA	Lucy Aikin
LC	*London Chronicle*
LEP	*London Evening Post*
LYL	Anna Letitia Barbauld, *A Legacy for Young Ladies*
M Rep	*The Monthly Repository of Theology and General Literature* (London)
M Rev	*The Monthly Review* (London)

MC	*Morning Chronicle* (London)
MJA	Lucy Aikin, *Memoir of John Aikin, M.D.*
MM	*The Monthly Magazine* (London)
MML	Lucy Aikin, *Memoirs, Miscellanies and Letters*
N & Q	*Notes and Queries*
NOS	*The New Oxford Shakespeare*
NYPL	New York Public Library
ODNB	*Oxford Dictionary of National Biography*
OED	*Oxford English Dictionary*
PA	*Public Advertiser* (London)
PML	Pierpont Morgan Library, New York
PUL	Princeton University Library
RB	Rochemont Barbauld
RO	Record Office (following name of city or county)
Rodgers	The Estate of Lady Rodgers, Sir Piers Rodgers, Executor
TNA	The National Archives, Kew, Surrey, UK
TUHS	*Transactions of the Unitarian Historical Society*
UCL	Library of University College, London University
WA	Warrington Academy
WL	Warrington Library, formerly Warrington Circulating Library, Warrington, Cheshire, UK
Works	*Works of Anna Letitia Barbauld*, ed. Lucy Aikin (2 vols, London, 1825)
WT	William Turner II (1761–1859)

VOLUME INTRODUCTION

Anna Letitia Barbauld was born the daughter and grand-daughter of teachers. From birth to age 42 she was environed by schools: first her father's school in the family house in Kibworth, then the academy for young men at Warrington, where her father taught Belles-Lettres and Divinity. Later the man she married, having resigned his prospects as a Church-of-England clergyman, kept a school. Teaching was a common occupation of male Dissenting intellectuals who were middle class, such as her grandfather, father, and husband. But for Barbauld, teaching was also a gender aspiration. In girlhood and young womanhood she had been surrounded by boys and young men, who, unlike girls, learned Latin and Greek as a matter of course. Because she was female, she was not automatically taught Latin and Greek; she had to plead, cajole, and lobby her father to help her learn Latin, and in all likelihood she never learned Greek. To her, being educated signified attaining to hard-won equality. For these reasons of family and gender, Barbauld engaged with learning and teaching throughout her life.

After their marriage, she and her husband moved to the village of Palgrave in Suffolk, where, for eleven years, they conducted a school for boys. Palgrave School rapidly achieved fame throughout East Anglia. Gradually it earned a national reputation, drawing pupils from London, Scotland, and even New York. In the summer of 1777, three years after their marriage, the Barbaulds adopted John Aikin's third son, her nephew Charles. One of their reasons for doing so, according to Anna Letitia, was that they wanted to try 'our own plans and schemes' in education, plans that could not be tried with their pupils, who were too old and were, after all, other people's children.[1] Anna Letitia wanted to teach a very young child; she had learned to read, herself, according to her mother, at age 2, and she wanted to teach her child to read at that early age. Her lessons for Charles 'from two to three years old' must have been written in the autumn of 1777, for by January 1778 she had sent them to her brother to have them printed.

Her decision to publish her lessons for Charles was momentous. Although many reading primers existed and many mothers wrote lessons for their children, the primers were always printed in tiny type and mothers

[1] ALB to JA, [summer 1776] (*Works*, 2:10).

did not attempt to publish what they wrote. Barbauld broke these conventions, both by publishing her lessons for Charles and by insisting that they be printed in large, easy-to-read type. Moreover, published primers traditionally began with alphabets and phonics—dreary lists of vowel-and-consonant combinations—and moved on to catechisms. Barbauld chose for Charles only words denoting people, events, things, and creatures he had experienced or could experience in daily life. *Lessons* departed from the norm in being realist and empiricist, and in publicizing transactions—quite likely actual transactions—between mother and child: 'Charles' is Charles, 'Mamma' is Anna Letitia, 'Papa' is Rochemont, and the rural setting is the village of Palgrave and its surroundings. Later volumes of *Lessons* take Charles farther afield and present more information in more systematic ways, but their method is always associative, always based on Charles's experience—of the pots and pans in the Barbauld kitchen, of the phases of the moon (as seen behind the nearby trees), of things dug up in the garden, of the plants and animals in the neighbourhood.[2] Their structure is progressive. On page one of *Two to Three* Charles spells a single word; at the end of *Three to Four* he is presumed able to read the prose poems uttered by Sun and Moon. The latter of these ranks among the finest things Barbauld ever wrote.

Until 1779, even Dissenting schoolmasters were obliged by law to teach the doctrines of the Church of England, so, from its beginning, religious instruction of some sort took place at Palgrave School. At the close of her 'Thoughts on the Devotional Taste', published late in 1775, Barbauld prophesied that:

[p]erhaps a time may come, when our worship . . . shall be new modelled by some free and enlarged genius. Perhaps the time may come, when the spirit of philosophy, and the spirit of devotion, shall join to conduct our public assemblies; when to all that is graceful in order and well-regulated pomp, we shall add whatever is affecting in the warmth of zeal, and all that is delightful in the beauty of holiness.[3]

Although she refers in this passage to adult assemblies, she had probably begun experimenting with a 'new modelled' worship for the boys at Palgrave; by January 1780 she had written six of the original twelve hymns for *Hymns in Prose*. Dissenting congregations enjoyed the freedom to compose their own liturgies; in writing her prose hymns, Barbauld was composing a liturgy for her congregation of boys.

She may well have come to see *Lessons* and *Hymns* as a progressive series while she was readying *Hymns* for the press. Reading primers conventionally

---

[2] On the method of association from Charles's experience in *Lessons* see Wharton, '"The Things Themselves"'.

[3] ALB, 'Thoughts on the Devotional Taste', 49–50.

proceeded from alphabets to religious instruction within the covers of a single volume; a progress from literacy to catechism was to be expected.[4] Moreover, Barbauld's methods for encouraging devotion—devotion, not niceties of doctrine—were the same as her methods for teaching reading: she appealed always to the child's experience of the world. She encouraged the child reader to see divine force at work in the lives of animals and plants and in the weather and the village itself. *Hymns* asks searching questions: 'Who is the shepherd's shepherd?' By what invisible powers do the things we see and touch come to exist? She challenged the child to imagine more than literal experience ('God was in the storm'), but still that literal experience is the beginning of wisdom. In Dissenting fashion, *Hymns* harnesses empiricism—science—to the project of worship.

Hymns in Prose was the best-known and most influential product of Barbauld's Palgrave years. It travelled to the United States, where it circulated so widely that every American writer from Emerson to Melville may be assumed to have read some version of it in childhood;[5] it was translated into French, Italian, German, Spanish, and even Hungarian and, thus, became essentially a work of European literature. Victorian editions were lavishly illustrated, in contradiction of Barbauld's Dissenting aesthetic; orthodox Christian redactors sometimes added hymns about the Incarnation and Crucifixion to adapt the work for religious conservatives.[6]

At Palgrave, Barbauld wrote and delivered lectures to her pupils, most of which probably perished along with other school materials in September 1940, when the London building in which a descendant kept them was bombed;[7] but among these lectures may have been those on 'Earth' and 'Plants' printed by Lucy Aikin after Barbauld's death. Barbauld also wrote short pieces and fables for the school. Some of these probably went into *Evenings at Home*, her brother's collection of tales, lectures, and dialogues written over the years for his children. Others may have been among the pieces gathered by Lucy Aikin in *A Legacy for Young Ladies*.[8] The present volume places these more or less speculatively into a section headed 'Palgrave School'.

After 1785, the year when Barbauld and her husband left Palgrave, she did no more classroom teaching. She continued, however, to take private

---

[4] The *Critical Review* perceived *Hymns* as 'a continuation' of *Lessons* (*C Rev* 52 [1781]:157).

[5] For editions of *Hymns* in the early United States, see Welch.

[6] A famous edition is the one published by John Murray in 1864, elaborately illustrated in the high Victorian style. An 1840 editor of *Hymns* undertook to add hymns about 'the divinity and incarnation of our Saviour' and 'the fall and consequent depravity of man' (*Chr Ref*, n.s. 8 [1841]:39).

[7] For details about the loss of family papers see *ALBVE*, xviii.

[8] One piece, 'Description of a Curious Animal', was definitely written at Palgrave.

pupils, teaching them not in classes but by writing to and for them. Most of those pupils who can be identified were the sons and daughters of family friends such as the Carrs of Hampstead—chiefly the daughters, for Barbauld devoted most of her teaching energy to the education of young women.[9] Barbauld may have taken her first female pupil informally while still at Palgrave: Judith Dixon, of Norwich, later Mrs. Beecroft, who was 14 when they met and remained a lasting friend. After settling in Hampstead in the later 1780s, Barbauld tutored Flora Wynch, probably a paying pupil. Later came Mary Anne Galton, whose mother pulled her back when Barbauld encouraged her to write for publication.[10] Lydia Rickards, from Birmingham, is Barbauld's best-documented pupil today, thanks to the recovery in 2011 of Barbauld's letters to her. Other pupils included the daughters of Susannah Taylor of Norwich, Grace Fletcher from Edinburgh ('I wished my dear child to have a high standard of intellectual and moral perfection, and in placing her with Mrs. Barbauld I had my wish accomplished'),[11] and S. S. S., who published a volume of 'young-adult' fiction called *Thornton Hall; or, Six Months at School* (1823) and dedicated it to Barbauld in thanks for 'that kind care which I experienced, during those happy days of my childhood which I passed under your friendly roof'.[12] Especially after her husband's death in 1808, teaching young women may well have been Barbauld's main source of income.

Barbauld taught some subjects—French and Italian, for example—probably by methodical exercises, but her principal way of teaching, and the one that survives, was by writing tutorials and 'fancy pieces', such as allegories, dream visions, and riddles: 'fancy' in the sense of imaginative exercise. Her tutorials—delivered in the form of letters to the pupil, such as those she wrote to Lydia Rickards on History, Language, and Homer—expound the subject, summing up what is known (usually with a sceptical turn), explaining its basic concepts, and urging its ethical and intellectual value. Barbauld's practice of writing tutorials in the form of letters actually

---

[9] Barbauld's views on women's education were once believed retrograde, a misconception based on a well-intended misrepresentation by Lucy Aikin. Aikin printed a letter that Barbauld had sent to Rochemont as having been sent to Elizabeth Montagu—a huge difference, in context. The letter rejected a proposal that Anna Letitia preside in an academy for young ladies. Aikin's motive in publishing the letter was almost certainly to shelter her aunt from Tory criticism. For details see *ALBVE*, 141–6.

[10] Barbauld's rebuff by Galton's mother has had to be inferred from Galton's much later, and well-muffled, account: see *ALBVE*, 495 and 667n13. For details on Rickards, see below.

[11] Fletcher, 91.

[12] *Thornton Hall*, Dedication. 'S.S.S.' was also the author of a guidebook 'addressed to the juvenile inhabitants of this city': *A Visit to Edinburgh; containing a Description of the Principal Curiosities and Public Buildings in the Scottish Metropolis* (Edinburgh: Fairbairn & Anderson, 1818). We have not further identified this author.

posted to a real recipient and not simply pro-forma letters (a known genre in the eighteenth century, exemplified, for instance, by Catharine Macaulay's *History of England*) creates difficulties for her present-day editors. This edition of Barbauld's *Collected Works* does not aim to publish her letters, and thus we have had to decide when a letter is actually a tutorial. We have taken pedagogic intent as our criterion, and have been influenced also by prior publication; but we know that in Barbauld's letters to young women, the line between pedagogy and pure epistolarity can be blurred. In theory, all of Barbauld's earlier letters to Lydia Rickards could be regarded as pedagogic, for by writing chatty descriptions of local landscape or the harvest, Barbauld could have intended to model concrete description and detailed attention to one's surroundings, a form of intelligence.

Riddles and other verbal games offered intellectual exercise, especially for women and children, that is to say, people who were not eligible for formal schooling by reason of sex or age, and they were popular entertainments even among adults. As Barbauld explained in 'On Riddles', such games engage the mind. Deciphering riddles is a means not only of intellectual but of ethical development, and understanding a riddle can make the difference between naïve folly (like that of the Young Mouse in *Evenings at Home*, who thinks a trap is a little house just for her, a gift from the family) and practical wisdom (like that of the Mother Mouse who knows that a trap is not a house and not a gift). Riddles can also reframe conventional perceptions to unsettle or broaden them, as when the Father in 'On Manufactures' asks Henry 'what are those two instruments you carry always about with you', thus startling Henry (and the reader) into perceiving human hands as tools. Further, riddles passed back and forth among women take on the character of a shared code. 'True Magicians', written for Sarah Grace Carr, exemplifies such a code: it images the arts and sciences as female figures who are powerful in themselves and can confer power upon a female aspirant. Presented as a dream vision, 'True Magicians' describes a college for women whose faculty are women, and who—like Barbauld herself, writing to Lydia Rickards about Homer—can conjure up the dead and make them perform. It does not say 'college', but, riddle-like, it describes the architectural setting of a college, shaded walks and spots for contemplation, and invites the reader to recognize what she is describing.

Barbauld seems to have thought of publishing some of these pieces. In 1813 she revised her letters to Lydia Rickards on history, perhaps with a view to giving them wider circulation; but if that was her plan, in the end she did not follow through with it. They and other pieces were gathered after her death by Lucy Aikin, chiefly in a volume entitled *A Legacy for Young Ladies*. A few pieces came to print by other routes; presumably they had circulated among friends of their original recipients. After their first publication in London, those pieces could cross the Atlantic and appear in American newspapers or be copied into American scrapbooks and manuscript albums. Barbauld's writings for young persons enjoyed wide popularity in the early United States as well as in Britain.

Had Lucy Aikin not squelched a growing movement to release Barbauld pieces to literary annuals and gift books, more of them might have appeared during the 1830s.[13] Probably, even today copies of unpublished Barbauld jeux-d'esprit and teaching pieces lie unidentified among the uncatalogued papers of descendants of the young men and women for whom she wrote them. One that remains lost was a response to or comment on Wollstonecraft's *Vindication of the Rights of Woman*, known today only from a tantalizing fragmentary description by Charles: 'a view of the female part of the creation a century hence on a g[eneral] revolution of manners which is to take place when Mrs Woolstonecraft has been su[. . .]'.[14]

Barbauld's fame as a teacher and writer for young people led to her being hired to review educational books. The *Annual Review* was a family project (its editor was her nephew, Arthur), and her contributions to that and to the *Monthly Review* reflect her belief that writing by women should be held to the same standards of judgement as writing by men. Apart from reviewing, Barbauld's only published educational work after *Evenings at Home*—other than additions to *Lessons* and *Hymns*—was an 1811 compilation, *The Female Speaker*, an anthology of extracts to be read aloud by young women so that they might find their voices—and, in the course of doing that, also become acquainted with some eminent writers.

Volume Structure

The structure of this volume is chronological, presenting Barbauld's writings for children and young persons in the order of their composition, as far as we can know or infer it. This aim entails breaking up the two collections, *Evenings at Home* and *A Legacy for Young Ladies*, to regroup their contents.

From *Evenings* we have conjecturally relocated six pieces to the present volume's section on Palgrave School. With very few known exceptions, the school's archive perished in the bombing of London in 1940; but

---

[13] Lucy Aikin wrote a tart letter to the *Monthly Repository* rebuking those who had released to print their copies of Barbauld verses which Aikin considered inferior to the contents of *Works* ('Mrs. Barbauld's MSS').

[14] CRA to ALB, 6 Dec. 1792 (quoted in *ALBVE*, 352).

because two pieces known today definitely date to Palgrave School, and because Barbauld devoted eleven important years of her life to the school, we aim to honour these efforts and to show the kinds of writing she penned for her pupils. Certainly the texts that appeared afterwards in *Evenings* could have been revised—one piece, 'Alfred', includes a passage that reads like a swipe at the 'Loyalist' craze of late 1792—but the *Evenings* texts are the only ones we have today, so there is no way to know whether or how they differ from what we presume were their Palgrave originals.

Breaking up *Evenings at Home* to relocate some of its contents in this way does little violence to *Evenings* itself. Barbauld's known part in this publication was small. She wrote fourteen pieces out of 99; the rest, according to Lucy Aikin, were John Aikin's. *Evenings* was a compilation of pieces most of which had been previously written, not—at least, as a whole—a new composition. *A Legacy for Young Ladies* has still less authorial integrity. *Legacy* was compiled by Lucy Aikin from Barbauld's papers after Barbauld's death. It brings together pieces from across Barbauld's writing life—from Palgrave School in around 1780 ('Description of a Curious Animal...') to at least 1813 (the revised form of letters to Lydia Rickards on History), and it does so with no apparent rationale. Although our resulting sequence is often unavoidably conjectural, to perpetuate the structure of *A Legacy for Young Ladies* would misrepresent the arc of Barbauld's writing career.

Thus, after *Lessons for Children* and *Hymns in Prose*, we group other pieces dating definitely or conjecturally to Palgrave School; then those pieces from *Evenings at Home* that we cannot date otherwise; then, in a section of 'Works of Imagination and Instruction', the contents of *Legacy*; then Barbauld's Preface to *The Female Speaker*, and a list of her selections for it. The volume closes with her reviews of educational books from the *Annual Review* and the *Monthly Review*. The recovery of the letters to Lydia Rickards confers upon the volume some important Barbauld holographs;[15] one of the riddles in 'On Riddles', originally published apart

---

[15] Thirty-nine Barbauld letters to Lydia Rickards remained with Lydia's collateral descendants (Lydia herself was childless) until early in 2011, when the last descendant died and the letters were put to auction (house of Dominic Winter, Cirencester, 11 May). They were purchased by Joanna Kafarowski; in 2016 she sold them to William McCarthy, who, in turn, sold them to the Carl H. Pforzheimer Collection of Shelley and His Circle at the New York Public Library. Jessica W. H. Lim published thirty-two of them in 'Unsettled Accounts: Anna Letitia Barbauld's Letters to Lydia Rickards' (*Tulsa Studies in Women's Literature*, Volume 38, Number 1, Spring 2019): 153–200. Thirty-two letters appear in 'Anna Letitia Barbauld Letters to Lydia Rickards, 1798–1815', ed. William McCarthy, *Romantic Circles Electronic Editions*. The remaining seven letters concerning education are published here for the first time.

from its essay in *Poems of Anna Letitia Barbauld* in 1994, is also given from holograph. With the exception of *Lessons for Children* as first printed, Barbauld did not attend to the texts of her writings for young persons as carefully as she did to the texts of her poems; she published them anonymously and did not claim copyright. Hence variant readings in successive editions are more likely to result from the oversights or habits of compositors than from revisions by her.

LESSONS FOR CHILDREN

INTRODUCTION

Lessons for Children originated as a family document, a series of lessons Barbauld composed for her nephew and newly adopted son, Charles Rochemont Aikin, in the autumn of 1777 when Charles was just over 2 years old. She wrote it to teach him to read, according to her belief that a toddler was capable of reading.[1] Many eighteenth-century mothers wrote lessons for their children; some survive to this day. Not at all common—unprecedented, so far as we know—was Barbauld's decision to publish hers. Nationally famous as a poet and essayist, writing lessons for a small child became the new turn in her literary career. *Lessons* was a highly innovative and original work: it included verbal exchanges between mother and child, drawn from everyday activities.

Publishing *Lessons* was such an unusual career move that Barbauld proceeded with great caution. She sent the manuscript to her brother in Warrington to have it printed by William Eyres, who had printed her previous books. No copy of Eyres's 1777 printing is known to have survived, but it seems to have followed what was then the convention in books for children—small type on small pages. Barbauld emphatically rejected that format. She wanted large type for ease of reading and other accommodations for her child readers. On 19 January 1778, she wrote: 'Charles's little book is very well, but my idea is not executed in it: I must therefore beg you will print one as soon as you can, on fine paper, on one side only, and more space and a clearer line for the chapters' (*Works*, 2:19).[2]

---

[1] According to Lucy Aikin, Barbauld herself had learned to read at age 2. None of Barbauld's manuscript lessons for Charles survive, but they may have looked like lessons she wrote many years later for Charles's daughter. One of those does survive and is reproduced as fig. 34 in *ALBVE*.

[2] By 'a clearer line for the chapters' Barbauld probably meant a better-inked rule between text segments. John Murray criticized Eyres for under-inking his work (Murray, Letterbook, 24 Sept. 1778). Thanks to Andrea Immel for this suggestion.

Eyres printed again, following her instructions. Joseph Johnson, Barbauld's London publisher, had *Lessons for Children, from Two to Three Years Old* entered in the Stationers' Register on 4 May 1778, under his own copyright.[3] Johnson advertised the little book in the *London Evening Post* and *London Chronicle* for 28–30 May; both advertisements studiously avoided identifying the author, either directly or by the hint of naming publications 'by Mrs. Barbauld'. Later that spring Barbauld sent her brother copy for a new volume of *Lessons*: 'You will see by the inclosed I have been employing my pen again for him [Charles], and again I must employ you to get it printed' (*Works*, 2:21, dated only 'Palgrave 1778'). On 12 June Johnson entered *Lessons for Children, of Three Years Old* in the Stationers' Register, again under his own copyright; no advertisement has surfaced, but this volume and *Two to Three* were reviewed in the *Monthly Review* for July and the *Critical Review* for August. Thomas Bentley, Wedgwood's partner and a Barbauld admirer, observed that 'It is pretty well known, tho' the Author's name does not appear to the work, that the rising generation are indebted to a lady of distinguished merit and genius, for these elementary lessons.'[4] London's *General Advertiser* for 16 November 1778 noticed *Two to Three* and *Three Years Old*: 'a very useful work, and much wanted.... It is said...to be written by the much admired and ingenious Mrs. Barbauld.' On 17 November the *Leeds Intelligencer* advertised *Two to Three* and *Three Years Old*, there listed, for the first time, in two parts: 'Lessons for Children of Three Years Old.—Part First' and 'Lessons for Children of Three Years Old, Part II'.[5] Finally, on 7 April 1779 Joseph Johnson entered *Lessons for Children, from Three to Four Years Old* in the Stationers' Register, again under his own copyright; and in May and June 1780 he advertised the entire set, 'In Four Parts, Price 6d. each, Lessons for Children,

---

[3] Perhaps she took her title from a work published earlier in the year by Newbery: *Spiritual Lessons for Children, adapted to each Letter in the Alphabet*. 'Spiritual' would probably have been understood to mean 'Methodist'. Barbauld's title conspicuously lacks 'Spiritual'; her *Lessons* were secular.

[4] Bentley (*M Rev*, 59:25). The *Westminster Magazine* for October noticed *Two to Three*, 'said to have been written by the ingenious Mrs *Barbauld*, for the use of her own infant son' (549).

[5] This is the earliest announcement of Part II known to us. We have not found an announcement in a London newspaper, not even the *London Evening Post*. Samuel Johnson's disparaging remark on *Lessons* ('see there! you are much better than a cat or a dog, for you can speak') may refer to *Two to Three* or to Part II of *Three Years Old*, but Boswell dated it 1775, three years too early (Boswell, 662).

from Two to Four Years of Age', in four London newspapers.[6] A year later Barbauld could bask in the praise of Vicesimus Knox, essayist and trend-setter: 'A poetess of our own times, remarkably distinguished by her taste and genius, has condescended to compose little books for the initiation of children in reading and they seem well adapted to effect her laudable purpose.'[7] 'Condescended' did imply a descent from her literary pedestal, and some thought Barbauld needed rescue from contempt.

Frances Burney, however, perceived *Lessons* as a 'new Walk'[8] in books for children. Thomas Bentley prized it for confining its vocabulary to words familiar to children, and he appreciated its progressive method, although he deprecated passages in which animals are made to speak. The *Critical Review* appreciated the 'chit-chat' of *Lessons*, its dialogical character.[9] Sarah Trimmer, although hostile to the Aikin-Barbauld circle's liberal politics, admired Barbauld 'for introducing a species of writing, in the style of *familiar conversation*, which is certainly much better suited to the capacities of young children than any that preceded it; and the infant readers are farther indebted to her for the happy thought of printing *first books*, in a large clear type'; Trimmer imitated *Lessons* in her own *Easy Introduction to the Knowledge of Nature*.[10] A writer for the *Gentleman's Magazine* in 1786 saw in *Lessons for Children* and *Hymns in Prose for Children*, as well as in several other works, a guide 'to every mother who wishes to acquire a proper and instructive method of conversing with her children. She might then render every walk which she takes with them in the fields not only conducive to their health and activity, but likewise to their improvement in useful knowledge.'[11] Richard Lovell Edgeworth, who with his daughter Maria would publish a leading treatise on education in 1798, was so impressed by *Lessons* that he laid aside a plan of his own to write a children's primer. When he came to write about books for children in *Practical Education*, Edgeworth declared the

---

[6] *SJC*, 11–13 and 18–20; *MC*, 15 May; *Gazetteer*, 19 May; *GEP*, 13–15 June. How many copies were sold is not known; twenty years later Johnson told Richard Lovell Edgeworth that 'a very large number indeed must be sold of a child's book before forty pounds are realised by it' (Johnson, 'Letterbook', fol. 32ᵛ).

[7] Knox, 20

[8] Burney, 4:187 (from 1798).   [9] *C Rev*, 46 (August 1778): 160.

[10] Trimmer, 1 (May–December 1802): 63–4.

[11] The *Gentleman's Magazine*, 56.2 (December 1786): 1025, dated Woodbridge, Dec. 3 [1786] and signed 'J. B.' The *Gentleman's Magazine* database identifies a 'J.B.' from Woodbridge as 'John Black' (Montluzin).

four volumes of *Lessons* 'by far the best books of the kind that have ever appeared.... The poetic beauty, and eloquent simplicity of many of Mrs. Barbauld's Lessons, cultivate the imagination of children, and their taste, in the best possible manner.'[12] (Edgeworth also criticized many details of *Lessons*. We print some of his objections in our notes.) By the end of the century books for children could be counted as 'literature', if they were well-written; in effect, Barbauld had enlarged the field. William Enfield remarked in 1796 while assessing Maria Edgeworth's *The Parent's Assistant* for the *Monthly Review*: 'it is not now deemed an unworthy employment for writers of the most distinguished abilities, to draw up instructive and amusing books even for children.... At present, writers of the first order do not feel themselves degraded by employing their talents in this way; and the public is well inclined to bestow due praise on such useful exertions.'[13]

John Aikin gave Barbauld a comprehensive appraisal of *Lessons* in the 'Preface' to his *Calendar of Nature: designed for the instruction and entertainment of young persons* (1784), a work confessedly based on hers:

Though some of the warm admirers of your poetry have censured you for employing talents of so superior a kind in the composition of books for children, yet, I believe, there are few parents who do not think themselves obliged to you for this condescension: and, if you are ambitious of higher approbation, you may assure yourself of that of the genuine philosopher, who must agree with you in thinking, that to lay a foundation for such a structure as that of the human mind cannot be an ignoble employment. Nor have your services in this important design been confined to your own exertions: it has been partly from your example, that others have been induced to consecrate respectable abilities to the same useful purpose; and the great superiority observable in the books for the instruction of children published within a few years past, to those of former periods, is owing to the superior literary rank of the authors.[14]

One of the most striking features of *Lessons* is its literary quality. Besides the lyrical beauty of the last vignettes in *Three to Four*—the prose poems uttered by Sun and Moon—there are many passages of

---

[12] Edgeworth, *Practical Education*, 317, 320–1. Twenty years earlier, Edgeworth had commented in detail on *Two to Three* (MS Eng. Misc. c. 895, Bod L). His criticisms of individual passages are often minute.

[13] Enfield, 89. A turn-of-the-century review of a French translation of *Lessons* speaks of the 'literary education of children' (*M Rev*, ns 27:465–6).

[14] Aikin, *Calendar*, [iii]–iv.

casual charm. For example, consider this one from *Lessons for Children, of Three Years Old*:

> April is come, and the birds sing, and the trees are in blossom, and flowers are coming out, and butterflies, and the sun shines. Now it rains. It rains and the sun shines. There is a rain-bow. O what fine colours! Pretty bright rain-bow! No, you cannot catch it, it is in the sky. (16)

In other passages, instruction takes delightfully whimsical forms:

> How many legs have you?
> Here is one, and here is another. Charles has two legs.
> How many legs has a horse?
> A horse has four legs.
> And how many has a dog?
> Four: and a cow has four; and a sheep has four; and puss has four legs.
> And how many legs have the chickens?
> Go and look.
> The chickens have only two legs.
> And the linnets, and the robins, and all the birds, have only two legs.
> But I will tell you what birds have got; they have got wings to fly with, and they fly very high in the air.
> Charles has no wings.
> No, because Charles is not a bird. (43–5)

One may imagine Mama giving Charles a hug or a tickle at the end of this dialogue. Other passages would probably be considered unsettling if not gruesome, by today's standards. For example, in one, Mama warns Charles about the reaper's scythe: 'Do not come near it, you will have your legs cut off' (21). The everyday world is full of delight but also fraught with danger. There was always more to *Lessons* than mere instruction in reading, and more than Barbauld claimed for it in her 'Advertisement'. She wanted Charles to grow up to be an informed member of society, one who would cherish beauty and care for the people around him.[15]

Lessons for Children was not, however, understood to address children of the working class. It was received, rather, as a book for 'the children of all people of fashion', in the words of a writer in *The Juvenile Magazine* in 1788; and a nineteenth-century chronicler of children's-book history, Charlotte Yonge, estimated that 'probably three-fourths of the gentry of

---

[15] For the intellectual and ethical substance of *Lessons*, see 'Mother of all Discourses', *ALBVE*, ch. 8, and Wharton. Barbauld's intellectual sources appear in our annotations.

the last three generations' learned to read from Mrs. Barbauld.[16] Children of the labouring class continued to be taught mostly from syllabaries and catechisms, usually inculcating Church-of-England orthodoxy.

The four volumes of *Lessons* were reprinted frequently and were known to be Barbauld's, even though her name never appeared on the title pages during her lifetime. Even so, our London 1781, presumed second edition copy of *Lessons for Children of Three Years Old*, Part II, contains an advertisement at the back for the first two volumes in the series along with the information that also at Joseph Johnson's shop in St. Paul's Churchyard 'may be had Mrs. Barbauld's Poems and Miscellaneous Pieces in Prose, price 3s. each, sewed'. For an 1808 edition Barbauld added much new material, perhaps at Johnson's request to renew copyright.[17] Variants in other editions, however, are not likely to be hers; their tendency is to update and 'normalize' the text verbally, replacing older or regional usages (such as *eat* for *ate* and *eaten*) with usages current at time of publication. The most conspicuous alterations in Barbauld's lifetime are those in the 1821 edition, perhaps the work of her nephew Arthur Aikin, who is known to have 'corrected' the text of *Evenings at Home*.[18]

TEXTUAL MATTERS

Up until recently the earliest known London-published copies of *Lessons* were a 1781–2 two-volume set of *Three Years Old*, sold to a private buyer by a Bath bookdealer;[19] the earliest available to the public was the British Library four-volume set dated 1787–8.[20] The 1779 Dublin editions of

---

[16] *The Juvenile Magazine*, 1 (March 1788): 135n; Yonge, 'Children's Literature of the Last Century', *Macmillan's Magazine*, 20 (1869): 234.

[17] Johnson owned the copyright to *Lessons*, and under provisions of copyright law, he had enjoyed two terms of fourteen years each from the time when all four volumes were advertised together (1780). To renew copyright he needed new material in the text (Mackinnon, 882).

[18] *Lessons for Children.... Part I. For Children from Two to Three Years Old* (London, 1821). On Arthur Aikin's alterations see our headnote to *Evenings*. The 1821 changes tend to update usage and even decor: e.g. 'Do not stand upon the hearth' (*Two to Three*, 7) becomes 'Stand upon the carpet'. Some might argue that Barbauld implied her work should be updated periodically by her intention to teach reading through children's knowledge of their surroundings, which of course change over time.

[19] Louise Ross.

[20] The Opie Collection (Bodleian Library) holds a 1784 copy of *Three to Four*.

Parts I and II of *Three Years Old* were also available. While doing research for this edition of Barbauld's *Collected Works*, Paula R. Feldman discovered copies from three of the four 1778–9 London first editions at the University of Glasgow Library, a second copy of one of those volumes at the University of Edinburgh Library, and a copy of a first edition of *Two to Three* (1778) at the John Rylands Library at Manchester University. These copies cast light on the early history of *Lessons*.

The Glasgow and Edinburgh first-edition copies of *Lessons* are more cleanly printed than copies of other editions, even when they do not differ textually from them. Further, the title page of Glasgow's *Lessons for Children, of Three Years Old* makes no mention of 'Part One' or 'Part Two': originally *Three Years Old* consisted of a single volume. A further surprise was revealed by collation of Glasgow *Two to Three* with Rylands *Two to Three*, both dated 1778. They are not identical: Rylands varies textually from Glasgow and thus represents a different setting of type, or at least a different state of the first-edition text. And finally, collation of Rylands *Two to Three* with the British Library copy (1787) of *Two to Three* suggests that the 1787 edition descended from the Rylands text, not from the Glasgow text.

The Rylands copy appears to have been published late in 1778, for the verso of its last page advertises *Three Years Old* in two parts, as did the *Leeds Intelligencer*. Dublin 'Part I' of *Three Years Old* presents a hybrid between Glasgow and 1788; although its arrangement of the text is almost identical to the arrangement in 1788, in fifty-one of sixty-seven textual variants it agrees with Glasgow rather than the British Library's 1788 copy.

We judge, then, that the Glasgow copies of *Two to Three*, *Three Years Old*, and *Three to Four* (and the Edinburgh copy of *Three Years Old*, from the same print run as its Glasgow counterpart) represent the earliest known printings of their respective titles, and that all subsequent printings, beginning even with Rylands *Two to Three*, progressively deteriorated the presswork. Pages became more crowded and type less carefully aligned. The deterioration is not grossly perceptible; in *Two to Three* the crowding reduced page numbers from fifty-eight (Glasgow) to fifty-six (Rylands and 1787). (An apparent exception is the 1788 *Three to Four*, eight pages *longer* than Glasgow *Three to Four*; but its extra length results from its use of catchwords, each of which gets a line to itself and thus reduces the typical page length from ten lines of text in Glasgow to nine in 1788.) The Glasgow and Edinburgh first-edition copies are the ones

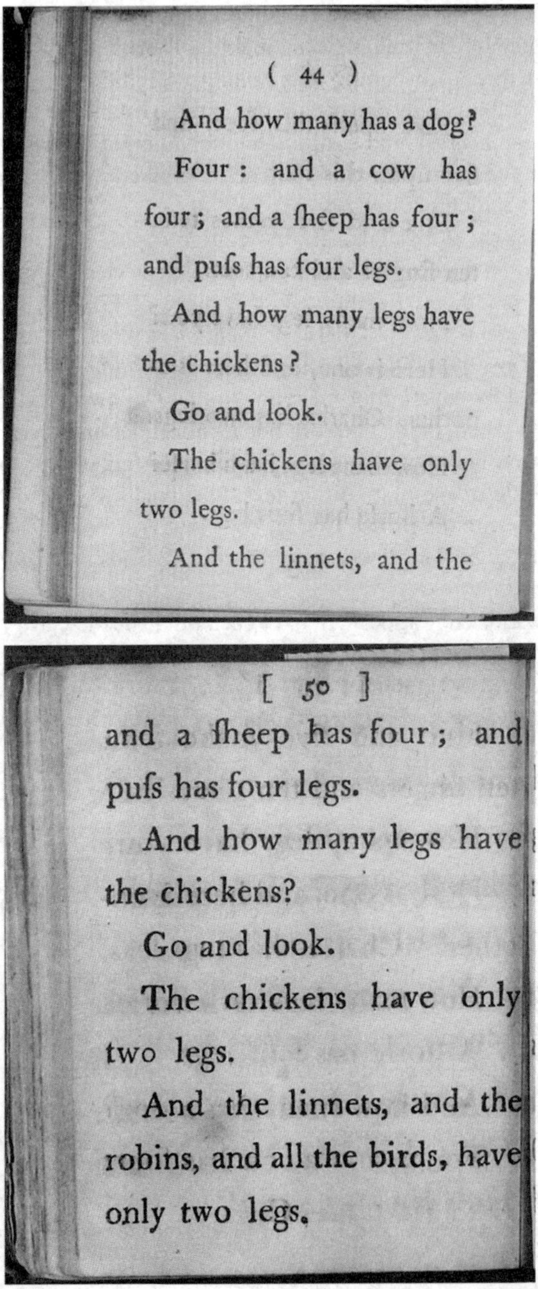

(44)

And how many has a dog?

Four: and a cow has four; and a ſheep has four; and puſs has four legs.

And how many legs have the chickens?

Go and look.

The chickens have only two legs.

And the linnets, and the

[50]

and a ſheep has four; and puſs has four legs.

And how many legs have the chickens?

Go and look.

The chickens have only two legs.

And the linnets, and the robins, and all the birds, have only two legs.

Fig. 1 Pages from *Lessons for Children, of Three Years Old*, London, 1778 (Glasgow RB4587) alongside the corresponding page, London 1812 (private collection).

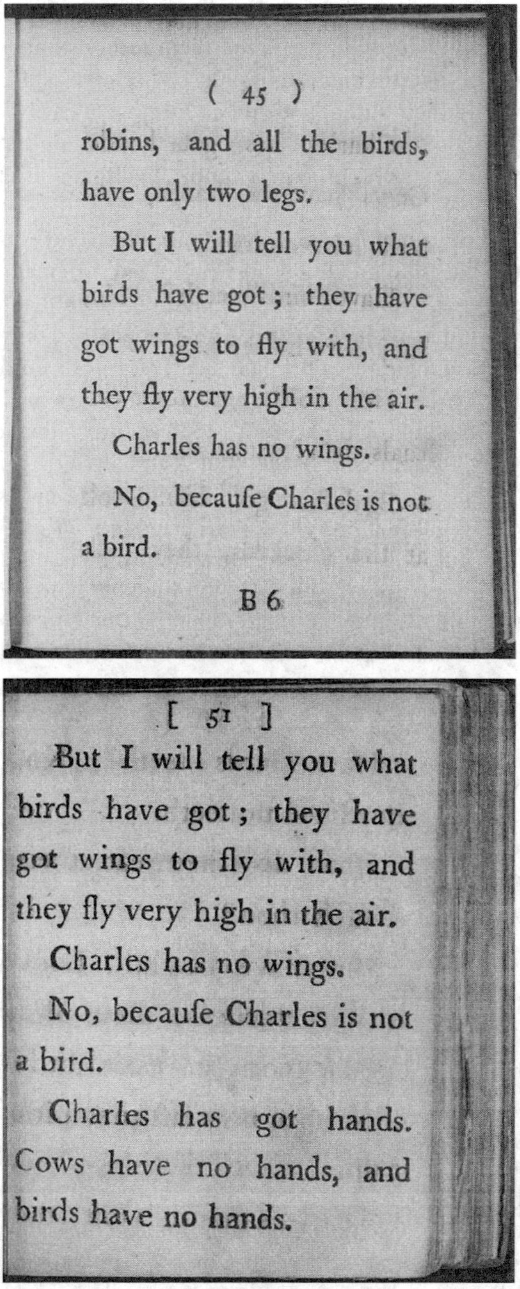

(45)

robins, and all the birds, have only two legs.

But I will tell you what birds have got; they have got wings to fly with, and they fly very high in the air.

Charles has no wings.

No, becaufe Charles is not a bird.

B 6

[51]

But I will tell you what birds have got; they have got wings to fly with, and they fly very high in the air.

Charles has no wings.

No, becaufe Charles is not a bird.

Charles has got hands. Cows have no hands, and birds have no hands.

Fig. 2   Pages from *Lessons for Children, of Three Years Old*, London, 1778 (Glasgow RB4587) alongside the corresponding page, London 1812 (private collection).

that most fully realize Barbauld's demand for 'clear type' and 'large spaces'. They also dutifully preserved their author's anonymity; they bear none of the advertisements for works 'by Mrs. Barbauld' that would have given away their author's identity. Once her identity was known, later printings could advertise, starting with the Rylands copy of *Two to Three*. The market success of *Lessons* contributed to the deterioration in its presswork.

For an 1808 edition of *Lessons* Barbauld introduced new material in all four volumes. Barbauld's additions in *Two to Three*, originally using only 463 distinct words, depart from the principle on which that first volume of *Lessons* was implicitly based: that Charles should read only words that refer to objects and events in his daily life. Just fifteen words in *Two to Three* are longer than two syllables, and they are all familiar words. In their far smaller word total, Barbauld's 1808 additions include fourteen words of more than three syllables, and many of those words denote places and people that 2- to 3-year-old Charles could not have experienced. The revisions in both volumes of *Three Years Old* are less open to this objection; but in *Three to Four*, some are plainly reminiscent of her pieces in *Evenings at Home*, which in 1808 were her most recently published writings for children. Perhaps her pieces in *Evenings* interfered with her memory of what she intended *Lessons* to do; by 1808 she had long been writing for young people instead of small children and that seems to have altered her style.

The three Glasgow first-edition copies supply the copy texts for three of the four volumes in the present edition. For 'Part II' of *Three Years Old*, in the absence of a surviving 1778 first-edition copy, we have chosen as copy text the London edition of 1781. A copy of this rare volume was discovered and purchased by Paula R. Feldman during the preparation of this volume; it is the earliest known surviving edition of this volume published by Joseph Johnson. Even though the extant Dublin edition of 1779 is earlier, we believe that this edition produced by Barbauld's own publisher has more textual authority. However, in a few places where the 1781 edition has pages with tears or excessive trimming, resulting in a loss of text, we have supplied what is missing using the 1779 Dublin edition, which we judge to be close to the first-edition text. To leave the texts of *Lessons* uninterrupted by superscripts, notes appear at the back of the book, cued to original page and line numbers.

We print the 1808 additions separately and cue them to the places in *Lessons* where they appear; we have not aimed to reproduce their lineation, though we do note their pagination. Bear in mind, however, that the 1808 text of *Lessons* was the one that became familiar to later generations—often, however, as the basis for repackaged versions. The compilers of the many volumes, both English and American, that imitated and borrowed from *Lessons* throughout the nineteenth century commingled Barbauld's writing with their own. Hence even her 1808 text did not come down to posterity in the form in which she left it.

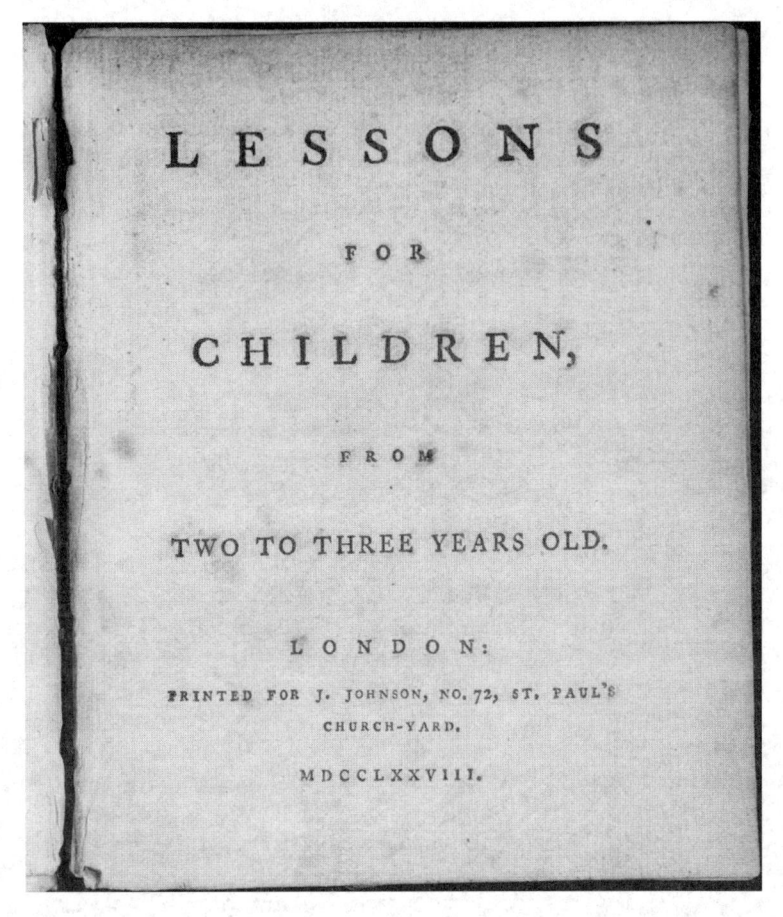

Fig. 3 *Lessons for Children, from Two to Three Years Old.* Title-page, London 1778, first edition (Glasgow University Library).

LESSONS

FOR

CHILDREN,

FROM

TWO TO THREE YEARS OLD

LONDON:
PRINTED FOR J. JOHNSON, NO. 72, ST. PAUL'S
CHURCH-YARD
MDCCLXXVIII

ADVERTISEMENT

This little publication was made for a particular child, but the public is welcome to the use of it. It was found, that amidst the multitude of books professedly written for children, there is not one adapted to the comprehension of a child from two to three years old. A grave remark, or a connected story, however simple, is above his capacity; and nonsense *is always below it; for Folly is worse than Ignorance. Another great defect is, the want of good paper, a clear and large type, and large spaces. They only who have actually taught young children can be sensible how necessary these assistances are. The eye of a child and of a learner cannot catch, as ours can, a small, obscure, ill-formed word, amidst a number of others all equally unknown to him.—To supply these deficiencies is the object of this book. The task is humble, but not mean; for to lay the first stone of a noble building, and to plant the first idea in a human mind, can be no dishonour to any hand.*

LESSONS
FOR CHILDREN,
FROM TWO TO THREE YEARS OLD

Come hither Charles,
 come to mamma.
Make haste.

(6)

Sit in mamma's lap.
Now read your book.
Where is the pin to point with?
Here is a pin.
Do not tear the book.
Only naughty boys tear books.
Charles shall have a pretty new lesson.

(7)

Spell that word. Good boy.
Now go and play.

Where is puss?
Puss is got under the table.
You cannot catch puss.
Do not pull her by the tail, you hurt her.

(8)

Stroke poor puss. You stroke her the wrong way. This is the right way.

But puss, why did you kill the rabbit?

You must catch mice, you must not kill rabbits.

Well, what do you say, did you kill the rabbit?

(9)

Why do you not speak, puss?

Puss cannot speak.

Will Charles feed the chickens?

Here is some corn for the pigeons. O pretty pigeons!

(10)

The sun shines. Open your eyes, little boy. Get up.

Maid, come and dress Charles.

Go down stairs. Get your breakfast.

Boil some milk for a poor little hungry boy.

(11)

Do not spill the milk.
Hold the spoon in the other hand.
Do not throw your bread upon the ground.
Bread is to eat, you must not throw it away.
Corn makes bread.
Corn grows in the fields.

(12)

Grass grows in the fields.
Cows eat grass, and sheep eat grass, and horses eat grass.
Little boys do not eat grass: no, they eat bread, and milk.

(13)

Papa, where is Charles?
Ah! where is the little boy?
Papa cannot find the little boy. Lie still. Do not stir.

Ah! here he is. He is under mamma's apron.
Ride upon papa's cane.

(14)

Here is a whip. Whip away.
Make haste, horse.
Come and give mamma three kisses.
One, two, three.
Little boys must always come when mamma calls them.
Blow your nose.
Here is a handkerchief.

(15)

Come, and let me comb your hair.
Stand still.
Here is the comb-case for you to hold.
Your frock is untied.
Pray clasp my shoe.
Somebody knocks at the door.
Open the door.

(16)

Come in.
Reach a chair.
Sit down.
Come to the fire.
How do you do?
Farewell.
Bring some coals. Make up the fire.
Sweep up the hearth.

(17)

Where is the brush.
Do not stand upon the hearth.
Do not meddle with the ink-horn.
See, you have inked your frock.
Here is a slate for you, and here is a pencil.

(18)

Now sit down on the carpet and write.
What is this red smooth stick?
It is sealing wax.

What is it for?
To seal letters with.
I want papa's watch.
No, you will break the glass.
You broke it once.

(19)
You may look at it.
Put it to your ear.
What does it say?
Tick, tick, tick.

There is a pretty butterfly.
Come shall we catch it?

(20)
Butterfly where are you going?
It is flown over the hedge.
He will not let us catch him.
There is a bee sucking the flowers.
Will the bee sting Charles?
No, it will not sting you if you let it alone.

(21)

Bees make wax and honey.
Honey is sweet.
Charles shall have some honey and bread for supper.
Caterpillars eat cabbages.
Here is a poor little snail crawling up the wall.
Touch him with your little finger.

(22)

Ah, the snail has crept into his shell.
His shell is his house. Good night, snail.
Let him alone, and he will soon come out again.

(23)

I want my dinner, I want pudding.
It is not ready yet.
It will be ready presently,

then Charles shall have his dinner.
Lay the Cloth.

(24)
Where are the knives and forks, and plates.
The clock strikes, take up the dinner.
May I have some meat?
No, meat is not good for little boys.
Here is some apple-dumpling for you, and some pota-

(25)
toes, and some beans, and carrots, and turnips, and rice pudding, and bread.
Here are cherries.
Do not swallow the stone.
I want some wine.
What, wine for little boys!
I never heard of such a

(26)

thing. No, you must not have wine. Here is water.
Do not stand so near the fire. Go on the other side.
Do not tread upon mamma's apron.
Go away now, I am busy.

(27)

Charles, what are eyes for?
To see with.
What are ears for?
To hear with.
What is tongue for?
To talk with.
What are teeth for?

(28)

To eat with.
What is nose for?
To smell with.
What are legs for?

To walk with.
Then do not make mamma carry you. Walk yourself. Here are two good legs.
Will you go abroad?

(29)

Fetch your hat.
Come let us go in the fields, and see the sheep, and the lambs, and the cows, and trees, and birds, and water.
There is a man on horseback.
Where are you going?
He does not mind us, he rides away.

(30)

Now he is a great way off.
Now we cannot see him at all.
There is a dog. The dog barks.
Well, do not be afraid, he will not hurt you.
Come hither, dog.

Let him lick your hand.
Poor Flora!

(31)

Charles is tired, come let us go home.

Ink is black, and papa's shoes are black.
Paper is white, and Charles's frock is white.
Grass is green.

(32)

Sky is blue.
Charles's shoes are red. Pretty red shoes!
Cowslip is yellow.
The table is brown.
White, black, red, green, blue, yellow, brown.

(33)

Pray give me a raisin.
Here is one.

I want another.
Here is another. One, two.
I want a great many, I want ten.
Here are ten. One, two, three,

(34)

four, five, six, seven, eight, nine, ten.
Now what will you do with all these raisins? Give Billy some, and sister Sally.
Good boy.
There is a pin.
Pick it up. Give it mamma.
O do not put it in your

(35)

mouth, that is a very, very naughty trick.
Stick it upon the pincushion.
Fetch the work-basket.
No, do not sit upon it, you will break it, sit upon your own little stool.
Mamma, what are you doing?

(36)

Making frocks for little Charles.

Lay by your work, mamma, and play with me.

It is winter now, cold winter.
There is ice in the pond.
It hails.

(37)

It snows.
Will you run out in the snow?
Go then.
Let us make snow-balls.
Pretty snow, how white it is, and how soft it is!
Bring the snow to the fire.
See, see how it melts. It is

(38)

all gone, there is nothing but water.

Shall we walk.
No, it is too dirty.

When Charles is a big boy, he shall have breeches, and a little pair of boots, and

(39)

then he shall go in the dirt; and he shall have a pretty little horse of his own, and a saddle, and bridle, and a whip, and then he shall ride out with papa.

When spring comes again there will be green leaves,

(40)

and flowers, daisies, and pinks, and violets, and roses, and there will be young lambs, and warm weather. Come again spring!

It rains hard.

See how it rains.

The ducks love rain.

(41)

Ducks swim, and geese swim.
Chickens do not swim.
Can Charles swim?
No.
If Charles goes in the water he will be drowned.
You shall learn to swim when you are as big as Billy.

(42)

Bring the tea-things.
Bring the little boy's milk.
Where is the bread and butter?
Where is the toast and the muffin?
Here is some bread for you.

(43)

Little boys do not eat butter.
Sop the bread in your tea.
The tea is too hot, you must not drink it yet.
You must wait a little.

Pour it into your saucer.
The sugar is not melted.
Who is that lady?
Do not you know?

(44)

Go and give her a kiss.
Pull off your hat.
Nobody wears a hat in the house.
Hats are to go abroad with.
Take me in your lap.
Come then.
Do you love mamma?
Poor mamma!

(45)

Charles has tumbled down.
Get up again then.
Never mind it.
What is the matter with your arm?
Puss has scratched it.
Poor arm, let me kiss it.

(46)

There, now it is well.
Puss did not intend it, she was only at play.
I have hit my head against the table, naughty table!
No, not naughty table, silly boy!
The table did not run a-

(47)

gainst Charles, Charles ran against the table.
The table stood still in its place.

I heard somebody cry just now, I wonder who it was.

(48)

It was some naughty boy, I fancy.
Good boys do not cry.
Little babies cry.

Little babies that cannot talk, nor run about, they can do nothing but cry.

Charles was a little baby once, and lay in a cradle.

(49)

Then I did cry.

Yes, but now you must not cry. Now you are a little boy and ride upon a stick.

See, here is Betty come from the fair.

What has she brought?

She has brought Charles a gun, and a sword, and a

(50)

hammer, and some gingerbread.

She is very good.

Thank you, Betty.

You must wear your sword by your side.

Charge your gun.

Now let it off. Pop!

(51)

Do not eat all the gingerbread now.

It will make you sick.

Give me some to lay by for to-morrow.

I will put it in the cupboard.

Your face is dirty.

Go and get your face washed.

(52)

Get your hands washed.

Now he is a clean boy.

Ah, here is money. What is this?

This is gold. This a guinea.

This white is silver: here is

(53)

a crown, here is a half crown, here is a shilling, here is a six-pence.

We will spin the half crown upon the table.

It is fallen down.
Pick it up.
Here is a half-penny for you.
I want some guineas.

(54)

No, mamma must have the guineas to buy beef and mutton with.

Here is a poor little boy at the door, he has no money at all, nor any thing to eat. Shall we give him a penny?

(55)

Yes.
Go then and give it him.

It is dark.
Bring candles.
Snuff the candles.
Shut the window-shutters.
Do not shut them yet. Look at the moon.

(56)

O bright moon! O pretty moon!

The moon shines at night, when the sun is gone to bed.

Is the sun gone to bed?

Then it is time for little boys to go to bed.

The chickens are gone to

(57)

bed, and the little birds are gone to bed, and the sun is gone to bed, and Charles must go to bed.

Poor little boy is sleepy.

I believe we must carry him up stairs.

Pull off his shoes.

(58)

Pull off his frock and petticoats.

Put on his night cap.

Cover him up.

Lay his little head upon the pillow.
Good night. Shut your eyes. Go to sleep.

THE END

1808 ADDITIONS
Cued by 1778 page numbers

[Between p. 12, 'bread and milk.' and p. 13, 'Papa', 1808 adds:]

(11)

Letters make syllables.
Syllables make words.
Several words make a sentence.
It is a pleasant thing to read well.
When you are older you shall

(12)

learn to write; but you must know how to read first.
Once Papa could not read, nor tell his letters.
Nobody knows any thing when he is just born.
If you learn a little every day, you will soon know a great deal.
Mamma, shall I ever have

(13)

learned all that there is to be learned?
No, never, if you were to live longer than the oldest man, but you may learn something every day.

[At p. 14, between 'Make haste, horse.' and 'Come and give' 1808 adds:]

I want to ride a live horse.

(15)

Saddle the horse for the little boy.
The horse prances, he tosses his head, he pricks up his ears, he starts.
Sit fast; take care he does not throw you; he ambles, he trots, he gallops. The horse stumbles. Down comes poor Charles in the

(16)

dirt.—Hark! the huntsman's horn sounds.
The hounds come by with their long sweeping ears.
The horses are in a foam.
See how they break down the farmers' fences.
Now they leap over the ditch. One, two, three.
They are all gone over.

(17)
They are running after the hare.
Poor little hare, I believe you must be caught.
In Germany they hunt the tusky boar.

Englishmen love roast beef and plum-pudding.

(18)
The Dutchman loves cheese and red herring.
The Frenchman loves soup and salad.
The Italian loves macaroni.
The German loves ham and pompernicle.
Turks sit cross-legged upon carpets.
Negroes are black, their hands

(19)
  are black, and their faces black, and all their bodies.
  It will not wash off; it is the colour of their skin. Negroes
  have flat noses and thick lips, and black hair, curled all over
  like wool.
The Indians, in North America, have copper-coloured skins.
Greenlanders drink train oil.

(20)
Russians travel in sledges over the ice.
Fire and smoke come out of Mount Vesuvius.
Dutchmen travel in boats upon canals.

[At p. 19, between 'Tick, tick, tick.' and 'There is a' 1808 adds:]

(25)
Squirrels crack nuts.
Monkeys are very comical.

(26)
You are very comical sometimes.
Kittens are playful.
Old cats do not play.
Mice nibble cheese.
There is an old rat in the trap.
He has fine whiskers, and a long tail.
He will bite hard, he will bite through wood.

(27)

Owls eat mice. Owls live in barns and hollow trees.
'Then nightly sings the staring owl, to whit, to whoo.'
Frogs live in marshes.
Do not kill that toad, it will not hurt you.
    See what a fine eye he has.

(28)

The snake has a new skin every year.
The snake lays eggs.
The snake will do you no harm.
The viper is poisonous.
An old fox is very cunning.
The lamb is gentle.
The ass is patient.
The deer are feeding in the park.

(29)

The flesh of cows makes beef.
The flesh of sheep makes mutton.
The flesh of calves makes veal.
The flesh of hogs makes pork.
The flesh of deer makes venison.
Rams have large twisted horns.
Bulls have short curled horns.
Stags have branching horns.

(30)

The chamois has spiral horns, like a cork-screw.
Is there not the horned owl?
Yes, it is called so, but he has not horns; he has only feathers that stand upright.

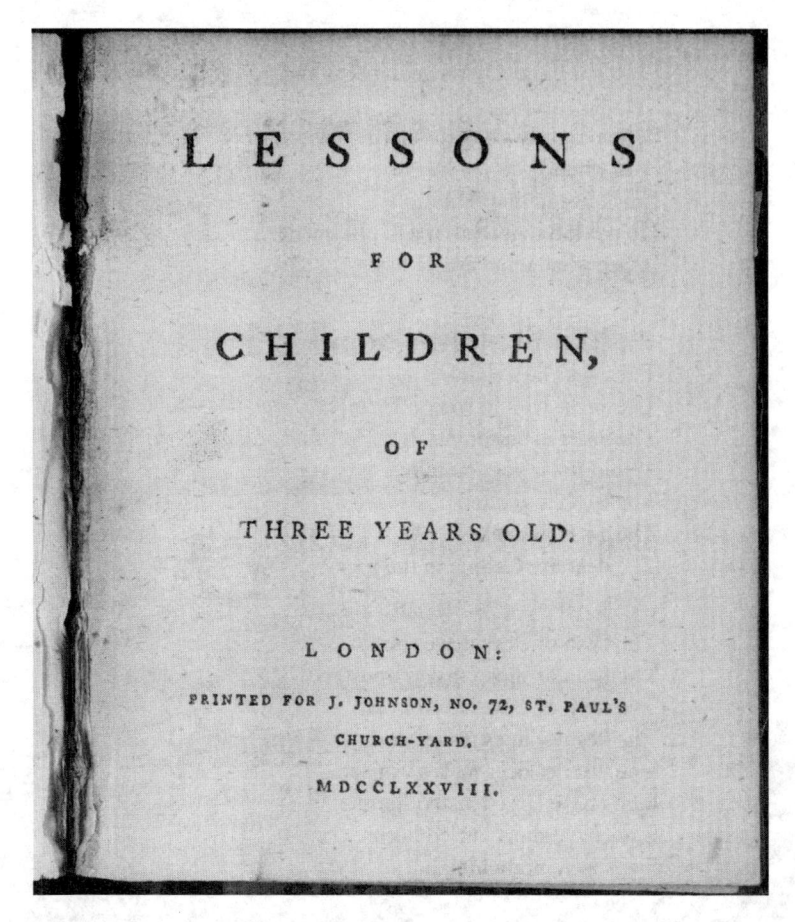

Fig. 4 *Lessons for Children, of Three Years Old*. Title-page, London 1778, first edition (Glasgow University Library).

LESSONS

FOR

CHILDREN,

OF

THREE YEARS OLD

LONDON:
PRINTED FOR J. JOHNSON, NO. 72, ST. PAUL'S
CHURCH-YARD
MDCCLXXVIII

LESSONS
FOR CHILDREN
OF THREE YEARS OLD

Good morrow, little boy! how do you do? Bring your little stool, and sit down by me, for I have

(4)

a great deal to tell you. I hope you have been a good boy, and read all the pretty words I wrote for you before. You have, you say; You have read them till you are tired, and you want some more new lessons. Come

(5)

then, sit down. Now you and I will tell stories.

What is to day, Charles?
To day is Sunday.
And what is to morrow?

To morrow will be Monday.

(6)

And what will the next day be?

The next day will be Tuesday.

And the next day?

Wednesday.

And the next?

Thursday.

And the next?

Friday.

(7)

And the next?

Saturday.

And what will come after Saturday?

Why then, Sunday will come again.

Sunday, Monday, Tuesday, Wednesday, Thursday, Friday, Saturday. That makes

(8)

seven days, and seven days make

A week.

And do you know how much four weeks make?

How much?

A month. And twelve months make a year—January, February, March, April, May, June, July, August,

(9)

September, October, November, December.

It is January. It is very cold. It snows. It freezes. There are no leaves upon the trees. The oil is frozen, and the milk is frozen, and the

(10)

river is frozen, and every thing.

All the boys are sliding. You must learn to slide. There is a man skaiting. How fast he goes! You shall have a pair of skates. Take care! there is a hole in the ice. Come in. It is four o'clock. It is dark. Light the can-

(11)

dles; and Ralph! get some wood from the wood-house, and get some coals, and make a very good fire.

February is very cold too, but the days are longer, and there is a yellow crocus com-

(12)

ing up, and the mezereon tree is in blossom, and there are some white snow-drops peeping up their little heads. Pretty white snow-drop, with a green stalk! May I gather it? Yes, you may, but you must always ask leave before you gather a flower. What a noise the rooks make!

(13)

Caw, caw, caw; and how busy they are! They are going to build their nests. There is a man plowing the field.

It is March. Now the wind blows! It will blow

(14)

such a little fellow as you away, almost. There is a tree blown down.

Here are some young lambs. Poor things! how they creep under the hedge. What is this flower? A primrose.

(15)

April is come, and the birds sing, and the trees are in blossom, and flowers are coming out, and butterflies, and the sun shines. Now it rains. It rains and the sun shines. There is a rain-

(16)

bow. O what fine colours! Pretty bright rain-bow! No, you cannot catch it, it is in the sky. It is going away. It fades. It is quite gone. I hear the cuckow. He says, cuckow! cuckow! He is come to tell us it is spring.

(17)

It is May. O pleasant May! Let us walk out in the fields. The hawthorn is in blossom. Let us go and get some out of the hedges. And here are daisies, and cowslips, and crow-flowers. We will make a nosegay.

(18)

Here is a bit of thread to tie it with. Smell! It is very sweet. What has Billy got? He has got a nest of young birds. He has been climbing a high tree for them. Poor little birds! they have no feathers. Keep them warm. You must feed them with a quill. You must give

(19)

them bread and milk. They are young goldfinches. They will be very pretty, when they have got their red head and yellow wings. Do not let them die. The little birds' papa and mamma will be very sorry if they come to die. O do not eat green

(20)

goose-berries! they will make you ill.

June is come. Get up! you must not lie so long in bed now; you must get up, and walk before breakfast. What noise is that? It is the mower whetting his

(21)

scythe. He is going to cut down the grass. And will he cut down all the flowers too? Yes, every thing. The scythe is very sharp. Do not come near it; you will have your legs cut off. Now we must make hay. Where is your fork, and rake? Spread the hay. Now make

(22)

it up in cocks. Now tumble on the hay cock. There! cover him up with hay. How sweet the hay smells! O, it is very hot! No matter; you must make hay while the sun shines. You must work well. See, all the lads and lasses are at work. They must have some beer,

(23)

and bread, and cheese. Now put the hay in the cart. Will you ride in the cart? Huzza! Hay is for papa's horse to eat in winter, when there is no grass.

Do you love strawberries and cream? Let us go then,

and gather some strawberries. They are ripe now. Here

(24)

is a very large one. It is almost too big to go into your mouth. Get me a bunch of currants. Strip them from the stalk. The birds have pecked all the cherries. Where is Charles? He is sitting under a rose-bush.

(25)

July is very hot indeed, and the grass and flowers are all burnt, for it has not rained a great while. You must water your garden, else the plants will die. Where is the watering-pot? Let us go under the trees. It is

(26)

shady there, it is not so hot. Come into the arbour. There is a bee upon the honeysuckle. He is getting honey. He will carry it to the hive. Will you go and bathe in the water? Here is water. It is not deep. Pull off your cloaths. Jump in. Do not be afraid. Pop your head

(27)

in. Now you have been long enough. Come out, and let me dry you with this towel.

It is August. Let us go into the corn fields to see if the corn is almost ripe. Yes, it is quite brown: it is ripe.

(28)

Farmer Diggory! you must bring a sharp sickle and cut

down the corn: it is ripe. Eat some, Charles; rub it in your hands. This is a grain of corn; this is an ear of corn; this stalk makes straw. Now it must be tied up in sheaves. Now put a great many sheaves together,

(29)

and make a shock. Put it in the cart, farmer Diggory! carry it to your barn to make bread. Sing harvest home! harvest home! There is a poor old woman, picking up some ears of corn; and a poor little girl that has no cloaths, hardly. They are gleaning. Give them your

(30)

handful, Charles. Take it, poor woman! it will help to make you a loaf. Poor woman! she is very old; she cannot run; she is sadly tired with stooping.

It is September. Hark! somebody is letting off a gun.

(31)
They are shooting the poor birds. Here is a bird dropped down just at your feet. It is all bloody. Poor thing! how it flutters. Its wing is broke. It cannot fly any further. It is going to die. What bird is it? It is a partridge. Are you not sorry, Charles! it was alive a little while ago.

(32)
Bring the ladder, and set it against the tree. Now bring a basket. We must gather apples. No, you cannot go up the ladder; you must have a little basket, and pick up apples under the

tree. Shake the tree. Down they come. How many have you got? We will have an

(33)

apple dumpling. Come, you must help to carry the apples into the apple chamber. Apples make cyder. You shall have some baked pears and bread for supper. Are these apples? No, they are quinces, they will make marmalade.

(34)

October is come, Charles; and the leaves are falling off the trees; and the flowers are all gone. No, here is an African marygold, and a China-aster, and a Michaelmas daisy. Will you have any nuts? Fetch the nut-

(35)

crackers. Peel this walnut. I will make you a little boat of the walnut shell. We must get the grapes, or else the birds will eat them all. Here is a bunch of black grapes. Here is a bunch of white ones. Which will you have? Grapes make wine.

(36)

What bird have you got there? It is dead, but it is very pretty. It has a scarlet eye, and red, and green and purple feathers. It is very large. It is a pheasant. He is very good to eat. We will pull off his feathers and tell Betty Cook to roast him. Here is a hare too. Poor

(37)

puss! The hounds did catch her.

Dark dismal November is come. No more flowers! no more pleasant sunshine! no more hay-making! The sky is very black; the rain

(38)

pours down. Well, never mind it. We will sit by the fire, and read, and tell stories, and look at pictures. Where is Billy, and Harry, and little Betsy? Now tell me who can spell best. Good boy! There is a clever fellow! Now you shall all have some cake.

(39)

It is December, and Christmas is coming, and Betty is very busy. What is she doing? She is paring apples, and chopping meat, and beating spice. What for, I wonder! It is to

(40)

make mince-pies. Do you love mince-pies? O they are very good! Little boys come from school at Christmas. Pray wrap them up warm, for it is very very cold. Well, Spring will come again sometime.

(41)

How many fingers have you got, little boy?

Here are four fingers on this hand; and what is this? Thumb. Four fingers and thumb, that makes five.

(42)

And how many on the other hand?

There are five too.

What hand is this?

This is the right hand.

And this? This is the left hand.

And how many toes have you got? Let us count.

(43)

Five upon this foot, and five upon this foot.

Five and five makes ten: ten fingers and ten toes.

How many legs have you?

Here is one, and here is another. Charles has two legs.

How many legs has a horse?

A horse has four legs.

(44)

And how many has a dog?

Four: and a cow has four; and a sheep has four; and puss has four legs.

And how many legs have the chickens?

Go and look.

The chickens have only two legs.

And the linnets, and the

(45)

robins, and all the birds, have only two legs.

But I will tell you what birds have got; they have got wings to fly with, and they fly very high in the air.

Charles has no wings.

No, because Charles is not a bird.

(46)

Charles has got hands. Cows have no hands, and birds have no hands.

Have birds teeth? No, they have no teeth.

How do they eat their victuals then?

Birds have got a bill. Look at the chickens, they pick

(47)

up the corn in their little bills. See how fast they pick it up.

Charles's mouth is soft; the chicken's bill is hard like bone.

How many legs have fishes?

(48)

Fishes have no legs at all.

How do they walk then?

They do not walk; they swim about in the water; they live always in the water.

Charles could not live under the water.

No, because Charles is not a fish.

Here is a fish that some-

(49)

body has caught. Poor little fish! throw it on the grass.

See how it flounces about! It has a hook in its gills. Take it by the tail. It is slippery, you cannot hold it. See, these are fins. It has got fins to swim with; and it has got scales, and sharp

(50)

teeth. It will be dead soon. It is going to die. It cannot stir any more. Now it is quite dead. The fish dies because it is out of the water, and Charles would die if he was in the water.

(51)

What has Charles got to keep him warm?

Charles has got a frock and warm petticoats.

And what have the poor sheep got; have they petticoats?

The sheep have got wool,

(52)

thick warm wool. Feel it. O, it is very comfortable! That is their petticoat.

And what have horses got?

Horses have got long hair; and cows have hair.

And what have birds got?

Birds have got feathers; soft, clean, shining feathers.

(53)

Birds build nests in trees; That is their house.

The wolf has a den; that is his house.

The dog has a kennel.

The bees live in a hive.

The pigs live in a stye.

Can you climb a tree?

No.

But you must learn then.

(54)

As soon as you have breeches you must learn to climb

trees.

Ask puss to teach you; she can climb. See, how fast she climbs! She is at the top. She wants to catch birds. Pray puss do not take the little birds that sing so merrily! She has got a spar-

(55)

row in her mouth. She has eat it all up. No, here are two or three feathers on the ground all bloody. Poor sparrow!

The dog barks. The hog grunts. The pig squeaks. The horse neighs. The cock

(56)

crows. The ass brays. The cat purrs. The kitten mews. The bull bellows. The cow lows. The calf bleats. Sheep bleat. The lion roars. The wolf howls. The tyger growls. The fox barks. Mice squeak. The frog croaks. The sparrow chirps. The swallow twitters. The rook caws.

(57)

The bittern booms. The pigeon cooes. The turkey gobbles. The peacock screams. The beetle hums. The grasshopper chirps. The duck quacks. The goose cackles. Monkeys chatter. The owl hoots. The screech-owl shrieks. The snake hisses. Charles talks.

(58)

Kites and hawks eat chickens.

Spiders make cobwebs; they catch flies in them and eat them up.

Owls fly in the night.

Butchers kill sheep.

(59)

The carpenter makes tables and boxes.

You shall have a box, with a lock and a key to it.

The carpenter has a saw, and a chisel, and a plane, and an adze, and a gimblet, and a turn-screw, and a hatchet, and a file, and a vice,

(60)

and pincers, and a hammer, and nails, and a mallet.

Charles's wooden horse is broke.

Well, take it to the carpenter's; let him mend it.

Charles has fallen down and broke his head.

Shall I take it to the carpenter's?

(61)

No, silly boy! Carpenters do not mend heads.

Shoe-makers make shoes.

Old people wear spectacles.

Good boys love to read.

The barber shaves.

Come papa! sit down; you must have your beard shaved.

Here is the soap, and the bason, and the razor.

Barber, do not cut papa.

Shall we go into the garden, and see the flowers, and the apple trees, and run about in the gravel walk?

Where is your roller? Come, roll the walk.

Work well, and perhaps I may give you a halfpenny a day. Every body works, but little babies; they cannot work.

If you are a good boy, you

(64)

shall have a little garden of your own, and a spade to dig with, and a hoe, and a rake, and a little wheelbarrow; and pray do not let me see any weeds in your garden; pull them all up. And you must make a little hedge about it, else the pigs will get in and spoil it. And

(65)

you must go to the gardener, and say, pray give me some seeds; and you must sow them. You must make a little hole in the ground, and put them in, and cover them up with mould, and they will grow. Here is some cress and mustard seed. Sow it, and we will have a sallad.

(66)

Water your garden. Charles, look at this gooseberry bush; it was but so high when we put it in the ground, and now it is a great deal taller; it is so high.

The gooseberry bush grows.

Does Charles grow?

Yes; Charles could not reach the table once, and

(67)

now he can reach higher a great deal.

Is the table taller than it was a great while ago?

No; the table does not grow.

Why does not the table grow, Charles?

(68)

Here is a lady-bird upon a leaf. It is red and has

black spots. Ah! it has wings. It is flown away. There is a black beetle. Catch it. How fast it runs! Where is it gone? Into the ground. It makes a little

(69)

hole and runs into the ground. Worms live in the ground.

It is cold, Charles, very cold! Pray what do they call it when it is so cold? They call it winter, you

(70)

know. I wonder what poor little boys do, that have no fire to go to, and no shoes and stockings to keep them warm, and no good papas and mammas to take care of them and give them victuals. Poor little boys! Do not cry, Charles, for here is a halfpenny, and when you see one of those poor little boys you shall give it him: he will go and buy a roll with it, for he is very hungry; and he will say, Thank you Charles, you are very good to me!

I will tell you what, Charles; it will be a great deal colder soon, and snow will come down. Then the pretty little robins will come and fly against the windows. Open the window. Well, what do you want, little robin? Only a few crumbs of bread. Give him some crumbs and he

(73)

will hop, hop, about the parlour, and sit upon the top of the screen, and sing— O he will sing all day long! Now pray do not let that wicked cat take him. No, puss! you must go and catch mice, you shall not eat poor robin. There was a cruel

(74)

naughty boy once—I will tell you a story about him.

There was a naughty boy; I do not know what his name was, but it was not Charles, nor George, nor Arthur, for those are all very pretty names: but there

(75)

was a robin came in at his window one very cold morning—shiver—shiver, and its poor little heart was almost frozen to death. And he would not give it the least little crumb of bread in the world, but pulled it about by the tail, and hurt it sadly, and

(76)

it died. Now a little while after the naughty boy's papa and mamma went away and left him; and then he could get no victuals at all, for you know he could not take care of himself. So he went about to every body—Pray give me something to eat, I am very hungry. And

(77)

every body said, No, we shall give you none, for we do not love cruel naughty boys. So he went about from one place to another, till at last he got into a thick wood of trees, for he did not know how to find his way any where; and then it grew dark, quite dark night.

(78)

So he sat down and cried sadly; and he could not get out of the wood; and I believe the bears came and eat him up in the wood, for I never heard any thing about him afterwards.

I will tell you another story.

(79)

There was a little boy; he was not a big boy, for if he had been a big boy I suppose he would have been wiser; but this was a little boy, not higher than the table, and his papa and mamma sent him to school.

(80)

It was a very pleasant morning; the sun shone, and the birds sung in the trees. Now this little boy did not much love his book, for he was but a silly little boy as I told you; and he had a great mind to play instead of going to school. And he saw a bee flying about, first upon

(81)

one flower and then upon another; so he said, Pretty bee! will you come and play with me? But the bee said, No, I must not be idle, I must go and gather honey. Then the little boy met a dog, and he said, Dog! will you play with me? But

(82)

the dog said, No, I must not be idle, I am going to catch a hare for my master's dinner, I must make haste and catch it. Then the little boy went by a hay-rick, and he saw a bird pulling some hay out of the hay-rick, and he said, Bird! will you come and play with me? But the bird

(83)

said, No, I must not be idle, I must get some hay to build my nest with, and some moss, and some wool. So the bird flew away. Then the little boy saw a horse, and he said, Horse! will you play with me? But the horse said, No, I must not

(84)

be idle, I must go and plough, or else there will be no corn to make bread of. Then the little boy thought with himself, what, is no body idle? then little boys must not be idle neither. So he made haste, and went to school, and learned his lesson very

(85)

well, and the master said he was a very good boy.

Farewel, Charles! good night.

THE END

1808 ADDITIONS
Cued by 1778 page numbers

[At p. 5, between 'tell stories.' and, 'What is to day?' 1808 adds:]

(4)

Look at puss! she pricks up her ears, and smells about.

(5)

She smells the mice. They are making a noise behind the wainscot. Puss wants to get into the closet. Let her in. The mice have been in the closet, and nibbled the biscuits. Ah! there is a mouse puts her tail through the hole of the wainscot. Take care, little mouse, puss will catch

(6)

you. Look, look, there she runs! See, puss springs upon her! puss has got the mouse; puss has given her a squeeze. She lets her run about a little. The poor mouse thinks to steal away by the side of the wainscot. Now puss springs again, and lays her paw upon her. I wish, puss, you would

(7)

not be so cruel. I wish you would eat her up at once.—It is cold night; it freezes. Let us catch puss. Come into this dark corner. Now rub her back while I hold her; rub hard. Stroke her fur the wrong way. Hark! it crackles; sparks come out. The cat's back is on fire.

(8)

This fire will not hurt her, nor you either. Now we will let her go; she begins to be angry.

Here is a piece of something you never saw before. What is it? It is amber; yellow transparent amber. Now rub it well in your hand, and I will show you

(9)

something. Have you rubbed it till it is warm? Now lay it upon the table. Put these straws near it. Move the amber gently. Hah! the amber draws the straws to it. Lift it up. The straws stick to the amber. What makes them do so?

[Between p. 40, 'some time.' and p. 41, 'How many', 1808 adds:]

(42)

Your papa's wife is your mother.
Your mamma's husband is your father.

(43)

Your papa's father is your grandfather.
Your papa's mother is your grandmother.
Your mamma's father and mother are your grandfather and grandmother.
Your papa's brother is your uncle.

(44)

Your papa's sister is your aunt.
Your mamma's brother and sister are your uncle and aunt.
You are your uncle's nephew.
Lucy is her uncle's niece.
Your papa's and mamma's child is your brother or sister.

(45)

Your uncle and aunt's child is your cousin.
Bring grandpapa his stick to walk with.
Set the arm-chair by the fire for grandmamma.
Your aunt knit these stockings for you.
Ask papa to play at hide and seek with you.

(46)

Hide yourself under mama's apron.
When your uncle comes you shall take a ride upon his horse.
Divide your cake with your brothers and sisters.
We will send for your cousins to play with you, and

(47)

then we shall have all the family together.

[Between p. 57, 'Charles talks.' and p. 58, 'Kites', 1808 adds:]

(63)

What is that spot of green light under the hedge? See, there is another, and another! Ah they move! how fast they run about! Is it fire? it is like wild fire; they are like little stars upon the ground.
Take one of them in your hand, it will not burn you.

(64)

How it moves about in my hand! my hand has fire in it. What is it?

Bring it into the house; bring it to the candle.

Ah, it is a little worm; it hardly shines at all, now.

It is called a glow-worm.

(65)

Do not you know the song of the fairies.

And when the sun does hide his head,
The glow-worm lights us home to bed.

In some countries there are insects which fly about in the Summer evenings, and give a great deal more light than the glow-worm:

you may see to read by two or three of them

(66)

together. They are called fire-flies.

A fine large moth has flown into the room.

He flutters about the candle; the light attracts him.

Pray do not burn yourself, pretty moth!

(67)

Put him away with your hand.

He will come again; I cannot hinder him.

He has scorched his long, slender feelers, and his silvery wings.

Why will you burn yourself, poor moth?

(68)

He will not be wise; he flies quite into the candle.

He is burnt to death.

The silly moth did not know what would hurt him.

No more do some little boys.

[Between p. 67, 'grow, Charles?' and p. 68, 'Here is a', 1808 adds:]

(78)

See, I have brought you something very pretty: look at this large round glass which is filled with water.

Ha! here are fish in it; beautiful, shining fish, with white, and crimson, and purple, and gold-coloured scales.

They are gold and silver fish.

(79)

How they swim about! how large they look when they are at the other end of the glass! See! see, now this fish looks as big again as it did just now.

That is because you see it through the water.

Are these fish found in the rivers?

They are not found in our

(80)

rivers; the gold and silver fish come from a great way off; they come from China.

Will they live in this glass?

Yes; and they will live almost without eating any thing at all. Sometimes they eat a little bread, but the water is nourishment enough for them for a long while.

(81)

They are very tender, and easily killed. Sometimes a hail-storm or a thunder cloud going over them will kill them in their own country.

Now set them in the window, in the warm sun.

Fig. 5 *Lessons for Children, of Three Years Old.* Title-page, Part II, London 1781, presumed second edition (private collection).

LESSONS

FOR

CHILDREN,

OF

THREE YEARS OLD

PART II

LONDON:
PRINTED FOR J. JOHNSON, NO. 72, ST. PAUL'S
CHURCH-YARD, 1781

[PRICE SIX-PENCE]

LESSONS
FOR CHILDREN,
OF THREE YEARS OLD

Charles, what a clever thing it is to read! A little while ago, you know, you could only read little words; and you were forced

(4)

to spell them—c–a–t, cat; d–o–g, dog. Now you can read pretty stories, and I am going to write you some.

Do you know why you are better than Puss? Puss can play as well as you; and Puss can drink milk, and lie upon the carpet; and she

(5)

can run as fast as you, and faster too, a great deal; and she can climb trees better;

and she can catch mice, which you cannot do. But can Puss talk? No. Can Puss read? No. Then that is the reason why you are better than Puss—because

(6)

you can talk and read. Can Pierrot, your dog, read? No. Will you teach him? Take the pin and point to the words. No—he will not learn. I never saw a little dog or cat learn to read. But little boys can learn. If you do not learn, Charles,

(7)

you are not good for half as much as a Puss. You had better be drowned.

What a clock is it, Charles? It is twelve o'clock.

It is noon. Come in the garden then. Now where is

(8)

the sun? Turn your face towards him. Look at the sun. That is South; always when it is twelve o'clock, and you look at the sun, your face is towards the South. Now turn to your left hand. Look forwards. That is East. In the morning, when

(9)

it is going to be light, you must look just there, and presently you will see the sun get up. Always in the morning look there for the sun; for the sun rises in the East. Now turn your back to the sun. Look straight forwards. That is North.

(10)

Now turn to your left hand. Look forwards. That is West. When you have had your supper, and it is going to be night, look for the sun just there. He is always there when he goes to bed; for the sun sets in the West. North, South, East, West.

(11)

The wind blows. Which way does the wind blow? Take out your handkerchief. Throw it up. The wind blows it this way. The wind comes from the north. The wind is north. It is a

(12)

cold wind. The wind was West yesterday, then it was warm.

Rain comes from the clouds. Look, there are black clouds. How fast they move along! Now they

(13)

have hid the sun. They have covered up the sun, just as you cover up your face when you throw a handkerchief over it. There is a little bit of blue sky still. Now there is no blue sky at all: it is all black with the clouds. It is very dark,

(14)

like night. It will rain soon. Now it begins. What large drops! The ducks are very glad, but the little birds are not glad; they go and shelter themselves under the trees. Now the rain is over. It was only a shower. Now the flowers smell sweet, and

(15)

the sun shines, and the little birds sing again, and it is not so hot as it was before it rained.

We will drink tea out of doors. Bring the tea-things. Come, fetch your hat. It

(16)

is very pleasant. But here is no table. What must we do? O, here is a large round stump of a tree, it will do very well for a table. But we have no chairs. Here is a seat of turf, and a bank almost covered with violets; we shall sit here, and you

(17)

and Billy may lie on the carpet. The carpet is in the parlour. Yes, there is a carpet in the parlour, but there is a carpet here too. What is it? The grass is the carpet out of doors. Pretty green soft carpet! and it is very large, for it

(18)

spreads every where, over all the fields, and over all the meadows: and it is very pleasant for the sheep and the lambs to lie down upon. I do not know what they would do without it, for they have no feather-bed to sleep upon.

(19)

It is a pleasant evening. Come hither, Charles, look

at the sun. The sun is in the West. Yes, because he is going to set. How pretty the sun looks! We can look at him now; he is not

(20)

so bright as he was at dinner-time, when he was up high in the sky. And how beautiful the clouds are! There are crimson clouds, and purple and gold-coloured clouds. Now the sun is going down a great pace. Now we can see only half

(21)

of him. Now we cannot see him at all. Farewel, sun! till to-morrow morning.

But now, Charles, turn your face the other way, to the East. What is it that shines so behind the trees? Is it a fire? No, it is the moon. It is very

(22)

large; and how red it is! like blood. The moon is round now, because it is full moon; but it will not be so round to-morrow night; it will lose a little bit: and the next night it will lose a little bit more; and more the next night; and so on,

(23)

till it is like your bow when it is bent: and it will not be seen till after you are in bed: and it will grow less and less, till in a fortnight there will be no moon at all. Then, after that, there will be a new moon; and you will see it in the afternoon; and

(24)

it will be very thin at first, but it will grow rounder and bigger every day, till at last, in another fortnight, it will be a full moon again like this, and you will see it rise again behind the trees.

(25)

Do you know what raisins are? They are grapes dried a great deal. Grapes, you know, grow upon vines; but raisins are made of larger grapes than those upon the vine in the garden: they

(26)

come from a great way off. Do you know what sugar comes from? Sugar comes from a cane like a walking stick, that grows in the ground; they squeeze the juice out, and boil it a great deal, and that makes sugar. And what is tea? Tea is a

(27)

leaf that grows upon a shrub, and that is dried a great deal.

Charles wants some bread and butter—But the bread is not baked. Then bid Christopher Clump heat his oven and bake it—But the

(28)

loaf is not kneaded. Then bid little Margery take the dough and knead it—But the flour is not ground. Then take it to the mill, and bid Roger the miller grind it—But the corn is not threshed. Then bid John Dobbins take his flail and thresh it—

(29)

But the corn is not reaped. Then bid Dick Clodpole take his sickle and cut it—But the wheat is not sown. Then bid Farmer Diggory take the seed and sow it—But the field is not plowed. Then bid Ralph Wiseacre take the horses and plow

(30)

it—But the plough is not made. Then go to Humphrey Hiccory the carpenter, and bid him make one—But there is never a plough-share. Then bid Firebrass the smith go to his anvil and beat one. —But we have no butter. Then go to market, Susan,

(31)

and buy some. But the butter is not churned. Then

take your churn, Dolly, and churn some—But the cow is not milked. Then take your pail, Cicely, and milk it—Now, Betty, pray spread Charles a slice of bread and butter:

(32)

Charles, do not you remember the caterpillar we put into a paper box, with some mulberry leaves for it to eat? Let us go and look at it. It is gone—here is no caterpillar—there is some-

(33)

thing in the box; what is it? I do not know. It is a little ball of yellow stuff. Let us cut it open, perhaps we may find the caterpillar. No, here is nothing but a strange little grub, and it is dead, I believe, for it does not move. Pinch it gently

(34)

by the tail. Now it stirs: it is not dead quite. Charles, this grub is your caterpillar; it is indeed. That yellow stuff is silk. The caterpillar spun all that silk, and covered itself up with it; and then it was turned into this grub. Take it, and lay it in the

(35)

sun; We will come and look at it again to-morrow morning—Well, this is very surprising! here is no grub at all to be found. Did not we put it on this sheet of paper last night? Yes we did. And no body has been in the room to meddle with it?

(36)

No, no body at all has been in the room. Is there nothing upon the sheet of paper? Yes, here is a white butterfly. I wonder how it came here; for the windows are shut. Perhaps the grub is turned into a butterfly. It is, indeed; and look, here

(37)

is the empty shell of the grub. Here is where the butterfly came out. But the butterfly is too big; this shell could not hold him. Yes, it did, because his wings were folded up, and he lay very snug. It is the same, I assure you, Charles;

(38)

all the pretty butterflies that you see flying about were

caterpillars once, and crawled on the ground.

Charles, you must not go out into the fields by yourself, nor without leave.

(39)
You are a very little boy, you know; and if you were to venture out by yourself you would be lost; then you would cry, and night would come, and it would be dark, and you could not find your way home, and you would have no bed; you would be

(40)
forced to lie down in the fields upon the wet cold grass, and perhaps you would die, and that would be a sad tale to tell.

I will tell you a story about a lamb. There was once a Shepherd, who had a great many sheep and lambs.

(41)

He took a great deal of care of them, and gave them sweet fresh grass to eat, and clear water to drink; and if they were sick he was very good to them; and when they climbed up a steep hill, and the lambs were tired, he used to carry them in his

(42)

arms; and when they were all eating their suppers in the field, he used to sit upon a stile, and play them a tune, and sing to them; and so they were the happiest sheep and lambs in the whole world. But every night this Shepherd used to pen them up

(43)

in a fold. Do you know what a sheep-fold is? Well, I will tell you. It is a place like the court; but instead of pales there are hurdles, which are made of sticks that will bend, such as osier twigs; and they are twisted and made very fast, so that no-

(44)

thing can creep in, and nothing can get out. Well, and so every night when it grew dark and cold, the Shepherd called all his flock, sheep and lambs, together, and drove them into the fold, and penned them up, and there they lay as snug and

(45)

warm and comfortable as could be, and nothing could

get in to hurt them, and the dogs lay round on the outside to guard them, and to bark if any body came near; and in the morning the Shepherd unpenned the fold, and let them all out again.

(46)

Now they were all very happy as I told you, and loved the Shepherd dearly, that was so good to them—all except one foolish little lamb. And this lamb did not like to be shut up every night in the fold; and she came to her mother, who

(47)

was a wise old sheep, and said to her, I wonder why we are shut up so every night! the dogs are not shut up, and why should we be shut up? I think it is very hard, and I will get away if I can, I am resolved, for I like to run about where I please,

(48)

and I think it is very pleasant in the woods by moonlight—Then the old sheep said to her, you are very silly, you little lamb, you had better stay in the fold. The Shepherd is so good to us, that we should always do as he bids us; and if you wander

(49)

about by yourself, I dare say you will come to some harm. I dare say not, said the little lamb: and so when the evening came, and the shepherd called them all to come into the fold, she would not come, but crept slily under a hedge and hid herself; and when

(50)

the rest of the lambs were all in the fold and fast asleep, she came out, and jumped, and frisked, and danced about; and she got out of the field, and got into a forest full of trees, and a very fierce wolf came rushing out of a cave and howled very

(51)

loud. Then the silly lamb wished she had been shut up in the fold; but the fold was a great way off—and the wolf saw her, and seized her, and carried her away to a dismal dark den, all covered with bones and blood; and there the wolf had two

(52)

cubs and the wolf said to them, Here, I have brought you a young fat lamb—and so the cubs took her, and growled over her a little while, and then tore her to pieces, and eat her up.

(53)
───

Gold is of a deep yellow colour. It is very pretty and bright. It is exceeding heavy; heavier than any thing else. Men dig it out of the ground. Shall I take my spade and get some? No,

(54)

there is none in the fields hereabouts: It comes from a great way off; and it lies deeper a great deal than you could dig with your spade. Guineas are made of gold; and half guineas. This watch is gold; and the looking glass frame, and the picture

(55)

frames are gilt with gold. Here is some leaf gold. What is leaf gold? It is gold beat very thin; thinner than leaves or paper.

Silver is white and shining. The spoons are silver; and the waiter is silver; and crowns, and half crowns,

(56)

and shillings, and sixpences are made of silver. Silver comes from a great way off too.

Copper is red. The kettles and pots are made of copper; and brass is made of copper. Brass is bright and yellow like gold almost.

(57)

This sauce-pan is made of brass; and the locks upon the door, and this candlestick.

What is this green upon the sauce-pan? It is rusty; the green is verdegris; it would kill you, if you were to eat it.

(58)

Iron is very hard. It is not pretty, but I do not know what we should do without it, for it makes us a great many things. Go and ask the cook whether she can roast her meat without a spit. Well, what does she say? She says she can-

(59)

not. But the spit is made of iron; and so are the tongs, and the poker, and shovel. Go and ask Dobbin if he can plow without the plough-share. Well, what does he say? He says No, he cannot. But the plough-share is made of iron. Will iron

(60)

melt in the fire? Put the poker in and try. Well, is it melted? No; but it is red hot, and soft; it will bend. But I will tell you, Charles; Iron will melt in a very very hot fire when it has been in a great while; then it will melt. Come,

(61)

let us go to the smith's shop. What is he doing? He has a forge: he blows the fire with a great pair of bellows to make the iron hot. Now it is hot. Now he takes it out with the tongs, and puts it upon the anvil. Now he beats it with a hammer.

(62)

How hard he works! The sparks fly about: pretty bright sparks! What is the blacksmith making? He is making nails, and horse shoes, and a great many things.

Steel is made of iron. Steel is very bright, and sharp, and hard.

(63)

Knives and scissars are made of steel.

Lead is soft, and very heavy. Here is a piece: lift it. There is lead in the casement; and the spout is lead, and the cistern is lead, and bullets are made of lead. Will lead melt in the fire?

(64)

Try: put some on the shovel: hold it over the fire.

Now it is all melted. Pour it into this bason of water. How it hisses? What pretty things it has made!

Tin is white and soft. It is bright too. The canisters, and the dripping pan, and

(65)

the reflector are all covered with tin.

Quicksilver is very bright like silver; and it is very heavy. See how it runs about! You cannot catch it. You cannot pick it up. There is quicksilver in the barometer.

(66)

Gold, Silver, Copper, Iron, Lead, Tin, Quicksilver. One, two, three, four, five, six, seven—What? Metals—They are all dug out of the ground.

(67)

Marble is dug out of the ground. It is very hard: you cannot cut it with a knife; but the stone cutter can cut it. There is white marble, and black, and green, and red, and yellow

(68)

marble. The chimney piece is made of marble, and the monument in the church.

Stones come out of the ground, and flints. Here are two flints: they are very hard: strike them both together. Ah! here is fire; here are sparks. Gravel is dug

(69)

out of gravel pits. They put it into carts, and then made gravel walks with it, or else mend the roads with it. Chalk and fuller's earth are dug out of the ground. Coals come out of the ground. Men dig great deep pits, and so they go down into them,

(70)

and get the coal with pick-axes, and bring it up. Those men are colliers: they are very black, but I do not know how we should do for coals to make fires without them. A great many things come out of the ground; sure it is very deep! Yes,

(71)

it is very deep. If you were to dig a hundred years, you would never come to the bottom, it is so deep.

Charles, here is a ring for you to play with. See how

it sparkles! Hold it against the sun. I see all colours in it. What is this bright

(72)

shining stone? It is a diamond. It is very hard; you may write upon the glass with it. A ruby is red; bright crimson red. An Emerald is green. A Topaz is yellow. A Sapphire is blue. The Amethyst is purple. The Garnet is red.

(73)

The Beryl is light green. All these are dug out of the earth. They are called jewels—precious stones. And here is a white round bead, which is very pretty; it is in an ear-ring. What is it? It is a pearl. And does that come out of the ground too.

(74)

No, it comes out of the sea. Pearls are found in oyster-shells.

Will stones melt in the fire? No.

Does glass come out of the ground? No. People make glass in a glass-house. They have great fires burning

(75)

all day and all night. You shall go to a glass-house some day and see them make it.

A tree has a root that goes under the ground a great way. The roots are like

(76)

its legs: the tree could not stand without it. Then the tree has a trunk; a large, thick, strait trunk. That is its body. Then the tree has branches. Those are like arms. They spread out very far. Then there are boughs; and upon the

(77)

boughs, leaves, and blossoms. Here is a blossom upon the apple-tree. Will the blossom be always upon the tree? No, it will fall off soon: perhaps it will fall off to-night. But then do you know what comes instead of the blossom? What? The

(78)

fruit. After the apple-blossoms, there will be apples. Then if the blossom falls off to-night, shall I come here and get an apple to-morrow? No, you must have patience: there will not be ripe apples a great while yet. There will be

(79)

first a little little thing hardly bigger than a pin's head. That will swell, and grow bigger every day, and harder, till at last it will come to be a great apple. But you must not eat it yet; you must let it hang till the sun has made it red, and till you

(80)

can pull it off easily. Now it is ripe: it is as red as your cheeks. Now gather it and eat it.

Has a flower a root too? Yes: here is a cowslip; we will pull it up. See, here are roots like strings; here is the stem of the cowslip;

(81)

here is the foot-stalk; here is the flower cup; here are the leaves of the flower; and a pretty flower it is: fine yellow with crimson spots. Here are the seeds. If the seeds are put in the ground, when they are ripe, another flower will grow up.

(82)

A she Horse is a Mare. A young Horse is a Colt. A very young Horse is a Foal.

A she Lion is a Lioness.

Tyger, Tygress.

Bull, Cow, Calf, Ox.

Boar, Sow, Pig, Hog.

(83)

Sheep, Ram, Ewe, Lamb, Wether.

Dog, Bitch, Puppy,

Whelp.

Cat, Kitten.

Cock, Hen, Chicken.

Gander, Goose, Gosling.

Drake, Duck, Duckling.

Eagle, Eaglet.

Stag, Buck, Doe, Hart, Hind, Fawn.

Hare, Leveret.

The Lion lives in a den. He is very strong. He has a great deal of thick yellow hair about his neck. That is his mane. He has very sharp claws; they would tear you to pieces. Look at him. He is very angry. See, he lashes his sides with his tail: his eyes sparkle like fire. He roars: how loud he roars! It is very terrible. He shows his sharp teeth.

(86)
His tongue is very rough. The Lion sleeps all day in his den. When it is night, he comes out, and prowls about to find something to eat. He eats cows, and sheep, and horses; and he would eat you too, if you were within his reach. The

(87)
Lioness has no mane. She is like a great dog. Any body would be afraid of a Lion if he was to come. Yes, any body would be afraid of a Lion, Charles: but you need not be afraid of dogs, they are good creatures. I will tell you a story.

(88)

There was once a little boy, who was a sad coward. He was afraid of every thing almost. He was afraid of the two little kids, Nanny and Billy, when they came and put their noses through the pales of the court; and he would not pluck Billy by the beard. What a silly

(89)

little boy he was! Pray what was his name? Nay, indeed I shall not tell you his name, for I am ashamed of him. Well, he was very much afraid of dogs too: he always cried if a dog barked, and ran away, and took hold of his mamma's apron like a baby. What a

(90)

foolish fellow he was! for dogs do not hurt, you know; they love little boys, and play with them. Did you ever see a dog eat up a little boy? No, never, I dare say. Well; so this simple little boy was walking by himself one day, and a pretty black dog came out of a

(91)

house, and said Bow, wow; bow, wow; and came to the little boy, and jumped upon him, and wanted to play with him; but the little boy ran away. The dog ran after him, and cried louder, Bow, bow, wow; but he only meant to say, Good-morrow, how do you

(92)

do? but this little boy was sadly frightened, and ran away as fast as ever he could, without looking before him, and he tumbled into a very dirty ditch, and there he lay crying at the bottom of the ditch, for he could not get out: and I believe he would have lain there all day, but

(93)

the dog was so good-natured, that he went to the house where the little boy lived, on purpose to tell them where he was. So when he came to the house, he scratched at the door, and said, Bow wow; for he could not speak any plainer. So they opened the door.

(94)

What do you want, you black dog? We do not know you. Then the dog went to Ralph the servant, and pulled him by the coat, and pulled him till he brought him to the ditch; and the dog and Ralph together got the little boy out of the ditch; but he was all over

(95)

mud, and quite wet, and every body laughed at him because he was a coward.

Now, Charles, my pen is tired, I cannot write any more at present, but if you are a good boy, perhaps I may write you some more stories another time. Farewel.

THE END

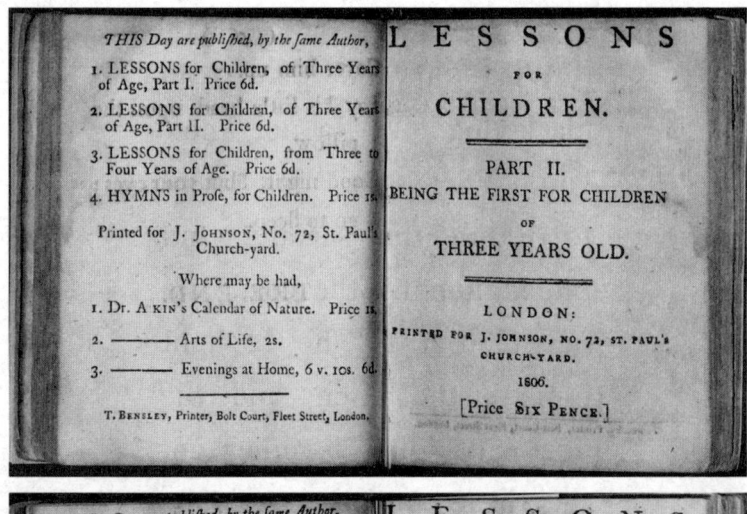

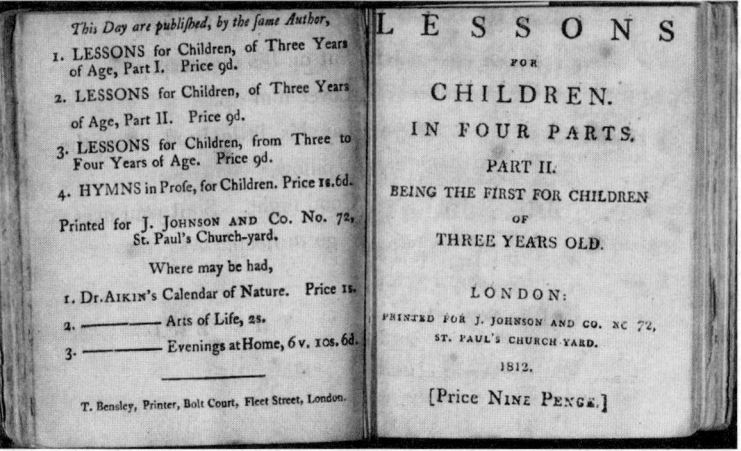

Fig. 6 *Lessons for Children, of Three Years Old.* Title-page, London 1806, with facing advertisements (private collection) along with *Lessons for Children, of Three Years Old*, Title-page, London 1812, with facing advertisements (private collection).

1808 ADDITIONS
Cued by 1781 page numbers

[between 'bread and butter' (p. 31) and 'Charles' (p. 32), 1808 adds:]

(30)

Little Birds eat seeds and fruits.
Partridges eat corn.
Wolves devour sheep.

(31)

Blackbirds peck cherries.
The Otter eats fish.
The Calf sucks milk.
The Weasel sucks eggs.
Squirrels crack nuts.
Foxes eat chickens.

Men eat every thing, corn, and fruit, and mutton, and fish, and eggs, and milk, and chickens.

---

(32)

The Tiger makes his lair in the thick forests, by the banks of the Ganges.

The Camelopard stalks over the vast plains of Africa; he lifts his long neck, and brouzes the trees as he walks.

(33)

The Ostrich runs swiftly over the burning sands of Monomotapa.

The Rhinoceros loves to wallow and roll himself in the wet mud, by the banks of large rivers, and in wet marshes.

The Chamois of Switzerland would pine if he could

(34)

not snuff the keen air of the mountains.

The little Ermine runs about in the frozen desarts of Siberia; she is white like the snow that is marked by her little feet.

The Humming-bird of Jamaica could not live in our woods; a frosty

(35)

night would kill him directly.

The Rein-deer lives in Lapland; he scrapes away the snow with his feet to get at a little moss which he lives upon; he would die if you were to expose him to the warm sun of Persia or Hindostan.

(36)

Wild Geese, and wild Ducks, and Plovers, live in fens and marshes.

Man can live every where, in cold Norway or Lapland, in hot Guinea or Persia; in hilly countries, or marshy plains; he can bear as much heat as the Ostrich, and as much cold as the Rein-deer.

(37)

The Sheep has a fleece to keep him warm.

The Beaver has a thick fur.

The Horse has hair, and a fine mane; how it flows over his neck, and waves in the wind.

The Ox has a thick hide.

(38)

The Ducks have feathers; thick, close feathers.

Puss has a warm fur; put your hands upon it, it is like a muff.

The snail has a shell to shelter him from the cold.

Has the little boy got any thing?

No; nothing but a soft

(39)

thin skin; a pin would scratch it and make it bleed, poor little naked boy!

But the little boy has got every thing; fur, and wool, and hair, and feathers; your coat is made of warm wool, shorn from the sheep, your hat is the fur of the rabbit and the beaver, and

(40)

your shoes are made of skin.

Look at this green tall plant; do you think it would make you a garment?

No indeed.

But your shirt is made of such a plant; your shirt was growing once in the fields.

(41)

In some countries they make clothes of the bark of trees.

Men can *make* things; the sheep and the ducks cannot spin and weave, that is the reason why the little boy has only his soft naked skin.

(42)

Come, let us go home, it is evening. See, Mamma! how tall my shadow is. It is like a great black giant stalking after me.

Your shadow is tall because the sun is low in the sky; it is near sunset. Look at your shadow to-morrow

(43)

at noon, and you will find it a great deal shorter.

In some countries the sun is directly over their heads at noon, and then they have no shadow at all.

If the sun were just over your head it would be hotter than you could bear.

Why is that? is not the

(44)

sun nearer us when it sinks down towards the fields, than when it is a great way up in the sky?

No; the sun does not really touch the fields, but he seems to do so, because you can see nothing between them.

But we are got home.

(45)

Come in. Now put your eye level with the table. Look at the globe that hangs at the other end of the room: Does it not appear to touch the table? Yes it does. But if it was held above the table it would not appear to touch. No. So it is with the Sun.

(46)

But why is it hotter when the sun is over our heads? Because his rays come directly down upon you. Come and stand just against the middle of this fire. Now stand at the same distance sideways. Did not you feel it hotter when you stood quite opposite?

Yes;

(47)

it scorched my face.—Well, at noon the sun sends down his scorching rays, like a number of burning arrows directly down upon you; but in the evening and the morning they come more slanting, and fewer of them reach you. That is the reason why it is hotter at

(48)

noon: the sun is always at the same distance, more thousands of miles off than you can count.

[Between 'eat her up' (p. 52) and 'Gold' (p. 53), 1808 adds:]

(68)

A Dog is a very good creature, he loves his master dearly, and remembers him a long while, even if he has not seen him for a great many, many years—I wish all little boys loved one another as well as a Dog loves his master—I

(69)

will tell you a story about a Dog—A great while ago there was a man called Ulysses, he lived in a little island called Ithaca; he was king of the island. And he had a Dog whose name was *Argus*, he was very fond of this dog, and used to take him out with him

(70)

when he went abroad; and Argus used to scour over the fields after any thing he saw, and gallop back again to his master swifter than a race-horse, and if his master only said 'Poor fellow!' and patted his head, he would be quite happy, and frisk, and bound

(71)

about him all day long, and he was well fed and taken great care of. But Ulysses went abroad to fight battles with his enemies, and he was ten years at war, and he was ten years more in getting home to his dear Ithaca, for he met with a great many

(72)

strange adventures by the way. Ten and ten, you know, make twenty, so he had been twenty years away. And when he came to Ithaca, he found that some bad people had taken possession of his palace, and he was afraid they would kill him. So he disguised

(73)

himself like a poor Beggar-man, and walked up to the gate with his stick in his hand.

Argus was lying in the sun upon a little straw. He was grown very old now, and could not frolick and bound as he used to do, and nobody had taken good care of him, so that

(74)

he was very weak and could hardly raise himself from his straw. However, he pricked up his ears at the sound of a footstep, and seeing a ragged fellow coming up to the gate was going to bark; but as Ulysses came nearer, he recollected his step, and looked up in

(75)

his face and knew his old master, though nobody else knew him. Then poor Argus roused himself, and just made shift to crawl towards him, and wagged his tail, and gazed joyfully in the face of Ulysses, and licked his hands, and then being quite weak and worn

(76)

out, fell down and died at his feet.

I heard a curious story the other day, which I am going to tell you. There was a Duck and a Drake who were very fond of each other. The Duck was sitting upon her eggs in the

(77)

duck-house, which was placed on a grass plot under the parlour windows, and the Drake was such a good husband that he staid with her all the time in the duck-house, sitting by her side and quacking to her; and though a Duck has not a very musical voice, I dare

(78)

say she thought his song as harmonious as the nightingale's. Well, at length the eggs were hatched, and the little ducklings came out, and then they turned the poor Drake out of the duck-house, for fear he should trample upon his children with his great splay

(79)

foot and hurt them. So he strolled about the grass plot. And next day he met a Hen with a brood of five little chickens. And he took the chickens, which were just hatched, for his own children. And he wanted to teach them to swim. For the Drake always takes that business upon himself. He leads his young ones to the water, and cuffs and bites them to make them go in, for they are afraid at first. So the Drake went up to these poor little chickens, and drove them before him down to the pond, which was at the bottom of the lawn. The Hen resisted and scuffled with him as well as she could, but the Drake was a great deal stronger than she, and nobody came to her assistance, though they saw from the house that something was the matter by her fluttering and screaming. But the Drake was resolved his little ones should learn to swim, so he pushed them along, with his wings spread out, till he made them all go into the pond, where they were all five found dead the next morning, and the Drake standing by, very much surprised I dare say that his children were so stupid as to let themselves be drowned rather than learn to swim.

    Yesterday is past, to *Day* is here, *To-morrow* is to come. When *To-morrow* is come, to *Day* will be *Yesterday*.
    I do not understand that.
    What is to day?
    Monday.
    And to-morrow?
    Tuesday.
    Then, on Tuesday, Monday will be *Yesterday*. I have heard a pretty riddle about that. What is that which was *To-morrow* and will be *Yesterday*?
    To Day.
    Yes. *To Day*, before it came, was called *To-morrow*, and when it is gone we shall call it Yesterday.
    Will *Yesterday* ever come again?

(86)

No never, nor to *Day*, so pray improve it. A great many Days will come, one after another, but none of them will be this Day that is now here.

If I have done any thing wrong yesterday must that always be?

What do you think, if

(87)

you write any thing with ink in this Book, can you blot it out again if it is bad?

No, I cannot.

And so if you have done something wrong yesterday, you cannot blot it out, it must stand in the book.

(88)

But I can write better in the next page.

That you may, and I hope you will; it is all that a little boy can do, or a great man either.

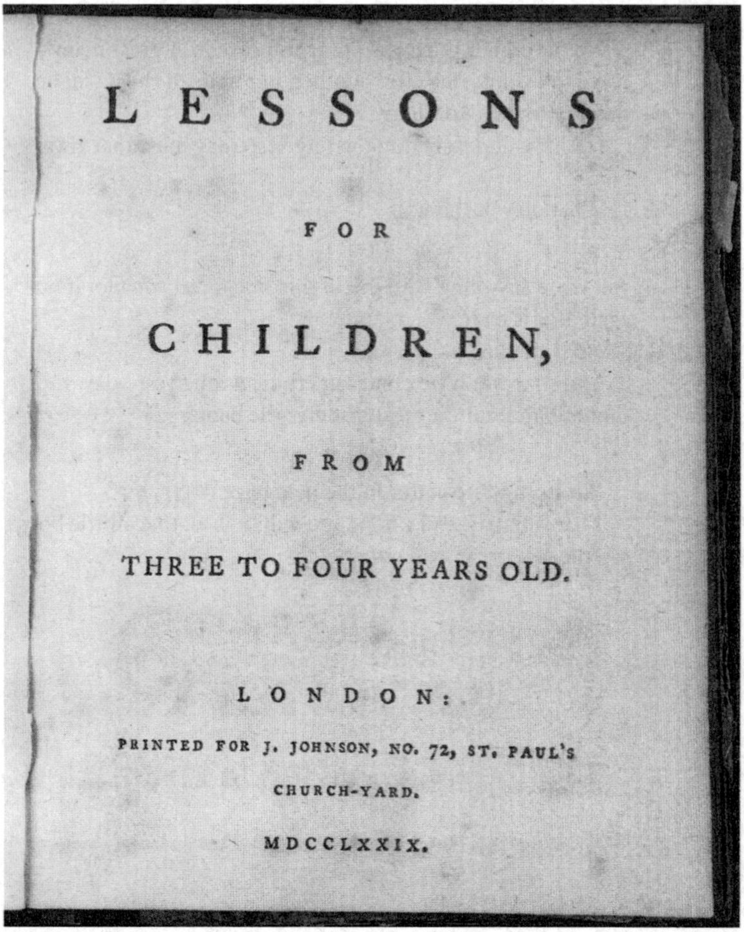

LESSONS

FOR

CHILDREN,

FROM

THREE TO FOUR YEARS OLD.

LONDON:
PRINTED FOR J. JOHNSON, NO. 72, ST. PAUL'S
CHURCH-YARD.
MDCCLXXIX.

Fig. 7 *Lessons for Children, from Three to Four Years Old.* Title-page, London 1779, first edition (Glasgow University Library).

LESSONS

FOR

CHILDREN,

FROM

THREE TO FOUR YEARS OLD

L O N D O N:
PRINTED FOR J. JOHNSON, NO. 72, ST. PAUL'S
CHURCH-YARD
MDCCLXXIX

LESSONS
FOR CHILDREN,
FROM THREE TO FOUR YEARS OLD

CHARLES, here are more stories for you,— stories about good boys, and

(4)

naughty boys, and silly boys; for you know what it is to be good now. And there is a story about two foolish cocks, that were always quarrelling, which is very naughty. You do not quarrel? No. I am glad of it; but if you see any little boys that quarrel, you may tell

(5)

them the story of the Two Cocks. This is it.

There was once a Hen, who lived in a farm-yard; and she had a large brood of chickens. She took a great deal of care of them, and gathered them under her wings every night, and fed

(6)

them, and nursed them very well: And they were all very good, except two Cocks, that were always quarrelling with one another. They were hardly out of the shell before they began to peck at each other; and when they grew bigger, they fought till they were all

(7)

bloody. If one picked up a barley-corn, the other always wanted to have it. They never looked pretty, because their feathers were pulled off in fighting till they were quite bare; and they picked at one another's eyes till they were both al-

(8)

most blind. The old Hen very often told them how naughty it was to quarrel so; but they did not mind her.

So one day these two Cocks had been fighting, as they always did; and the biggest Cock, whose name was Chanticlear, beat the other, and crowed over him,

(9)

and drove him quite out of the yard. The Cock that had been beat slunk away, and hid himself; for he was vexed he had been conquered, and he wanted sadly to be revenged: but he did not know how to manage it, for he was not strong enough

(10)

himself. So after thinking a great deal, he went to an

old sly Fox that lived near, and said to him, Fox, if you will come with me, I will show you where there is a large fat Cock in a farm-yard; and you may eat him up if you will. The Fox was very glad, for he was

(11)

hungry enough, and he said, Yes, I will come with all my heart, and I will not leave a feather of him. So they went together, and the Cock shewed Reynard the way into the farm-yard; and there was poor Chanticlear asleep upon the perch. And

(12)

the Fox seized him by the neck, and eat him up; and the other Cock stood by and crowed for joy. But when the Fox had done, he said,

Chanticlear was very good, but I have not had enough; and so he flew upon the other Cock, and eat him up too in a moment.

(13)

I will tell you a story.

There was a little boy whose name was Harry; and his papa and mamma sent him to school. Now Harry was a clever fellow, and loved his book; and he

(14)

got to be first in his class. And his mamma heard that he had got first in his class. So his mamma got up one morning very early, and called Betty the maid, and said, Betty, I think we must make a cake for Harry, for he has learned his book very well. And Betty said, Yes,

(15)

with all my heart. So they made a nice cake. It was very large, and stuffed full of plums, and sweetmeats, orange and citron; and it was iced all over with sugar: it was white and smooth on the top like snow. So this cake was sent to the school.

(16)

When little Harry saw it, he was very glad, and jumped about for joy, and he hardly stayed for a knife to cut a piece, but gnawed it like a little dog. So he eat till the bell rang for school, and after school he eat again, and he eat till he went to bed; nay, his bed-fellow told me

(17)

that he laid his cake under his pillow, and sat up in the night to eat some. So he

eat till it was all gone.—
But presently after this little
boy was very sick and ill,
and every body said, I wonder what is the matter with
Harry? he used to be so
brisk, and play about more

(18)

nimbly than any of the boys;
and now he looks pale and
is very ill. And somebody
said, Harry has had a rich
cake, and eat it all up very
soon, and that has made him
ill. So they sent for Dr.
Camomile, and he gave him
I do not know how much
bitter stuff. Poor Harry did

(19)

not like it at all, but he was
forced to take it or else he
would have died, you know.
So at last he got well again,
but his mamma said she

would send him no more cakes.

Now there was another boy, who was one of Harry's school-fellows: his name

(20)

was Peter; the boys used to call him Peter Careful. And Peter had written his mamma a very neat pretty letter—there was not one blot in it all. So his mamma sent him a cake. Now Peter thought with himself, I will not make myself sick with this good cake, as silly Harry

(21)

did; I will keep it a great while. So he took the cake, and tugged it up stairs. It was very heavy: he could hardly carry it. And he locked it up in his box, and once a day he crept slily up stairs, and eat a very little piece, and then locked his box again. So he kept it

(22)

several weeks, and it was not gone, for it was very large; but, behold! the mice got into his box and nibbled some. And the cake grew dry and mouldy, and at last was good for nothing at all. So he was obliged to throw it away and it grieved him to the very

(23)

heart, and no body was sorry for him.

Well; there was another little boy at the same school, whose name was Billy. And one day his mamma sent him a cake, because she loved him dearly, and he loved her dearly. So when the cake came, Billy said to his school-

(24)

fellows, I have got a cake, come let us go and eat it. So they came about him like a parcel of bees; and Billy took a slice of cake himself, and then gave a piece to one, and a piece to another, and a piece to another, till it was almost gone. Then Billy put the rest by, and said,

(25)

I will eat it to morrow. So he went to play and the boys all played together very merrily. But presently after an old blind Fiddler came into the court. He had a long white beard; and because he was blind, he had a little dog in a string to lead him. So he came into the court,

(26)

and sat down upon a stone, and said, My pretty lads,

if you will, I will play you a tune. And they all left off their sport, and came and stood round him. And Billy saw that while he played the tears ran down his cheeks. And Billy said, Old man, why do you cry? And

(27)

the old man said, Because I am very hungry—I have no body to give me any dinners or suppers—I have nothing in the world but this little dog; and I cannot work. If I could work, I would. Then Billy went without saying a word, and fetched the rest of his cake which

(28)

he had intended to have eaten another day, and he said, Here old man! here is some cake for you. The old man said, Where is it? for I am blind, I cannot see it. So Billy put it into his hat. And the Fiddler thanked him, and Billy was more

(29)

glad than if he had eaten ten cakes.

Pray which do you love best? do you love Harry, or Peter, or Billy best?

Little boy, come to me. Tell me how far from home have you been in your life?

(30)

I think I should like to go a great long way with you, and see what we could see: for there are a great many places in the world besides home. Bring your hat. Good bye Papa. Farewel, Billy, and Harry, and every body. We are going a great way off. And we shall go

(31)

down the lane, and through the church-yard, and by the corner house, and over the stile, till we have got quite into the fields. How pretty the fields will look! for it will be summer days again before we go. And there will be yellow flowers, and white flowers, and grass,

(32)

and trees, and hedges; and the grasshoppers will chirp, chirp, under our feet. Do not try to catch them; it will only hinder us, and we have a great way to go.

Pray what are those pretty creatures that look so meek and good-natured, and have soft thick white wool upon

(33)

their backs, like a great coat; and make a noise like the little baby when it cries? Those are sheep, and lambs. And what are those creatures with horns, that are bigger than the sheep? Some of them are black, and some red: they make a loud noise,

(34)

but they do not look as if they would hurt any body. Those are cows that give milk. Stroke them. Poor cows! Stand still and look back. Now we cannot see papa's house at all; and we can see only the top of the church steeple. Let us go a little farther. Now look

(35)

back. Now we cannot see the church at all. Farewell!

We are going a great way. Shall we ever come back again? Yes, we shall come back again; but we must go on now. Come, make haste.

What is that tall thing,

(36)

that has four great arms which move very fast? I believe if I was near it they would strike me down. It is a Wind-mill. Those arms are the sails. The wind turns them round. And what is a Wind-mill for? It is to grind corn. You could have no bread if the

(37)

corn were not ground. Well, but here is a river; how shall we do to get over it? Why do not you see how those ducks do? they swim over.

But I cannot swim. Then you must learn to swim, I believe: it is too wide to jump over. O here is a

(38)

Bridge! Somebody has made a bridge for us quite over the river. That somebody was very good, for I do not know what we should have done without it; and he was very clever too. I wonder how he made it. I am sure I could not make such a bridge.

(39)

Well, we must go on, on, on; and we shall see more rivers, and more fields, and towns bigger than our town a great deal—large towns, and fine churches, streets and people—more than there is at the fair. And we shall have a great many high hills

(40)

to climb. I believe I must get somebody to carry the little boy up those high hills. And sometimes we shall go through dusty sandy roads; and sometimes through green lanes, where we shall hear the birds sing. Sometimes we shall go over wide commons, where we shall see no

(41)

trees, nor any house; and large heaths, where there is hardly any grass—only some purple flowers, and a few black-nosed little sheep. Hah! did you see that pretty brown creature that ran across the path? Here is another; and look! there is another:

(42)

there are a great many. They are Rabbits. They live here, and make themselves houses in the ground. This is a rabbit-warren.

Now we are come amongst a great many trees—more trees than there are in the orchard by a great many;

(43)

and taller trees. There is oak, and ash, and elm. This is a Wood. What great boughs the trees have! like thick arms. The sun cannot shine amongst the trees, they are so thick. Look, there is a squirrel! jumping from one tree to another.

(44)

He is very nimble. What a pretty tail he has!

Well; when we have gone on a great many days, through a great many fields, and towns, we shall come to a great deep water; bigger a great many times than the river; for you can see over the river, you know—you

(45)

can see fields on the other side: but this is so large, and so wide, you can see nothing but water, water, as far as ever you can carry your eyes. And it is not smooth, like the river; it is all rough, like the great pot in the kitchen when it

(46)

is boiling. And it is so deep, it would drown you if you were as tall as two church steeples. I wonder what they call this great water!

There is an old, old fisherman, sitting upon a stone drying himself; for he is very wet. I think we will ask him. Pray, fisherman!

(47)

what is this great water? It is the Sea: did you never hear of the sea? What! is this great water the same sea that is in our map at home? Yes, it is. Well, this is very strange! we are come to the sea that is in our map. But it is very little in the

(48)

map. I can lay my finger over it. Yes; it is little in the map, because every thing is little in the map: the towns are little, and the rivers are little.

Pray, Fisherman, is there any thing on the other side

of this sea? Yes; fields, and towns, and people. Will

(49)

you go and see them? I should like to go very well; but how must we do to get over? for there is no bridge here. Do not you see those great wooden boxes that swim upon the water? They are bigger than all papa's house. There are tall poles in the middle, as high as a

(50)

tree. Those are masts. See! now they are spreading the sails. Those white sheets are the sails. They are like wings. These wooden boxes are like houses with wings. Yes, and I will tell you what, little boy! they are made on purpose to go over the sea; and the

(51)

wind blows them along faster than a horse can trot. What do they call them? They call them Ships. You have seen a ship in a picture. Shall we get in? What have those men in the ship got on? They have jackets and trowsers on, and checked shirts. They are sailors. I think

(52)

we will make you a sailor; and then instead of breeches you must have a pair of trowsers. Do you see that sailor, how he climbs up the ropes? He is very nimble. He runs up like a monkey. Now he is at the top of the mast. How little he looks! But we must get in. Come,

(53)

make haste: they will not stay for us. What are you

doing? picking up shells! We must get into a boat first, because the ship is not near enough. Now we are in.

Now we are upon the great sea. Blow, blow wind! Sail away ship! There are

(54)

little rooms in the ship. Those little rooms are called cabins. Let us walk about, and look at the ship. Why, you cannot walk steady: I am afraid you are tipsy! Because the ship rolls about. But the sailors can walk steady. The sea is not like the river; it is greenish. Well;

(55)

here is water enough if we should be thirsty. Yes, here is water enough; but you would not like to drink it. It is salt and bitter. You could not drink it. How fast we go! Now the fields are a great way off. Now we cannot see any green fields at all, nor any houses,

(56)

nor any thing but the great deep water. It is water all round as far as ever we can see. Yes, and sky; we can see the sky too. All sky over our heads, and all water every where round us! Do not be afraid, little boy! Blow, blow, wind! sail away ship! I see some

(57)

things in the sea at a great distance. Those are more ships and boats. How very small they are! they look like nut shells in a great pond. O, now we are coming to the green fields and towns on the other side of the sea! I can see them a little. Now I can see them

(58)

very plain. And here is a little piece of green land, with the water running all round it. That is an island. A piece of land with water all round it, is an island. But we are not going there; we are going to the great land.

Now we are at the land.

(59)

Get out of the ship. Pray what country is this? This is France. France! why France is in the map too. And pray what is the name of that country we came from, where we live, and where papa lives? It is England. And the deep sea is between France and Eng-

(60)

land? Yes, you know it is so in the map.

O, France is a pretty place! It is warmer than our country: and here are pretty flowers, and fine fruit, and large grapes. I never saw such large grapes in all my life. And the vines grow in the fields; they do not grow

(61)

against walls, as our vines do. And there are a great many people, men, and women, and little boys and girls, singing, and dancing about, and so merry! nothing can be like it. I think we will live here, and send for papa and Arthur. Let us go and talk with those

(62)

people. Here, you little girl! pray give us some of your nice fruit. *Serviteur Monsieur.* What do you say, little girl? I do not understand you. I cannot help that. Here is an old man cutting the vines; we will speak to him. Pray, old man, will you give us some

(63)

of your fruit? We are come a great way to see you. *Serviteur Monsieur.* What do you say? We do not know what *Serviteur Monsieur* is. It is French. But we do not understand French. I cannot help that; you must go home and learn. And why do you speak French? Be-

(64)

cause this is France. Did not you know that every body speaks French in France? Ha, ha, ha! He, he, he! Ho, ho, ho! Here is a foolish little boy come a great way over the sea, and does not know that every body speaks French in France. Ha, ha, ha! He,

(65)

he, he! Ho, ho, ho! Here is a foolish little boy come a great way over the sea, and does not know that every body speaks French in France. Ha, ha, ha! He, he, he! Ho, ho, ho!— What shall we do, little boy? every body laughs at

(66)

us; and all the little birds twitter and chirp at us. We

will go home again. Farewel, France! We will not go to France again till papa has taught us to talk French. Let us get into the ship again. Blow, wind! sail away, ship! Now we are got back again. Pray, papa, teach the little boy French before he goes a great way abroad again.

You know how many legs a Horse has? Yes, a Horse has four legs. And do you know what an animal is called that has four legs? It is called a Quadruped. The cow is a quadruped; and the dog, and the lion, and all the beasts. But birds are not quadrupeds, for they have only two legs. Some quadrupeds have hoofs. The Horse has hoofs; so has the

(69)

Ass, and the Cow: but the Dog has no hoofs; the Dog has toes with claws; so the dog is not hoofed, but digitated; and the cat, and the squirrel, and a great many more are digitated. The hoof of the horse is whole, it is all in one piece;

(70)

but the hoof of the cow is parted, as if it were two hoofs. That is being cloven-footed; the hoof is cloven. The cow, and the sheep, and the hog, and the stag are all cloven-footed; but the horse, and the ass, have whole hoofs.

(71)

The Ass says, I am a Quadruped; I am a very patient good creature. I have hoofs, and very long ears. I bray very loud. The horse is frightened when I bray, and starts back; but

(72)
I am very meek, and never hurt any thing. My young ones are colts: I suckle them. I am not so big as a horse, and I cannot gallop fast, but I work very hard. Sometimes I carry little boys on my back, two or three at a time, and they whip me, and prick my sides, to

(73)
make me go faster. I carry greens to market, and tur-

nips, and potatoes; and sometimes I carry a great load of pans, and mugs, and pots, with which my back is almost broke; and I get nothing for my dinner but a few prickly thistles, and

(74)

some coarse grass from off the common: and I have no stable to go into as a horse has; I always lie out in the fields, in the snow, and in the rain; but I am very contented. I give milk, as well as the cow; and my milk is very good for people that

(75)

are sick, to make them well again.

Ha! what is there amongst the furze? I can see only its eyes. It has very large full eyes. It is a Hare. It is in its form, squatting

(76)

down amongst the bushes to hide itself, for it is very fearful. The Hare is very innocent and gentle. Its colour is brown; but in countries which are very cold it turns white as snow. It has a short bushy tail; its lip is parted, and very hairy; and it always moves its lips.

(77)

Its hind legs are very long, that it may run the better. The Hare feeds upon herbs, and roots, and the bark of young trees, and green corn; and sometimes it will creep through the hedge, and steal into the gardens, to eat pinks, and a little parsley;

(78)

and it loves to play and skip about by moon-light, and to bite the tender blades of grass when the dew is upon them; but in the day-time it sleeps in its form. It sleeps with its eyes open, because it is very fearful and timid; and when it hears the least noise, it starts and

(79)

pricks up its large ears. And when the huntsman sounds his horn, and the poor harmless hare hears the dogs coming, then it runs away very swiftly strait forward, stretching its legs, and leaves them all behind. But the dogs pursue her, and she grows

(80)

tired, and cannot run so fast as at first. Then she

doubles, and turns, and runs back to her form, that the hounds may not find her; But they run with their noses to the ground, smelling, till they have found her out. So when she has run five or six miles, at last

(81)

she stops, and pants for breath, and can run no further. Then the hounds come up, and tear her, and kill her. Then when she is dead, her little limbs which moved so fast, grow quite stiff, and cannot move at all. A snail could go faster than a hare when it is

(82)

dead: and its poor little heart, that beat so quick, is quite still and cold; and its round full eyes are dull and dim;

and its soft furry skin is all torn and bloody. It is good for nothing now, but to be roasted.

(83)

All birds that swim in the water are web-footed. Their toes are joined together by a skin that grows between them; that is being web-footed; and it helps the birds to swim well, for then

(84)

their feet are like the fins of a fish.

The swan says, My name is Swan. I am a large bird, larger than a goose. My bill is red, but the sides of it are black, and I have black about my eyes. My legs are dusky, but my feet are red, and I am web-footed.

(85)

My body is all white, as white as snow, and very beautiful. I have a very long neck. I live in rivers and lakes. I eat plants that grow in the water, and seeds, and little insects, and snails. I do not look pretty when I walk upon the ground, for I cannot walk well at all;

(86)

but when I am in the water, swimming smoothly along, arching my long neck, and dipping my white breast, with which I make way through the water, I am the most graceful of all birds. I build my nest in a little island amongst the reeds and rushes. I make it of sticks

(87)

and long grass: it is very large and high. Then I lay

my eggs, which are white, and very large, larger a great deal than a goose's egg; and I sit upon them for two months; then they are hatched, and my young ones come out. They are called cygnets. They are

(88)

not white at first, but greyish. If any body was to come near me when I am in my nest, sitting upon my eggs, or when I have my young ones, I should fly at him; for I am very fierce to defend my young, and if you were to come to take them away, I should beat

(89)

you down with my strong pinion, and perhaps break your arm. I live a very great while.

The Sun says, My name is Sun. I am very bright. I rise in the east; and when I rise, then it is day. I look

(90)

in at your window with my bright golden eye, and tell you when it is time to get up; and I say, Sluggard, get up: I do not shine for you to lie in your bed and sleep, but I shine for you to get up, and work, and read, and walk about. I am a great traveller, I travel all

(91)

over the sky; I never stop, and I never am tired. I have a crown upon my head of bright beams, and I send forth my rays every where. I shine upon the trees, and the houses, and upon the water; and every thing looks sparkling and beautiful when I shine upon it. I give you

(92)

light, and I give you heat, for I make it warm. I make the fruit ripen, and the corn ripen. If I did not shine upon the fields, and upon the gardens, nothing would grow. I am up very high in the sky, higher than all trees, higher than the clouds, higher than every thing.

(93)

I am a great way off. If I were to come nearer you I should scorch you to death, and I should burn up the grass, for I am all made of hot glowing fire. I have been in the sky a great while. Four years ago, there was no Charles; Charles was not alive then, but there was a

(94)

Sun. I was in the sky before papa and mamma were alive, a great many long years ago; and I am not grown old yet. Sometimes I take off my crown of bright rays, and wrap up my head in thin silver clouds, and then you may look at me; but when there are no clouds,

(95)

and I shine with all my brightness at noon-day, you cannot look at me, for I should dazzle your eyes, and make you blind. Only the Eagle can look at me then: the Eagle with his strong piercing eye can gaze upon me always. And when I am going to rise in the

(96)

morning, and make it day, the Lark flies up in the sky to meet me, and sings sweetly in the air: and the Cock crows loud to tell every body that I am coming. But the Owl and the Bat, fly away when they see me, and hide themselves in old walls and hollow trees; and the Lion

(97)

and the Tiger go into their dens and caves, where they sleep all the day. I shine in all places. I shine in England, and in France, and in Spain, and all over the earth. I am the most beautiful and glorious creature that can be seen in the whole world.

(98)

The Moon says, My name is Moon. I shine to give you light in the night, when the sun is set. I am very beautiful and white like silver. You may look at me always, for I am not so bright as to dazzle your eyes, and I never scorch you. I am mild and gentle.

(99)

I let even the little glow-worms shine, which are quite dark by day. The stars shine all round me, but I am larger and brighter than the stars, and I look like a large pearl amongst a great many small sparkling diamonds. When you are asleep, I shine through your curtains with my gentle beams, and I say,

(100)

Sleep on, poor little tired boy, I will not disturb you. The nightingale sings to me, who sings better than all the birds of the air. She sits upon a thorn, and sings melodiously all night long, while the dew lies upon the grass and every thing is still and silent, all around.

THE END

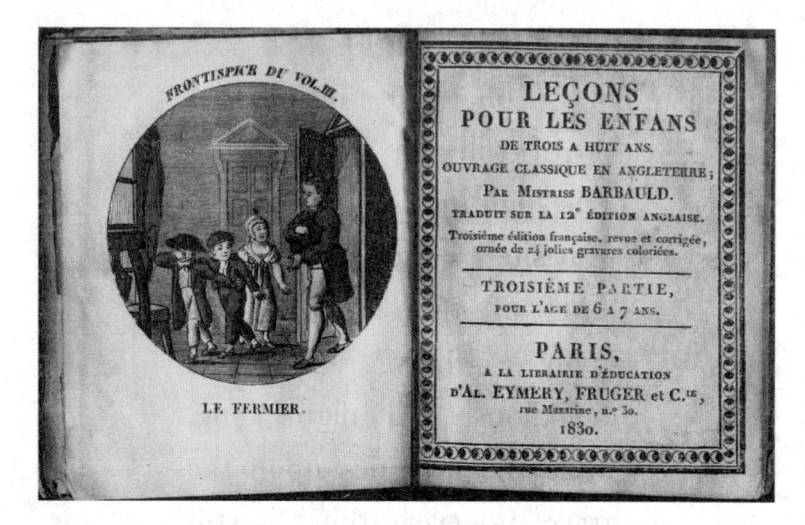

Fig. 8 *Leçons pour les enfans*. Paris. 1830 Title-page with frontispiece (private collection)

1808 ADDITIONS
Cued by 1779 page numbers

[At p. 67, between 'abroad again' and 'You know', 1808 adds:]

(68)

I will tell you a story about two little boys, Sam and Harry.—One fine summer's day Sam was walking home from school, over the fields. He sauntered slowly along, for it was very pleasant, and he was reading in a pretty story-book which he had

(69)

just bought with his week's money, and sometimes he lay down under a tree and read, and the birds sang over his head, and he was a happy little boy. Well, at length, he got over a stile and came to the high road, and there was a gate across the road, and a blind

(70)

beggar stood holding the gate open, and said, Pray bestow a halfpenny. But Sam gave him nothing. What! did Sam give the poor blind beggar nothing? No, because he had nothing to give, for, as I told you, he had spent his money. So he walked

(71)

through and looked rather sorrowful. And in a minute or two afterwards, a smart curricle came driving down to the gate, and Harry and his Mamma were in it. And the blind man stood and held his hat. Let us give the poor blind man something, said Harry

(72)

immediately to his Mamma. So his Mamma gave him a handful of halfpence which she had just received from the last turnpike man. And Harry took them eagerly, but instead of putting them into the poor man's hat, which he held out for them, he threw the whole hand-

(73)

ful as far as he could scatter them into the hedge. The poor man could not find them there you know, and looked very melancholy; but Sam, who had turned his head to look at the fine curricle, saw Harry fling the halfpence, and came back, and looked

(74)

carefully in the hedge, and in the grass, and all about, till, one by one, he had found all the halfpence; and, besides the trouble he had, it took him so much time, that he almost lost his dinner by coming too late. Now pray which do you think was most kind

(75)

to the poor blind man, Harry or Sam? I know very well which he thanked most in his heart.

[Between 1779 p. 70, 'whole hoofs', and p. 71, 'The Ass says', 1808 adds:]

(79)

What a pretty sight a poultry-yard is! There is the Hen chuckling, the Cock strutting about, the Peacock spreading his tail, the Drake shewing his fine plumage as he sails in the pond, the Turkey gobbling, and the Guinea Hens crying, "Come back, Come

(80)

back," for which reason in Norfolk they call them *Comebacks*. But these fowls are very jealous of a new comer, and often treat him very ill. I will tell you a little story about that.—There was a gentleman who had a yard full of all these kinds of fowls, and

(81)

they lived very sociably together, but one day the gentleman bought a Bantam Cock, and sent him in among them. He was very finely mottled and feathered down to the toes; but, for some reason or other, the rest took a dislike to him. I think it very probable

(82)

the Bantam might be saucy, and give himself airs, for a Bantam is a great coxcomb, and struts about, and seems to think himself as tall as a Turkey Cock. Well, somehow he had affronted them, so all the fowls in the yard got together, and made a circle round him,

(83)

and a couple of Guinea fowls took him by the wings, and dragged him to the pond, where they fairly gave him a good ducking, and all the fowls that stood by seemed much pleased with the operation. But when the master of the yard was told of it next

(84)

day, he ordered his man John to take the two Guinea fowls and give them a ducking in the same pond, which was done, and I dare say you think they were served very right.

(85)

I will tell you another story. William and Edward were two clever little boys, and not at all ill-natured, but they were very fond of sport, and they did not care whether people were hurt or no, provided they could but laugh. So one fine sum-

(86)

mer's day, when they had said their lessons, they took a walk through the long grass in the meadows. William began to blow the Dandelions, and the feathered seeds flew in the wind like arrows, but Edward said, Let us tie the grass, it will be very good

(87)

sport to tie the long grass over the path, and to see people tumble upon their noses as they run along, and do not suspect any thing of the matter. So they tied it in several places, and then hid themselves to see who would pass. And presently a

(88)

farmer's boy came trudging along, and down he tumbled, and lay sprawling on the ground, however he had nothing to do but to get up again, so there was not much harm done this time. Then there came Susan the milk-maid, tripping along with her milk-

(89)

pail upon her shoulders, and singing like a lark. When her foot struck against the place where the grass was tied, down she came with her pail rattling about her shoulders, and her milk was all spilt upon the ground. Then Edward said, Poor Susan! I think

(90)

I should not like to be served so myself, let us untie the grass. No, no, said William, if the milk is spilt there are some pigs that will lick it up, let us have some more fun, I see a man running along, as if he were running for a wager, I am sure he will

(91)

fall upon his nose. And so the man did, and William and Edward both laughed; but when the man did not get up again they began to be frightened, and went up to him and asked him if he was hurt. O masters, said the man, some thoughtless boys, I do not

(92)

know who they are, have tied the grass together over the path, and as I was running with all my might it threw me down, and I have sprained my ancle so that I will not be able to walk for a month. I am very sorry, said Edward, have you a great deal of

(93)

pain? O yes, said the man, but that I do not mind, but I was going in a great hurry to fetch a surgeon to bleed a gentleman who is in a fit, and they say he will die if he is not bled. Then Edward and William both turned pale as ashes, and said, Where does the

(94)

surgeon live? we will go for him, we will run all the way. He lives at the next town, said the man, but it is a mile off, and you cannot run so fast as I should have done; you are only boys. Where must we tell the surgeon to come to? said William. He must

(95)

come to the white house, at the end of the long chesnut avenue, said the man: he is a very good gentleman that lives there. O it is papa! it is our dear papa! said the two boys. Oh papa will die, what must we do!—I do not know whether their papa

(96)

died or no, I believe he got well again; but I am sure of one thing, that Edward and William never tied the grass to throw people down again as long as they lived.

---

(97)

See! I have brought you a picture, what is it a picture of?
It is a picture of a horse.
Is it *like* a horse?
O yes, very like. How well he holds his head. What a fine mane. How

(98)

he stretches out his legs. He is galloping along very fast indeed.

What is the word that is written under?

That is *Horse* too.

Is that *like* a horse?

I do not know. I do not quite understand the question, it *means* horse.

(99)

If you were to shew it a Frenchman that had not learned English, would he know that it means horse?

No, not till he was told.

If you were to ask him what word means Horse, what would he say?

He would say *Cheval*.

But if you were to shew

(100)

him this picture, would he know what it is?

Yes, directly.

Or an Italian, or a Spaniard, or a German?

Yes, any body would know it directly, without being told.

If you were to take this picture and cut it in pieces,

(101)

what would you have?

I should have the head in one piece, and the legs in another, and the body in another.

And the legs would be like legs, would they not, and the body like a body?

Yes.

But if you were to take

(102)

the *word* horse, and cut it in pieces, what would you have?

I should have letters h, and o, and r, and s, and e.

Would those letters be the legs and head?

No, they would mean nothing.

Could you have known

(103)

that the word horse means a horse before you were told?

No, I remember learning to read it, I did not know it before.

But you would always have known the *picture* of a horse; your little cousin that cannot read at all, and can hardly speak, knows that, and tries to neigh when he sees it. Nay, animals will know a picture if it is very well done; there is a story of a man that painted a bunch of grapes so very well that the birds came and pecked at it; but do you think you could have taught a bird to read?

No indeed.

Well, then, you see that the *picture* of a horse is really *like* a horse, but the *word* is not. The word only means horse, because people choose to make it so; any other letters would have done as well. If they had chosen that RAB should mean horse, it would have meant horse; but nobody could make the picture of an eagle to be the picture of a horse, because a picture must be *like* the thing it is a picture of.

Words are arbitrary marks of our ideas, but you cannot understand that sentence yet, I have tried to explain the *thing*.

HYMNS
IN
PROSE
FOR CHILDREN.

BY THE AUTHOR OF

LESSONS FOR CHILDREN.

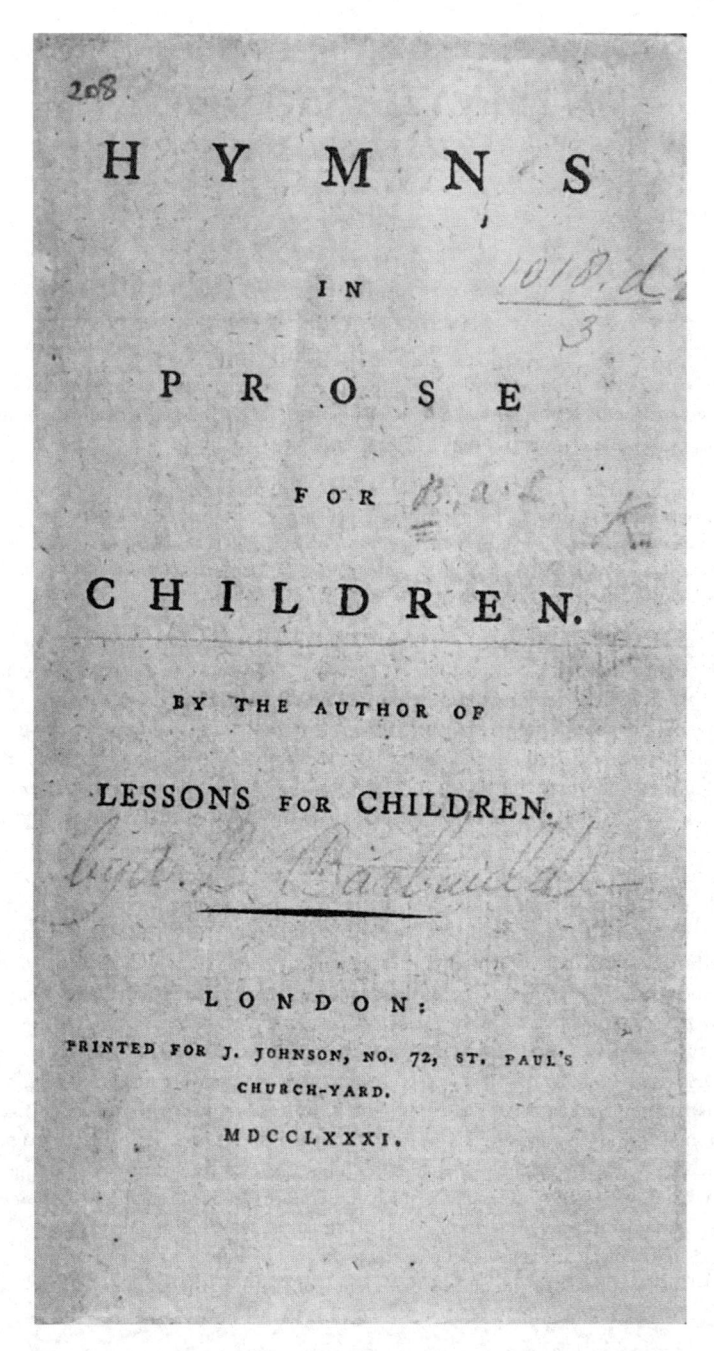

LONDON:
PRINTED FOR J. JOHNSON, NO. 72, ST. PAUL'S
CHURCH-YARD.
MDCCLXXXI.

Fig. 9 Title page to the first edition of *Hymns in Prose for Children* (British Library).

HYMNS IN PROSE FOR CHILDREN

INTRODUCTION

Barbauld's most famous and most influential work originated as devotional exercises for the boys at Palgrave School. By January 1780 she had written six of the original twelve hymns and sent her brother copies:

I have not yet hymns enow to make a book even a Lilliputian one, & I do not know how many you have so pray tell me in your next. I will give you the first lines. *Come let us praise God for he is exceeding great. Come let us go forth into the fields. Come & I will shew you what is beautiful. Behold the shepherd of the flock. Child of reason whence comest thou? Child of mortality whence comest thou?* (Letter to JA, 19 January 1780)

Thus Hymns I–IV, VI, and X (in the 1781 numbering) must date to 1779 or earlier; she could well have written them at the same time she was writing *Lessons* for Charles. Schools were required to teach religion, and these hymns were intended for that purpose. John Aikin received them enthusiastically and urged her to publish them, but she did not feel ready.[1] When, exactly, she composed the remaining hymns is unknown. But on 22 August 1781, Joseph Johnson entered *Hymns in Prose for Children. By the Author of Lessons for Children*, with a preface signed 'A.L.B.' in the Stationers' Register under his own copyright. The *London Magazine* listed it among new publications for August and September, and the *Critical Review* for August 1781 noticed it, observing that the volume 'is intended to give the young reader a proper idea of the Creator and his works. It is the production of Mrs. Barbauld, and is written with that delicacy of style and sentiment which appears in all the compositions of that ingenious lady'.[2] The earliest advertisement we have found appeared in the *London Packet* for 15–18 February 1782.

To public perception, and as a sequence of texts, *Hymns in Prose* continued *Lessons for Children* by moving from elementary reading to elementary religious instruction. Such a move was conventional, for reading primers progressed from alphabets and phonics directly to catechisms or Bible stories. Barbauld based her reading pedagogy on the principle that children's texts should present only ideas that they are ready to understand. She had therefore excluded religion from *Lessons*. She designed *Hymns* for older children to implant religious ideas, and to do so using the child's own experience of the world, as *Lessons* had done.

Hymns appeals to the child's experience of Nature (the animals, plants, and weather that figure in her text) and village life (which provides, in Hymn VIII, an

---

[1] Letter to ALB, 18 February 1780; Letter to JA, 15 April 1780.
[2] 50:441; 52:156–7.

analogy of the world under Divine governance). In itself this was not novel, for her predecessor, Isaac Watts, had urged teachers of religion to invoke Nature as a means to know God; moreover, Dissenting belief valued the systematic knowledge of Nature revealed by Science for manifesting God's design of the universe. *Hymns* depends on an associationist psychology that derives ultimately from David Hartley (1705–57) but probably came to Barbauld through Hartley's admirer, her friend Joseph Priestley, whose sermon 'On Habitual Devotion' (1767) had inspired her poem, 'An Address to the Deity'. Priestley advised cultivating devotion by association: 'In the course of your usual employments, omit no proper opportunity of turning your thoughts towards God. Habitually regard him as *the ultimate cause*, and *proper author* of every thing you see.'[3] Early association was believed crucial to forging a person's habits of thought and feeling; hence Barbauld writes in her Preface, 'a child, to feel the full force of the idea of God, ought never to remember the time when he had no such idea'.

Barbauld conceived *Hymns* as a liturgy and an act of religious renovation. 'Perhaps a time may come', she had written in 'Thoughts on the Devotional Taste' (1775), 'when our worship...shall be new modelled by some free and enlarged genius. Perhaps the time may come, when the spirit of philosophy, and the spirit of devotion, shall join to conduct our public assemblies' (50). She composed *Hymns* for alternate recitation by the 'congregation' (her pupils); perhaps she acted as leader of the congregation. Its devotional character arises from its 'measured prose', her term for a style that is meant to suggest the English Bible. Doctrinally, *Hymns* departs from its most popular predecessor, Isaac Watts's *Divine Songs...for the Use of Children* (1715), a work she praises and dismisses in her Preface. She encourages a benevolent idea of religion that derived ultimately from the ethics of Francis Hutcheson (1694–1746), the Scottish philosopher who urged an optimistic view of human motivation and of God. Humans, Hutcheson argued, are the fundamentally good creatures of a kind and loving creator. Hence, *Hymns* is entirely free of any suggestion of sin. It invites the child reader to associate God with the beauties and pleasures of the natural world; Barbauld attaches religion not just to Science, but almost to pleasure. Only late in *Hymns* does the reader encounter the limits of the natural and human worlds—their being subject to mortality—and the consequent need for an unlimited, spiritual world.

Hymns made a deep impression on readers of all ages over several generations. 'I do not wonder you were struck with Mrs. Barbauld's Hymns', wrote Elizabeth Carter to a friend. 'They are all excellent, but there are some passages amazingly sublime.'[4] Mary Wollstonecraft recommended *Hymns* in her *Thoughts on the Education of Daughters* (1787): they 'would contribute', she thought, 'to make the Deity obvious to the senses'.[5] Thomas De Quincey recalled that *Hymns* 'left upon my childish recollection a deep impression of solemn beauty and simplicity'.[6] Harriet Martineau had been greatly affected at age 8: 'parts of [*Hymns*]...I dearly loved: but other parts made me shiver with awe'.[7] Another woman remembered

---

[3] JP, 'On Habitual Devotion', 114.
[4] *Series of Letters*, 2:346.   [5] Wollstonecraft, *Works*, 4:10.
[6] De Quincey, 11:127n.   [7] Martineau, 1:34.

that, 'when a little girl...I used to retire to a quiet room...and read [*Hymns*] aloud, in a solemn voice, page after page....The grave and well sustained rhythm had a charm for my ear;...and the elevated and reverent spirit of the compositions evoked similar feelings in my own breast' (S.A.A.).

Hymns enjoyed at least twenty editions during Barbauld's lifetime and remained in print in England for more than 120 years, and in the United States, where it may have been initially even more popular, for more than eighty. It was translated into French, Italian, Spanish, German, and Hungarian; in 1816 an English-language edition appeared in Calcutta. Anthologies reprinted selections. The hymns were sometimes turned into verse; Felicia Hemans was one reader who versified them.[8] The influence of *Hymns* on nineteenth-century Anglo-American culture is incalculable. The American Unitarian William Peabody was confident in 1826 that 'thousands look back [to *Hymns*] as the source of much happiness and devotion'.[9] Its literary influence has been traced in William Blake's *Songs of Innocence*[10] and William Wordsworth's 'Ode: Intimations of Immortality'.[11] Barbauld's measured prose impressed even Modernist commentators: extracts from *Hymns in Prose* 'might easily today be mistaken for simple passages from [the Symbolist poet Maurice] Maeterlinck', opined the *Cambridge History of English Literature* in 1914.[12] Echoes of *Hymns* are present in the poems of T. S. Eliot: compare the opening phrases of Hymns IV, VII, and IX with *Prufrock*'s 'Let us go, then, you and I', and *The Waste Land*'s 'Come in under the shadow of this red rock'.

The doctrinal optimism of *Hymns* caused consternation in strict religious circles. When 10-year-old Mary Howitt was enrolled in a Quaker school in 1809 her copy of *Hymns* was confiscated.[13] In 1840, an unnamed clergyman's wife undertook to rescue *Hymns* for orthodoxy by adding materials about sin and salvation: 'The divinity and incarnation of our Saviour, the fall and consequent depravity of man, are topics which are quite as well adapted to the capacities of children as many of those subjects of which Mrs. Barbauld has treated. The present edition is, therefore, undertaken to supply the deficiency which has been so long felt.'[14] Sarah Trimmer, who appraised children's books for the orthodox in *The Guardian of Education*, admired *Hymns* hugely but criticized it for 'doctrinal errors'. Because Trimmer spoke for orthodoxy, we quote some of her comments in our notes to the text.

TEXTUAL MATTERS

Hymns in Prose was a small book, like *Lessons for Children*, printed in large type with typically eleven or twelve lines per page, a format specifically designed for child readers; if Barbauld came to regard *Hymns* as a sequel to *Lessons*, its readers would have been age 4 or older. We suggest the format of the original by printing the text in larger than normal type. In 1814 Barbauld added three hymns, perhaps, as with *Lessons* in 1808, to secure copyright, or to counter a pirated edition

---

[8] Nicholson Papers 920 NIC 29, Liverpool RO. [9] Peabody, 310.
[10] Summerfield, 216–19. [11] Zall. [12] 11:384.
[13] Feldman, 325. [14] Quoted in R., Review of *Hymns in Prose*, 39.

(Edinburgh, 1813). The additions are less discordant with the original text of *Hymns in Prose* than are the additions to *Lessons*, but they depart from the liturgical character of the original and interrupt its implicit narrative from birth and Creation to death and Apocalypse. Therefore, we print them separately. Our copy text is the 1781 first edition; for the three hymns that were added in 1814, our copy text is the 16th edition, enlarged, London, 1814. To leave the texts of *Hymns in Prose* uninterrupted by superscripts, notes appear at the back of the book, cued to the hymn and line numbers.

PREFACE

Among the number of Books composed for the use of Children; though there are many, and some on a very rational plan, which unfold the system, and give a summary of the doctrines of religion; it would be difficult to find one calculated to assist them in the devotional part of it, except indeed Dr. Watts' Hymns for Children. These are in pretty general use, and the author is deservedly honoured for the condescension of his Muse, which was very able to take a loftier flight. But it may well be doubted, whether poetry ought to be lowered to the capacities of children, or whether they should not rather be kept from reading verse, till they are able to relish good verse: for the very essence of poetry is an elevation in thought and style above the common standard; and if it wants this character, it wants all that renders it valuable.

 The Author of these Hymns has therefore chosen to give them in prose. They are intended to be committed to memory, and recited. And it will probably be found, that the measured prose in which such pieces are generally written, is nearly as agreeable to the ear as a more regular rhythmus. Many of these Hymns are composed in alternate parts, which will give them something of the spirit of social worship.

 The peculiar design of this publication is, to impress devotional feelings as early as possible on the infant mind; fully convinced as the author is, that they cannot be impressed too soon, and that a child, to feel the full force of the idea of God, ought never to remember the time when he had no such idea—to impress them by connecting religion with a variety of sensible objects; with all that he sees, all he hears, all that affects his young mind with wonder or delight; and thus by deep, strong, and permanent associations, to lay the best foundation for practical devotion in future life. For he who has early been accustomed to see the Creator in the visible appearances of all around him, to feel his continual presence, and lean upon his daily protection—though his religious ideas may be mixed with many improprieties, which his correcter reason will refine away—has made large advances towards that habitual piety, without which religion can scarcely regulate the conduct, and will never warm the heart.

A. L. B.

HYMNS IN PROSE FOR CHILDREN

HYMN I

Come, let us praise God, for he is exceeding great; let us bless God, for he is very good.

He made all things; the sun to rule the day, the moon to shine by night.

He made the great whale, and the elephant; and the little worm that crawleth on the ground.

The little birds sing praises to God, when they warble sweetly in the green shade.

The brooks and rivers praise God, when they murmur melodiously amongst the smooth pebbles.

I will praise God with my voice; for I may praise him, though I am but a little child.

A few years ago, and I was a little infant, and my tongue was dumb within my mouth:

And I did not know the great name of God, for my reason was not come unto me.

But now I can speak, and my tongue shall praise him; I can think of all his kindness, and my heart shall love him.

Let him call me, and I will come unto him: let him command, and I will obey him.

When I am older, I will praise him better; and I will never forget God, so long as my life remaineth in me.

HYMN II

Come, let us go forth into the fields, let us see how the flowers spring, let us listen to the warbling of the birds, and sport ourselves upon the new grass.

The winter is over and gone, the buds come out upon the trees, the crimson blossoms of the peach and the nectarine are seen, and the green leaves sprout.

The hedges are bordered with tufts of primroses, and yellow cowslips that hang down their heads; and the blue violet lies hid beneath the shade.

The young goslings are running upon the green, they are just hatched, their bodies are covered with yellow down; the old ones hiss with anger if any one comes near.

The hen sits upon her nest of straw, she watches patiently the full time, then she carefully breaks the shell, and the young chickens come out.

The lambs just dropt are in the field, they totter by the side of their dams, their young limbs can hardly support their weight.

If you fall, little lambs, you will not be hurt; there is spread under you a carpet of soft grass, it is spread on purpose to receive you.

The butterflies flutter from bush to bush, and open their wings to the warm sun.

The young animals of every kind are sporting about, they feel themselves happy, they are glad to be alive,—they thank him that has made them alive.

They may thank him in their hearts, but we can thank him with our tongues; we are better than they, and can praise him better.

The birds can warble, and the young lambs can bleat; but we can open our lips in his praise, we can speak of all his goodness.

Therefore we will thank him for ourselves, and we will thank him for those that cannot speak.

Trees that blossom, and little lambs that skip about, if you could, you would say how good he is; but you are dumb, we will say it for you.

We will not offer you in sacrifice, but we will offer sacrifice for you, on every hill, and in every green field, we will offer the sacrifice of thanksgiving, and the incense of praise.

HYMN III

Behold the Shepherd of the flock, he taketh care for his sheep, he leadeth them among clear brooks, he guideth them to fresh pasture; if the young lambs are weary, he carrieth them in his arms; if they wander, he bringeth them back.

But who is the shepherd's shepherd? who taketh care for him? who guideth him in the path he should go? and if he wander, who shall bring him back?

God is the shepherd's shepherd. He is the Shepherd over all; he taketh care for all; the whole earth is his fold: we are all his flock; and every herb, and every green field is the pasture which he hath prepared for us.

The mother loveth her little child; she bringeth it up on her knees; she nourisheth its body with food; she feedeth its mind with knowledge: if it is sick, she nurseth it with tender love; she watcheth over it when asleep; she forgetteth it not for a moment; she teacheth it how to be good; she rejoiceth daily in its growth.

But who is the parent of the mother? who nourisheth her with good things, and watcheth over her with tender love, and remembereth her every moment? Whose arms are about her to guard her from harm? and if she is sick, who shall heal her.

God is the parent of the mother; he is the parent of all, for he created all. All the men, and all the women who are alive in the wide world, are his children; he loveth all, he is good to all.

The king governeth his people; he hath a golden crown upon his head, and the royal sceptre is in his hand; he sitteth upon a throne, and sendeth forth his commands; his subjects fear before him; if they do well, he protecteth them from danger; and if they do evil, he punisheth them.

But who is the sovereign of the king? who commandeth him what he must do? whose hand is stretched out to protect him from danger? and if he doeth evil, who shall punish him?

God is the sovereign of the king; his crown is of rays of light, and his throne is amongst the stars. He is King of kings, and Lord of lords: if he biddeth us live, we live; and if he biddeth us die, we die: his dominion is over all worlds, and the light of his countenance is upon all his works.

God is our Shepherd, therefore we will follow him: God is our Father, therefore we will love him: God is our King, therefore we will obey him.

HYMN IV

Come, and I will shew you what is beautiful. It is a rose fully blown. See how she sits upon her mossy stem, like the queen of all the flowers! her leaves glow like fire; the air is filled with her sweet odour; she is the delight of every eye.

She is beautiful, but there is a fairer than she. He that made the rose, is more beautiful than the rose: he is all lovely; he is the delight of every heart.

I will shew you what is strong. The lion is strong; when he raiseth up himself from his lair, when he shaketh his mane, when the voice of his roaring is heard, the cattle of the field fly, and the wild beasts of the desert hide themselves, for he is very terrible.

The lion is strong, but he that made the lion is stronger than he: his anger is terrible; he could make us die in a moment, and no one could save us out of his hand.

I will shew you what is glorious. The sun is glorious. When he shineth in the clear sky, when he sitteth on his bright throne in the heavens, and looketh abroad over all the earth, he is the most excellent and glorious creature the eye can behold.

The sun is glorious, but he that made the sun is more glorious than he. The eye beholdeth him not, for his brightness is more dazzling than we could bear. He seeth in all dark places; by night as well as by day; and the light of his countenance is over all his works.

Who is this great name, and what is he called, that my lips may praise him?

This great name is God. He made all things, but he is himself more excellent than all which he hath made: they are beautiful, but he is beauty; they are strong, but he is strength; they are perfect, but he is perfection.

HYMN V

The glorious sun is set in the west; the night-dews fall; and the air which was sultry, becomes cool.

The flowers fold up their coloured leaves; they fold themselves up, and hang their heads on the slender stalk.

The chickens are gathered under the wing of the hen, and are at rest: the hen herself is at rest also.

The little birds have ceased their warbling; they are asleep on the boughs, each one with his head behind his wing.

There is no murmur of bees around the hive, or amongst the honeyed woodbines; they have done their work, and lie close in their waxen cells.

The sheep rest upon their soft fleeces, and their loud bleating is no more heard amongst the hills.

There is no sound of a number of voices, or of children at play, or the trampling of busy feet, and of people hurrying to and fro.

The smith's hammer is not heard upon the anvil; nor the harsh saw of the carpenter.

All men are stretched on their quiet beds; and the child sleeps upon the breast of its mother.

Darkness is spread over the skies, and darkness is upon the ground; every eye is shut, and every hand is still.

Who taketh care of all people when they are sunk in sleep; when they cannot defend themselves, nor see if danger approacheth?

There is an eye that never sleepeth; there is an eye that seeth in dark night, as well as in the bright sun-shine.

When there is no light of the sun, nor of the moon; when there is no lamp in the house, nor any little star twinkling through the thick clouds; that eye seeth every where, in all places, and watcheth continually over all the families of the earth.

The eye that sleepeth not is God's; his hand is always stretched out over us.

He made sleep to refresh us when we are weary: he made night, that we might sleep in quiet.

As the mother moveth about the house with her finger on her lips, and stilleth every little noise, that her infant be not disturbed; as she draweth the curtains around its bed, and shutteth out the light from its tender eyes; so God draweth the curtains of darkness around us; so he maketh all things to be hushed and still, that his large family may sleep in peace.

Labourers spent with toil, and young children, and every little humming insect, sleep quietly, for God watcheth over you.

You may sleep, for he never sleeps: you may close your eyes in safety, for his eye is always open to protect you.

When the darkness is passed away, and the beams of the morning-sun strike through your eye-lids, begin the day with praising God, who hath taken care of you through the night.

Flowers, when you open again, spread your leaves, and smell sweet to his praise.

Birds, when you awake, warble your thanks amongst the green boughs; sing to him, before you sing to your mates.

Let his praise be in our hearts, when we lie down; let his praise be on our lips, when we awake.

HYMN VI

Child of reason, whence comest thou? What has thine eye observed, and whither has thy foot been wandering?

I have been wandering along the meadows, in the thick grass; the cattle were feeding around me, or reposing in the cool shade; the corn sprung up in the furrows; the poppy and the harebell grew among the wheat; the fields were bright with summer, and glowing with beauty.

Didst thou see nothing more? Didst thou observe nothing beside? Return again, child of reason, for there are greater things than these.—God was among the fields; and didst thou not perceive him? his beauty was upon the meadows; his smile enlivened the sun-shine.

I have walked through the thick forest; the wind whispered among the trees; the brook fell from the rocks with a pleasant murmur; the squirrel leapt from bough to bough; and the birds sung to each other amongst the branches.

Didst thou hear nothing, but the murmur of the brook? no whispers, but the whispers of the wind? Return again, child of reason, for there are greater things than these.—God was amongst the trees; his voice sounded in the murmur of the water; his music warbled in the shade; and didst thou not attend?

I saw the moon rising behind the trees: it was like a lamp of gold. The stars one after another appeared in the clear firmament. Presently I saw black clouds arise, and roll towards the south; the lightning streamed in thick flashes over the sky; the thunder growled at a distance; it came nearer, and I felt afraid, for it was loud and terrible.

Did thy heart feel no terror, but of the thunderbolt? Was there nothing bright and terrible, but the lightning? Return, O child of reason, for there are greater things than these.—God was in the storm, and didst thou not perceive him? His terrors were abroad, and did not thine heart acknowledge him?

God is in every place; he speaks in every sound we hear; he is seen in all that our eyes behold: nothing, O child of reason, is without God;—let God therefore be in all thy thoughts.

HYMN VII

Come, let us go into the thick shade, for it is the noon of day, and the summer sun beats hot upon our heads.

The shade is pleasant, and cool; the branches meet above our heads, and shut out the sun, as with a green curtain; the grass is soft to our feet, and a clear brook washes the roots of the trees.

The sloping bank is covered with flowers: let us lie down upon it; let us throw our limbs on the fresh grass, and sleep; for all things are still, and we are quite alone.

The cattle can lie down to sleep in the cool shade, but we can do what is better; we can raise our voices to heaven; we can praise the great God who made us. He made the warm sun, and the cool shade; the trees that grow upwards, and the brooks that run murmuring along. All the things that we see are his work.

Can we raise our voices up to the high heaven? can we make him hear who is above the stars? We need not raise our voices to the stars, for he heareth us when we only whisper; when we breathe out words softly with a low voice. He that filleth the heavens is here also.

May we that are so young, speak to him that always was? May we that can hardly speak plain, speak to God?

We that are so young, are but lately made alive; therefore we should not forget his forming hand, who hath made us alive. We that cannot speak plain, should lisp out praises to him who teacheth us how to speak, and hath opened our dumb lips.

When we could not think of him, he thought of us; before we could ask him to bless us, he had already given us many blessings.

He fashioneth our tender limbs, and causeth them to grow; he maketh us strong, and tall, and nimble.

Every day we are more active than the former day, therefore every day we ought to praise him better than the former day.

The buds spread into leaves, and the blossoms swell to fruit; but they know not how they grow, nor who caused them to spring up from the bosom of the earth.

Ask them, if they will tell thee; bid them break forth into singing, and fill the air with pleasant sounds.

They smell sweet; they look beautiful; but they are quite silent: no sound is in the still air; no murmur of voices amongst the green leaves.

The plants and the trees are made to give fruit to man; but man is made to praise God who made him.

We love to praise him, because he loveth to bless us; we thank him for life, because it is a pleasant thing to be alive.

We love God, who hath created all beings; we love all beings, because they are the creatures of God.

We cannot be good, as God is good, to all persons every where; but we can rejoice, that every where there is a God to do them good.

We will think of God when we play, and when we work; when we walk out, and when we come in; when we sleep, and we wake, his praise shall dwell continually upon our lips.

HYMN VIII

See where stands the cottage of the labourer, covered with warm thatch; the mother is spinning at the door; the young children sport before her on the grass; the elder ones learn to labour, and are obedient; the father worketh to provide them food: either he tilleth the ground, or he gathereth in the corn, or shaketh his ripe apples from the tree: his children run to meet him when he cometh home, and his wife prepareth the wholesome meal.

The father, the mother, and the children, make a family; the father is the master thereof. If the family is numerous, and the grounds large, there are servants to help to do the work: all these dwell in one house; they sleep beneath one roof; they eat of the same bread; they kneel down together and praise God every night and every morning with one voice; they are very closely united, and are dearer to each other than any strangers. If one is sick, they mourn together; and if one is happy, they rejoice together.

Many houses are built together; many families live near one another; they meet together on the green, and in pleasant walks, and to buy and sell, and in the house of justice; and the sound of the bell calleth them to the house of God, in company.

If one is poor, his neighbour helpeth him; if he is sad, he comforteth him. This is a village; see where it stands enclosed in a green shade, and the tall spire peeps above the trees. If there be very many houses, it is a town—it is governed by a magistrate.

Many towns, and a large extent of country, make a kingdom: it is enclosed by mountains; it is divided by rivers; it is washed by seas; the inhabitants thereof are countrymen; they speak the same language; they make war and peace together—a king is the ruler thereof.

Many kingdoms, and countries full of people, and islands, and large continents, and different climates, make up this whole world—God governeth it. The people swarm upon the face of it like ants upon a hillock: some are black with the hot sun; some cover themselves with furs against the sharp cold; some drink of the fruit of the vine; some the pleasant milk of the cocoa-nut; and others quench their thirst with the running stream.

All are God's family; he knoweth every one of them, as a shepherd knoweth his flock: they pray to him in different languages, but he understandeth them all; he heareth them all; he taketh care of all; none are so great, that he cannot punish them; none are so mean, that he will not protect them.

Negro woman, who sittest pining in captivity, and weepest over thy sick child; though no one seeth thee, God seeth thee; though no one pitieth thee, God pitieth thee: raise thy voice, forlorn and abandoned one; call upon him from amidst thy bonds, for assuredly he will hear thee.

Monarch, that rulest over an hundred states; whose frown is terrible as death, and whose armies cover the land, boast not thyself as though there were none above thee:—God is above thee; his powerful arm is always over thee; and if thou doest ill, assuredly he will punish thee.

Nations of the earth, fear the Lord; families of men, call upon the name of your God.

Is there any one whom God hath not made? let him not worship him: is there any one whom he hath not blessed? let him not praise him.

HYMN IX

Come, let us walk abroad; let us talk of the works of God.

Take up a handful of the sand; number the grains of it; tell them one by one into your lap.

Try if you can count the blades of grass in the field, or the leaves on the trees.

You cannot count them, they are innumerable; much more the things which God has made.

The fir groweth on the high mountain, and the grey willow bends above the stream.

The thistle is armed with sharp prickles; the mallow is soft and woolly.

The hop layeth hold with her tendrils, and claspeth the tall pole; the oak hath firm root in the ground, and resisteth the winter storm.

The daisy enamelleth the meadows, and groweth beneath the foot of the passenger: the tulip asketh a rich soil, and the careful hand of the gardener.

The iris and the reed spring up in the marsh; the rich grass covereth the meadows; and the purple heath-flower enliveneth the waste ground.

The water-lilies grow beneath the stream; their broad leaves float on the surface of the water: the wall-flower takes root in the hard stone, and spreads its fragrance amongst broken ruins.

Every leaf is of a different form; every plant hath a separate inhabitant.

Look at the thorns that are white with blossoms, and the flowers that cover the fields, and the plants that are trodden in the green path. The hand of man hath not planted them; the sower hath not scattered the seeds from his hand, nor the gardener digged a place for them with his spade.

Some grow on steep rocks, where no man can climb; in shaking bogs, and deep forests, and desert islands: they spring up every where, and cover the bosom of the whole earth.

Who causeth them to grow every where, and bloweth the seeds about in winds, and mixeth them with the mould, and watereth them with soft rains, and cherisheth them with dews? Who fanneth them with the pure breath of Heaven; and giveth them colours, and smells, and spreadeth out their thin transparent leaves?

How doth the rose draw its crimson from the dark brown earth, or the lily its shining white?

How can a small seed contain a plant? How doth every plant know its season to put forth? They are marshalled in order: each one knoweth his place, and standeth up in his own rank.

The snow-drop, and the primrose, make haste to lift their heads above the ground. When the spring cometh, they say, here we are! The carnation waiteth for the full strength of the year; and the hardy laurustinus cheereth the winter months.

Every plant produceth its like. An ear of corn will not grow from an acorn; nor will a grape stone produce cherries; but every one springeth from its proper seed.

Who preserveth them alive through the cold of winter, when the snow is on the ground, and the sharp frost bites on the plain? Who saveth a small seed, and a little warmth in the bosom of the earth, and causeth them to spring up afresh, and sap to rise through the hard fibres?

The trees are withered, naked, and bare; they are like dry bones. Who breatheth on them with the breath of spring, and they are covered with verdure, and green leaves sprout from the dead wood?

Lo, these are a part of his works; and a little portion of his wonders.

There is little need that I should tell you of God, for every thing speaks of him.

Every field is like an open book; every painted flower hath a lesson written on its leaves.

Every murmuring brook hath a tongue; a voice is in every whispering wind.

They all speak of him who made them; they all tell us, he is very good.

We cannot see God, for he is invisible; but we can see his works, and worship his foot-steps in the green sod.

They that know the most, will praise God the best; but which of us can number half his works?

HYMN X

Child of mortality, whence comest thou? why is thy countenance sad, and why are thine eyes red with weeping?

I have seen the rose in its beauty; it spread its leaves to the morning sun—I returned, it was dying upon its stalk; the grace of the form of it was gone; its loveliness was vanished away; the leaves thereof were scattered on the ground, and no one gathered them again.

A stately tree grew on the plain; its branches were covered with verdure; its boughs spread wide and made a goodly shadow; the trunk was like a strong pillar; the roots were like crooked fangs.—I returned, the verdure was nipt by the east wind; the branches were lopt away by the ax; the worm had made its way into the trunk, and the heart thereof was decayed; it mouldered away, and fell to the ground.

I have seen the insects sporting in the sun-shine, and darting along the stream; their wings glittered with gold and purple; their bodies shone like the green emerald: they were more numerous than I could count; their motions were quicker than my eye could glance—I returned, they were brushed into the pool; they were perishing with the evening breeze; the swallow had devoured them; the pike had seized them: there were none found of so great a multitude.

I have seen man in the pride of his strength; his cheeks glowed with beauty; his limbs were full of activity; he leaped; he walked; he ran; he rejoiced in that he was more excellent than those—I returned, he lay stiff and cold on the bare ground; his feet could no longer move, nor his hands stretch themselves out; his life was departed from him; and the breath out of his nostrils:—therefore do I weep, because DEATH is in the world; the spoiler is among the works of God: all that is made, must be destroyed; all that is born, must die.

HYMN XI

I have seen the flower withering on the stalk, and its bright leaves spread on the ground—I looked again, and it sprung forth afresh; the stem was crowned with new buds, and the sweetness therefore filled the air.

I have seen the sun set in the west, and the shades of night shut in the wide horizon: there was no colour, nor shape, nor beauty, nor music; gloom and darkness brooded around—I looked, the sun broke forth again from the east, and gilded the mountain tops; the lark rose to meet him from her low nest, and the shades of darkness fled away.

I have seen the insect, being come to its full size, languish, and refuse to eat: it spun itself a tomb, and was shrouded in the silken cone; it lay without feet, or shape, or power to move—I looked again, it had burst its tomb; it was full of life, and sailed on coloured wings through the soft air; it rejoiced in its new being.

Thus shall it be with thee, O man! and so shall thy life be renewed.

Beauty shall spring up out of ashes, and life out of the dust.

A little while shalt thou lie in the ground, as the seed lieth in the bosom of the earth: but thou shalt be raised again; and, if thou art good, thou shalt never die any more.

Who is he that cometh to burst open the prison doors of the tomb; to bid the dead awake, and to gather his redeemed from the four winds of heaven?

He descendeth on a fiery cloud; the sound of a trumpet goeth before him; thousands of angels are on his right hand.

It is Jesus, the Son of God; the saviour of men; the friend of the good.

He cometh in the glory of his Father; he hath received power from on high.

Mourn not therefore, child of immortality!—for the spoiler, the cruel spoiler that laid waste the works of God, is subdued: Jesus hath conquered death:—child of immortality! mourn no longer.

HYMN XII

The rose is sweet, but it is surrounded with thorns: the lily of the valley is fragrant, but it springeth up amongst the brambles.

The spring is pleasant, but it is soon past: the summer is bright, but the winter destroyeth the beauty thereof.

The rainbow is very glorious, but it soon vanisheth away: life is good, but it is quickly swallowed up in death.

There is a land, where the roses are without thorns, where the flowers are not mixed with brambles.

In that land, there is eternal spring, and light without any cloud.

The tree of life groweth in the midst thereof; rivers of pleasures are there, and flowers that never fade.

Myriads of happy spirits are there, and surround the throne of God with a perpetual hymn.

The angels with their golden harps sing praises continually, and the cherubim fly on wings of fire!

This country is Heaven: it is the country of those that are good; and nothing that is wicked must inhabit there.

The toad must not spit its venom amongst turtle doves; nor the poisonous hen-bane grow amongst sweet flowers.

Neither must any one that doeth ill, enter into that good land.

This earth is pleasant, for it is God's earth, and it is filled with many delightful things.

But that country is far better: there we shall not grieve any more, nor be sick any more, nor do wrong any more; there the cold of winter shall not wither us, nor the heats of summer scorch us.

In that country there are no wars nor quarrels, but all love one another with dear love.

When our parents and friends die, and are laid in the cold ground, we see them here no more; but there we shall embrace them again, and live with them, and be separated no more.

There we shall meet all good men, whom we read of in holy books.

There we shall see Abraham, the called of God, the father of the faithful; and Moses, after his long wanderings in the Arabian desert; and Elijah, the prophet of God; and Daniel, who escaped the lion's den; and there the son of Jesse, the shepherd king, the sweet singer of Israel.

They loved God on earth; they praised him on earth; but in that country they will praise him better, and love him more.

There we shall see Jesus, who is gone before us to that happy place; and there we shall behold the glory of the high God.

We cannot see him here, but we will love him here: we must be now on earth, but we will often think on heaven.

That happy land is our home: we are to be here but for a little while, and there for ever, even for ages of eternal years.

THE END

1814 ADDITIONS

[The following three hymns appeared for the first time in the 16th edition, enlarged, published in London in 1814 (our copy text) and numbered X–XII; original Hymns X–XII were renumbered XIII–XV.]

HYMN X

Look at that spreading oak, the pride of the village green! its trunk is massy, its branches are strong. Its roots, like crooked fangs, strike deep into the soil, and support its huge bulk. The birds build among the boughs; the cattle repose beneath its shade; the neighbours form groups beneath the shelter of its green canopy. The old men point it out to their children, but they themselves remember not its growth: generations of men one after another have been born and died, and this son of the forest has remained the same, defying the storms of two hundred winters.

Yet this large tree was once a little acorn; small in size, insignificant in appearance; such as you are now picking up upon the grass beneath it. Such an acorn, whose cup can only contain a drop or two of dew, contained the whole oak. All its massy trunk, all its knotted branches, all its multitude of leaves were in that acorn; it grew, it spread, it unfolded itself by degrees, it received nourishment from the rain, and the dews, and the well adapted soil, but it was all there. Rain, and dews, and soil, could not raise an oak without the acorn; nor could they make the acorn any thing but an oak.

The mind of a child is like the acorn; its powers are folded up, they do not yet appear, but they are all there. The memory, the judgment, the invention, the feeling of right and wrong, are all in the mind of a child; of a little infant just born; but they are not expanded, you cannot perceive them.

Think of the wisest man you ever knew or heard of; think of the greatest man; think of the most learned man, who speaks a number of languages and can find out hidden things; think of a man who stands like that tree, sheltering and protecting a number of his fellow men, and then say to yourself, the mind of that man was once like mine, his thoughts were childish like my thoughts, nay, he was like the babe just born, which knows nothing, remembers nothing, which cannot distinguish good from evil, nor truth from falsehood.

If you had only seen an acorn you could never guess at the form and size of an oak: if you had never conversed with a wise man, you could form no idea of him from the mute and helpless infant.

Instruction is the food of the mind; it is like the dew and the rain and the rich soil. As the soil and the rain and the dew cause the tree to swell and put forth its tender shoots, so do books and study and discourse feed the mind, and make it unfold its hidden powers.

Reverence therefore your own mind; receive the nurture of instruction, that the man within you may grow and flourish. You cannot guess how excellent he may become.

It was long before this oak shewed its greatness; year after year passed away, and it had only shot a little way above the ground, a child might have plucked it up with his little hands; it was long before any one called it a tree; and it is long before the child becomes a man.

The acorn might have perished in the ground, the young tree might have been shorn of its graceful boughs, the twig might have bent, and the tree would have been crooked, but if it grew at all it could have been nothing but an oak, it would not have been grass or flowers, which live their season and then perish from the face of the earth.

The child may be a foolish man, he may be a wicked man, but he must be a man; his nature is not that of any inferior creature, his soul is not akin to the beasts which perish.

O cherish then this precious mind, feed it with truth, nourish it with knowledge; it comes from God, it is made in his image; the oak will last for centuries of years, but the mind of man is made for immortality.

Respect in the infant the future man. Destroy not in the man the rudiments of an angel.

HYMN XI

The golden orb of the sun is sunk behind the hills, the colours fade away from the western sky, and the shades of evening fall fast around me.

Deeper and deeper they stretch over the plain; I look at the grass, it is no longer green; the flowers are no more tinted with various hues; the houses, the trees, the cattle, are all lost in the distance. The dark curtain of night is let down over the works of God; they are blotted out from the view, as if they were no longer there.

Child of little observation! canst thou see nothing because thou canst not see grass and flowers, trees and cattle? Lift up thine eyes from the ground shaded with darkness, to the heavens that are stretched over thy head; see how the stars one by one appear and light up the vast concave.

There is the moon bending her bright horns like a silver bow, and shedding her mild light, like liquid silver over the blue firmament.

There is Venus, the evening and the morning star; and the Pleiades, and the Bear that never sets, and the Pole star that guides the mariner over the deep.

Now the mantle of darkness is over the earth; the last little gleam of twilight is faded away; the lights are extinguished in the cottage windows, but the firmament burns with innumerable fires; every little star twinkles in its place. If you begin to count them they are more than you can number; they are like the sands of the sea shore.

The telescope shows you far more, and there are thousands and ten thousands of stars which no telescope has ever reached.

Now Orion heaves his bright shoulder above the horizon, and Sirius, the dog star, follows him, the brightest of the train.

Look at the milky way, it is a field of brightness; its pale light is composed of myriads of burning suns.

All these are God's families; he gives the sun to shine with a ray of his own glory; he marks the path of the planets, he guides their wanderings through the sky, and traces out their orbit with the finger of his power.

If you were to travel as swift as an arrow from a bow, and to travel on further and further still, for millions of years, you would not be out of the creation of God.

New suns in the depth of space would still be burning round you, and other planets fulfilling their appointed course.

Lift up thine eyes, child of earth, for God has given thee a glimpse of heaven.

The light of one sun is withdrawn, that thou mayest see ten thousand. Darkness is spread over the earth, that thou mayest behold, at a distance, the regions of eternal day.

This earth has a variety of inhabitants; the sea, the air, the surface of the ground, swarm with creatures of different natures, sizes, and powers; to know a very little of them is to be wise among the sons of men.

What then, thinkest thou, are the various forms and natures and senses and occupations of the peopled universe?

Who can tell the birth and generation of so many worlds? who can relate their histories? who can describe their inhabitants?

Canst thou measure infinity with a line? canst thou grasp the circle of infinite space?

Yet these all depend upon God, they hang upon him as a child upon the breast of its mother; he tempereth the heat to the inhabitant of Mercury; he provideth resources against the cold in the frozen orb of Saturn. Doubt not that he provideth for all beings that he has made.

Look at the moon when it walketh in brightness; gaze at the stars when they are marshalled in the firmament, and adore the Maker of so many worlds.

HYMN XII

It is now Winter, dead Winter. Desolation and silence reign in the fields, no singing of birds is heard, no humming of insects. The streams murmur no longer; they are locked up in frost.

The trees lift their naked boughs like withered arms into the bleak sky; the green sap no longer rises in their veins; the flowers and the sweet smelling shrubs are decayed to their roots.

The sun himself looks cold and chearless; he gives light only enough to show the universal desolation.

Nature, child of God, mourns for her children. A little while ago, and she rejoiced in her offspring; the rose shed its perfume upon the gale; the vine gave its fruit; her children were springing and blooming around her, on every lawn and every green bank.

O Nature, beautiful Nature, beloved child of God, why dost thou sit mourning and desolate? Has thy father forsaken thee, has he left thee to perish? Art thou no longer the object of his care?

He has not forsaken thee, O Nature; thou art his beloved child, the eternal image of his perfections; his own beauty is spread over thee, the light of his countenance is shed upon thee.

Thy children shall live again, they shall spring up and bloom around thee; the rose shall again breathe its sweetness on the soft air, and from the bosom of the ground verdure shall spring forth.

And dost thou not mourn, O Nature, for thy human births; for thy sons and thy daughters that sleep under the sod; and shall they not also revive? Shall the rose and the myrtle bloom anew, and shall man perish? Shall goodness sleep in the ground, and the light of wisdom be quenched in the dust, and shall tears be shed over *them* in vain?

They also shall live; their winter shall pass away; they shall bloom again. The tears of thy children shall be dried up when the eternal year proceeds. Oh come that eternal year!

PALGRAVE SCHOOL

INTRODUCTION

From July 1774 through June 1785 Anna Letitia and Rochemont Barbauld kept a school in the village of Palgrave in Suffolk, just south of the region's market town, Diss, in Norfolk. Their pupils ranged in age from 3 to 18.[1] The school's archive remained in the Aikin family and came into the possession of Charles William Brodribb, a direct descendant of John Aikin's son and Barbauld's nephew, Charles, a pupil at the school. The archive included a single issue of a 'weekly chronicle' or school newspaper composed at least in part by Barbauld; many issues of it must once have existed, and perhaps the verses she composed for or about pupils first appeared there. The archive perished on the night of 25 September 1940, when Brodribb's London residence was damaged by bombing. Brodribb's essay, 'Mrs. Barbauld's School', the first detailed account of the school, was the only one based on the archive.

The Barbaulds ran the school as a community with elements of a republic. Pupils elected a 'captain' of the school from among themselves, thus learning forms and ethics of representative government. Those forms and ethics were set forth in the following document.[2]

Privileges and Duties of the Captain of Palgrave School

The Captain shall take his place wherever he chooses at dinner and supper, and wherever the boys are assembled together he shall always have a place at the fire in the school or hall.

He shall have a right to the sitting-room above stairs.

He shall arbitrate in all disputes amongst the boys, reserving, however, a right of appeal to Mr. Barbauld.

If any presents of fruit, etc., are made to the school he shall divide them and claim a double share himself.

The Captain shall hold himself obliged to set a good example in the school, both in morals and diligence, to protect the younger ones from oppression, to preserve

---

[1] Ninety-five of the pupils have been identified, at least by surname; the total, over eleven years, is estimated to be 130. For subsequent accounts of the school, based in part on documents held elsewhere, see McCarthy, '"Celebrated Academy"', and *ALBVE*, ch. 8.

[2] Published by Brodribb from a manuscript 'preserved in [Barbauld's] handwriting'. The whereabouts of that holograph are today unknown. Our copy text is Broadribb's published transcription.

order; and as far as is in his power to prevent anything from being done which may throw dishonour on the society. It will be the Captain's business to deliver the sense of the school when any favours are to be asked of Mr. Barbauld or any other person; or when any thing is to be said which relates to the whole body.

The office of Captain will continue for one session only; he is to be chosen by a majority of votes, Mr. Barbauld always reserving to himself a negative on the candidate.

If the Captain should be guilty of falsehood, breach of trust, oppression, habitual indolence, or any other capital fault, he will be immediately degraded from his dignity.

Form of declaration for voters: I, A.B., promise on the honour of a gentleman that I will give my vote unbiassed by any motives but a serious and deliberate regard for the merits of the candidates.

Form of engagement for the Captain: I, A.B., engage on the honour of a gentleman to conduct myself in the office I am elected to in such a manner as may best promote the reputation, order, happiness and improvement of the society to which I belong.

*It is expected that the Captain be never seen without his badge at home or abroad.

The course of study at Palgrave included the customary Latin and Greek Classics, History, English Composition, and Science; the last three were Barbauld's province. It is impossible to tell whether her lectures on 'Earth' and 'Plants', published long afterwards in *A Legacy for Young Ladies*, were delivered at the school or addressed to individual pupils outside the school, contemporaneously or years later; they are at least consistent with what we know of Barbauld's pedagogy there. A fragment in Barbauld's hand on Arabian history looks like notes for a lecture:

Ismael Abulfeda Prince of Hamah & descended from brother of Saladin b at Damascus 1273 d 1333. Skilled in medicine philosophy & Poetry, but chiefly known by his his^y & geograph^y works. Designs of publish^g his works have failed both in France & England. Michaelis has lately pub^d his Geo^y of Egypt. He brought his General His. down to latter years of his life, of which only portions have been given to the world, his acc^t *of Mahomet* by Gagnier printed Oxford folio 1723. his his. *of the Arabian Caliphs* to 406 Hegira Leipsic 1754, & narrative circumstances relating to Saladin annexed by Schultens to Bohaddin's life of Saladin. He did not possess his dominions till established in them by sultan of Egypt 13 years before his death[.][3]

Every May near the end of term Palgrave boys performed plays. The playbill survives for William Mason's *Caractacus* (see Fig. 10). At the school examinations

---

[3] Warrington Library MS 269, fol. 5, endorsed by Lucy Aikin 'Handwriting of Mrs Barbauld'; reprinted in McCarthy, '"Celebrated Academy"', 326.

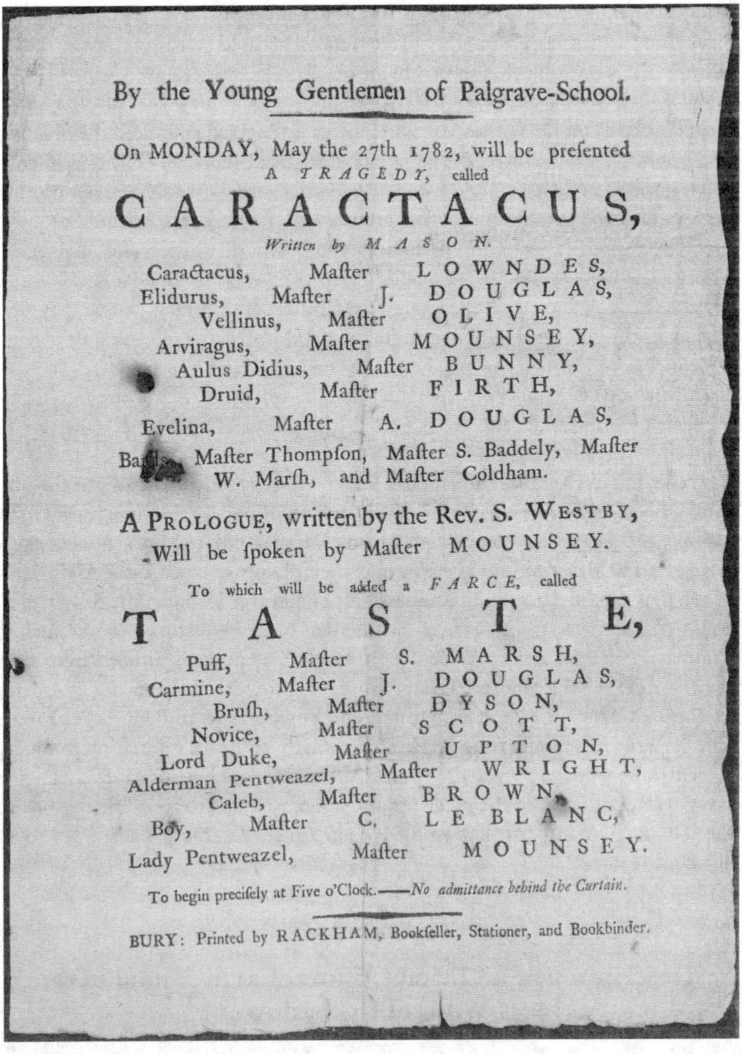

By the Young Gentlemen of Palgrave-School.

On MONDAY, May the 27th 1782, will be presented
A *TRAGEDY*, called

CARACTACUS,

Written by MASON.

Caractacus, Master LOWNDES,
Elidurus, Master J. DOUGLAS,
Vellinus, Master OLIVE,
Arviragus, Master MOUNSEY,
Aulus Didius, Master BUNNY,
Druid, Master FIRTH,
Evelina, Master A. DOUGLAS,
Bards, Master Thompson, Master S. Baddely, Master W. Marsh, and Master Coldham.

A PROLOGUE, written by the Rev. S. WESTBY, Will be spoken by Master MOUNSEY.

To which will be added a *FARCE*, called

TASTE,

Puff, Master S. MARSH,
Carmine, Master J. DOUGLAS,
Brush, Master DYSON,
Novice, Master SCOTT,
Lord Duke, Master UPTON,
Alderman Pentweazel, Master WRIGHT,
Caleb, Master BROWN,
Boy, Master C. LE BLANC,
Lady Pentweazel, Master MOUNSEY.

To begin precisely at Five o'Clock.——*No admittance behind the Curtain.*

BURY: Printed by RACKHAM, Bookseller, Stationer, and Bookbinder.

Fig. 10 Playbill for Palgrave School productions of *Caractacus* by William Mason and *Taste* by Samuel Foote, 27 May 1782 (MS MC 257/63/1/3, Norfolk RO). Courtesy of the Norfolk Record Office.

before Christmas the boys recited verses or scenes from plays. Besides adapting plays from Shakespeare and other playwrights, Barbauld sometimes wrote scenes herself, so it is probable that she wrote the playlets 'Canute's Reproof' and 'Alfred' (published in *Evenings at Home*) for performance at Palgrave. Especially in France, plays figured as tools of education, and liberals in England embraced the practice: *Le Théatre de l'Education* by the French educationist Stéphanie Félicité de Genlis was translated in 1781 as *The Theatre of Education*, and Barbauld and her brother were approached to translate another French work for children, Arnaud Berquin's *Ami des Enfans* (1782–4), a periodical composed of stories and dialogues.[4] Afterwards, these works inspired John Aikin's *Evenings at Home*. 'It is hoped', explained the preface to *The Theatre of Education*, 'that young people may find lessons in [these playlets], both entertaining and instructive. Besides, in playing these pieces, in learning them by heart, several advantages may be found; such as, engraving excellent principles upon their minds, exercising their memories, forming their pronunciation, and giving them a graceful pleasing manner' ('Preface of the Editor', de Genlis, 1:4).

According to Brodibb, the school's weekly newspaper contained puzzles and word games, sometimes derived from the names of pupils. So the solution to 'A man behind a cave' is 'Denman'. (Thomas Denman entered the school at age 3 in 1782.) The description that follows is the only prose piece Lucy Aikin published that can be dated without question to Palgrave School ('Mr. B.'s menagerie'). It describes a pupil there in the idiom of Natural History—works such as Thomas Pennant's *British Zoology* (1768–70). The pupil is either Philip Gell (1775–1842) or his more famous younger brother, William (1777–1836), explorer of Troy and Pompeii, author, and chamberlain to Princess Caroline. The Gells were a family from Derbyshire, which enjoyed a reputation for being romantically wild; so a 'creature' from Derbyshire could be imagined as a noble savage. Barbauld wrote the piece around 1780, perhaps to welcome the boy to the school. The only text known today is in *Legacy for Young Ladies*, pp. 70–2, our copy text.

Description of a Curious Animal Lately Found in the Wilds of Derbyshire

This little creature, which seems a very beautiful specimen of the species to which it belongs, is about the size of a common monkey, which it likewise much resembles in its agility and various tricks. The eye is very lively, wild, and roving; teeth white and sharp; body covered with a woolly integument, except the head and fore feet; hair rude and tangled, hangs

---

[4] For details about *L'Ami des Enfans* and Barbauld, see the notes to her 'Letter to Recommend French Authors'.

about the shoulders and covers the forehead as low as the eyes, rest of the face naked; skin soft and white; cheeks full and of a glowing red; under lip swelled and pouting; paws white with streaks of brown; claws long, toes of the hind feet joined together.

Habits.—This animal walks, indifferently, on two or on four feet, feeds itself with its fore feet, makes a chattering noise, climbs, leaps and runs, and has a spring in its muscles equal to an antelope; has a wonderful suppleness in its limbs, which it can twist into various attitudes, all surprisingly graceful; is always in motion, except when basking by the fire, of which it is very fond in winter. Will often shake its hair over the whole face, which gives it a look of peculiar wildness. Is very good-natured and playful, caressing to its keeper and every one who takes notice of it. Is however easily put in a passion, and when angry makes a threatening noise, but is soon put to flight by the least show of resistance. If seized, kicks with its hind legs: is however tolerably docile, considering how lately it has been caught. Feeds on fruits, roots, or flesh; will eat cakes or nuts out of the hand. To be seen at the Rev. Mr. B's menagerie, with many other young animals equally curious.

SCIENCE LECTURES

One of Barbauld's subjects at Palgrave School was Natural Science. Much of her teaching may have been empirical, consisting of experiments such as those Joseph Priestley conducted with friends as spectators, but much of it was inspirational. Among liberals, Science figured as a spiritual discipline. Thus the Scottish mathematician Colin Maclaurin declared that the scientist, 'while he contemplates and admires so excellent a system, cannot but be himself excited and animated to correspond with the general harmony of nature'.[5] Benjamin Stillingfleet (1702–71), who introduced the work of Carl Linnaeus to British botany, described the solar year as 'formed by the Creator'.[6] For him as for other liberals, there was no contradiction between Science and Religion. Later Barbauld was to inform a prospective pupil that ignorance of 'the great laws of the universe' is 'unpardonable', for knowledge of them is knowledge of the Divine plan (see 'On Female Studies').

Lucy Aikin published 'Earth' and 'On Plants' without a date, but they can reasonably be regarded as Palgrave lectures. In them Barbauld retailed up-to-date information about their subjects and sought to arouse reverence for the natural world: they are spiritual meditations as much as lectures. Similar pieces by John Aikin would appear in *Evenings at Home* (1792–6), for example, 'The Leguminous

---

[5] 'A General View of Sir Isaac Newton's Method', in Broadie, 782.
[6] Stillingfleet, 252.

Plants' (3:82–92). Copy texts: 'Earth': *Legacy for Young Ladies*, pp. 112–16; 'On Plants': *Legacy for Young Ladies*, pp. 105–10.

Earth

All the different substances which we behold have by the earliest philosophers been resolved into four elements,—*Earth, Water, Air,* and *Fire*. These, combined with endless diversity, in their various dance, under the direction of the great First Mover, form this scene of things,—so complex, so beautiful, so infinitely varied!

Earth is the element which on many accounts claims our chief notice. It forms the bulk of that vast body of matter which composes our globe; and, like the bones to the human body, it gives firmness, shape, and solidity to the various productions of Nature. It is ponderous, dull, unanimated, ever seeking the lowest place; and, except moved by some external impulse, prone to rest in one sluggish mass. Yet when fermented into life by the quickening power of vegetation,—in how many forms of grace and beauty does it rise to the admiring eye! How gay, how vivid with colours! how fragrant with smells! how rich with tastes,—luscious, poignant, sapid, mild, pungent, or saccharine! Into what delicate textures is it spread out in the thin leaf of the rose, or the light film of the floating gossamer! How curious in the elegant ramifications of trees and shrubs, or the light dust which the microscope discovers to contain the seed of future plants!

Nor has Earth less of magnificence, in the various appearances with which upon a larger scale its broad surface is diversified;—whether we behold it stretched out into immense plains and vast savannahs, whose level green is only bounded by the horizon; or moulded into those gentle risings and easy declivities whose soft and undulating lines court the pencil of the landscape-painter; or whether, swelled into bulk enormous, it astonishes the eye with vast masses of solid rock and long-continued bulwarks of stone. Such are the Pyrenees, the Alps, the Andes, which stand the everlasting boundaries of nations; and, while kingdoms rise and fall, and the lesser works of nature change their appearance all around them, immoveable on their broad basis, strike the mind with an idea of stability little short of eternal duration.

If from the mountains which possess the middle of Earth we bend our course to the green verge of her dominions, the utmost limits of her shores, where land and water, like two neighbouring potentates, wage eternal war,—with what steady majesty does she repel the encroachments of the ever-restless ocean, and dash the turbulence of waves from her strong-ribbed sides!

Nor do thy praises end here:—With a kind of filial veneration I hail thee, O universal mother of all the elements,—to man the most mild, the most beneficent, the most congenial! Man himself is formed from thee: on thy maternal breast he reposes when weary; thy teeming lap supplies him with never-failing plenty: and when for a few years he has moved about upon thy surface, he is gathered again to thy peaceful bosom, at once his nurse, his cradle, and his grave.

Who can reckon up the benefits supplied to us by this parent Earth,— ever serviceable, ever indulgent! with how many productions does she reward the labour of the cultivator! how many more does she pour out spontaneously! How faithfully does she keep, with what large interest does she restore, the seed committed to her by the husbandman! What an abundance does she yield, of food for the poor, of delicacies for the rich! Her wealth is inexhaustible; and all that is called riches amongst men consists in possessing a small portion of her surface.

How patiently does she support the various burdens laid upon her! We tear her with ploughs and harrows, we crush her with castles and palaces; nay we penetrate her very bowels, and bring to light the veined marble, the pointed crystal, the ponderous ores and sparkling gems, deep hid in darkness the more to excite the industry of man. Yet, torn and harassed as she might seem to be, our mother Earth is still fresh and young, as if she but now came out of the hands of her Creator. Her harvests are as abundant, her horn of plenty as overflowing, her robe as green, her unshorn tresses (the waving foliage of brown forests) as luxuriant; and all her charms as blooming and full of vigour. Such she remains, and such we trust she will remain, till in some fated hour the more devouring element of fire, having broke the bonds of harmonious union, shall seize upon its destined prey, and all nature sink beneath the mighty ruin.

On Plants

Plants stand next to animals in the scale of existence: they are, like them, organized bodies; like them, increase by nutrition, which is conveyed through a system of tubes and fine vessels, and assimilated to their substance; like them, they propagate their race from a parent, and each seed produces its own plant; like them, they grow by insensible degrees from an infant state to full vigour, and after a certain term of maturity decay and die. In short, except the powers of speech and locomotion, they seem to possess every characteristic of sentient life.

A plant consists of a root, a stem, leaves, and a flower or blossom.

The root is bulbous, as the onion; long, like a parsnip or carrot; or branched out into threads, as the greater number are, and particularly all the large ones;—a bulbous root could not support a large tree.

The stem is single or branched, clinging for support or upright, clothed with a skin or bark.

The flower contains the principle of reproduction, as the root does of individuality. This is the most precious part of the plant, to which every thing contributes. The root nourishes it, the stem supports, the leaves defend and shelter it: it comes forth but when Nature has prepared for it by showers and sun and gentle soothing warmth;—colour, beauty, scent adorn it; and when it is complete, the end of the plant's existence is answered. It fades and dies; or, if capable by its perennial nature of repeating the process, it hides in its inmost folds the precious germ of new being, and itself almost retires from existence till a new year.

A tree is one of the most stately and beautiful objects in God's visible creation. It does not admit of an exact definition, but is distinguished from the humbler plant by its size, the strength of its stem, which becomes a trunk, and the comparative smallness of the blossom. In the fruit-trees, indeed, the number of blossoms compensates for their want of size; but in the forest-trees the flower is scarcely visible. Production seems not to be so important a process where the parent tree lives for centuries.

Every part of vegetables is useful. Of many the roots are edible, and the seeds are generally so; of many the leaves, as of the cabbage, spinach; the buds, as of the asparagus, cauliflower; the bark is often employed medicinally, as the quinquina and cinnamon.

The trunk of a tree determines the manner of its growth, and gives firmness: the foliage serves to form one mass of a number of trees; while the distinct lines are partly seen, partly hidden. The leaves throw over the branches a rich mantle, like flowing tresses; they wave in the wind with an undulatory motion, catch the glow of the evening sun, or glitter with the rain; they shelter innumerable birds and animals, and afford variety in colours, from the bright green of spring to the varied tints of autumn. In winter, however, the form of each tree and its elegant ramifications are discerned, which were lost under the flowing robe of verdure.

Trees are beautiful in all combinations: the single tree is so; the clump, the grove, rising like an amphitheatre; the flowing line that marks the skirts of wood and the dark, deep, boundless shade of the forest; the green line of the hedge-row, the more artificial avenue, the Gothic arch of verdure, the tangled thicket.

Young trees are distinguished by beauty, in maturity their characteristic is strength. The ruin of a tree is venerable even when fallen: we are then more sensible of its towering height: we also observe the root, the deep fangs which held it against so many storms, and the firmness of the wood; a sentiment of pity mixes too with our admiration. The trees in groves and woods shed a brown religious horror,[1] which favoured the religion of the ancient world. Trees shelter from cutting winds and sea air; they preserve moisture: but if too many, in their thick and heavy mass lazy vapours stagnate; their profuse perspiration is unwholesome;[2] they shut out the golden sun and ventilating breeze.

It should seem as if the number of trees must have been diminishing for ages, for in no cultivated country does the growth of trees equal the waste of them. A few gentlemen raise plantations, but many more cut down; and the farmer thinks not of so lofty a thing as the growth of ages. Trees are too lofty to want the hand of man. The florist may mingle his tulips and spread the paper ruff on his carnations; he may trim his mount of roses and his laurel hedge: but the lofty growth of trees soars far above him. If he presumes to fashion them with his shears, and trim them into fanciful or mathematical shapes, offended taste will mock all his improvements. Even in planting he can do little. He may succeed in fancying a clump or laying out an avenue, and may perhaps gently incline the boughs to form the arch; but a forest was never planted.

FABLES

Although none of Barbauld's fables can be assigned with certainty to Palgrave School, it is reasonable to suppose that she wrote them for pupils there. Fables were a staple of eighteenth-century education and popular wisdom literature, and were used at Palgrave: in November 1783 Rochemont Barbauld ordered six copies of 'Clarke's Esop' in Latin and English (*Fabulæ Æsopi selectæ... With an English Translation... by H. Clarke*, 1774); earlier that year pupil George Aikin, one of Barbauld's nephews, was reading *Fables Choisies*[7]—probably Louis Chambaud's (London, 1751), for in later years Barbauld '[took] it for granted the young pupil has read Chambauld's *Fables Choisies*, or some elementary book of the same nature' (see, in the Appendix, her 'Letter to Recommend French Authors'). Fables could be devices for teaching a classical language, or for inculcating ethical views and practical wisdom, their traditional purpose. The same story line and set of characters (usually two, and usually in opposition to each other: the Cock and the Fox, for instance, or the Man and the Dog) could be adapted to make various ethical points.

Barbauld's 'The Pine and the Olive' looks like a critique of Stoicism, but actually compares bad Stoicism (mere obduracy and pride) to good Stoicism, such as the

---

[7] ALB to JA, in McCarthy, '"Celebrated Academy"', 330.

Greek philosopher Epictetus expounds: the true philosopher, says Epictetus (in Elizabeth Carter's 1758 version), 'adapt[s] his Will to whatever happens. So that none of the Things which happen, may happen against our Inclination; nor those which do not happen, be wished for by us.'[8] The Olive accommodates herself to change; the Pine refuses. A predecessor in Antoine Houdart de la Motte, *One Hundred New Court Fables* (1721), is 'The Peach Tree and the Mulberry Tree'. Lucy Aikin published 'The Pine and the Olive', without date, in *Legacy for Young Ladies* (pp. 23–5), our copy text.

Palgrave School numbered among its pupils sons of gentry and even of aristocracy. Barbauld might have composed, or adapted, 'The River and the Brook' for their particular benefit, although the sociopolitical ethic which that fable inculcates would have been suitable for all. Alone among her fables this one may be traced, in outline if not in detail and moral, to a model in H. Clarke's *Aesop*: 'Fable CXXIX. Of the River provoking his Spring with Reproaches'. Lucy Aikin published it, without date, in *Legacy for Young Ladies* (pp. 209–10), our copy text.

Four fables were first published in *Evenings at Home*, volumes I and II (1793): 'The Wasp and Bee' (I:20–1); 'The Goose and Horse' (II:56–8), 'The Flying Fish' (II:119–20), 'The Phenix and Dove' (II:137–9). Our copy texts are from these first editions. 'Confidence and Modesty: A Fable' was first published in *Legacy for Young Ladies* (pp. 235–8), our copy text.

The Pine and the Olive: A Fable

A Stoic, swelling with the proud consciousness of his own worth, took a solitary walk; and straying amongst the groves of Academus, he sat down between an Olive and a Pine tree. His attention was soon excited by a murmur which he heard among the leaves. The whispers increased; and listening attentively, he plainly heard the Pine say to the Olive as follows: "Poor tree! I pity thee; thou now spreadest thy green leaves and exultest in all the pride of youth and spring; but how soon will thy beauty be tarnished! The fruit which thou exhaustest thyself to bear, shall hardly be shaken from thy boughs before thou shalt grow dry and withered; thy green veins, now so full of juice, shall be frozen; naked and bare thou wilt stand exposed to all the storms of winter, whilst my firmer leaf shall resist the change of the seasons. *Unchangeable* is my motto, and through the various vicissitudes of the year I shall continue equally green and vigorous as I am at present."

The Olive, with a graceful wave of her boughs, replied: "It is true thou wilt always continue as thou art at present. Thy leaves will keep that sullen and gloomy green in which they are now arrayed, and the stiff regularity of thy branches will not yield to those storms which will bow down many of the feebler tenants of the grove. Yet I wish not to be like thee. I rejoice when nature rejoices; and when I am desolate, nature mourns with me. I fully

[8] Carter, *Epictetus*, 159.

enjoy pleasure in its season, and I am contented to be subject to the influences of those seasons and that economy of nature by which I flourish. When the spring approaches, I feel the kindly warmth; my branches swell with young buds, and my leaves unfold; crowds of singing birds which never visit thy noxious shade, sport on my boughs, my fruit is offered to the Gods and rejoices men; and when the decay of nature approaches, I shed my leaves over the funeral of the falling year, and am well contented not to stand a single exemption to the mournful desolation I see everywhere around me."

The Pine was unable to frame a reply; and the philosopher turned away his steps rebuked and humbled.

The River and the Brook: A Fable

There was once a River which was very large, and flowed through a great extent of country which it rendered fruitful and pleasant. It was some miles broad at its mouth; it was navigable for a long way up the stream, and ships of large burthen floated on its bosom. The River, elated with its own consequence, despised all the little brooks and streams which fell into it; and swelling above its banks with pride, said to them—"Ye petty and inconsiderable streams, that hasten to lose your names and your being in my flood, how little does your feeble tribute increase my greatness! whether you withhold or bring it I feel no increase and shall perceive no diminution."

"Proud stream!" replied a little Brook which lifted up its head and murmured these words,—"dost thou not know that all thy greatness is owing to us whom thou despisest?"

The River, mindless of this reproof, in wanton pride overflowed its banks. But the next summer proving a very hot one, all the little streams were dried up, and the River was so far dried that men and cattle could wade over it; and a strong wind bringing a heap of dust across its stream, it was lost in the sands and never heard of afterwards.

The Wasp and Bee: A Fable

A Wasp met a Bee, and said to him, Pray, can you tell me what is the reason that men are so ill-natured to me, while they are fond of you? We are both very much alike, only that the broad golden rings about my body make me much handsomer than you are: we are both winged insects, we both love honey, and we both sting people when we are angry; yet men always hate me, and try to kill me, though I am much more familiar with them than you are, and pay them visits in their houses, and at their tea-table, and at all their meals: while you are very shy, and hardly ever come near them: yet they build you curious houses, thatched with straw, and take care of, and feed you, in the winter very often:—I wonder what is the reason.

The Bee said, because you never do them any good, but, on the contrary, are very troublesome and mischievous; therefore they do not like to see you; but they know that I am busy all day long in making them honey. You had better pay them fewer visits, and try to be useful.

The Goose and Horse: A Fable

A Goose, who was plucking grass upon a common, thought herself affronted by a Horse who fed near her, and in hissing accents thus addressed him. "I am certainly a more noble and perfect animal than you, for the whole range and extent of your faculties is confined to one element. I can walk upon the ground as well as you; I have besides wings, with which I can raise myself in the air; and when I please, I can sport in ponds and lakes, and refresh myself in the cool waters: I enjoy the different powers of a bird, a fish, and a quadruped."

The Horse, snorting somewhat disdainfully, replied, "It is true you inhabit three elements, but you make no very distinguished figure in any one of them. You fly, indeed; but your flight is so heavy and clumsy, that you have no right to put yourself on a level with the lark or the swallow. You can swim on the surface of the waters, but you cannot live in them as fishes do; you cannot find your food in that element, nor glide smoothly along the bottom of the waves. And when you walk, or rather waddle, upon the ground, with your broad feet and your long neck stretched out, hissing at every one who passes by, you bring upon yourself the derision of all beholders. I confess that I am only formed to move upon the ground; but how graceful is my mane![a] how well turned my limbs! how highly finished my whole body! how great my strength! how astonishing my speed! I had far rather be confined to one element, and be admired in that, than be a Goose in all."

The Flying Fish

The Flying Fish, says the fable,[3] had originally no wings; but being of an ambitious and discontented temper, she repined at being always confined to the waters, and wished to soar in the air. "If I could fly like the birds," said she, "I should not only see more of the beauties of nature, but I should be able to escape from those fish which are continually pursuing me, and which render my life miserable." She therefore petitioned Jupiter for a

---

[a] We have editorially corrected 'make', a printer's error, to 'mane'.

pair of wings: and immediately she perceived her fins to expand. They suddenly grew to the length of her whole body, and became at the same time so strong as to do the office of a pinion. She was at first much pleased with her new powers, and looked with an air of disdain on all her former companions; but she soon perceived herself exposed to new dangers. When flying in the air, she was incessantly pursued by the tropic bird, and the Albatross; and when for safety she dropped into the water, she was so fatigued with her flight, that she was less able than ever to escape from her old enemies the fish. Finding herself more unhappy than before, she now begged of Jupiter to recal his present; but Jupiter said to her, "When I gave you your wings, I well knew they would prove a curse; but your proud and restless disposition deserved this disappointment. Now, therefore, what you begged as a favour, keep as a punishment!"

The Phenix and Dove

A Phenix, who had long inhabited the solitary deserts of Arabia, once flew so near the habitations of men as to meet with a tame Dove, who was sitting on her nest, with wings expanded, and fondly brooding over her young ones, while she expected her mate, who was foraging abroad to procure them food. The Phenix, with a kind of insulting compassion, said to her, "Poor bird, how much I pity thee! confined to a single spot, and sunk in domestic cares, thou art continually employed either in laying eggs or in providing for thy brood; and thou exhaustest thy life and strength in perpetuating a feeble and defenceless race. As to myself, I live exempt from toil, care, and misfortune. I feed upon nothing less precious than rich gums and spices; I fly through the trackless regions of the air, and when I am seen by men, am gazed at with curiosity and astonishment; I have no one to controul my range, no one to provide for; and when I have fulfilled my five centuries of life, and seen the revolutions of ages, I rather vanish than die, and a successor without my care, springs up from my ashes. I am an image of the great sun whom I adore; and glory in being, like him, single and alone, and having no likeness."

The Dove replied, "O Phenix, I pity thee much more than thou affectest to pity me! What pleasure canst thou enjoy, who livest forlorn and solitary in a trackless and unpeopled desert; who hast no mate to caress thee, no young ones to excite thy tenderness and reward thy cares, no kindred, no society amongst thy fellows. Not long life only, but immortality itself would be a curse, if it were to be bestowed on such uncomfortable terms. For my part, I know that my life will be short, and therefore I employ it in raising a numerous posterity, and in opening my heart to all the sweets of domestic happiness. I am beloved by my partner; I am dear to man; and shall leave marks behind me that I have lived. As to the sun, to whom thou hast presumed to compare thyself, that glorious being is so totally different from, and so infinitely superior to, all the creatures upon earth, that it does not become us to liken ourselves to him, or to determine upon the manner of his existence. One obvious difference, however, thou mayest remark; that the sun, though alone, by his prolific heat, produces all things, and though he shines so high above our heads, gives us reason every moment to bless his beams; whereas thou, swelling with thy imaginary greatness, dreamest away a long period of existence, equally void of comfort and usefulness."

Confidence and Modesty: A Fable

When the Gods, knowing it to be for the benefit of mortals that the few should lead and that the many should follow, sent down into this lower world Ignorance and Wisdom, they decreed to each of them an attendant and guide, to conduct their steps and facilitate their introduction. To Wisdom they gave Confidence, and Ignorance they placed under the guidance of Modesty. Thus paired, the parties travelled about the world for some time with mutual satisfaction.

Wisdom, whose eye was clear and piercing, and commanded a long reach of country, followed her conductor with pleasure and alacrity. She saw the windings of the road at a great distance; her foot was firm, her ardour was unbroken, and she ascended the hill or traversed the plain with speed and safety.

Ignorance, on the other hand, was short-sighted and timid. When she came to a spot where the road branched out in different directions, or was obliged to pick her way through the obscurity of the tangled thicket, she was frequently at a loss, and was accustomed to stop till some one appeared, to give her the necessary information, which the interesting countenance of her companion seldom failed to procure her.

Wisdom in the mean time, led by a natural instinct, advanced towards the temple of Science and Eternal Truth. For some time the way lay plain before her, and she followed her guide with unhesitating steps: but she had not proceeded far before the paths grew intricate and entangled; the meeting branches of the trees spread darkness over her head, and steep mountains barred her way, whose summits, lost in clouds, ascended beyond the reach of mortal vision. At every new turn of the road her guide urged her to proceed; but after advancing a little way, she was often obliged to measure back her steps, and often found herself involved in the mazes of a labyrinth which, after exercising her patience and her strength, ended but where it began.

In the mean time Ignorance, who was naturally impatient, could but ill bear the continual doubts and hesitation of her companion. She hated deliberation, and could not submit to delay. At length it so happened that she found herself on a spot where three ways met, and no indication was to be found which might direct her to the right road. Modesty advised her to wait; and she had waited till her patience was exhausted.—At that moment Confidence, who was in disgrace with Wisdom for some false steps he had led her into, and who had just been discarded from her presence, came up, and offered himself to be her guide. He was accepted. Under his auspices Ignorance, naturally swift of foot, and who could at any time have outrun Wisdom, boldly pressed forward, pleased and satisfied with her new companion. He knocked at every door, visited castle and convent, and introduced his charge to many a society whence Wisdom found herself excluded.

Modesty, in the mean time, finding she could be of no further use to her charge, offered her services to Wisdom. They were mutually pleased with each other, and soon agreed never to separate. And ever since that time Ignorance has been led by Confidence, and Modesty has been found in the society of Wisdom.

DRAMATICS

Two playlets probably written for Palgrave School concerned the ethics of government, and particularly of kingship. Both drew from legendary episodes in English history retailed in the popular *History of England* (1726–31) by Paul Rapin de Thoyras. 'Canute's Reproof' draws on the legend that Saxon king Canute rebuked his idolatrous courtiers by showing them that he could not command the tide. Rapin tells the story:

> One Day, as he was walking by the Sea-side,[9] they that were with him extoll'd him to the Skies, and even proceeded so far as to compare him with God himself. Offended at these extravagant Praises, and willing to make them sensible of their Folly and Impiety, he order'd a Chair to be brought him, and seating himself in a Place where the Tide was about to flow, he turn'd to the Sea, and said; *O Sea, thou art under my Dominion, and the Land I sit on, is mine: I charge thee not to presume to approach any farther, nor to dare to wet the Feet of thy Sovereign.* Having said this, he sat still for some time, as if he expected the Sea shou'd obey his Commands. But as the Tide came rolling on as usual, he took Occasion from thence to let his base Flatterers know, that the Titles of *Lord* and *Master* belong only to him whom the Land and the Sea obey. It is said, from that Moment he wou'd never wear his Crown again....[10]

'Alfred' draws on the legend that Saxon King Alfred took refuge in disguise after losing his kingdom to Danish invaders. As retold by Rapin:

[9] At Southhampton. [*Rapine's note.*]   [10] Rapin, 2.i, p. 43.

Such was his [Alfred's] Distress, that he was forc'd to go and conceal himself at a *Neat-herd's* in the Isle of *Athelney* in *Somersetshire*.... In this Place the King lay conceal'd for some time, from his Friends as well as Enemies, without being so much as known by the *Neat-herd's* Wife, who employ'd him about her little Houshold Affairs. She having one day set a Cake on the Coals, and being busied about something else, the Cake happen'd to be burnt; upon which she fell a scolding at the King for his Carelessness in not looking after the Cake, which she told him he cou'd eat fast enough.[11]

Alfred was restored to his throne by the valour of loyal subordinates; the Danes were driven from England, and the nation recovered.

Barbauld's 'Alfred' also glances at a masque by James Thomson and David Mallet based on this story (*Alfred: A Masque*, 1740). In their admiring version, the peasants with whom Alfred takes refuge can tell by his countenance that he is of high birth. Alfred's name and legend were often invoked in the eighteenth century by liberals such as Thomson, for whom Alfred was a hero of unselfish patriotism. Barbauld's 'Alfred' follows Rapin's story and makes fun of the Thomson-Mallet work, but not of Alfred. It may have been written as an after-piece to a serious play put on by the boys, and perhaps during the American War, which caused economic distress in Britain.

Both playlets were published in John Aikin's *Evenings at Home*, 1 (1793): 'Canute' (pp. 102–5) and 'Alfred' (pp. 32–42). Our copy texts are from this first edition.

Canute's Reproof to his Courtiers

Persons

Canute, King of England.
Oswald, Offa, Courtiers.

Scene—*The Sea-Side, near Southampton.*
The tide coming in.

Canute. Is it true, my friends, what you have so often told me, that I am the greatest of monarchs?

Offa. It is true, my liege; you are the most powerful of all kings.

Oswald. We are all your slaves; we kiss the dust of your feet.

Offa. Not only we, but even the elements, are your slaves. The land obeys you from shore to shore; and the sea obeys you.

Canute. Does the sea, with its loud boisterous waves, obey me? Will that terrible element be still at my bidding?

Offa. Yes, the sea is yours; it was made to bear your ships upon its bosom, and to pour the treasures of the world at your royal feet. It is boisterous to your enemies, but it knows you to be its sovereign.

Canute. Is not the tide coming up?

Oswald. Yes, my liege; you may perceive the swell already.

---

[11] 1:330–1 and 331n.

Canute. Bring me a chair then; set it here upon the sands.

Offa. Where the tide is coming up, my gracious lord?

Canute. Yes, set it just here.

Oswald (aside). I wonder what he is going to do!

Offa (aside). Surely he is not such a fool as to believe us!

Canute. O mighty Ocean! thou art my subject; my courtiers tell me so, and it is thy bounden duty to obey me. Thus, then, I stretch my sceptre over thee, and command thee to retire. Roll back thy swelling waves, nor let them presume to wet the feet of me, thy royal master.

Oswald (aside). I believe the sea will pay very little regard to his royal commands.

Offa. See how fast the tide rises!

Oswald. The next wave will come up to the chair. It is a folly to stay; we shall be covered with salt water.

Canute. Well, does the sea obey my commands? If it be my subject, it is a very rebellious subject. See how it swells, and dashes the angry foam and salt spray over my sacred person. Vile sycophants! did you think I was the dupe of your base lies? that I believed your abject flatteries? Know, there is only one Being whom the sea will obey. He is Sovereign of heaven and earth, King of kings, and Lord of lords. It is only he who can say to the ocean, "Thus far shalt thou go, but no farther, and here shall thy proud waves be stayed." A king is but a man; and man is but a worm. Shall a worm assume the power of the great God, and think the elements will obey him? Take away this crown, I will never wear it more. May kings learn to be humble from my example, and courtiers learn truth from your disgrace!

Alfred, a Drama

Persons of the Drama

Alfred, King of England.
Gubba, a Farmer.
Gandelin, his Wife.
Ella, an Officer of Alfred.

Scene—*The Isle of Athelney*.

Alfred. How retired and quiet is every thing in this little spot! The river winds its silent waters round this retreat; and the tangled bushes of the thicket fence it in from the attack of an enemy. The bloody Danes have not yet pierced into this wild solitude. I believe I am safe from their pursuit. But I hope I shall find some inhabitants here, otherwise I shall die of hunger.— Ha! here is a narrow path through the wood; and I think I see the smoke of a cottage rising between the trees. I will bend my steps thither.

Scene—Before the cottage.
Gubba *coming forward.* Gandelin *within.*

Alfred. Good even to you, good man. Are you disposed to shew hospitality to a poor traveller?

Gubba. Why truly there are so many poor travellers now a days, that if we entertain them all, we shall have nothing left for ourselves. However, come along to my wife, and we will see what can be done for you.

Wife, I am very weary; I have been chopping wood all day.

Gandelin. You are always ready for your supper, but it is not ready for you, I assure you: the cakes will take an hour to bake, and the sun is yet high; it has not yet dipped behind the old barn. But who have you with you, I trow?[4]

Alfred. Good mother, I am a stranger; and entreat you to afford me food and shelter.

Gandelin. Good mother, quotha! Good wife, if you please, and welcome. But I do not love strangers; and the land has no reason to love them. It has never been a merry day for Old England since strangers came into it.

Alfred. I am not a stranger in England, though I am a stranger here. I am a true born Englishman.

Gubba. And do you hate those wicked Danes, that eat us up, and burn our houses, and drive away our cattle?

Alfred. I do hate them.

Gandelin. Heartily! He does not speak heartily, husband.[5]

Alfred. Heartily I hate them; most heartily.

Gubba. Give me thy hand then; thou art an honest fellow.

Alfred. I was with King Alfred in the last battle he fought.

Gandelin. With King Alfred? heaven bless him!

Gubba. What is become of our good King?

Alfred. Did you love him, then?

Gubba. Yes, as much as a poor man may love a king; and kneeled down and prayed for him every night, that he might conquer those Danish wolves; but it was not to be so.

Alfred. You could not love Alfred better than I did.

Gubba. But what is become of him?

Alfred. He is thought to be dead.

Gubba. Well, these are sad times; heaven help us! Come, you shall be welcome to share the brown loaf with us; I suppose you are too sharp set to be nice.[6]

Gandelin. Ay, come with us; you shall be as welcome as a prince! But hark ye, husband; though I am very willing to be charitable to this stranger (it would be a sin to be otherwise), yet there is no reason he should not do something to maintain himself: he looks strong and capable.

Gubba. Why, that's true. What can you do, friend?

Alfred. I am very willing to help you in any thing you choose to set me about. It will please me best to earn my bread before I eat it.

Gubba. Let me see. Can you tie up faggots neatly?

Alfred. I have not been used to it. I am afraid I should be awkward.

Gubba. Can you thatch? There is a piece blown off the cow-house.

Alfred. Alas, I cannot thatch.

Gandelin. Ask him if he can weave rushes: we want some new baskets.

Alfred. I have never learned.

Gubba. Can you stack hay?

Alfred. No.

Gubba. Why, here's a fellow! and yet he hath as many pair of hands as his neighbours. Dame, can you employ him in the house? He might lay wood on the fire, and rub the tables.

Gandelin. Let him watch these cakes, then: I must go and milk the kine.

Gubba. And I'll go back and stack the wood, since supper is not ready.

Gandelin. But pray observe, friend! do not let the cakes burn; turn them often on the hearth.

Alfred. I shall observe your directions.

Alfred *alone.*

Alfred. For myself, I could bear it; but England, my bleeding country, for thee my heart is wrung with bitter anguish!—From the Humber to the Thames[7] the rivers are stained with blood!—My brave soldiers cut to pieces!—My poor people—some massacred, others driven from their warm homes, stripped, abused, insulted:—and I, whom heaven appointed their shepherd, unable to rescue my defenceless flock from the ravenous jaws of these devourers!—Gracious heaven! if I am not worthy to save this land from the Danish sword, raise up some other hero to fight with more success than I have done, and let me spend my life in this obscure cottage, in these servile offices: I shall be content, if England is happy.

O! here comes my blunt host and hostess.

Enter Gubba *and* Gandelin.

Gandelin. Help me down with the pail, husband. This new milk, with the cakes, will make an excellent supper: but, mercy on us, how they are burnt! black as my shoe; they have not once been turned: you oaf, you lubber, you lazy loon—

Alfred. Indeed, dame, I am sorry for it; but my mind was full of sad thoughts.

Gubba. Come, wife, you must forgive him; perhaps he is in love. I remember when I was in love with thee—

Gandelin. You remember!

Gubba. Yes, dame, I do remember it, though it is many a long year since; my mother was making a kettle of furmety[8]—

Gandelin. Pr'ythee, hold thy tongue, and let us eat our suppers.

Alfred. How refreshing is this sweet new milk, and this wholesome bread!

Gubba. Eat heartily, friend. Where shall we lodge him, Gandelin?

Gandelin. We have but one bed, you know; but there is fresh straw in the barn.

Alfred (aside). If I shall not lodge like a king, at least I shall lodge like a soldier. Alas! how many of my poor soldiers are stretched on the bare ground!

Gandelin. What noise do I hear? It is the trampling of horses. Good husband, go and see what is the matter.

Alfred. Heaven forbid my misfortunes should bring destruction on this simple family! I had rather have perished in the wood.

Gubba *returns, followed by* Ella *with his sword drawn.*

Gandelin. Mercy defend us, a sword!

Gubba. The Danes! the Danes! O do not kill us!

Ella (kneeling). My Liege, my Lord, my Sovereign; have I found you!

Alfred (embracing him). My brave Ella!

Ella. I bring you good news, my Sovereign! Your troops that were shut up in Kinworth Castle made a desperate sally—the Danes were slaughtered. The fierce Hubba lies gasping on the plain.[9]

Alfred. Is it possible! Am I yet a king?

Ella. Their famous standard, the Danish raven, is taken; their troops are panic struck; the English soldiers call aloud for Alfred. Here is a letter which will inform you of more particulars. *(Gives a letter.)*

Gubba (aside). What will become of us! Ah, dame, that tongue of thine has undone us!

Gandelin. O, my poor dear husband! we shall all be hanged, that's certain. But who could have thought it was the King?

Gubba. Why, Gandelin, do you see, we might have guessed he was born to be a King, or some such great man, because, you know, he was fit for nothing else.

Alfred (coming forward). God be praised for these tidings! Hope is sprung up out of the depths of despair. O, my friend! shall I again shine in arms,—again fight at the head of my brave Englishmen,—lead them on to victory! Our friends shall now lift their heads again.

Ella. Yes, you have many friends, who have long been obliged, like their master, to sculk in deserts and caves, and wander from cottage to cottage. When they hear you are alive, and in arms again, they will leave their fastnesses, and flock to your standard.

Alfred. I am impatient to meet them: my people shall be revenged.

Gubba and Gandelin (throwing themselves at the feet of Alfred).
O, my lord—

Gandelin. We hope your majesty will put us to a merciful death. Indeed, we did not know your majesty's grace.

Gubba. If your majesty could but pardon my wife's tongue: she means no harm, poor woman!

Alfred. Pardon you, good people! I not only pardon, but thank you. You have afforded me protection in my distress; and if ever I am seated again on the throne of England, my first care shall be to reward your hospitality.[10] I am now going to protect *you*. Come, my faithful Ella, to arms! to arms! My bosom burns to face once more the haughty Dane; and here I vow to heaven, that I will never sheath the sword against these robbers, till either I lose my life in this just cause, or

> Till dove-like Peace return to England's shore,
> And war and slaughter vex the land no more.[11]

FROM *EVENINGS AT HOME*

INTRODUCTION

In 1792 Barbauld's brother, John Aikin, inspired by a recent French work, *Les Veillées du Chateau* (*Evenings at the Castle*, 1784), a collection of stories and dialogues for children by Stéphanie-Félicité de Genlis, gathered pieces he had written over the years for his own children into a collection he titled *Evenings at Home*.[1] Entered in the Stationers' Register on 28 January 1793 by Joseph Johnson under his own copyright and published initially in two volumes, *Evenings* eventually reached six volumes and ninety-nine pieces; Barbauld contributed fourteen of them, all but one in the first two volumes (LA, 'Memoir', xxxvi–vii n.). 'I am glad you & my father are again favouring the younger part of society', wrote Charles to Barbauld on 6 December 1792; 'I suppose many of the pieces will not [be] new to me' (quoted in *ALBVE*, 324). Some pieces, such as 'Things by their Right Names', Barbauld may well have written for Charles; others were probably composed for pupils at Palgrave School. At least one, 'The Four Sisters', was sent directly to John Aikin, no doubt for his children's amusement but also for his own. The dialogue 'On Manufactures' can be dated to 1792, soon after the death of Richard Arkwright.

Evenings was an immediate success, enjoying thirteen London editions in Barbauld's lifetime as well as reprints in the United States from 1797 on; it remained more or less continually in print, in whole or in part and in various repackagings, until the early twentieth century. Reviews were few but friendly: 'We have pursued our ingenious author with great pleasure through his several volumes.... [A]mong the various publications for the use of young persons that have fallen under our notice, we have not met with one equally pleasant and useful' (*C Rev*, ns 17 [August 1796]: 442). Educational progressives such as Maria Edgeworth and her father admired *Evenings* and learned from it; educational conservatives such as Sarah Trimmer, who monitored children's books for *The*

---

[1] By the time edition 1 of Volume 6 appeared, editions 2 and 3 of Volumes 1–2 had been published (1794, 1795). Thus, the bibliographical history of *Evenings* was complicated from its beginning by overlapping and composite editions—which, today, are unevenly available. The thirteenth edition was advertised as 'carefully revised and corrected throughout' by Arthur Aikin (*Morning Post*, 13 March 1823). Arthur Aikin's text was reprinted with further changes by Lucy Aikin in 1826, but her edition (the fourteenth, in four volumes) assumes importance from its first publication of 'Live Dolls' (1:84–94).

Each edition appears to have been reset from its predecessor, with occasional small corrections and the usual minor variants resulting from errors. Edition 7 is repaginated as well as reset. Small verbal variants in editions after the first cannot be traced to Barbauld with any confidence; they could as well be John Aikin's, or alterations by Joseph Johnson's printer. Our copy text for all pieces from *Evenings* is ed. 1 of each volume that contains her work.

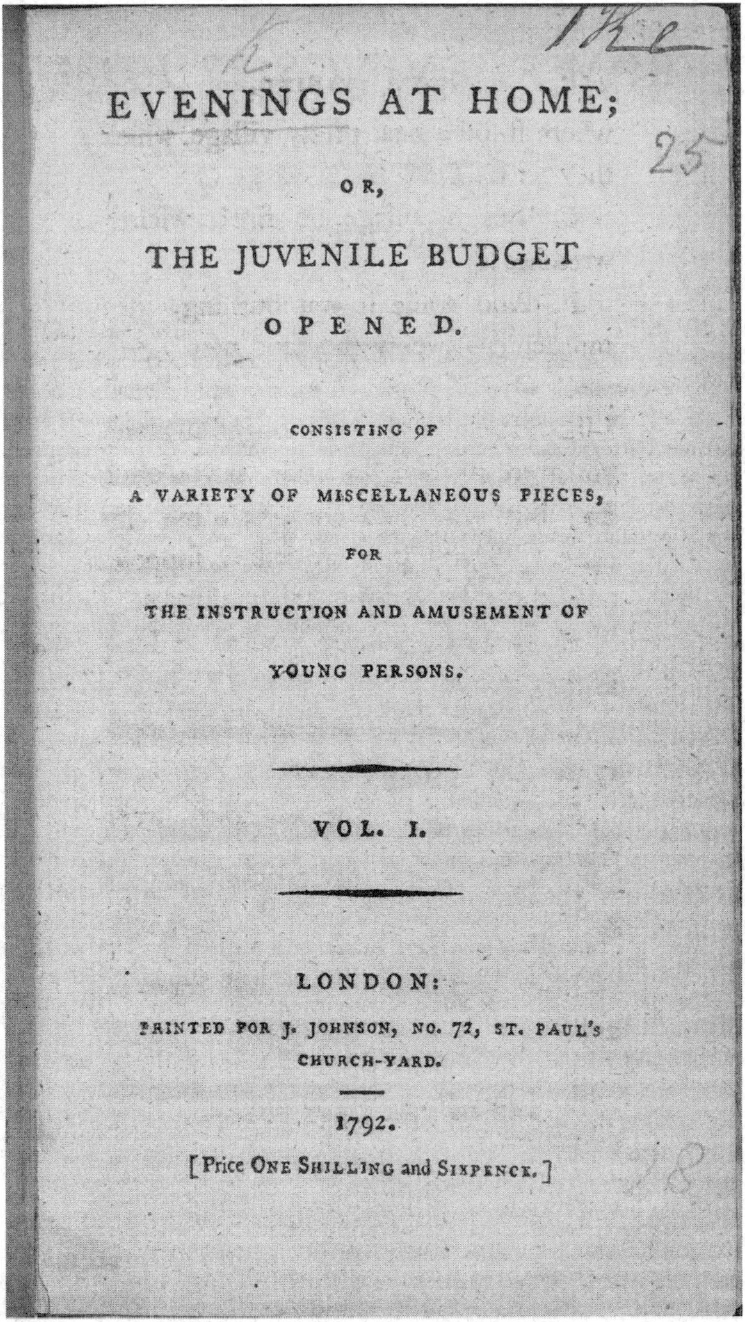

EVENINGS AT HOME;

OR,

THE JUVENILE BUDGET OPENED.

CONSISTING OF

A VARIETY OF MISCELLANEOUS PIECES,

FOR

THE INSTRUCTION AND AMUSEMENT OF

YOUNG PERSONS.

VOL. I.

LONDON:

PRINTED FOR J. JOHNSON, NO. 72, ST. PAUL'S
CHURCH-YARD.

1792.

[Price ONE SHILLING and SIXPENCE.]

Fig. 11 *Evenings at Home*. Title-page of Volume 1. British Library, first edition. © The British Library Board (Shelfmark 0 1031.d.15).

Guardian of Education, thought it insufficiently Christian if not actually subversive of the Bible. Liberal politics were indeed integral to *Evenings*, and Lucy Aikin characterized it well: 'the morality which [the pieces] inculcate is not that of children merely, but of men and citizens;... it engages the youthful feelings in the cause of truth, of freedom, and of virtue' (LA, *MJA*, 1:159).

Probably as a result of Joseph Johnson's advertising, *Evenings* was often ascribed in its entirety to Barbauld. (Johnson's ad in the *London Chronicle*, 18–20 June 1793, listed *Evenings* along with other Barbauld titles and made no reference to John Aikin.) Lucy Aikin's list of Barbauld's contributions was intended to correct that impression; it provides our only specific information about the authorship of *Evenings*. Although Charles's observation to Anna Letitia that she and his father were again 'favouring the younger part of society' could suggest that *Evenings* was undertaken as a joint work, and although Barbauld and her brother did co-write a tale about a shepherd they called Hidallan, sending it back and forth in letters (ALB to JA, 9 Sept. 1775, in *Works*, 2:5–7), there is currently no reason to believe that Barbauld's part in *Evenings* exceeded the fourteen pieces listed by Lucy Aikin. Our copy text for each of these pieces is the 1793 first edition.

Copy texts: *Evenings at Home*, first edition (1793); 'The Young Mouse' (1:18–20); 'The Masque of Nature' (1:124–7); 'Things by their Right Names' (1:150–2); 'On Manufactures' (2:97–118); 'The Manufacture of Paper' (2:140–8); 'A Lesson in the Art of Distinguishing' (2:121–36); 'The Four Sisters' (6:30–8). One poem published in *Evenings at Home*, 'Animals, and their Countries', appears in Volume 1.

The Young Mouse.
A Fable

A young Mouse lived in a cupboard where sweetmeats were kept; she dined every day upon biscuit, marmalade, or fine sugar. Never any little Mouse had lived so well. She had often ventured to peep at the family while they sat at supper; nay, she had sometimes stole down on the carpet, and picked up the crumbs, and nobody had ever hurt her. She would have been quite happy, but that she was sometimes frightened by the cat, and then she ran trembling to her hole behind the wainscot. One day she came running to her mother in great joy; Mother! said she, the good people of this family have built me a house to live in; it is in the cupboard: I am sure it is for me, for it is just big enough: the bottom is of wood, and it is covered all over with wires; and I dare say they have made it on purpose to screen me from that terrible cat, which ran after me so often: there is an entrance just big enough for me, but puss cannot follow; and they have been so good as to put in some toasted cheese, which smells so deliciously, that I should have run in directly and taken possession of my new house, but I thought I would tell you first, that we might go in together, and both lodge there to-night, for it will hold us both.

My dear child, said the old Mouse, it is most happy that you did not go in, for this house is called a trap, and you would never have come out again, except to have been devoured, or put to death in some way or other. Though man has not so fierce a look as a cat, he is as much our enemy, and has still more cunning.

The Masque of Nature

Who is this beautiful Virgin that approaches, clothed in a robe of light green? She has a garland of flowers on her head, and flowers spring up wherever she sets her foot. The snow which covered the fields, and the ice which was in the rivers, melt away when she breathes upon them. The young lambs frisk about her, and the birds warble in their little throats to welcome her coming; and when they see her, they begin to choose their mates, and to build their nests. Youths and maidens, have ye seen this beautiful Virgin? If ye have, tell me who is she, and what is her name.

Who is this that cometh from the south, thinly clad in a light transparent garment? Her breath is hot and sultry; she seeks the refreshment of the cool shade; she seeks the clear streams, the crystal brooks, to bathe her languid limbs. The brooks and rivulets fly from her, and are dried up at her approach. She cools her parched lips with berries, and the grateful acid of all fruits; the seedy melon, the sharp apple, and the red pulp of the juicy cherry, which are poured out plentifully around her. The tanned haymakers welcome her coming; and the sheep-shearer, who clips the fleeces of his flock with his sounding shears. When she cometh, let me lie under the thick shade of a spreading beech tree,—let me walk with her in the early morning, when they dew is yet upon the grass,—let me wander with her in the soft twilight, when the shepherd shuts his fold, and the star of evening appears. Who is she that cometh from the south? Youths and maidens, tell me, if you know, who is she, and what is her name.

Who is he that cometh with sober pace, stealing upon us unawares? His garments are red with the blood of the grape, and his temples are bound with a sheaf of ripe wheat. His hair is thin and begins to fall, and the auburn is mixed with mournful grey. He shakes the brown nuts from the tree. He winds the horn, and calls the hunters to their sport. The gun sounds. The trembling partridge and the beautiful pheasant flutter, bleeding in the air, and fall dead at the sportsman's feet. Who is he that is crowned with the wheat-sheaf? Youths and maidens, tell me, if ye know, who is he, and what is his name.

Who is he that cometh from the north, clothed in furs and warm wool? He wraps his cloak close about him. His head is bald; his beard is made of sharp icicles. He loves the blazing fire high piled above the hearth, and the wine sparkling in the glass. He binds skates to his feet, and skims over the frozen lakes. His breath is piercing and cold, and no little flower dares to peep above the surface of the ground, when he is by. Whatever he touches turns to ice. If he were to stroke you with his cold hand, you would be quite stiff and dead, like a piece of marble. Youths and maidens, do you see him? He is coming fast upon us, and soon he will be here. Tell me, if you know, who is he, and what is his name.

Things by their Right Names[12]

Charles. Papa, you grow very lazy. Last winter you used to tell us stories, and now you never tell us any; and we are all got round the fire quite ready to hear one. Pray, dear papa, let us have a very pretty one?

Father. With all my heart—What shall it be?

C. A bloody murder, papa!

F. A bloody murder! well then—Once upon a time, some men, dressed all alike....

C. With black crapes over their faces.

F. No; they had steel caps on:—having crossed a dark heath, wound cautiously along the skirts of a deep forest...

C. They were ill-looking fellows, I dare say.

F. I cannot say so; on the contrary, they were tall personable men as most one shall see:—leaving on their right hand an old ruined tower on the hill...

C. At midnight, just as the clock struck twelve; was it not, papa?

F. No, really; it was on a fine balmy summer's morning:—and moved forwards, one behind another....

C. As still as death, creeping along under the hedges.

F. On the contrary—they walked remarkably upright; and so far from endeavouring to be hushed and still, they made a loud noise as they came along, with several sorts of instruments.

C. But, papa, they would be found out immediately.

F. They did not seem to wish to conceal themselves; on the contrary, they gloried in what they were about.—They moved forwards, I say, to a large plain, where stood a neat pretty village, which they set on fire....

C. Set a village on fire? wicked wretches!

F. And while it was burning, they murdered—twenty thousand men.

C. O fie! papa! You do not intend I should believe this! I thought all along you were making up a tale, as you often do; but you shall not catch me this time. What! they lay still, I suppose, and let these fellows cut their throats!

F. No, truly—they resisted as long as they could.

C. How should these men kill twenty thousand people, pray?

F. Why not? the *murderers* were thirty thousand.

C. O, now I have found you out! You mean a BATTLE.

F. Indeed I do. I do not know of any *murders* half so bloody.

On Manufactures

Father.—Henry.

Hen. My dear father, you observed the other day that we had a great many *manufactures* in England. Pray what is a Manufacture?

Fa. A Manufacture is something made by the hand of man. It is derived from two Latin words, *manus*, the hand, and *facere*, to make. Manufactures are therefore opposed to *productions*, which latter are what the bounty of nature spontaneously affords us; as fruits, corn, marble.

Hen. But there is a great deal of trouble with corn: you have often made me take notice how much pains it costs the farmer to plough his ground, and put the feed in the earth, and keep it clear from weeds.

Fa. Very true; but the farmer does not *make* the corn; he only prepares for it a proper soil and situation, and removes every hindrance arising from the hardness of the ground, or the neighbourhood of other plants, which might obstruct the secret and wonderful process of vegetation; but with the vegetation itself he has nothing to do. It is not *his* hand that draws out the slender fibres of the root, pushes up the green stalk, and by degrees the spiky ear; swells the grain, and embrowns it with that rich tinge of tawny russet, which informs the husbandman it is time to put in his sickle: all this operation is performed without his care or even knowledge.

Hen. Now then I understand; corn is a *Production*, and bread a *Manufacture*.

Fa. Bread is certainly, in strictness of speech, a Manufacture; but we do not in general apply the term to any thing in which the original material is so little changed. If we wanted to speak of bread philosophically, we should say, it is a *preparation* of corn.

Hen. Is sugar a Manufacture?

Fa. No, for the same reason. Besides which, I do not recollect the term being applied to any article of food; I suppose from an idea that food is of too perishable a nature, and generally obtained by a process too simple to deserve the name. We say, therefore, sugar-works, oil-mills, chocolate-works; we do not say a beer-manufactory, but a brewery; but this is only a nicety of language, for properly all those are manufactories, if there is much of art and curiosity in the process.

Hen. Do we say a manufactory of *pictures*?

Fa. No; but for a different reason. A picture, especially if it belong to any of the higher kinds of painting, is an effort of genius. A picture cannot be produced by any given combinations of canvas and colour. It is the hand, indeed, that executes, but the head that works. Sir Joshua Reynolds could not have gone, when he was engaged to paint a picture, and hired workmen, the one to draw the eyes, another the nose, a third the mouth;[13] the whole must be the painter's own, that particular painter's, and no other; and no one who has not his ideas can do his work. His work is therefore nobler, of a higher species.

Hen. Pray give me an instance of manufacture?

Fa. The making of watches is a manufacture: the silver, iron, gold, or whatever else is used in it, are productions, the material of the work; but it is by the wonderful art of man that they are wrought into the numberless wheels and springs of which this complicated machine is composed.

Hen. Then is there not as much art in making a watch as a picture? Does not the head work?

Fa. Certainly, in the original invention of watches, as much, or more, than in painting; but when once invented, the art of watch-making is capable of being reduced to a mere mechanical labour, which may be exercised by any man of common capacity, according to certain precise rules, when made familiar to him by practice. This, painting is not.

Hen. But, my dear father, making of books surely requires a great deal of thinking and study; and yet I remember the other day at dinner a gentleman said that Mr. Pica had *manufactured* a large volume in less than a fortnight.

Fa. It was meant to convey a satirical remark on his book, because it was compiled from other authors, from whom he had taken a page in one place, and a page in another; so that it was not produced by the labour of his brain, but of his hands. Thus you heard your mother complain that the London cream was *manufactured*; which was a pointed and concise way of saying that the cream was not what it ought to be, nor what it pretended to be; for cream, when genuine, is a pure production; but when mixed up and adulterated with flour and isinglass, and I know not what, it becomes a

Manufacture. It was as much as to say, art has been here, where it has no business; where it is not beneficial, but hurtful. A great deal of the delicacy of language depends upon an accurate knowledge of the specific meaning of single terms, and a nice attention to their relative propriety.

Hen. Have all nations Manufactures?

Fa. All that are in any degree cultivated; but it very often happens that countries naturally the poorest have manufactures of the greatest extent and variety.

Hen. Why so?

Fa. For the same reason, I apprehend, that individuals, who are rich without any labour of their own, are seldom so industrious and active as those who depend upon their own exertions: thus the Spaniards, who possess the richest gold and silver mines in the world, are in want of many conveniences of life which are enjoyed in London and Amsterdam.

Hen. I can comprehend that; I believe if my uncle Ledger were to find a gold mine under his warehouse, he would soon shut up shop.

Fa. I believe so. It is not, however, easy to establish Manufactures in a *very poor* nation; they require science and genius for their invention, art and contrivance for their execution; order, peace, and union, for their flourishing; they require a number of men to combine together in an undertaking, and to prosecute it with the most patient industry; they require, therefore, laws and government for their protection. If you see extensive Manufactures in any nation, you may be sure it is a civilized nation; you may be sure property is accurately ascertained and protected. They require great expences for their first establishment, costly machines for shortening manual labour, and money and credit for purchasing materials from distant countries. There is not a single Manufacture of Great Britain which does not require, in some part or other of its process, productions from the different parts of the globe; oils, drugs, varnish, quick-silver, and the like; it requires, therefore, *ships* and a friendly intercourse with foreign nations to transport commodities, and exchange productions. We could not be a manufacturing, unless we were also a commercial nation. They require time to take root in any place, and their excellence often depends upon some nice and delicate circumstance; a peculiar quality, for instance, in the air, or water, or some other local circumstance not easily ascertained. Thus, I have heard, that the Irish women spin better than the English, because the moister temperature of their climate makes their skin more soft and their fingers more flexible: thus again we cannot dye so beautiful a scarlet as the French can, though with the same drugs, perhaps on account of the superior purity of their air. But though so much is necessary for the perfection of the more curious and complicated

Manufactures, all nations possess those which are subservient to the common conveniences of life—the loom and the forge, particularly, are of highest antiquity.

Hen. Yes; I remember Hector bids Andromache return to her apartment, and employ herself in weaving with her maids; and I remember the shield of Achilles.[14]

Fa. True; and you likewise remember, in an earlier period, the fine linen of Egypt; and, to go still higher, the working in brass and iron is recorded of Tubal Cain before the flood.[15]

Hen. Which is the most important, Manufactures or Agriculture?

Fa. Agriculture is the most *necessary*, because it is first of all necessary that man should live; but almost all the enjoyments and comforts of life are produced by Manufactures.

Hen. Why are we obliged to take so much pains to make ourselves comfortable?

Fa. To exercise our industry. Nature provides the materials for man. She pours out at his feet a profusion of gems, metals, dyes, plants, ores, barks, stones, gums, wax, marbles, woods, roots, skins, earths, and minerals of all kinds. She has likewise given him tools.

Hen. I did not know that Nature gave us tools.

Fa. No! what are those two instruments you carry always about with you, so strong and yet so flexible, so nicely jointed, and branched out into five long taper, unequal divisions, any of which may be contracted or stretched out at pleasure; the extremities of which have a feeling so wonderfully delicate, and which are strengthened and defended by horn?

Hen. The hands.

Fa. Yes. Man is as much superior to the brutes in his outward form, by means of the hand, as he is in his mind by the gifts of reason. The trunk of the elephant comes perhaps the nearest to it in its exquisite feeling and flexibility (it is, indeed, called his hand in Latin), and accordingly that animal has always been reckoned the wisest of brutes. When Nature gave man the hand, she said to him, 'Exercise your ingenuity, and work.' As soon as ever man rises above the state of a savage, he begins to contrive and to make things, in order to improve his forlorn condition; thus you may remember Thomson represents Industry coming to the poor shivering wretch, and teaching him the arts of life:

> Taught him to chip the wood, and hew the stone,
> Till by degrees the finish'd fabric rose;
> Tore from his limbs the blood-polluted fur,
> And wrapt them in the woolly vestment warm,
> Or bright in glossy silk and flowing lawn.[16]

Hen. It must require a great deal of knowledge, I suppose, for so many curious works; what kind of knowledge is most necessary?

Fa. There is not any which may not be occasionally employed; but the two sciences which most assist the manufacturer are *mechanics* and *chemistry*. The one for building mills, working of mines, and in general for constructing wheels, wedges, pullies, &c. either to shorten the labour of man, by performing it in less time, or to perform what the strength of man alone could not accomplish:—the other in fusing and working ores, in dying and bleaching, and extracting the virtues of various substances for particular uses: making of soap, for instance, is a chemical operation; and by chemistry an ingenious gentleman has lately found out a way of bleaching a piece of cloth in eight and forty hours, which by the common process would have taken up a great many weeks.[17]—You have heard of Sir Richard Arkwright who died lately—[18]

Hen. Yes, I have heard he was at first only a barber, and shaved people for a penny a-piece.

Fa. He did so; but having a strong turn for mechanics, he invented, or at least perfected, a machine, by which one pair of hands may do the work of twenty or thirty; and, as in this country every one is free to rise by merit, he acquired the largest fortune in the country, had a great many hundreds of workmen under his orders, and had leave given him by the King to put *Sir* before his name.

Hen. Did that do him any good?

Fa. It pleased him, I suppose, or he would not have accepted of it; and you will allow, I imagine, that if titles are used, it does honour to those who bestow them, that they are given to such as have made themselves noticed for something useful.—Arkwright used to say, that if he had time to perfect his inventions, he would put a fleece of wool into a box, and it should come out broad cloth.

Hen. What did he mean by that; was there any fairy in the box to turn it into broad cloth with her wand?

Fa. He was assisted by the only fairies that ever had the power of transformation, Art and Industry: he meant that he would contrive so many machines, wheel within wheel, that the combing, carding, and other various operations should be performed by mechanism, almost without the hand of man.

Hen. I think, if I had not been told, I should never have been able to guess that my coat came off the back of the sheep.

Fa. You hardly would; but there are Manufactures in which the material is much more changed than in woollen cloth. What can be meaner in appearance than sand and ashes? Would you imagine any thing beautiful could be made out of such a mixture? Yet the furnace transforms this into that transparent crystal we call *glass*,[19] than which nothing is more sparkling, more brilliant, more full of lustre. It throws about the rays of light as if it had life and motion.

Hen. There is a glass-shop in London, which always puts me in mind of Aladdin's palace.[20]

Fa. It is certain that if a person ignorant of Manufacture were to see one of our capital shops, he would think all the treasures of Golconda[21] were centered there, and that every drop of cut glass was worth a prince's ransom.—Again, who would suppose, on seeing the green stalks of a plant, that it could be formed into a texture so smooth, so snowy-white, so firm, and yet so flexible as to wrap round the limbs and adapt itself to every movement of the body? Who would guess this fibrous stalk could be made to float in such light undulating folds as in our lawns and cambrics; not less fine, we presume, than that transparent drapery which the Romans called *ventus textilis, woven wind.*

Hen. I wonder how any body can spin such fine thread.

Fa. Their fingers must have the touch of a spider, that, as Pope says,

'Feels at each thread, and lives along the line;'[22]

and indeed you recollect that Arachne *was* a spinster. Lace is a still finer production from flax, and is one of those in which the original material is most improved. How many times the price of a pound of flax do you think that flax will be worth when made into lace?

Hen. A great many times, I suppose.

Fa. Flax at the best hand is bought at fourteen-pence a pound. They make lace at Valenciennes, in French Flanders, of ten guineas a yard, I believe indeed higher, but we will say ten guineas; this yard of lace will weigh probably not more than half an ounce: what is the value of half an ounce of flax? reckon it.

Hen. It comes to one farthing and three quarters of a farthing.

Fa. Right; now tell me how many times the original value the lace is worth.

Hen. Prodigious! it is worth 5760 times as much as the flax it is made of.[23]

Fa. Yet there is another material that is still more improveable than flax.

Hen. What can that be?

Fa. Iron. The price of pig-iron is ten shillings a hundred weight; this is not quite one farthing for two ounces: now you have seen some of the beautiful cut steel that looks like diamonds.

Hen. Yes, I have seen buckles, and pins, and watch-chains.

Fa. Then you can form an idea of it; but you have seen only the most common sorts. There was a chain made at Woodstock, in Oxfordshire, and sent to France, which weighed only two ounces, and cost 170l.[24] Calculate how many times *that* had increased its value.

Hen. Amazing! It was worth 163,600 times the value of the iron it was made of.

Fa. This is what Manufactures can do; here man is a kind of creator, and, like the great Creator, he may please himself with his work, and say it is good. In the last-mentioned Manufacture, too, that of steel, the English have the honour of excelling all the world.

Hen. What are the chief Manufactures of England?

Fa. We have at present a greater variety than I can pretend to enumerate, but our staple Manufacture is woollen cloth. England abounds in fine pastures and extensive downs, which feed great numbers of sheep; hence our wool has always been a valuable article of trade; but we did not always know how to work it. We used to sell it to the Flemish or Lombards, who wrought it into cloth; till in the year 1326, Edward the Third invited some Flemish weavers over to teach us the art; but there was not much made in England till the reign of Henry the Seventh.[25] Manchester and Birmingham are towns which have arisen to great consequence from small beginnings, almost within the memory of old men now living; the first for cotton and muslin goods, the second for cutlery and hardware, in which we at this moment excel all Europe. Of late years, too, carpets, beautiful as fine tapestry, have been fabricated in this country. Our clocks and watches are greatly esteemed. The earthen-ware plates and dishes, which we all use in common, and the elegant set for the tea-table, ornamented with musical instruments, which we admired in our visit yesterday, belong to a very extensive manufactory, the seat of which is at Burslem in Staffordshire. The principal potteries there belong to one person, an excellent chymist, and a man of great taste; he, in conjunction with another man of taste who is since dead, has made our clay more valuable than the finest porcelain of China.[26] He has moulded it into all the forms of grace and beauty that are to be met with in the precious remains of the Greek and Etruscan artists. In the more common articles he has penciled it with the most elegant designs, shaped it into shells and leaves, twisted it into wicker-work, and trailed the ductile foliage round the light basket. He has filled our cabinets and chimney-pieces with urns, lamps, and vases, on which are lightly traced, with the purest simplicity, the fine forms and floating draperies of Herculaneum. In short, he has given to our houses a classic air, and has made every saloon and every dining-room schools of taste. I should add that there is a great demand abroad for this elegant Manufacture. The

Empress of Russia has had some magnificent services of it; and the other day one was sent to the King of Spain, intended as a present from him to the Archbishop of Toledo, which cost a thousand pounds.[27] Some morning you shall go through the rooms in the London Warehouse.

Hen. I should like very much to see Manufactures, now you have told me such curious things about them.

Fa. You will do well; there is much more entertainment to a cultivated mind in seeing a pin made, than in many a fashionable diversion which young people half ruin themselves to attend.[28] In the mean time I will give you some account of one of the most elegant of them, which is *paper*.

Hen. Pray do, my dear father.

Fa. It shall be left for another evening, however, for it is now late. Good night.

The Manufacture of Paper

F. I will now, as I promised, give you an account of the elegant and useful manufacture of *Paper*, the basis of which is itself a manufacture. This delicate and beautiful substance is made from the meanest and most disgusting materials, from old rags, which have passed from one poor person to another, and at length have perhaps dropped in tatters from the child of the beggar. These are carefully picked up from dunghills, or bought from servants by Jews, who make it their business to go about and collect them.[29] They sell them to the rag-merchant, who gives from two-pence to four-pence a pound, according to their quality; and he, when he has got a sufficient quantity, disposes of them to the owner of the paper-mill. He gives them first to women to sort and pick, agreeably to their different degrees of fineness: they also with a knife cut out carefully all the seams, which they throw into a basket for other purposes: they then put them into the dusting-engine, a large circular wire sieve, from whence they receive some degree of cleansing. The rags are then conveyed to the mill. Here they were formerly beat to pieces with vast hammers, which rose and fell continually with a most tremendous noise that was heard from a great distance. But now they put the rags into a large trough or cistern, into which a pipe of clear spring water is constantly flowing. In this cistern is placed a cylinder, about two feet long, set thick round with rows of iron spikes, standing as near as they can to one another without touching. At the bottom of the trough there are corresponding rows of spikes. The cylinder is made to whirl round with inconceivable rapidity, and with these iron teeth rends and tears the cloth in every possible direction; till, by the assistance of the water, which continually flows through the cistern, it is thoroughly masticated, and reduced to a fine pulp; and by the same process all its impurities are cleansed away, and it is restored to its original whiteness. This process takes about six hours. To improve the colour they then put in a little smalt,[30] which gives it that bluish cast which all Paper has more or less: the French Paper has less of it than ours. This fine pulp is next put into a copper of warm water. It is the substance of paper, but the form must now be given it: for this purpose they use a mould. It is made of wire, strong one way, and crossed with finer. This mould they just dip horizontally into the copper, and take it out again. It has a little wooden frame on the edge, by means of which it retains as much of the pulp as is wanted for the thickness of the sheet, and the superfluity runs off through the interstices of the wires. Another man instantly receives it, opens the frame, and turns out the thin sheet, which has now shape, but not consistence, upon soft felt, which is placed on the ground to receive it. On that is placed another piece of felt, and then another sheet of Paper, and so on till they have made a pile of forty or fifty. They are then pressed with a large screw-press, moved by a long lever, which forcibly squeezes the water out of them, and gives them immediate consistence. There is still however, a great deal to be done. The felts are taken off and thrown on one side, and the Paper on the other, from whence it is dexterously taken up with an instrument in the form of a T, three sheets at a time, and hung on lines to dry. There it hangs for a week or ten days, which likewise further whitens it; and any knots and roughnesses it may have are picked off carefully by the women. It is then sized. Size is a kind of glue; and without this preparation the Paper would not bear ink; it would run and blot as you see it does on grey Paper.[31] The sheets are just dipped into the size, and taken out again. The exact degree of sizing is a matter of nicety, which can only be known by experience. They are then hung up again to dry, and when dry taken to the finishing-room, where they are examined anew, pressed in the dry presses, which gives them their last gloss and smoothness; counted out into quires, made up in reams, and sent to the stationer's, from whom we have it, after he has folded it again and cut the edges; some too he makes to shine like satin, by glossing it with hot plates. The whole process of Paper-making takes about three weeks.

H. It is a very curious process indeed. I shall almost scruple for the future to blacken a sheet of Paper with a careless scrawl, now I know how much pains it costs to make it so white and beautiful.

F. It is true that there is hardly any thing we use with so much waste and profusion as this manufacture; we should think ourselves confined in the use of it, if we might not tear, disperse, and destroy it in a thousand ways; so that it is really astonishing from whence linen enough can be procured to answer so vast a demand. As to the coarse brown papers, of which an astonishing quantity is used by every shopkeeper in packages, &c. these are made chiefly of oakum, that is, old hempen ropes. A fine Paper is made in China of silk.

H. I have heard lately of woven Paper; pray what is that? they cannot weave Paper, surely!

F. Your question is very natural. In order to answer it, I must desire you to take a sheet of common Paper, and hold it up against the light. Do not you see marks in it?

H. I see a great many white lines running along lengthways, like ribs, and smaller that cross them. I see, too, letters and the figure of a crown.

F. These are all the marks of the wires; the thickness of the wire prevents so much of the pulp lying upon the sheet in those places, consequently wherever the wires are, the Paper is thinner, and you see the light through more readily, which gives that appearance of white lines. The letters too are worked in the wire, and are the maker's name. Now to prevent these lines, which take off from the beauty of the Paper, particularly of drawing Paper, there have been lately used moulds of brass wire exceeding fine, of equal thickness, and woven or latticed one within another; the marks, therefore, of these are easily pressed out, so as to be hardly visible; if you look at this sheet you will see it is quite smooth.

H. It is so.

F. I should mention to you, that there is a discovery very lately made, by which they can make Paper equal to any in whiteness, of the coarsest brown rags, and even of dyed cottons; which they have till now been obliged to throw by for inferior purposes. This is by means of manganese, a sort of mineral, and oil of vitriol; a mixture of which they just pass through the pulp, while it is in water, for otherwise it would burn it, and in an instant it discharges the colours of the dyed cloths, and bleaches the brown to a beautiful whiteness.[32]

H. That is like what you told me before of bleaching cloth in a few hours.

F. It is indeed founded upon the same discovery. The Paper made of these brown rags is likewise more valuable, from being very tough and strong, almost like parchment.

H. When was the making of Paper found out?

F. It is a disputed point, but probably in the fourteenth century.[33] The invention has been of almost equal consequence to literature, as that of printing itself; and shows how the arts and sciences, like children of the same family, mutually assist and bring forward each other.

A Lesson in the Art of Distinguishing

F. Come hither, Charles; what is that you see grazing in the meadow before you?

C. It is a horse.

F. Whose horse is it?

C. I do not know; I never saw it before.

F. How do you know it is a horse, if you never saw it before?

C. Because it is like other horses.

F. Are all horses alike, then?

C. Yes.

F. If they are all alike, how do you know one horse from another?

C. They are not quite alike.

F. But they are so much alike, that you can easily distinguish a horse from a cow?

C. Yes, indeed.

F. Or from a cabbage?

C. A horse from a cabbage! Yes, surely I can.

F. Very well; then let us see if you can tell how a horse differs from a cabbage?

C. Very easily; a horse is alive.

F. True; and how is every thing called, which is alive?

C. I believe all things that are alive are called *animals*.

F. Right; but can you tell me what a horse and a cabbage are alike in?

C. Nothing, I believe.

F. Yes, there is one thing in which the slenderest moss that grows upon the wall is like the greatest man or the highest angel.

C. Because God made them.

F. Yes; and how do you call every thing that is made?

C. A creature.

F. A horse then is a creature, but a living creature; that is to say, an animal.

C. And a cabbage is a dead creature; that is the difference.

F. Not so, neither; nothing is dead that has never been alive.

C. What must I call it then, if it is neither dead nor alive?

F. An inanimate creature; there is the animate and the inanimate creation. Plants, stones, metals, are of the latter class, horses belong to the former.

C. But the gardener told me some of my cabbages *were* dead, and some were alive.

F. Very true. Plants have a *vegetative* life, a principle of growth and decay; this is common to them with all organized bodies; but they have not sensation, at least we do not know they have—they have not *life*, therefore, in the sense in which animals enjoy it.

C. A horse is called an animal, then.

F. Yes; but a salmon is an animal, and so is a sparrow; how will you distinguish a horse from these?

C. A salmon lives in the water and swims; a sparrow flies, and lives in the air.

F. I think a salmon could not walk upon the ground, even if it could live out of the water.

C. No, indeed; it has no legs.

F. And a bird would not gallop like a horse.

C. No; it would hop away upon its two slender legs.

F. How many legs has a horse?

C. Four.

F. And an ox?

C. Four likewise.

F. And a camel?

C. Four still.

F. Do you know any animals which live upon the earth that have not four legs?

C. I think not; they have all four legs; except worms, and insects, and such things.

F. You remember, I suppose, what an animal is called that has four legs; you have it in your little books.[34]

C. A quadruped.

F. A horse then is a *quadruped*: by this we distinguish him from birds, fishes, and insects.

C. And from men.

F. True; but if you had been talking about birds, you would not have found it so easy to distinguish them.

C. How so! a man is not at all like a bird.

F. Yet an ancient philosopher could find no way to distinguish them, but by calling man *a two-legged animal without feathers*.[35]

C. I think he was very silly; they are not at all alike, though they have both two legs.

F. Another ancient philosopher, called Diogenes, was of your opinion. He stript a cock of his feathers, and turned him into the school where Plato, that was his name, was teaching, and said, Here is Plato's man for you.

C. I wish I had been there, I should have laughed very much.

F. Probably. Before we laugh at others, however, let us see what we can do ourselves. We have not yet found any thing which will distinguish a horse from an elephant, or from a Norway rat.

C. O, that is easy enough. An elephant is very large, and a rat is very small; a horse is neither large nor small.

F. Before we go any further, look what is settled on the skirt of your coat.

C. It is a butterfly; what a prodigious large one! I never saw such a one before.

F. Is it larger than a rat, think you?

C. No, that it is not.

F. Yet you called the butterfly large, and the rat small.

C. It is very large for a butterfly.

F. It is so. You see, therefore, that large and small are *relative terms*.

C. I do not well understand that phrase.

F. It means that they have no precise and determinate signification in themselves, but are applied differently according to the other ideas which you join with them, and the different positions in which you view them. This butterfly, therefore, is *large*, compared with those of its own species, and *small* compared with many other species of animals. Besides, there is circumstance which varies more than the size of individuals. If you were to give an idea of horse from its size, you would certainly say it was much bigger than a dog; yet if you take the smallest Shetland horse, and the largest Irish greyhound, you will find them very much upon a par: size, therefore, is not a circumstance by which you can accurately distinguish one animal from another; nor yet is colour.

C. No; there are black horses, and bay, and white, and pied.

F. But you have not seen that variety of colours, in a hare, for instance.

C. No, a hare is always brown.

F. Yet if you were to depend upon that circumstance, you would not convey the idea of a hare to a mountaineer, or an inhabitant of Siberia; for he sees them white as snow. We must, therefore, find out some circumstances that do not change like size and colour, and I may add shape, though they are not so obvious, nor perhaps so striking. Look at the feet of quadrupeds; are they all alike?

C. No; some have long taper claws, and some have thick clumsy feet without claws.

F. The thick feet are horny; are they not?

C. Yes, I recollect they are called hoofs.

F. And the feet that are not covered with horn, and are divided into claws, are called *digitated*, from *digitus*, a finger; because they are parted like fingers. Here, then, we have one grand division of quadrupeds into *hoofed* and *digitated*. Of which division is the horse?

C. He is hoofed.

F. There are a great many different kinds of horses: did you ever know one that was not hoofed?

C. No, never.

F. Do you think we run any hazard of a stranger telling us, Sir, horses are hoofed indeed in your country, but in mine, which is in a different climate, and where feed them differently, they have claws?

C. No, I dare say not.

F. Then we have got something to our purpose; a circumstance easily marked, which always belongs to the animal, under every variation of situation or treatment. But an ox is hoofed, and so is a sheep; we must distinguish still farther. You have often stood by, I suppose, while the smith was shoeing a horse. What kind of a hoof has he?

C. It is round, and all in one piece.

F. And is that of an ox so?

C. No, it is divided.

F. A horse, then, is not only hoofed, but *whole-hoofed*. Now how many quadrupeds do you think there are in the world that are whole-hoofed?

C. Indeed I do not know.

F. There are, among all animals that we are acquainted with, either in this country or in any other, only the horse, the ass, and the zebra, which is a species of wild ass. Now, therefore, you see we have nearly accomplished our purpose; we have only to distinguish him from the ass.

C. That is easily done, I believe; I should be sorry if any body could mistake my little horse for an ass.

F. It is not so easy, however, as you imagine; the eye readily distinguishes them by the air and general appearance, but naturalists have been rather puzzled to fix upon any specific difference, which may serve the purpose of a definition. Some have, therefore, fixed upon the ears, others on the mane and tail. What kind of ears has an ass?

C. O, very long clumsy ears. Asses' ears are always laughed at.

F. And the horse?

C. The horse has small ears, nicely turned, and upright.

F. And the mane, is there no difference there?

C. The horse has a fine long flowing mane; the ass has hardly any.

F. And the tail; is it not fuller of hair in the horse than in the ass?

C. Yes; the ass has only a few long hairs at the end of his tail; but the horse has a long bushy tail, when it is not cut.

F. Which, by the way, it is pity it ever should. Now, then, observe what particulars we have got. *A horse is an animal of the quadruped kind, whole-hoofed, with short erect ears, a flowing mane, and a tail covered in every part with long hairs.*[a] Now is there any other animal, think you, in the world that answers these particulars?

C. I do not know; this does not tell us a great deal about him.

F. And yet it tells us enough to distinguish him from all the different tribes of the creation which we are acquainted with in any part of the earth. Do you know now what we have been making?

C. What?

F. A DEFINITION. It is the business of a definition to distinguish precisely the thing defined from every other thing, and to do it in as few terms as possible. Its object is to separate the subject of definition, first, from those with which it has only a general resemblance; then, from those which agree with it in a greater variety of particulars; and so on, till by constantly throwing out all which have not the qualities we have taken notice of, we come at length to the individual or the species we wish to ascertain. It is a kind of chase, and resembles the manner of hunting in some countries, where they first enclose a very large circle with their dogs, nets, and horses; and then, by degrees, draw their toils closer and closer, driving their game before them till it is at length brought into so narrow a compass, that the sportsmen have nothing to do but to knock down their prey.

C. Just as we have been hunting this horse, till at last we held him fast by his ears and his tail.

F. I should observe to you, that in the definition naturalists give of a horse, it is generally mentioned that he has six cutting teeth in each jaw; because this circumstance of the teeth has been found a very convenient one for characterising large classes: but as it is not absolutely necessary here, I have omitted it; a definition being the more perfect the fewer particulars you make use of, provided you can say with certainty from those particulars, 'The object so characterised must be this, and no other whatever'.

C. But, papa, if I had never seen a horse, I should not know what kind of animal it was by this definition.

F. Let us hear, then, how you would give me an idea of a horse.

C. I would say it was a fine large prancing creature, with slender legs and an arched neck, and a sleek smooth skin, and a tail that sweeps the

---

[a] 'hairs': The copy text (first edition, 1793) has 'ears' but the second edition has 'hairs.' We have emended the text to correct this printer's error.

ground, and that he snorts and neighs very loud, and tosses his head, and runs as swift as the wind.

F. I think you learned some verses upon the horse in your last lesson: repeat them.

C. The wanton courser thus with reins unbound
Breaks from his stall, and beats the trembling ground;
Pamper'd and proud, he seeks the wonted tides,
And laves, in height of blood, his shining sides;
His head, now freed, he tosses to the skies;
His mane dishevel'd o'er his shoulders flies;
He snuffs the females in the distant plain,
And springs, exulting, to his fields again.
                                    Pope's *Homer*.[36]

F. You have said it very well; but this is not a *Definition*, it is a *Description*.

C. What is the difference?

F. A description is intended to give you a lively picture of an object, as if you saw it; it ought to be very full. A definition gives no picture to those who have not seen it; it rather tells you what its subject is not, than what it is, by giving you such clear specific marks, that it shall not be possible to confound it with any thing else; and hence it is of the greatest use in throwing things into classes. We have a great many beautiful descriptions from antient authors so loosely worded that we cannot certainly tell what animals were meant by them, whereas if they had given us definitions, three lines would have ascertained their meaning.

C. I like a description best, papa.

F. Perhaps so; I believe I should have done the same at your age. Remember, however, that nothing is more useful than to learn to form ideas with precision, and to express them with accuracy: I have not given you a definition to teach you what a horse is, but to teach you to *think*.

The Four Sisters

'The Four Sisters' pre-dates 'The King in his Castle' and was written, probably as much for Lucy Aikin's enjoyment as for John Aikin's, between 1793 and late 1795. The first date is inferred, because it did not appear in Volume 1 of *Evenings at Home* and the second date is inferred because it appeared in Volume 6, reviewed in February 1796.

Two manuscript copies of this piece are known today: one by Matthew Nicholson, a graduate of Warrington Academy (Liverpool RO MS 920 NIC 22/2/6), and a copy in an unidentified hand—the same hand that copied 'The

King in his Castle' (Osborn Files 711, Beinecke). In both, the piece is addressed 'to Dr. Aikin', and both differ frequently from the *Evenings at Home* text, agreeing with each other against it. Their many verbal variants are of the kind that accrue in copies of copies; apart from the closing paragraph, no variant suggests an authorial original that differed from the *Evenings at Home* text, even though the ultimate source of the copies may well have been the manuscript Barbauld sent to her brother. The *Evenings at Home* text (6:30–8) probably derives more directly than either manuscript from Barbauld's untraced holograph. Thus, we have adopted it as our copy text.

I am one of four Sisters; and having some reason to think myself not well used either by them or by the world, I beg leave to lay before you a sketch of our history and characters. You will not wonder there should be frequent bickerings amongst us, when I tell you that in our infancy we were continually fighting; and so great was the noise, and din, and confusion, in our continual struggles to get upper-most, that it was impossible for any body to live amongst us in such a scene of tumult and disorder—These brawls, however, by a powerful interposition, were put an end to;[37] our proper place was assigned to each of us, and we had strict orders not to encroach on the limits of each other's property, but to join our common offices for the good of the whole family.

My first sister, (I call her the first, because we have generally allowed her the precedence in rank,) is, I must acknowledge, of a very active sprightly disposition; quick and lively, and has more brilliancy than any of us: but she is hot: every thing serves for fuel to her fury when it is once raised to a certain degree, and she is so mischievous whenever she gets the upper hand, that, notwithstanding her aspiring disposition, if I may freely speak my mind, she is calculated to make a good servant, but a very bad mistress.

I am almost ashamed to mention, that notwithstanding her seeming delicacy, she has a most voracious appetite,[38] and devours every thing that comes in her way; though, like other eager thin people, she does no credit to her keeping. Many a time has she consumed the product of my barns and storehouses, but it is all lost upon her. She has even been known to get into an oil-shop or tallow-chandler's[39] when every body was asleep, and lick up with the utmost greediness whatever she found there. Indeed, all prudent people are aware of her tricks, and though she is admitted into the best families, they take care to watch her very narrowly. I should not forget to mention, that my sister was once in a country where she was treated with uncommon respect; she was lodged in a sumptuous building, and had a number of young women of the best families to attend on her, and feed her, and watch over her health: in short, she was looked upon as something more than a common mortal. But she always behaved with great severity to her maids, and if any of them were negligent of their duty, or made a slip in their own conduct, nothing would serve her but burying the poor girls alive.[40] I have myself had some dark hints and intimations from the most respectable authority, that she will some time or other make an end of me.[41] You need not wonder, therefore, if I am jealous of her motions.

The next sister I shall mention to you, has so far the appearance of Modesty and Humility, that she generally seeks the lowest place. She is indeed of a very yielding easy temper, generally cool, and often wears a sweet placid smile upon her countenance; but she is easily ruffled, and when worked up, as she often is, by another sister, whom I shall mention to you by and by, she becomes a perfect fury. Indeed she is so apt to swell with sudden gusts of passion, that she is suspected at times to be a little lunatic.[42] Between her and my first mentioned sister, there is a more settled antipathy than between the Theban pair;[43] and they never meet without making efforts to destroy one another. With me she is always ready to form the most intimate union, but it is not always to my advantage. There goes a story in our family, that when we were all young, she once attempted to drown me. She actually kept me under a considerable time, and though at length I got my head above water, my constitution is generally thought to have been essentially injured by it ever since.[44] From that time she has made no such atrocious attempt, but she is continually making encroachments upon my property; and even when she appears most gentle, she is very insidious, and has such an undermining way with her, that her insinuating arts are as much to be dreaded as open violence. I might indeed remonstrate, but it is a known part of her character, that nothing makes any lasting impression upon her.

As to my third sister, I have already mentioned the ill offices she does me with my last mentioned one, who is entirely under her influence. She is besides of a very uncertain variable temper, sometimes hot, and sometimes cold, nobody knows where to have her. Her lightness is even proverbial, and she has nothing to give those who live with her more substantial than the smiles of courtiers. I must add, that she keeps in her service three or four rough blustering bullies with puffed cheeks,[45] who, when they are let loose, think they have nothing to do but to drive the world before them. She sometimes joins with my first sister, and their violence occasionally throws me into such a trembling, that, though naturally of a firm constitution, I shake as if I was in an ague fit.[46]

As to myself, I am of a steady solid temper; not shining indeed, but kind and liberal, quite a Lady Bountiful. Every one tastes of my beneficence, and I am of so grateful a disposition, that I have been known to return an hundred-fold for any present that has been made me. I feed and clothe all my children, and afford a welcome home to the wretch who has no other home. I bear with unrepining patience all manner of ill usage; I am trampled upon, I am torn and wounded with the most cutting strokes; I am pillaged of the treasures hidden in my most secret chambers; notwithstanding which, I am always ready to return good for evil, and am continually subservient to the pleasure or advantage of others; yet, so ungrateful is the world, that because I do not possess all the airiness and activity of my sisters, I am stigmatised as dull and heavy. Every sordid miserly fellow is called by way of derision one of *my* children; and if a person on entering a room does but turn his eyes upon me, he is thought stupid and mean, and not fit for good company. I have the satisfaction, however, of finding that people always incline towards me as they grow older; and that those who seemed proudly to disdain any affinity with me, are content to sink at last into my bosom. You will probably wish to have some account of my person. I am not a regular beauty; some of my features are rather harsh and prominent, when viewed separately; but my countenance has so much variety of expression, and so many different attitudes of elegance, that those who study my face with attention, find out continually new charms; and it may be truly said of me, what Titus says of his mistress, and for a much longer space,

> Pendant cinq ans entiers tous les jours je la vois,
> Et crois toujours la voir pour la premiere fois.[47]
>
> For five whole years each day she meets my view,
> Yet every day I seem to see her new.

Though I have been so long a mother, I have still a surprising air of youth and freshness, which is assisted by all the advantages of well chosen ornament, for I dress well, and according to the season.

This is what I have chiefly to say of myself and my sisters. To a person of your sagacity it will be unnecessary for me to sign my name. Indeed, one who becomes acquainted with any one of the family, cannot be at a loss to discover the rest, notwithstanding the difference in our features and characters.[48]

WORKS OF IMAGINATION AND INSTRUCTION

INTRODUCTION

Barbauld continued to teach after leaving Palgrave. Some was probably unpaid, for the benefit of friends such as the Carr family of Hampstead and their children. But the parents of Flora Wynch, although Barbauld friends, agreed to pay Barbauld 50 guineas for Flora's instruction, and other friends may have done so too.[1] After Barbauld's death Lucy Aikin gathered from her papers and published under the title *A Legacy for Young Ladies* thirty-five instructional pieces also meant to amuse, written at various times in her aunt's life, for girls and young women. Aikin observed that 'Some of them enforce moral truths; others contain instruction in history and other branches of the graver studies of youth; but the greater number are of a light and elegant cast, adapted to exercise the ingenuity and amuse the fancy while they refine the taste' and their 'allegorical or enigmatical style' are 'peculiarly adapted to her genius'.[2]

The pieces in verse, other than 'On Riddles', appear in Volume 1. Of the pieces in prose, only two, 'On Fashion' and 'Epitaph on a Goldfinch', are known to have been published in Barbauld's lifetime.[3] Several pieces could have been lectures delivered at Palgrave School; 'Description of a Curious Animal' (*Legacy for Young Ladies*, 70–2) definitely belongs to Palgrave. Those pieces appear in our 'Palgrave School' section. Pieces in dialogue, such as 'On Expense', in which a parent explains a subject to a child, are generically identical to dialogues in *Evenings at Home*, but had they been written prior to *Evenings* they probably would have appeared there. Other pieces cannot be traced to any specific occasion or addressee; Barbauld may have written some for herself alone.

Those, however, 'in the form of letters', Aikin explained in her Preface, 'were all addressed to different ladies whom [Barbauld] favoured with her friendship'.[4] At the time those pieces were written their addressees were not 'ladies' but girls: daughters of Barbauld friends, or pupils such as Flora Wynch (the addressee of 'On Fashion') and Lydia Rickards. Barbauld's relations with these young women

---

[1] Pieces by Barbauld may survive to this day, unidentified among the papers of families whose children she taught.
[2] LA, 'Preface', *LYL*, iv; LA, 'Memoir', lxix.
[3] 'On Fashion' appears in Volume 4 of this edition, among essays from the *Monthly Magazine*.
[4] *A Legacy for Young Ladies*, iv–v.

could have been both pedagogic and social: a girl might have begun as Barbauld's pupil and have become a friend, as Rickards did. Barbauld delivered much of her post-Palgrave teaching in the form of written tutorials, essays, or jeux d'esprit given or sent to pupils. The fact that Aikin found copies among Barbauld's papers may have meant that Barbauld regarded them as potentially publishable.

The dates of many of the pieces in this section can be identified or conjectured from their references and allusions and appear in date order; those whose dates cannot be determined are given following the dated ones and in the order in which they appear in the Lucy Aikin volumes.

Copy texts: 'Description of Two Sisters' (*Legacy*, pp. 187–90); 'Allegory on Sleep' (*Legacy*, pp. 214–20); 'Zephyrus and Flora' (*Works* [1825], 2:268–71); 'On the Classics' (*Legacy*, pp. 73–94); 'Atalanta' (*Legacy*, pp. 85–8); 'Arion' (*Legacy*, pp. 88–90); 'Venus and Adonis' (*Legacy*, pp. 91–4); 'The King in his Castle' (*Legacy*, pp. 34–40); 'Live Dolls' (*Evenings at Home*, 14th edn (1826): 1:84–94).

Description of Two Sisters

That it is addressed to 'dear Cousin' and that it opens by alluding to their conversation about 'beauties' (meaning, in the context, women deemed especially handsome) suggests that this piece may date to the Warrington years. The cousin would be Elizabeth Belsham (1743–1819), who visited Warrington probably as early as the mid-1760s and certainly in 1772. This would be Barbauld's earliest surviving jeu d'esprit, the work not of a teacher to a pupil but of one young woman to another. The 'beauties' mentioned in the opening sentence could be the sisters Sarah and Elizabeth Rigby, admired by Aikin and subjects of verses by her. Copy text: *Legacy for Young Ladies*, pp. 187–90.

Dear Cousin,

Our conversation last night upon beauties, put me in mind of two charming sisters, with whom I think you must be acquainted as well as I, though they were not in your list of belles. Their charms are very different however; the youngest is generally thought the handsomest, and yet other beauties shine more in her company than in her sister's; whether it be that her gay looks diffuse a lustre on all around, while her sister's beauty has an air of majesty which strikes with awe, or that the younger sets every one she is with in the fairest light, and discovers perfections which were before concealed, whilst the elder seems only solicitous to set off her own person and throw a shade upon every one else: yet, what you will think strange, it is she who is generally preferred for a confidant; for her sister, with all her amiable qualities, cannot keep a secret.

O! what an eye the younger has, as if she could look a person through; yet modest is her countenance, even and composed her pace, and she treads so softly—"Smooth sliding without step," as Milton says.[49] She seldom meets you without blushing,—her sister cannot blush,—she dresses very gaily, sometimes in clouded silks,[50] which indeed she first brought into fashion, but blue is her most becoming colour, and she generally appears in it. Now and then, she wears a very rich scarf, or sash, braided with all manner of colours.

The elder, like the Spanish ladies, dresses in black in order to set off her jewels, of which she has a greater quantity than Lady ———,[51] and, if I might judge, much finer. I cannot pretend to give you a catalogue of them; they are of all sizes, and set in all figures: her enemies say she does well to adorn her dusky brow with brilliants, and that without them she would be but little taken notice of; but certain it is, she has inspired more serious and enthusiastic passions than her sister, whose admirers are often fops more in love with themselves than with her. A learned clergyman some time ago fell deeply in love with her, and wrote a fine copy of verses on her;[52] and what was worst, her sister could not go into company without hearing them.

One thing they quite agree in,—not to go out of their way or alter their pace for any body. Once or twice indeed I have heard that the younger ......, but it was a great while ago, and she was not so old then, and so was more complaisant. She is generally waked with a fine concert of music, the other prefers a good solo....[53]

But see, the younger beauty looks pale and sick,—she faints,—she is certainly dying,—a slight blush still upon her cheek,—it fades, fast, fast.—She is gone, yet a sweet smile overspreads her countenance. Will she revive? Shall *I* ever see her again? Who can tell me?

Allegory on Sleep

'Miss D****' may be Judith Dixon (1762–1833+), afterwards Beecroft, of Norwich, whom Barbauld met when Dixon was 14 and with whom she established a mentoring relationship that, as often between Barbauld and her pupils, ripened into friendship. Thus 'Allegory on Sleep' might be dated to around 1778. The title may be Lucy Aikin's. Copy text: *Legacy for Young Ladies*, pp. 214–20.

My Dear Miss D****.

The affection I bear you, and the sincere regard I have for your welfare, will I hope excuse the liberty I am going to take in remonstrating against the indulgence of a too partial affection which I see with sorrow is growing upon you every day.

You start at the imputation: but hear me with patience; and if your own heart, your own reason, does not bear witness to what I say, then blame my suspicions and my freedom.

But need I say much to convince you of the power this favoured lover, whose name I will not mention, has over you, when at this very moment he absorbs all your faculties, and engrosses every power of your mind to such a degree as leaves it doubtful whether this friendly admonition will reach your ear, lost as you are in the soft enchantment? Is it not evident that in his presence you are dead to every thing around you? The voice of your nearest friends, your most sprightly and once-loved amusements, cannot draw your attention; you breathe, you exist, only for him. And when at length he has left you, do not I behold you languid, pale, bearing in your eyes and your whole carriage the marks of his power over you? When we parted last night, did not I see you impatient to sink into his arms? Have you never been caught reclined on his bosom, on a soft carpet of flowers, on the banks of a purling stream, where the murmuring of the waters, the whispering of the trees, the silence and solitude of the place, and the luxurious softness of every thing around you, favoured his approach and disposed you to listen to his addresses? Nay, in that sacred temple which ought to be dedicated to higher affections, has he never stolen insensibly on your mind, and sealed your ears against the voice of the preacher, though never so persuasive? Has not his influence over you greatly increased within these few weeks? Does he not every day demand, do you not every day sacrifice to him, a larger portion of your time?

Not content with your devoting to him those hours

"When business, noise, and day are fled,"[54]

does he not encroach upon the morning watches, break in upon your studies, and detain your mind from the pursuit of knowledge and the pursuit of pleasure,—of all pleasure but the enervating indulgence of your passion?

Diana, who still wishes to number you in her train, invites you to join in her lively sports; for you Aurora bathes the new-born rose in dew, and streaks the clouds with gold and crimson; and Youth and Health offer a thousand innocent pleasures to your acceptance.

And, let me ask you, what can you find in the company of him with whom you are thus enamoured, to make you amends for all that you give up for his sake? Does he entertain you with any thing but the most incoherent rhapsodies, the most romantic and visionary tales? To believe the strange, improbable and contradictory things he tells you, requires a credulity beyond that of an infant. If he has ever spoken truth, it is mixed with so much falsehood and obscurity, that it is esteemed the certain sign of a weak mind to be much affected with what he says.

As I wish to draw a true portrait, I will by no means disguise his good qualities; and shall therefore allow that he is a friend to the unhappy and the friendless, that his breast is the only pillow for misfortune to repose on, and that his approaches are so gentle and insinuating as in some moments to be almost irresistible. If he is at all disposed to partiality, it is in favour of the poor and mean, with whom he is generally thought to associate more readily than with the rich. Yet he dispenses favours to all: and those who are most disposed to rebel against his power and treat him with contempt, could never render themselves quite independent of him.

He is of a very ancient family, and came in long before the Conquest.[55] He has a half-brother, somewhat younger than himself, who has made his name very famous in the world: he is a tall meagre figure, with a ghastly air and a most forbidding countenance; he delights in slaughter, and has destroyed more men than Caesar or Alexander.

He who is the subject of my letter is fond of peace, sleek and corpulent, with a mild heavy eye and a physiognomy perfectly placid; yet with all this opposition of feature and character, there is such a resemblance between them (as often happens in family likenesses), that in some lights and attitudes you can scarce distinguish the one from the other.

To finish the description of your lover,—he is generally crowned with flowers, but of the most languid kind, such as poppies and cowslips; and he is attended by a number of servants, thin and light-footed, to whom he does not give the same livery; for some are dressed in the gayest, others in the most gloomy habits imaginable, but all fantastic.

He is subject to many strange antipathies, and as strange likings. The warbling of the lark, to others so agreeable, is to him the harshest discord, and Peter could not start more at the crowing of a cock.[56] The slightest accident, the cry of an infant, a mouse behind the wainscot, will oftentimes totally disconcert and put him to flight, and at other times he will not regard the loudest thunder. His favourite animal is the dormouse, and his music the dropping of water, the low tinkling of a distant bell, the humming of bees, and the hollow sound of the wind rustling through the trees.

But I have now said enough to let you into the true character of this powerful enchanter. You will answer, I know, to all this, that he begins by enslaving every faculty that might resist him, and that his power must be already broken before Reason can exert herself. You will perhaps likewise tell me (and I must acknowledge the justice of the retort), that I myself, though my situation affords a thousand reasons to resist him which do not take place with you, have been but too sensible of his attractions.

With blushes I confess the charge. At this moment, however, the charm is broken, and Reason has her full empire over me. Let me exhort you therefore... But why exhort you to what is already done? for if this letter has made its way to your ear, if your eye is now perusing its contents, the spell is dissolved, and you are no longer sunk in the embraces of *Sleep*.

Zephyrus and Flora

Letter to Mrs. W——

'Mrs. W——' is Rhoda Crocket Wynch (1754–1846), wife of William Wynch (1750–1819). The Wynches were neighbours of the Barbaulds in Hampstead in the later 1780s. Their daughter, Flora (1776–1842), in August 1787 became Barbauld's private pupil (ALB, Letters to JA, 16 Aug. and 5 Sept. 1787). For her Barbauld wrote 'On Fashion'. With her and William Wynch Barbauld visited Scotland from September to October 1794 (see her 'Lines to Mr W——, on his forty-fifth Birthday'). On 27 January 1795 Flora married James Willis, consul-general in Africa (*GM*, 65:82). Her parents remained friends with the Barbaulds; Rochemont's diary records social visits for June 1802 (*ALBVE*, 407).

This fable must pre-date 19 July 1788; by that date the Wynches had moved to London: 'Mr Wynch is returned from the Indies & tho I most heartily share in the joy of his wife, it has deprived us of the most agreeable neighbour by far that we had, & we no longer see our light graceful Flora dancing about & tripping about us in the fields with nymph like step. She is after a while however to attend me again, from London' (ALB, Letter to JA, 19 July [1788]). 'Zephyrus and Flora' alludes to the mythological tale of Zephyrus, Greek god of the west wind and of spring, who abducted Chloris (Flora in Roman mythology), goddess of flowers, raped and later married her. (Ovid tells the story in the *Fasti*, Book 5.) A fable of the arrival of Spring and a testimony to Barbauld's delight in young Flora Wynch (and to Flora's own delight in Spring), it also parodies the kind of letter a nosey but well-intentioned neighbor would have written to warn a parent about a child's behaviour. Copy text: *Works* (1825), 2:268–71, the only text known.

Dear Madam,

I think it my duty, as well from the high esteem I bear yourself, as from the tender and solicitous affection I feel for your lovely daughter, to inform you of an affair between her and one who has lately been fluttering about her; and for whom, young as she is, she seems to have conceived an extraordinary inclination. Of this you will be convinced, madam, when I assure you she often walks in the fields purposely to meet him; and that on her return I have seen her lips and cheeks improved in their colour by his kisses. It is but within these few weeks that this lover of hers has frequented the environs of Hampstead, for he spent the winter between Lisbon and the Canary Islands; and since his return, which by her has been passionately longed for, her fondness for walking has been much more apparent. Her excursions to the Heath, and her parties to West-end,[57] particularly when she gave me the slip the other day, have been all planned with the hope of meeting him. Nor can I wonder, indeed, that she admires so pretty a fellow; for he is a light airy being like herself, as playful and as frolicsome. He dresses in a light garment of the thinnest blue silk, fluttering in a thousand different folds, and by way of epaulette two silver wings peeping above his shoulders. His breath is made up of sighs, and perfumed with violets; and his whispers, especially at this season of the year, have a certain prevailing languishment and softness in them, that few can resist. He is fond of caressing the opening roses; and no birthnight beau is more powerfully scented with Mareschal powder than he is with every blossom of the spring.[58] But then he is a general lover, inconstant as he is gay; noted for levity, here today and gone tomorrow, hovering about every beautiful object without attaching himself to one. To fix him would be as difficult as to arrest a sunbeam or to hold a wave between your fingers. Yet I am sorry to say, madam, your daughter absolutely courts this *volage*,[59] and allows him liberties which a prudent mother like yourself must tremble at. He delights to play with her fair hair; sometimes he throws it over her forehead, and almost covers her face with it. Sometimes he takes a single lock, and plays it about her temples; now he spreads her tresses all over her graceful shoulders; and then lifts them up, or gently parts them, to discover the elegant turn and whiteness of her neck, giving them all the while a thousand kisses. Why need I mention what passes before your eyes, under your own window? It is there that I have seen him busied in wafting her to and fro with an easy motion, when her light form dances through the air in the swing you have lately put up, while he catches her fluttering garment and throws it into every varying fold his fancy dictates. It may be, however, that you may not think these sportive liberties of great consequence to one so young as your daughter is: but I am not without apprehensions that he may some day or other absolutely run away with her. I the rather fear this, as a brother of his, a rough blustering fellow, did once carry off a young lady whose parents had rejected his addresses, as is well known to all who are acquainted with the anecdotes of the family.⁶⁰ It is true, he that I speak of has neither the strength nor the impetuosity of his brother; but when I consider the peculiar lightness and airiness of the nymph in question, the enterprise appears to me very practicable.

I have only to add, that his amour with *Flora*⁵ is of long standing; and so little is it a secret in the world that every schoolboy is acquainted with it.⁶¹ I doubt not, madam, but you will take the measures your prudence must suggest on this occasion. All my motive in this affair has been to prove with how much zeal and affection I am,

dear madam,
Your devoted and obedient.

On the Classics

Barbauld was ambivalent towards the Greek and Latin classics. She knew Latin works in the original, having persuaded her father to teach her Latin, despite her gender, and the Greek probably in translation. The classics formed an essential part of a literary education, and she shared the general belief in their cultural primacy; but she also thought a good effect of the French Revolution would be a decline in 'classical learning' and a proportionate rise in the importance of more modern sciences: 'All the kindred studies of the cloister must sink, and we shall live no longer on the lean relics of antiquity' (ALB to JA, 1791; *Works*, 2:159). In this tutorial on the classics she retails customary views which she shared, at least until the Revolution.

Lucy Aikin published the piece without a date. Its reference to Sir William Jones (d. 1794) as if he were still active, and its mentions of Erasmus Darwin and William Cowper, whose reputations peaked in the 1790s, argue composition in the early '90s. 'Subjoined' suggests a written tutorial rather than a lecture. Thus the piece might have been composed for Flora Wynch at Hampstead. Copy text: *Legacy for Young Ladies*, pp. 73–94.

The authors known by the name of the Greek and Roman Classics have laid the foundation of all that is excellent in modern literature; and are so frequently referred to both in books and conversation, that a person of a cultivated mind cannot easily be content without obtaining some knowledge of them, even though he should not be able to read them in their original tongues. A clear and short account of these authors in a chronological series, together with a sketch of the character of their several

---

⁵ The name of this young lady was Flora. [*Lucy Aikin's note.*]

productions, for the use of those who have either none or a very superficial knowledge of the languages they are written in, is, as far as I know, a desideratum which it is much to [be] wished that some elegant scholar should supply: in the mean time a few general remarks upon them may be not unacceptable.

In the larger sense of the word, an author is called a Classic when his work has stood the test of time long enough to become a permanent part of the literature of his country. Of the number of writings which in their day have attained a portion of fame, very few in any age have survived to claim this honourable distinction. Every circumstance which gave temporary celebrity must be forgotten; party must have subsided; the voice of friends and of enemies must be silent; and the writer himself must have long mouldered in the dust, before the gates of immortality are opened to him. It is in vain that he attempts to flatter or to soothe his contemporaries, they are not called to the decision; his merits are to be determined by a race he has never seen; the judges are not yet born who are to pronounce on the claims of Darwin and of Cowper.[62] The severe impartiality of Posterity stands aloof from every consideration but that of excellence, and from her verdict there is no appeal.

It is true, indeed, that amidst the revolutions of ages, particularly before the invention of printing, accidental circumstances must often have had great influence in the preservation of particular writings: and we know and lament that many are lost which the learned world would give treasures of gold to recover. But it cannot easily happen that a work should be preserved without superior merit; and indeed we know from the testimony of antiquity, that the works which have come down to us, and which we read and admire, are in general the very works which by the Greeks and Romans themselves were esteemed most excellent.

It is impossible to contemplate without a sentiment of reverence and enthusiasm, these venerable writings which have survived the wreck of empires; and, what is more, of languages; which have received the awful stamp of immortality, and are crowned with the applause of so many successive ages. It is wonderful that words should live so much longer than marble temples;—words, which at first are only uttered breath; and, when afterwards enshrined and fixed in a visible form by the admirable invention of writing, committed to such frail and perishable materials: yet the light paper bark floats down the stream of time, and lives through the storms which have sunk so many stronger built vessels. Homer is read, though *The grass now grows where Troy town stood*:[63] and nations once despised as barbarous appretiate the merit of Cicero's orations on the banks of the Thames, when the long honours of the Consulate are vanished,[64] and the language of Rome is no longer spoken on the shores of the Tiber.

> Still green with bays each ancient altar stands,
> Above the reach of sacrilegious hands;
> Secure from flames, from envy's fiercer rage,
> Destructive war and all-involving age.
> See from each clime the learn'd their incense bring,
> Hear in all tongues consenting Paeans ring![65]

It is owing to the preservation of a few books of the kind we are speaking of, that at the revival of letters the world had not to go back to the very beginnings of science. When the storm of barbaric rage had past over and spent itself, they were drawn from the mould of ruins and dust of convents, and were of essential service in forming our taste and giving a direction to the recovered energies of the human mind. Oral instruction can benefit but one age and one set of hearers; but these silent teachers address all ages and all nations. They may sleep for a while and be neglected; but whenever the desire of information springs up in the human breast, there they are with their mild wisdom ready to instruct and please us. The Philosopher opens again his school; his maxims have lost nothing of their truth: the harmony of the Poet's numbers, though locked up for a time, becomes again vocal; and we find that what was nature and passion two thousand years ago, is nature and passion still.

Books are a kind of perpetual censors on men and manners; they judge without partiality, and reprove without fear or affection. There are times when the flame of virtue and liberty seems almost to be extinguished amongst the existing generation; but their animated pages are always at hand to rekindle it. The Despot trembles on his throne, and the bold bad man turns pale in his closet at the sentence pronounced against him ages before he was born.

In addition to their intrinsic value, there is much incidental entertainment in consulting authors who flourished at so remote a period. Every little circumstance becomes curious as we discover allusions to customs now obsolete, or draw indications of the temper of the times from the various slight hints and casual pieces of information which may be gathered up by the ingenious critic. Sometimes we have the pleasure of being admitted into the cabinet of a great man, and leaning as it were over his shoulder while he is pouring himself out in the freedom of a confidential intercourse which was never meant to meet the eye even of his contemporaries. At another time we are delighted to witness the conscious triumph of a genius who, with a generous confidence in his powers, prophesies his own immortality, and to feel as we read that his proud boast has not been too presumptuous. Another advantage of reading the ancients is, that we trace the stream of ideas to their spring. It is always best to go to the fountain head. We can never have a just idea of the comparative merit of the moderns, without knowing how much they have derived from imitation. It is amusing to follow an idea from century to century, and observe the gradual accession of thought and sentiment; to see the jewels of the ancients new set, and the wit of Horace sparkling with additional lustre in the lines of Pope.[66]

The real sources of History can only be known by some acquaintance with the original authors. This indeed will often be found to betray the deficiency of our documents, and the difficulty of reconciling jarring accounts. It will sometimes unclothe and exhibit in its original bareness what the art of the moderns has drest up and rounded into form. It will show the unsightly chasms and breaks which the modern compiler passes over with a light foot; and perhaps make us sceptical with regard to many particulars of which we formerly thought we had authentic information. But it is always good to know the real measure of our knowledge. That knowledge would be greater, if the treasures of antiquity had come to us undiminished: but this is not the case. Besides the loss of many mentioned with honour by their contemporaries, few authors are come down to us entire; and of some exquisite productions only fragments are extant. The full stream of narration is sometimes suddenly checked at the most interesting period, and the sense of a brilliant passage is clouded by the obscurity of a single word. The literary productions are come to us in a similar state with the fine statues of antiquity: of which some have lost an arm, others a leg; some a little finger only: scarce any have escaped some degree of mutilation; and sometimes a trunk is dug up so shorn of its limbs, that the antiquaries are puzzled to make out to what god or hero it originally belonged. To the frequent loss of part of an author must be added the difficulty of deciphering what remains.

Ancient manuscripts are by no means easy to read. You are not to imagine, when you see a fair edition of Virgil, or Horace, divided into verses and accurately pointed, that you see it in any thing like its original state. The oldest manuscripts are written wholly in capitals, and without any separation of letters into words. Passing through many hands, they have suffered from the mistakes or carelessness of transcribers; by which so great an obscurity is thrown on many passages, that very often he who makes the happiest guess is the best commentator. But this very obscurity has usefully exercised the powers of the human mind. It became a great object, at the revival of letters, to compare different readings; to elucidate a text by parallel passages; to supply by probable conjecture what was necessary to make an author speak sense; and by every possible assistance of learning and sound criticism, together with typographical advantages, to restore the beauty and splendour of the classic page. Verbal criticism[67] was at that time of great and real use; and those who are apt to undervalue it, are little aware how much labour was requisite to reduce the confused or mutilated work of a thousand years back to form and order.

This task was well fitted for an age recently emerged out of barbarism. The enthusiastic admiration with which men were struck on viewing the master-pieces of human genius, and even the superstitious veneration with which they regarded every thing belonging to them, tended to form their taste by a quicker process than if they had been left to make the most of their own abilities. By degrees the moderns felt their own powers; they learned to imitate, and perhaps to excell what before they idolized. But a considerable period had passed before any of the modern languages were thought worthy of being the vehicle of the discoveries of science or even of the effusions of fancy. Christianity did not as might have been expected, bring into discredit the pagan philosophy. Aristotle reigned in the schools, where he was regarded with a veneration fully equal to what was expressed for the sainted fathers of the church; and as to the mythology of the ancients, it is so beautiful that all our earlier poetry has been modeled upon it. Even yet, the predilection for the Latin language is apparent in our inscriptions, in the public exercises of our schools and universities, and the general bent of the studies of youth. In short, all our knowledge and all our taste has been built upon the foundation of the ancients; and without knowing what they have done, we cannot estimate rightly the merit of our own authors.

It may naturally be asked why the Greek and Roman writers alone are called by the name of Classics. It is true the Hebrew might be esteemed so, if we did not receive them upon a higher ground of merit.[68] As to the Persian and Arabic with other languages of countries once highly cultivated, their authors are not taken into the account, partly because they are understood by so few, and partly because their idioms and modes of expression, if not of feeling, are so remote from ours that we can scarcely enter into their merits. Their writings are comprehended under the name of Oriental literature. It has been more cultivated of late, particularly by Sir William Jones;[69] and our East India possessions will continue to draw our attention that way: but curiosity is gratified rather than taste. We are pleased indeed with occasional beauties, sometimes a pure maxim of morality and sometimes a glowing figure of speech; but they do not enter into the substance of the mind, which ever must be fed and nourished by the classic literature of Greece and Rome.

I shall subjoin a few specimens of the mythological stories of the ancients.

Atalanta[70]

Atalanta was a beautiful young woman, exceedingly swift of foot. She had many lovers; but she resolved not to marry till she could meet with one who should conquer her in running. A great many young men proposed themselves, and lost their lives; for the conditions were, that if they were overcome in the race they should be put to death. At length she was challenged by Hippomenes, a brave and handsome youth. "Do you know," said Atalanta, "that nobody has yet been found who excells me in swiftness, and that you must be put to death if you do not win the race? I should be sorry to have any more young men put to death."—"I am not afraid," said Hippomenes; "I think I shall win the race and win you too."

So the ground was marked out and the day appointed, and a great number of spectators gathered together; and Atalanta stood with her garments tucked up, and Hippomenes by her, waiting impatiently for the signal. At length it was given; and immediately they both started at the same instant, and ran with their utmost speed across the plain. But Atalanta flew like the wind, and soon outstripped the young man. Then Hippomenes drew from his vest a golden apple, which had been given him by Venus from the gardens of the Hesperides, and threw it from him with all his force. The virgin saw it glittering as it rolled across the plain, and ran out of the course to pick it up. While she was doing so, Hippomenes passed her, and the spectators shouted for joy. However, Atalanta redoubled her speed, soon overtook Hippomenes, and again got before him. Upon this, Hippomenes produced another golden apple, and threw it as before. It rolled a great way out of the course, and the virgin was thrown very far behind by picking it up. She had great difficulty this time to recover her lost ground, and the spectators shouted "Hippomenes will win! Hippomenes will win!" But Atalanta was so light, so nimble, and exerted herself so much, that at length she passed him as before, and flew as if she had wings towards the goal. And now she had but a little way to run; and the people said, "Poor Hippomenes! he will lose after all, and be put to death like the rest;—see, see how she gains ground of him! how near the goal she is! Atalanta will win the race." Then Hippomenes took another golden apple,—it was the last he had, and prayed to Venus to give him success, and threw it behind him. Atalanta saw it, and considered a moment whether she should venture to delay herself again by picking it up. She knew she ran the risk of losing the race, but she could not withstand the beautiful glittering of the apple as it rolled along; and she said to herself, "I shall easily overtake Hippomenes, as I did before." But she was mistaken; for they had now so little a way to run, that though she skimmed along the plain like a bird, and exerted all her strength, she was too late. Hippomenes reached the goal before her: she was obliged to own herself conquered, and to marry him according to the agreement.

Arion[71]

Arion was a poet of Lesbos, who sung his own verses to his harp. He had been a good while at the court of Periander tyrant of Corinth, and had acquired great riches, with which he was desirous to return to his native country. He therefore made an agreement with a captain of a ship to carry him to Mitylene in Lesbos, and they set sail. But the captain and crew, tempted by the wealth which he had on board, determined to seize his gold and throw him into the sea. When poor Arion heard their cruel intention, he submitted to his fate, for he knew he could not resist, and only begged they would allow him to give them one tune upon his harp before he died. This they complied with; and Arion, standing on the deck, drew from his harp such melodious strains, accompanied with such moving verses, that any body but these cruel sailors would have been touched with them. When he had finished they threw him into the sea, where they supposed he was swallowed up: but that was not the case; for a dolphin, which had been drawn towards the ship by the sweetness of Arion's voice, swam to him, took him gently upon his back, conveyed him safely over the waves, and landed him at Tenaera, whence he returned to Periander. Periander was very much surprised to see him come again in such a forlorn and destitute condition, and asked him the reason. Arion told his story. Periander bade him conceal himself till the sailors should return from their voyage, and he would do him justice. When the ship returned from its voyage, Periander ordered the sailors to be brought before him, and asked them what they had done with Arion. They said he had died during the voyage, and that they had buried him. Then Periander ordered Arion to appear before them in the clothes he wore when they cast him into the sea. At this plain proof of their guilt they were quite confounded, and Periander put them all to death. It is said further, that the dolphin was taken up into the heavens and turned into a constellation.—It is a small constellation, of moderate brightness, and has four stars in the form of a rhombus; you will find it south of the Swan, and a little west of the bright star Alcair.

Venus and Adonis[72]

The goddess Venus loved Adonis, a mortal. Beautiful Venus loved the beautiful Adonis. She often said to him, "O Adonis! be content to lie crowned with flowers by the fresh fountains, and to feed upon honey and nectar, and to be lulled to sleep by the warbling of birds; and do not expose your life by hunting the tawny lion or the tusky boar, or any savage beast. Take care of that life, which is so dear to Venus!" But Adonis would not listen to her. He loved to rise early in the morning while the dew was upon the grass, and to beat the thickets with his well-trained hounds, whose ears swept the ground. With his darts he pierced the nimble fawns and the kids with budding horns, and brought home the spoil upon his shoulders. But one day he wounded a fierce bristly boar; the arrow stuck in his side, and made the animal mad with pain: he rushed upon Adonis, and gored his thigh with his sharp tusks. Beautiful Adonis fell to the ground like a lily that is rooted up by a sudden storm: his blood flowed in crimson streams down his fair side; and his eyelids closed, and the shades of death hovered over his pale brow.

In the mean time the evening came on, and Venus had prepared a garland of fresh leaves and flowers to bind around the glowing temples of Adonis when he should come hot and tired from the chase, and a couch of rose-leaves to rest his weary limbs: and she said, "Why does not Adonis come! Return, Adonis! let me hear the sound of your feet! let me hear the voice of your dogs! let them lick my hands, and make me understand that their master is approaching!"—But Adonis did not return; and the dark night came, and the rosy morning appeared again, and still he did not appear. Then Venus sought him in the plains and through the thickets, and amidst the rough brakes; and her veil was torn with the thorns, and her feet bruised and bleeding with the sharp pebbles; for she ran hither and thither like a distracted person. And at length upon the mountain she found him whom she loved so dearly: but she found him cold and dead, with his faithful dogs beside him.

Then Venus rent her beautiful tresses, and beat her breast, and pierced the air with her loud lamentations: and the little Cupids that accompany her broke their ivory bows for grief, and scattered upon the ground the arrows of their golden quivers: and they said, "We mourn Adonis; Venus mourns for beautiful Adonis; the Loves mourn along with her. Beautiful Adonis lies dead upon the ground, his side gored with the tooth of a boar,—his white thigh with a white tooth. Venus kisses the cold lips of Adonis; but Adonis does not know that he is kissed, and she cannot revive him with her warm breath."

Then Venus said, "You shall not quite die, my Adonis! I will change you into a flower." And she shed nectar on the ground, which mixed with the blood, and presently a crimson flower sprung up in the room of Adonis; and also the river was tinged with his blood and became red.

And every year, on the day that Adonis died, the nymphs mourned and lamented for him, and ran up and down shrieking, and crying "Beautiful Adonis is dead!"

The King in his Castle

Barbauld sent this piece to young Lucy Aikin not long after she sent 'The Four Sisters' to John, for she opens it by asking Lucy if she has 'made out who the four Sisters are'; hence it probably dates to the early or mid-'90s. A manuscript text (Osborn Files, Folder 713, Beinecke) in the same unknown hand as 'The Four Sisters' may derive from a circulating copy of Barbauld's original. Because the piece was addressed to Lucy and published by her, we assume that the *Legacy* text is closer than the Beinecke copy to Barbauld's original. Copy text: *Legacy for Young Ladies*, pp. 34–40.

My Dear Lucy,

Have you made out who the four Sisters are?[6] If you have, I will tell you another story. It is about a monarch who lives in a sumptuous castle, raised high above the ground and built with exquisite art. He takes a great deal of state upon him, and, like Eastern monarchs, transacts every thing by means of his ministers; for he never appears himself, and indeed lives in so retired a manner, that though it has often excited the curiosity of his subjects, his residence is hidden from them with as much jealous care as that of Pygmalion was from the Tyrians;[73] and it has never been discovered with any certainty which of the chambers of the castle he actually inhabits, though by means of his numerous spies he is acquainted with what passes in every one of them.

But I must proceed to give you some account of his chief ministers; and I will begin with two who are mutes. Their office is to bring him quick and faithful intelligence of all that is going forward; this they perform in a very ingenious manner. You have heard of the Mexicans, who, not having the

---

[6] See this piece in *Evenings at Home*. [*Lucy Aikin's note*.]

art of writing, supplied the deficiency by painting every thing they have a mind to communicate;[74] so that when the Spaniards came amongst them, they sent regular accounts to the king of their landing and all their proceedings, in very intelligible language, without writing a single word. Now this is just the method of these two mutes; they are continually employed in making pictures of every thing that passes, which they do with wonderful quickness and accuracy, all in miniature, but in exact proportion, and coloured after life. These pictures they bring every moment to a great gate of the palace, where the king receives them.

The next I shall mention are two drummers. These have each a great drum, on which they beat soft or loud, quick or slow, according to the occasion. They often entertain the king with music; besides which they are arrived at such wonderful perfection upon their instrument, and make the strokes with such precision, that by the different beats, accompanied by proper pauses and intervals, they can express any thing they wish to tell;— and the king relies upon them as much as upon his mutes. There is a sort of covered way made in the form of a labyrinth from the station of the drummers to the inner rooms of the palace.

There is a pair of officers,—for you must know, the officers[75] go mightily by pairs,—whose department it is to keep all nuisances from the palace. They are lodged for that purpose under a shed or penthouse built with that view before the front of the palace: they likewise gather and present to the monarch sweet odours, essences and perfumes, with which he regales himself: they likewise inspect the dishes that are served up at his table; and if any of them are not fit to be eaten, they give notice for their removal; and sometimes, if any thing offensive is about to enter the palace, they order the agents to shut two little doors which are in their keeping, and by that means prevent its entrance.

The agents are two very active officers of long reach and quick execution. The executive part of government is chiefly intrusted to them; they obey the king's commands with a readiness and vigour truly admirable; they defend the castle from all assaults, and are vigilant in keeping at a distance every annoyance. Their office is branched out into ten subordinate ones, but in cases which require great exertion they act together.

I must not omit the beef-eaters.[76] These stand in rows at the great front gate of the palace, much as they do at St. James's,[77] only that they are dressed in white. Their office is to prepare the viands for the king, who is so very lazy and so much accustomed to have every thing done for him, that, like the king of Bantam[78] and some other Eastern monarchs, he requires his meat to be chewed before it is presented to him.

Close by the beef-eaters lives the king's orator, a fat portly gentleman, something of a Dutch make, but remarkably voluble and nimble in his motions notwithstanding.[79] He delivers the king's orders and explains his will. This gentleman is a good deal of an epicure, which I suppose is the reason he has his station so near the beef-eaters. He is a perfect connoisseur in good eating, and assumes a right of tasting all the dishes; and the king pays the greatest regard to his opinion. Justice obliges me to confess that this orator is one of the most flippant and ungovernable of the king's subjects.

Among the inferior officers are the porters, two stout lusty fellows who carry the king about from place to place (for I am sure you are by this time too well acquainted with his disposition to suppose he performs that office for himself); but as most great men's officers have their deputies, so these lazy porters are very apt to get their business done by deputy, and to have people to carry *them* about.

I should never have done if I were to mention all the particulars of the domestic establishment and internal oeconomy of the castle, which is all arranged with wonderful art and order; how the outgoings are proportioned to the income, and what a fellow-feeling there is between all the members of the family from the greatest to the meanest. The king, from his high birth, on which he values himself much,—being of a race and lineage quite different from any of his subjects,—and from his superior capacity, claims the most absolute obedience; though, as is frequently the case with kings, he is in fact most commonly governed by his ministers, who lead him where they please without his being sensible of it.—As you, my dear Lucy, have had more conversation with this king than most of your age have been honoured with, I dare say you will be at no loss in pointing him out. I therefore add no more but that I am

Yours, &c.

Live Dolls

The addressee of this piece is not identified, but it can plausibly be dated to the late 1790s by reference to an innovation in doll-making. Eliza is surprised by her new doll's ability to open its eyes. A dialogue about a new doll appears in Part II of Ellenor Fenn's *The Infant's Friend* (1797):

> Is your's a wax doll?
> Does she open her eyes?
> Has she a cloak?—and a bonnet? (p. 52)[7]

---

[7] Thanks to Andrea Immel for this reference.

LIVE DOLLS

'Live Dolls' describes a ladies' sewing circle to benefit the poor, probably one that Barbauld had heard of or visited. The piece was found by Lucy Aikin among Barbauld's papers and would have suited *Legacy*, but Aikin assigned it to a new edition of *Evenings at Home* which she promised in 1825: 'In a new edition, will be added, Live Dolls' (LA, 'Memoir', xxxvii n). Copy text: *Evenings at Home*, 14th edn (1826): 1:84–94, its first appearance in print, according to Aikin ('Preface', I: vi).

Mrs. Lacour was accustomed to lay out for her daughter, a girl about eight years old, a great deal of money in play-things. One morning Eliza (that was her name) was in raptures over a new wax doll, which her mamma had given two guineas for in Fleet-street.[80] By means of a concealed wire, it had been made to open and shut its eyes, to the no small surprise of the little girl, not unmixed with a certain degree of terror, when her mother first exhibited the phaenomenon; but having had the principle explained to her, she had spent the greatest part of the morning in moving the wires up and down, and making them alternately open and shut the eye-lids. It is true the mechanism had one defect, which we record, in hopes the ingenuity of future doll-makers may find a remedy for it. The doll shut her eyes after the manner of a bird, by drawing up the membrane over the eye, instead of letting the eye-lid fall over it, as is the custom in human creatures; but as Eliza had not studied comparative anatomy, this slight irregularity was not noticed. She was still in raptures over her new acquisition, when she was surprised with a visit from Mrs. Dorcas, a maiden sister of her father's, who sometimes called upon her.[81] "Look here, my dear aunt," said she, "what a charming doll I have got; see, now its eyes are shut, now they are open again, how curious! I dare say you cannot guess how I do it. I can hardly help fancying it alive. To-morrow I shall begin to dress it, for it must have a fine worked cap with a laced border, and a long muslin robe and shoes. I do not know whether it should have shoes yet, for it is only a baby; and I shall lay it in the cradle, and rock it,—and when I want it to go to sleep; its eyes shall be shut, and in the morning they shall be open again, just as if it were really alive: I wish it could eat and drink,—why could they not make its mouth to open?"

Mrs. D. Your doll is very pretty, indeed, and I commend you for intending to make its clothes yourself, but would not you like better to have a real live doll to dress?

Eliza. O yes! that I should, indeed, but I believe—I am afraid there is no such doll.

Mrs. D. I will find you such a one if you will dress it.

Eliza. And will it open its mouth and eat?

Mrs. D. Yes it will.

Eliza. And can it speak too?

Mrs. D. I do not say it can speak yet; it has not been taught; but you shall hear its voice, and you shall see it breathe: your doll does not breathe. (Eliza took her doll and placed her hand upon its waxen bosom, as if she expected to feel it heave.) And the clothes you will make will warm it too. A wax doll is not warmed by its clothes. Your doll is as cold when she is wrapped up in a quilt and placed in the cradle, as if she were laid naked upon a marble slab.

Eliza. Is she?

Mrs. D. Yes; you may convince yourself of that whenever you please; but this live doll will not only be warmed by the clothes you make, but, perhaps, she may die if you do not make them.

Eliza. O! do not let her die, I will set about making the clothes directly.

Mrs. D. Then come along with me.

Eliza sallied forth with her aunt Dorcas: she was all the way silent, and breathless with expectation: after leading her through a few streets, her aunt stopped at a house, and asked to be shown into the work-room. It was a room where a number of young girls were sitting at a long table, with cheerful and busy looks. The table was covered with work-bags, needle-cases, thread-papers, and such like sewing implements, and spread with flannel, calico, dimity, and old linen; one of the girls was making a cap, another a petticoat, a third a frock, the elder ones were cutting out the cloth, some of the little ones were stretching out their hands to hold a skein of thread for the others to wind; not one was unemployed. "What are they all doing?" said Eliza.

Mrs. D. They are all working for live dolls.

Eliza. But where are the dolls?

Mrs. D. You cannot see them yet; they would suffer if the clothes were not prepared for them before they came.

Eliza. But here are no laces nor worked muslins; here is nothing very pretty.

Mrs. D. No, because pretty things seldom have the property of keeping the wearers warm.

Eliza. But who are they working for?

At that instant a woman with a child upon her bosom, pale, but with a countenance shining with joy and gratitude, entered the work-room, pouring out her thanks to the good young ladies, as she truly called them, for their well-timed bounty. "But for you," she said, "this dear little infant might perhaps have perished, or at least its little limbs would have been chilled with cold for want of good and substantial clothing. My husband was ill, and could not work, and I had no money to buy any thing but necessary food. If I could have bought the materials, or if you had given them me, I could not have cut them out and contrived them, and made them up myself; for I was never taught to be handy at my needle, as you have been, ladies. I was only set to coarse work. Look what a sweet little infant it is, and how comfortable he looks. God bless you, dear ladies! and make you all happy wives and mothers, when the time comes!" The girls, with great pleasure, rose when she had finished her address to them; and after congratulating the mother, took the infant, and handing it from one to another, kissed and played with it. Eliza, too, advanced, but timidly, and as if she had not yet earned a right to caress it. "Approach, my niece," said Mrs. Dorcas, "kiss the lips of this infant, and imbibe that affection which is one of the characteristics of your sex. Women are made to love children, and they should begin to love them while they themselves are children; nor is there any surer way of learning to love a being, than by doing good to it. You see now why I brought you hither. This is the live doll I promised you: its limbs are not the work of a clumsy mechanic, they are fashioned by consummate wisdom and skill, and it will not always remain as it is; this little frame has a principle of improvement in it—it has powers that will unfold themselves by degrees—the limbs will stretch and grow; after a while it will walk, it will speak, it will play, it will be like one of you. How precious then is the life of such a creature! But it has pleased the Creator of all things that this excellent being should come into the world naked and helpless; it has neither hair, nor wool, nor fur, nor feathers to keep it warm; if not clothed and cherished, it would soon be killed with the cold. It is therefore very desirable to help those poor people who cannot afford to clothe their infants, lest so admirable a work of God as a human creature should perish for want of care. There is a great deal of pain and danger in bearing children in any situation of life; but when people are poor as well as sick, the distress is very much increased. These good young ladies, Eliza, have formed a society among themselves for making baby-linen for the poor. Nobody bid them do it; it was entirely of their own accord. They have agreed to subscribe a penny a week out of their little pocket money. A penny is a very small matter; girls who have a great deal of money, perhaps would not suppose it worth thinking about, but a great many pennies every week will in time come to a sum that is not so contemptible. With this they buy the materials, such as warm flannels, coarse printed cottons, and dimity. Their mammas give them, every now and then, some fine old linen and cast-off clothes; but the value of their work is a great deal more than that of the materials: if they did not cut and contrive, and make them up, they would be of little service comparatively to the poor people; besides, the doing so will make them clever managers when they come to have children of their own. None of these good girls are above fourteen; and they have clothed a number of little helpless infants, and made, as you have seen, the mothers' hearts very glad. Now, if you wish it, I dare say they will let you work with them; but here is no finery,—and if you like better to work for your wax-doll, do so." "O, no!" said Eliza, "the live doll for me;" and she bespoke a place at the long work-table.

The Rich and the Poor: A Dialogue

The mother's critique of Fashion at the end of this dialogue aligns it with Barbauld's 'Fashion: a Vision', published in 1796 but written several years earlier, and with the critique of Fashion in 'Remarks on the Inequality of Conditions', published in 1807 but possibly written in 1802. The following dialogue could have been inspired by a letter about charity-schools for girls by Barbauld's acquaintance Catharine Cappe, published in John Aikin's *Monthly Magazine* in May 1798, or by the general interest in the subject to which Cappe refers: 'it appears, from the attention paid to many late publications on similar subjects, that there is a disposition in the public mind, to take under consideration whatever may have the benefit of the poorer classes for its object' (Cappe, 'Letter', 319). 'The poorer classes' was a subject of national discussion in the 1790s. John Aikin saw the nation divided almost into two 'species', 'the inhabitant of the splendid square, and the tenant of the gloomy alley' (JA, 'On the Inequality of Conditions', 207–8). In Barbauld's dialogue, the mother instructs her naïve daughter on the difference between 'paupers' and the ranks of people who can support themselves.

Barbauld's reference to 'Lady Selina' calls to mind Selina Hastings, Countess of Huntingdon (1707–91), a devout Methodist and patron of the Wesleys. Perhaps the name functions here as a synecdoche for 'Methodist', for in the later eighteenth and early nineteenth centuries, they believed in teaching the children of the poor to be religious and submissive (see Thompson, *The Making of the English Working Class*, ch. 11). 'Lady Mary', founder of the charity school in this dialogue, is not identified and may well be fictional. 'Harriet' is also the name of the daughter in Barbauld's dialogue 'On Expense'. Copy text: *Legacy for Young Ladies*, pp. 57–69.

Mamma! said Harriet Beechwood, I have just heard such a proud speech of a poor man! you would wonder if you heard it.

Not much, Harriet; for pride and poverty can very well agree together:—but what was it?

Why, mamma, you know the charity-school that Lady Mary has set up, and how neat the girls look in their brown stuff gowns and little straw bonnets.

Yes, I think it a very good institution; the poor girls are taught to read and spell and sew, and what is better still, to be good.

Well, mamma, Lady Mary's gardener, a poor man who lives in a cottage just by the great house, has a little girl; and so, because she was a pretty little girl, Lady Mary offered to put her into this school;—and do you know he would not let her go!

Indeed!

Yes: he thanked her, and said, "I have only one little girl, and I love her dearly; and though I am a poor man, I had rather work my fingers to the bone than she should wear a charity dress."

I do not doubt, my dear Harriet, that a great many people will have the same idea of this poor man's behaviour which you have; but for my own part, I am inclined to think it indicates something of a noble and generous spirit.

Was it not proud to say she should not wear a charity dress?

Why should she?—would you wear a charity dress?

O, mamma, but this is a poor man!

He is able to pay for her learning, I suppose; otherwise he would certainly do wrong to refuse his child the advantage of instruction because his feelings were hurt by it.

Yes, he is going to put her to Dame Primmer's across the Green; she will have half a mile to walk.

That will do her no hurt.

But he is throwing his money away; for he might have his little girl taught for nothing; and as he is a poor man he ought to be thankful for it.

Pray what do you mean by a poor man?

O, a man—those men that live in poor houses, and work all day, and are hired for it.

I cannot tell exactly how you define a poor house: but as to working, your papa is in a public office, and works all day long, and more hours certainly than the labourer does; and he is hired to it, for he would not do the work but for the salary they give him.

But you do not live like those poor people, and you do not wear a check apron like the gardener's wife.

Neither am I covered with lace and jewels like a duchess: there is as much difference between our manner of living and that of many people above us in fortune, as between ours and this gardener's whom you call poor.

What is being poor then? is there no such thing?

Indeed I hardly know how to answer your question: rich and poor are comparative terms; and provided a man is in no want of the necessaries of life and is not in debt, he can only be said to be poor comparatively with others, of whom the same might be affirmed by those who are still richer.

But to whatever degree of indigence you apply the term, you must take care not to confound a *poor man* with a *pauper*.

What is a pauper? I thought they had been the same thing?

A pauper is one who cannot maintain himself, and who is maintained by the charity of the community. Your gardener was not a pauper; he worked for what he had, and he paid for what he had; and therefore he had a right to expect that his child should not be confounded with the children of the idle, the profligate, and the dissolute, who are maintained upon charity. I wish the lower classes had more of this honourable pride.

Is it a crime to be a pauper?

To be a pauper is often the consequence of vice; and where it is not, it justly degrades a man from his rank in society. If the gardener's daughter were to wear a kind of charity badge, the little girls she plays with would consider her as having lost her rank in society. You would not like to lose your rank, and to be thrust down lower than your proper place in society. There are several things it would not at all hurt you to do, which you would not choose to do on this account. For instance, to carry a bandbox through the street;[82]—yet it would not hurt you to carry a bandbox, you would carry a greater weight in your garden for pleasure.

But I thought gardeners and such sort of people had no rank?

That is a very great mistake. Every one has his rank, his place in society; and so far as rank is a source of honourable pride, there is less difference in rank between you and the gardener, than between the gardener and a pauper. Between the greater part of those we call different classes, there is only the difference of less and more; the spending a hundred, or five hundred, or five thousand a year; the eating off earthenware, or china, or plate: but there is a real and essential difference between the man who provides for his family by his own exertions, and him who is supported by charity. The gardener has a right to stretch out his nervous arm and to say, "This right hand, under Providence, provides for myself and my family; I earn what I eat, I am a burthen to no one, and therefore if I have any superfluity I have a right to spend it as I please, and to dress my little girl to my own fancy."

But do you not think, mamma, that a brown stuff gown and a straw bonnet would be a much properer dress for the lower sort of people than any thing gaudy? If they are much dressed, you know, we always laugh at their vulgar finery.

They care very little for your laughing at them; they do not dress to please you.

Whom do they dress to please?

Whom do you dress to please?

You, my dear mamma, and papa.

Not entirely, I fancy;—you tell me the truth, but not the whole truth. Well, they dress to please their papas and mammas, their young companions, and their sweethearts.

I have often heard Lady Selina say, that if all the lower orders were to have a plain uniform dress, it would be much better; and that if a poor person is neat and clean, it is quite enough.

Better for whom?—enough for whom? for themselves, or for us? They have a natural love of ornament as well as we have. It is true they can do our work as well in a plainer dress; but when the work is done and the time of enjoyment comes,—in the dance on the green, or the tea-party among their friends,—who shall hinder them from indulging their taste and fancy, and laying out the money they have so fairly earned in what best pleases them?

But they are not content without following our fashions; and they are so ridiculous in their imitations of them. I was quite diverted to see Molly the pastrycook's girl tossing her head about in a hat and ribbon which I dare say she thought very fashionable; but such a caricature of the mode—I was so diverted.

You may be diverted with a safer conscience when I assure you that the laugh goes round. London laughs at the country, the court laughs at the city, and I dare say your pastrycook's girl laughs at somebody who is distanced by herself in the race of fashion.

But every body says, and I have heard you say, mamma, that the kind of people I mean, and servants particularly, are very extravagant in dress.

That unfortunately is true: they very often are so, and when they marry they suffer for it severely; but do not you think many young ladies are equally so? Did you not see at your last dancing-school ball many a girl whose father cannot give her a thousand pounds, covered with lace and ornaments?[83]

It is very true.

Are not duchesses driven by extravagance to pawn their plate and jewels?

I have heard so.

The only security against improper expense is dignity of mind, and moderation: these are not common in any rank; and I do not know why we should expect them to be more common among the lower and uneducated classes than among the higher.—To return to your gardener. He has certainly a right to dress his girl as he pleases without asking you or me: but I shall think he does not make a wise use of that right if he lays out his money in finery, instead of providing the more substantial comforts and enjoyments of life. And I should think exactly the same of my neighbour in the great house in the park.

Have servants a rank?

Certainly; and you will find them very tenacious of it. A gentleman's butler will not go behind a coach; a lady's maid will not go on an errand.

Are they not very saucy to refuse doing it, if they are ordered?

No; if they refuse civilly. They are hired to do certain things, not to obey you in every thing. There are many ranks above, but there are also many ranks below them; and they have both the right and the inclination to support their place in society.

But their masters would respect them the more if they did not stand upon these punctilios.

But I have told you it is not our approbation they seek. When the lower orders mix with the higher, it is to maintain themselves and get money; and if they are honest, they will do their work faithfully: but it is amongst their equals that they seek for affection, applause, and admiration; and there they meet with it. It matters very little in what rank a man is, provided he is esteemed and reckoned a man of consequence there. The feelings of vanity are exactly the same in a countess's daughter dancing at court, and a milkwoman figuring at a country hop.

But surely, mamma, the countess's daughter will be more really elegant?

That will depend very much upon individual taste. However, the higher ranks have so many advantages for cultivating taste, so much money to lay out in decoration, and are so early taught the graces of air and manner to set off those decorations, that it would be absurd to deny their superiority in this particular. But Taste has one great enemy to contend with.

What is that?

Fashion,—an arbitrary and capricious tyrant, who reigns with the most despotic sway over that department which Taste alone ought to regulate. It is Fashion that imprisons the slender nymph in the vast rotunda of the hoop and loads her with heavy ornaments, when she is conscious, if she dared rebel, she should dance lighter and look better in a dress of one tenth part of the price. Fashion sometimes orders her to cut off her beautiful tresses, and present the appearance of a cropped school-boy; and though this is a sacrifice which a nun going to be profest looks upon as one of the severest she is to make, she obeys without a murmur. The winter arrives, and she is cold; but Fashion orders her to leave off half her clothes, and be abroad half the night. She complies, though at the risk of her life. A great deal more might be said about this tyrant; but as we have had enough of grave conversation for the present, we will here drop the subject.

Epitaph on a Goldfinch

"Epitaph on a Goldfinch" is one of several pieces Barbauld wrote advocating for more humane treatment of animals and one of only two pieces collected in *Legacy* that is known to have been previously published—twice, in 1798, in a volume called *Moral Philosophy* and in *Exercises for the Memory and Understanding*, edited by Thomas and John Holland, where it is titled 'Epitaph on a Green-Finch'. All three texts are formatted like epitaphs, but their lineations differ greatly.[8] The *Moral Philosophy* text is likely to have been printed from a circulating copy, but the Hollands could have had its text from their brother-in-law William Turner, who collected Barbauld's writings. Because the *Legacy* text was most likely printed from a Barbauld holograph, we have chosen it for our copy text: *Legacy for Young Ladies*, pp. 183–4.

        Here lieth,
aged three moons and four days,
the body of RICHARD ACANTHIS,
a young creature
of unblemished life and character.
He was taken in his callow infancy,
from under the wing
of a tender parent,
by the rough and pitiless hands
of a two-legged animal
without feathers.
Though born with the most aspiring dispositions,
and unbounded love of freedom,
he was closely confined in a grated prison,
and scarcely permitted to view those fields,
to the possession of which
he had a natural and undoubted
charter.
Deeply sensible of this infringement
of his native and inalienable rights,
he was often heard to petition for redress;
not with rude and violent clamours,
but
in the most plaintive notes
of melodious sorrow.
At length,

---

[8] *Legacy*'s is forty-two lines, *Exercises* and *Moral Philosophy*, thirty four.

wearied with fruitless efforts to escape,
his indignant spirit
burst the prison which his body could not,
and left behind
a lifeless heap of beauteous feathers.
Reader,
if suffering innocence can hope for retribution,
deny not to the gentle shade
of this unfortunate captive
the natural though uncertain hope
of animating some happier form,
or trying his new-fledged pinions
in some humble Elysium;
beyond the reach of Man,
the tyrant
of this lower universe.

The Misses

(Addressed to a Careless Girl)

The identity of 'Anne', the addressee of this piece, is not definitively known. However, in 1891 Edith Cordelia Rickards identified the addressee of 'an amusing letter on the Misses, to one of Mrs. Barbauld's pupils' as a Mrs. Benyon.[9] An undated Barbauld note to a Mrs. Benyon has survived (Houghton Library, Harvard) and perhaps this is the addressee. Another possibility might be Anne Finch, Joseph Priestley's grand-daughter (1788–1809), who visited Barbauld in the late 1790s while her mother, Priestley's daughter Sarah, was seeking medical care. If so, 'The Misses' would have been addressed to a girl of 9 or 10. We also do not know whether or not the Rickards copy was in Barbauld's hand, like her letters to Lydia Rickards. Unfortunately it is not among the Rickards letters at the New York Public Library, and its whereabouts is currently unknown.

'The Misses' came to print late in 1829. It was published first in *The Juvenile Forget Me Not. A Christmas and New Year's Gift, or Birthday Present for the Year 1830*, ed. [Anna Maria] Mrs. S.[amuel] C.[arter] Hall[10] and was reprinted shortly afterwards in the *Lady's Magazine* (for 30 November). The piece also appeared in the 23 January 1830 issue of the *Columbian Star and Christian Index* (Boston), p. 57. *Eliza Cook's Journal* published a copy in 1849, and Grace Ellis reprinted *The*

---

[9] See the note by Rickards, who dated the piece 1798 or '99 and seems to have had a copy in her collection of Barbauld's letters to Lydia Rickards Withering, held today at the Pforzheimer Collection, NYPL.

[10] London: N. Hailes, Fred. Westley and A. H. Davis, and R. Jennings, [1829], pp. 1–8.

Juvenile Forget Me Not text in America in her *Memoir of Mrs. Barbauld*.[11] Our copy text is *The Juvenile Forget Me Not* for 1830 [1829].

We were talking last night, my dear Anne, of a family of Misses, whose acquaintance is generally avoided by people of sense. They are most of them old maids, which is not very surprising, considering that the qualities they possess are not the most desirable for a helpmate. They are a pretty numerous clan, and I shall endeavour to give you such a description of them as may enable you to decline their visits; especially as, though many of them are extremely unlike in feature and temper, and, indeed, very distantly related, yet they have a wonderful knack at introducing each other; so that, if you open your doors to one of them, you are very likely, in process of time, to be troubled with the whole tribe.

The first I shall mention, and, indeed, she deserves to be mentioned first—for she was always fond of being a ringleader of her company, is *Miss Chief*. This young lady was brought up, until she was fourteen, in a large rambling mansion in the country, where she was allowed to romp all day with the servants and idle boys of the neighbourhood. There she employed herself in the summer, in milking into her bonnet, tying the grass together across the path to throw people down; and in winter, making slides before the door for the same purpose, and the accidents these gave rise to always procured her the enjoyment of a hearty laugh. She was a great lover of fun; and at Christmas time distinguished herself by various tricks, such as putting furze[84] balls into the beds, drawing off the clothes in the middle of the night, and pulling people's seats from under them. At length, as a lady, who was coming to visit the family, mounted on rather a startish[85] horse, rode up to the door, Miss Chief ran up and unfurled an umbrella full in the horse's face, which occasioned him to throw his rider, who broke her arm; after this exploit, miss was sent off to a boarding school; here she was no small favourite with the girls, whom she led into all manner of scrapes; and no small plague to the poor governess, whose tables were hacked, and beds cut, and curtains set on fire continually. It is true miss soon laid aside her romping airs and assumed a very demure appearance; but she was always playing one sly trick or another, and had learned to tell lies, in order to lay it upon the innocent.

---

[11] *Eliza Cook's Journal* (London), 21 July 1849; *Memoir of Mrs. Barbauld* (Boston, 1874), 2:374–80. Earlier American reprints appeared in the *Louisville Public Advertiser*, 19 Feb. 1830, *Southern Times* (Columbia, SC), 19 April 1830, and [North] *Carolina Observer*, 13 May 1830. An unknown hand copied the piece into an album composed of 'letters of advice to young ladies' (MS Osborn d498, Beinecke). The MS copy is shorter than the printed text and may be American: it uses American spellings (*-or*) in places where *JFMN* uses British (*-our*).

At length she was discovered in writing anonymous letters, by which whole families in the town had been set at variance; and she was then dismissed the school with ignominy. She has since lived a very busy life in the world; seldom is there a great crowd of which she does not make one, and she has even frequently been taken up for riots, and other disorderly proceedings, very unbecoming in one of her sex.

The next I shall introduce to your acquaintance is a city[86] lady, *Miss Management*, a very stirring, notable woman, always in a bustle, and always behindhand. In the parlour, she saves candle ends; in the kitchen, every thing is waste and extravagance; she hires her servants at half wages, and changes them at every quarter;[87] she is a great buyer of cheap bargains, but as she cannot always use them, they grow worm and moth eaten on her hands; when she pays a long score to her butcher, she wrangles for the odd pence, and forgets to add up the pounds. Though it is her great study to save, she is continually outrunning her income, which is partly owing to her trusting a cousin of hers, *Miss Calculation*, with the settling her accounts, who, it is very well known, could never be persuaded to learn perfectly her Multiplication Table, or state rightly a sum in the Rule of Three.[88]

Miss Lay and *Miss Place* are sisters, great slatterns: when Miss Place gets up in the morning she cannot find her combs, because she has put them in her writing box. Miss Lay would willingly go to work, but her housewife[89] is in the drawer of the kitchen dresser, her bag hanging on a tree in the garden, and her thimble any where but in her pocket. If Miss Lay is going a journey the keys of her trunk are sure to be lost. If Miss Place wants a volume out of her bookcase, she is certain not to find it along with the rest of the set. If you peep into Miss Place's dressing room, you find her drawers filled with foul linen, and her best cap hanging upon the carpet broom. If you call Miss Lay to take a lesson in drawing, she is so long in gathering together her pencils, her chalk, her India rubber, and her drawing paper, that her master's hour is expired before she has well got her materials together.

Miss Understanding. This lady comes of a respectable family, and has a half sister distinguished for her good sense and solidity, but she herself, though not a little fond of reasoning, always takes the perverse side of any question; she is often seen with another of her intimates, *Miss Representation*, who is a great tale bearer, and goes about from house to house telling people what such a one and such a one said of them behind their backs. Miss Representation is a notable story teller, and can so change, enlarge, and dress up an anecdote, that the person to whom it happened shall not know it again: how many friendships have been broken by these two or turned into bitter enmities! The latter lady does a great deal of varnish work, which wonderfully sets off her paintings, for she pretends to use the pencil, but her productions are such miserable daubings, that it is the varnish alone which makes them pass to the most common eye. Though she has of all sorts, black varnish is what she uses most. As I wish you very much to be on your guard against this lady, whenever you meet her in company, I must tell you she is to be distinguished by a very ugly leer; it is quite out of her power to look straight at any object.

Miss Trust, a sour old creature, wrinkled and shaking with the palsy. She is continually peeping and prying about, in the expectation of finding something wrong; she watches her servants through the keyhole, and has lost all her friends by little shynesses, that have arisen no one knows how; she is worn away to skin and bone, and her voice never rises above a whisper.

Miss Rule. This lady is of a very lofty spirit, and had she been married, would certainly have governed her husband; as it is, she interferes very much in the management of families; and, as she is very highly connected, she has as much influence in the fashionable world as amongst the lower orders. She even interferes in political concerns, and I have heard it whispered that there is scarcely a cabinet in Europe where she has not some share in the direction of affairs.

Miss Hap and *Miss Chance.* These are twin sisters, so like as scarcely to be distinguished from each other; their whole conversation turns upon little disasters. One tells you how her lap-dog spoiled a new Wilton carpet;[90] the other how her new muslin petticoat was torn by a gentleman's setting his foot upon it. They are both left handed, and so exceedingly awkward and ungainly, that if you trust either of them with but a cup and saucer you are sure to have them broken. These ladies used frequently to keep days for visiting, and as people were not very fond of meeting them, many used to shut themselves up and see no company on those days, for fear of stumbling upon either of them; some people, even now, will hardly open their doors on Friday[91] for fear of letting them in.

Miss Take. This lady is an old doting woman, who is purblind, and has lost her memory; she invites her acquaintance on wrong days, calls them by wrong names, and always intends to do just the contrary thing to what she does.

Miss Fortune. This lady has the most forbidding look of any of the clan, and people are sufficiently disposed to avoid her as much as it is in their power to do; yet some pretend that notwithstanding the sternness of her countenance on the first address, her physiognomy softens as you grow more familiar with her, and though she has it not in her power to be an agreeable acquaintance, she has sometimes proved a valuable friend. There are lessons which none can teach so well as herself, and the wisest philosophers have not scrupled to acknowledge themselves the better for her company. I may add, that, notwithstanding her want of external beauty, one of the best poets in our language fell in love with her, and wrote a beautiful ode in her praise.[92]

TEACHING LETTERS TO LYDIA RICKARDS

Barbauld's best-documented pupil today is Lydia Rickards (1784–1867), who later married William Withering, son of the famous botanist. Lydia came from Birmingham in 1797.[1] Barbauld's surviving holograph letters to her run from June 1798 to January 1815 and are held today by the Carl H. Pforzheimer Collection of Shelley and His Circle at the New York Public Library.[2] The first of those surviving letters (Misc. MS 4337) is clearly pedagogical in purpose.[3]

In 1891 Lydia's collateral descendant Edith Cordelia Rickards published three articles about Lydia and the letters. She recounted that Lydia was eleven and the only child of a widowed mother when she first became Barbauld's pupil: 'The friendship begun, lasted for more than twenty years.... The Barbaulds and Lydia and her mother were living at Hampstead at that time, so that it was easy for the little girl to become a day-pupil at her teacher's house. It was no wonder that they soon became tenderly attached to one another, for Lydia was gentle and affectionate, and Mrs. Barbauld had just the qualities that would win a young girl's enthusiasm.'[4] In 1815 Lydia suffered an attack of 'severe' fever[5] that left her mentally incapacitated for the rest of her life.

Some letters are known today only from Edith Cordelia Rickards' *Monthly Packet* articles.[6] In November 1891, Rickards published extracts from the whole series of Barbauld's letters to Lydia in *Murray's Magazine*.[7] Until 2016 those published extracts were the only form in which the letters were known. They are superseded today by the original letters held by the New York Public Library Pforzheimer Collection.

---

[1] Information on the family appears in *Burke's Landed Gentry of Great Britain*, s.v. 'Rickards of South Hill'; Lydia's birth and death dates come from endorsements on her Will (MS Lee Crowder, Bundle 837a, Birmingham Public Library).

[2] Jessica W. H. Lim published thirty-two of these Barbauld letters to Lydia Rickards in 'Unsettled Accounts: Anna Letitia Barbauld's Letters to Lydia Rickards' (*Tulsa Studies in Women's Literature*, 38.1 (2019): 153–200). William McCarthy later published a corrected edition of these letters in 'Anna Letitia Barbauld Letters to Lydia Rickards, 1798–1815', *Romantic Circles Electronic Editions*; romantic-circles.org. The teaching letters published in our volume are not included in either of these publications.

[3] It is a copy, rather than an original, of a Barbauld letter to Mr. Douce, which we have titled 'A Letter Recommending French Books'; we believe that it documents Barbauld's recommendations of books for Lydia's tutor to have her read.

[4] *Monthly Packet* (London), ns 1 (1891): 276.

[5] Withering Family Letters: Mrs. James Watt to William Withering, 18 Nov. 1815.

[6] *Monthly Packet* (London), ns 1 (1891): 276–85 (March), and 514–23 (May).

[7] 10:706–26.

[Dressing Table Ornaments][8]

My Dear Little Friend,—

    I send you a set of boxes for your dressing-table, full of valuable ornaments, which I beg you will use constantly, as they are exceedingly becoming, and will, I am sure, wear well.

A mirror.
Humility.

A fine eye-water.	A lip-salve.
Benevolence.	*Cheerfulness.*
A wash to smooth wrinkles.	A mixture giving sweetness to the voice.
Contentment.	*Mildness and Truth.*
A pair of earrings.	A genuine and universal beautifier.
Attention.	*Good Humour.*
Best white paint.	Best rouge.
Innocence.	*Modesty.*

Never rise from your table without being adorned by these, and then you will be in a proper dress for any company whatever, and cannot fail of appearing lovely and being admired.[93]

A Letter from Miss Susan Slipslop to Miss Fanny Flippant[94]

Mrs Barbauld recommends to the notice of Miss R. the enclosed epistle, and if her critical ear should be offended with any violations of grammar or faults of orthography upon the reading it, she begs she will do Miss Slipslop the favour of correcting them, marking at the same time the nature of the fault, whether it sins against Grammar or against idiom; whether it is faulty from a want of correctness or of elegance, and in every case substituting the proper expression.

To Miss Fanny Flippant

My Dear Miss,—

    Tho I don't owe you no letter, for I am sure I have wrote last to you, yet as Miss Lucy is going home, and she will take it for me, and being determinated not to miss this opportunity, for you must know I hate to correspond

---

[8] Copy text: *Monthly Packet* (London), ns 1 (1891): 277

without I can write my letters all out of my own head, and my Governess nor nobody shan't see this. We have had a grete ball here, and the most genteelest company I ever see'd here, but poor Caroline has tore her new gownd. We was just going to begin Coatiluns, and she had not drawed it up, and her pardner trod upon it. It was trimm'd with the beautifulest lace which her Unkle had gave her. I danced with Harry, who looks more handsomer than ever. Don't you think the time passes very pleasant when one has a good pardner, We talked a great deal about Maria of Richmond, for you know Harry comes from there. She is monstrous pretty, and I kept plaguing Harry about her. Maria is staying at Richmond, because the hair is so soft, for she is very cricklish[95] in her health and has had a deal of Doctoring lately. Her Mama is larning her to paint. Do you like Richmond. Its a place as I never was att; for as often as I have rid, I have never took a ride that way. So you are larning to play upon the musick, and I should never have knowed nothing about it, if the musick master had not lett it out. I wish I might larn after the Vocation. My Bedfellow is gone home. She was come for, yesterday, so I laid with Miss Lucy last night, and the window was broke, and I had such a rheumatise, I could hardly rise myself in my bed. I have the pleasure to tell you that I can speak French quite perfect; for we always do speke it, because we must not speke nothing else, for you know there is no use speaking English att schole, for that comes into one's head quite natural. And I can understand all our Misses, but there was a Mountsier[96] came the other day, jabbering to my Governess, and I could not understand him att all, for his French was quite different to ours, I believe because he spoke so fast.

Now Goodbye,
Susan Slipslop.

[Dated 6 June 1798][9]

Dorking June 6th

My dear Lydia,

I thank you for your pretty French letter which I would send back corrected if I had any franks; as it is, I will keep it till we meet—Your observations on the history you have read are very just, & shew that you not only treasure up facts in your memory, but that your mind receives the impressions those facts are calculated to make—Nothing exercises the moral feelings more profitably than History. When we study those parts of science

---

[9] Copy text holograph letter NYPL Pforzheimer Collection, New York Public Library, Misc. MS 4337. Addressed to 'Miss Rickards at Mrs. Hunt's Crescent near Birmingham'.

which relate to inanimate nature, our sagacity is called forth & our taste is gratified, but that lively interest is wanting which results from contemplating the actions & fortunes of our fellow creatures. On the other hand when we enter with vivacity into the transactions which pass before our eyes, our feelings are apt to be mingled with the bitterness of party or tinged with private partialities & resentments. In History alone nothing checks the freedom of disenssion you may take the side of the Greeks or of the Persians without giving offence to any body, & if you can pick up any anecdotes relative to the coterie of Aspasia[97] or the toilette of Semiramis[98] they may be circulated without occasioning any scandal—I hope you are all enjoying the country as much as we do, but begging your pardon I doubt whether you have so fine a one to enjoy, & this I may say without any disparagement of yours for the face of the country about Box hill[99] is I believe allowed to be one of the finest in England. Add to this that its beautiful swells & hollows are improved to the best advantage in the numerous gentlemen's seats which every where embellish the prospect. Amongst these Mr Locke's[100] has the preeminence for the admirable disposition of the walks & points of view, & the artful manner in which the different shades of green relieve one another so as to produce the most picturesque effect. Indeed modern English Gardening is the art of Landscape painting only the artist uses real trees & turf & water instead of canvass & a box of colours but he considers every effect of light & shade the disposition of every tree & almost of every bough. His keeping,[101] his foregrounds & his backgrounds are all disposed by the same rules of art which the Painter observes. Mr Locke had a consultation of Painters to determine in what spot of the grounds his house ⟨shoul⟩ would be built to most advantage—I wish you would give me [your] opinion in your next letter <u>what constitutes that beauty in a landscape with which we are all so much charmed</u>; how much of it is owing to colour, to form, to contrast, to motion &c[102]—This is a very good country for botanizing. We have had several specimens of the various species of the Orchis, many of which (formed it should seem in the sportiveness of nature) bear a whimsical resemblance to some animal or part of animal. There is the <u>bee Orchis</u> & the <u>fly Orchis</u>, each of which might deceive the eye with the semblance of those insects whose name they [MS obscured] & there is another, the root of which is exactly like a child's; or if you will a fairy's <u>hand</u>.[103] I hardly know what to tell you about my Brother; a while ago we thought him mending, he is just now not so well. ⟨Vicica⟩ Vicissitudes more anxious than uniform illness! He seems to take comfort in our company. I will wait therefore till I have another letter from [MS torn] [be]fore I fix our return, as it is possible <u>you</u> may have plans which may delay you[.] Remember me affectionately to

Mrs Rickards & Miss H[unt].[104] tell Mrs Rickards she has had an escape of increasing her family by the servant she dismissed. She has acknowledged to Mrs. Carr[105] that she is five months gone with child. Excuse me f[or no]t having written sooner & believe [me dear] Lydia Your very aff[te] friend AL Barbauld

LETTERS ON GRAMMAR, HISTORY, AND HOMER

After Lydia turned 16 Barbauld wrote for her a series of letters on Grammar, History, and Homer. In doing so she re-enacted Hester Mulso Chapone's instructional letters to her niece, which Chapone afterwards published to great acclaim as *Letters on the Improvement of the Mind* (1773). Barbauld knew Chapone personally and wrote a memoir of her for the *Monthly Magazine* (1802), in which she spoke respectfully of *Letters*:

It is distinguished by sound sense, a liberal, as well as a warm, spirit of piety, and a philosophy applied to its best use, the culture of the heart and affections. It has no shining eccentricities of thought, no peculiarities of system; it follows experience as its guide, and is content to produce effects of acknowledged utility, by known and approved means.[10]

Nevertheless, when she addressed the same topics—especially History, its materials and methods—Barbauld often tacitly dissented from Chapone's views. Her dissent is evident in her assumption that a young woman can be assumed capable of understanding and remembering detailed and precise information. For another example, compare Barbauld's statement of the date of the Hegira with Chapone's, below. (The comparison is striking also in the different manners in which Chapone and Barbauld speak of Mohammed.) However, Barbauld often agrees with her friend Joseph Priestley, who had taught history at Warrington Academy and published his lectures.[11] Barbauld's instruction in history derives much from his works.

Barbauld dated only the letter on grammar (6 November 1800), but she wrote both it and the third letter on history on paper watermark-dated 1799. The whole series may date between 1800 and 1802.[12] The letters bear no addresses or postmarks, but even if sent through the post, these are properly tutorials, similar in kind to the lectures Barbauld had delivered at Palgrave School. Those on history she may have thought of publishing, for on 18 May 1813 she thanked Lydia 'for

---

[10] *Monthly Magazine*, 13 [Feb. 1802]: 39. See Volume IV.

[11] *Lectures on History and General Policy* (1788). Earlier, Priestley had published *A Chart of Biography* (1765) and *A Description of a New Chart of History, containing a View of the principal Revolutions of Empire that have taken place in the World* (1769).

[12] The third letter on history—the letter that deals with geography—may draw on a book published in March 1800 or in 1802.

sending me the letters. What an immense study History is now become!"[13] The *Legacy* texts of Letters I–III differ from the texts of the letters sent to Rickards in ways that suggest authorial revision. Our copy texts for 'The Uses of History' letters are the holograph manuscripts rather than the later *Legacy* texts (117–48). Letter IV is known today only from Aikin's text, which is necessarily our copy text (*Legacy*, 148–64). After copying them, Barbauld returned the letters to Lydia. The texts of Letters I–III on history and the letter on grammar were published by E. C. Rickards in the *Monthly Packet* (1891), 277–85 and 515–21. However, our copy text for the letter on grammar is Barbauld's holograph (NYPL Pforzheimer Collection Misc. MS 4343).

The letter on Homer is published here for the first time from Barbauld's holograph, the only text known (NYPL Pforzheimer Collection Misc. MS 4347).

[On Grammar]

Novr 6. 1800

My dear Lydia,

As the gradual opening of your mind begins to render you in some measure capable of ⟨entering⟩ comprehending abstract ideas, it seems to me a proper time to turn your attention to the principles of Grammar; both as they regard language in general, & the language of our native country in particular. I know indeed that the principles of English Grammar are among the first lessons now taught to young people destined to receive a liberal education—in my opinion erroneously, since, if studied in its principles, hardly any science is more abstruse & metaphysical;[106] if in their exemplification by particular ^rules^ a previous knowledge ⟨is⟩ be required of different languages. For we become so habituated to the modes of speech in which from infancy we have expressed ourselves, that we can scarcely conceive they have only an arbitrary connection with the meanings they signify, till, by comparing them with other & different modes ^we become able to dissect ⟨our language to⟩ & anaylise our expressions, & thus^ ⟨we⟩ to gain an idea of the elements of language in general—

A child who has heard no language but its own, probably imagines the word red as naturally expresses that colour, as the picture of a bird expresses a bird; &, in an age somewhat more advanced, the various inflexions used to express comparison, number, sex, & the like in our native tongue, & the order in which we place our words, seem to an uninstructed person to be inherent in the nature of language itself. Language therefore is not taught by Grammar but Grammar is taught by Languages—

---

[13] At that time Barbauld was thinking about History; her 'Dialogue in the Shades' between Clio and Mercury refers to the French army's disastrous retreat from Russia at the end of 1812.

[ON GRAMMAR]

The faculty of Speech supereminently distinguishes man from all his fellow inhabitants of this globe, & to it, more than to any other circumstance ⟨does⟩ is he indebted for the superiority he enjoys over them. For without this he would be confined to his own solitary crude ideas, incapable of profiting, either by the ⟨communication⟩ ^discoveries^ of his companions, or ⟨of⟩ by that accumulated & still accumulating store of information, delivered down from age to age by oral or written communications—It is indeed true that all the more perfect animals are endowed with powers of imparting to each other their sensations, sometimes in a very forcible manner; but their scanty tones of expression do not amount to any thing deserving the high appellation of <u>language</u>—Neither indeed are their powers of expression only scanty, since in that case they would probably enlarge them in course of time, as, amongst us, languages are rendered more copious & perfect by use & civilization, but there is an essential difference in their nature. Language, properly so called, teaches to express ideas by <u>arbitrary</u> sounds: this the brute animals do not; or if, in some dubious instances they seem to affix a meaning to such sounds, as when a dog answers to his name, or a horse to the words by which he is commanded to stop or to go on, it is in consequence of the associations impressed upon them in their commerce with man, & the lesson is never communicated to their offspring or to other individuals. The language of the brutes seems to consist in the expression of their feelings by correspondent tones, & from being more natural is less perfect than ours. In man, laughing, screaming, & other spontaneous noises which strongly indicate the state of mind, have no pretensions to be called speech; for Speech is the child of intellect not of passion. Language is therefore a thing of convention, not an effect of instinct; not produced perfect, but, like all the other inventions of man, improveable & rising by degrees from the most imperfect rudiments of the Indian dialects ^or the barbarous slang of a Gipsey^ to the tongue of a Cicero or a Milton, rich, copious, accurate & discriminating, containing ⟨in⟩ ^within^ its ample bosom, clothing from its ⟨spacious wareh⟩ ^immense^ storehouse^s^ all the ideas of a Newton, the feelings of a Rousseau; the wisdom of the wise, the treasures of the learned, & the sweet reciprocations of confidential ⟨friendship⟩ ^intercourse^. Language is at once the cause & effect; ⟨as⟩ it is the measure & gage of national improvement; it expands itself with the rising genius of a people, is rough when they are barbarous, polished when they are elegant; betrays by its derivations ^& foreign idioms^ the sources of their acquirements; changes with their changing manners, becomes tinged with their very humours, & ⟨peculiar⟩ & reflects, ⟨seriously⟩ as in a faithful mirror, not only their sentiments & ideas, but their peculiar modes of feeling & apprehending. The compass of a man's language is the compass of his knowledge, the measure of his mind; for language has very much the nature of a garment we read of in the fairy tales, which had the gift of adapting itself to every shape, & enlarged or contracted its folds to suit the dimensions of the wearer—

—The physical means by which nature has enabled man, & him alone, to raise so wonderful a structure, consists in the capacity of uttering <u>articulate</u> sounds. An articulate sound is a sound produced by the tongue, teeth, palate, lips; the human organs of speech. These are susceptible of greater variety & more accurate distinctions that the mere emission of breath by the voice, ⟨in comm⟩ by which are produced the lowing of a cow, the bleating of a sheep, & similar expressions belonging to the animal tribe—It is however very doubtful whether in all cases this difference proceeds from a different organization, & not rather from that unknown something in the <u>intellect</u> of man which gives him so decided a superiority. For there are animals that approach so near to man in their structure both internal & external, that it is difficult to discover what secret bar, what invisible spell forbids them to imitate his utterance, if they possessed sufficient intelligence to do it. The Indians indeed imagine that the tribe of monkeys could speak if they chose it.[107] As to those animals, by us means the nearest to man in their outward appearance, who are said to <u>talk</u>, if accurately attended to, they will be found rather to imitate the tones of the human voice than properly to articulate—They do not pronounce the consonants, in which articulation consists[.] Hence their ⟨speech is⟩ ^phrases are^ hardly intelligible to those who do not know the particular tones that have been taught with them.

We should now proceed to investigate the elements of which language is composed, but enough for the present. Let us remember that Language is <u>arbitrary</u> is <u>peculiar to man</u> & is composed of <u>articulate sounds</u>.

   Farewell
   ALB.

On the Uses of History

Letter 1st[14]
My dear Lydia,

 I was told the other day that you have not forgotten a promise of mine to correspond with you upon some subject which might be worth

---

[14] Our copy text is the holograph letter, New York Public Library, NYPL Pforzheimer Collection MS MISC 4344, four pages. Barbauld wrote at the head of this letter 'Letter 1st', presumably in 1813 when preparing to copy it.

discussing, & relative to your pursuits. I have often recollected it also, & as promises ought not only to be recollected but fulfilled, I will without further preface throw together some thoughts on History, a study that I know you value as it deserves,[108] & I trust it will not be disagreeable to you, if you should find some observations which your own mind may have suggested, or which you may recollect to have heard from me in some of those hours which we spent together with mutual pleasure. Much has been said of the uses of History, they are no doubt many but do not apply equally to all, but it is quite sufficient to make it a study worth our pains & time, that it satisfies the desire which naturally arises in every intelligent mind to know the transactions of the country—of the globe in which he lives[.] Facts, as facts, interest our curiosity & engage our attention. ⟨Suppose⟩

Suppose a person placed in a part of the country where he was a total stranger, he would naturally ask, who are the chief people of the place, what family they are of, have any of their ancestors have been famous & for what. If he see a ruined Abbey, he will enquire what the building was used for, & if he be told it is a place where people got up at midnight to sing psalms & scourged themselves in the day, he will ask how there came to be such people, or why there are none now. If he observes a dilapidated castle which appears to have been battered by violence, he will ask in what quarrel it suffered, & why they built formerly structures so different from any we see now. If any part of the inhabitants should speak a different language from the rest, or have some singular customs among them, he would suppose they came originally from some remote part of the country, & would inform himself, if he could, of the cause of their peculiarities. If he ⟨was⟩ were of a curious temper, he would not rest till he had informed himself who every estate in the parish belonged to, what hands they had gone thro, how one man got this field by marrying an heiress, & the other lost that meadow by a ruinous law suit—As a man of spirit he would feel delighted on hearing the relation of the opposition made by an honest yeoman to an over bearing rich man on the subject of an accustomed path way or right of common.[109] If he should find the town or village ⟨was⟩ were divided into parties, he would take some pains to trace the original cause of their dissension, & to find out, if possible, who had the right on his side. Circumstances would often occur to excite his attention, if he saw a bridge he would ask when & by whom it was built. If in digging in his garden he should find utensils of a singular form & construction, or a pot of money with a stamp & legend quite different from the common coin, he would be led to enquire when they were in use & to whom they had belonged. His curiosity would extend itself by degrees. If a brook ran thro the meadows he would be pleased to trace it till it swelled into a river, & the river till it lost itself in the sea, he would be asking whose seat he saw upon the edge of the distant forest, & what sort of Country lay behind the range of hills that bounded his utmost view. If any strangers came to visit or reside in the place where he lived he would be questioning them about the country they came from, their connections & alliances & the remarkable transactions that had taken place within their memory or that of their parents—The answers to these questions would insensibly grow up into <u>History</u>, which, as you see, does not originate in abstruse speculation, but grows naturally out of our situation & relative connections. It gratifies a curiosity which all feel in some degree, but which spreads & enlarges itself with the cultivation of our powers, till at length it embraces the whole globe which we inhabit—To know is as natural to the mind as to see is to the eye and knowledge is itself an ultimate end. But tho this may be esteemed an ultimate & sufficient end, the study of History is important to various purposes. Few pursuits tend more to enlarge the mind. It gives us, & it only can give us an extended knowledge of human nature, not human nature as it exists in one age or climate or particular spot of earth, but human nature under all the various circumstances by which it can be affected. It shows us what is radical & what is adventitious in it, that man is still man in Turkey & in Lapland, as a subject in Russia or a member of a wandering tribe in India, in antient Athens or modern Rome, yet that his character ⟨is⟩ ^is susceptible of violent changes, & becomes^ moulded into infinite diversities by the influence of government climate civilization wealth & poverty. By showing us how man has acted it shews us ⟨how he⟩ to a certain degree how he will ever act in given circumstances; & general rules & maxims are drawn from it for the service of the lawgiver & the statesman. Here I must observe however that with regard to <u>events</u> a knowledge of History does not seem to give us any great advantage in foreseeing & preparing for them. The deepest politician with all his knowledge of the revolutions of past ages, could probably no more have predicted the course & termination of the late French Revolution than a common man. The state of our own national debt has baffled calculation, the course of ages has presented nothing like it. Who could have pronounced that the struggle of the Americans would be successful, that of the Poles unsuccessful?[110] Human characters indeed act always alike, but events depend upon circumstances as well as characters, & circumstances are infinitely various & changed by the slightest causes. A battle won or lost may decide the fate of an empire, but a battle may be won or lost by a shower of snow being blown to the east or the west, by a horse (the general's) losing his shoe, by a bullet or an arrow taking a direction a tenth of an inch one way or the other. The whole course of the French affairs might have been changed if the king had not stopped to breakfast, or if the post master at Varennes had not happened to know him.[111] These are particulars which no man can foresee, & therefore no man can with precision foresee events. The rising up of certain characters at particular periods, ranks among those unforeseen circumstances that powerfully influence events. Often does a single man as Epaminondas illustrate his country & leave a long track of light after him to future ages,[112] & who can tell how much even America owed to the accident of being served by such a man as Washington. There are always many probable events, all that History enables the politician to do is to predict that one or other of them will take place, if so & so it will be this, if so & so it will be that, but which he cannot tell. There are always combinations of circumstances which have never met before from the creation of the world, & which mock all power of calculation. But let the circumstances be known & the characters upon the stage, & history will tell him what to expect from them. It will tell him with certainty, for instance, that a treaty extorted by force from distress will be broken when opportunity offers, that if the Church & the monarch are united they will oppress, if at variance they will divide the people, that a powerful nation will make its advantage of the divisions of a weaker which applies for its assistance————It is another advantage of History that it stores the mind with facts that apply to most subjects which occur in conversation among enlightened people, whether morals commerce languages the belle lettres be the object of discussion, it is history that must supply her large store house of proofs & illustrations. A man or ^a^ woman may decline without blame many subjects of literature, but to be ignorant of history is not permitted to any one of a cultivated mind—It may be reckoned among its advantages that this study naturally increases the love of every man to his Country. We can only love what we know. It is by becoming acquainted with the long line of patriots heros & distinguished men that we learn to love the country which has produced them. As a man learns to value himself upon his family who can walk thro a long gallery of pictures, & see among his ancestors Admirals Generals & Bishops distinguished for learning & successful enterprize, so in loving England we love the long train of patriots poets or warriors the Sidneys Hampden's & Milton's who have defended or adorned it—But I must conclude this letter already perhaps too long tho I have not got to the end of my subject, it will give me soon another opportunity of subscribing myself

Your ever aff[ectiona]te Friend
A L Barbauld

On the Uses of History[15]

Letter 2ᵈ

I left off, my dear Lydia, with mentioning among the advantages of an accquaintance with History, that it fosters the sentiments of patriotism. What is a man's country? To the unlettered peasant who has never left his native village, that village is his country, & consequently all of it he can love. The man who mixes in the world, & has a large accquaintance with the characters existing, along with himself, upon the stage of it has a wider range. His idea of a country extends to its civil polity, its military triumphs, the eloquence of its courts & the splendor of its capital. All the great & good characters he is accquainted with, swell his idea of its importance, & endear to him the society of which he is a member—But how wonderfully does this idea expand, & how majestic a form does it put on, when History conducts our retrospective view thro past ages.—How much more has the man to love, how much to interest him in his Country in whom her image is identified with the virtues of an Alfred, with the exploits of the Henrys & Edwards, with the fame & fortunes of the Sidneys & Hampdens,[113] the Lockes & Miltons that have illustrated her annals. Like a man ^of noble birth^ who walks up & down in a long gallery of portraits, & is able to say "This my progenitor was admiral in such a sea fight; that my great uncle was general in such an engagement, he on the right hand held the seals in such a reign, that lady in so singular a costume was a celebrated beauty two hundred years ago, this little man in the black cap & peaked beard was one of the luminaries of his age, & suffered for his religion["][114]—he learns to value himself upon his ancestry, & to feel interested for the honour & prosperity of the whole line of descendants. Could a Swiss, think you, be so good a patriot who had never heard of the name of William Tell, or an Hollander who was unacquainted with the glorious struggles which freed his nation from the tyranny of the duke of Alva?[115] The man conversant in History has been long acquainted with his country. He knew her in the infancy of her greatness, has seen her, perhaps, in the wattled huts & slender canoes in which Caesar discovered her;[116] he has watched her rising fortunes, has trembled at her dangers, rejoiced at her deliverances, & shared with honest pride triumphs that were celebrated ages before he was born. He has traced her gradual improvement thro many a dark & turbulent period, many a storm of civil warfare to the fair reign of her liberty & law,

---

[15] Barbauld headed the holograph of this letter 'Letter 2ᵈ On the Uses of History', presumably in 1813 when preparing to copy it. Our copy text is the holograph letter in the NYPL Pforzheimer Collection, New York Public Library MS 4345.

to the fulness of her prosperity & the amplitude of her fame——Or, should our patriot have his lot cast in some age & country which has declined from this high station of pre-eminence, should he observe the gathering glooms of superstition & ignorance ready to close again over the bright horizon; Should liberty lie prostrate at the feet of a despot, & the golden stream of commerce, diverted into other channels, leave nothing but beggary & wretchedness around him—even then, in these ebbing fortunes of his country, History, like a faithful menter, would tell him how high the tide had once risen, he would not tread unconsciously the ground where the Muses & the Arts had once resided, like the goat that stupidly browses upon the fane of Minerva[117]—even then the name of his country will be dear & venerable to him—he will muse over her fallen greatness, sit down under the shade of her never dying laurels, build his little cottage amidst the ruins of her towers & temples, & contemplate with tenderness & respect the decaying age of his once illustrious parent.

But if an acquaintance with history thus increases a rational love of our country, it also tends to check those low, illiberal, vulgar prejudices which adhere to the uninformed of every nation. Travelling will also cure them, but to travel is not within the power of every one. There is no use, but a great deal of harm in fostering a contempt for other nations, in an arrogant assumption of superiority, & the clownish sneer of ignorance at every thing in laws government or manners which is not fashioned after our partial ideas & familiar usages. A well informed person will not be apt to exclaim at every event out of the common way, that nothing like it has ever happened since the creation of the world, that such atrocities are totally unheard of in any age or nation; sentiments we have all of us so often heard of late on the subject of the French Revolution, when in fact we can scarcely open a page of their history without being struck with similar & equal enormities.[118]

Indeed party spirit is very much cooled & checked by an acquaintance with the events of past times. When we see the mixed ⟨motives, plans, skills wherein the partial success of the best schemes⟩ & imperfect virtue of the most distinguished characters, the variety of motives, some pure & some impure, which influence political conduct, the partial success of the wisest schemes, & the frequent failure of the fairest hopes, we shall find it more difficult to chuse a side & to keep up an interest towards it in our minds, than to restrain our feelings & language within the bounds of good sense & moderation—This, by the way, makes it particularly proper that <u>Ladies</u> who interest themselves in the events of public life should have their minds cultivated by an acquaintance with history, without which they are apt to let the whole warmth of their natures flow out,

^upon party matters,^ in an ardour more honest than wise, & more zealous than candid—

—With regard to the moral uses of History what has been just mentioned may stand for one. It serves also, by exercise, to strengthen the moral feelings—The traits of generosity, heroism, disinterestedness, magnanimity are scattered over it like sparkling gems, & arrest the attention of the most common reader—It is wonderfully interesting to follow the revolutions of a great state, particularly when they lead to the successful termination of some glorious contest—Is it true? a child asks when you tell him a wonderful story that strikes his imagination[.] The writer of fiction has the unlimited command of events & of characters, yet that single circumstance of truth, that the events related really come to pass, that the heroes brought upon the stage really existed, counterbalances with respect to interest, all the advantages of the former, & in a mind a little accustomed to exertion will throw the advantage on the side of the historian. The more History approaches to Biography the more interest it excites. Where the materials are meagre & scanty, the antiquarian & the chronologer may dwell upon the page, but it will seldom excite the glow of admiration or draw the delicious tear sensibility——I must acknowledge however in order to be candid that the emotions excited by the actions of our species are not always of so pleasing ^or so edifying^ a nature. The miseries & the vices of man form a large part of the picture of human society; the pure mind is disgusted by depravity, the existence of which it could not have imaged to itself, & the feeling heart is cruelly lacerated by the sad repetition of wrongs & oppression, chains & slaughter, & sack & massacre which assail it in every page.[119] Till the mind has gained some strength so ugly a picture should ⟨[?]⟩ ^hardly^ be presented to it. Chosen periods of history may be selected for youth, as the society of chosen characters precedes, in well regulated education, a more indiscriminate acquaintance with the world. In favour of a more extended view I can only say that truth is truth, man must be shewn as the being he really is, or no real knowledge is gained. If a young person were to read only the <u>Beauties of History</u>[120] or, according to M[m]e Genlis' scheme, stories & characters in which all that was vicious should be left out, he might as well, for any real acquaintance with life he would gain, have been reading all the while Sir Charles Grandison or the Princess of Cleves. One consoling idea will present itself with no small degree of probability on comparing the annals of past & present times, that of a tendency to amelioration, at least it is evidently so in those Countries with which we are most connected—But the only balm that can be poured ^with full effect^ into the feeling mind which bleeds for the folly & wickedness of man is the belief that all events are directed &

controuled by supreme wisdom & goodness.¹²¹ Without this persuasion the world becomes a desart, & its devastators the wolves & tigers that prowl in it—— It is needless to insist on the uses of History to those whose situation in life gives them room to expect that their actions may one day become the objects ^of it^. Besides the immediate necessity to them of the knowledge it supplies, it affords the strongest motives for their conduct of hope & fear. The solemn ⟨request⟩ ^award^, the incorruptible tribunal, & the severe soul searching inquisition of posterity is calculated to strike an awe into their souls. They cannot take refuge in oblivion. It is not permitted them to die. They must be the objects of gratitude or detestation as long as the world stands. They may flatter themselves that ^they^ have silenced the voice of truth, they may forbid papers & pamphlets & conversation,¹²² an unseen hand is all the while tracing out their history, & often their minutest actions in indelible characters & it will ^soon^ be held up for the judgement of the world at large—

—^Lastly^, This permanency of human characters tends to cherish in the mind the hope & belief of ⟨immortality⟩ an existence after death. If we had no notices from the page of History of those races of men that have lived before us, they would seem to be completely swept away, & we should no more think of enquiring ⟨after⟩ what human beings filled our place upon the earth a thousand harvests ago, than we should think about the generations of cattle that at that time grazed the marshes of the Tiber, or the venerable ancestors of the goats that are browsing upon mount Hymettus[.]¹²³ No vestige would remain of one any more than of the other, & we might more ⟨easily⟩ ^pardonably^ fall into the opinion that they both had shared a similar fate. But when we see illustrious characters continuing to live on in the eye of posterity, their memories still fresh, & their noble actions shining with all the vivid colouring of truth & reality, ages after the very dust of their tombs is scattered, high conceptions kindle within us, & feeling one immortality, we are led to hope for another. We find it hard to persuade ourselves that the man who like Antoninus¹²⁴ or Socrates fills the world with the sweet perfume of his virtue—the martyr or the patriot to whom posterity is doing the justice which was denied ⟨them⟩ him by ^his^ contemporaries, should all the while himself be blotted out of existence, that he should be benefiting mankind & doing good, so long after he is capable of receiving any, that we should be so well acquainted with him, & that he should never know any thing of us. That one who is an active agent in the world, instructing informing it, inspiring friendship, making disciples—should be nothing—this does not seem probable. The records of time suggest to us Eternity. Farewell   ALB

[Geography, Letter III][16]

My dear Lydia,

We have considered the uses of History. I would now direct your attention to those collateral branches of science which are necessary for the profitable understanding of it. It is impossible to understand one thing well without understanding to a certain degree many other things. There is a mutual dependance between all the parts of knowledge. This is the reason that a child never fully comprehends what he is taught. He receives an idea, but not the full idea, perhaps not the principal, of what you want to teach him, but as his mind opens, this idea enlarges, & receives accessory ideas, till slowly & by degrees he is master of the whole. This is particularly the case in History: you may recollect probably that the mere <u>adventure</u> was all you entered into in those portions of it which were presented to you at a very early age. You could understand nothing of the springs of action, nothing of the connection of events with the intrigues of cabinets, with religion, with commerce, nothing of the state of the world at different periods of society & improvement, & as little could you grasp the measured distances of time & space which are set between them. This you could not do, not because the history was not related with clearness, but because you were destitute of other knowledge——

The first studies which present themselves as accessories in this light are <u>Geography</u> & <u>Chronology</u>, which have been called the two eyes of History.[125] When was it done? Where was it done? are the two first questions you would ask ⟨of⟩ ^concerning^ any fact that was related to you; without these two particulars there can be no precision or clearness——
Geography is best learned along with History, for if the first explains history, the latter gives interest to Geography, which without it is but a dry list of names. For this reason if a young person begin⟨s⟩ with antient history, I should think it adviseable, after a slight general acquaintance with the globe to confine his Geography to the period & country of which he is reading, & it ⟨is⟩ ^would be^ a desireable thing to have maps adapted to each remarkable period in the great empires of the world. These should not contain any towns, or be divided into any provinces, which were not known at that period. A map of Egypt for instance, calculated for its antient monarchy, should have Memphis marked in it, but not Alexandria, because the two capitals did not exist together. A map of Judea for the time of Solomon, or any period of its monarchy should not exhibit the name of

---

[16] Our copy text is the holograph letter in the New York Public Library, Pforzheimer Collection MS 4346.

[GEOGRAPHY, LETTER III]

Samaria, nor the villages of Bethlehem & Nazareth, but each Country should have the towns & divisions, as far as they are known, calculated for the period the map was meant to illustrate.[126] Thus Geography, civil Geography, would be seen to grow out of History, & the mere view of the map would suggest the political state of the world at ⟨the⟩ any period. It would be a pleasing speculation to see how the arbitrary divisions of kingdoms & provinces ⟨shift & change⟩ ^vary & become obsolete^ & large towns flourish & fall again into ruins, while the great natural features, the mountains & rivers & seas remain unchanged, by whatever name we please to call them, whatever Empire incloses them within its temporary boundaries. We have it is true antient & modern maps, but the one set includes every period from the creation of the world to the provinciating the Roman Empire under Trajan, & the other takes in all the rest.[127] About half a dozen sets for the antient states & empires, & as many for the modern⟨s⟩, would be sufficient to exhibit the most important changes & would be ^as^ many as we should be able to give with any clearness——The young Student should make it an invariable rule never to read History without a map before him, to which should be added plans of towns harbours &c These should be conveniently placed under the eye, separate if possible from the book he is reading, that by frequent glancing upon them, the image of the Country may be indelibly impressed on his imagination. Besides the necessity of maps for understanding History, the memory is wonderfully assisted by the local association which they supply. The battles of Issus & the Granicus[128] will not be confounded by those who have taken the pains to trace the rivers on whose banks they were fought, the exploits of Hannibal are connected with a view of the Alps, & the idea of Leonidas is inseparable from the straits of Thermopyle. The greater accuracy of maps, & still more the facility, from the arts of printing & engraving, of procuring them, is an advantage the moderns have over the antients. They have been perfected by slow degrees. The Egyptians & Chaldeans studied the science of mensuration & the first map (rude enough no doubt) is said to have been made by order of Sesostris when he become master of Egypt. Commerce & war have been the two parents of this science. Pharaoh Necho ordered the Phoenicians whom he sent round Africa, to make a survey of the coast,[129] this they finished in 3 years. Darius got the Ethiopic sea & the mouth of the Indus to be surveyed. That maps were known in Greece you no doubt recollect from the pretty story of Socrates & Alcibiades.[130] Anaximander[131] a disciple of Thales is said to have made the first sphere, & first delineated what was then known of the countries of the earth. He flourished ⟨in the year⟩ 547 Before Christ. Herodotus mentions a map of brass or copper which was ⟨shewn⟩ presented by

Aristagoras tyrant of Miletus to Cleomenes king of Sparta, in which he had described the known earth with its seas & rivers.[132] Alexander the great in his expedition into Asia took two Geographers with him & from their itineraries many things have been copied by succeeding writers[.] From Greece the science of Geography passed to Rome. The enlightened policy of the Romans cultivated it as a powerful means of extending & securing their dominion. One of the first things they did was to make roads, for which it was necessary to have the country measured. They had a custom when they had conquered a country to have a painted map of it always carried aloft in their triumphs. The great historian Polybius reconnoitred under a commission from Scipio Emilianus the coasts of Africa Spain & France, & measured the distances of Hannibal's march over the Alps & Pyrenees.[133] Julius Caesar employed men of science to survey & measure the globe & his own commentaries show his attention to this part of knowledge. Strabo, a great Geographer whose works are extant, flourished under Augustus, Pomponius Mela in the 1st Century.[134] Many of the Roman itineraries which are still extant, show the systematic care ⟨with⟩ which they bestowed on a science so necessary for the orderly distribution & government of their large dominions. But still it was late before Geography was settled upon its true basis, astronomical observations. The greater part of the early maps were laid down in a very loose inaccurate manner, & where particular parts were done with the greatest care, yet if the longitude & latitude were wanting, their relative situation to the rest of the earth could not be known. Some attempts had indeed been made by Hipparchus & Possidonius Greek philosophers to settle the parallels of latitude by the length of the days, but the foundation they had laid was neglected till the time of Ptolemy who flourished at Alexandria about 150 after Christ under Adrian & Antoninus Pius. This is he from whom the Ptolemaic system took its name. He diligently compared & revised the antient maps & Charts, correcting their errors & supplying their defects & by the reports of travellers & navigators, the measured or reputed distances of maps & itineraries, & astronomical calculations all digested together, he reduced Geography into a regular system, & laid down the situation of places according to minutes & degrees of longitude & latitude as we now have them. His maps were in general use till the last three or four Centuries, in which time the progress of the moderns in the knowledge of the globe we inhabit have thrown at a great distance all the antient geographers.[135] We are now, some few breaks & chasms excepted, pretty well acquainted with the outline of the globe ^& with those parts of it with which we are connected by our commercial or political relations^ but we are still profoundly ignorant of the interior of Africa, of South America &

the western part of North America. We know little of Thibet & the central parts of Asia, & have as yet only touched upon the great continent of New Holland.¹³⁶ The best antient maps are those of D'Anville.¹³⁷ It has required great learning & proportionate skill to bring together the scattered notices which are found in various authors, and to fix the position of places which have been long ^ago^ destroyed; very often the Geographer has no other guide than the relation of the historian that such a place is within 6 or 8 days journey from another place. In some instances the maps of Ptolemy are lately come into repute again, as in his delineation of the course of the Niger, which is thought to be favoured by modern discoveries. Major Rennel has done much to improve the Geography, ⟨particularly that⟩ of India.¹³⁸ There are many valuable maps ^scattered^ in voyages & travels, & many of the Atlases contain a collection sufficient for all common purposes, but a complete collection of the best maps & charts with plans of harbours towns &c, becomes an object of even princely expence—The French have taken the lead in this, as in many other branches of science. The late Empress of Russia caused a geographical survey to be taken of her dominions, which has much improved our knowledge of the north east regions of Europe & Asia—¹³⁹ We have some elegant maps by Arrowsmith, but Cary's when completed will be the best Atlas that has been published—¹⁴⁰

Yours affectionately A L Barbauld

[Chronology] Letter IV[17]

Dear Lydia,

Geography addresses itself to the eye, and is easily comprehended: to give a clear idea of Chronology is somewhat more difficult. It is easy to define it by saying it gives an answer to the question, when was it done? but the meaning of the *when* is not quite so obvious. A date is a very artificial thing, and the world had existed for a long course of centuries before men were aware of its use and necessity. *When* is a relative term; the most natural application of it is, how long ago, reckoning backwards from the present moment? Thus if you were to ask an Indian when such an event happened, he would probably say—So many harvests ago, when I could but just reach the boughs of yonder tree;—in the time of my father, grandfather, great-grandfather; still making the time then present to him the date from which he sets out. Even where a different method is well understood, we use in

---

[17] Our copy text is *A Legacy for Young Ladies*, pp. 148–64, the only text known.

more familiar life this natural kind of chronology—The year before I was married,—when Henry, who is now five years old, was born,—the winter of the hard frost. These are the epochs which mark the annals of domestic life more readily and with greater clearness, so far as the real idea of time is concerned, than the year of our Lord, as long as these are all within the circle of our personal recollection. But when events are recorded, the relator may be forgotten, and the *when* again occurs: "When did the historian live? I understand the relative chronology of his narration; I know how the events of it follow one another; but what is their relation to general chronology, to time as it relates to me and to other events?"

To know the transactions of a particular reign, that of Cyrus for instance, in the regular order in which they happened in that reign, but not to know where to place them with respect to the history of other times and nations, is as if we had a very accurate map of a small island existing somewhere in the boundless ocean, and could lay down all the bearings and distances of its several towns and villages, but for want of its longitude and latitude were ignorant of the relative position of the island itself. Chronology supplies this longitude and latitude, and fixes every event to its precise point in the chart of universal time. It supplies a common measure by which I may compare the relator of an event with myself, and his *now* or *ten years ago* with the present *now* or *ten years*, reckoning from the time in which I live.

In order to find such a common measure, men have been led by degrees to fix upon some one known event, and to make that the center from which, by regular distances, the different periods of time are reckoned, instead of making the present time, which is always varying, and every man's own existence, the center.

The first approach to such a mode of computing time is to date by the reigns of kings; which, being public objects of great notoriety, seem to offer themselves with great advantage for such a purpose. The scripture history, which is the earliest of histories, has no other than this kind of successive dates: "Now it came to pass in the fifth year of the king Hezekiah." "And the time that Solomon reigned in Jerusalem over all Israel was forty years: and Solomon slept with his fathers; and Rehoboam his son reigned in his stead."[141] From this method a regular chronology might certainly be deduced, if we had the whole unbroken series; but unfortunately there are many gaps and chasms in history; and you easily see that if any links of the chain are wanting, the whole computation is rendered imperfect. Besides, it requires a tedious calculation to bring it into comparison with other histories and events. To say that an event happened in the tenth year of the reign of king Solomon, gives you only an idea of the time relative to the histories of that king, but leaves you quite in the dark as to its relation with the time you live in, or with the events of the Roman history.

We want therefore an universal date, like a lofty obelisk seen by all the country round, from and to which every distance should be measured. The most obvious that offers itself for this purpose is the creation of the world, an event equally interesting to all; to us the beginning of time, and from which therefore time would flow regularly down in an unbroken stream from the earliest to the latest generations of the human race. This would probably therefore have been made use of, if the date of the creation itself could be ascertained with any exactness; but as chronologers differ by more than a thousand years as to the time of that event, it is necessary previously to mention what system is made use of; which renders this æra obscure and inconvenient. It has therefore been found more convenient, in fact, to take some known event within the limit of well-authenticated history, and to reckon from that fixed point backwards and forwards. As we cannot find the head of the river, and know not its termination, we must raise a pillar upon its banks, and measure our distances from that, both up and down the stream.[142] This event ought to be important, conspicuous, and as interesting as possible, that it may be generally received; for it would spare a great deal of trouble in computation if all the world would make use of the same date. This however has never been the case, chance and national vanity having had their full share in settling them.

The Greeks reckoned by olympiads, but not till more than sixty years after the death of Alexander the Great. The Olympic games were the most brilliant assembly in Greece, the Greeks were very fond of them, they began 776 years before Christ, and each olympiad includes four years. Some of the earlier Greek historians digested their histories by ages, or by the succession of the priestesses of Juno at Argos; others by the archons of Athens or the kings of Lacedaemon. Thucydides uses simply the beginning of the Peloponnesian war, the subject of his history; for, writing to his contemporaries, it seems not to have occurred to him that another date would ever be necessary. The Arundelian marbles, composed sixty years after the death of Alexander the Great, reckon backwards from the then present time.[143]

The Roman æra was the building of their city, the eternal city as they loved to call it.

The Mahometans date from the Hegira, or flight of Mahomet from Mecca his birth-place, to Medina, A.D. 622; and they have this advantage, that they began almost immediately to use it.[144]

The æra used all over the Christian world is the birth of Christ. This was adopted as a date about A.D. 360; and though there is an uncertainty of a few years, which are in dispute, the accuracy is sufficient for any present purpose.

The reign of Nabonassar the first king of Babylon, of Yesdigerd the last king of Persia,—who was conquered by the Saracens,—and of the Seleucidae of Syria, have likewise furnished æras.

Julius Scaliger formed an æra which he called the *Julian period*, being a cycle of 7980 years, produced by multiplying several cycles into one another, so as to carry us back to a period 764 years before the creation of the world. This æra, standing out of all history, like the fulcrum which Archimedes wished for, and independent of variation or possibility of mistake, was a very grand idea; and in measuring every thing by itself, measured it by the eternal truth of the laws of the heavenly bodies. But it is not greatly employed, the common æra serving all ordinary purposes. In modern histories the olympiads, Roman æras, and others, are reduced, in the margin, to the year of our Lord, or of the creation.[145]

Such is the nature of æras, now in such common use that we can with difficulty conceive the confusion in which, for the want of them, all the early part of history is involved, and the strenuous labours of the most learned men which have been employed in arranging them and reducing history to the order in which we now have it.[146]

The earliest history which we possess, as we have before observed, is that of the Jewish scriptures; these carry us from the creation to about the time of Herodotus: having no date, we are obliged to compute from generations, and to take the reigns of kings where they are given. But a great schism occurs at the very outset. The Septuagint translation of the Mosaic history into Greek, which was made by order of Ptolemy Philadelphus, differs from the Hebrew text by 1400 years from the creation to the birth of Abraham.

The chronology of the Assyrian and Babylonish monarchies is involved in inextricable difficulties; nor are we successful in harmonizing the Greek with the oriental writers of history. The Persian historians make no mention of the defeat of Xerxes by the Greeks, or that of Darius by Alexander. All nations have had the vanity to make their origin mount as high as possible; and they have often invented series of kings, or have reckoned the contemporary individuals of different dynasties as following each other in regular succession, as if one should take the kings of the Heptarchy[147] singly instead of together.

You will perhaps ask, if we have no æras, what have we to reckon by? We have generations and successions of kings. Sir Isaac Newton, who joined wonderful sagacity to profound learning and astronomical skill, made very great reforms in the ancient chronology. He pointed out the difference between generations and successions of kings. A generation is not the life of man; it is the time that elapses before a man sees his successor; and this, reckoning to the birth of the eldest son, is estimated at about thirty years. The succession of kings would seem at first sight to be the same, and so it had been reckoned; but Newton corrected it, on the principle that kings are often cut off prematurely in turbulent times, or are succeeded either by their brothers, or by their uncles, or others older than themselves. The lines of kings of France, England, and other countries within the range of exact chronology, confirmed this principle. He therefore rectified all the ancient chronology according to it; and with the assistance of astronomical observations he found reason to allow, as the average length of a reign, about eighteen or twenty years.[148]

But after all, great part of the chronology of ancient history is founded upon conjecture and clouded with uncertainty.

Although I recommend to you a constant attention to chronology, I do not think it desirable to load your memory with a great number of specific dates, both because it would be too great a burthen on the retentive powers, and because it is, after all, not the best way of attaining clear ideas on the subjects of history. In order to do this, it is necessary to have in your mind the relative situation of other countries at the time of any event recorded in one of them. For instance, if you have got by heart the dates of the accession of the kings of Europe, and want to know whether John lived at the time of the crusades, and in what state the Greek empire was, you cannot tell without an arithmetical process, which perhaps you may not be quick enough to make. You cannot tell whether Constantinople had been taken by the Turks when the Sicilian Vespers happened;[149] for each fact is insulated in your mind; and indeed your dates give you only the dry catalogue of accessions. Nay, you may read separate histories, and yet not bring them together if the countries be remote. Each exists in your mind separately, and you have at no time the state of the world. But you ought to have an idea at once of the whole world, as far as history will give it. You do not see truly what the Greeks were, except you know that the British Isles were then barbarous.[150]

A few dates therefore, perfectly learned, may suffice, and will serve as landmarks to prevent your going far astray in the rest: but it will be highly useful to connect the histories you read in such a manner in your own mind, that you may be able to refer from one to the other, and to form them all into a whole. For this purpose, it is very desirable to observe and retain in your memory certain coincidences, which may link, as it were, two nations together. Thus you may remember that Haroun al Raschid sent to Charlemagne the first clock that was seen in Europe.[151] If you are reading the history of Greece when it flourished most, and want to know what the Romans were doing at the same time, you may recollect that they sent to Greece for instruction when they wanted to draw up the laws of the Twelve Tables. Solon and Crœsus connect the history of Lesser Asia with that of Greece. Egbert was brought up in the court of Charlemagne; Philip Augustus of France and Richard I. of England fought in the same crusade against Saladin. Queen Elizabeth received the French ambassador in deep mourning after the massacre of St. Bartholomew.[152]

It may be desirable to keep one kingdom as a meter for the rest. Take for this purpose first the Jews, then the Greeks, the Romans, and, because it is so, our own country: then harmonize and connect all the other dates with these.

That the literary history of a nation may be connected with the political, study also biography, and endeavour to link men of science and literature and artists with political characters. Thus Hippocrates was sent for to the plague of Athens; Leonardo da Vinci died in the arms of Francis I. Often an anecdote, a smart saying, will indissolubly fix a date.

Sometimes you may take a long reign, as that of Elizabeth or Louis XIV., and making that the center, mark all the contemporary sovereigns, and also the men of letters. Another way is, to make a line of life, composed of distinguished characters who touch each other. It will be of great service to you in this view to study Dr. Priestley's biographical chart; and of still greater, to make one for yourself, and fill it by degrees as your acquaintance with history extends. Marriages connect the history of different kingdoms; as those of Mary queen of Scots and Francis II., Philip II. and Mary of England.

These are the kind of dates which make every thing lie in the mind in its proper order; they also take fast hold of it. If you forget the exact date by years, you have nothing left; but of circumstances you never lose all idea. As we come nearer to our own times, dates must be more exact: a few years more or less signify little in the destruction of Troy, if we knew it exactly; but the conclusion of the American war should be accurately known, or it will throw other events near it into confusion.

In so extensive a study no auxiliary is to be neglected: Poetry impresses both geography and history in a most agreeable manner upon those who are fond of it. Thus,

> "...... fair Austria spreads her mournful charms,
> The queen, the beauty, sets the world in arms."

A short, lively character in verse is never forgotten:

> "From Macedonia's madman to the Swede."[153]

Historic plays deeply impress, but should be read with caution. We take our ideas from Shakespeare more than history: he, indeed, copied pretty exactly from the chroniclers, but other dramatic writers have taken great liberties both with characters and events.

Painting is a good auxiliary; and though in this country history is generally read before we see pictures, they mutually illustrate one another: painting also shows the costume. In France, where pictures are more accessible, there is more knowledge generally diffused of common history. Many have learned scripture history from the rude figures on Dutch tiles.[154]

I will conclude with the remark, that though the beginner in history may and ought to study dates and epochas for his guidance, chronology can never be fully possessed till after history has been long studied and carefully digested.

Farewell; and believe me
Yours affectionately.

[On Homer][18]

My dear Lydia,

I am glad to see that you read with interest, in its English dress, the Iliad of Homer, as it is a Poem not only worthy of admiration on its own account but is also an object of great curiosity, as being the first Epic Poem that ever was written, at least the first which we have any account of—An Epic Poem is a series of adventures, wrought into one story, told in verse & embellished with all the ornaments of fancy. The chief interest is generally thrown upon one character, commonly called the hero of the Poem; at least the attention must be directed to one great event, to the accomplishment of which the various incidents are made subservient. Wonderful adventures, the display of character, & the richest poetical ornaments must combine to render a work of this description excellent in its kind. When so executed, it is esteemed one of the master-pieces of human genius. In order to enhance the wonderful, the interposition of some kind of superior beings has generally been introduced; this is called the <u>Mythology</u> of the poem, & some esteem it essential to the Epic[155]——We know very little about Homer. His birth place has been warmly contested. He was undoubtedly a Greek, & probably of lesser Asia. Smyrna & the island of Chios seem to have the best claim to the honour of being his native soil. He had certainly travelled a great deal; neither the knowledge of events nor the geography of countries was at that time to be gained by sitting at home &

---

[18] '[On Homer]': Our copy text is the holograph manuscript in the New York Public Library, Pforzheimer Collection Misc. MS 4347. It is published here for the first time.

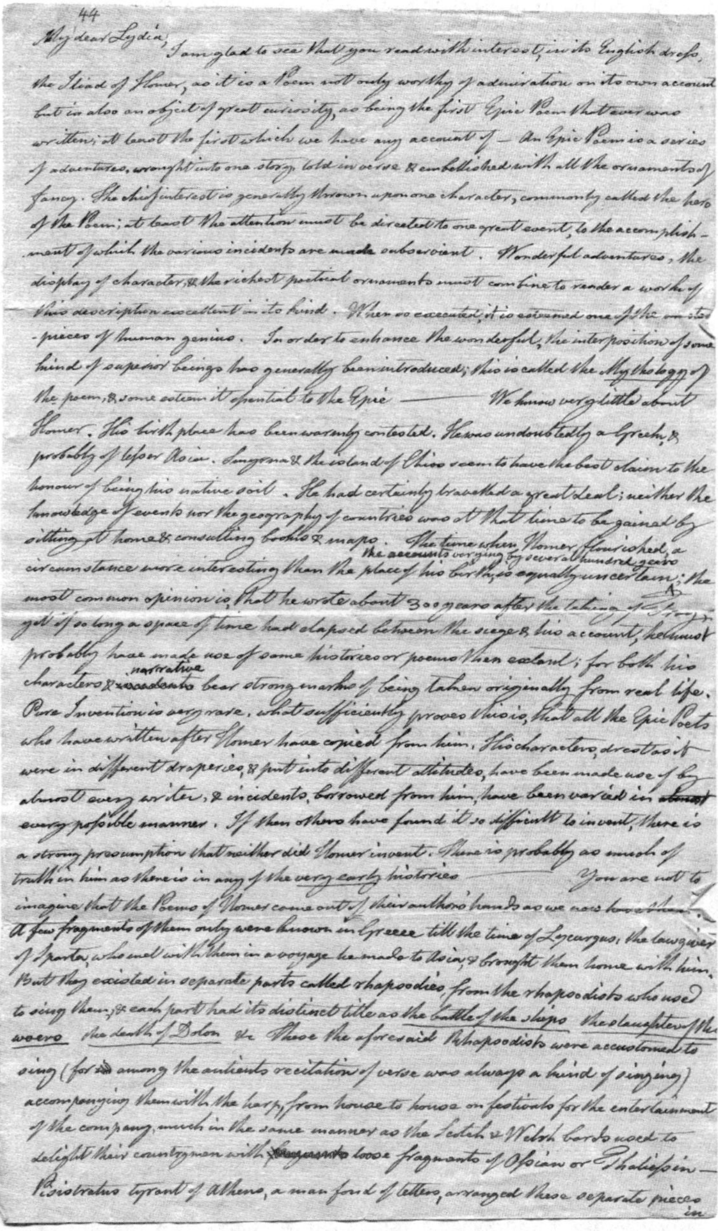

Fig. 12 First page of Barbauld's Letter to Lydia Rickards on Homer. New York Public Library MS 4347.

consulting books & maps. The time when Homer flourished, a circumstance more interesting than the place of his birth, is equally uncertain ^the accounts varying by several hundred years^; the most common opinion is that he wrote about 300 years after the taking of Troy, yet if so long a space of time had elapsed between the siege & his account, he must probably have made use of some histories or poems then extant; for both his characters & ⟨incidents⟩ ^narrative^ bear strong marks of being taken originally from real life. Pure Invention is very rare, what sufficiently proves this is, that all the Epic Poets who have written after Homer have copied from him. His characters, drest as it were in different draperies, & put into different attitudes, have been made use of by almost every writer, & incidents, borrowed from him, have been varied in ⟨almost⟩ every possible manner. If then others have found it so difficult to invent, there is a strong presumption that neither did Homer invent. There is probably as much of truth in him as there is in any of the very early histories——You are not to imagine that the Poems of Homer came out of their author's hands as we now have them.[156] A few fragments of them only were known in Greece till the time of Lycurgus, the lawgiver of Sparta, who met with them in a voyage he made to Asia, & brought them home with him. But they existed in separate parts called rhapsodies, from the rhapsodists who used to sing them; & each part had its distinct title as the battle of the ships the slaughter of the woers the death of Dolon &c[.] These the aforesaid Rhapsodists were accustomed to sing (for ⟨in⟩ among the antients recitation of verse was always a kind of singing) accompanying them with the harp, from house to house on festivals for the entertainment of the company, much in the same manner as the Scotch & Welsh bards used to delight their countrymen with ⟨fragments⟩ loose fragments of Ossian or Thaliessin[157]—Pisistratus tyrant of Athens, a man fond of letters, arranged these separate pieces in the best manner he could, gave the two Poems the name of the Iliad & Odyssey & divided each of them into twenty four books. From that time the name of Homer became more & more celebrated, his works were carefully preserved in libraries, they were ⟨appealled⟩ appealed to as authority in questions of Geography & History & as the number of his commentators increased he was considered as a repository of all kinds of science—His works were revised by that great critic & universal genius Aristotle, & his pupil Alexander the great thought he could not put to a worthier use the rich casket of Darius than by making it the repository of this correct edition.[158] In short all manner of honours were paid this venerable father of Poetry by antiquity, even to the erecting temples to his honour—In later times the very idea of Epic Poetry & the laws of that species of composition have been drawn from his works, & they have afforded a storehouse of images & beauties of every kind which all succeeding writers have largely made use of

> Hither, as to their fountain, other stars
> Repairing, in their golden urns draw light.[159]

Besides the two great works already mentioned some smaller pieces are extant which are also attributed to Homer, whether with truth is uncertain. The battle of the Frogs & Mice is a very pretty piece of mock heroic, & therefore more likely to be written in later times, for it is a kind of parody of Homer's manner.[160] We see many busts of Homer, & there are medals in existence ^which were^ struck for him at Chios & Smyrna, in none of which we must look for an in[di]vidual resemblance, as they were doubtless executed long after his death, but they show the venerable idea ⟨that⟩ under which the bard presented himself to their imaginations & exactly answer to Pope's lively painting of him,

> Father of verse; in holy fillets drest,
> His silver beard waved gently oe'r his breast;
> Tho blind, a boldness in his looks appears,
> In years he seems, but not impaired by years.[161]

With regard to the blindness ⟨which tradition⟩ he is supposed to have been afflicted with, if the tradition be true, at best it could not have taken place till, like our own Milton, he had stored his mind with all the images of the beautiful the grand & the picturesque which the ample scenes of nature afford[.]

 I am Dear
  Your aff[ectiona]te
   ALB.

[A Letter Recommending French Books]

The collection of Barbauld's surviving letters to Lydia Rickards includes a copy by an unidentified hand of 'A letter of Mrs Barbauld[']s to Mr Douce recommending some french Books'. He may well have been the 'J. Douse' who called on the Barbaulds on 11 June 1802 (RB, Diary) and to whom Barbauld wrote on 17 October [1810], recommending books on ancient history for young readers (*GC*, 232). The letter is undated, but the paper is watermarked 1794. It shows Barbauld's wide acquaintance with French literature and recommends books which were used at Palgrave School as well as books which Barbauld may be assumed to have recommended to her private female pupils. The fact that the letter belongs to the collection of Barbauld's letters to Lydia suggests that it may have been intended for the guidance of a tutor who oversaw Lydia's reading before Barbauld took over supervising her studies; Douce would have been that tutor. The letter would then date to around 1795 and is published here for the first time.[19]

Sir

With regard to french books taking it for granted the young pupil has read Chambauld[']s Fables Choisies, or some elementary book of the same nature, she may read with advantage <u>Le Magazin des Enfants</u> by M[adam]e le Prince de Beaumont, a work which contains a very agreeable mixture of Geography sacred History instructive Dialogue & entertaining stories the whole adapted to Children from 6 to 10 years old according to their proficiency well calculated to form the heart and the manners. <u>Berquin[']s Ami des Enfants</u> contains a number of charming stories in elegant & modern french, all ⟨in⟩tending to impress on the heart the purest word[s] & the most refined sentiments of virtue & benevolence. man[y] of them are in Dialogue the Incidents are well imagined and many of them very affecting, the manners and language of Children are hapily seized. It must be remember'd they are french Children. It is not a book of Instruction, the object is to form the heart. The first vols are the best[.] Berquin has also written <u>L'Ami des adol[es]cens</u> but not with equal spirit. No books for young people have been more read of late than those of M[adam]e de Genlis they may properly succeed Berquin[']s. Her <u>Theodore & Adele</u> is a system of education written for parents & not for Children[.] It is very entertaining however & many young people read it I think her system has many objectionable things in it in point of morality. Her <u>Veillées du Chateau</u> is written for Children or rather some of them for young people of 14 or 15, there is a great deal of fancy and ingenuity in them. All her works have something of an overstrain'd morality ⟨in them⟩ particularly in the article of obedience or rather devotion to parents which however most will think an fault on the right side; She has ⟨also⟩ likewise written <u>Theatre d'Education</u>, a set of Dramas intended for young people to act. The French is elegant but the manners of ^the Country are still more apparent than those in^ Berquin & therefore to us accustomed to much simpler, they will appear affected. Fontenelle[']s <u>Pluralités des monde[s]</u> has long been consider'd as a model of the graces & playfulness of Dialogue applied to [the] purpose of instruction and is well worth reading tho' as a mere book of Astronomy Modern times have supplied many more perfect.

---

[19] Our copy text is NYPL Pforzheimer Collection Misc. MS 4379. One sheet folded into two leaves; watermark: Britannia seated in frame, with date 1794. No date for the text. The hand is unidentified.

Le Spectacle de la Nature[162] stands on pretty much the same footing. It is a book of Natural History, not scientific in the style of modern systems, but one in which the habits and manners of animals are so pleasingly delineated that many young people have been indebted to that book for their early love of so engaging a Science—You will no doubt wish to introduce the young ladies to an early acquaintance with History. For this purpose Voltaire[']s His[toire] de Charles 12 & Vertot[']s[163] Revolutions de Portugal & Revolutions de Suede are very proper as being separate pieces of as forbidding length & written, the 2 first especially with so much life & spirit that a romance is not more entertaining. When the study of general History is enter'd upon, there is none better adapted for Children than Rollin's Histoire Ancienne[164] tho' I should be inclin'd to stop at the death of Alexander lest the his[tory] of his successors should be found too dry for a child.—Vertot[']s Revolutions Romaines is well executed & interesting. Rousseau's lettres botaniques[165]—is the only publication I recollect of that enchanting author which can be recommended to Children. It is certainly an excellent introduction to that fashionable Science. Buffon the celebrated naturalist has many passages of great beauty and desireable for young people but I do not know that there is any french abridgement of his work the whole is only fit for a Library.[166] The Telemaque of Fenelon well deserves the rank it has long held among the French Classics. The most brilliant imagination, the purest moral[s] full of sweetness & amenity, a stile that has all the richness and melody of Poetry & yet [is] so easy as to suit the beginner in French[.] Charicterise this work which has been called an Epic Poem in Prose.—Perhaps however it may be as well to leave out on the first reading some of the graver political parts into which a Child cannot ^so^ well enter.—Marmontel[']s Belisaire is another didactic Romance of great merit & a pure stile, but still more of it is political. Les Incas is a very beautiful work of the same Author, with more of fancy & variety than the former. It may perhaps be thought an Objection that it has a love Story which tho' perfectly pure is given in glowing colours. There is also an exceptionable Chapter describing the promiscuous dances of the Indian. M[adam]e Sévigne's lettres[167] have always been esteemed models of the easy epistolary stile, part of them for the whole would be tedious may be read along with Voltaire's Siècle de Louis 14th among elegant books of amusement may be selected Les Lettres Peruviennes[168] by [Madame de Graffigny] Paul et Virginie by M[onsieu]r de la Pierre[169] & la Chamière Indienne by the same Author they both besides the merit of the story have that of giving lively & beautiful descriptions of nature in the tropical climates. Fenelon[']s tales I might have mention'd before as they suit an earlier age. La Galatée of Florian[170] is a pretty pastoral imitated from the

[A LETTER RECOMMENDING FRENCH BOOKS]

Spanish of Cervantes. I mention last the Poets and Dramatic writers as it is in that order they ought to be taken. Fables de la Fontaine are indeed given to Children, the subject is particularly pleasing to them. the stile is difficult but full [of] beauties ⟨particularly pleasing to them⟩ peculiar to himself, and as a fabulist he is allow'd to be unequalled in any Country; The great comic writer Moliere is equally original in his work[.] His best pieces are Le Misanthrope, L'Avare, Le Bourgeois Gentilhomme, Les femmes Savantes, Le Malade Imaginaire. Corneille, Racine & Voltaire are the 3 Tragedians principally read. There is a select Vol. of Corneille containing Le Cid & a few others of his best plays which are all it is particularly desirable to read of that Author[.] His french is a little antiquated. Racine is a standard for the elegance and sweetness of his Verse. All his plays are finish'd with a high polish but Britanicus Phædre Iphigenie and Bajazet are among his Master pieces. Athalie & Esther may be particularly recommended to young ladies as they were written to be acted by such. Voltaire is somewhat more negligent in his Verse but has a great deal of strength & spirit. he make[s] more use of Modern History & has formed himself in some measure by the English Theatre[.] Mahomet, Semiramis, Merope, Lazare & Alzire may be selected to give a taste of this Author. It may be observed that there is an Advantage particularly to girls in the French Drama which is that both their Comedies & Tragedies are much Chaster than ours. L'Henriade de Voltaire is an historical Poem not without beauties yet on the whole scarcely worth reading except as being the only poem the French boast of under the name of Epic. The VerVert of Gresset[171] is a charming little poem of the same nature with Mason's English Garden. his descriptions of natural beauties are very good and were in a manner new to the French. Boileau I take next as his excellent Satires require a knowledge of life and manners which a very young person can hardly be supposed to possess, he abounds in good sense and is besides one of their best Versifiers. There is a Collection called Pieces Choisies in 6 Vol. which contains very judicious specimens of the best French Authors.[172] I have omitted to mention two tracts of Fenelon which have merit, Traité sur l'existence d'un Dieu & Education d'une fille.

FROM *A LEGACY FOR YOUNG LADIES*

Pic-nic

The *OED* dates the first appearance of the word *pic-nic* in English to 1802 (earlier occurrences are in French). Because the daughter in this dialogue has only 'lately' heard the word, the dialogue may date to around 1802–3. The evening party it describes—in which news from Germany, galvanism, a poet, and aesthetics all figure—calls to mind volume 13 (1802) of the *Monthly Magazine* under John Aikin's editorship, which contains a notice of a Royal Academy exhibition, reviews of new books including poetry, a report of literary affairs in Germany, and a 'history' of galvanism. Galvanism continued to be a topic of interest in the *Monthly Magazine* into 1803. In January of that year a demonstration was performed in London on the body of an executed criminal; the *Monthly Magazine* reported inferences drawn from 'the late important and striking experiments in Galvanism' (15:160).

That 'Lady Isabella' presides over the gathering with quiet skill also calls to mind a Bluestocking evening at Elizabeth Montagu's: 'How easily and effectually', wrote Hannah More, 'may a well-bred woman promote the most useful and elegant conversation, almost without speaking a word!'[1]

The addressee and occasion of this dialogue are not known. Copy text: *Legacy for Young Ladies*, pp. 192–7.

Pray, mamma, what is the meaning of *pic-nic*? I have heard lately once or twice of a *pic-nic supper*, and I cannot think what it means; I looked for the word in Johnson's Dictionary and could not find it.

I should wonder if you had, the word was not coined in Johnson's time; and if it had, I believe he would have disdained to insert it among the legitimate words of the language.[173] I cannot tell you the derivation of the phrase; I believe pic-nic is originally a cant word, and was first applied to a supper or other meal in which the entertainment is not provided by any one person, but each of the guests furnishes his dish. In a pic-nic supper one supplies the fowls, another the fish, another the wine and fruit, &c.; and they all sit down together and enjoy it.

A very sociable way of making an entertainment.

Yes, and I would have you observe that the principle of it may be extended to many other things. No one has a right to be entertained gratis in society;

---

[1] Quoted in Major, 'The Politics of Sociability', 178.

he must expend if he wishes to enjoy.—Conversation, particularly, is a picnic feast, where every one is to contribute something, according to his genius and ability. Different talents and acquirements compose the different dishes of the entertainment, and the greater variety the better; but every one must bring something, for society will not tolerate any one long who lives wholly at the expense of his neighbours. Did not you observe how agreeably we were entertained at Lady Isabella's party last night?

Yes: one of the young ladies sung, and another exhibited her drawings; and a gentleman told some very good stories.

True: another lady who is very much in the fashionable world gave us a great deal of anecdote; Dr. R., who is just returned from the continent, gave us an interesting account of the state of Germany;[174] and in another part of the room a cluster was gathered round an Edinburgh student and a young Oxonian, who were holding a lively debate on the power of galvanism. But Lady Isabella herself was the charm of the party.

I think she talked very little; and I do not recollect any thing she said which was particularly striking.

That is true. But it was owing to her address and attention to her company that others talked and were heard by turns; that the modest were encouraged and drawn out, and those inclined to be noisy restrained and kept in order. She blended and harmonized the talents of each; brought those together who were likely to be agreeable to each other, and gave us no more of herself than was necessary to set off others. I noticed particularly her good offices to an accomplished but very bashful lady and a reserved man of science, who wished much to be known to one another, but who would never have been so without her introduction. As soon as she had fairly engaged them in an interesting conversation she left them, regardless of her own entertainment, and seated herself by poor Mr.———, purely because he was sitting in a corner and no one attended to him. You know that in chemical preparations two substances often require a third, to enable them to mix and unite together. Lady Isabella possesses this amalgamating power:—this is what she brings to the pic-nic. I should add, that two or three times I observed she dexterously changed topics, and suppressed stories which were likely to bear hard on the profession or connexions of some of the company. In short, the party which was so agreeable under her harmonizing influence, would have had quite a different aspect without her. These merits, however, might easily escape a young observer. But I dare say you did not fail to notice Sir Henry B———'s lady, who was declaiming with so much enthusiasm, in the midst of a circle of gentlemen which she had drawn round her, upon the *beau ideal*.[175]

No indeed, mamma; I never heard so much fire and feeling:—and what a flow of elegant language! I do not wonder her eloquence was so much admired.

She has a great deal of eloquence and taste; she has travelled, and is acquainted with the best works of art. I am not sure, however, whether the gentlemen were admiring most her declamation or the fine turn of her hands and arms. She has a different attitude for every sentiment. Some observations which she made upon the beauty of statues seemed to me to go to the verge of what a modest female will allow herself to say upon such subjects,—but she has travelled. She was sensible that she could not fail to gain by the conversation while beauty of form was the subject of it.

Pray what did———, the great poet, bring to the pic-nic, for I think he hardly opened his mouth?

He brought his fame. Many would be gratified with merely seeing him who had entertained them in their closets; and he who had so entertained them had a right to be himself entertained in that way which he had no talent for joining in.—Let every one, I repeat, bring to the entertainment something of the best he possesses, and the pic-nic table will seldom fail to afford a plentiful banquet.

Letter from Grimalkin to Selima

This letter from an old mother cat to her adolescent daughter parodies the language and style of the conduct books for young women that had become ubiquitous by 1800: such works as James Fordyce's *Sermons to Young Women* (1766, a book Barbauld especially resented), John Gregory's *A Father's Legacy to his Daughters* (1774), the Rev. John Bennett's *Letters to a Young Lady* (1789), and Thomas Gisborne's *Enquiry into the Duties of the Female Sex* (1797). Besides signifying 'an old female cat', Grimalkin pejoratively signifies an irritable, elderly woman. This piece was written in or after 1802, the year of publication of Elizabeth Hamilton's *Letters on the Elementary Principles of Education*, which it mentions and which Barbauld reviewed. Copy text: *Legacy for Young Ladies*, pp. 198–204.[2]

My Dear Selima,

As you are now going to quit the fostering cares of a mother, to enter, young as you are, into the wide world, and conduct yourself by your own prudence, I cannot forbear giving you some parting advice in this important æra of your life.

---

[2] Reprinted in the *Eclectic Review*, ns 25 (1826): 79–85, a review of *Legacy*: 'The following playful letter... is more in the manner of Cowper,—or of Jane Taylor.'

Your extreme youth, and permit me to add, the giddiness incident to that period, make me particularly anxious for your welfare. In the first place then, let me beg you to remember that life is not to be spent in running after your own tail. Remember you were sent into the world to catch rats and mice. It is for this you are furnished with sharp claws, whiskers to improve your scent, and with such an elasticity and spring in your limbs. Never lose sight of this great end of your existence.[176] When you and your sister are jumping over my back, and kicking and scratching one another's noses, you are indulging the propensities of your nature, and perfecting yourselves in agility and dexterity. But remember that these frolics are only preparatory to the grand scene of action. Life is long, but youth is short. The gaiety of the kitten will most assuredly go off. In a few months, nay even weeks, those spirits and that playfulness, which now exhilarate all who behold you, will subside; and I beg you to reflect how contemptible you will be, if you should have the gravity of an old cat without that usefulness which alone can ensure respect and protection for your maturer years.

In the first place, my dear child, obtain a command over your appetites,[177] and take care that no tempting opportunity ever induces you to make free with the pantry or larder of your mistress. You may possibly slip in and out without observation; you may lap a little cream, or run away with a chop without its being missed: but depend upon it, such practices sooner or later will be found out; and if in a single instance you are discovered, every thing which is missing will be charged upon you. If Mrs. Betty or Mrs. Susan[178] chooses to regale herself with a cold breast of chicken which was set by for supper,—you will have clawed it; or a raspberry cream,—you will have lapped it. Nor is this all. If you have once thrown down a single cup in your eagerness to get out of the storeroom, every china plate and dish that is ever broken in the house, you will have broken it; and though your back promises to be pretty broad, it will not be broad enough for all the mischief that will be laid upon it. Honesty you will find is the best policy.

Remember that the true pleasures of life consist in the exertion of our own powers. If you were to feast every day upon roasted partridges from off Dresden china, and dip your whiskers in syllabubs and creams, it could never give you such true enjoyment as the commonest food procured by the labour of your own paws. When you have once tasted the exquisite pleasure of catching and playing with a mouse, you will despise the gratification of artificial dainties.

I do not with some moralists call cleanliness a half virtue only. Remember it is one of the most essential to your sex and station;[179] and if ever you should fail in it, I sincerely hope Mrs. Susan will bestow upon you a good whipping.

Pray do not spit at strangers who do you the honour to take notice of you. It is very uncivil behaviour, and I have often wondered that kittens of any breeding should be guilty of it.

Avoid thrusting your nose into every closet and cupboard,—unless indeed you smell mice; in which case it is very becoming.

Should you live, as I hope you will, to see the children of your patroness, you must prepare yourself to exercise that branch of fortitude which consists in patient endurance: for you must expect to be lugged about, pinched and pulled by the tail, and played a thousand tricks with; all which you must bear without putting out a claw: for you may depend upon it, if you attempt the least retaliation you will for ever lose the favour of your mistress.

Should there be favourites in the house, such as tame birds, dormice, or a squirrel, great will be your temptations. In such a circumstance, if the cage hangs low and the door happens to be left open,—to govern your appetite I know will be a difficult task. But remember that nothing is impossible to the governing mind; and that there are instances upon record of cats who, in the exercise of self-government, have overcome the strongest propensities of their nature.

If you would make yourself agreeable to your mistress, you must observe times and seasons. You must not startle her by jumping upon her in a rude manner: and above all, be sure to sheathe your claws when you lay your paw upon her lap.

You have like myself been brought up in the country, and I fear you may regret the amusements it affords; such as catching butterflies, climbing trees, and watching birds from the windows, which I have done with great delight for a whole morning together. But these pleasures are not essential. A town life has also its gratifications. You may make many pleasant acquaintances in the neighbouring courts and alleys. A concert upon the tiles in a fine moonlight summer's evening may at once gratify your ear and your social feelings. Rats and mice are to be met with everywhere: and at any rate you have reason to be thankful that so creditable a situation has been found for you; without which you must have followed the fate of your poor brothers, and with a stone about your neck have been drowned in the next pond.

It is only when you have kittens yourself, that you will be able to appretiate the cares of a mother. How unruly have you been when I wanted to wash your face! how undutiful in galloping about the room instead of coming immediately when I called you! But nothing can subdue the affections of a parent. Being grave and thoughtful in my nature, and having the advantage of residing in a literary family, I have mused deeply on the subject of education; I have pored by moonlight over Locke, and Edgeworth, and Mrs. Hamilton, and the laws of association:[180] but after much cogitation I am only convinced of this, that kittens will be kittens, and old cats old cats. May you, my dear child, be an honour to all your relations and to the whole feline race. May you see your descendants of the fiftieth generation. And when you depart this life, may the lamentations of your kindred exceed in pathos the melody of an Irish howl.[181]

Signed by the paw of your affectionate mother,

Grimalkin

True Magicians

To Miss C.

'Miss C.' is Sarah Grace Carr (b. 1794), eldest daughter of Thomas William and Frances Carr, close friends of the Barbaulds in Hampstead. This piece can be provisionally dated from Barbauld's mention of Epsom in a letter to Lydia Rickards of 17 October 1803: 'Mr Barbauld & myself spent one week of quiet & domestic enjoyment, which was also brightened by fine weather at Epsom with the Carrs.' The piece cannot date later than October 1805, when the Battle of Trafalgar ended Britain's need for the blockade of French ports mentioned in the text. Copy text: *Legacy for Young Ladies*, pp. 1–16.

My Dear Sarah,

I have often reflected, since I left you, on the wonderful powers of magic exhibited by you and your sister.[182] The dim obscurity of that grotto hollowed out by your hands under the laurel hedge, where you used to mix the ingredients of your incantations, struck us with awe and terror; and the broom which you so often brandished in your hands made you look very like witches indeed. I must confess, however, that some doubts have now and then arisen in my mind, whether or no you were truly initiated in the secrets of your art; and these suspicions gathered strength after you had suffered us and yourself to be so drenched as we all were on that rainy Tuesday; which to say the least was a very odd circumstance, considering you had the command of the weather.—As I was pondering these matters alone in the chaise between Epsom and London, I fell asleep and had the following dream.

I thought I had been travelling through an unknown country, and came at last to a thick wood cut out into several groves and avenues, the gloom of which inspired thoughtfulness, and a certain mysterious dread of unknown powers came upon me. I entered however one of the avenues, and found it terminated in a magnificent portal, through which

I could discern confusedly among thick foliage, cloistered arches and Grecian porticoes, and people walking and conversing amongst the trees. Over the portal was the following inscription: "*Here dwell the true magicians. Nature is our servant. Man is our pupil. We change, we conquer, we create.*"

As I was hesitating whether or no I should presume to enter, a pilgrim who was sitting under the shade offered to be my guide, assuring me that these magicians would do me no harm, and that so far from having any objection to be observed in their operations, they were pleased with any opportunity of exhibiting them to the curious. In therefore I went, and addressed the first of the magicians I met with, who asked me whether I liked panoramas. On replying that I thought them very entertaining, she took me to a little eminence and bade me look round. I did so, and beheld the representation of the beautiful vale of Dorking, with Norbury-park and Box-hill to the north, Riegate to the east, and Leith tower with the Surry hills to the south.[183] After I had admired for some time the beauty and accuracy of the painting, a vast curtain seemed to be drawn gradually up, and my view extended on all sides. On one hand I traced the windings of the Thames up to Oxford, and stretched my eye westward over Salisbury Plain, and across the Bristol Channel into the romantic country of South Wales; northward the view extended to Lincoln cathedral, and York minster towering over the rest of the churches. Across the Sussex downs I had a clear view of the British Channel, and the opposite coast of France, with its ports blockaded by our fleets. As the horizon of the panorama still extended, I spied the towers of Notre Dame, and the Tuilleries, and my eye wandered at large over "The vine-covered hills and gay regions of France,"[184] quite down to the source of the Loire. At the same time the great Atlantic ocean opened to my view; and on the other hand I saw the lake of Geneva, and the dark ridge of mount Jura, and discovered the summits of the Alps covered with snow; and beyond, the orange groves of Italy, the majestic dome of St. Peter's, and the smoking crater of Vesuvius. As the curtain still rose, I stretched my view over the Mediterranean, the scene of ancient glory, the Archipelago studded with islands, the shores of the Bosphorus, and the gilded minarets and cypress groves of Constantinople. Throwing back a look to the less attractive north, I saw pictured the rugged, broken coast of Norway, the cheerless moors of Lapland, and the interminable desolation of the plains of Siberia. Turning my eye again southward, the landscape extended to the plains of Barbary, covered with date-trees; and I discerned the points of pyramids appearing above the horizon, and saw the Delta and the seven-mouthed Nile. In short, the curtain still rose, and the view extended further and further till the panorama took in the whole globe. I cannot express to you the pleasure I felt as I saw mountains, seas, and islands, spread out before me. Sometimes my eye wandered over the vast plains of Tartary, sometimes it expatiated in the savannahs of America. I saw men with dark skins, white cotton turbans wreathed about their heads, and long flowing robes of silk; others almost naked under a vertical sun. I saw whales sporting in the northern seas, and elephants trampling amidst fields of maize and forests of palm-trees. I seemed to have put a girdle about the earth,[185] and was gratified with an infinite variety of objects which I thought I never could be weary of contemplating. At length, turning towards the magician who had entertained me with such an agreeable exhibition, and asking her name, she informed me it was *Geography*.

My attention was next arrested by a sorceress, who, I was told, possessed the power of calling up from the dead whomsoever she pleased, man or woman, in their proper habits and figures, and obliging them to converse and answer questions. She held a roll of parchment in her hand, and had an air of great dignity. I confess that I felt a little afraid; but having been somewhat encouraged by the former exhibition, I ventured to ask her to give me a specimen of her power, in case there was nothing unlawful in it. "Whom," said she, "do you wish to behold?" After considering some time, I desired to see Cicero the Roman orator. She made some talismanic figures on the sand, and presently he rose to my view, his neck and head bare, the rest of his body in a flowing toga, which he gathered round him with one hand, and stretching out the other very gracefully, he recited to me one of his orations against Catiline [*see Fig. 13*]. He also read to me, which was more than I could in reason have expected, several of his familiar letters to his most intimate friends. I next desired that Julius Cæsar might be called up: on which he appeared, his hair nicely arranged, and the fore part of his head, which was bald, covered with wreaths of laurel; and he very obligingly gave me a particular account of his expedition into Gaul. I wished to see the youth of Macedon,[186] but was a little disappointed in his figure, for he was low in stature and held his head awry; but I saw him manage Bucephalus with admirable courage and address, and was afterwards introduced with him into the tent of Darius, where I was greatly pleased with the generosity and politeness of his behaviour. I afterwards expressed some curiosity to see a battle, if I might do it with safety, and was gratified with the sea-fight of Actium. I saw, after the first onset, the galleys of Cleopatra turning their prows and flying from the battle, and Antony, to his eternal shame, quitting the engagement and making sail after her. I then wished to call up all the kings of England, and they appeared in order one after the other, with their crowns and the insignia of their dignity, and walked over the stage for my amusement, much like the

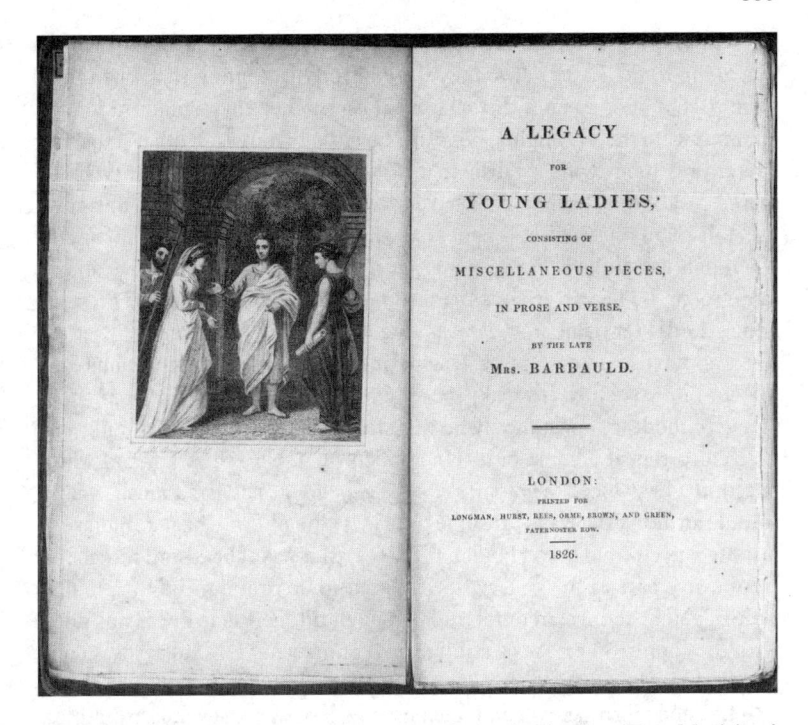

Fig. 13   Frontispiece to *A Legacy for Young Ladies*, to illustrate 'True Magicians' and Title-page (private collection).

descendants of Banquo in Macbeth.[187] Their queens accompanied them, trailing their robes upon the ground, and the bishops with their mitres, and judges, and generals, and eminent persons of every class. I asked many questions as they passed, and received a great deal of information relative to the laws, manners, and transactions of past times. I did not, however, always meet with direct answers to my questions. For instance, when I called up Homer, and after some other conversation asked him where he was born, he only said, "Guess!" And when I asked Louis the Fourteenth who was the man in the iron mask, he frowned and would not tell me.[188] I took a great deal of pleasure in calling up the shades of distinguished people in different ages and countries, making them stand close by one another, and comparing their manners and costume. Thus I measured Catherine of Russia against Semiramis, and Aristotle against Lord Bacon.[189] I could have spent whole years in conversation with so many celebrated persons, and promised myself that I would often frequent this obliging magician. Her name, I found, was in heaven *Clio*, on earth *History*.

I saw another who was making a charm for two friends, one of whom was going to the East Indies: they were bitterly lamenting that when they were parted at so great a distance from each other they could no longer communicate their thoughts, but must be cut off from each other's society. Presenting them with a talisman inscribed with four-and-twenty black marks, "Take this," she said; "I have breathed a voice upon it: by means of this talisman you shall still converse, and hear one another as distinctly when half the globe is between you, as if you were talking together in the same room." The two friends thanked her for such an invaluable present, and retired. Her name was *Abracadabra*.[190]

I was next invited to see a whispering-gallery of a most curious and uncommon structure. To make the experiment of its powers, a young poet of a very modest appearance, who was stealing along in a retired walk, was desired to repeat a verse in it. He applied his lips to the wall, and whispered in a low voice, "*Rura mihi et rigui placeant in vallibus amnes.*"[191] The sound ran along the walls for some time in a kind of low whisper; but every minute it grew louder and louder, till at length it was echoed and re-echoed from every part of the gallery, and seemed to be pronounced by a multitude of voices at once, in different languages, till the whole dome was filled with the sound. There was a strong smell of incense. The gallery was constructed by *Fame*.

The good pilgrim next conducted me to a cave where several sorceresses, very black and grim, were amusing themselves with making lightning, thunder, and earthquakes. I saw two vials of cold liquor mixed together, and flames burst forth from them. I saw some insignificant-looking black grains, which would throw palaces and castles into the air. I saw—and it made my hair stand on end—a headless man who lifted up his arm and grasped a sword.[192] I saw men flying through the air, without wings, over the tops of towns and castles, and come down unhurt. The cavern was very black, and the smoke and fires and mephitic blasts and sulphureous vapours that issued from it gave the whole a very tremendous appearance. I did not stay long, but as I retired I saw *Chemistry* written on the walls in letters of flame, with several other names which I do not now remember.

My companion whispered me that some of these were suspected of communication with the evil genii, and that the demon of War had been seen to resort to the cave. "But now," said the pilgrim, "I will lead you to enchanters who deserve all your veneration, and are even more beneficent than those you have already seen." He then led me to a cavern that opened upon the sea shore: it blew a terrible storm, the waves ran mountains high, the wind roared, and vessels were driven against each other with a terrible shock. A female figure advanced and threw a little oil upon the waves; they immediately subsided, the winds were still, the storm was laid, and the vessels pursued their course in safety. "By what magic is this performed?" exclaimed I. "The magician is *Meekness*," replied my conductor: "she can smooth the roughest sea, and allay the wildest storm."

My view was next directed to a poor wretch who lay groaning in a most piteous manner, and crushed to the earth with a mountain on his breast: he uttered piercing shrieks, and seemed totally unable to rise or help himself. One of these good magicians, whose name I found was *Patience*, advanced and struck the mountain with a wand; on which, to my great surprise, it diminished to a size not more than the load of an ordinary porter, which the man threw over his shoulders with something very like a smile, and marched off with a firm step and very composed air.

I must not pass over a charmer of a very pleasing appearance and lively aspect. She possessed the power (a very useful one in a country so subject to fogs and rains as this is) of gilding a landscape with sunshine whenever she breathed upon it. Her name was *Cheerfulness*. Indeed you may remember that your papa brought her down with him on that very rainy day when we could not go out at all, and he played on his flute to you, and you all danced.

I was next struck, on ascending an eminence, with a most dreary landscape. All the flat country was one stagnant marsh. Amidst the rushy grass lay the fiend Ague, listless and shivering: on the bare and bleak hills sat Famine, with a few shells of acorns before her, of which she had eaten the fruit. The woods were tangled and pathless; the howl of wolves was heard. A few smoky huts, or caves, not much better than the dens of wild beasts, were all the habitations of men that presented themselves. "Miserable country!" I exclaimed; "step-child of nature!" "This," said my conductor, "is Britain as our ancestors possessed it." "And by what magic," I replied, "has it been converted into the pleasant land we now inhabit?" "You shall see," said he. "It has been the work of one of our most powerful magicians. Her name is *Industry*." At the word she advanced and waved her wand over the scene. Gradually the waters ran off into separate channels, and left rich meadows covered with innumerable flocks and herds. The woods disappeared, except what waved gracefully on the tops of the hills, or filled up the unsightly hollows. Wherever she moved her wand, roads, bridges, and canals laid open and improved the face of the country. A numerous population, spread abroad in the fields, were gathering in the harvest. Smoke from warm cottages ascended through the trees, pleasant towns and villages marked the several points of distance. Last, the Thames was filled with forests of masts, and proud London appeared with all its display of wealth and grandeur.

I do not know whether it was the pleasure I received from this exhilarating scene, or the carriage having just got upon the pavement, which awakened me; but I determined to write out my dream, and advise you to cultivate your acquaintance with all the *true Arts of Magic*.

On Female Studies

We do not know the identity of this letter's addressee. Barbauld had not yet met her: she was evidently a new or prospective pupil. Hence Barbauld writes more circumspectly than she did with young women she knew, and probably also with an eye to the girl's mother. Even so, Letter I offers views similar to those of Mary Wollstonecraft in *A Vindication of the Rights of Woman* (1792). Barbauld's keeping copies of the two letters that set forth these views may indicate that she thought of publishing them; or she may have anticipated reusing them to address other new pupils whom she had not yet met. They outline a program of study analogous to that of Hester Chapone in *Letters on the Improvement of the Mind*. Together with the letters to Lydia Rickards on History and the essay on Friendship, they can be seen as materials towards a book Barbauld did not write but may have thought of writing: an updated version of Chapone's *Letters*. Perhaps Lucy Aikin regarded *Legacy* as serving this purpose.

These letters can be dated, speculatively, to 1803 or soon after, for Barbauld's reference to Isaac Newton in the second letter runs parallel to Lady Mary Wortley Montagu's counsel in a letter to her daughter published in 1803. In its review of *Legacy* the *Eclectic Review* praised the 'short but excellent letters on Female Studies, marked by all the correct feeling and discrimination of the Writer' (82). Lucy Aikin found these letters among Barbauld's papers and published them in *A Legacy for Young Ladies*. As they are the only texts known today, they serve as our copy texts (pp. 41–56).

Letter I

My dear Young Friend,

If I had not been afraid you would feel some little reluctance in addressing me first, I should have asked you to begin the correspondence between us; for I am at present ignorant of your particular pursuits: I cannot guess whether you are climbing the hill of science, or wandering among the flowers of fancy; whether you are stretching your powers to embrace the planetary system, or examining with a curious eye the delicate veinings of a green leaf, and the minute ramifications of a sea-weed; or whether you are toiling through the intricate and thorny mazes of grammar. Whichever of these is at present your employment, your general aim no doubt is the improvement of your mind; and we will therefore spend some time in considering what kind and degree of literary attainments sit gracefully upon the female character.

Every woman should consider herself as sustaining the general character of a rational being, as well as the more confined one belonging to the female sex; and therefore the motives for acquiring general knowledge and cultivating the taste are nearly the same to both sexes. The line of separation between the studies of a young man and a young woman appears to me to be chiefly fixed by this,—that a woman is excused from all professional knowledge. Professional knowledge means all that is necessary to fit a man for a peculiar profession or business. Thus men study in order to qualify themselves for the law, for physic, for various departments in political life, for instructing others from the pulpit or the professor's chair. These all require a great deal of severe study and technical knowledge; much of which is nowise valuable in itself, but as a means to that particular profession. Now as a woman can never be called to any of these professions, it is evident you have nothing to do with such studies. A woman is not expected to understand the mysteries of politics, because she is not called to govern; she is not required to know anatomy, because she is not to perform surgical operations; she need not embarrass herself with theological disputes, because she will neither be called upon to make nor to explain creeds.

Men have various departments in active life; women have but one, and all women have the same, differently modified indeed by their rank in life and other incidental circumstances. It is, to be a wife, a mother, a mistress of a family.[193] The knowledge belonging to these duties is your professional knowledge, the want of which nothing will excuse. Literary knowledge therefore, in men, is often an indispensable duty; in women it can be only a desirable accomplishment. In women it is more immediately applied to the purposes of adorning and improving the mind, of refining the sentiments, and supplying proper stores for conversation. For general knowledge women have in some respects more advantages than men. Their avocations often allow them more leisure; their sedentary way of life disposes them to the domestic quiet amusement of reading; the share they take in the education of their children throws them in the way of books. The uniform tenor and confined circle of their lives makes them eager to diversify the scene by descriptions which open to them a new world; and they are eager to gain an idea of scenes on the busy stage of life from which they are shut out by their sex. It is likewise particularly desirable for women to be able to give spirit and variety to conversation by topics drawn from the stores of literature, as the broader mirth and more boisterous gaiety of the other sex are to them prohibited. As their parties must be innocent, care should be taken that they do not stagnate into insipidity. I will venture to add, that the purity and simplicity of heart which a woman ought never, in her freest commerce with the world, to wear off; her very seclusion from the jarring interests and coarser amusements of society,—fit her in a peculiar manner for the worlds of fancy and sentiment, and dispose her to the quickest relish of what is pathetic, sublime, or tender. To you, therefore, the beauties of poetry, of moral painting, and all in general that is comprised under the term of polite literature, lie particularly open, and you cannot neglect them without neglecting a very copious source of enjoyment.

Languages are on some accounts particularly adapted to female study, as they may be learnt at home without experiments or apparatus, and without interfering with the habits of domestic life; as they form the style, and as they are the immediate inlet to works of taste. But the learned languages, the Greek especially, require a great deal more time than a young woman can conveniently spare. To the Latin there is not an equal objection; and if a young person has leisure, has an opportunity of learning it at home by being connected with literary people, and is placed in a circle of society sufficiently liberal to allow her such an accomplishment, I do not see, if she has a strong inclination, why she should not make herself mistress of so rich a store of original entertainment:—it will not in the present state of things excite either a smile or a stare in fashionable company. To those who do not intend to learn the language, I would strongly recommend the learning so much of the grammar of it as will explain the name and nature of cases, genders, inflexion of verbs, &c.; of which, having only the imperfect rudiments in our own language, a mere English scholar can with difficulty form a clear idea. This is the more necessary, as all our grammars, being written by men whose early studies had given them a partiality for the learned languages, are formed more upon those than upon the real genius of our own tongue.

I was going now to mention French, but perceive I have written a letter long enough to frighten a young correspondent, and for the present I bid you adieu.

Letter II

French you are not only permitted to learn, but you are laid under the same necessity of acquiring it as your brother is of acquiring Latin. Custom has made the one as much expected from an accomplished woman, as the other from a man who has had a liberal education. The learning French, or indeed any language completely, includes reading, writing, and speaking it. But here I must take the liberty to offer my ideas, which differ something from those generally entertained, and you will give them what weight you think they deserve. It seems to me that the efforts of young ladies in learning French are generally directed to what is unattainable;

and if attained, not very useful,—the speaking it. It is utterly impossible, without such advantages as few enjoy, to speak a foreign language with fluency and a proper accent; and if even by being in a French family some degree of both is attained, it is soon lost by mixing with the world at large. As to the French which girls are obliged to speak at boarding-schools, it does very well to speak in England, but at Paris it would probably be less understood than English itself.[194]

I do not mean by this to say that the speaking of French is not a very elegant accomplishment; and to those who mean to spend some time in France, or who being in very high life often see foreigners of distinction, it may be necessary; but in common life it is very little so: and for English people to meet together to talk a foreign language is truly absurd. There is a sarcasm against this practice as old as Chaucer's time—

> "....Frenche she spake ful fayre and fetisely,
> After the schole of Stratford atte Bowe,
> For Frenche of Paris was to her unknowe."[195]

But with regard to reading French, the many charming publications in that language, particularly in polite literature, of which you can have no adequate idea by translation, render it a very desirable acquisition. Writing it is not more useful in itself than speaking, except a person has foreign letters to write; but it is necessary for understanding the language grammatically and fixing the rules in the mind. A young person who reads French with ease and is so well grounded as to write it grammatically, and has what I should call a good English pronunciation of it, will by a short residence in France gain fluency and the accent; whereas one not grounded would soon forget all she had learned, though she had acquired some fluency in speaking. For speaking, therefore, love and cultivate your own: know all its elegancies, its force, its happy turns of expression, and possess yourself of all its riches. In foreign languages you have only to learn; but with regard to your own, you have probably to unlearn, and to avoid vulgarisms and provincial barbarisms.

If after you have learned French you should wish to add Italian, the acquisition will not be difficult. It is valuable on account of its poetry, in which it far excels the French,—and its music. The other modern languages you will hardly attempt, except led to them by some peculiar bent.

History affords a wide field of entertaining and useful reading. The chief thing to be attended to in studying it, is to gain a clear well-arranged idea of facts in chronological order, and illustrated by a knowledge of the places where such facts happened. Never read without tables and maps: make abstracts of what you read. Before you embarrass yourself in the detail of this, endeavour to fix well in your mind the arrangement of some leading facts, which may serve as landmarks to which to refer the rest. Connect the history of different countries together. In the study of history the different genius of a woman I imagine will show itself. The detail of battles, the art of sieges, will not interest her so much as manners and sentiment; this is the food she assimilates to herself.

The great laws of the universe, the nature and properties of those objects which surround us, it is unpardonable not to know: it is more unpardonable to know, and not to feel the mind struck with lively gratitude. Under this head are comprehended natural history, astronomy, botany, experimental philosophy, chemistry, physics. In these you will rather take what belongs to sentiment and to utility than abstract calculations or difficult problems. You must often be content to know a thing is so, without understanding the proof. It belongs to a Newton to prove his sublime problems, but we may all be made acquainted with the result.[196] You cannot investigate; you may remember. This will teach you not to despise common things, will give you an interest in every thing you see. If you are feeding your poultry, or tending your bees, or extracting the juice of herbs, with an intelligent mind you are gaining real knowledge; it will open to you an inexhaustible fund of wonder and delight, and effectually prevent you from depending for your entertainment on the poor novelties of fashion and expense.

But of all reading, what most ought to engage your attention are works of sentiment and morals. Morals is that study in which alone both sexes have an equal interest; and in sentiment yours has even the advantage. The works of this kind often appear under the seducing form of novel and romance: here great care, and the advice of your older friends is requisite in the selection. Whatever is true, however uncouth in the manner or dry in the subject, has a value from being true: but fiction in order to recommend itself must give us *la belle Nature*.[197] You will find fewer plays fit for your perusal than novels, and fewer comedies than tragedies.

What particular share any one of the studies I have mentioned may engage of your attention will be determined by your peculiar turn and bent of mind. But I shall conclude with observing, that a woman ought to have that general tincture of them all which marks the cultivated mind. She ought to have enough of them to engage gracefully in general conversation. In no subject is she required to be deep,—of none ought she to be ignorant. If she knows not enough to speak well, she should know enough to keep her from speaking at all; enough to feel her ground and prevent her from exposing her ignorance; enough to hear with intelligence, to ask questions with propriety, and to receive information where she is not qualified to give it. A woman who to a cultivated mind joins that quickness of intelligence and delicacy of taste which such a woman often possesses in a superior degree, with that nice sense of propriety which results from the whole, will have a kind of *tact* by which she will be able on all occasions to discern between pretenders to science and men of real merit. On subjects upon which she cannot talk herself, she will know whether a man talks with knowledge of his subject. She will not judge of systems, but by their systems she will be able to judge of men. She will distinguish the modest, the dogmatical, the affected, the over-refined, and give her esteem and confidence accordingly. She will know with whom to confide the education of her children, and how to judge of their progress and the methods used to improve them. From books, from conversation, from learned instructors, she will gather the flower of every science; and her mind, in assimilating every thing to itself, will adorn it with new graces. She will give the tone to the conversation even when she chooses to bear but an inconsiderable part in it. The modesty which prevents her from an unnecessary display of what she knows, will cause it to be supposed that her knowledge is deeper than in reality it is:—as when the landscape is seen through the veil of a mist, the bounds of the horizon are hid. As she will never obtrude her knowledge, none will ever be sensible of any deficiency in it, and her silence will seem to proceed from discretion rather than a want of information. She will seem to know every thing by leading every one to speak of what he knows; and when she is with those to whom she can give no real information, she will yet delight them by the original turns of thought and sprightly elegance which will attend her manner of speaking on any subject. Such is the character to whom profest scholars will delight to give information, from whom others will equally delight to receive it:—the character I wish you to become, and to form which your application must be directed.

On Expense

A Dialogue

This dialogue may be conjecturally dated between 1800 (the year when the panorama depicting the capture of Seringapatam went on view) and July 1805, when Barbauld read William Roscoe's four-volume *History of the Life and Pontificate of Leo X*, in which Pope Leo X is defended from the charge of gluttony quoted against him in Pierre Bayle's *Encyclopédie*. Barbauld has a character repeat the charge, which she probably would not have done had she read Roscoe's defence. As no holograph manuscript is known to have survived, our copy text of 'On Expense' is from the first edition of *Legacy for Young Ladies* (pp. 253–65).

You seem to be in a reverie, Harriet; or are you tired with your long bustling walk through the streets of London?

Not at all, papa; but I was wondering at something.

A grown person even cannot walk through such a metropolis without meeting with many things to wonder at. But let us hear the particular subject of your admiration;—was it the height and circumference of St. Paul's, or the automatons, or the magical effect of the Panorama that has most struck you?[198]

No, papa; but I was wondering how you who have always so much money in your pockets can go through the streets of London, all full of fine shops, and not buy things: I am sure if I had money I could not help spending it all.

As you never have a great deal of money, and it is given you only to please your fancy with, there is no harm in your spending it in any thing you have a mind to; but it is very well for you and me too that the money does not *burn* in my pocket as it does in yours.

No, to be sure you would not spend all your money in those shops, because you must buy bread and meat, but you might spend a good deal. But you walk past just as if you did not see them: you never stop to give one look. Now tell me really, papa, can you help *wishing* for all those pretty things that stand in the shop-windows?

For all! Would you have me wish for all of them? But I will answer you seriously. I do walk by these tempting shops without wishing for any thing, and indeed in general without seeing them.

Well, that is because you are a man, and you do not care for what I admire so very much.

No, there you are mistaken; for though I may not admire them so very much as you say you do, there are a vast number of things sold in London which it would give me great pleasure to have in my possession. I should greatly like one of Dollond's best reflecting telescopes. I could lay out a great deal of money, if I had it to spare, in books of botany and natural history.[199] Nay, I assure you I should by no means be indifferent to the fine fruit exposed at the fruit-shops; the plums with the blue upon them as if they were just taken from the tree, the luscious hot-house grapes, and the melons and pineapples. Believe me, I could eat these things with as good a relish as you could.

Then how can you help buying them, when you have money; and especially, papa, how can you help thinking about them and wishing for them?

London is the best place in the world to cure a person of extravagance, and even of extravagant wishes. I see so many costly things here which I know I could not buy, even if I were to lay out all the money I have in the world, that I never think of buying any thing which I do not really want.

Our furniture, you know, is old and plain. Perhaps if there were only a little better furniture to be had, I might be tempted to change it; but when I see houses where a whole fortune is laid out in decorating a set of apartments, I am content with chairs whose only use is to sit down upon, and tables that were in fashion half a century ago. In short, I have formed the habit of *self-government*, one of the most useful powers a man can be possessed of. Self-government belongs only to civilized man,—a savage has no idea of it. A North-American Indian is temperate when he has no liquor; but as soon as liquor is within his reach, he invariably drinks till he is first furious and then insensible.[200] He possesses no power over himself, and he literally can no more help it, than iron can help being drawn by the loadstone.

But he seldom gets liquor, so he has not a habit of drinking.

You are right; he has not the habit of drinking, but he wants the habit of self-control: this can only be gained by being often in the midst of temptations, and resisting them. This is the wholesome discipline of the mind. The first time a man denies himself any thing he likes and which it is in his power to procure, there is a great struggle within him, and uneasy wishes will disturb for some time the tranquillity of his mind. He has gained the victory, but the enemy dies hard. The next time he does not wish so much, but he still thinks about it. After a while he does not think of it; he does not even see it. A person of moderate fortune, like myself, who lives in a gay and splendid metropolis, is accustomed to see every day a hundred things which it would be madness to think of buying.

Yes; but if you were very rich, papa—if you were a lord?

No man is so rich as to buy every thing his unrestrained fancy might prompt him to desire. Hounds and horses, pictures and statues and buildings, will exhaust any fortune. There is hardly any one taste so simple or innocent, but what a man might spend his whole estate in it, if he were resolved to gratify it to the utmost. A nobleman may just as easily ruin himself by extravagance as a private man, and indeed many do so.

But if you were a king?

If I were a king, the mischief would be much greater; for I should ruin not only myself, but my subjects.

A king could not hurt his subjects, however, with buying toys or things to eat.

Indeed but he might. What is a diamond but a mere toy? but a large diamond is an object of princely expense. That called the Pitt diamond was valued at 1,000,000*l*. It was offered to George the Second, but he wisely thought it too dear.[201] The dress of the late queen of France was thought by the prudent Necker a serious object of expense in the revenues of that large kingdom;[202] and her extravagance and that of the king's brothers had a great share in bringing on the calamities of the kingdom. As to eating, you could gratify yourself with laying out a shilling or two at the pastry-cook's: but Prince Potemkin, who had the revenues of the mighty empire of Russia at command, could not please his appetite without his dish of sterlet soup, which cost every time it was made above thirty pounds; and he would send one of his aids-de-camp an errand from Yassy to Petersburg, a distance of nearly 700 miles, to fetch him a tureen of it. He once bought all the cherries of a tree in a green-house at about half-a-crown a piece.[203] The Roman empire was far richer than the Russian, and in the time of the Emperors was all under the power of one man. Yet when they had such gluttons as Vitellius and Heliogabalus, the revenue of whole provinces was hardly sufficient to give them a dinner: they had tongues of nightingales, and such kind of dishes, the value of which was merely in the expense.[204]

I think the throat of the poor little nightingales might have given them much more pleasure than the tongue.

True: but the proverb says, The belly has no ears.[205] In modern Rome, Pope Adrian, a frugal Dutchman, complained of the expense his predecessor Leo X. was at in peacock sausages.[206] The expenses of Louis XIV. were of a more elegant kind;—he was fond of fine tapestry, mirrors, gardens, statues, magnificent palaces. These tastes were becoming in a great king, and would have been serviceable to his kingdom if kept within proper limits: but he could not deny himself any thing, however extravagant, that it came into his mind to wish for; and indeed would have imagined it beneath him to think at all about the expense: and therefore while he was throwing up water fifty feet high at his palaces of Versailles and Marli, and spouting it out of the mouths of dolphins and tritons, thousands of his people in the distant provinces were wanting bread.

I am sure I would not have done so to please my fancy.

Nor he neither perhaps, if he had seen them; but these poor men and their families were a great way off, and all the people about him looked pleased and happy, and said he was the most generous prince the world had ever seen.

Well, but if I had Aladdin's lamp I might have every thing I wished for.

I am glad at least I have driven you to fairyland. You might no doubt with the lamp of Aladdin, or Fortunatus's purse, have everything you wished for;[207] but do you know what the consequence would be?

Very pleasant, I should think.

On the contrary; you would become whimsical and capricious, and would soon grow tired of every thing. We do not receive pleasure long from any thing that is not bought with our own labour: this is one of those permanent laws of nature which man cannot change; and therefore pleasure and exertion will never be separated even in imagination in a well-regulated mind. I could tell you of a couple who received more true enjoyment of their fortune than Aladdin himself.

Pray do.

The couple I am thinking of lived about a century ago in one of our rich trading towns, which was just then beginning to rise by manufacturing tapes and inkle.[208] They had married because they loved one another; they had very little to begin with, but they were not afraid, because they were industrious. When the husband had come to be the richest merchant in the place, he took great pleasure in talking over his small beginnings; but he used always to add, that poor as he was when he married, he would not have taken a thousand pounds for the table his dame and he ate their dinner from.

What! had he so costly a table before he was grown rich?

On the contrary, he had no table at all; and his wife and he used to sit close together, and place their dish of pottage upon their knees;—their knees were the table. They soon got forward in the world, as industrious people generally do, and were enabled to purchase one thing after another: first perhaps a deal table; after a while a mahogany one; then a sumptuous sideboard. At first they sat on wooden benches; then they had two or three rush-bottomed chairs; and when they were rich enough to have an armchair for the husband, and another for a friend, to smoke their pipes in, how magnificent they would think themselves! At first they would treat a neighbour with a slice of bread and cheese and a draught of beer; by degrees with a good joint and a pudding; and at length with all the delicacies of a fashionable entertainment: and all along they would be able to say, "The blessing of God upon our own industry has procured us these things." By this means they would relish every gradation and increase of their enjoyments: whereas the man born to a fortune swallows his pleasures *whole*, he does not *taste* them. Another inconvenience that attends the man who is born rich is, that he has not early learned to deny himself. If I were a nobleman, though I could not buy every thing I might fancy for myself, yet playthings for you would not easily ruin me, and you would probably have a great deal of pocket-money; and you would grow up with a confirmed habit of expense and no ingenuity, for you would never try to make any thing, or to find out some substitute if you could not get just the thing you wanted. That is a very fine cabinet of shells which the young heiress showed you the other day: it is perfectly arranged and mounted with the utmost elegance and yet I am sure she has not half the pleasure in it, which you have had with those little drawers of shells of your own collecting, aided by the occasional contributions of friends, which you have arranged for yourself and display with such triumph. And now, to show you that I do sometimes think of the pleasures of my dear girl, here is a plaything for you which I bought while you were chatting at the door of a shop with one of your young friends.

A magic-lantern![209]—how delightful! O, thank you, papa! Edward, come and look at my charming magic-lantern.

The End

On Riddles

'On Riddles' appears to be a letter Barbauld sent or gave to 'young friends' home from school for the Christmas season. It might be dated 1811, because Barbauld sent a copy of one of the riddles to a Mrs. Smith on 12 December 1811. However, Barbauld tells her readers that the riddles 'will be new' to them, and one of the riddles had been published in 1801, suggesting perhaps an earlier date. Knowledge of her readers' identity could help to date the piece.[3] 'On Riddles' was first published in *Legacy for Young Ladies*.[4] The second edition transferred a fifth riddle, the poem 'An unfortunate maid', to the end of 'On Riddles'. The four riddles that close the essay in the first edition of *Legacy* circulated independently.[5] Riddle II ('Ye youths and ye virgins') exists in a Barbauld holograph appended to her letter to a Mrs. Smith, of Tetbury, postmarked 12 December 1811 (Hyde Collection, Houghton Library, Harvard). Riddle III ('I never talk') is probably not by Barbauld.[6] Riddle IV ('We are spirits') also exists in Barbauld's holograph, a variant text titled 'Riddle' on an undated, trimmed leaf showing only a partial watermark (Harry Ransom Research Center, University of Texas). This text varies

---

[3] The number of siblings suggests that the recipients may have been the Carr family of Hampstead, whose eldest child, Sarah, was born in 1794, and youngest in 1804; that could date the piece to around 1810, when the youngest Carr turned 6. Or, if the essay dates to 1811, it could have been written for a Stoke Newington family, the Rivazes, with whom Barbauld was close and to whom she presented an 'Enigma' early in 1811.

[4] An abridged text (from 'Finding out riddles' through 'ashamed of reading them') was reprinted in *The Fashionable Puzzler; or, Book of Riddles...Selected by an American Lady. With Remarks on Riddles, By the late Mrs. Barbauld* (New York, 1835), pp. [vii]–viii.

[5] In *PALB* they are Poems 153–6. Riddle I ('I often murmur', Poem 153) was published in the *Monthly Visitor*, 14 (July 1801): 262, attributed to Barbauld, as the first of several 'Enigmas &c. for Solution'; the variants suggest that the *Monthly Visitor* text derived from a circulating copy. A copy of Riddle II at the Beinecke Library (Osborn Poetry Box V/71) bears a note by the unidentified copyist: 'This Riddle sent by Mrs Barbauld to Mrs Smith accompanied by a letter, in consequence of the latter having expressed the wish to have something of her's in her own handwriting.' Another text, whether from *Legacy* or from another manuscript copy is not known, appears in Emily Taylor's *Memories of some Contemporary Poets* (1868), 15–16. Le Breton appears to have reprinted Riddle IV (pp. 217–18, titled 'Enigma') from *Legacy*.

[6] See 'Rejected Attributions' in Volume 1.

from the *Legacy* text, and varies also from the earliest published text, in Maria Edgeworth, *Harry and Lucy Concluded; being the Last Part of Early Lessons* (1825), 3:208–9, published presumably from a copy Barbauld sent to Edgeworth in 1823 (see Le Breton 1874, p. 184).

Our copy text for the essay and Riddles I–III are from *Legacy for Young Ladies* (pp. 26–32) with variants for Riddle II from the Hyde holograph. For Riddle IV the copy text is the holograph manuscript emended by verbal changes in Edgeworth (*HLC*) and *Legacy* that appear to be revisions.

My Dear Young Friends,

I presume you are now all come home for the holidays, and that the brothers and sisters and cousins, papas and mammas, uncles and aunts, are all met cheerfully round a Christmas fire, enjoying the company of their friends and relations, and eating plum pudding and mince pie. These are very good things; but one cannot always be eating plum pudding and mince pie: the days are short, and the weather bad, so that you cannot be much abroad; and I think you must want something to amuse you. Besides, if you have been employed as you ought to be at school, and if you are quick and clever, as I hope you are, you will want some employment for that part of you which thinks, as well as that part of you which eats; and you will like better to solve a riddle than to crack a nut or a walnut. Finding out riddles is the same kind of exercise to the mind which running and leaping and wrestling in sport are to the body. They are of no use in themselves,—they are not work, but play; but they prepare the body, and make it alert and active for any thing it may be called to perform in labour or war. So does the finding out of riddles, if they are good especially, give quickness of thought, and a facility of turning about a problem every way, and viewing it in every possible light. When Archimedes coming out of the bath cried in transport, "*Eureka!*" (I have found it!) he had been exercising his mind precisely in the same manner as you will do when you are searching about for the solution of a riddle.[210]

And pray, when you are got together, do not let any little Miss or Master say, with an affected air, "O! do not ask me; I am so stupid I never can guess." They do not mean you should think them stupid and dull; they mean to imply that these things are too trifling to engage their attention. If they are employed better, it is very well; but if not, say, "I am very sorry indeed you are so dull, but we that are clever and quick will exercise our wits upon these; and as our arms grow stronger by exercise, so will our wits."

Riddles are of high antiquity, and were the employment of grave men formerly. The first riddle that we have on record was proposed by Sampson at a wedding feast to the young men of the Philistines, who were invited upon the occasion. The feast lasted seven days; and if they found it out within the seven days, Sampson was to give them thirty suits of clothes and thirty sheets; and if they could not guess it, they were to forfeit the same to him. The riddle was; "Out of the eater came forth meat, and out of the strong came forth sweetness." He had killed a lion, and left its carcase: on returning soon after, he found a swarm of bees had made use of the skeleton as a hive, and it was full of honeycomb. Struck with the oddness of the circumstance, he made a riddle of it. They puzzled about it the whole seven days, and would not have found it out at last if his wife had not told them.[211]

The Sphinx was a great riddle-maker. According to the fable, she was half a woman and half a lion. She lived near Thebes, and to every body that came she proposed a riddle; and if they did not find it out, she devoured them. At length Œdipus came, and she asked him, "What is that animal which walks on four legs in the morning, two at noon, and three at night?" Œdipus answered, Man:—in childhood, which is the morning of life, he crawls on his hands and feet; in middle age, which is noon, he walks erect on two; in old age he leans on a crutch, which serves for a supplementary third foot.[212]

The famous wise men of Greece did not disdain to send puzzles to each other. They are also fond of riddles in the East. There is a pretty one in some of their tales.—"What is that tree which has twelve branches, and each branch thirty leaves, which are all black on one side and white on the other?"—The tree is the year; the branches the months; the leaves black on one side and white on the other signify day and night.[213] Our Anglo-Saxon ancestors also had riddles, some of which are still preserved in a very ancient manuscript.[214]

A riddle is a description of a thing without the name: but as it is meant to puzzle, it appears to belong to something else than what it really does, and often seems contradictory; but when you have guessed it, it appears quite clear. It is a bad riddle if you are at all in doubt when you have found it out whether you are right or no. A riddle is not verbal, as charades, conundrums, and rebuses are: it may be translated into any language, which the others cannot. Addison would put them all in the class of false wit: but Swift, who was as great a genius, amused himself with making all sorts of puzzles;[215] and therefore I think you need not be ashamed of reading them. It would be pretty entertainment for you to make a collection of the better ones,—for many are so dull that they are not worth spending time about. I will conclude by sending you a few which will be new to you.

I

    I often murmur, yet I never weep;
    I always lie in bed, yet never sleep;
    My mouth is wide, and larger than my head,
    And much disgorges though it ne'er is fed;
    I have no legs or feet, yet swiftly run,   5
    And the more falls I get, move faster on.

II

Ye youths and ye virgins, come list to my tale,
With youth and with beauty my voice will prevail.
My smile is enchanting, and golden my hair,
And on earth I am fairest of all that is fair;   10
But my name it perhaps may assist you to tell,
That I'm banish'd alike both from heaven and hell.
There's a charm in my voice, 'tis than music more sweet,
And my tale oft repeated, untired I repeat.
I flatter, I soothe, I speak kindly to all,   15
And wherever you go, I am still within call.
Tho' I thousands have blest, 'tis a strange thing to say,
That not one of the thousands e'er wishes my stay,
But when most I enchant him, impatient the more,
The minutes seem hours till my visit is o'er.   20
In the chase of my love I am ever employ'd,
Still, still he's pursued, and yet never enjoy'd;
O'er hills and o'er valleys unwearied I fly,
But should I o'ertake him, that instant I die;
Yet I spring up again, and again I pursue,   25
The object still distant, the passion still new.
Now guess,—and to raise your astonishment most,
While you seek me you have me, when found I am lost.

III

    I never talk but in my sleep;
    I never cry, but sometimes weep;   30
    My doors are open day and night;

Substantive Variants
1 yet] though *Monthly Visitor*
6 get] have *Monthly Visitor* / faster] swifter *Monthly Visitor*
18 That] Hyde] There's *Legacy for Young Ladies*

Old age I help to better sight;
I, like camelion, feed on air,
And dust to me is dainty fare.

IV

We are spirits all in white, 35
On a field as black as night;
There we dance and sport and play,
Changing every changing day.
Yet with us is wisdom found,
As we move in mystic round. 40
Mortal! wouldst thou count the grains
That Ceres heaps on Lybian plains,
Or leaves that sallow Autumn strews,
Or the stars that Herschel views,
Or find how many drops would drain 45
The wide-scooped bosom of the main,
Or measure central depths below,
Ask of us and thou shalt know.
With fairy feet we compass round
The pyramid's capacious mound, 50
And step by step ambitious climb
The cloud-capt mountain's height sublime;
Riches, tho we do not use,
Tis ours to gain, and ours to lose.
From Araby the blest we came, 55
In every land our tongue's the same;
And if our number you require,
Go count the bright Aonian quire.
Would'st thou cast a spell to find
The track of light, the speed of wind? 60
Or, when the snail, with creeping pace,
Shall the swelling globe embrace?
Mortal! ours the potent spell,
Ask of us, for we can tell.

---

40 in] *HLC, Legacy for Young Ladies*] our *MS*
41 count] know *HLC, Legacy for Young Ladies*
42 Lybian] Lybya's *Legacy for Young Ladies*
43 sallow] yellow *HLC, Legacy for Young Ladies*
50 mound] bound *Legacy for Young Ladies*   51 And] Or *HLC, Legacy for Young Ladies*
57 require] *HLC, Legacy for Young Ladies*] enquire *MS*
63 potent] powerful *HLC, Legacy for Young Ladies*

Letter of a Young King

The 'Young King' is the New Year, and he tells us his predecessor died 'last night precisely at twelve o'clock'. May Hill, mentioned in the text, lies near the village of Longhope, between Gloucester and Ross-on-Wye; the Barbauld friends who lived near enough to appreciate the reference were the Estlins, who lived in Bristol. They visited her in Stoke Newington at New Year's 1814; she thanked them for their visit on 6 January (ALB to Mrs. Estlin, MS, Fales Library, New York University). This allegorical piece might plausibly be dated to that visit. The date is further supported by reference to the onset of frost and fog (see note below). Our copy text is *A Legacy for Young Ladies* (pp. 95–102).[7]

Madam,

Amidst the mutual compliments and kind wishes which are universally circulated at this season, I hope mine will not be the least acceptable; and I have thought proper to give you this early assurance of my kind intentions towards you, and the benefits I have in store for you: for though I am appointed your sovereign; though your fates and fortune, your life and death, are at my disposal; yet I am fully sensible that I was created for my subjects, not my subjects for me; and that the end of my very existence is to diffuse blessings on my people.

My predecessor departed this life last night precisely at twelve o'clock. He died of a universal decay; nature was exhausted in him, and there was not vital heat sufficient to carry on the functions of life; his hair was fallen, and discovered his smooth, white, bald head; his voice was hoarse and broken, and his blood froze in his veins: in short, his time was come. And to say truth he will not be much regretted; for of late he had been gloomy and vapourish, and the sudden gusts of passion he had long been subject to were worked up into such storms it was impossible to live under him with comfort.[216]

With regard to myself, I am sensible the joy expressed at my accession is sincere, and that no young monarch has ever been welcomed with warmer demonstrations of affection. Some have ardently longed for my coming, and all view my approach with pleasure and cheerfulness; yet such is the uncertainty of popular favour, that I well know that those who are most eager and sanguine in expressing their joy will soonest be tired of my company. You yourself, madam, though I know that at present you regard me with kindness, as one from whom you expect more happiness than you have yet enjoyed, will probably after a short time wish as much to part with me, and transfer the same fond hopes and wishes to my successor. But

[7] Reprinted in the *Eclectic Review*, ns 25 (1826): 83–5.

though your impatience may make me a very troublesome companion, it will not in the least hasten my departure; nor can all the powers of earth oblige me to resign a moment before my time. In order, therefore, that you may form proper expectations concerning me, I shall give you a little sketch of my temper and manners, and I will acknowledge that my aspect at present is somewhat stern and rough; but there is a latent warmth in my temper which you will perceive as we grow better acquainted, and I shall every day put on a milder and more smiling look: indeed I have so much fire, that I may chance sometimes to make the house too hot for you; but in recompense for this inequality of temper I am kind and bountiful as a giving God: I come full-handed, and my very business is to dispense blessings;—blessings of the basket and the store; blessings of the field and of the vineyard; blessings for time and for eternity. There is not an inhabitant of the globe who will not experience my bounty; yet such is the ingratitude of mankind, that there is scarcely one whom I shall not leave in some degree discontented.

Whimsical and various are the petitions which are daily put up to me from all parts; and very few of the petitioners will be satisfied; because they reject and despise the gifts I offer them with open hand, and set their minds on others which certainly will not fall to their share. Celia has begged me on her knees to find her a lover: I shall do what I can; I shall bring her the most magnificent shawl that has appeared in Europe. For Dorinda, who has made the same petition, I have two gifts,—wisdom and grey hairs; the former I know she will reject, nor can I force her to wear it; but the grey hairs I shall leave on her toilette whether she will or no. The curate Sophron expects I shall bring him a living: I shall present him with twins as round and rosy as an apple.[217] Nor can I listen to the entreaty of Dorimant, whose good father being a little asthmatic, he has desired me to push him into his grave as we walk up May hill together: but I shall marry him to a handsome lively girl, who will make a very pretty stepmother to the young gentleman.[218] It is in vain for poor Sylvia to weary me as she does with prayers to restore to her her faithless lover: but I shall give her the choice of two, to replace him. Codrus[219] has asked me if he may bespeak a suit of black: but I can tell him his little wife will outlive me and him too: I have offered the old man a double portion of patience, which he has thrown away very pettishly. Strephon has entreated me to take him to Scotland with his mistress: I shall do it; and he will hate my very name all his life after.[220]

The wishes of some are very moderate;—Fanny begs two inches of height, and Chloe that I would take away her awkward plumpness; Carus a new equipage, and Philida a new ball-dress. A mother brought me her son the other day, made me many compliments, and desired me to teach him every thing; at the same time begging the youth to throw away his marbles, which he had often promised to part with as soon as he saw me:—but the boy held them fast, and I shall teach him nothing but to play at taw.[221] Many ladies have come to me with their daughters in their hands, telling me they hope their girls, under me, will learn prudence: but the young ladies have as constantly desired me to teach prudence to their grandmothers, whom it would better become, and to bring them new dances and new fashions. In short, I have scarcely seen any one with whom I am likely entirely to agree, but a stout old farmer who rents a small cottage on the green. He was leaning on his spade when I approached him. As his neighbour told him I was coming, he welcomed me with a cheerful countenance; but at the same time bluntly told me he had not expected me so soon, being too busy to pay much attention to my approach. I asked him if I could do any thing for him. He said he did not believe me better or worse than those who had preceded me, and therefore should not expect much from me; that he was happy before he saw me, and should be very well contented after I left him: he was glad to see me, however, and only begged I would not take his wife from him, a thin withered old woman who was eating a mess of milk at the door. "And I shall be glad too," said he, "if you will fill my cellar with potatoes." As he applied himself to his spade while he said these words, I shall certainly grant his request.

I shall now tell you, that great and extensive as my power is, I shall possess it but a short time. However the predictions of astrologers are now laughed at, nothing is more certain than what I am going to tell you. A scheme of my nativity has been cast by the most eminent astronomers, who have found, on consulting the stars and the aspect of the heavenly bodies, that Capricornus will be fatal to me: I know that all the physicians in the world cannot protract my life beyond that fatal period. I do not tell you this to excite your sensibility,—for I would have you meet me without fondness and part with me without regret; but to quicken you to lay hold on those advantages I am able to procure you; for it will be your own fault if you are not both wiser and better for my company. I have likewise another request to make to you,—that you will write my epitaph: I may make you happy, but it depends on you to make me famous. If, after I am departed, you can say my reign was distinguished by good actions and wise conversations, and that I have left you happier than I found you, I shall not have lived in vain. My sincere wishes are, that you may long outlive me, but always remember me with pleasure. I am, if you use me well,

> Your friend and servant,
> The New Year.

Knowledge and Her Daughter

A Fable

Lucy Aikin published this piece in *Works*, 2:350–51, which is our copy text. As a fable, it might have been written for Palgrave School. Its occasion, date, and addressee, if any, are unknown.

Knowledge, the daughter of Jupiter, descended from the skies to visit man. She found him naked and helpless, living on the spontaneous fruits of the earth, and little superior to the ox that grazed beside him. She clothed and fed him; she built him palaces; she showed him the hidden riches of the earth, and pointed with her finger the course of the stars as they rose and set in the horizon. Man became rich with her gifts, and accomplished from her conversation. In process of time Knowledge became acquainted with the schools of the philosophers; and being much taken with their theories and their conversation, she married one of them. They had many beautiful and healthy children; but among the rest was a daughter of a different complexion from all the rest, whose name was Doubt. She grew up under many disadvantages; she had a great hesitation in her speech; a cast in her eye, which, however, was keen and piercing; and was subject to nervous tremblings. Her mother saw her with dislike: but her father, who was of the sect of the Pyrrhonists,[222] cherished and taught her logic, in which she made a great progress. The Muse of History was much troubled with her intrusions: she would tear out whole leaves, and blot over many pages of her favourite works. With the divines her depredations were still worse: she was forbidden to enter a church; notwithstanding which, she would slip in under the surplice, and spend her time in making mouths at the priest. If she got at a library, she destroyed or blotted over the most valuable manuscripts. A most undutiful child; she was never better pleased than when she could unexpectedly trip up her mother's heels, or expose a rent or an unseemly patch in her flowing and ample garment. With mathematicians she never meddled; but in all other systems of knowledge she intruded herself, and her breath diffused a mist over the page which often left it scarcely legible. Her mother at length said to her, "Thou art my child, and I know it is decreed that while I tread this earth thou must accompany my footsteps; but thou art mortal, I am immortal; and there will come a time when I shall be freed from thy intrusion, and shall pursue my glorious track from star to star, and from system to system, without impediment and without check."

A Lecture on the Use of Words

The use, or misuse, of words that this dialogue addresses is the imprecise use of 'excessively' by stylish young women in the late eighteenth and early nineteenth centuries. Barbauld may be nodding to Frances Burney's novel *Cecilia* (1782), which she loved. In that work, Lady Honoria declares: 'I am always excessively rejoiced' and 'I shall be excessively happy'; she describes her father, when he is angry, as looking 'so excessively hideous'.[8] Similarly, Jane Austen pokes fun at imprecise language in her parody of the Gothic novel, *Northanger Abbey* (wr. 1798 or 1799; pub. 1816). Henry Tilney teases Catherine Morley on her use of language, when she asks 'do not you think Udolpho the nicest book in the world?' He replies, 'The nicest;—by which I suppose you mean the neatest. That must depend upon the binding.' Eleanor, his sister, explains, 'The word "nicest," as you used it, did not suit him; and you had better change it as soon as you can, or we shall be overpowered with Johnson and Blair all the rest of the way.'[9] Copy text: *A Legacy for Young Ladies*, pp. 17–22.

My dear mamma, who worked you this scarf? it is excessively pretty.

I am sorry for it, my dear.

Sorry, mamma! are you sorry it is pretty?

No, but I am sorry if it is *excessively* pretty.

Why so?—a thing cannot be too pretty, can it?

If so, it cannot be excessively pretty. Pray what do you mean by excessively pretty?

Why excessively pretty means—it means very pretty.

What does the word excessively come from? What part of speech is it? You know your grammar?

It is an adverb: the words that end in *ly* are adverbs.

Adverbs are derived from adjectives by adding *ly*, you should have said;—excessive, excessively. And what is the noun from which they are both derived?

Excess.

And what does excess mean?

It means too much of any thing.

You see then that it implies a fault, and therefore cannot be applied as a commendation. We say a man is excessively greedy, excessively liberal; a woman excessively fine: but not that a man is excessively wise, a woman excessively faithful to her husband; because in these there is no excess: nor is there in beauty, that being the true and just proportion which gives pleasure.

---

[8] 1796 edition, 3:167, 277, 237.

[9] Austen, Jane. Cambridge Edition of the *Works of Jane Austen, Northanger Abbey*, Cambridge University Press, 2006, 109.

But we say excessively kind.

We do, because kindness has its limits. A person may be too kind to us, who exposes himself to a great and serious inconvenience to give us a slight pleasure: we also may mean by it exceeding that kindness which we have a claim to expect. But when people use it, as they often do, on the slightest occasion, it is certainly as wrong as excessively pretty.

But, mamma, must we always consider so much the exact meaning of words? Every body says excessively pretty, and excessively tall, and infinitely obliged to you.—What harm can it do?

That every body does it I deny; that the generality do it is very true; but it is likewise true, that the generality are not to be taken as a pattern in any thing. As to the harm it does,—in the first place it hurts our sincerity.

Why, it is not telling a lie sure?

Certainly I do not mean to say it is; but it tends to sap and undermine the foundations of our integrity, by making us careless, if not in the facts we assert, yet in the measure and degree in which we assert them. If we do not pretend to love those we have no affection for, or to admire those we despise, at least we lead them to think we admire them more and love them better than we really do; and this prepares the way for more serious deviations from truth. So much for its concern with morality:—but it has likewise a very bad effect on our taste. What, think you, is the reason that young people, especially, run into these vague and exaggerated expressions?

What is vague, mamma?

It means what has no precise, definite signification. Young people run into these, sometimes indeed from having more feeling than judgement, but more commonly from not knowing how to separate their ideas and tell what it is they are pleased with. They either do not know, or will not give themselves the trouble to mark, the qualities, or to describe the scenes which disgust or please them, and hope to cover their deficiency by these overwhelming expressions; as if your dress-maker, not knowing your shape, should make a large loose frock that would cover you over were you twice as tall as you are. Now you would have shown your taste if in commending my scarf you had said that the pattern was light, or it was rich, or that the work was neat and true; but by saying it was excessively pretty, you showed you had not considered what it was you admired in it. Did you never hear of the countryman who said "there will be monstrous few apples this year, and those few will be huge little."[223] Poets run into this fault when they give unmeaning epithets instead of appropriate description;—young ladies, when in their letters they run into exaggerated expressions of friendship.

You have often admired in this painting the variety of tints shaded into one another. Well! what would you think of a painter who should spread one deep blue over all the sky, and one deep green over the grass and trees? would not you say he was a dauber? and made near objects and distant objects, and objects in the sun and objects in the shade, all alike? I think I have some of your early performances in which you have coloured prints pretty much in this style; but you would not paint so now?

No, indeed.

Then do not talk so: do not paint so with words.

The Morning Repast

This description of breakfast defamiliarizes the ordinary by rendering it in the vocabulary of epic; the effect is similar to that of enigma. The occasion and date of the piece are unknown. Lucy Aikin published it in the first edition of *A Legacy for Young Ladies* (pp. 185–6), our copy text; it was dropped from the second edition, perhaps to save further repagination after the transfer of 'An unfortunate maid' to the essay 'On Riddles'.

When Apollo had left the bed of Thetis, and with his fiery horses was prancing up the eastern hills, we shook off the chains of Somnus, and having attired ourselves and performed the usual ablutions, descended into the hall of banquets. The table was covered with the finest looms of Ireland, and spread with a variety of cates well calculated to incite the lazy appetite.

Our nostrils were regaled by the grateful steams of the sun-burnt berry of Mocha, sent forth from vases formed of the precious metal of Potosi.[224] The repast was rendered more substantial by the gifts of Ceres and of Pales, and painted vessels of porcelain were filled with the infusion of the Indian leaf, rendered more grateful by the saccharine juices of the American cane, and crowned with rich streams pressed from the milky mother of the herd.

Our company then separated to pursue their various occupations.

On Friendship

Advice concerning 'the regulation of the heart and affections' (Hester Chapone's phrase, in *Letters on the Improvement of the Mind*) was a staple of conduct books addressed to young women, among which Chapone's *Letters* (1773) enjoyed pre-eminence. Barbauld knew Chapone, wrote the *Monthly Magazine*'s memoir of her after her death (1802), and regarded *Letters* with critical respect. In this essay or letter 'On Friendship' Barbauld agrees in general with Chapone's advice on the choice of friends, but tacitly dissents from many of her prescriptions: for example, that a young woman should choose her friends among women older and wiser than herself. Fundamentally, Barbauld resists the very idea of *choosing* a friend; to list, as Chapone does, principles on which a young woman should choose is to hyper-rationalize the life of the emotions. Our copy text is *Legacy for Young Ladies*, pp. 226–34.

Friendship is that warm, tender, lively attachment which takes place between persons in whom a similarity of tastes and manners, joined to frequent intercourse, has produced an habitual fondness for each other. It is not among our duties, for it does not flow from any of the necessary relations of society; but it has its duties when voluntarily entered into. In its highest perfection it can only, I believe, subsist between two; for that unlimited confidence and perfect conformity of inclinations which it requires, cannot well be found in a larger number: besides, one such friendship fills the heart, and leaves no want or desire after another.

Friendship, where it is quite sincere and affectionate, free from affectation or interested views, is one of the greatest blessings of life. It doubles our joys, and it lessens our sorrows, when we are able to pour both into the bosom of one who takes the tenderest part in all our interests, who is to us as another self. We love to communicate all our feelings; and it is in the highest degree grateful where we can do it to one who will enter into them all; who takes an interest in every thing that befalls us; before whom we can freely indulge even our little weaknesses and foibles, and show our minds as it were undrest; who will take part in all our schemes, advise us in any emergency; who rejoices in our company, and who, we are sure, thinks of us in our absence.

With regard to the choice of friends, there is little to say; for a friend was never chosen. A secret sympathy, the attraction of a thousand nameless qualities; a charm in the expression of the countenance, even in the voice, or the manner, a similarity of circumstances,—these are the things that begin attachment, which is fostered by being in a situation which gives occasion for frequent intercourse; and this depends upon chance. Reason and prudence have, however, much to do in restraining our choice of improper or dangerous friends. They are improper if our line of life and pursuits are so totally different as to make it improbable we shall long keep up an intimacy, at least without sacrificing to it connexions of duty; they are dangerous if they are in any respect vicious.

It has been made a question whether friendship can subsist amongst the vicious.[225] If by vicious be meant those who are void of the social, generous, and affectionate feelings, it is most certain it cannot; because these make the very essence of it. But it is very possible for persons to possess fine feelings, without that steady principle which alone constitutes virtue; and it does not appear why such may not feel a real friendship. It will not indeed be so likely to be lasting, and is often succeeded by bitter enmities.

The duties of friendship are, first, sincere and disinterested affection. This seems self-evident: and yet there are many who pretend to love their friends, when at the same time they only take delight in them, as we delight in a fine voice or a good picture. If you love your friend, you will love him when his powers of pleasing and entertaining you have given way to malady or depression of spirits; you will study *his* interest and satisfaction, you will be ready to resign his company, to promote his advantageous settlement at a distance residence, to favour his connexion with other friends;— these are the tests of true affection: without such a disposition, you may enjoy your friend, but you do not love him.

Next, friendship requires pure sincerity and the most unreserved confidence. Sincerity every man has a right to expect from us, but every man has not a right to our confidence: this is the sacred and peculiar privilege of friendship; and so essential is it to the very idea of this connexion, that even to serve a friend without giving him our confidence, is but going half way;—it may command gratitude, but will not produce love. Above all things, the general tenour of our thoughts and feelings must be shown to our friends exactly as they are; without any of those glosses, colourings, and disguises which we do, and partly must, put on in our commerce with the world.

Another duty resulting from this confidence is inviolable secrecy in what has been entrusted to us. To every one indeed we owe secrecy in what we are formally entrusted with; but with regard to a friend, this extends to the concealing every thing which in the fullness of his heart and in the freedom of unguarded conversation he has let drop, if you have the least idea it may in any manner injure or offend him. In short, you are to consider yourself as always, to him, under an implied promise of secrecy; and should even the friendship dissolve, it would be in the highest degree ungenerous to consider this obligation as dissolved with it.

In the next place, a friend has a right to our best advice on every emergency; and this, even though we run the risk of offending him by our frankness. Friends should consider themselves as the sacred guardians of each other's virtue; and the noblest testimony they can give of their affection is the correction of the faults of those they love. But this generous solicitude must be distinguished from a teazing, captious, or too officious notice of all the little defects and frailties which their close intercourse with each other brings continually into view: these must be overlooked or borne with; for as we are not perfect ourselves, we have no right to expect our friends should be so.

Friends are most easily acquired in youth, but they are likewise most easily lost: the petulance and impetuosity of that age, the eager competitions and rivalships of an active life, and more especially the various changes in rank and fortune, connexions, party, opinions, or local situation, burst asunder or silently untwist the far greater part of those friendships which, in the warmth of youthful attachment, we had fondly promised ourselves should be indissoluble.[226]

Happy is he to whom, in the maturer season of life, there remains one tried and constant friend: their affection, mellowed by the hand of time, endeared by the recollection of enjoyments, toils, and even sufferings shared together, becomes the balm, the consolation, and the treasure of life. Such a friendship is inestimable, and should be preserved with the utmost care; for it is utterly impossible for any art ever to transfer to another the effect of all those accumulated associations which endear to us the friend of our early years.[227]

These considerations should likewise induce us to show a tender indulgence to our friends, even for those faults which most sensibly wound the feeling heart,—a growing coldness and indifference. These may be brought on by many circumstances, which do not imply a bad heart; and provided we do not by bitter complaints and an open rupture preclude the possibility of a return, in a more favourable conjuncture the friendships of our youth may knit again, and be cultivated with more genuine tenderness than ever.

I must here take occasion to observe, that there is nothing young people ought to guard against with more care than a parade of feeling, and a profusion of exaggerated protestations. These may sometimes proceed from the amiable warmth of a youthful heart; but they much oftener flow from the affectation of sentiment, which is both contemptible and morally wrong.

All that has been said of the duties or of the pleasures of friendship in its most exalted sense, is applicable in a proportionate degree to every connexion in which there exists any portion of this generous affection: so far as it does exist in the various relations of life, so far it renders them interesting and valuable; and were the capacity for it taken away from the human heart, it would find a dreary void, and starve amidst all the means of enjoyment the world could pour out before it.

The Death-Bed

At Palgrave School Barbauld occasionally thought of writing plays, an interest she may have retained throughout her life. She envied Hannah More's success on the stage (ALB to JA, 19 Jan. 1778; *Works*, 2:18). This piece appears to be a fragment of a play, but its occasion and date are unknown. The *Eclectic Review* reprinted this piece in its review of *A Legacy for Young Ladies*, from which we take our copy text (pp. 239–40).

[A little Parlour with deal Floor[228]; a Bed with a clean Quilt, in which lies the Grandmother.]

I had more pain when I brought you into the world than now.

Shall I lay on more clothes?

Yes, on my feet.

Are they warmer?

No. When your father died was the greatest grief I ever knew. Well! we began life together, and lived hardly enough. I have often thought since, I could not do it again. But we loved one another. I am sure I could never have recovered his loss but for the care necessary to take for you: and one friend helped, and another friend, so I struggled through. Yet, my child, I would not live it again; the tired traveller would not measure back his steps.

If I were to live, I should grow worse and worse, deafer, and blind. I have read of a country where they keep their ancestors' mummies,—living mummies would be worse.

Your father's Bible,—your ages are all down in it,—never sell it.

I have loved you all equally.... And yet I am not sure.... Poor Tommy was so long sick, and would come to nobody but me....

Jenny, you may marry the shoemaker.—And now, if I could but see my poor naughty Emma!.....

You will save nothing by me but water-gruel and an egg or two,—care indeed, but that produces love.

You will not quarrel for my inheritance. The Squire,—it has gone to my heart when he has said, My old mother keeps me out of my estate.[229]—Let my ring be buried with me.

A Dialogue of the Dead, between Helen, and Madame Maintenon

In her 'Memoir' of Barbauld Lucy Aikin recounts that Barbauld 'early read, with great delight, though in an English translation, the Dialogues of Lucian' (LA, 'Memoir', lxix). Barbauld also read the Lucianic dialogues of Bernard le Bouvier de Fontenelle, a copy of whose *Entretiens sur la Pluralité des Mondes* (1686) she was given at age 7. In his *Dialogues of the Dead, Ancient and Modern* (English translation 1685), Fontenelle imitated Lucian in setting up witty dialogic encounters between famous ancients and famous moderns who could be paralleled, and who would then contest with each other whose life, customs, or experiences were better or worse. Barbauld's dialogue between Helen of Troy and the wife of Louis XIV compares two legends of female influence and concludes that neither makes for woman's happiness. Helen, wife of Greek king Menelaus, was the legendary cause of the Trojan War, subject of the *Iliad*. Françoise d'Aubigné, marquise de Maintenon, known as Madame de Maintenon (1635–1719), became the secret wife of King Louis XIV but was never officially acknowledged as Queen of France. Barbauld probably read about her in Book II of the *Memoirs* (1788) of the Duc de Saint-Simon, but Maintenon's letters had been published much earlier (1753).

Lucy Aikin published this dialogue without date in *A Legacy for Young Ladies*, our copy text (pp. 241–50).

Helen.—Whence comes it, my dear Madame Maintenon, that beauty, which in the age I lived in produced such extraordinary effects, has now lost almost all its power?

Maint.—I should wish first to be convinced of the fact, before I offer to give you a reason for it.

Helen.—That will be very easy; for there is no occasion to go any further than our own histories and experience to prove what I advance. You were beautiful, accomplished, and fortunate; endowed with every talent and every grace to bend the heart of man and mould it to your wish: and your schemes were successful; for you raised yourself from obscurity and dependence to be the wife of a great monarch.—But what is this to the influence my beauty had over sovereigns and nations! I occasioned a long ten years war between the most celebrated heroes of antiquity; contending kingdoms disputed the honour of placing me on their respective thrones; my story is recorded by the father of verse; and my charms make a figure even in the annals of mankind. You were, it is true, the wife of Louis XIV and respected in his court; but you occasioned no wars; you are not spoken of in the history of France, though you furnish materials for the memoirs of a court.[230] Are the love and admiration that were paid you merely as an amiable woman to be compared with the enthusiasm I inspired, and the boundless empire I obtained over all that was celebrated, great, or powerful in the age I lived in?

Maint.—All this, my dear Helen, has a splendid appearance, and sounds well in a heroic poem; but you greatly deceive yourself if you impute it all to your personal merit. Do you imagine that half the chiefs concerned in the war of Troy were at all influenced by your beauty, or troubled their heads what became of you, provided they came off with honour? Believe me, love had very little to do in the affair: Menelaus sought to revenge the affront he had received; Agamemnon was flattered with the supreme command; some came to share the glory, others the plunder; some because they had bad wives at home, some in hopes of getting Trojan mistresses abroad; and Homer thought the story extremely proper for the subject of the best poem in the world. Thus you became famous: your elopement was made a national quarrel; the animosities of both nations were kindled by frequent battles: and the object was not the restoring of Helen to Menelaus, but the destruction of Troy by the Greeks.—My triumphs, on the other hand, were all owing to myself, and to the influence of personal merit and charms over the heart of man. My birth was obscure, my fortunes low; I had past the bloom of youth, and was advancing to that period at which the generality of our sex lose all importance with the other; I had to do with a man of gallantry and intrigue, a monarch who had been long familiarized with beauty, and accustomed to every refinement of pleasure which the most splendid court in Europe could afford; Love and Beauty seemed to have exhausted all their powers of pleasing for him in vain: yet this man I captivated, I fixed; and far from being content, as other beauties had been, with the honour of possessing his heart, I brought him to make me his wife, and gained an honourable title to his tenderest affection.—The infatuation of Paris reflected little honour upon you. A thoughtless youth, gay, tender, and impressible, struck with your beauty, in violation of all the most sacred laws of hospitality carries you off, and obstinately refuses to restore you to your husband. You seduced Paris from his duty,—I recovered Louis from vice; you were the mistress of the Trojan prince, I was the companion of the French monarch.

Helen.—I grant you were the wife of Louis, but not the queen of France. Your great object was ambition, and in that you met with but a partial success:—my ruling star was love, and I gave up every thing for it. But tell me, did not I show my influence over Menelaus in his taking me again after the destruction of Troy?

Maint.—That circumstance alone is sufficient to show that he did not love you with any delicacy. He took you as a possession that was restored to him, as a booty that he had recovered; and he had not sentiment enough to care whether he had your heart or not. The heroes of your age were capable of admiring beauty, and often fought for the possession of it; but they had not refinement enough to be capable of any pure, sentimental attachment or delicate passion. Was that period the triumph of love and gallantry, when a fine woman and a tripod were placed together for prizes at a wrestling-bout, and the tripod esteemed the more valuable reward of the two?[231] No; it is our Clelia, our Cassandra, and Princess of Cleves that have polished mankind and taught them how to love.[232]

Helen.—Rather say you have lost sight of nature and the passion, between bombast on one hand and conceit on the other. Shall one of the cold temperament of France teach a Grecian how to love? Greece, the parent of fair forms and soft desires, the nurse of poetry, whose soft climate and tempered skies disposed to every gentler feeling, and tuned the heart to harmony and love!—was Greece a land of barbarians? But recollect, if you can, an incident which showed the power of beauty in stronger colours than when the grave old counsellors of Priam on my appearance were struck with fond admiration, and could not bring themselves to blame the cause of a war that had almost ruined their country:—you see I charmed the old as well as seduced the young.

Maint.—But I, after I was grown old, charmed the young; I was idolized in a capital where taste, luxury and magnificence were at the height; I was celebrated by the greatest wits of my time, and my letters have been carefully handed down to posterity.[233]

Helen.—Tell me now sincerely, were you happy in your elevated fortune?

Maint.—Alas! Heaven knows I was far otherwise: a thousand times did I wish for my dear Scarron[234] again. He was a very ugly fellow it is true, and had but little money; but the most easy, entertaining companion in the world: we danced, laughed and sung; I spoke without fear or anxiety, and was sure to please. With Louis all was gloom, constraint, and a painful solicitude to please—which seldom produces its effect: the king's temper had been soured in the latter part of life by frequent disappointments; and I was forced continually to endeavour to procure him that cheerfulness which I had not myself. Louis was accustomed to the most delicate flatteries; and though I had a good share of wit, my faculties were continually on the stretch to entertain him,—a state of mind little consistent with happiness or ease: I was afraid to advance my friends or punish my enemies. My pupils at St. Cyr[235] were not more secluded from the world in a cloister than I was in the bosom of the court; a secret disgust and weariness consumed me. I had no relief but in my work and books of devotion; with these alone I had a gleam of happiness.

Helen.—Alas! one need not have married a great monarch for that.

Maint.—But deign to inform me, Helen, if you were really as beautiful as fame reports? for to say truth, I cannot in your shade see the beauty which for nine long years had set the world in arms.

Helen.—Honestly, no; I was rather low, and something sunburnt: but I had the good fortune to please; that was all. I was greatly obliged to Homer.

Maint.—And did you live tolerably with Menelaus after all your adventures?

Helen.—As well as possible. Menelaus was a good-natured domestic man, and was glad to sit down and end his days in quiet. I persuaded him that Venus and the Fates were the cause of all my irregularities, which he complaisantly believed. Besides, I was not sorry to return home: for to tell you a secret, Paris had been unfaithful to me long before his death, and was fond of a little Trojan brunette whose office it was to hold up my train; but it was thought dishonourable to give me up. I began to think love a very foolish thing: I became a great housekeeper, worked the battles of Troy in tapestry, and spun with my maids by the side of Menelaus, who was so satisfied with my conduct, and behaved, good man, with so much fondness, that I verily think this was the happiest period of my life.

Maint.—Nothing more likely: but the most obscure wife in Greece could rival you there.—Adieu! you have convinced me how little fame and greatness conduce to happiness.

THE FEMALE SPEAKER;

OR,

MISCELLANEOUS PIECES,

IN

PROSE AND VERSE,

SELECTED FROM THE BEST WRITERS,

AND

ADAPTED TO THE USE OF YOUNG WOMEN.

BY

ANNA LÆTITIA BARBAULD.

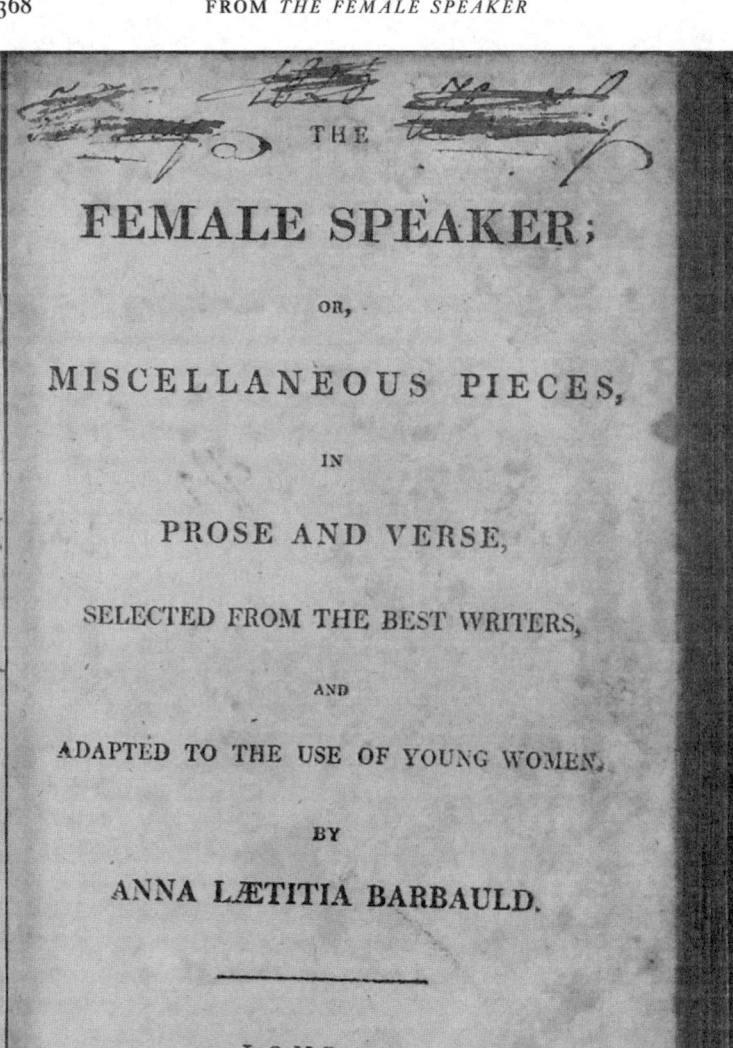

LONDON:
PRINTED FOR J. JOHNSON AND CO.,
ST. PAUL'S CHURCHYARD.
1811.

Fig. 14 Title-page of *The Female Speaker*, first edition (private collection).

FROM *THE FEMALE SPEAKER*

Introduction

In February 1811 Joseph Johnson's successor published *The Female Speaker; or, Miscellaneous Pieces, in Prose and Verse, Selected from the Best Writers, and Adapted to the Use of Young Women*, by Anna Lætitia Barbauld.[1] This genre had two precursors: *The Speaker* (1774) by Barbauld's friend William Enfield, and *The Female Reader* (1789) by Barbauld's acquaintance Mary Wollstonecraft (using the pseudonym 'M. Cresswick'). Enfield aimed to instruct young men who might one day speak in public. Although young women generally lacked the opportunity to speak in public, they could recite at home, in family and social gatherings, in Quaker houses of worship, and of course they could read, as Wollstonecraft's title asserted. Barbauld's title glanced at Enfield's and hence at speaking, but also at Wollstonecraft's and at women's intellectual cultivation. Like Enfield's and Wollstonecraft's, Barbauld's anthology consisted of selections from other writers arranged in rhetorical or generic categories; her original contributions to it were the Preface and a reprint of her poem 'An Address to the Deity'. A list of the writers from whom Barbauld selected, arranged under the headings and the titles her anthology used, follows the text of her 'Preface'. Our copy text is from the 1811 first edition (pp. iii–vi).

The contents of *The Female Speaker* were in part Barbauld's own choices and in part hereditary, included because Barbauld must have known them to be expected, even though in some instances (Fordyce, for example) she herself disliked them. It was conventional to give young people essays taken from periodicals such as the *Spectator*. (Barbauld edited a three-volume collection of that and other Addison-Steele series.) As the Edgeworths observed in *Practical Education*, 'these are books with which all libraries are furnished' (p. 341). The grouping of contents into numbered 'Books' with category headings was also customary.[2] The volume begins with 'Book I. Select Sentences' (pp. 1–15), composed of unattributed extracts of prose and verse, usually drawn from—or, in context, acting as—wisdom literature. Many are biblical, from Proverbs; verse passages come from Shakespeare, Pope, Young, Goldsmith, Cowper, Dryden, and others. One or more of the passages in prose may be hers, but none have been identified. 'Book II. Moral and Didactic Pieces' (pp. 16–100) includes, along with traditional choices from Dodsley, Fordyce, Gregory, Thomson, Swift, Pope, Cowper, Akenside, and

---

[1] A second London edition appeared in 1816, issued by Baldwin, Cradock, and Joy; R. Hunter, successor to Joseph Johnson; Longman, Hurst, Rees, Orme, and Brown; and Law and Whittaker. The Boston firm of Wells and Lilly also brought out an edition in 1824.

[2] For further discussion of Barbauld's choices see *ALBVE*, 500–2.

others, selections from Hannah More, Hester Chapone, Catharine Talbot, John Aikin, and Barbauld's own 'Address to the Deity'. 'Book III. Narrative Pieces' (pp. 101–202) selects passages from Benjamin Franklin, Addison, Johnson, Maria Edgeworth, and Swift, among others. 'Book IV. Descriptive and Pathetic' (pp. 203–304) includes extracts from works as diverse as Gibbon's *Decline and Fall of the Roman Empire*, Buffon's *Natural History*, Goldsmith's *Animated Nature*, Ovid's *Metamorphoses*, Spenser's *Faerie Queene*, Darwin's *The Botanic Garden*, and Lucy Aikin's *Epistles on Women*, among others. 'Book V. Dialogues' (pp. 305–71) has selections from Milton's *Comus* and various Shakespeare plays, along with John Gay's *The Shepherd's Week*, Sheridan's *The Rivals*, Otway's *Venice Preserv'd*, and others. The last book, 'Epistles' (pp. 372–421) includes excerpts of letters by, among others, Cowper, Gray, and Montagu.

Preface of the Editor

The following Selection, intended for the use of young females, belongs to the class of those useful and unpretending publications, which industry, joined to some degree of taste, may always supply, and for which the routine of education, particularly in schools, will always create a demand. It is impossible to supply the pupils of a school with any great variety of original authors, and yet it is very desirable, that they should be early introduced to a number of the best authors at least in their own language. When the sources are opened to them, they may take fuller draughts at their leisure. A taste for fine writing cannot be cultivated too early; and the surest mode of cultivating it is by reading much at that period of life, when what is read is indelibly impressed upon the memory, and by reading nothing, which does not deserve to be so impressed. How strongly are moral sentiments or descriptions of nature fixed upon the mind by passages which we have admired in early youth, and which, whenever we meet with them at any distant time, raise, almost mechanically, the emotions we then experienced! The maxims first recommended by beauty of diction become, perhaps, the guides of our after life; and the feelings, introduced through the medium of the imagination, influence the heart in the intercourses of society.

It is, perhaps, an error in modern education, liberally conducted as at present it is towards females, that they spend too much time in learning of languages, and too little in reading of authors; so that, when they have gone through their course of education, they have a general acquaintance with, perhaps, three or four languages, and know little of the best productions in their own. If they have time to pursue their studies, they may supply the deficiency; but if the happiest destination of a woman be fulfilled, they become early engaged in domestic cares and duties, their acquirements stop short at the threshold of knowledge, and the real furniture of their minds is less rich, than that of a girl, who, educated at home and with little expense, but supplied with a judicious variety of English classics, has learnt less, but read more. It may be questioned, whether the practice, now so much in fashion, of teaching the learned languages to young women indiscriminately, can answer the time and pains, which must be employed about it. If a girl has a decided turn for literature, and a genius, which may perhaps impel her, at some period of her life, to give her own thoughts to the public, they will certainly enlarge the sphere of her ideas; but they can be of little use to those, who, in their own language, joined to that of the French, have more than enough to employ all the time they ever will or ought to devote to reading. That a girl should be put to read Virgil or Horace, who is unacquainted with Pope or Boileau, is surely a solecism in education.

The greatest part of this Selection is calculated for *recital* as well as for reading, an exercise, the editor takes the liberty to say, which is too much neglected. Graceful reading is a most pleasing, and it is a scarce accomplishment, and it is seldom attained without some practice in reciting; which necessarily demands a full, distinct utterance, and those tones and cadences, which bring out the sense of the author and the harmony of his periods. Finished verse, particularly, loses half its charms when it is only submitted to the eye; and if Poetry has been divorced from Music, it ought at least to have the music of a well modulated voice, regulated by a well informed taste. Many English ladies profess to want courage to recite, or even to read aloud a copy of verses in a social party; nor can it be denied, that bashfulness, and shrinking from display, is one strong characteristic of our nation: yet it is somewhat difficult to conceive, that a young lady shall have courage enough to stand up, by the side of a professional singer, and entertain a large and mixed audience, for an hour together, and yet be too modest to read or recite, by her father's fireside, amidst a circle of his friends, a passage of twenty lines from Milton or Cowper.

The editor has only to add, that this Collection, being intended chiefly for females, she has considered that circumstance, not only in having a more scrupulous regard to delicacy in the pieces inserted, but in directing her choice to subjects more particularly appropriate to the duties, the employments, and the dispositions of the softer sex. The pieces in Dr. Enfield's Speaker have been rather avoided, as that excellent collection is well known.

Independently of the pleasure, which a young mind of feeling and taste must derive from a familiarity with the most striking passages of our best authors, the advantage of it in future life is not small. They are equally relished in age as in youth. Whoever has been conversant with them in early youth, has laid up in her mind treasures, which, in sickness and in sorrow, in the sleepless night and the solitary day, will sooth the mind with ideas dear to its recollection; will come upon it like the remembrance of an early friend, revive the vivid feelings of youth, feed the mind with hope, compose it to resignation, and perhaps dismiss the parting breath with those hallelujahs on the tongue, which awoke the first feelings of love and admiration in the childish bosom.

REVIEWS OF EDUCATIONAL BOOKS

Introduction

Three generations of the Aikin family wrote journal reviews. The Reverend John, John M.D., and John's son Arthur all wrote for Ralph Griffiths' *Monthly Review*, and John M.D. is thought to have written, over the initials 'D.M.', for Joseph Johnson's *Analytical Review* (Roper, 282). In 1802 Arthur Aikin signed with Longmans to edit a massive new periodical, the *Annual Review*, which undertook to survey, by categories in one large octavo yearly volume, the publications of an entire year. The *Annual Review* ran to seven volumes, 1803–9; its contents were anonymous, as was customary for reviews at the time.

That Barbauld contributed to the *Annual Review* is certain. Lucy Aikin acknowledged that 'she reluctantly took part of the poetry and polite literature in one or two of the earliest volumes' (*MML*, 163–4); John Kenrick, citing a letter from Arthur Aikin, stated that Barbauld 'wrote the leading articles in poetry and belles letters' (Kenrick, 60). Because reviews were not signed, hers can be identified only by testimony or inference. Two reviews identified by testimony and published in volume 1 total thirteen pages. The *Annual* paid its reviewers at the rate of 7.5 to 8 guineas per printed sheet, and in an octavo volume one printed sheet comprised sixteen pages. Longman's Joint Commission and Divide Ledger for 1803–7 shows payment to Barbauld of £30 for reviews in Volume 1; if she were paid at the higher rate, she must have produced copy totaling around fifty-seven printed pages (more than three and a half sheets). The two known reviews account for thirteen pages, leaving some forty-four pages attributable to her only by inference. Reviews of books by Elizabeth Hamilton and William Barrow included in the present volume are attributed to her for reasons explained in notes.

In 1809 Barbauld began writing for the *Monthly Review*, then under the editorship of George Edward Griffiths, son of Ralph Griffiths, the *Monthly*'s founder. Again, her reviews were unsigned. They are known today because Griffiths, in his own set of the *Monthly* (now at the Bodleian Library), identified each review by a short form of its author's name: Barbauld was 'Mrs. Bar.' Between July 1809 and October 1815, when he stopped noting reviewers' names, Griffiths identified Barbauld as the author of 349 reviews; her subjects were Education (also called School Books), Poetry, and Novels. Her reviews appeared in the 'Monthly Catalogue' section of the issues that carried them; they are short, often no more than a few sentences, and total barely more than 129 pages. Griffiths paid his reviewers 5 guineas per printed sheet (Roper, 39), so Barbauld's 349 reviews, filling in total about eight sheets, would have earned her between £42 and £43, a small sum for the number of years over which she wrote them and the number of books she had to read and review.

The *Annual*'s and the *Monthly*'s are the only known texts of Barbauld's reviews, and the texts of the *Monthly*'s may not accurately represent the copy she sent to Griffiths. Griffiths imposed on his staff a strict policy of uniformity in style and sentiment: 'In such a work as the Monthly Review', he explained to one of his more eccentric writers, William Taylor, 'the ostensible editor is alone responsible for the style, and the avowed proprietor alone amenable for the sentiments; *his* property and *his* person solely being affected by its success or its failure. Consequently the editor and proprietor *must* have the unlimited power of approving or rejecting that style and that sentiment for which only he, or they, will be answerable' (quoted in Nangle, xi).[1] Hence, expressions in Barbauld's reviews such as 'the fair writer' (surely a male reviewer's phrase, not hers) and opinions that contradict those she expressed elsewhere (such as the censure of Maria Edgeworth's *Tales of Fashionable Life* in her *Monthly* review of it and her defence of the same work in a letter to *The Gentleman's Magazine*) may be results of Griffiths' interventions in the copy she sent him. Or she may have complied in advance with his insistence on uniformity, regarding the reviews as hired and therefore made to order. For either reason, or both, when the sentiments in her reviews diverge from those in her other writings contemporary with them, the reviews should not be assumed to express Barbauld's personal judgements. Our notes to the reviews attempt to identify, where possible, the authors whose books Barbauld reviewed.

Copy texts

Annual Review: *Letters on the Elementary Principles of Education*. By Elizabeth Hamilton, Author of the *Memoirs of Modern Philosophers*, &c. 2 vol. 8 vo. pp. 431 and 455 1 (1802); 568–76; *An Essay on Education; in which are particularly considered the Merits and the Defects of the Discipline and Instruction in our Academies. By the Rev.* WILLIAM BARROW, LL.D. F.A.S. Author of the *Bampton Lecture* for 1799, and late Master of the Academy in Soho-Square, London. 12mo. 2 vols. pp. 314 and 333 1 (1802): 576–8.

Monthly Review: *Tales of the Hermitage, Variety* ns 60 (Oct. 1809): 216, 220; *Important Studies for the Female Sex* ns 61 (Jan. 1810): 103; *Soirées d'Automne* ns

[1] See Nangle's discussion of Griffiths's attitude and its effects on the *Monthly Review* (Nangle, vii–xii). We know that Griffiths intervened in a few of Barbauld's reviews, because he annotated his interventions in the printed texts. We don't know to what extent he intervened in the manuscript copy sent to him; nor do we know how much time elapsed between reviewers' submissions of copy for a given volume and the publication of the volume. We can only trust that Griffiths correctly identified his reviewers.

63 (Sept. 1810): 101–2; *History of Rome* (Oct. 1810): 206–7; *The World Displayed* ns 63 (Oct. 1810): 207; *A History of France, Guy's School Geography, Perambulations in London, Lessons for Children* (Dec. 1810): 433–4, 434, 441–2; *Moral Truths, Guy's New British Spelling Book, Il vero modo, The Juvenile Spectator,* Mylius's *School Dictionary, The French Student's Vade Mecum, Contes à ma Fille, True Stories, Poetry for Children* ns 64 (Jan. 1811): 96, 97, 97–8, 98, 98–9, 99, 102; *Instructive Tales* (Feb. 1811): 219–20; *The First Book of Poetry, The Poetical Class Book, True Stories* (April 1811): 434–5, 435, 436; *An Introduction to Geography, Practical English Prosody, Key to Practical English Prosody, A Sequel to the Poetical Monitor, Familiar Letters, Manuel Epistolaire* ns 65 (Aug. 1811): 433, 433–4, 434; *Simple Pleasures, A New Introduction to Reading* ns 66 (Oct. 1811): 209–10, 210; *Chronology* (Nov. 1811): 332; *Dix's Juvenile Atlas, Guy's New British Reader, Juvenile Correspondence, Sermon sur les Devoir, English Exercises, Evening Entertainments, The Elements of Conversations* (Dec. 1811): 437, 437–8, 438, 438–9; *Choix de Biographie* (Supplement): 544; *New Dialogues, School of Instruction, The Accomplished Youth* ns 67 (March 1812): 319, 332; *On the Education of Daughters, Rules for English Composition, Miscellaneous English Exercises, Elements of French Grammar, A Dictionary of the Idioms* ns 68 (May 1812): 107, 107–8, 108; *The Mirror of the Graces* (June 1812): 221; (July 1812): 336; *The Cabinet of Entertainment* ns 69 (Sept. 1812): 98–9; *A Series of Tales, Thoughts on Education, First Lessons in English Grammar, The French Scholar's Depository* (Nov. 1812): 327, 327–8; *A Father's Bequest to his Son, Eastern Tales* (Dec. 1812): 445; *The Parent's Offering, A New System of English Grammar* ns 70 (April 1813): 438–9, 439; *The Deserted Village School, Fables in Verse, Conseils à ma Fille, The Juvenile Spectator, The Lady-Birds' Lottery, A Guide to Tutors, Diurnal Readings* ns 71 (June 1813): 209, 213, 213–14, 214, 222; *Elements of Universal Geography, The School Cyphering Book* (August 1813): 432–3, 433, *The Geographical Primer, The New Young Man's Companion, An English Vocabulary* ns 72 (Nov. 1813): 327; *The Female Class-Book, Grammatical Questions on the English Grammar, Scriptural Stories* ns 73 (Jan. 1814): 98, 98–9; *The Mother's Fables, The Nursery Companion, The Decoy, Maternal Sollicitude, French Phraseology, Maxims, Reflections,* and *Biographical Anecdote* (Feb. 1814): 210, 212, 212–13, 213, 219; *Punctuation* (April 1814): 437; *The History of Thomas Dellow* ns 74 (May 1814): 111; *Sir Hornbook, The Elements of Arithmetic, The Spanish Guitar, Difficult Pronunciation* (June 1814): 214, 217, 217–18; *Letters addressed to Two absent Daughters* (July 1814): 325–6; *A Treatise on Politeness, Natural History of Quadrupeds, Rules for English Composition, Méthode Pratique* (Aug. 1814): 438, 438–9, 439; *The English Pronouncing Spelling-Book, Ellen, Introduction to the Diurnal Readings, An Introduction to the Epistolary Style of the French, New Orthographical Exercises, A First or Mother's Dictionary, The Juvenile Arithmetic, A French Dictionary* ns 76 (Jan. 1815): 102, 102–3, 103, 103–4, 104; *Mentor and Amander* (Feb. 1815): 211; *Rules for pronouncing and reading the French Language, Original Letters of Advice, A Synopsis of French Grammar* ns 77 (June 1815): 210, 211; *A Grammar of the French Language,* A *Key to the Re-translation of the*

English Examples in the French Grammar, A copious Collection of instructive and entertaining Exercises, A Key to the copious Collection of instructive and entertaining Exercises, Tables of the different Parts of Speech in French, Practical Hints to Young Females (July 1815): 324, 324–5, 325.

Reviews in the *Annual Review*

Letters on the Elementary Principles of Education. By Elizabeth Hamilton, Author of the *Memoirs of Modern Philosophers*, &c. 2 vol. 8vo. pp. 431 and 455.[236]

Few practical subjects have more employed the thoughts and the pen, than the important subject of education; so much has been written, and by authors of such distinguished abilities, that one might naturally suppose little remained to be said upon so beaten a subject, yet such is the deep interest inspired by the successive generation of helpless and innocent human beings that come into life under the necessity of receiving from other and imperfect human beings all their ideas, habits, and associations; such is the immense difference between man and man according as the process he goes through is favourable or unfavourable to his improvement in knowledge and virtue; such waste of genius, such wrecks of innocence, such cruel disappointment of early hopes do we see around us, that a speculative mind will be continually turning its thoughts towards some new plan of instruction, some peculiar system of management which is to remedy every preceding defect, and by assiduous and unremitting care, prolonged from infancy through youth, to build up a perfect man. Much of this sanguine hope is probably fallacious. The workman by his rules can make a machine with accuracy, and which shall fully answer his purpose, but the human mind is submitted to so many influences, the far greater part of them beyond the controul of the parent, that no certain receipt for making a wise and virtuous man will ever be found, and hence a degree of disappointment will attend every system that has been tried, and a degree of new hope every one that is untried. By education much however may be done, though not every thing, and it is perhaps more powerful to harm than to benefit; it is therefore at least desirable that bad systems should be exploded; an elegant shape may be formed without stays, but an ill made pair is sure to ruin one. It is a commendation of Miss Hamilton's treatise, considered in a practical light, that it offers no peculiar system, holds out no views of extraordinary proficiency by uncommon methods, runs into no eccentricities; forbids nothing which is commonly reckoned salutary, recommends nothing which does not approve itself to common sense, and instead of sparkling with the fire of genius, holds out the sober lamp of truth and experience; the popularity it has gained does credit, therefore, to the public taste. This popularity has, we apprehend, been very much promoted by the judicious moderation with which it treats the important article of religion. It is well known, that two treatises on education, each of great merit, which have lately appeared, have exhibited a marked difference in this respect, the one bringing forward religious tenets with a zeal and fervour which many will term enthusiastic, the other carefully abstaining from all mention of them.[237] Miss Hamilton observes that mean which is likely to be most agreeable to the generality of serious and moderate people; her religion is rational and liberal; she is pious without being severe, and a friend to enquiry without its leading her away from the common and most approved systems. The method Miss Hamilton proposes to herself is, first, to examine the principles of the human mind, as far as education is concerned, and to that and the practical inferences arising from them the first volume is devoted. The grand principle the author makes use of for explaining every phænomenon is the law of association, a very important principle certainly, and one that has been often discussed by philosophical writers.[238] We think, in the present treatise, too much is made of it, and that the term is often used where habit would have been more proper; neither does the author give any clear definition of it, though we are particularly led to expect one from the observation, "that she has been assured, that however familiar the use of the term might be to a certain class of readers, to such as had never heard of any other associations than those of the loyal volunteers, it was to the last degree perplexing." If the doctrine was so new to many of her readers, certainly they had a right to expect an accurate definition of a term on which is made to depend the whole of the reasoning in all of the first volume; yet for such a definition we looked through the subsequent pages in vain; we find indeed, in allusion to the volunteer associations,[239] that, "the associations which take place in our ideas are seldom volunteers but are united by laws which are to the last degree arbitrary, and that their union, when once formed, is no longer at the will of a superior, but frequently remains indissoluble notwithstanding the commands issued by reason for disbanding them." We also find some appropriate instances of association, but still no definition, such as would give a person who had never before heard of the term, a just idea of it. But we find the author saying in the next page, "Of systems I have none save the system of Christianity." What has the system of Christianity to do with a treatise which professes to examine philosophically the principles of the human mind, and thence to deduce our opinions and actions? Christianity has no system of the kind, it directs our faith and practice, but it does not in the least degree assist the investigations of the metaphysical reasoner. If therefore, Miss Hamilton choose to spread a philosophic and scholastic air over her work, to talk about association, perception, generalization of ideas, abstraction of ideas, &c. she ought to recollect, that instead of boasting that she has no system, it is incumbent upon her to have one, and most certainly in these points and many others that she treats of, she will not find it in the New Testament. Indeed, without undervaluing the philosophy of this part of the work, we think its merit consists still more in the maxims of sound sense and experience, and the familiar illustrations it contains, than in those observations which have an air of greater abstruseness; neither is it for want, as Miss Hamilton seems to suppose, of clear ideas of the laws of mind, that mistakes are made in education; for all practical purposes the laws of mind are sufficiently understood by the most illiterate; and the nursery-maid who gives a child sweetmeats[240] to make it fond of her, or whips it to make it fear her, understands perfectly well the nature of the law of association, though probably she never heard of the term. The first chapters (letters they are called) of the work, show the influence of early associations in inspiring aversion or terror: permanent associations depend either on the strength of the original impression, or on the frequency of the repetition; to the former class belong those of the painful kind; timidity ought not to be encouraged in females, as it is almost always accompanied by an extreme regard to self, and incapacitates for benevolent exertion; striking instances of each kind are given. The author goes on to observe on the danger of early antipathies, on behaviour to servants, in which she opposes a doctrine of Miss Edgeworth's, which has been generally thought exceptionable.[241] The following observations are not only excellent, but give an amiable idea of the author:

> "Whatever tends to inspire children with an high opinion of their own comparative importance; whatever annexes to the idea of situation, independent of worth or virtue, ideas of contempt or complacency, will certainly counteract our design of inspiring them with humility. The light in which children are generally taught to consider servants, must infallibly, at a very early age, produce this high opinion of their own comparative importance; an importance which they must attach to situation, and which must therefore be necessarily productive of the pride of rank and power.—A pride which we would vainly endeavour to reconcile with true christian humility. Would we make a proper use of the instruments which nature so kindly affords us, in the helplessness of infancy, we should find a powerful assistance in laying the foundation of this inestimable virtue. Why should we not teach them to accept the services their tender age requires, with meekness and gratitude? Might not this first exercise of the social and benevolent affections, produce effects upon the mind so advantageous to the character, as completely to counterbalance all

the evils which can arise from occasional intercourse with domestics? But are these evils certain and unavoidable? Is it impossible to procure attendants for our children, of uncorrupted minds and undepraved manners? I cannot believe it. The corruption and depravity of servants is a general theme. From whence does it proceed, but from the corruption and depravity of their superiors? Governed by the selfishness of luxury and pride, we concern ourselves no further with the morals of our domestics than is necessary to the preservation of our property. No qualities are regarded in them, but such as contribute to the gratification of our ease or convenience. Their virtues are unrewarded by our esteem; their vices, provided they do not immediately injure us, unpunished by our disapprobation.

Whatever may be our own opinions concerning religion, we all agree that a notion of a Deity, and a fear of future punishment, is necessary to the vulgar; and yet who, in this age of philosophy and refinement, makes the religious instruction of their servants any part of their concern? Pride prevents us from undertaking what policy would dictate. We feel it too mortifying to represent to beings so much beneath us, that we are the creatures of the same GOD; that we are to be judged by the same laws; and that in a few fleeting years no other distinction shall be found between us except that of virtue. The moral precepts of our religion, it may not indeed be convenient to dwell upon, as we must blush to recommend rules to their practice, which seldom govern our own. The golden precept of *doing as we would be done by*, may, perhaps, sometimes occur to us in our transactions with our equals; but it seems as if we had some clause of exception with regard to our behaviour to those of an inferior station. We consider not them as beings endowed with passions and feelings similar to our own. Wrapt up in our prerogative, we provoke the one with impunity and insult the other without remorse. If we cannot read a chapter of the New Testament in their presence which does not libel our conduct, it is no wonder that we decline the task of religious instruction. But why, after this, declaim against the ignorance and depravity of servants? Those who have had sufficient energy to obey the call of principle in their domestic regulations: those who have considered the moral qualities of their servants as no less important than their abilities, and who to instruction and precept, have added the weight of example; have generally found that worth is to be met with in every station. People of moderate fortune have indeed here, as in many other respects, a manifest advantage. The size of their establishments does not swell beyond the possibility of inspection. The conduct and character of every individual of their families is, or ought to be, known to them. But, alas! the indolence of luxury is no longer confined within the walls of palaces! It pervades all ranks in society. What more common, than to hear ladies, even of moderate fortune, declare they have not a servant on whose truth or honesty they can depend; but that they do not change, because they know it impossible to get better? Were I to speak from experience, I should question this impossibility; for in the course of my life it has been my fate, both in town and country, in the corruption of the metropolis and the secluded scenes of retirement, to meet with servants, the excellence of whose moral characters entitled them to my esteem. The attendant of my infancy still possesses the regard, the gratitude, and veneration of my heart. She is now advancing into the vale of years, and I firmly believe will go to the great audit with a conscience that has never been stained by deceit, equivocation, or falsehood; nor is it improbable, that, I may, perhaps, be more indebted for my love of truth to her example than to all the precepts of my instructors. And yet she was but the orphan daughter of a poor servant! It must be, however, confessed, that the principles of religion were early and deeply implanted in her mind."[242]

The important subject of religion is next treated on, and the author very properly insists upon the desireableness of connecting all ideas of the Supreme Being and his laws with exhilarating and chearful impressions, and avoiding that air of gloom which is so frequently cast on such subjects: "the religious instruction of children ought to be chiefly addressed to the heart." In all this part the ideas are sound and liberal. It may be remarked, however, that the use of religion being principally as a restraining power, all those who believe and obey will be benefited by it, though the gloomy tinge which has been spread over it may hinder them from enjoying its consolatory influences; if their opinions direct them right in matters of practice, they will "depart from evil," though they may not be able "to rejoice in the Lord."[243] Proceeding to moral from divine, we have a number of good observations on the method of cultivating the benevolent affections in children, and inducing such an orderly quiet behaviour as may tend to the comfort of those about them, without encroaching on their natural vivacity. The author is an advocate for the good old system of implicit and early obedience, and throws strong and just blame on those parents who, in order to avoid a little present trouble, allow their children to grow selfish and ungovernable, till they are obliged at length, as the most unreasonable indulgence must stop somewhere, to use those severe methods of correction which completely sour their tempers. Her reasonings are enlivened with many entertaining anecdotes both of warning and example. The pernicious influences of partiality in parents are next considered, and particularly of a partiality not uncommon, that, towards the male part of their offspring, which coinciding with the opinion of the world, tends not only to degrade the female sex in their own eyes and in those of their brothers, but also to degrade and throw a shade upon those virtues, supposed to belong peculiarly to the sex.

"With a contempt for the female sex, on an account of this fancied inferiority, has been associated a contempt for those moral qualities which are allowed to constitute the perfection of the female character. Meekness, gentleness, temperance and chastity; that command over the passions which is obtained by frequent self-denial; and that willingness to sacrifice every selfish wish, and every selfish feeling, to the happiness of others, which is the consequence of subdued self-will, and the cultivation of the social and benevolent affections; are considered as feminine virtues, derogatory to the dignity of the manly character. Nay, further. By this unfortunate association has religion itself come into disgrace; devotional sentiment is considered as a mere adjunct of female virtue, suitable to the weakness of the female mind, *and for that reason* disgraceful to the superior wisdom of man. At the thought of *judgment to come* women, like Felix, may learn to tremble; and, in order to avert the consequences of divine displeasure, may study the practice of that righteousness and temperance recommended by the apostle to his royal auditor. But while the christian graces are associated with that contempt which the idea of inferiority inspires, neither righteousness, nor temperance, nor judgment to come, will be considered as worthy of consideration in the mind of man. This unhappy prejudice is in some respects far less injurious to the female than to the male. The obedience which they are taught to pay to authority, the submission with which they are made to bow to arrogance and injustice, produce habits of self-denial favourable to disinterestedness, meekness, humility, and generosity; dispositions which are allied to every species of moral excellence. And so seldom do these amiable dispositions fail to be produced by the subjugation of self-will, in females who have been properly educated, that in combating the prejudice which throws contempt upon the female character, I shall be found to plead the cause of the other sex rather than of my own. Every prejudice founded in selfishness and injustice inevitably corrupts the mind, and every act of tyranny resulting from it debases the human character: but submission "for conscience sake," even to the highest degree of tyranny and injustice, is an act, not of meanness, but of magnanimity. Instead of murmuring at the circumstances under which they are placed, women ought early to be taught to turn those very circumstances to their advantage, by rendering them conducive to the cultivation of all the milder virtues."[244]

Every judicious reader will concur with the author, in the commendation of temperance and indifference to a certain degree (for we must not counteract nature) towards the gratifications of the palate, but we fear few must expect to meet with such children, as it seems have fallen under the observation of the author, who "having had from five years of age a liberal supply of pocket-money, can aver that in all that period they never laid out one farthing in the purchase of fruit, cake, or sweetmeat for their own eating; but with infinite pleasure can dwell on little acts of infant charity, when the pure heart, first felt the glow of sympathy, and rejoiced in conscious benevolence." We are pretty sure at least that those self-denying infants were not boys. We are pleased with the following instance of sagaciousness, sharpened by early necessity, placed in opposition to the effect of provision made by toys and play-things for the amusement of the rich.

"It is they alone (the poor) who are permitted to feel and enjoy the rich provision made by nature for their instruction in its full extent. Accordingly, we shall find that the children of peasants of the lowest class, nay, even the children of gypsies, have at three years of age, a greater stock of ideas, acquired from the examination of sensible objects, and are infinitely more capable of taking care of themselves, than children of the higher ranks at six.

On a woody and steep declivity of the Cotteswold hills, where they project into the vale of Gloucester, stands a small cot inhabited by a poor widow, or rather a deserted wife, who was left with two infants, for whose provision she exerted herself in the labours of the field, and being a woman of remarkable strength and dexterity, she found constant employment with the neighbouring farmers. Soon as her youngest boy was weaned, she consigned him to the care of his brother, not three years of age. After having cut the brown bread which was to supply them with food for the day, and given necessary instructions to the elder boy, who was to act as cook, housekeeper, and nurse, she left them generally about five in the morning, and seldom returned till night. At the time I first saw this little pair (which I frequently did every day for weeks together, when on a visit to a family in the neighbourhood,) the eldest was near five, and the youngest about two years of age. Each might have sat for the picture of an infant Hercules. By living almost constantly in the open air, they had acquired a degree of hardiness and vigour, seldom to be met with at that early age; and by experience had become so well acquainted with the objects around them, and with the nature of every danger to which they were exposed, that though often on the edge of precipices which would make a fine lady shudder with horror, and where a fine little master would most probably have broken his neck, I never heard of their meeting with the smallest accident or disaster. When the hours of meal arrived, the elder, who never for a moment forsook his little charge, took him into the cot, and seating him in a corner, proceeded to make a fire of sticks, which he managed with great dexterity.

The brown bread was then crumbled down boiled with water, and sweetened with a very little very coarse sugar. This plain, but from its effects evidently wholesome viand, he then placed on the floor, and sitting down betwixt it and his brother, gave him alternate spoonful with himself till all was finished.

'Take care, Dan,' said a lady who once happened to step into the cottage at the beginning of this operation, 'Take care that you don't scald your brother's mouth.' 'No fear o' that,' returned the boy, 'for I's always takes un first to self.' "[245]

Whatever tends to promote pride and vanity, whether arising from wealth, birth, acquirements, or personal appearance is next gone through, and the volume concludes with a sensible critique on books for children, and the supposed modern improvements in the art of teaching.[246]

The second volume is devoted to an examination of the principles upon which we ought to proceed in the improvement of the intellectual faculties. It is therefore not any particular course of study which is intended to be pointed out, but a due attention to the unfolding the powers of the mind according to the order prescribed by nature. The powers are perception, attention, conception, judgment, and abstraction, all which prepare the mind for the cultivation of taste and imagination. These are treated on in the order given, and remarks on the power of reflection close the series. As this treatise, though relating to both sexes, is chiefly intended for the benefit of women, they are exhorted in the following spirited manner not to relinquish the privilege of exercising those rational faculties which are common to both the sexes.

> "If in analysing the faculties of the human mind, we find that Providence has made a manifest distinction betwixt the sexes, by leaving the female soul destitute of any of the intellectual powers, it will become us to submit to the divine decision. But if, upon enquiry, we find that no such partiality has been shewn by heaven; it is incumbent upon us to consider, by what right we take upon us to despise the gift of GOD."[247]

The power of perception, that is, the power of receiving ideas by sensible objects, is the first that opens in children, and indeed the foundation of all their knowledge; the vigour and clearness of this power depends partly on the perfection of the senses, but also very much on the faculty of attention, which therefore parents ought to take pains to exercise in their children: that the senses may be sharpened to almost an unlimited degree by attention, is exhibited in those who, having lost one sense, are obliged to depend on the remaining ones; on the other hand people who live in towns often become short-sighted for want of distant objects on which to exercise their powers. We cannot here help noticing what appears to us a fastidious piece of refinement in the philosophic author, who while she is recommending the assiduous culture of all the other senses, seems to think that of *taste* beneath the notice of a rational being. It is surely worthy our attention, in the first place, because of the actual pleasure it procures us, a pleasure by no means to be despised; and in the next place, to females at least it is a very necessary sense in the important part of their household duties. The author is fond of Milton; we wonder she does not recollect, that Eve was *exact of taste and elegant*, and that she was able, when her husband saw company, that is to say, when he entertained the angel, to bring

"Taste after taste upheld with kindliest change,"[248]

which she could hardly have done if she had despised the cultivation of that faculty. Attention is roused by the passions, and the passions, on the other hand, are increased by attention. By the attention which a delicate state of health demands, a disposition to selfishness is frequently produced. The instinctive perception which persons who have what is called a natural antipathy to any object, have of it, is accounted for by supposing, that the attention, sharpened by aversion, renders the smell surprizingly acute with regard to that particular object. The attention of children should be exercised on common things before they learn to read. The advantage of the institution of the Sabbath is derived from its breaking the trains of thought which otherwise, by constant attention, would grow too strong, and turning them into different channels.

Conception, or the power of forming ideas of absent objects, or of combining them, comes next to be considered. This depends, in a great measure, on accuracy of perception. Children should be accustomed to describe what they have seen or heard; they should be led to observation, and not read a multitude of books. The following observations on the languid and low spirited, appear to us very judicious.

> "Mothers, I apprehend, are seldom aware of the important consequences which result from their conduct to beings of this description. There is something so amiable and endearing in the gentleness which commonly attends this languor of spirits, that it naturally inspires tenderness. This tenderness is increased by that helplessness which clings to the maternal bosom for support. But if this tenderness be not enlightened and guided by reason, it will prepare a never ending fund of misery for its unhappy object.
>
> The inevitable effect of indulgence in generating selfishness, I have explained at large in the former volume: and as selfishness is the never-failing concomitant of the disposition above described; it follows, that it is the particular duty of the parent to guard against nurturing and increasing this natural tendency.
>
> From the languid flow of ideas in the low-spirited, proceeds an indolence of mind, which terminates in torpid apathy. Selfishness is then the sole spring of action: benevolence may dwell upon the tongue; but no feelings, no affections, but such as are connected with self-love, ever touch the heart. Such an one finds friendship necessary to his support, to his comfort, nay, to his very existence. He therefore clings to his friends with fondness; but what consolation, what comfort, what support does he afford them in return? Does he enter with the same interest into the feelings of others, with which he expects others to enter into his? No. But this deficiency of feeling does not proceed from a want of benevolence or of attachment. It proceeds from a want of conception with regard to every thing that does not concern self. How would many of our acquaintances start at the picture that is here drawn, if applied to themselves! Let us make a more useful application of it to those who are yet at a period of life when the evils I have here pourtrayed, admit of remedy.
>
> In the education of children who indicate a tendency to this disposition, whether such tendency be hereditary or acquired, particular pains should be taken to lead the mind to attend to the feelings of others. Whatever services, whatever attentions they exact from others, they should be obliged in their turn to pay. If they are once permitted to imagine, that from the softness and delicacy

of their dispositions, they have any right of exemption from the rule of 'doing to others as they would have others do by them,' they are inevitably ruined. It is essential, in such cases, to use every means to increase the flow of ideas. Lively and exhilarating images ought incessantly to be presented to the mind; and instead of encouraging that disposition to study, which frequently appears prematurely in such persons, the mind ought to be roused to active and vigorous exertion. Whatever knowledge it acquires, it ought to be made freely to communicate, for unless this be done, reading will be, to such a mind, only another mode of indulging indolence. To conquer the indolence that invariably adheres to such dispositions, every effort ought to be made. These efforts ought to be unceasing; and their efficacy will be much encreased by frequently changing the attention from object to object. The variety and beauty of the material world will be here powerfully assistant to the tutor's views. While the perceptive faculties are thus exercised, the mind cannot sink into apathy, or indulge in the luxury of indolent reverie. It will, by these means, likewise acquire that command of attention which is in all cases so eminently useful."[249]

The author afterwards points out the different kinds of memory, and gives directions for inspiriting the dull, and restraining the too lively, and dwells with earnestness on the importance of laying deep the foundations of knowledge. Poetry ought not to be presented to children till they have acquired a large stock of visible ideas.

"Let us suppose a little girl, whose acquaintance with natural objects extends to the grass-plot which ornaments the centre of some neighbouring square. In order to cultivate a taste for descriptive poetry, she is enjoined the task of getting by heart Gray's celebrated elegy, which abounds in imagery at once natural and affecting. Let us follow her in the conceptions she forms from it. Two lines will be sufficient example:

'The curfew tolls the knell of parting day,
The lowing herd winds slowly o'er the lea.' "[250]

After mentioning *curfew* and *parting day* as difficulties to the child, though first admits of an easy explanation, and the last she may surely have seen from her grass plot, Miss Hamilton adds what we cannot at all understand, except she has herself, probably from some local meaning of the word, fallen into the astonishing mistake of supposing *herd* to mean *herdsman*.

"What does she make, what *can* she make, of the succeeding line? A *herd* she has probably heard of, as one who takes care of sheep, goats, or other animals; but why the herd should *low*, is certainly beyond her comprehension. How, or in what manner, he *winds*, is equally so."[251]

If Miss Hamilton really has made this mistake, we should be glad to know how she herself interprets the *lowing* of the herdsman, for we profess ourselves as much at a loss here as the child. Whatever becomes of this illustration, with the general idea we entirely agree, that natural objects ought to be presented to children, and engage their attention as much as possible, and before they read descriptive poetry; yet, where it happens, as it often does in towns, that such objects do not frequently occur, the reverse of the method may have its advantages, for by previously uniting the object with moral, historical, or other interesting ideas, a child is led to view it with a much more lively feeling than if he had received the idea of it only from his eye. A boy who should have read Thomson's beautiful description of *the huge elephant, wisest of brutes*,[252] will see it afterwards with much more pleasure than if he had read no such passage: and Miss Hamilton herself observes, how much Blouzelind had previously interested her in the sound of the *wether's bell*.[253]

The next attribute of mind that comes to be considered is *judgment*. It is recommended here also to give the child ample time to form its own reasonings, and not to conduct him prematurely to the result. Arithmetic is recommended as a most useful branch of knowledge: and it is asked, why the female sex should be so utterly precluded as they generally are, from it? We did not know they were so. Accustoming women to the early exercise of judgment, is recommended as a means of keeping them in the path of virtue. Novel reading, and *educating youth by means of pretty stories*, are condemned, and every thing that tends to bring forward the imagination before the judgment. Miss Hamilton expresses her opinion, that the mode of education in the sixteenth and seventeenth centuries, and even the heavy needle work in fashion in those times, was more favourable to bringing forward the powers of the mind than the kind of culture bestowed at present upon young ladies.

> "If the higher powers of the mind were not called forth, the first and most essential faculties were so cultivated as to produce that equality which is always favourable to the production of common sense; and in the early cultivation of these first faculties, a foundation was laid for the perfection of all the higher powers of the mind, wherever a superior degree of mental culture was bestowed. Of this we have a decisive proof in the many illustrious instances of female learning and genius, which adorned the sixteenth and seventeenth centuries.
>
> It was not by means of pretty story books, abridgments, and beauties of history, nor yet by scraps of poetry selected from the best authors, that a Lady Jane Gray, or a Lady Anne Askew, attained those high accomplishments, and that intellectual energy, which has rendered them the admiration of succeeding ages."[254]

Of the mode of education of these illustrious ladies and their contemporaries, our accounts are very scanty, but if we are to judge of their literary merit by any thing they have produced, we imagine Miss

Hamilton herself will not bring them into comparison with the female writers of the eighteenth century. Let the education be judged of by its fruits. As to Lady Jane Grey, her fame is chiefly owing to her rank and her misfortunes.[255]

The next chapter is devoted to the best mode of giving instruction to the poor, particularly in bible knowledge.

Imagination and taste are next considered. The furniture of imagination must arise from having laid in a stock of clear, accurate, and distinct ideas; taste must depend on proper associations, and a devotional spirit is favourable to it. The author is not a friend, any more than Mrs. H.[annah] More, to bestowing the time which is generally bestowed on female accomplishments, and seems to prefer that general cultivation which enlarges the mind.

> "The mother who is superior to the chains of fashion, and who is capable of taking an extensive view of the probabilities of human life, as well as of weighing the talents of her children with accurate impartiality, will decide with wisdom and precision, on the value of those accomplishments which must inevitably be purchased at the expence of a large portion of time and attention. Does the mind appear destitute of that energy which is necessary to give a zest to the intellectual pleasures? she will readily perceive the advantage which may be derived to such a mind, from having at all times the power of gratifying itself by an elegant and innocent amusement. But if her children possess sufficient intellectual vigour to find full employment from other sources, she will, perhaps, content herself with cultivating in them that taste for the fine arts in general, which will at all times ensure them the most exquisite gratification.
>
> To such minds, sources of delight open on every side. Every scene in nature presents some object calculated to call forth trains of ideas, which either interest the heart, or amuse the fancy. But if the time in which the mind ought naturally to be employed in accumulating those ideas, be devoted to acquiring a facility of execution at a musical instrument, it is evident no such ideas can be called forth. I once travelled 400 miles in company with an accomplished young gentleman, who made, in the course of the journey, but one solitary observation, and that was called forth by an extensive moorish fen, where, he said, he was sure was abundance of snipes! Read the observations of St. Fond, on going over the same ground, and observe the rich variety of ideas presented to the man of science by objects which are to the vulgar eye barren of delight. Follow the elegant Gilpin through the same tour, and mark the emotions which the various scenery of natural landscape excites in the mind of the man of taste. Who that is capable of weighing the value of the mind's enjoyment in the scale of truth and reason, will not instantly perceive how much the balance preponderates in favour of those who have such a rich variety of associations, when put in competition with the superficially accomplished? Let science and taste unite in the same mind, and you prepare materials for a constant feast."[256]

The power of *abstraction* comes next to be treated of, or the power of generalising our ideas, and forming principles of action. A mistress of a large family, as Miss Hamilton well observes, "has occasion for a comprehensive view of the effect to be produced, an accurate conception of the powers of each individual agent, and a just notion of how it can be employed to the best advantage, and a distinct view of how the whole is to be set in motion, so as most easily to produce the desired effect." A woman left in a state of widowhood, has still more occasion for this power. We meet with many good observations on this head; with the following we cannot equally concur.

> "Before your pupils enter upon speculative enquiry, it is above all things essential, that their judgment should be exercised in ascertaining the limits of human knowledge. All speculations concerning what is placed beyond the reach of the human faculties, ought to be avoided, for from them no possible advantage can be derived. They must ever end, as they begin, in uncertainty and doubt; but far from being a harmless waste of time, they frequently excite the violence of prejudice and animosity."[257]

Part of this assertion may be very true, but it is difficult to imagine how a pupil *before* he *enters* upon enquiry, can exercise his judgment in ascertaining limits which it is necessary to have travelled to those limits in order to ascertain. He may, indeed, and, in many cases, ought to allow himself to be directed, in such points, by the judgment of others; but if such knowledge is to be the result of his own, it is the very last he will acquire. It is vain to think of cultivating judgment and stimulating enquiry, and, at the same time, dictating to that judgment, and saying to enquiry, hitherto shalt thou go, and no further: the greater part of the world do, and ought to take opinions upon trust; but whoever, whether man or woman, enquires, must lay their account with a certain portion of doubt and uncertainty; and they who set them about it, must lay *their* account with seeing them rest in conclusions often very different from the preconceived opinions they began with.

The subject of the last chapter is *reflection*, or the power which the mind possesses of examining its own operations. The author seems to mean by it self-examination, and the directing all the powers which the mind has unfolded to the culture of the heart. The chapter has an excellent moral tendency, but, considered as a philosophical investigation, it is not very clear.

We have now gone through these volumes, and it only remains to express our satisfaction with their general contents. Objections might be made to many parts of the theory, and particularly this, that in fact the different powers open much more nearly together than the theory seems to imply. A child, for instance, exercises the power of *abstraction* as soon, at least, as he understands that the word *cat* means *cats* in general, and not merely an individual, and of judgment when he compares distances, &c.; but without dwelling on these remarks, we with pleasure repeat, that the sound sense, and judicious observations the reader will meet with, the just estimate of life, and the spirit of piety and virtue breathed through the whole; a piety strict without being gloomy, and a virtue firm, but not ascetic, must make the work be numbered among those publications calculated to bring to their author the best reward, the consciousness of having done good.

An Essay on Education; in which are particularly considered the Merits and the Defects of the Discipline and Instruction in our Academies. By the Rev. WILLIAM BARROW, LL.D. F.A.S. Author of the *Bampton Lecture* for 1799, *and late Master of the Academy in Soho-Square, London.* 12mo. 2 vols. pp. 314 and 333.[258]

Among the treatises on education, few, comparatively, have been written by those who have actually engaged in it as a business. Systems for home education, however elaborate or ingenious, do not apply to the generality of youth (we mean to speak of boys only), who ever have, and, probably, ever must be brought up under the discipline of schools public or private. What those schools are, and what they should be, the advantages enjoyed, and the risks incurred by the scholars, the grievances of the masters, and the frequent disappointment of the parents, are here set forth in a manner which shews the publication to the result of sound sense and real experience. Dr. Barrow speaks with just indignation against those seminaries, so frequent in the vicinity of London, where the master himself possesses no qualification for his office, but the skill of conducting a boarding house; where, consequently, the parent loses his money, and the scholar his time; and the servility, the false pretensions, and the impositions on one side, are fairly traced to their true source, the parsimony of parents, who will not give, in the first instance, that liberal stipend which would engage a man of letters, and preclude the necessity of encreasing it by mean arts. Of the little respect which, in proportion to its utility, the character of a schoolmaster obtains among the other classes of society, of the difficulties thrown in his way by the folly, suspicion, or illiberal behaviour of parents, Dr. Barrow speaks with an acuteness of feeling which is evidently not the result of observation alone.

> "They (these grievances) exhaust that patience in the teacher, which ought to be reserved for the instruction and benefit of his pupils; they sometimes render his temper so irritable, that he can hardly be considered as fit for his own

profession: they accelerate that injury to his health, which his labours would naturally occasion, and render him the sooner unequal to his task. Above all, they have driven many to endeavour to make an academy merely an occupation of profit; to look upon their pupils, not so much as youth to be educated, as instruments of gain; to practise all those artifices which have been so justly censured; all that delusion which the people seemed to court, and without which they would not be contented. Is it to be wondered then, that, in this case, as in almost every thing human, evils become reciprocally the cause and effect of each other! Unprincipled schoolmasters provoke illiberal treatment, and illiberal treatment makes unprincipled schoolmasters. Is it to be wondered, that so few men of spirit and talents engage in the profession; or that they escape from it, as soon as a decent subsistence can elsewhere be found! In enumerating what were in his judgment the requisite qualifications of an instructor of youth, Quintilian has drawn such a literary and moral character, as would, indeed, do honour to any profession; but which human frailty forbids us to hope, will frequently be found: yet the idea of the ancient rhetorician, however exalted, seems by no means equal to the popular expectation of the present day. If we consult the sentiments and conduct of the less intelligent and less liberal part of the community, it will appear that the master of an academy is required to possess, like the hero of a romance, not only talents and virtues, above the ordinary endowments of humanity, but such contrarieties of excellence, as seem incompatible with each other. He is required to possess spirit enough to govern the most refractory of his pupils, and meanness enough to submit to the perpetual interference of their friends; such delicacy of taste as may enable him to instruct his scholars in all the elegancies of polite literature, and robust strength enough to bear, without fatigue, the most incessant exertions. He is required to possess learning sufficient to relish the eloquence of Cicero and Demosthenes; and good nature to listen, without weariness, to a grandmother blazoning the merits of her heir; skill adequate to the performance of his task, and patience to be instructed how to perform it. He is required to possess judgment enough to determine the most proper studies, and the most suitable destinations for his pupils; and complaisance at all times to submit his own opinion to the opinions of those who have employed him; moral principle enough to ensure on all occasions the faithful discharge of his duties; and forbearance to hear those principles continually suspected, and his diligence and fidelity called in question. It is expected that he shall be daily exposed to the severest trials of his temper, but neither require, nor be allowed any indulgence for its occasional excesses; and that he be able to secure all the good effects of discipline, without the use of the only means which ever yet procured them. He is expected to feel that conscious dignity which science confers upon its possessor; and yet to descend without reluctance to teach infants their alphabet; to possess generosity enough to maintain his pupils liberally without a liberal stipend; and insensibility enough to permit his demands to be taxed by those by whom they ought to be most readily and gratefully discharged.

That many parents appear to expect this variety of talents in the teachers of their sons, the masters of academies know to their sorrow and their cost; but where such constellations of excellence are to be found, it is surely needless to enquire. The glasses of Herschel,[259] in the search would *sweep the regions of space* in vain."[260]

With regard to his own system, Mr. Barrow is a declared enemy to all the softnesses and indulgences of modern life, to that relaxation of parental and magisterial authority, which is generally allowed to have taken place of late years: he speaks (we had almost said *con amore*) in favour of the good old practice of flogging, "without the use or the fear of which," he says, (perhaps with some truth) "no good classic scholar was ever yet made." He sets his face against all those novelties which so many ingenious people have deemed improvements in the mode of instruction, against the deceptive system of *playing children into learning*, or *reasoning them into obedience*, against *infant libraries filled with natural history, and French philanthropy*, which, he complains, *have superseded the bible and the catechism;* against *playing tricks with electrical machines, and studying the botanical names of weeds under a hedge*, instead of applying to mathematics, or Greek and Latin; and, indeed, we must so far agree with this author, that if the great object of the first eighteen or twenty years of life be to make a youth thorough master of two dead languages, the slow and steady method of our great schools, cannot be much improved upon. Mr. Barrow, however, is candid enough to tell us, that an education at the great schools is a very improper introduction to a mercantile life.

The following remarks are worth the notice of those parents who are ambitious of sending their sons to Eton or Westminster.

"Our public schools, properly so called, are unsuitable places of education for those who are designed for any private station, for the retirement and tranquillity of the country, or the patient diligence of trade. Young men do not there learn the sciences best adapted to such persons; and they usually acquire notions, habits, and connexions, and sometimes vices too, incompatible with their future destination. The mechanic does not willingly receive his apprentice, nor the merchant select his clerk, from amongst the pupils of a public school; nor has the pupil of a public school more inclination than aptitude to become the clerk or the apprentice. Our academies are the places where education suitable to such stations is to be sought; and in many of them it may undoubtedly be found. Sometimes, indeed, an attempt is made to unite the advantages of both. For, in the conduct of education, what absurdity can be named, which human folly has not, in some instance, endeavoured to reduce to practice? From a principle of mistaken pride, from the hope and prospect of valuable connexions, or from some other personal or general motive, a youth is not unfrequently fixed for a few years, at Eton or Westminster, and afterwards placed at an academy, to learn the qualifications requisite for trade. But the first part of this scheme usually frustrates the last. The master of an academy generally finds a youth of this description amongst the most turbulent and refractory of his pupils. He comes prepared to despise alike the persons, the instructions, and the authority of his teachers; and determines not to submit to what he deems the intolerable confinement and degrading drudgery of his destined occupation. He insists, too resolutely to be refused, on an appointment in the navy or the army; and leaves his parents to repent at leisure the disappointment of their hopes, and the folly of their plan."[261]

The author proceeds to give his sentiments on various points, some adapted to different modes of education, others, as health and morals, common to all, and the reader will find many excellent remarks mingled with notices of elementary books, and directions in the mode of communicating knowledge, which, from an experienced teacher, are valuable hints.[262] These, we must be allowed to think, would have been more extensively useful, had not the author shewn himself so decidedly hostile to the principles of free enquiry and civil liberty. The leaven of high church politics pervades every chapter. Mr. Barrow, as a scholar, ought to know how inimical it would eventually prove to the interests of literature, if, as he strenuously urges, no man were allowed to teach without taking out a license from the bishop of the diocese. A zeal for establishments both in church and state, seems paramount to every other consideration. The study of the French language is discouraged, lest their books should corrupt the principles of youth; and boys are to be taught religion at school, because *Christianity is a part of the laws of the land.* It cannot be wondered at, that with such sentiments he speaks in terms of pointed disapprobation of *those members of the church of England who send their children to dissenting schools.*[263] We could suggest to him one reason for this practice. It is because in many towns the established clergy want either the sobriety, the literature, or, at least, the necessity for exertion, requisite to make them able to fulfil, and willing to undertake the task. In his last chapter, *on the effects of the French revolution*, the author is much too angry to philosophise well.

We observe a singular error of the press, in one of these chapters. It is said, that at one period there prevailed, as we are told by Locke, in his treatise on education, so general a passion for literature, among the ingenuous youth of *Portugal*, that it was as difficult to restrain them as to excite others. Never having heard this anecdote of the Portuguese youth, we were at first rather startled, till it occurred, that the author must have meant *Port Royal*.[264]

We cannot dismiss these volumes without observing, that they are well written, and in a stile flowing and dignified.

REVIEWS IN THE *MONTHLY REVIEW*

Tales of the Hermitage, in English and Italian, translated by V. Peretti. 2d Edition. 12mo. 3s. sewed. Duhlau, & Co. 1809.

Signor Peretti has already distinguished himself by the publication of a very useful Italian grammar;[265] and this translation of some Tales, written by an English lady,[266] will be a valuable present to youthful students of the Italian language. The nature of the Tales, which are intended merely for the amusement of children, will probably prevent them from circulating beyond the school-room: but a perusal of them might be more extensively advantageous in teaching the pronunciation of Italian. In the preface, several plain and important rules for placing the accents are laid down, while every word throughout the Tales is accented so as to indicate the pronunciation which it requires: the English and Italian are printed opposite to each other; and the corresponding paragraphs are judiciously *numbered*, to prevent any difficulty to the most ignorant, in tracing their affinity.

Variety, or Selections and Essays, consisting of Anecdotes, curious Facts, interesting Narratives, with occasional Reflections. By Priscilla Wakefield.[267] 12mo. 4s. Boards. Darton and Harvey. 1809.

These Essays seem in every respect calculated to fulfil the intention of the compiler, by instructing without wearying, and amusing without weakening the minds of her young readers; and we can safely recommend 'Variety' as a very judicious and entertaining little work.

Important Studies for the Female Sex, in Reference to modern Manners. By Mrs. Cockle.[268] 12mo. 7 s. Boards. Chapple.

In this well-written little work, a great part of the chapter on 'Temper' is much to be commended both for its style and its sentiments; and the story of 'Mrs Orville,' though not new, is so impressively related as to enforce the moral which it illustrates. The fair writer also gives some useful advice with respect to the oeconomy of time, and the appropriation of every hour to some destined employment. She is rather complimentary to those contemporaries of her own sex, who have written on the subject of education: but she is sometimes in danger of inculcating such motives for the actions which she recommends, as (we hope) would not be encouraged by the authors whom she takes for her models. Thus, page 58, she assures her young friend that 'the tear of benevolence, or the blush of modesty, those interesting testimonies of the worth of the heart, are far more *attractive* than the diamond which glitters in the tiara as a rival to the one, or the rouge which is resorted to as a substitute for the other;'—and in page 139, she bids the matron 'recollect that the interesting and gentle graces of the mother present in that moment' (i.e. when she is nursing) 'a more *attractive* picture, a more powerful *charm* than fashion ever bestowed, with all the adventitious aids of dress or beauty.'

Such considerations as these, improperly understood and applied, may destroy the artlessness of compassion, and vitiate the purity of maternal tenderness. If 'the tear of benevolence' be 'resorted to' as an *attraction*, and the youthful mother be instructed to mingle coquetry with her duties, the readers of this book will be still farther from 'simplicity and godly sincerity'[269] than they were before Mrs. Cockle undertook to improve them. It is, however, but just to acknowledge that the instances which we have quoted are the only cases in which we remarked a defective morality, and that the general tenor of the work is rational and instructive.

Soirées d'Automne, &c. i.e. Autumnal Evenings, or Vice punished and Virtue rewarded. For the Instruction of Youth and the Use of Schools. By Mlle. G. Bertholet. 12mo. 4s. 6d. Boards. Dulau and Co. 1810.[270]

The introductory dialogues, with which this work commences, are rather dull and superfluous, and seem to be written merely in imitation of Madame de Genlis's *Veillées du Chateau*:[271] but Mlle. Bertholet has told the history of Joseph and his brethren in a very animated and interesting manner. She appears, however, to think that a love-story is indispensable to the effect of a tale; and she has accordingly heightened the picture of Joseph's grief at his banishment from his father, by describing him as being torn also from the amiable *Semira* at the very moment when Hymen prepared to crown their mutual love.—Perhaps, in strict critical severity, we should object to the mention of *Hymen*'s Pagan name among these pious Israelites. At any rate, this introduction of a fictitious fair one causes improbabilities, while it lessens Joseph's merit in resisting the blandishments of *Zora*; so that, instead of appearing as the triumphant servant of God, he becomes a mere faithful Corydon to the amiable Semira.—A story which has already been related in history, or in holy writ, should not be altered, even if it may be amplified; and therefore we hesitate in commending the writer for having softened the character of Potiphar's wife. Instead of the recorded *intreaty*, the *Zora* of the present performance only takes hold of Joseph's garment in order to tell him that he is made free; while he is so fearful of temptation that he will not stay to hear her. *His coat of many colours* is also changed into a wedding robe, woven by Semira.

We must have been, 'like Niobe, all tears,'[272] to have sympathized in the numerous weepings of Joseph and his brethren; and we suspect that the writer has fallen into this sentimental error by endeavouring to copy the style of Gesner,[273] instead of trusting to her own. Her language, however, is pure and elegant: the incidents which she imagines are generally probable and pleasing; and the whole composition seems to be judiciously adapted to its professed end,—'the amusement and instruction of youth.'

History of Rome, from the Building of the City to the Ruin of the Republic. Illustrated with Maps and other Plates. For the Use of Schools and young Persons. By Edward Baldwin, Esq. 12mo. 4s. bound. Godwin. 1809.

The plan of this history is new, and claims some attention. Mr. Baldwin (as the author calls himself)[274] thinks that many details and dates are wearisome to young people; and he has therefore merely related the most remarkable anecdotes of Roman virtue, such as the generosity of Camillus, the patriotism of the Decii, the disinterestedness of Fabricius, and the continence of Scipio, &c. He has proceeded only as far as to the Destruction of the Republic, though he might have collected instances of magnanimity during the reigns of the emperors. The words and actions of Titus, Vespasian, and Trajan, &c. would have furnished him with many impressive passages; while the cruelties of Claudius and Nero serve to make Arria's heroism and Seneca's resignation more conspicuous. The work cannot fail of being interesting and in a certain degree useful to young readers, since it tends to inspire noble and generous sentiments; and it may excite a relish for the study of history, previously to the necessity of proceeding more methodically. We anticipate, however, the danger that this method of *skimming the cream* will make longer books on the same subjects appear tasteless.

The World Displayed: or the characteristic Features of Nature and Art exhibited: on a new Plan. Intended for Youth in general, &c. By John Greig, Teacher of Mathematics, and Author of "The Heavens displayed,"—"Lady's Arithmetic," &c.[275] 12mo. pp. 664. 8s. 6d. Boards. Cradock and Joy. 1810.

Geography and Biography, Chemistry and History, Botany and Mineralogy, have all contributed their portion of striking facts, remarkable discoveries, amusing experiments, and natural productions, in order to render this work worthy of attention; and it appears calculated to excite as well as to gratify the curiosity of young people on all the subjects of which it treats.

The Junior Class Book; or Reading Lessons for every Day in the Year. Selected from the most approved Authors, for the Use of Schools. By William Frederick Mylius.[276] 12mo. pp. 367. 4s. bound. Godwin. 1809.

This is an amusing compilation;[277] and we think that it is calculated, by the variety of its subjects, to inspire a taste for reading in those who are too young or too volatile to attend to a more connected work.

A History of France, from the Commencement of the Reign of Clovis, in 481, to the Peace of Campo Formio in 1797. After the Manner of *The History of England, in a Series of Letters from a Nobleman to his Son*. 12mo. pp. 444. 5s. 6d. Boards. Darton and Co. 1809.[278]

This history is written in a clear and lively manner, the principal events of each reign are detailed with perspicuity, the dates are carefully specified, and the author has even found room to embellish his work with many judicious remarks and entertaining anecdotes. As a book of reference, it would have been improved by the addition of an alphabetical index. In its present state, however, it is well calculated for the instruction of young persons; and in this point of view we approve the manner in which it is arranged: each division being of a reasonable length, and not so much extended as to exhaust the attention or fatigue the memory. Yet since it is impossible to suppose that the History of France should really have been detailed in a series of familiar epistles, we can find nothing sufficiently animating in the commencements of 'My dear Boy,' or in the conclusions of 'Your's affectionately,' to reconcile us to this little subterfuge.

Guy's School Geography, on a new and easy Plan, comprising not only a complete general Description, but much topographical Information, &c. By Joseph Guy, Author of 'the Pocket Encyclopedia.'[279] &c. 12mo. 3s. bound. Cradock and Joy. 1810.

The different parts of this work are arranged with judgment and perspicuity; and while the larger print comprehends every thing which it is absolutely necessary for the young geographical student to learn, the smaller type contains much valuable and amusing information. The price is very moderate, the size of the book is not alarming, and we think that it will prove an useful acquisition to those for whose assistance it is intended.

Lessons for Children, by Mrs. Fenwick, in Three Parts.[280] 12mo. 1s. each. Godwin. 1809.

These little stories are progressive; and those which are contained in the first part are adapted to the comprehension of *very* young children, whose amusement has not of late been so much consulted as that of their elder brothers and sisters.

The tales are both moral and entertaining; and the type is large and clear.

Perambulations in London and its Environs. Comprehending an historical Sketch of the ancient State and Progress of the British Metropolis, a concise Description of its present State, Notices of eminent Persons, and a short Account of the surrounding Villages. In Letters designed for Young Persons, by Priscilla Wakefield.[281] 12mo. 6s. 6d. Boards. Darton and Co. 1809.

The industry, which must have been exerted in collecting the materials for this volume, is equalled by the good sense with which they are selected and arranged. We know not a publication on the same subject which affords so much information in so little compass, and adapted not only to the gratification of harmless curiosity, but also to that of antiquarian research; since it relates the time and the occasion on which every public or remarkable building was founded, while the historical events or anecdotes which are connected with them are judiciously introduced. We have received entertainment from the perusal of this work, and we cannot recommend it too highly to our young readers; nor indeed, to all those who wish to be concisely acquainted with the history, manufactures, and institutions of the British Metropolis.

Moral Truths, and Studies from Natural History. Intended as a Sequel to the Juvenile Journal, or Tales of Truth. By Mrs Cockle.[282] 12mo. 7s. Boards. Chapple. 1810.

Copious extracts from the writings of Darwin, Paley,[283] &c. impart an adventitious value to this work, while the compiler herself is intitled to praise for her manner of selecting and connecting these materials. Her plan for a journal or diary to be kept by a little girl is in itself good, and we think that our young friends can glean nothing that will not be pleasant and profitable from this publication.

Guy's New British Spelling Book, or an easy Introduction to Spelling and Reading, in Seven Parts, &c. &c. 12mo. 1s. 6d. bound. Cradock. 1809.[284]

This spelling book promises to be as useful as any that we have seen. The reading lessons are amusing, the columns of spelling are well arranged, and the whole is in general divested of needless perplexities.

Il vero modo di piacere in Compagnia, &c. By Carlo Monteggia.[285] 12mo. pp. 315. Boards. Colburn. 1810.

In composing a book for children, their amusement should be consulted as much as their instruction, or the work will be in danger of having only the first pages cut open. Signor Monteggia has been aware of this necessity; and though his subject is unpromising, he has introduced so many "antient saws and modern instances,"[286] in order to enliven his observations on polite behaviour, that he escapes being wearisome: while the opposite pages of Italian and French are sufficiently alike to assist the reader, without losing the idiom of either language by injudicious similarity. On the whole, therefore, we think so favourably of this performance, that we do not hesitate in recommending it to our young readers, who are studying the Italian language.

The Juvenile Spectator. Being Observations on the Tempers, Manners, and Foibles of various young Persons. By Arabella Argus. 12mo. 4s. 6d. bound. Dartons. 1810.

Mrs. Argus, as this writer chooses to be called,[287] appears to be well acquainted with the dispositions and habits of young people, and her work will afford pleasure to a sensible child by the natural anecdotes and good humoured advice which it contains: but she might perhaps have rendered it more acceptable if she had enlivened it with a few Tales, in imitation of her predecessors, Isaac Bickerstaff and Adam Fitz Adam,[288] &c.; and she would have made it more useful, if she had paid greater attention to the propriety of her style. For instance, she says, 'You will let Lucy and *I* know how you spend this dollar;'—'there *is* a thousand *ways* in which news may be brought,' &c. —She talks also of *naming* circumstances, instead of *mentioning* them; and she speaks of one boy in the following enigmatical manner: 'He is going to school to-morrow; where I hope he will acquire steadiness of character, at present his most predominant defect!'

Mylius's School Dictionary of the English Language. Intended for those by whom a Dictionary is used as a Series of daily Lessons. In which such Words as are pedantical, vulgar, indelicate, and obsolete are omitted; and such only are preserved as are purely and simply English, or are of necessary Use and universal Application. The second Edition: To which is prefixed a New Guide to the English Tongue. By Edward Baldwin,[289] Esq. 12mo. 2s. 6d. bound. Godwin. 1809.

Mr. Mylius makes a just distinction between an interpreting and an elementary Dictionary; and the plan of his present publication is rational, though its execution is not quite unexceptionable: since his care to exclude such words as are 'indelicate' has not been equalled by his attention in rejecting all which are 'vulgar or obsolete.'

The 'Essay on the English Language,' prefixed to this edition, is ingenious, and shews that the writer has studied his subject: but, as he ought to have furnished an example as well as a rule of luminous expression, he should either not have introduced the word *paradigm*, with some others, or he should have caused them to be explained in the columns of the dictionary, which are debased by many expletives that have no right to insertion; such as *Mewl*, to *squall* as a child,—*Screetch*, to shriek;—*Snack*, a share;—*Swash*, to make a great *clatter* or noise, &c. &c.

The French Student's Vade Mecum, or Indispensable Companion. In which are displayed the different Cases of Persons and Things, as required by all the French Verbs and Adjectives: the different Prepositions which they govern, those required by the Substantives, and the different Moods which must follow the Conjunctions. By the Rev. P. C. Le Vasseur, a Native of France, and Chaplain of the Cathedral of Lisieux. 12mo. 3s. Boards. Longman and Co. 1809.

Although this publication may be useful to such persons as wish to acquire the habit of speaking French grammatically, yet, as the French words are placed *first*, the student can only learn their cases and government, without receiving any assistance in finding expressions for his ideas; and many words are introduced which are not used in conversation, and should therefore have been distinguished as technical or obsolete, lest they should be injudiciously applied.—However, as the size of this work is convenient, and as the plan is in some respects dissimilar from that of other elementary books in the same language, it may prove an advantageous addition to their number.

Contes à ma Fille; &c. *i.e.* Tales for my Daughter. By J. N. Bouilly, Member of the Philotechnic Society,[290] &c., in Paris. 2 Vols. 12mo. 8s. Boards. Colburn. 1811.

These tales are the production of a man of letters who has devoted himself to the instruction of his daughter; and they will be acceptable to all those who have undertaken a similar task, from the amusing variety of their subjects, and the moral lessons which they convey. The story of M. de Malesherbe's roses, which is beautiful, we believe to be founded on facts;[291] and *Les Papillotes, La Piece d'Or,* and *Le Journal des Modes*, are very ingenious and original: but we think that M. Bouilly expatiates too much on the *beauty* and the *attire* of his little heroines, and represents the parents as employing unnecessary *finesse* in correcting their foibles. One father instructs his servants in a line of conduct which may have a proper influence on the pride of his daughter; and another causes himself to be imprisoned during six months, in the hope that his Cornelia will learn to read during his detention. These schemes are too romantic and insincere to succeed in real life; and they remind us of Rousseau's visionary contrivance for reproving Emilius, which was to station at every corner of the street some obliging butchers and bakers, who were all prepared to make the required speeches, as if by accident, when the boy passed near them.[292]

True Stories; or interesting Anecdotes of young Persons: designed through the Medium of Example to inculcate Principles of Virtue and Piety. By the Author of "Lessons for young Persons in humble Life."[293] 12mo. 4s. 6d. Longman and Co. 1810.

We are sorry to perceive that, in this work, the writer is rather too melancholy in his selection; the greatest part of the present publication consisting of examples of learning and virtue in young persons who have perished in early life.[294] The consumption which carried off Edward the Sixth makes way for the scaffold of Lady Jane Grey, and these are followed by the histories of Henry Prince of Wales and the Countess of Suffolk, &c.: so that this portion of the volume will afford the same sort of information which may be gained by reading the monumental inscriptions in Westminster Abbey, but without the amusement of gazing on cloistered arches, and "painted windows richly dight."[295] Young people require to be entertained as well as admonished; and one striking or interesting anecdote will often make more impression, and excite them to emulation more effectually, than a volume of death-bed scenes, or melancholy panegyrics penned by surviving friends. We must, however, applaud the compiler for the purity of his language, and the morality which is observable in the choice of his subjects. A knowledge of history, as well as of biography, may be promoted by his work; and if he succeeds in engaging the attention of his young readers, their time will be advantageously employed.

Poetry for Children. Entirely original. By the Author of Mrs. Leicester's School.[296] 2 Vols. 12mo. 3s. half bound. Godwin. 1809.

Nothing can be either more natural or more engaging than the subjects of these little poems; and they will teach children to be happy by making them reflect on their own comforts, and by exciting them to promote the happiness of others. The versification, indeed, is too puerile: but it is impossible even for adult readers to be uninterested by the touching juvenile traits and anecdotes which these volumes contain. We hear that they are production of *Miss Lambe*, whose brother published "Tales from Shakspeare;" and we think that this lady will be intitled to the gratitude of every mother whose children obtain her compositions.

Instructive Tales. By Mrs. Trimmer.²⁹⁷ Collected from the Family Magazine. 12mo. 4s. Boards. Hatchard. 1810.

In their present compact form, these Tales constitute a very rational and consistent publication for the use of the lower class of people. The counsel which they inculcate is pious, wise, and practicable; the rules given in the Appendix for the management of infants, sick persons, &c. are valuable; and the stories themselves are amusing and intelligible. We are convinced, therefore, that the circulation of this little work will be beneficial to those for whose service it is intended.—Since its publication, the worthy lady who penned it has been called to reap the eternal reward of a well spent life.

The language is not an object of criticism in a composition of this nature, and intended for such a purpose: but were it designed for the toilette of the lady of fashion instead of the cottage of the labourer, (with whom a familiarity and colloquiality of expression will form a recommendation,) we should animadvert on a variety of inelegant phrases which occur in it;—such as *cutting a figure, living in style.* &c. &c.²⁹⁸

The First Book of Poetry, for the Use of Schools. Intended as Reading Lessons for the younger Classes. By William Frederick Mylius.²⁹⁹ 12mo. 3s. Bound. Godwin. 1811.

This volume is a sort of introduction to Mr. Mylius's 'Poetical Class Book;' and among the variety of poems and extracts which it contains, it has the merit of offering none that can be unintelligible or uninteresting to the very young readers for whom the work is intended.

The compiler has shewn as much good sense as taste in the choice of his subjects, and we apprehend that his industry cannot fail of being rewarded by the improvement of those for whose service it is exerted.

The Poetical Class Book: or Reading Lessons for every Day in the Year. Selected from the most popular English Poets, ancient and modern. For the Use of Schools. By William Frederick Mylius. 12mo. 5s. Bound. Godwin.

The propriety of accustoming young persons to read poetry aloud is generally acknowledged; and the present selection will be useful, not only in giving them a taste for this kind of reading, but in teaching them to understand the merits and to distinguish the manner of our most eminent poetical authors, at the same time that they will be enriching their memories with many of the most pleasing and beautiful passages contained in their works.—We think that the methodical arrangement of the extracts must increase the utility of this compilation.

True Stories, or interesting Anecdotes of Children; designed, through the Medium of Example, to inculcate Principles of Virtue and Piety. By the Author of 'Lessons for Young Persons in humble Life.'[300] 12mo. 2s. 6d. Boards. Longman and Co. 1810.

These little anecdotes are related in simple and pleasing language, and they receive value from their authenticity as well as their morality. They will form an agreeable addition to many youthful libraries, and the compiler has displayed judgment in the greater part of the selection.

An Introduction to Geography. Intended chiefly for the Use of Schools. With a large Collection of Geographical Questions and Exercises, an Outline of the Solar System, and a Selection of the most useful Problems on the Globes. By Isaac Payne.[301] 2d Edition, considerably enlarged and improved. 12mo. 5s. Darton and Harvey. 1809.

We have already noticed this work with commendation; (see M. Rev. Vol. lii, p. 108.)[302] and in the present edition some errors of the first have been corrected, and many additions and improvements are made. Among these, the plan of exercising the learner's memory, by the questions at the end of the book, seems new and judicious; and the Historical Sketches are concise and well written, though we consider it as a defect that they are not all carried up to the same period; the account of Sweden going no farther than to the freedom obtained by Gustavus Vasa, and that of Italy terminating with the surrender of Rome to the Pope by Charlemagne, while the history of France leaves off with the Death of Louis XVI., and those of Holland and of Spain are continued to the placing of Bonaparte's brothers on the thrones of those countries.[303] Altogether, we may recommend this as a well arranged and compendious introduction to geography; containing very little superfluous matter, and affording more useful information than is often found in a work of so limited a compass.

Practical English Prosody and Versification; or Descriptions of the different Species of English Verse, with Exercises in Scanning and Versification. Gradually accommodated to the Capacities of Youth at different Ages, &c. &c. By John Carey, LL.D.[304] 12mo. 4s. bound. Gillet.

Dr. Carey disclaims all intention of making poets and poetesses by this publication; professing that his aim is only 'to teach the learner to read poetry with propriety, and to improve his style for prose-composition:'— but it seems scarcely necessary to go through a whole book of scanning-exercises in order to gain a knowledge of the metrical feet; and in Lindley Murray's English Grammar,[305] not to mention others, we have already a reasonable number of exercises on this very plan. However, Dr. Carey's work is the most compendious of the kind which we have seen; his examples are collected with much industry; and his explanations may be useful not only to readers of poetry, but to those composers of "splay-foot verse"[306] who wish to learn the common rules of metre.

Key to Practical English Prosody and Versification. By J. Carey, LL.D.[307] 12mo. 2s. 6d. Gillet. 1809.

This is a necessary appendage to the "Practical English Prosody," as containing all the exercises of the latter, properly filled up and arranged, so that the student will be enabled to correct his own mistakes.

A Sequel to the Poetical Monitor, consisting of Pieces select and original, adapted to improve the Minds and Manners of young Persons. By Elizabeth Hill. 12mo. 3s. bound. Longman and Co. 1811.

It is no slight praise to say that this publication forms an appropriate sequel to the excellent selection for still younger readers, which Mrs. Hill lately produced, and which we announced in one of our former Numbers.[308]

Almost all the poems in the present volume are transcribed from authors whose names alone would suffice to recommend them;[309] they are classed according to their subjects, which include most topics of moral contemplation; and we think that it is an additional proof of the compiler's good taste, that most of the compositions with which she presents us are short and complete: while the few extracts which she makes from longer works are better calculated to stand alone than such mutilations usually appear.

Familiar Letters, addressed to Children and young Persons of the middle Ranks. 12mo. 3s. Boards. Darton and Harvey. 1811.

Though the style of this writer is neither forcible nor fluent, her work[310] is recommended by a spirit of rational piety and benevolent solicitude; and it contains advice on the regulation of the mind and conduct, which may be useful to young persons in every rank of life. Some poetical sketches are introduced; among which we were pleased with a hymn, (page 116.) derived from the pen of the late Professor Carlyle.[311]

Manuel Epistolaire, or, the Young Lady's Assistant in writing French Letters. 2d Edition. 12mo. 5s. sewed. Deconchy. 1810.

This work appears to be well adapted for the purpose which it is meant to fulfil. The "Essay upon the general principles of the Epistolary Art," with which it commences, is written with judgment and acuteness; the chapter relative to French epistolary forms is useful and perspicuous; and although the subjects for letters which the author furnishes are trifling, they will be serviceable from his having subjoined the idiomatic French expressions at the end of each: while his extracts from celebrated French letter-writers are calculated to form the style and improve the taste of the reader.

Simple Pleasures. Designed for young Persons above twelve Years of Age. By Miss Venning.[312] 12mo. 3s. 6d. bound. Harris. 1811.

When country-walks and a game at chess were proposed to the Regent Duke of Orleans, the reason which he alleged for declining them was, "*qu'il n'aimoit pas les plaisirs innocens*";[313] and this answer involuntarily occurred to us as we perused the volume of 'Simple Pleasures' with which Miss Venning has provided us. This work is, however, intended for readers between the ages of twelve and fourteen years; and to such it will certainly be innoxious, and may perhaps prove both instructive and amusing. The fair author has composed it according to the plans and hints contained in Mr. Edgeworth's book on "Practical Education:"[314] but she carries his system too far when she describes a girl who receives exactly the same education as her brother, and is afterward taken into partnership with him, and made a clerk in her father's counting house!

A New Introduction to Reading; containing many useful Exercises, or Lessons, adapted to the Capacities of Children of either Sex, from six to twelve Years of Age. By the Rev. G. J. Davies, A.M.[315] 12mo. 2s. bound. Lackington and Co. 1811.

The materials of this little book are not original, but the plan of it is in some measure new; since the compiler has arranged his reading and spelling-lessons so as to furnish progressive studies during a long period of education. His selections appear well adapted both to amuse and to improve the pupil; and, notwithstanding the great number of schoolbooks which already exist, we think that no parent or teacher can regret that the present publication is added to the list.

Chronology, or the Historian's Companion: being an authentic Register of Events, from the earliest Period to the present Time. Comprehending an Epitome of universal History, antient and modern, with a copious List of the most eminent Men in all ages of the World. By Thomas Tegg.[316] 12mo. 6s. bound. Tegg. 1811.

It appears to us that Mr. Tegg has inserted every event which we can reasonably expect to find in a work of this size, while his arrangements are judicious, and his little volume will be found both portable and useful: but, from a laudable desire to furnish as much information as was admissible, he has introduced some derivations of old phrases and contradictions of vulgar errors which have no connection with chronology, and very little with common sense. Many names which occur in this publication are also printed inaccurately; such as *Spencer* for *Spenser*, the poet;—*Le Seuer* for *Le Sueur*,—*Conimbra* for *Coimbra*,—*Herrin hunters* for *Herren huters*, or Moravian brethren; &c. &c.

Dix's Juvenile Atlas; containing 44 Maps, with plain Directions for copying them. Designed for the junior Classes. 4to. 10s. 6d. and 14s. coloured. Darton and Harvey. 1811.

Mr. Dix[317] *directs* that the copyist should trace these maps through transparent paper, and pierce holes with a needle in order to draw a parallelogram. We do not consider these mechanical methods as very improving; but, the maps being mere outlines of each country, without any subdivisions or cities marked, the work may perhaps be rendered useful by requiring students to fill up their copies, and to insert some of the names and boundaries which Mr. Dix has omitted.

Guy's New British Reader, or Sequel to his New British Spelling Book, containing a great Variety of easy Lessons, selected from approved authors; exhibiting a very easy Gradation, and adapted to the junior Classes of Ladies and Gentlemen's Schools. By Joseph Guy, Author of "the Pocket Cyclopedia", "School Geography", &c.[318] 120. Cradock and Joy, &c. 1811.

Mr. Guy's title-pages usually contain a minute description of his works, while his prefaces bestow on them an elaborate commendation. He has certainly furnished some useful books for children; and although the present selection may not be, as he asserts, 'the only one in which are concentrated those objects which every teacher must desire to see united,' it appears to be well arranged, and to offer amusement and instruction in all the extracts of which it is composed.

Juvenile Correspondence, or Letters designed as Examples of the epistolary Style for Children of both Sexes. By Lucy Aikin. 12mo. 1s. 6d. Johnson and Co. 1811.

Miss Aikin has ably surmounted what she states to be the chief difficulty of her undertaking, viz. 'to render these letters better than children's and yet like children's.' They possess amusement and variety, yet are still so natural that many youthful scribes may derive assistance from them. We think, however, that some of the expressions are too familiar; such as 'these children *came to be reckoned* the cleverest;' (p. 3.) 'the clock of St. Paul's is a *monstrous thing;*' (p. 109.) &c.; and we object to the anecdote of Edward's dashing a rat against the wall in p. 16., and to the story of the fox and the wolf, (p. 67.) as being likely to excite ideas of cruelty and cunning, which would be contrary to the general tendency of this ingenious performance.

Sermon sur les Devoirs de la Jeunesse, &c.; i.e. A Sermon on the Duties of Youth, translated from the English of Dr. Blair, by M. Lenoir, Professor of the French Language, Author of "*Les Fastes Britanniques,*" &c. 12mo. Pamphlet. Dulau and Co.

In this translation of Blair's excellent discourse on the duties of youth,[319] the meaning and spirit of the original are well preserved; and it will therefore be acceptable to all who cannot read the sermon in English, as well as to those students of the French language for whose service it seems to have been more expressly intended.

English Exercises, for teaching grammatical Composition on a new Principle. By John Fenwick.[320] 12mo. 2s. 6d. Sherwood and Co. 1811.

Mr. Fenwick objects to the method of giving children exercises in false grammar to correct, lest their ear should be habituated to its errors; and he has therefore invented a mode of exercising young grammarians, by putting every word in the sentence that is declinable and is varied into its root, and requiring them, with the help of certain directions, to restore the sense. His plan appears to be deserving of attention.

Evening Entertainments; or Delineations of the Manners and Customs of various Nations, interspersed with Geographical Notices, Historical and Biographical Anecdotes, and Descriptions in Natural History. Designed for the Instruction and Amusement of Youth. By G. B. Depping.[321] 2 Vols. 12mo. Boards. Colburn. 1811.

We are told by Mr. Depping that he proposes 'to unfold all the advantages with which the teaching of geography is capable of furnishing parents and instructors of youth;' and in pursuance of this plan he has written a series of conversations, in which an intelligent father is supposed to describe to his children every thing remarkable which he has learned or observed in the course of his travels. The dialogues consequently impart so much general knowledge and amusing information, that we think the author has not only established his proposition, but has produced a very entertaining and valuable book for children.

The Elements of Conversation, French and English. By C. Gros.[322] 12mo. 2s. 6d. Dulau and Co. 1811.

It appears to us that M. Gros has composed an ample and useful collection of French and English dialogues, by which the colloquial idioms and peculiarities of the French language may be in a great measure learned, and in which all the most usual topics of conversation are introduced.

Choix de Biographie, &c. i.e. Biographical Selections, antient and modern, for the Use of Youth: or Notices respecting the most celebrated Men of various Nations, with their Portraits neatly engraved (in outline) from the best Originals. By C.P. LANDON, Painter, &c.[323] 12mo. 2 Vols. Paris. 1810. Imported by Dulau. Price 1l.8s. Boards.

M. LANDON's *Historical Gallery of celebrated Men* was announced in the Appendix to our xlixth Vol. p. 544. (N.S.); and, as he rightly observes, that work being much too voluminous and costly for the use of young people, he has formed the present abridgment of it for their benefit. It is still an elegant production, in which the biographical sketches, though necessarily very brief, are written with simplicity, and are much embellished by the portraits affixed to each. Some of the heads, such as those of Mohammed and Confucius, are evidently *ben trovati*:[324] but others are well drawn from antique sculpture and original paintings, and confer great interest on the publication.

In the account of Dr. *Franklin* a ludicrous error occurs by assigning the year 1705 (1725) to his acquaintance with Sir *Isaac Newton*, when the Doctor's birth had been accurately dated in 1706. High praise is given to the talents of *Garrick*; whose remains were deposited in Westminster Abbey, 'where the ashes of heroes, and of men whose talents have rendered them celebrated, repose by the side of those of their sovereigns.' This idea is repeated when speaking of *Shakspeare*; of whom it is said that his most distinguished pieces are *Othello*, the *Merry Wives of Windsor*, (here improperly rendered *les Commères*, or *Gossips*,) *Hamlet*, *Macbeth*, *Julius Cæsar*, *Henry IV.* and *Richard III.*; and it is added 'the most sublime beauties sparkle in his plays, by the side of the most ridiculous extravagancies, and never did genius shew itself more unequal; never did it fall so low, after having taken so elevated a flight.'—Our great lexicographer and moralist *Johnson* is strangely overlooked.

New Dialogues, in French and English: containing Exemplifications of the Parts of Speech, and the auxiliary and active Verbs; with familiar Conversations on the following Subjects, History, Arithmetic, Botany, Astronomy, The Comet, The Opera, Singing, Hippodramatic Performances, Italian, Painting, Music, &c. &c. &c. By W. Keegan, Author of "*Le Négociant Universel*," &c.[325] 12mo. Common Paper, 3s. Fine, 4s. Boosey. 1811.

We agree with Mr. Keegan in wishing that more instructive subjects should be found for French and English dialogues than the directions to tradesmen, valets, and washerwomen, of which they usually consist; and as in the present work an attempt is made to convey some information, we recommend it to those who are in the habit of committing French conversations to memory.

School of Instruction: a Present, or Reward, to those Girls who have left their Sunday-School with Improvement and a good Character. By a Lady. 8vo. 2s. Ryan. 1812.

We have seldom seen instructions for the young, the poor, and the ignorant, which were more pleasingly simple or more laudably pious than these Exhortations. They are transcripts of weekly lectures delivered by the author to the children of a Sunday-school; and we think that they may be useful to many who are engaged in a similar good work.

The Accomplished Youth: containing a familiar View of the true Principles of Morality and Politeness. 12mo. 2s. 6d. Boards. Crosby and Co. 1811.

Too many Chesterfieldian documents[326] are here interspersed with the writings of Blair, Raleigh, and Mme. de Lambert:[327] but this little book offers a great variety of useful counsel, and is farther recommended by its portable size and moderate price.

Instinct displayed, in a Collection of Well-authenticated Facts, exemplifying the extraordinary Sagacity of various Species of the Animal Creation. By Priscilla Wakefield.[328] 12mo. pp. 311. 5s. 6d. Boards. Darton and Harvey. 1811.

By collecting instances of animal sagacity, Mrs. Wakefield not only affords her young readers a rational amusement, but a powerful incentive to humanity. We applaud her attention in selecting, for this pleasing little volume, only such facts as have been attested by persons deserving of credit, and her candour in detailing them precisely in the same form in which they were communicated to her: but we confess our incredulity respecting the musical taste of a dog, who (see page 192.) is said to have *beaten time* with his tail to the Piano-forte.

On the Education of Daughters; translated from the French of the Abbé Fenelon, afterward Archbishop of Cambray.[329] 12mo. 2s. 6d. Boards. Darton. 1812.

This little treatise by the venerable Fenelon is written in a spirit of such benevolent piety, and contains such excellent practical advice, that we do not hesitate in recommending it to the perusal of mothers, while we applaud the care and accuracy with which the translator has given the sense of the original.

Rules for English Composition, and particularly for Themes; designed for the Use of Schools, and in Aid of Self-Instruction. By John Rippingham.[330] 12mo. 3s. 6d. Boards. Longman and Co. 1812.

Mr. Rippingham presents his readers with a sensible explanation of the nature of themes, and a few useful directions for their composition. The examples, which occupy the largest portion of his book, are taken chiefly from the writings of Addison, Johnson, and Blair;[331] and they are so judiciously analyzed, that we think this work will prove adapted to the purposes for which it is intended.

Miscellaneous English Exercises. Consisting of selected Pieces of Prose and Poetry, written in false Spelling, false Grammar, and without Stops, calculated to convey Amusement and Instruction to young Minds, as well as to promote Improvement in the Orthography of our own Language. By the Rev. Wm. Jillard Hort.[332] 12mo. 3s. 6d. Boards. Longman and Co. 1812.

When works like the present are employed in the education of children, much depends on the intelligence and care of the teacher; and we cannot recommend these exercises indiscriminately, lest the pupil, who has toiled through a volume in which every sentence is purposely rendered erroneous in grammar and spelling, should be in danger of retaining the faults which he was desired to correct, and thus create more trouble and confusion than if he had merely been desired to rectify his own mistakes.[333]

Elements of French Grammar, more especially designed for the Use of the Gentlemen Cadets of the Royal Military Academy at Woolwich. By Lewis Catty, First French Master in the above Academy.[334] 12mo. 4s. Robinson. 1812.

Elementary books, grammars, and exercises, multiply so fast on us, that, if any person inquires the reason for these numerous publications on the same subject, we are tempted to answer, like Peter Pindar's vender of razors, that they were "made to sell."[335] We can, however, advise the purchase of the present work by those who are not already provided with French grammars, since it appears to be clear and comprehensive, and it contains some useful observations on the rules.

A Dictionary of the Idioms of the French and English Languages. By a Society of Masters. 12mo. 4s. 6d. bound. Sherwood and Co. 1812.

The plan of this work appears to be new, and we think that it might be very useful to those who study the French language, if it were arranged with more circumspection: but, for the service of learners, those phrases which are provincial, or obsolete, and only found in books, ought to have been distinguished from such as may be used in conversation. Some sentences are inserted which we believe to be equally inadmissible in writing and in speaking; thus, in page 101., '*Elle est forte sur le piano-forte, sur la harpe,*' &c. is a common expression: but nobody would say, '*Elle est forte* sur la musique,' or '*C'est un homme* de frit,' p. 104. In page 28. a separate explanation is required for the quotation from Racine, viz.

> *Tous les plus gros Monsieurs me parloient chapeau-bas,*
> *Monsieur de petit Jean, ah! gros comme le bras;*[336]

because the expression "*gros comme le bras*" has not the same meaning with those of '*à bras raccourci,*' and '*à tour de bras,*' which precede it.—In page 31. the following sentence, '*Cela le rendit bien camus,*' which (if it be ever used) signifies, "That made him look very foolish," is thus translated: 'His nose was finely pulled;'—*un nez camus* literally means a flat nose.—On the whole, we would recommend a careful revision of this Dictionary; since we applaud the ingenuity of the idea, and the industry which has already been exerted in collecting the idioms.

The Mirror of the Graces; or the English Lady's Costume; combining and harmonizing Taste and Judgment, Elegance and Grace, Modesty, Simplicity, and Œconomy, with Fashion in Dress, &c., with useful Advice on Female Accomplishments, Politeness, and Manners, &c. &c. By a Lady of Distinction. 2d Edition. 12mo. 7s. 6d. Boards. Crosby and Co. 1811.

The author of this book descends to all the minutiæ of dress and colours, descants on short stays and long stays, prescribes the number and length of her fair readers' petticoats, and concludes with recipes for improving their complexions, and removing their corns. We shall scarcely be expected to examine seriously a work of this description: but we think that some of the observations on propriety in dress and in dancing evince good taste and good sense.

The Cabinet of Entertainment, a new and select Collection of Ænigmas, Charades, Rebuses, &c., with Solutions. 12mo. 4s. Boards. Colburn. 1811.

To such persons as love "to clear these ambiguities,"[337] this publication offers a fund of harmless amusement, and it is one of the most select yet ample collections of ænigmas and charades which we remember to have seen.

Observations on the most important Subjects of Education: containing many useful Hints to Mothers, but chiefly intended for private Governesses. 12mo. 5s. 6d. Boards. Darton, Harvey, and Co. 1812.

This fair writer[338] evinces piety and good sense; and her observations on obedience to parents, as well as on attention to the minor duties and daily courtesies of life are excellent; though too much resembling the remarks of Mrs. H. More, on the same subject,[339] to be original. It is indeed difficult to furnish new or striking remarks on the hackneyed topic of education; yet we think that a young instructress may find this volume useful from the judicious and practical advice which it contains.

A Series of Tales from a Preceptor to his Pupils. Written for the Instruction and Admonition of Youth of both Sexes. Rendered from the German of the celebrated Adlerjung. By Wm. Wennington.[340] 12mo. 7s. Boards. Chapple. 1811.

Whatever spirit or interest these tales may possess in the original, it is completely lost in this very lame translation; and the stories contain anecdotes of licentiousness and depravity which it would be wiser to keep from the knowledge of youth than to press on their notice: lest they should resemble the Cock in the fable, whose curiosity was excited by the description of danger, and who, after having fallen into the Well, exclaimed,

"But for my mother's prohibition,
I ne'er had been in this condition!"[341]

Thoughts on Education, in two Parts: the first on general Education, and the second on that of Females. By Agnes Sophia Semple, Daughter of the late Rev. Dr. Henry Hunter.[342] 12mo. pp. 307. 7s. Boards. Murray. 1812.

If "authors before they write *would* read,"[343] many might be assisted by the observations of others, and some few would be deterred from publishing their own by perceiving how "stale and unprofitable"[344] they were likely to appear. In the present instance, Mrs. Semple avows 'that she had read but few writers on education;' and those whose researches have been more extensive will find no obvious improvement of system or novelty of idea elicited in her work, although it contains several views of the subject, and is enlivened by agreeable anecdotes and quotations. Rousseau's opinion, that religious instruction should be deferred till the pupil has attained his fifteenth or eighteenth year,[345] is ably combated at p. 189.; and the strictures on Fordyce's Sermons to Young Women, p. 270., are not without foundation.[346]

We also agree with the fair writer in regretting that music, drawing, and dancing, are not more frequently taught by females, since such employments would furnish a respectable addition to the few resources which women possess for their own maintenance: but we cannot refine as she does on the impropriety of the contrary method, nor 'consider as dangerous to the purity of youth the liberties which a dancing and music-master may and sometimes must take in directing the performance of their pupils.'

First Lessons in English Grammar, adapted to the Capacities of Children from Six to Ten Years old. 12mo. 9d. Longman and Co. 1812.

This little book is well adapted to the instruction of very young children, the different parts of speech being explained in short and simple lessons; and the ingenious illustration of them at page 37., taken from Abbé Bossuet's Grammar,[347] is likely to captivate the pupil's attention, and to remain in his memory.

The French Scholar's Depository; in which are gradually developed the most important Elements of French Conversation. By Anne Lindley, Author of "A Preparatory French Grammar," and "The Translator's Assistant." 12mo. 1s. 6d. Darton and Harvey. 1811.

The plan of this work is so judiciously arranged, that, if it were more carefully printed, it might be very useful: but, among other errors, we find at page 3., '*de la soi,*' for *de la soie:* p. 6. '*n'étois je frivole,*' for *n'étois je pas frivole*: p. 8. '*des tortine,*' for *des tartines*: p. 13. '*Conjugez,*' for *conjuguez*: p. 30. '*dancer,*' for *danser*: p. 38. '*un conturiere,*' for *une couturiere*: p. 57. '*bien dorme,*' for *bien dormi*: p. 65.' *avoir droite,*' for *avoir droit*: p. 77. '*couillir,*' for *cueillir,* &c. &c.—Some of the sentences are so incorrect, that we know not whether the blame of them should rest with the author or the printer; such are the following phrases, page 6., '*n'etoient ils pas obligeant*': p. 63. '*comme le tems passé,*' for 'how time slips away;' and p. 77., '*plusieurs d'autres choses.*'

A Father's Bequest to his Son, containing Rules for Conduct through Life. Intended as a Companion to Gregory's "Father's Legacy."[348] 12mo. 4s. 6d. Boards. Chapple. 1811.

In this little production, the strictures on reading are excellent: but the course of study recommended to a son would be equally eligible for a daughter; and in the advice on 'Domestic Habits,' we trace an indulgence and deference for the fair sex which even lead us to suspect that the writer belongs to it. The work, however, displays rational sentiments and liberal principles, and may be perused with safety and advantage by every class of readers.

Eastern Tales; or Moral Allegories: illustrative of the Manners and Customs of Oriental Nations, and designed for the Instruction and Amusement of Youth. 12mo. 5s. Boards. Chapple. 1811.

So many eastern tales have been published since the Arabian Nights' Entertainments first appeared,[349] that it seems to be a work of supererogation to spin out more: but the present stories are moral, and may possibly amuse young readers whose taste for oriental fictions has not been palled by repetition.

The Parent's Offering, or Tales for Children. By Mrs. Caroline Barnard.[350] Small 12mo. 2 Vols. Godwin. 1813.

In these tales, our young readers will find considerable variety and interest, together with some humour and a good moral tendency. In the story of Helen Holmes, however, the character of *Louisa* displays a want of feeling and of gratitude which is scarcely possible in early youth, and which is not sufficiently punished; and we question whether the author judges wisely in displaying to children such faults and vices as they are not likely to commit.—To the composers of juvenile books, we would say with a French writer,

> —*N'enseignons que le bien:*
> *Le mal s'apprend tout seul.*[351]

A New System of English Grammar; with Exercises and Questions for Examination: interspersed with critical Notes and explanatory Observations, chiefly of a practical Nature. Also an Appendix, containing an extensive Collection of Vulgar Anglicisms, Scotticisms, Examples of bad Arrangement, of Ambiguity, &c. and Elements of English Composition. With a Key to the Exercises. By William Angus, A.M., Teacher of English, &c. 12mo. Printed at Glasgow; and sold in London by Cowie and Co.

The chief merit which the author claims for this grammar is that it contains in one volume such exercises and explanations as have been published by others in three and even four separate tracts. We think that mere beginners will find Mr. Angus's 'Orthographical Rules' more puzzling than a common spelling-book: but the work is compendious, and well calculated for those who are somewhat advanced in the study of English grammar. The list of Scotticisms may be usefully studied by the young North Briton, who is desirous of writing English without those peculiarities.

The Deserted Village School, a Poem.[352] 8vo. 2s. Longman and Co. 1812.

We should be glad to see the pleasantry of this writer more worthily employed, than in ridiculing the zeal for promoting the education of the poor which now pervades the kingdom. Few persons seem to question the expediency of teaching children of all ranks to read and write; and, since the old "Village Schools" were insufficient for this purpose, it may be well to assist or supersede them by later inventions. At any rate, and without engaging deeply in controversy with the author, we deem his fears about the alphabet perfectly futile, and can assure him that learning to trace the letters in sand is not 'a slippery knowledge gained too soon;' as well as that, if he chuses to 'peep' at some of Dr. Bell's school-mistresses,[353] 'amidst their pigmy throng,' he may still see 'high spectacled her *reverential* nose,' as he informs us was the case with his favourite dame in days of yore.

Fables in Verse; from Aesop, La Fontaine, and others. By Mary Anne Davis.[354] 12mo. Boards. Harris. 1813.

As a work intended for children, these fables have considerable merit; since they are written with a pleasantry which must make them attractive, and the moral lessons which they convey are adapted to young people: while the author's poetical style is easy, and sufficiently harmonious.

Conseils à ma Fille; ou nouveaux Contes; i.e. Advice to my Daughter, or more Tales. By J. N. Bouilly, Author of 'Tales for my Daughter.' 12mo. pp. 319. Boards. Colburn. 1813.

This volume may be considered as a sequel to the former production of the same author, which was mentioned in the M.R. for Jan. 1811, since M. Bouilly still offers his advice under the attractive form of tales.[355] In some of these compositions, however, the *dénouement* is too theatrical; many of the characters are such as will scarcely be found in real life; and in the story intitled '*Les Presomptions*,' the mistakes of the two sisters are exaggerated till they become unnatural. Yet, as this work uniformly inculcates lessons of practical morality, while it offers an agreeable variety of anecdotes, it may be read with amusement and advantage.

The Juvenile Spectator. Part II. Containing some Account of Old Friends, and an Introduction to a few Strangers. By Arabella Argus.[356] 12mo. Darton. 1812.

We noticed this writer's first volume in the Review for January, 1811, and we announce with pleasure the second part of so pleasing a work.

The idea of a Spectator for children is ingenious; and the trifling faults and unpleasant habits to which they are liable are here displayed in a good-humoured and amusing manner. We cannot, however, congratulate Mrs. Argus on having attained the grammatical accuracy to which we counselled her to aspire. In page 38., we read the following sentence:

'The last *twelve months has* made;' and in page 142., 'Whose amiable mind and excellent character *has* excited,' &c.

The Lady-Birds' Lottery; or the Fly's Alphabet. By Queen Mab. Pocket 4to. 1s. Longman and Co. 1813.

Although it is beyond the comprehension of those children who have still the alphabet to learn, this ingenious performance may afford amusement in the nursery, and procure additional popularity for *Queen Mab*.[357]

A Guide to Tutors, Parents, and private Students, in the Selection of Elementary School Books, in every Branch of Education, by the late Rev. Joshua Collins.[358] A new Edition, revised and enlarged, by the Rev. Samuel Catlow, late Master of the Seminary at Wimbledon, &c. 12mo. 1s. 6d. Longman and Co.

Elementary books for children are now published in such numbers, that a work like the present becomes desirable to assist the choice of teachers, by pointing out some of the most eligible performances in the different branches of education. Messrs. Collins and Catlow are too fond of recommending *selections* of history and poetry, instead of entire works which might be read with still greater advantage: but, on the whole, they have executed their task with ability, and have produced an useful little volume.

Diurnal Readings; being Lessons for every Day in the Year; compiled from the most approved Authorities, and calculated to combine Entertainment with Instruction. 12mo. 6s. bound. Sherwood and Co. 1812.

This volume offers much variety, and contains some useful and many amusing extracts from recent publications. Those from the writings of Dr. Buchanan and Dr. Clarke will be found particularly interesting:[359] but the details from Prud'homme (mis-spelt *Proudhomme*, at page 290.) of the atrocities committed during the French Revolution, and the account of an impalement, from Stockdale, in page 268., with some other passages in the same style, are so horrible that perhaps the eye of youth should not be unnecessarily shocked with them. The description of "The Burning of Hindoo Women," in page 321., is copied from Southey's "Curse of Kehama," and not from the "Asiatic Researches," as is erroneously stated;[360] and the name of *Nealliny* is in this transcript changed to *Nealing*.

Elements of Universal Geography, ancient and modern, containing a Description of the Boundary, Chief Cities, Sea Ports, Rivers, Mountains, Religion, Population, Climate, Historical Events, &c. &c., of the several Countries, States, &c., in the known World: to which are added, Historical,

Classical, and Mythological Notes, by A. Picquot.[361] 12mo. pp. 312. 5s. 6d. Lackington and Co., 1812.

M. Picquot apologizes for verbal inaccuracies, by stating that he writes for the first time in a language not his own; and he thus not only accounts for some quaint expressions, but excites our surprize at the general propriety of his style. His book offers considerable information; and the Synopsis of Antient Geography is ingenious, though in course somewhat conjectural. Too much is perhaps attempted at once; and the mixture of history and mythology with the geographical lessons may confuse those who attempt to commit the whole to memory.

The School Cyphering Book, for Beginners; containing all the Variety of Sums and Questions usually proposed in the first five Rules of Arithmetic; viz. Notation, Addition, Subtraction, Multiplication, and Division. With a complete Set of Arithmetical Tables. By Joseph Guy, Author of a "Pocket Cyclopedia," "School Geography," &c. &c.[362] 4to. 3s. 6d. Boards. Cradock and Joy. 1811.

This seems to be a plain useful cyphering book; and the questions to be resolved at the end of each rule are well selected. Mr. Guy's method of furnishing printed sums to beginners will certainly save trouble. A *Key* to this book is published, and may be purchased separately.

The Geographical Primer; designed for the younger Classes of Learners, and calculated to advance them by natural and easy Gradations to a perfect Acquaintance with the Elements of the Science; with an Appendix, containing 1400 Questions on the principal Maps. By. J. H. Wiffen.[363] 12mo. pp. 216. Darton, junior. 1812.

These lessons, being concise, are advisable for young beginners; and it may be considered as an improvement that, in naming the principal cities and towns in England, the rivers are also mentioned, on which several of those places are situated: as 'Chester on the Dee,' 'Reading on the Thames,' (and Kennet,) &c.: but we were surprised to see that the *Liffey* is omitted among the rivers of Ireland.

The New Young Man's Companion; or the Youth's Guide to general Knowledge, designed chiefly for the Benefit of private Persons of both Sexes, and adapted to the Capacities of Beginners. By John Hornsey, Author of "A short Grammar of the English Language," &c. &c.[364] 12mo. 4s. Boards. Longman and Co. 1811.

An useful compendium of information on various subjects, of which a part is original, and the rest is judiciously chosen from other works. The student, however, would be led into a slight breach of *etiquette* if he addressed a letter to '*The Honourable* Sir A.B., Bart.,' or to '*The Honourable* Sir A.B., Knight,' in compliance with Mr. Hornsey's directions in page 79., Baronets and Knights not being *consequently* Honourable.

An English Vocabulary, in which the Words are arranged indiscriminately, designed as a Sequel to "The Scholars' Spelling Assistant," for the Purpose of grounding young Persons more effectually in Spelling and Pronunciation: to which are added, Miscellanies on the most useful and interesting Subjects. By Thomas Carpenter, Author of "The Youth's Guide to Business," &c.[365] 12mo. 2s. bound. Longman and Co. 1813.

The *indiscriminate* arrangement of words in this spelling-book can be no recommendation, since children perhaps learn and retain most easily those lessons in which their ear is assisted by similarity of sounds. The letters before each word, denoting the part of speech to which it belongs, may be considered as an improvement; and the explanations will be useful where they are likely to be intelligible, although some of them are better fitted to exercise the memory than to increase the knowledge of the pupil. Thus, '*spurious*' is illustrated by a longer word, and said to mean '*illegitimate;*' '*bust*' is stated to be 'the figure or portrait of a person in *relievo;*' and '*history*' is described as 'a very useful species of instruction, which may properly be called the common school of mankind.' Such definitions are not sufficiently clear for those who have yet the rudiments of arts and sciences to learn.

The Female Class-Book; or Three Hundred and Sixty-five Reading Lessons, adapted to the Use of Schools, &c. By Martin Smart. 12mo. 6s. bound. Lackington and Co. 1813.

As this compilation contains a variety of extracts,[366] among which many are pleasing and none are reprehensible, it may be recommended to those who determine to employ young persons in reading scraps and quotations, instead of perusing entire works, and following up the subjects on which they may have begun to gain instruction.

Grammatical Questions on the English Grammar, being an easy Method to interrogate Young Persons in Classes, and useful to Teachers and others, to Examine the Progress of Education on that Subject. By the Reverend Christopher Muston, Preceptor of the Boarding School, Epping, Essex. 12mo. Robins and Sons. 1813.

The above title is somewhat deficient in perspicuity; and the grammatical questions, to which it refers, would have been more generally useful to teachers if answers had been annexed to them. They may, however, certainly save some trouble by suggesting topics of examination.

Scriptural Stories, for very Young Children. By the Author of "The Decoy,"[367] "Natural History of Quadrupeds," &c. With Copper-plates. 12mo. 1s. Darton and Co. 1813.

This little book has an affectionate simplicity of style, which will make it attractive and intelligible to young children: it also conveys excellent admonitions, and gives a clear account of several scriptural histories.

The Mother's Fables, in Verse. Designed, through the Medium of Amusement, to convey to the Minds of Children some useful Precepts of Virtue and Benevolence. 12mo. 1s. 6d. Boards. Darton and Co. 1812.

We approve this writer's[368] plan of 'preceding every fable by a childish anecdote which illustrates the moral,' and can recommend the little volume as offering an agreeable variety of subjects. 'The Frog's Song,' page 33., is original; and Aesop's Fable of 'The Gnat and the Bull' is versified with considerable pleasantry. We doubt, however, whether cuckoos and tom-tits are to be found in the native groves of the *mocking-bird*, although placed there by the author of these ingenious little pieces: see page 3.[369]

The Nursery Companion; or, Rules of English Grammar, in Verse. By a Lady. Pocket 4to. Pp. 23. Crosby. 1813.

These lines have perhaps as much melody as the subject would admit; and the composition is lively and ingenious. The work may therefore be useful, if the attraction of rhyme be found to recommend the dry study of grammar, and to atone for the additional intricacy which it here receives from the unavoidable transpositions occurring in verse.

The Decoy; or an agreeable Method of teaching Children the Elementary Parts of English Grammar by Conversations and familiar Examples.[370] Small 12mo. 1s. Darton and Co. 1813.

We may recommend this little book as an useful present to the nursery; the dialogues being simple and amusing, and explaining clearly the nature of the different parts of speech. [ns 73 (February 1814): 212]

Maternal Sollicitude for a Daughter's best Interests. By Mrs. Taylor, of Ongar.[371] 12mo. 5s. Boards. Taylor and Hessey. 1814.

The subjects of these essays are well chosen, and ingeniously diversified; and the fair writer displays a degree of piety, with a knowledge and application of the Scriptures, which increases the value of her work. Yet the comparison, in page 111., may be deemed rather strained between Solomon's knowledge of trees and plants,[372] and a young lady's improvement of days and moments; and in page 155. a trifling mistake occurs in a passage beginning thus:—'The being who *ushers* forth from under the paternal roof.' It was probably intended to have been, 'The being who *rushes* forth,'[373] &c.

French Phraseology. 2d Edition. 12mo. Law. 1814.

Though an accurate knowledge of the peculiarities of any language is best obtained by reading and conversation, yet, as the present collection of French idioms is compendious and methodical, it will be useful for occasional reference. The corresponding French and English expressions are accurately discriminated, excepting the very few instances which we must notice as erroneous.

In page 10. "*Ecrire au courant de la plume*" is rendered thus: "To write *currente calamo,*" which Latin phrase should have been "translated for the country gentlemen,"[374] or rather it ought not to have been inserted in this book of elementary instruction. Page 21. '*un maitre ès arts*' is probably misprinted for *des arts*; as in page 94. '*amiable*' is twice put for the French '*aimable.*' The expression in page 83., '*Elle n'a point de naturel,*' may be said to mean, *She has no simplicity*, rather than 'she has no natural affection,' as it is here explained; and in page 99. '*La contention d'esprit*' is obscurely translated by 'great application or exertion of mind.'

Maxims, Reflections, and Biographical Anecdotes. Selected for the Use of Young Persons. By James Hews Bransby.[375] 12mo. 2s. half-bound. Johnson and Co. 1813.

This selection is deficient in arrangement, the passages in each section having no obvious connection with each other: but they all inculcate laudable sentiments, and may therefore be safely put into the hands of young people.

Punctuation; or an Attempt to facilitate the Art of Pointing, on the Principles of Grammar and Reason. For the Use of Schools, and the Assistance of general Readers. By S. Rousseau.[376] 12mo. 5s. Boards. Longman and Co. 1813.

Some advantage may certainly be derived from the perusal of these hints, although the examples are needlessly multiplied, and in a few instances the writer's grammar is inaccurate. Thus, (in p. 105.) he says,[377] '*every verse* in the Psalms, the Te Deum, and some other parts of the Liturgy of the Church of England, *are* divided by a colon;' and in page

146. the following sentence is incorrect: 'we do not see but such a mode of punctuation is allowable.' Some errors occur also in the quotations; such as in page 47., 'Nor cast *me* longing ling'ring look behind;' and, page 63., 'And bathed in *fragment* oils that breathed of Heaven.' These mistakes may be attributable to the printer, but they ought to have been rectified. It is to be observed, also, that the author has borrowed too largely from preceding writers, without due acknowledgement.

The History of the distressing Loss and happy Recovery of little Thomas Dellow, who was stolen from St. Martin's Lane, Upper Thames Street, London, on the 18th of November 1811, and discovered at Gosport in Hampshire on the 28th of December following. 12mo. 1s. Darton, Harvey, and Darton. 1812.

This little tract details all the circumstances yet known, relative to a strange affair by which the public was considerably interested;[378] and the narrative will excite sympathy in those young readers who may meet with it.

Sir Hornbook; or Childe Launcelot's Expedition; a Grammatico-Allegorical Ballad.[379] Pocket 4to. 1s. 6d. Sharpe and Hailes. 1814.

This little poem is not sufficiently plain to be substituted for the first pages of an English Grammar, but it is written with spirit, and it will both exercise and reward the ingenuity of its young readers.

The Elements of Arithmetic, being a full, clear, and comprehensive Introduction to the Science of Numbers. For the Use of Schools and Private Tuition. In five Parts, each published separately. By E. Ward, Teacher of Writing, Geography, and Mathematics.[380] 12mo. Part I. 10d. Part II. 1s. 3d. Wilkie and Robinson. 1813.

Mr. Ward's publication is judiciously divided into separate parts; each being of small size and price. The first and second carry the student as far as Compound Division, and explain the first four Rules of Arithmetic with clearness and accuracy. They contain many useful tables, and good practical questions: but the *Addition and Subtraction Table*, (Part I.) which is recommended to be learned by heart, appears to us to be quite unnecessary, and calculated only to puzzle the learner.

The Spanish Guitar; a Tale, for the Use of Young Persons. By Elizabeth Isabella Spence, Author of "Caledonian Excursion," "The Curate and his Daughter," &c. 12mo. 3s. Boards. Chapple. 1814.

would employ: such as 'ben't for be not;' —'d for had;'—'D' for do;'—'d'os for does;'—'do't for do it;'—'ha'n't for have not;'—'Gi me for give me;'—'t' th' for to the,' &c.

The English Pronouncing Spelling-Book, on a Plan entirely new, calculated to correct Provincialisms, &c. By Thomas West.[390] 12mo. bound. Darton and Co. 1812.

On recurring to the above title, we were ready to exclaim, like Sterne, after he had repeated the text of one of his sermons, '*That I deny;*'[391] since we discover nothing 'entirely new' in the plan of this publication, though it is a good spelling-book, containing many reading-lessons of very short words, and therefore well calculated for the use of young beginners.

Ellen; or The Young Godmother, a Tale for Youth, by Alicia Catherine Mant.[392] 12mo. bound. Law. 1814.

The opening of this little tale is pleasing both by its novelty and its morality, and the latter recommendation is preserved throughout the work: but, after the commencement, instead of displaying the peculiar situation and duties of a young godmother, the writer diverges into hackneyed improbabilities, such as making a father who was supposed to be dead suddenly re-appear, and find a son who was said to have been dead also, &c. Some few incorrect sentences occur, as, (page 67.) 'Ellen happy *of* an opportunity,' &c. P. 97. 'They were gratified by receiving dispatches from Henfield, and *of* learning that their friends were all well,' &c.

Introduction to the Diurnal Readings, being choice Pieces in Prose and Verse, adapted to the Capacities of Youth; in which is employed a certain Mark, to point out the intermediate and almost imperceptible Pauses observed by good Readers and Speakers. By Thomas Haigh, A.M. Master of the Boarding-School, Kitts End, Barnet. 12mo. 3s. bound. Sherwood and Co. 1814.

To the selection of these little pieces[393] we offer no objection, but we think that the subdivision of sentences, introduced by the editor, is troublesome and fanciful; as it is more desirable to vary the tone and accent than to suspend the breath in reading those short passages which are not interrupted by commas, and as the mechanical part of these inflexions must be learnt orally, and therefore cannot be communicated by Mr. Haigh's proposed *hiatus*.

An Introduction to the Epistolary Style of the French; or a Selection of familiar Notes and Letters in French; for the Use of Schools, with an alphabetical Index, explanatory of the Words and idiomatical Expressions.[394]

By George Saulez, D.F.I.M. Farnham, Surrey, Author of "Theory and Practice of the French Language," &c. 12mo. bound. Law. 1814.

This selection presents considerable variety, and is well calculated to assist young people in acquiring a good French epistolary style. In a few instances, however, we discovered errors of the press which may mislead, as (p. 12.) '*La compagnie*' for *la compagne;* (ib.) '*la compagne*' for *la campagne*; (p. 60) '*Monsieurs P.*' for *Monsieur P* &c.

New Orthographical Exercises, with the correct Orthoëpy of every Word, for the Use of Foreigners, and Schools in general. By Alexander Power, Master of the Commercial Academy, Ashford, Kent.[395] 12mo. bound. Law. 1814.

We have already objected to the plan of giving passages erroneously spelt, as exercises to children, who may probably retain some of the faults which they are desired to correct, and which might not otherwise have occurred to them. Those teachers, however, who approve of this method, will deem the present an eligible publication; since the proper accent is added to each word, and a kind of scale of the vowels is added which will afford some assistance in the pronunciation.—In p. 99. a letter 'from Lord Chesterfield to Dr. R. C.' is made to begin and end with "My dear Lord."

A First or Mother's Dictionary for Children; containing upwards of 3800 Words which occur most frequently in Books and conversation, simply and familiarly explained, &c. By Anna Brownell Murphy.[396] 12mo. 4s. 6d. bound. W. Darton.

This dictionary is formed on the same plan with an ingenious little glossary which Miss Edgeworth added to one of her juvenile stories;[397] and, though the present collection of words might with advantage have been made more copious, yet the explanations given are so well suited to the capacities of children that we have no hesitation in recommending the work.

The Juvenile Arithmetic, or Child's Guide to Figures; being an easy Introduction to Joyce's Arithmetic, and various others now in Use. By a Lady. 12mo. 1s. Souter. 1814.

As this little tract may be serviceable from the attractive form of dialogues, in which the lessons are conveyed, and from the clearness and simplicity with which it explains the first four rules of arithmetic, it is adapted to the perusal of juvenile accomptants.

A French Dictionary, on a Plan entirely new; wherein all the Words are so arranged, and divided, as to render their Pronunciation both Easy and Accurate, &c. By William Smith, A.M. 8vo. 8s. 6d. Boards. Law. 1814.

Mr. Smith's ingenious scheme for teaching the pronunciation of the French language, by analogy, may claim attention from such persons as learn French by an English fire-side; though we believe that no exhibition of similar sounds in English will enable them to speak French so well as they may hope to do it by practice and oral instruction.

Mentor and Amander; or, a Visit to Ackworth School, with descriptive Notes. By a late Teacher.[398] Crown 8vo. 1s. Darton. 1814.

We are disposed to agree with Mentor in his abhorrence of severe corporeal punishment for children; and, for the sake of giving publicity to his mild suggestions, we should be glad to recommend this simple and rather pleasing description of the school at Ackworth, instituted by the Society of Friends.

Rules for pronouncing and reading the French Language. By the Rev. Israel Worsley.[399] 12mo. 2s. Longman and Co. 1814.

Rules for pronouncing are here, as they must always be, insufficient; and Mr. Worsley's directions seem particularly vague. For instance, in page 14. he says that the *g* is mute in *rang* and *sang*, whereas those words have a different sound from that which they would receive without the *g*. In page 27. we are told merely that '*mienne, sienne, tienne*, are not nasal sounds;' when it should have been stated that *no* French words terminating with a double *n* and *e* final are to be considered as nasal sounds. In the list of particles, it is probably from an error of the press that *du* is directed to be employed as a substitute for *de la*: the term should be *de le*, because *de la* is correct before a noun feminine, when *du* would be improper. In page 42. the particle *que* is not added to the potential mood, which is thus written by Mr. Worsley:

> *Je parle*, I may or can speak,
> *Je parlasse*, I might or could speak,

yet nobody would speak correctly who should speak thus; and the omission of *que* may mislead learners, though it is, for the sake of brevity, in the conjugation of verbs, tolerated by grammarians.

We agree with Mr. W. in advising the student to 'begin soon to read,' since we believe that, in acquiring any language, this is the best method: but we cannot see the necessity for removing every flower from the road to learning; nor for chusing, according to Mr. W's advice, 'such books as are least interesting, in order that the attention may not be drawn from the rules of pronunciation'.

Original Letters of Advice to a Young Lady. By the Author of "The Polite Reasoner."[400] 12mo. 2s. 6d. bound. Souter. 1814.

In this specimen of book-making, four pages are occupied by a part of the 40th chapter of Isaiah, 'given in case the reader should not have *that book* immediately at hand;'[401] and the writer is mistaken in ascribing to Dr. Garnett the eastern tale of *Zadig and the Basilisk*:[402] but we will not trouble our readers with the numerous inaccuracies which abound in these letters, because they are compensated by no attractions: the ideas and advice are equally common-place, and perhaps have been "ne'er so *ill* expressed"[403] in any recent work on similar subjects.

A Synopsis of French Grammar, comprehending the most useful and necessary Rules in Chambaud's Grammar, and many other Points and Peculiarities on the French Language. By P. F. Merlet.[404] 12mo. 2s. Longman and Co. 1815.

It may be objected against this little book that it refers continually to Chambaud's Grammar, instead of 'comprehending the most useful rules' in that work; and we attempted in vain to *practise* M. Merlet's directions for pronouncing the French particles *un* and *on*, in articulating which he enjoins his reader to 'emit the second sound from the pit of the stomach, and to convey it through the nose.' The best part of the treatise is the 'selection of words and phrases which, occurring often in English, have a particular acceptation in French.' These are stated to have been taken from *Le Manuel Epistolaire*, of which M. Merlet does not inform us who is the author:[405] but the opposition and variation of several phrases in the two languages are here so clearly shewn, that this selection merits attention; and, though not so copious as it might be wished, it will be found decidedly useful.

A Grammar of the French Language, in which the Rules are illustrated by Examples selected from the best Authors, by C. Laisné, Teacher of Languages, &c.&c.[406] 12mo. 5s. Boards. Dulau and Co.

In the present work, as well as in his Spanish and Portugueze grammars, (See our Rev. Vol. lxv. N.S. pp. 106, 107.) M. Laisné judiciously "avoids all tedious disquisitions on the principles of general grammar," and gives examples from the writings of esteemed authors, instead of the dialogues which are usual in similar publications. His extracts are generally well chosen: but a little more discrimination was necessary between those idiomatic phrases which should be read merely in order to be understood, and those which may be adopted in conversation. This observation applies particularly to the passages from Don Quixote and Gil Blas;[407] which, as they are here given, may lead a student into the egregious mistake of mixing with the polished language of Buffon and Fenelon[408] such inelegant proverbial expressions as the following: p. 231., '*trouver une franche lippée,*' to feast for nothing; p. 234. '*lui donne le croc en jambe,*' tripped up his heels; p. 235., '*bien jouer des machoires,*' to make a good use of one's teeth; '*pour me tirer les vers du nez,*' to press me, &c. &c.,

A Key to the Re-translation of the English Examples in the French Grammar, intended to serve as a Test of Accuracy. By C. Laisné. 12mo. Dulau and Co. 1814.

This companion to the preceding grammar will be particularly useful to those who study French without the constant help of a master.

A copious Collection of instructive and entertaining Exercises on the French Language, with the different Parts of Speech and Rules of Grammar prefixed to every Article. By C. Laisné. 12mo. 4s. 6d. Boards. Longman and Co. 1814.

Since these passages are selected from the works of St. Pierre, Buffon, Mme. de Sevigné, &c. they may be considered as examples of correct and elegant French writing; and they are so disposed as to furnish separate exercises on all the different parts of speech, which we consider as an ingenious and improving arrangement.

A Key to the copious Collection of instructive and entertaining Exercises on the French Language, or the original French of the English Examples faithfully transcribed. By C. Laisné. 12mo. 4s. 6d. Boards. Longman and Co. 1814.

In this companion to the above work, we have noticed a few typographical errors besides those which are mentioned among the errata. For instance, in page 53. '*Le Roi l'a* (la) *fit mettre.*' Page 62., '*On peut trouver un verre* (ver) *sous la dure coque d'une aveline,*' &c.

Tables of the different Parts of Speech in French. By C. Laisné. On Sheets, in a Pocket Case. 4s. 6d. Dulau and Co.

These tables may be found useful, because they comprize the rudiments of the French language in a small compass, and in the convenient form of a grammatical pocket-companion.

Practical Hints to Young Females, on the Duties of a Wife, a Mother, and a Mistress of a Family. By Mrs. Taylor, of Ongar. Author of "Maternal Solicitude for a Daughter's best Interests."[409] 12mo. 5s. Boards. Taylor and Hessey. 1815.

We have pleasure in recommending this little work, in which a sensible practice is founded on Christian principles, and in which the several subjects are judiciously distributed, and treated in a manner which must interest as well as convince. Yet we must observe that Mrs. Taylor has not quite exhausted the topic of domestic duties; and it will perhaps be wished that, in those chapters which treat of family-economy and the management of children, she had descended more into particulars, and, in addition to her valuable general remarks, had furnished some suggestions for particular situations, as well as more advice relative to those cares and arrangements which usually devolve on young mistresses of families with slender incomes.

EXPLANATORY NOTES

Lessons for Children

LESSONS FOR CHILDREN, FROM TWO TO THREE YEARS OLD

To avoid interrupting the text of *Lessons for Children* with distracting superscripts, we have keyed each explanatory note to the original page number. Because each page has few lines of text, we have omitted line numbers in the margin, as well. So the note below tied to 'is got' appeared on page seven (7) of the original publication and line 4, or '7.4'.

Advertisement.6 'nonsense...*Ignorance*': By 'nonsense' Barbauld likely meant the silly ways adults often spoke to children, and probably also techniques for 'alluring children to read' such as 'the Cuz's Chorus', a device for teaching phonics by solmization syllables (*A Pretty Play-Thing for Children of all Denominations*, 1759+; imperfect copy in Cotsen Children's Library, PUL).

7.4 'is got': Joseph Priestley judged this seeming regionalism to be arguably better English than 'has got': 'It seems not to have been determined by the English grammarians, whether the passive participles of verbs neuter require the auxiliary *am* or *have* before them.... The French would say, *what is become*; and in this instance, perhaps, with more propriety' (Priestley, *Rudiments*, 127–8).

8.4–5 'why did you kill the rabbit?': Richard Lovell Edgeworth objected strongly to this sentence: 'The Idea of killing is in itself very complex and if explained serves only to excite terror. And how can a child be made to comprehend why a Cat *should* catch mice & not kill Rabbits; indeed I know of no reason why this species of Honesty is to be expected from an Animal of Prey' (Edgeworth, Letter, fol. 54ᵛ; Edgeworth repeated this objection almost unchanged, but in a different context, in *Practical Education*, 318).

9.2 'Puss cannot speak': A major theme of *Lessons* is the idea that what distinguishes human beings from animals is that humans can speak and animals cannot. Lacking speech, Puss also lacks moral sense and cannot take responsibility for her actions. Barbauld linked speech and ethics. The idea goes back to Aristotle and appears again in the *Essai sur l'origine des connoissances humaines* by Étienne Bonnot de Condillac (1746; translated into English as *An Essay on the Origin of Human Knowledge*, 1756).

10.2 'Get up': 'Mrs. Barbauld has judiciously chosen to introduce a little boy's daily history in these books; all children are extremely interested for Charles, and they are very apt to expect, that every thing which happens to him is to happen to them' (Edgeworth, *Practical Education*, 318–19).

11.8 'Corn': Grain (the US equivalent is 'wheat'). The following passage (through 'bread and milk') proceeds associatively: from bread to the product that makes bread, to where that product is found, to what else is found there. The theory of association goes back to John Locke, but David Hartley proposed a renovated version in *Observations on Man* (1749), a book that greatly impressed Joseph Priestley. See Wharton, 113–14: Barbauld's text 'gradually spread[s itself] out over the material and the everyday, mirroring the mind's own development' by association of ideas (114).

14.3–4 'three kisses': In nursery games, events such as kisses often occur in threes: e.g. 'Kiss me three times' in 'Father Francis' (Opie and Opie, p. 8).

23.1 'I want my dinner...ready yet': Edgeworth objected to Charles's demand for dinner: 'Does Charles take it for granted, that what he eats is his own, and that he *must* have his dinner' (Edgeworth, *Practical Education*, 318) Edgeworth apparently thought *Lessons* endorsed this behaviour, but 'It is not ready yet' subjects Charles's demand to the discipline of reality.

34.5 'Billy...and sister Sally': Sally is unidentified. In 1778 Charles did not have a sister. Several pupils at Palgrave School were named William.

43.1 'Little boys...butter': Edgeworth remarked that 'Charles must know that some little boys do eat butter' and that 'this mode of expression, "Nobody does that!"...lays the foundation for prejudice in the mind' (Edgeworth, *Practical Education*, 319). Barbauld may have been remembering 'when butter was forbid' to her in childhood: see 'Washing-Day', l. 65.

47.3–4 'The table did not...place': This passage is a nod to Elizabeth Carter's *Epictetus*: 'In Infancy...if we happen to stumble, our Nurse doth not chide *us*, but beats the Stone. Why: what Harm hath the Stone done? Was it to move out of its Place, for the Folly of your Child?...It is he whom you are to correct and improve' (Carter, *Epictetus*, 276–7).

56.4–5 'when the Sun...bed': Edgeworth objected to this passage: 'When the sun is out of sight, would be more correct....Every thing relative to the system of the universe is above the comprehension of a child, we should, therefore, be careful to prevent his forming erroneous opinions' (Edgeworth, *Practical Education*, 320). Elizabeth Hamilton disagreed: ' "The moon shines at night when the sun is gone to bed," is an expression in one of Mrs. Barbauld's excellent little books for children, and objected to by Miss Edgeworth on account of the erroneous opinion it conveys. With all due deference to an authority so respectable, I much question, whether the idea excited by the expression above quoted can make more than a momentary impression on the most juvenile pupil; while the false opinions that may be formed of the tutor's motive for obliterating the reprobated line, will probably give birth to pride and suspicion, passions that are neither transient nor innoxious. To preserve the tender mind from false and erroneous notions upon every subject, appears at first sight to be very desirable; but to do so effectually, we must shut up the organs of sense, for by the impressions made upon these, thousands of erroneous notions are every day received, at a period when the judgment is immatured by experience, and the mind incapable of reflection. But as these impressions are slight, the associations formed by their means are transient, and may therefore be easily changed.

We may obliterate lines, and cut out whole pages, of the books we put into our children's hands, in the manner recommended by Miss Edgeworth, and yet find it impossible to prevent the misconceptions of infant inexperience, for these will often attach false ideas to a word or sentence which appears to us clear and intelligible' (Hamilton, 1:409–10). See Barbauld's review of Hamilton's *Letters on the Elementary Principles of Education*.

1808 additions, cued by 1778 page numbers

19.2–4 'Negroes...wool': Barbauld may be referencing 'Blackface' characters in plays such as Charles Dibdin's long-running *The Islanders* ('it will not wash off'). While such depictions are repugnant today, Barbauld was ahead of her time in describing differences of skin-colour and other traits as facts of nature, with the aim of broadening the child's awareness of and acceptance of human diversity.

19.6 'train oil': Oil obtained from whale blubber (*OED*, citing van Leeuwenhoek, 1712).

27.3–4 'Then nightly...whoo': *Love's Labours Lost*, NOS V.ii.917–18.

LESSONS FOR CHILDREN, OF THREE YEARS OLD, PART I

8.3 'A week': 'The enumeration of the months in the year, the days in the week, of metals, &c. are excellent lessons for a child who is just beginning to learn to read' (Edgeworth, *Practical Education*, 320).

9.3 'It is January': Barbauld's traversal of the months from January to December loosely adapts the 'Calendar of Flora' in Benjamin Stillingfleet's *Miscellaneous Tracts relating to Natural History, Husbandry, and Physick. To which is added the Calendar of Flora* (1762), the work that introduced Swedish innovations in Botany to English readers. The 'Calendar' notes not just the times when plants flower but also other seasonal phenomena: for example, for December 22, '*Butter shrinks and separates from the sides of the tub*' (Stillingfleet, 261); for March 25, '*Roads very dirty and full of water*' (262); and for April 6, '*The* FLY *creeps forth*' (262). Calendars of the seasons were not in themselves a new thing; Ovid's *Fasti* details the events of the year day by day, Stillingfleet quotes Pliny's remark that '*Some people...think the appearance of the butterfly the surest sign of Spring*' (262), and Barbauld's beloved James Thomson had, of course, written *The Seasons*. Nevertheless, John Aikin credited Barbauld with having started something in *Lessons*: his *Calendar of Nature* (1784) was confessedly based on the 'description of the several months, formed of some of the most striking circumstances attending each' (JA, *Calendar*, v). Aikin's son Arthur revised his *Calendar* under the title *The Natural History of the Year* (1799), and Leigh Hunt, in turn, paid it homage in *The Months, descriptive of the successive Beauties of the Year* (1821). In 1831, William Howitt published *The Book of the Seasons, or the Calendar of Nature*.

11.1 'Ralph': This could be a generic name or the name of a servant in the Barbauld household.

11.5–12.1 'February...coming up': Edgeworth quotes a shortened version of this sentence in *Practical Education*, 1:63.

12.3–4 'snow-drops...heads': The snow-drop figures in Barbauld's poem 'The Invitation'. The boys at Palgrave School planted snow-drops (S. W. Rix, 3:).

18.3 'Billy': This may be a Palgrave School pupil.

22.6–7 'make hay...shines': Barbauld shows how this familiar saying is grounded in farming practice.

28.1 'Diggory': Probably a generic name; it does not appear among names of Palgrave landholders.

29.5 'harvest home': William Hone quotes Leigh Hunt: '"This is the month of harvest....Harvest-home is still the greatest rural holiday in England, because it concludes at once the most laborious and the most lucrative of the farmer's employments, and unites repose and profit"' (Hone, 1059).

37.1 puss: An affectionate name for a hare (*OED*).

38.6 'Betsy': No girls are known to have attended Palgrave School. 'Betsy' may have been a neighbourhood child, or, like 'Anna' in Barbauld's poem 'A School Eclogue', she may be fictional.

45.3–9 'But I will tell you...is not a bird': This and the following lessons pursue the theme that humans and animals essentially differ, but that each is endowed with specific abilities and gifts that serve analogous ends. 'No, because Charles is not a bird' may be a nod to Pope's *Essay on Man*: 'Why has not Man a microscopic eye? / For this plain reason, Man is not a Fly' (i.193–4; Pope, 511).

65.9 'cress...seed': Palgrave boys did grow gardens with cresses and mustard plants (*ALBVE*, 595 n. 5).

73.6–9 'No, puss...robin': Concern for animal welfare in the later eighteenth century tended to focus on birds. In *Exercises for the Memory and Understanding* (1798) the Hollands write approvingly of a boy who 'beat the cat' for trying to catch a bird (Holland, 119). See Barbauld's 'Epitaph on a Goldfinch'.

74.6–8 'George...names': George and Arthur Aikin, Charles's brothers, were pupils in the school.

74.8–78.7 'there was a robin....afterwards': 'The description...of the naughty boy who tormented the robin, and who was afterwards supposed to be eaten by bears, is more objectionable than any in the book' (Edgeworth, *Practical Education*, 318). A later compiler changed this story to give it a happier ending: the boy is taken in by 'a poor man who was passing that way' (*Lessons for Children, by Mrs. Barbauld*, 67).

1808 additions, cued by 1778 page numbers

65.2–3 And when...bed': From an anonymous popular poem, 'Song. The Fairies', found in *Elegant Extracts* and elsewhere: 'And if the moon doth hide her head, / The glow-worm lights us home to bed' (Knox, 3:891).

LESSONS FOR CHILDREN, OF THREE YEARS OLD, PART II

27.9–31.9 'Charles wants some bread....bread and butter': In detailing the different trades and operations necessary to produce a slice of bread and butter,

EXPLANATORY NOTES 433

this lesson adapts a dialogue by James Harris in 'Concerning Happiness' (Harris, *Three Treatises*, 150–1). Barbauld follows Harris in demonstrating the interdependence of human beings in society. She had read Harris's exposition of Stoicism in her teens, at around the time she read Epictetus (*ALBVE*, 51–3).

38.3–4 'caterpillars...ground': Caterpillars served both as a subject of scientific inquiry and as another occasion of teaching respect for animals; see the headnote to Barbauld's poem 'The Caterpillar'.

52.7 'eat her up': Lucy Aikin's friend Catherine Sharpe reported how strongly her step-brother responded to this and another story in *Lessons*: '[William] will sit and read Mrs Barbauld's stories of the little lamb, & the Robin starved [to] death till he sobs so he cannot go on. I have several times been obliged to send him to play in the middle of reading to recover himself' (Sharpe). See *Lessons for Children, of Three Years Old*, part I, 74–8.

75.1–4 'You shall go...make it': Glass-making was one of Warrington's industries; Barbauld had probably witnessed the process.

75.5–7 'A tree...way': See Barbauld's piece about 'Trees' in the Palgrave School section of this volume.

85.6 'his eyes sparkle like fire': In 1794, William Blake may have been recalling this passage when he asked 'Tyger, tyger burning bright....In what distant deeps or skies, / Burnt the fire of thine eyes?'

88.8 'court': The forecourt, presumably the area fronting or adjoining the Palgrave School house, which was also the Barbauld residence (see fig. 32 in *ALBVE*).

1808 additions, cued by 1781 page numbers

33.1–2 'Monomotapa': A region in southeast Africa on the 1794 map of *Africa, with all its States, Kingdoms, Republics, Regions, Islands, &c., improved and inlarged from D'Anville's Map...By S. Boulton*. It included present-day Zimbabwe, Lesotho, Swaziland, and Mozambique, and parts of Namibia, Botswana, Zambia, and South Africa.

75.4–76.1 'Ulysses...at his feet': Barbauld retells the episode of Ulysses' arrival home, from the *Odyssey*, Book xvii.

LESSONS FOR CHILDREN, FROM THREE TO FOUR YEARS OLD

5.1–2 'the story of the Two Cocks': Versions of a story about a Cock and a Fox proliferated in the eighteenth century. Elements of this one occur in a popular collection by Samuel Croxall (*c.* 1690–1752) 'The Fighting Cocks', *Fables of Aesop and Others* (1722).

13.1 'I will...story': Parents of Palgrave School students sent food gifts. This story is a variation on folk tales in which events occur in threes. See also Barbauld's 'Petition of a Schoolboy', a poem written in the voice of a boy asking for a cake from home.

25.6 'court': The forecourt of the Palgrave schoolhouse.

31.1–5 'down the lane...fields': An 1812 Enclosure Survey map of Palgrave shows features that correspond approximately to Barbauld's description. See Palgrave Enclosure Survey 1812. B150/1/312 Suffolk Records Office.

37.1–38.1 'here is a river...a Bridge': If they are walking north, the river is the Waveney and the bridge Cock Street Bridge (W. P. Rix, 10; today Denmark Bridge). Mention of the bridge reinforces Barbauld's theme that humans benefit from living in society.

42.2 'Rabbits': Norfolk, the county on the other side of the Waveney, had a large population of rabbits.

55.2–4 'water...not like to drink it': Perhaps Coleridge remembered this sentence in *The Rime of the Ancient Mariner*: 'Water, water every where, / Nor any drop to drink!' (II:37–38).

61.9 'Arthur': Arthur Aikin, Charles's older brother and a pupil at Palgrave School.

62.3–4 '*Serviteur Monsieur*': 'Your servant, Sir', a polite way of expressing non-comprehension.

66.5–6 'papa...French': Rochemont's native language was French.

68.2–3 'Quadruped': 'The classification of animals into quadrupeds, bipeds, &c. is another useful specimen of the manner in which children should be taught to generalize their ideas' (Edgeworth, *Practical Education*, 320).

71.1 'The Ass says': Barbauld's making animals speak (a traditional device in fable) distressed Thomas Bentley, otherwise her admirer: 'Why will this good Lady go contrary to Nature, and persist in making dumb animals speak?' (Bentley [1779], 488). It did not disturb Richard Lovell Edgeworth: 'Poetic descriptions of real objects are well suited to children' (*Practical Education*, 321).

74.8–75.2 'my milk...well again': The use of asses' milk for nutrition dates to ancient Egypt. French naturalist Georges-Louis LeClerc (1707–88) had reasserted its value.

82.6 'torn and bloody': 'The pathetic description of the poor timid hare running from the hunters, will leave an impression upon the young and humane heart, which may perhaps save the life of many a hare' (Edgeworth, *Practical Education*, 320). In Coleridge's periodical *The Watchman*, 'Felix' praises Barbauld for 'teach[ing] lessons of compassion towards animals' (Coleridge, 268).

89.5–6 'My name is Sun': Sarah Trimmer remarked disapprovingly that in making Sun and Moon speak, Barbauld made them behave like pagan deities (Trimmer, *Guardian*, 2:45).

95.7–9 'Eagle...always': The myth that eagles can gaze at the sun goes back at least to Pliny (first century CE).

1808 additions, cued by 1779 page numbers

71.2 *curricle*: 'A superior kind of two-wheeled carriage' (W. Felton, 1794, quoted in *OED*) designed to be drawn by two horses abreast. It was considered a particularly genteel form of transportation.

104.4 'pecked at it': Pliny the elder tells the story in *Naturalis Historia* of Zeuxis (fl. late fifth century BCE), who painted grapes so realistic that birds flew down to peck at them.

107.2 'explain the *thing*': See Barbauld's explanation of language to 16-year-old Lydia Rickards in her letter on Grammar.

Hymns in Prose for Children

Preface.17 'social worship': The term preferred by Rational Dissenters such as Barbauld to signify formal religious services.

Hymn I.3–4 'rule...by night': An example of Barbauld's stylistic method in *Hymns*: she weaves a phrase from the King James Bible ('to rule the day', Genesis 1:16) into her own sentence to produce the effect of biblical idiom. The opening of Hymn I as a whole holds the same place in *Hymns* that Genesis holds in the Bible; thus *Hymns* begins with the Creation.

I.16 'reason...me': See 'my reason returned unto me' (Daniel 4:36).

Hymn II.18 'chickens come out': A hatching chick breaks its own shell. Barbauld's error suggests that she may never have carefully observed the process.

II.33 'We can thank him...better': As in *Lessons*, so here Barbauld asserts the ontological superiority of humans over other creatures, by virtue of their having language. But with that superiority comes an obligation to speak for the other creatures ('we will thank him for those that cannot speak,')—an unorthodox view, as Sarah Trimmer noticed.

II.43 'we will offer sacrifice for you': Sarah Trimmer, who defended orthodox Christianity in *The Guardian of Education*, objected to this passage: '[N]or do we read in Scripture that human beings, who stand in constant need of a Mediator themselves, have ever been appointed to officiate as *Priests* for any of the brute creation' (Trimmer, 2:47).

Hymn III.1 This hymn is a reworking for the child's comprehension of Psalm 23.

III.43 'King...lords': See Revelation 17:14.

III.45–6 'light of his countenance' occurs in several psalms: see 4:6, 44:3, 89:15, and 90:8.

Hymn IV.23–4 'most excellent...behold': Sarah Trimmer objected: 'We think that children from this description may be apt to form an idea of the sun as an *intelligent being*. Neither can this bright luminary be properly called "the *most excellent creature the eye can behold*," because this epithet, in respect to the visible creation, is appropriate to MAN' (Trimmer, 2:47).

Hymn V.19–20 'hammer is not heard...carpenter': Barbauld echoes Revelation 18:22 ('And the voice of harpers, and musicians, and of pipers and trumpeters, shall be heard no more at all in thee; and no craftsman...shall be found any more in thee; and the sound of a millstone shall be heard no more at all in thee'), transposing it into terms appropriate to village life.

V.29 'never sleepeth': See Psalm 121:4, 'He who keeps Israel will neither slumber nor sleep.' A famous hymn in the *Book of Common Prayer* begins, 'There is an eye that never sleeps.' It was originally published on 28 Sept. 1839 in the *Scottish Christian Herald* by John Aikman Wallace and was probably inspired by this Barbauld hymn.

V.65 'praise': Cf. Psalms 34:1, 35:28, 51:15, 119:171, and 138:1.

Hymn VI.1 'Child of reason': Benjamin Whichcote (1609–83) invoked this phrase to oppose Puritan ideas of human depravity and argue in favour of religious toleration. However, in this hymn Barbauld uses it to criticize lack of religious imagination: The 'child of reason' sees nothing in natural phenomena beyond the phenomena themselves and needs to learn Joseph Priestley's discipline of seeing God in everything (JP, 'On Habitual Devotion'; see also Barbauld's 'Address to the Deity').

VI.11–12 'Return again': Several biblical texts use the phrase 'turn again' (often in the sense of reforming one's life). For 'Greater things than these' see John 1:50.

VI.37 'God...storm': Cf. Nahum 1:3: 'the Lord hath his way in the whirlwind and in the storm, and the clouds are the dust of his feet.'

Hymn VII.28 'Made us alive': See I Samuel 2:6 ('The Lord killeth, and maketh alive') and I Corinthians 15:22 ('even so in Christ shall all be made alive', signifying 'reborn'). Barbauld introduces the child to biblical metaphor by using phrases whose literal meaning the child can understand.

VII.62 'walk out...come in': A child would understand this phrase in its literal sense as daily coming and going. But in the Bible 'walk' carries metaphoric meaning, usually signifying the manner in which one lives (e.g. 'walk[ing] in darkness' [1 John 1:6]).

Hymn VIII: This hymn in its entirety reproduces in concrete form Francis Hutcheson's outline of 'Our Duties toward Mankind' in his *Short Introduction to Moral Philosophy* (1747). Hutcheson's outline begins with the nuclear family and moves outward through a series of (implied) analogies to 'all mankind, or all...intelligent natures'; it closes with 'tender compassion toward any that are in distress' (Hutcheson, 81–2).

VIII.54–9 'Negro woman...thee': Moira Ferguson suggests that this, Barbauld's first expression of Abolitionist sentiment, was prompted by a much-publicized 1773 visit to London of the African-American poet Phillis Wheatley (Ferguson, 132). Mary Wollstonecraft reprinted this passage in her anthology, *The Female Reader* (1789).

Hymn IX.48–9 'They are marshaled in order': Here, as elsewhere in *Hymns*, Botany provides evidence of God. Barbauld adapts Benjamin Stillingfleet's 'Introduction' to *The Calendar of Flora*: 'Every flower has its appointed season....Again in another season we see others rising in their room, and that...by so regular and constant a law, according to the direction of their natures, that it seems impossible for any one to behold this series and variety, without the highest admiration' (Stillingfleet, 252).

IX.62 'saveth': 'soweth', the reading introduced in 1814 (and accepted in the Broadview Barbauld), seems correct until one notices that the preceding verb is 'preserveth'.

IX.67 'dry bones': See Ezekiel 37:1–10.

Hymn X.39 'must die': The 1784 edition added the following: 'Let me alone, for I will weep yet longer.' See *Much Ado about Nothing*, NOS, IV.i.256: 'Yea, and I will weep a while longer'.

Hymn XI.13–19 'I have seen the insect...new being': Barbauld cites processes in the natural world to introduce the child to the spiritual idea of resurrection.

XI.28–38 'Burst open the prison doors of the tomb' suggests the Resurrection. 'To gather...heaven' and 'He descendeth on a fiery cloud' together almost

EXPLANATORY NOTES   437

quote Matthew 24:30–1; 'He cometh...power from on high' condenses
Mark 8:30 and Revelation 1:7. These four paragraphs were among the passages
Elizabeth Carter thought 'amazingly sublime'.

Hymn XII.47 'son of Jesse': David, said to be the author of Psalms.

1814 Additions

Hymn XI.11–14 'Lift up thine eyes...concave': As Hymn IX encouraged devotion through Botany, this hymn encourages devotion through Astronomy. A book Barbauld had been given at age 7, *Entretiens sur la Pluralité des Mondes* (1686), by Bernard le Bouvier de Fontenelle, invoked Astronomy to encourage awe at the diversity of the Creation. In the eighteenth century the *Entretiens* became a standard text for the education of young people.

XI.15–16 'moon...silver bow': See Charlotte Smith, 'To the Moon', in *Elegiac Sonnets* (1784): 'Queen of the silver bow!'

Hymn XII.15–16 'Has thy father forsaken thee': See Matthew 27:46.

Palgrave School

1 'brown religious horror': Poetical. The *OED* quotes Dryden's translation of the *Aeneid*: 'which thick with Shades, and a brown Horror, stood' (7:41).

2 'unwholesome': Before contagious diseases such as malaria and cholera were understood to be transmitted through germs, the miasma theory was used to explain epidemics. Noxious vapours or miasmas, generated by rotting organic matter, it was said, caused illness.

3 'says the fable': See Aesop's fable 'The Flying Fish and the Dolphin'.

4 'I trow': *OED* cites examples in which 'I trow' is only an interjection in a question.

5 'Heartily!...husband': Gandelin voices doubt of the stranger's loyalty. 'Hearty' affirmations of loyalty by residents of counties around England were published prominently in newspapers late in 1792, in response to vigilante persecution of suspected dissidents.

6 *sharp set*: 'Eager or keen for food, very hungry' (*OED*).

7 'From the Humber to the Thames': The East Midlands and East Anglia.

8 *furmety*: 'Frumenty', a dish made of wheat boiled in milk and sweetened (*OED*).

9 'Your troops...gasping on the plain': Alfred's army, besieged in Kinworth Castle by the Danish invader Hubba, made a desperate sally that surprised the Danes. '*Hubba* was slain, and his famous Standard, called *Reafan*, or the *Raven*, fell into the hands of the *English*' (Rapin, 1:332). In Thomson and Mallet: 'Behold the warrior bright with Danish spoils!— / The *raven* droops his wings' and 'The valiant Hubba bites the bloody field' (Thomson, *Works*, 2:240, 241).

10 'hospitality': In Thomson and Mallet, 'Thy rural entertainment was sincere, / Plain, hospitable, kind: such as, I hope, / Will ever mark the manners of this nation' (Thomson, *Works*, 2:243).

11 'Till...no more': These lines do not occur in Thomson's *Alfred*. Closing a scene or a play with a couplet was common stage procedure; hence this couplet may be original with Barbauld. Possibly she alludes to *Orlando Furioso*:

'And with the whole old warfare vex the land; / And that it better were to sue for peace'.

From *Evenings at Home*

12 'Things by their Right Names' incurred strong censure from Sarah Trimmer in *The Guardian of Education*: 'Evidently designed to impress children with the idea that all *warriors* are *murderers*. But to call a battle a "*bloody murder*", when the cause on one side or other is justifiable, is *not* "calling things by their *right names*"; if it were, then the people of Israel, when they went against the idolatrous nations to extirpate them from the earth, were *bloody murderers*, though they acted by the express command of the LORD GOD' (Trimmer, 2 [1803]: 308). On the other hand, Sarah J. Hale concludes the preface to *Things by Their Right Names: And Other Stories, Fables, and Moral Pieces* (1839) with the hope that 'our young readers will *study* this volume, thoroughly; there is scarcely an article in it, but deserves to be repeatedly read, till the whole is fixed in the heart as well as mind.' See also Penny Mahon, '"Things by Their Right Names": Peace Education in *Evenings at Home*', in *Children's Literature*, 28 (2000), 164–74.
13 'the one to draw the eyes, ... a third the mouth': It was standard in the workshops of the most esteemed painters to assign lower paid artist/workers with painting backgrounds, lace, ornaments, etc. Reynolds delegated the painting of costume in his portraits to 'professional drapery painters, notably Peter Toms and George Roth, who also painted drapery for Hudson' (*ODNB*).
14 'Hector...Achilles': In the *Iliad*, Book 6, Hector bids Andromache return to the women's chambers. Book 18 describes the shield of Achilles.
15 'Tubal Cain': An 'instructor of every artificer in brass and iron' (Genesis 4:22).
16 'Taught...lawn': Thomson, *The Seasons*: 'Autumn', ll. 82–6.
17 'an ingenious gentleman...weeks': Presumably Claude-Louis Berthollet (1749–1822), who in 1785 introduced the use of chlorine for bleaching. 'The common process' used sunlight to bleach cloth.
18 'Arkwright': Sir Richard Arkwright (1732–92, knighted 1786) adapted earlier inventions and, by making them more efficient, organized cloth-weaving into a factory system (*ODNB*). The claim that he could put wool into a box and have it come out broadcloth, though not true, was a boast of his system's efficiency. Barbauld may have read *The Case of Mr. Richard Arkwright and Co.* (1782) or may have heard stories of his youth from mutual acquaintances, the Gell and Wedgwood families.
19 'furnace...*glass*': Barbauld would most likely have witnessed glass-making at Warrington, which had a glass factory.
20 'Aladdin's palace': In 'Aladdin, or the Wonderful Lamp' in the *Arabian Nights*, the lamp's magical powers allow Aladdin to marry the Princess of Cathay and build a palace for her reception.
21 'treasures of Golconda': That is to say, great wealth. Before 1725, all diamonds originated in India, and the finest of those were mined in the kingdom of Golconda.

EXPLANATORY NOTES 439

22 'Feels... line': Pope, *Essay on Man*, i.218 (Pope, 512). Arachne in Greek myth competed with Athena in weaving and was turned into a spider (Ovid, *Metamorphoses*, 6:129–45).

23 '5760 times... made of': A passage in Adam Smith's *Wealth of Nations* (1776) might have suggested this calculation: 'The person who works the lace of a pair of fine ruffles... will sometimes raise the value of perhaps a pennyworth of flax to thirty pounds sterling' (Smith, 667).

24 'There was a chain... 170l.': 'Woodstock [in Oxfordshire] has two manufactures; those of polished steel and gloves, from which it derives considerable benefit. The articles of polished steel are entirely made from the old nails of horses' shoes, which are formed into small bars before applied to the various purposes of delicate workmanship. The lustre of the article thus tediously wrought is eminently fine, and the polish is restored at a trifling expense, however great the apparent injury committed by rust. The price obtained for some specimens of the Woodstock steel will convey an idea of the skill and labour bestowed. A chain, weighing only two ounces, was sold in France for 170 pounds sterling' (Brewer, 384). While the last sentence in Brewer is almost identical to Barbauld's, Brewer did not begin publishing *The Beauties of England and Wales* before 1801, so she cannot have taken it from him. Most likely the two share a common untraced source.

25 'in the year 1326... Henry the Seventh': Barbauld's source was not Rapin, whose *History of England* she had consulted on other occasions. Perhaps she drew from David Hume's *History of England*: 'Edward [III] endeavoured to introduce and promote the woollen manufacture by giving protection and encouragement to foreign weavers, and by enacting a law, prohibiting every one to wear any cloth but of English make' (Hume, *History*, 2:523).

26 'a man of great taste... China': Josiah Wedgwood (1730–95) and his partner, Thomas Bentley (1730–80), founded the manufactory that created British jasper ware. Wedgwood belonged to the circle that included Joseph Priestley, Wedgwood's son attended Warrington Academy, and his portrait subjects for cameos included Barbauld herself. On a visit to London in June 1774 the Barbaulds saw, at the London warehouse and showrooms of Wedgwood and Bentley in Great Newport Street, the 952-piece table service commissioned from Wedgwood by the Russian empress Catherine. The Wedgwood warehouse moved in 1787 to Greek Street, Soho, and in 1797 to St. James's Square.

27 'a thousand pounds': The Archivist at the Wedgwood Museum, Lucy Lead, has reported finding no record of a sale to the King of Spain, although the absence of a record does not, she says, mean that there was no sale (communication to William McCarthy, 12 December 2017).

28 'more entertainment to a cultivated mind': See ch. 1 of Smith's *Wealth of Nations*, in which he illustrates division of labor from the 'very trifling manufacture' of pin-making (Smith, 14).

29 'old rags': Rag-collecting was one of the few trades open to poor London Jews in Barbauld's time. Anti-Semitism, like anti-Catholicism, was a standard feature of British culture.

EXPLANATORY NOTES

30 'smalt': Blue glass, pulverized for use as a colouring agent (*OED*).
31 'grey Paper': Paper of low quality made from discoloured or coloured rags that remained unbleached; many books were supplied by booksellers in grey paper wrappers before purchasers had them finely bound in leather.
32 'beautiful whiteness': Black oxide of manganese, oil of vitriol (sulphuric acid), water, and common salt produce muriatic acid, a bleach.
33 'fourteenth century': In fact, paper was invented in China in the early second century BCE, and the manufacturing of paper had spread to Spain by 1144 and to Italy by 1276. Germany established its first paper mill in 1389 and Belgium in 1405. See https://www.cabinet.ox.ac.uk/origins-paper.
34 'your little books': Assuming that 'C.' in 'The Art of Distinguishing' is Charles, the books would be *Lessons for Children*. The word 'quadruped' appears in *Three to Four*, 68.
35 '*a two-legged...feathers*': Plato described man as 'animal bipes implume', a definition that Diogenes ridiculed by plucking a chicken and bringing it into the Academy, proclaiming, 'This is Plato's man.' See Diogenes Laertius, *Lives of Eminent Philosophers*, Book 6, Chapter 2.
36 'The wanton...fields again': Pope's *Iliad*, 6:652–9.
37 'the noise, and din...were put an end to': Barbauld's description of the primal chaos derives from Ovid, *Metamorphoses*, 1:1–31. All the elements were originally 'at odds, for...cold things strove with hot, and moist with dry' until 'God—or kindlier Nature—composed this strife' (Loeb translation).
38 'she has a most voracious appetite': Conduct books for young women strongly discouraged appetite: 'the luxury of eating...in *your* sex...is beyond expression indelicate and disgusting' (Gregory, 28).
39 'tallow-chandler': A maker of cheap candles. Chandlers' shops were frequent sites of fires.
40 'she was lodged...alive': The Roman goddess Vesta, a fire deity, had a temple consecrated to her and was attended by young virgins selected for purity of character. The punishment for misconduct by a Vestal virgin was, as Barbauld states, to be buried alive. An indication that Barbauld could shock her readers is the variant text of this punishment in both MS copies: 'nothing would serve her but turning the poor girls away.'
41 'make an end of me': 2 Peter 3:7: 'the heavens and the earth...are...reserved unto fire against the day of judgment.' In Barbauld's allegory, the Earth will be destroyed by Fire. Cf. her 'Hymn I.'
42 'lunatic': Besides 'insane', a second meaning (now obsolete) was 'influenced by the moon' (*OED*), as are tides.
43 'the Theban pair': In Greek mythology, Oedipus, King of Thebes, had two sons, Polynices and Eteocles. After Oedipus died, Eteocles and Polynices agreed to share the throne, but when Eteocles refused to yield it to his brother, Polynices returned to Thebes with an army. The brothers died fighting against each other, a battle memorialized in Aeschylus's tragedy, *Seven Against Thebes*.

44 'to drown me...injured by it ever since': A reference to the biblical Flood, perhaps by way of Thomas Burnet's interpretation in *The Theory of the Earth* (1691): 'this unshapen Earth we now inhabit, is the Form it was found in when the Waters had retir'd' (13).

45 'puffed cheeks': The 'bullies' are the Four Winds (North, East, South, and West), often represented in the corners of maps as faces with puffed cheeks.

46 'shake...fit': Earthquakes, which in ancient Greek science were thought to result from movements of hot subterranean winds.

47 'pendant...fois': Slightly misquoted from Racine, *Bérénice* (1670), II.ii.

48 'This is what...characters': In place of this paragraph the MS copies read, 'Of you Sir I have no complaints to make. I know that you are one of my most constant admirers, & have even attempted to delineate some striking lines of my countenance,—But what most attaches me to you is your having sent from time to time so many of your friends to lodge with me;—for this mark of our kindness I am Sir with an affection truly maternal Yours &c.' The Nicholson MS adds the signature, 'A.L. Barbauld'. John Aikin had 'delineated' some of Earth's features in *The Calendar of Nature* (1785); Barbauld's comment that he 'sent so many...friends to lodge with me' refers to Aikin's medical practice, the joke being that doctors kill more patients than they save.

Works of Imagination and Instruction

49 'smooth...step': *Paradise Lost*, 8:302 (Adam's description of a divine apparition).

50 'clouded silks': Printed silk taffeta or silk woven with a fancy yarn in which 'two single yarns in different colors are plied together. Each one alternately forms the core and covers (clouds) the other ply in the core' (Tortora and Johnson, 128–9). Gowns made of clouded silk were popular beginning around 1765.

51 'Lady ———': If this piece dates to the Warrington years, 'Lady ———' could be a local magnate such as the Countess of Stamford, to whose daughter, Lady Mary West, Anna Letitia Aikin was to dedicate *Poems*.

52 'A learned clergyman...verses on her': The Rev. Edward Young, author of *Night Thoughts* (1742–5).

53 'the younger' and 'good solo...': Both ellipses occur in the copy text. The first alludes to Ovid's tale of Dawn, or Eos (Aurora in Latin), carrying off the young man Cephalus (*Metamorphoses*, Book 7); the second may be an abridgement by Lucy Aikin. The 'fine concert of music' would be morning birdsong, the 'solo' the song of the nightingale.

54 'When...fled': Isaac Watts, 'Meditation in a Grove' (*Horae Lyricae: Poems*, 3rd edn, 1715, 115–16), slightly misquoted. Thanks to Kurt Milberger for this reference.

55 'long before the Conquest': The Norman Conquest (1066). The phrase was often used to boast of a family's antiquity.

56 'Peter...cock': For the story of Peter's denial of Jesus, see Matthew 26:75: 'And Peter remembered the word of Jesus, which said unto him, Before the cock crow, thou shalt deny me thrice. And he went out, and wept bitterly.'

57 'Heath...West-end': Hampstead Heath. West End Lane ran through the centre of Hampstead to a small village called 'West End' surrounded by farmland.

58 'birthnight': 'The evening of a royal birthday' (*OED*), for which fashionable people would dress their best. Barbauld alludes to Pope, *The Rape of the Lock*, i.23: 'A Youth more glitt'ring than a *Birth-night Beau*' (Pope, 219). 'Mareschal powder': a fashionable sweet-scented powder.

59 '*volage*': Light-minded (an adjective in *OED*, but used here as a noun).

60 'blustering fellow...family': Boreas (the North Wind), enraged by her rejection, carried off Orythia (Ovid, *Metamorphoses*, Book 6, the 'anecdotes of the family' in Barbauld's phrase).

61 'every schoolboy is acquainted with it': The story of Zephyrus and Flora was familiar to Barbauld's readers from having read Ovid.

62 'Darwin and of Cowper': Erasmus Darwin (1731–1802) and William Cowper (1731–1800) were two of the most highly regarded English poets of the 1780s and '90s.

63 '*The grass...stood*': Gay, *The Shepherd's Week* (1714): 'Sixth Pastoral: Saturday; or the Flights', l. 120 ('And how the grass now grows where Troy Town stood?').

64 'the Consulate': Cicero held the high office of consul of Rome in 63–62 BCE, but was best remembered later for his writings.

65 'Still green...ring!': Pope, *Essay on Criticism*, i.181–6 (Pope, 150).

66 'Horace...Pope': Alexander Pope's *Imitations of Horace* (1733–8) were not translations, but used Horace as a model.

67 'Verbal criticism': The determining of which parts of a text are its author's and which are not.

68 'receive...merit': i.e. as sacred texts.

69 'Jones': Sir William Jones (1746–94), linguist, founded the Royal Asiatic Society in 1784 and translated Sanskrit texts. He is considered the father of Indo-European comparative grammar (*ODNB*).

70 'Atalanta': The story of Atalanta is told in Ovid's *Metamorphoses*, Book 10. Barbauld alludes to it in *An Address to the Opposers of the Repeal of the Corporation and Test Acts* (1790), using it as a metaphor for temptations felt by Dissenters to go over to the Established Church.

71 Arion, a Greek musician and poet is said to have lived in the late seventh century BCE. The story of Arion and the dolphin is told by Herodotus in his *History* (1.23–4). The small constellation Delphinus is in the northern sky near Aquarius and Pegasus.

72 Ovid tells the story of Venus and Adonis in *Metamorphoses*, Book 10.

73 'Pygmalion...Tyrians': In Virgil's *Aeneid*, Book 1, Pygmalion, brother of Dido, daughter of the king of Tyre, murders Dido's husband to seize his gold, and hides the murder and the gold from Dido: 'Some tale, some new pretense, he daily coin'd. / To soothe his sister, and delude her mind' (Dryden translation).

74 'painting...communicate': 'Picture-writing' was a form of communication used in Mexico from the Pre-Colombian through the Colonial Period. William Robertson described it in his *History of America* (1777): by pictures

the Mexicans 'could exhibit a more complex series of events in progressive order, and describe, by a proper disposition of figures, the occurrences of a king's reign from his accession to his death.... They represent *things*, not *words*' (Robertson, 3.204–5).

75 'officers': The copy text reads 'offices'; we have corrected this printer's error.
76 'beef-eaters': A popular name for the Yeomen of the Guard.
77 'St. James's': A royal palace in London.
78 'King of Bantam': The Bantam (or Banten) Sultanate (1552–1813) was centred in Banten, a port for the spice trade in Java.
79 'Dutch': Implying (opprobriously) a heavy, sluggish build (*OED*); also an allusion to the notoriety of Dutch feasting.
80 'two guineas...Fleet Street': Mrs. Lacour shops in fashionable streets. Two guineas (£2 and 2 shillings) in 1797 was a huge sum to spend on a toy. By pointed contrast, membership in the charity sewing-group described later is a penny a week.
81 'Mrs. Dorcas': In Acts 9:36, a woman named Dorcas is 'full of good works and alms-deeds.' Mrs. Dorcas will introduce Eliza to a Dorcas Society, an association devoted to making clothes for the poor.
82 'carry a bandbox...street': A box for collars, hats, and other lightweight apparel that would be carried by a servant.
83 'a thousand pounds': To put this figure in perspective, in 1806, Charles Robert Maturin was paid a salary of 100 pounds a year as a curate. In the 1820s 'Living in a small village in Wales, without the expense of a carriage, fine clothes, wine, a large staff of servants and other costly items, [the poet Felicia] Hemans could comfortably support a middle class household [of 8] on 100 pounds per year' (Paula R. Feldman, 'The Poet and the Profits: Felicia Hemans and the Literary Marketplace', *Keats-Shelley Journal*, 46 (1997) 156 n. 12). In Lord Byron's time, roughly when *Legacy* was published, 'A senior officer on half pay, who would be expected to support his family in the style of a gentleman, received one hundred shillings per week, or 260 pounds per year' (William St. Clair, 'The Impact of Byron's Writings', in *Byron: Augustan and Romantic*, ed. Andrew J. Rutherford (New York: St. Martin's, 1990).
84 'furze': Gorse; '*Ulex europæus*, a spiny evergreen shrub with yellow flowers, growing abundantly on waste lands throughout Europe' (*OED*).
85 'startish': 'Apt to start or jib' (*OED*). The *OED* quotations apply the word to horses.
86 'city': Presumably, as in 'the City' (of London), i.e. middle class.
87 'half wages...quarter': She pays servants half a year's wages on hiring them but changes her servants every three months.
88 'Rule of three': 'A method of finding a fourth number from three given numbers, of which the first is in the same proportion to the second as the third is to the unknown fourth' (*OED*). It was a customary rule in the study of arithmetic.
89 'housewife': 'A pocket-case for needles, pins, thread, scissors, etc.' and, in this sense, usually pronounced 'huzziff' (*OED*). Harriet Martineau, who admired Barbauld enormously, nevertheless repeated a story that 'she was

not much of a needlewoman. There is a tradition that the skeleton of a mouse was found in her workbag' (Martineau, 'What Women Are Educated For', 177).
90 'Wilton carpet': Carpets made in Wilton, Wiltshire, were of high quality and costly.
91 'open...Friday': A day for visits and receptions (*OED*, s.v. 'Friday').
92 'one of the best poets...ode in her praise': Thomas Gray's 'Ode to Adversity' (1753).

Teaching Letters to Lydia Rickards

93 'eye-water...rouge': 'Eye-water' was widely advertised as 'an infallible Cure for all Disorders in the Eyes' (*London Daily Advertiser*, 25 Oct. 1796). The Cosmetic Warehouse in the Strand advertised 'a real French Vegetable White...which possesses the most beautiful properties of White Paint, without...its pernicious qualities' (*Morning Post*, 4 April 1793).
94 Copy text: *Monthly Packet* (London), ns 1 (1891): 521–2. Edith Cordelia Rickards dated the original of this letter '1797 or 98' in a MS note on Barbauld's letters to Lydia. In this letter Barbauld improved on a teaching technique she had used at Palgrave School. There she herself had corrected her pupils' exercises (see William Taylor's recollection in McCarthy, '"Celebrated Academy"', 307); here she invites Lydia to do the correcting. Years later, reviewing a volume of similar exercises in the *Monthly Review* (the Rev. William Jillard Hort's *Miscellaneous English Exercises* [*M Rev*, ns 68, May 1812: 107–8], she expressed concern lest students be corrupted by the errors they were meant to correct.
95 'cricklish': Presumably derived from 'crick', a spasmodic pain in the neck (*OED*).
96 'Mountsier': A corruption of 'mounseer', an archaic anglicized pronunciation of 'monsieur', which survived throughout the 19th century (*OED*).
97 'Aspasia': Consort of Pericles, famed for learning and wit (*c*.470–410 BCE).
98 'Semiramis': Legendary founder of Nineveh (ninth century BCE).
99 'Box hill': A celebrated tourist sight near the village of Dorking in Surrey. When she wrote this letter Barbauld was staying nearby, as a companion to her brother during his convalescence from a serious illness. See the headnote to 'The Cottage that Stands at the Foot of the Hill'.
100 'Locke': William Lock, whose estate at Norbury attracted artists and writers. See Vittoria Caetani, *The Locks of Norbury: The Story of a Remarkable Family in the XVIIIth and XIXth Centuries* (London, 1940).
101 'keeping': 'The maintenance of the proper relation between the representations of nearer and more distant objects in a picture; hence, in more general sense, "the proper subserviency of tone and colour in every part of a picture, so that the general effect is harmonious to the eye" (Fairholt); the maintenance of harmony of composition' (*OED*).

102 'I wish... motion &c.': The letter in which Lydia complied with this request has not surfaced, but Barbauld's comment on it does: 'I think you are a very good landscape-painter, & I hope you will sometime draw them with a pencil as well as a pen, only your <u>cascades</u> must not <u>gently distil</u>, but rush foaming down the steep, the greater passion they put themselves into, the better. I think too you might be satisfied with <u>one navigable river</u> instead of <u>some</u>[.] I am sure we should think ourselves very magnificent with <u>one</u> here. There is one thing I beg you will take care of in your landscapes, & that is to keep them in constant verdure. Ours are so burnt up at this moment that the <u>russet grass</u>, the <u>brown meadow</u>, the <u>tawny slope</u> are epithets much more characteristic of the objects which meet our eyes at present, than if <u>green</u> were applied to every one of them. The Summer has appeared this year in all the strength & glow of warmer climates, the true child of the sun as Thomson calls him.

In pride of youth and felt thro nature's depth

I cannot help wishing some of these chalky hills were covered with vines; I have no doubt but they would ripen. It appears that there were formerly vineyards in Britain, probably introduced by the Romans, & many places still bear the name of the <u>vineyard</u>. I believe however I need not regret it for the sake of the inhabitants, as the peasants in a vine Country are generally poor: corn is on the whole a richer produce' (ALB to Lydia, 17 June 1798; MS Misc. 4338, Pforzheimer Collection, NYPL).

103 'the Orchis... hand': A species of orchid-like plant found in temperate regions; its flowers have been fancied to resemble various creatures (*OED*).

104 'Miss H[unt]': According to the address panel, this letter made its way to Lydia Rickards via the attention of 'Mrs Hunt's / Crescent / near / Birmingham'.

105 'Mrs. Carr': Frances Carr, whose family in Hampstead were close friends of the Barbaulds.

106 'Abstruse & metaphysical' may be a swipe at James Harris's *Hermes; or, A Philosophical Inquiry concerning Universal Grammar*, a work of linguistic speculation that Barbauld thought pedantic (ALB, Letter to JA, 6 June 1787). The idea of language that Barbauld emphasizes, that it is unique to humans and consists of arbitrary signs, was available to her in previous work on language. One book that she is likely to have known is the *Essai sur l'Origine des Connoissances Humaines* (1746) by Étienne-Bonnot de Condillac. Condillac distinguishes three kinds of signs, of which the second is the vocal response to a stimulus such as pain and the third and highest 'les signes d'institution, ou ceux que nous avons nous-mêmes choisis, & qui n'ont qu'un rapport arbitraire avec nos idées' (Condillac, 65 [Part I, ch. iv]; 'instituted signs, or those that we have ourselves chosen and that have only an arbitrary relation to our ideas' [tr. Aarsleff, 36]). Another work Barbauld is likely to have known is *Of the Origin and Progress of Language* (1773–92) by James Burnet, Lord Monboddo. Like Condillac, Monboddo regards language as a distinctively human invention, but he allows that animals have powers of communication

among themselves and, as the title of his work implies, he treats language as having progressed from cruder to more refined states, an idea with which Barbauld agrees.

107 'monkeys...it': Barbauld read books about India with interest, and her brother translated a prefatory essay to his friend Thomas Pennant's *Indian Zoology* (2nd edn, 1790); but this assertion about monkeys does not appear there. She may have read it in Buffon, who says of monkeys (but without reference to Indians): 'la langue du singe a paru aux Anatomistes aussi parfaite que celle de l'homme: le singe parleroit donc s'il pensoit' (Buffon, 2:439; 'the tongue of the monkey has appeared to anatomists as perfect as that of Man; thus the monkey could speak if he thought of speaking').

108 'I know...deserves': See Barbauld's letter to Lydia Rickards, 6 June 1798. Gibbon's *Decline and Fall* was among the books Barbauld had previously recommended that Lydia read (Rickards, 709).

109 'right of common': Common grazing land, which was being gradually enclosed for private use by wealthy families.

110 'that of the Poles unsuccessful': The second Russo-Prussian Partition of Poland (1793) provoked a Polish national uprising under the leadership of Tadeusz Kosciuszko in 1794. Initially successful, it was defeated by Russian troops in October.

111 'post master...know him': The attempt of the French royal family to escape from France (June 1791) ended at the village of Varennes, where the king stopped for breakfast and was recognized by the postmaster there from his image on the coinage.

112 'Epaminondas': In the fourth century BCE Epaminondas led Thebes to victory over Sparta and instituted powerful new military tactics. His 'greatness lay in his qualities of mind and character which so impressed his fellow-countrymen' (Howatson, 212).

113 'Alfred...Hampdens': Alfred, ninth-century king of the West Saxons, an icon of patriotism to British liberals (see Barbauld's 'Alfred, a Drama'); English Kings Henry IV (1399–1413) and V (1413–22), admired warriors and subjects of Shakespeare plays; Algernon Sidney (1622–83), Whig politician executed by Charles II; and John Hampden (1594–1643), Parliamentary leader who vigorously attacked policies of Charles I. Sidney and Hampden became heroes in the pantheon of Whig Dissent for their resistance to arbitrary rule by Stuart kings.

114 'black cap and peaked beard...religion': The man would have been a Dissenting minister under Charles II, ejected from the Church of England and further penalized by such laws as the Five-Mile Act (1662), which prohibited a Dissenting minister from settling within five miles of his last parish. Barbauld may have had in mind the eminent Rev. Richard Baxter (1615–91).

115 'William Tell...Duke of Alva': William Tell, legendary Swiss hero, who symbolized for British liberals Swiss resistance to French invasion of the cantons in 1798. His legend was an inspiration to nationalist revolutions in the early nineteenth century. Fernando Alvarez de Toledo, 3rd Duke of Alba ('Alva' in

EXPLANATORY NOTES 447

Dutch) (1507–82), a Spanish general and repressive governor of the Netherlands (1567–73), persecuted Protestants and committed atrocities. In 1572 the Gueux, Dutch guerrillas, assisted by William, Prince of Orange and his brother, Louis of Nassau, captured part of Zeeland and Holland.

116 'Caesar discovered': Julius Caesar invaded Britain in 55 and 54 BCE during the Gallic Wars. He writes about the Britons he encountered in his *Bello Gallico*, Book IV, 22–31.

117 'goat...Minerva': Minerva was the Roman name for Athena, goddess of wisdom; goats browsing on the site of her temple would be unaware of its past glory.

118 'sentiments...enormities': Barbauld argues much as Charles James had done in *Audi Alteram Partem* (1793 edn). James acknowledged the horrors of the Prison Massacre in Paris but reminded readers that the French monarchy had perpetrated similar horrors—as, he noted, had the English monarchy. See Barbauld's translation of Rabaut St. Etienne's *Adresse aux Anglois*.

119 'the feeling heart...in every page': Cf. Priestley: 'They are rather melancholy reflections, which the view of such a chart of history as this is apt to excite in the minds of persons of feeling and humanity. What a number of revolutions are marked upon it!...What torrents of human blood has the restless ambition of mortals shed, and in what complicated distress has the discontent of powerful individuals involved a great part of their species!' (JP, *Description*, 17).

120 'Beauties of History': *The Beauties of History* (1772), a selection of 'great moments' by the Rev. William Dodd (1729–77). In her pedagogical novel *Adèle et Théodore* (1782) French educationist Stéphanie Félicité de Genlis proposed that education should be conducted in a totally arranged environment, to exclude bad influences. *The Princess of Cleves* (1678) by Madame de La Fayette was a work of romance; Samuel Richardson's *Sir Charles Grandison* (1753–4) aimed to depict an ideal man.

121 'all events...goodness': Cf. Priestley: '[L]et not the dark strokes which disfigure the fair face of an historical chart affect our faith in the great and comfortable doctrine of an over-ruling Providence. While we look upon this chart,...let us not forget...that the Most High ruleth in the kingdoms of men....Let us remember that his views are always great and kind, however they may appear to our narrow comprehension' (JP, *Description*, 17–18).

122 'forbid...conversation': Barbauld refers to 'Pitt's Reign of Terror', the British government's crackdown on Reformist opinion in 1792–4. The 'Royal Proclamation against Seditious Writings and Publications' of May 1792 criminalized Reformist writings priced for wide circulation; in 1793 'disloyal expressions' in coffee-house conversation could lead to prosecution and prison. See *ALBVE*, 344–5.

123 'mount Hymettus': Hymettus overlooks Athens and was famed in the classical world for its honey and marble (Howatson, 291). Goats, a metaphor for historical oblivion earlier, here signify unimportance.

124 'Antoninus': Antoninus Pius (86–161 CE), mild-mannered Roman emperor who guided the empire through a period of internal peace and prosperity.

After his wife died, he founded in her memory a charitable institution for the daughters of the poor.

125 'the two eyes of History': A proverbial expression, repeated, for example, in Lord Chesterfield's *Letters to his Son*: 'Chronology and geography are called the two eyes of history, because history can never be clear, and well understood, without them' (Chesterfield, 98–9).

126 'calculated for the period...illustrate': The concept of the 'historical atlas' Barbauld describes emerged gradually during the seventeenth and eighteenth centuries. An example is Guillaume Delisle's *Theatrum Historicum ad annum Christi quadringentesimu* (1705), 'in which the condition of both the Roman Empire and the barbarians living around it is placed before the eyes' (Goffart, ch. 3, fig. 12). Previous maps showed chronologically separate events as if they were simultaneous.

127 'one set...all the rest': A map purporting to show the ancient world from the Flood (in the Book of Genesis) to the reign of the emperor Trajan (98–117 CE) would span around 2,500 years; 'all the rest' would span about 1,700 years. Chapone gives '2350 years...from the deluge to our Saviour's birth' (Chapone, 205); the Septuagint dates the death of Noah to 2780 BCE (JP, *Description*, 70).

128 'The battles of Issus & the Granicus': At the Battle of Issus (5 November 333 BCE, in Turkey near the River Pinarus) Alexander the Great defeated the Persian army under King Darius III. At the Battle of Granicus (May 334 BCE, on the Granicus River, east of the Dardanelles), Alexander defeated Memnon of Rhodes.

129 'Pharaoh Necho...coast': Barbauld took the history of ancient map-making either from Herodotus or from a new book (announced in the *St. James's Chronicle* for 13–15 March 1800), James Rennell's *The Geographical System of Herodotus, Examined; and Explained, by a Comparison with those of other Ancient Authors, and with Modern Geography* (1800), which includes a chapter 'Concerning the Circumnavigation of Africa, by the Ships of Pharaoh Necho, King of Egypt'. She knew Rennell's work on India.

130 'Socrates & Alcibiades': Plato and Plutarch both recount that Alcibiades was a soldier in the Potidaea campaign. Socrates was his comrade and tent mate. Socrates defended Alcibiades when he was wounded. But neither account mentions maps.

131 'Anaximander': A Greek philosopher who first developed a systematic philosophical view of the world or cosmology (610–546 BCE). He wrote about astronomy and geography, drew a map of the known world, and may also have built a celestial globe. He was either a student or colleague of the Greek philosopher Thales of Miletus (*Britannica*).

132 'Herodotus...rivers': According to Rennell: 'Herodotus says...that Aristagoras appeared before the king of Sparta, "with a tablet of brass in his hand, upon which was inscribed *every known part of the habitable world, the seas, and the rivers*"' (Rennell, 326).

133 'Polybius...Pyrenees': Polybius (*c.* 200–after 118 BCE), historian of Rome, during captivity there found a patron in Scipio Aemilianus, with whom he

EXPLANATORY NOTES 449

witnessed the capture of Carthage (Howatson, 452). The Carthaginian general Hannibal had led an army over the Alps to attack Rome.

134 'Julius Caesar... 1ˢᵗ Century': The famous opening sentence of Julius Caesar's *Commentaries on the Gallic War*, 'Gallia est omnis divisa in partes tres', evinces interest in Geography. Strabo (64 BCE–24+ CE) wrote *Geography* in seventeen books, for centuries a standard text. Pomponius Mela was author of 'the earliest surviving Latin work on geography', *De situ orbis* (*c*.43 CE) (Howatson, 541, 455).

135 'antient geographers': Barbauld's account of the importance of Claudius Ptolemy's *Cosmographia* is correct: his treatise introduced 'the use of a grid of latitude and longitude, an extensive set of coordinates, and the goal of uniformity of scale, projection, and coverage' (Goffart, 14).

136 'New Holland': Australia, where the British Government had opened a prison colony in 1788.

137 'D'Anville': Jean-Baptiste Bourguignon d'Anville (1697–1782), eminent geographer and cartographer, a catalogue of whose many works was published in 1802 (*Notice des Ouvrages de M. D'Anville*, Paris, 1802). He 'won his most enduring fame in mapping ancient lands' (Goffart, 20).

138 'Major Rennel': James Rennell's *A Bengal Atlas* (1781) and *Memoir of a Map of Hindoostan* (1782).

139 'late Empress': Catherine II (1729–96) ordered a general land survey that permanently fixed the boundaries of aristocrats' estates.

140 'the best... published': The letter Barbauld sent to Rickards mentions two contemporary cartographers: Aaron Arrowsmith (1750–1823), who established his reputation in 1790 with a world map based on Mercator's projection, and Matthew Carey (1760–1839), who published the first American atlas (1795).

141 'Now it came... in his stead': 2 Kings 18:9 and 1 Kings 11:43, loosely quoted.

142 'stream': The metaphor of a stream occurs in Priestley, in whose *Chart* time is represented as 'flow[ing] uniformly' and '*laterally*, like a river' (JP, *Description*, 8), a representation that addresses the problem of competing chronologies Barbauld describes.

143 'The Greeks... present time': The substance of this paragraph comes from Andrew Reid's *Abstract of Sir Isaac Newton's Chronology of Ancient Kingdoms* (1732) and all but copies one sentence: 'The Arundelian marbles were composed 60 years after the death of Alexander the Great... [and] reckon backward from the time then present' (Reid, 8). The Arundelian marbles were antiquities collected by Thomas, Earl of Arundel, and given in 1667 by his grandson to the University of Oxford.

144 'The Mahometans... use it': Barbauld's instruction quietly dissents from Chapone's. 'The next epocha', Chapone writes, 'is the year 622—for the ease of memory say 600—when Mahomet, by his successful imposture, became the founder of the Saracen empire' (Chapone, 205). Chapone is nervous about straining a girl's memory. She also repeats the then-customary Christian characterization of Mohammed as an 'impostor'.

145 'in the margin': In Gibbon's *Decline and Fall* (1776–88) dates are given in the margins.

146 'labours... now have it': Her treatment of Chronology is a major point on which Barbauld dissents from Chapone, who asserts that 'Chronology may be naturally divided into three parts, *the Ancient—the Middle—*and *the Modern*' (Chapone, 194). Barbauld declares at the outset that 'a date is a very artificial thing'. Chapone lists the 'eras' of history as if they were objectively real and known; Barbauld declares them the results of 'strenuous labours' to 'reduc[e] history to the order in which we now have it'. She views many dates in ancient history as arbitrary, uncertain, and the result of conjecture.

147 'the Heptarchy': The seven small kingdoms of England dating from the fifth-century Anglo-Saxon settlement until England's unification in the early tenth century.

148 'eighteen or twenty years': Barbauld's account of Newton's calculations draws on Andrew Reid's *Abstract*. Priestley, too, drew on Newton's chronology for his *Chart of Biography* (1765).

149 'You cannot... happened': The Sicilian Vespers rebellion against the rule of the French King Charles I took place on 30 March 1282 in Sicily. The Siege of Constantinople by Sultan Mehmed II, ruler of the Ottoman Turks, took place in 1453.

150 'you ought to have... barbarous': Priestley, too, urged the value of comparing different states of civilization at the same period: 'when we are contemplating what was doing in any one part of the world, we cannot help wishing to know what was carrying on in other parts, at the same time' (JP, *Description*, 13). He designed his *Chart of History* to facilitate such comparisons.

151 'the first clock... in Europe': Barbauld may have read about this clock, sent by Harun al-Rashid in 799, in *An Essay Toward a History of the Origin and Progress of Clock and Watch-making* (1797) by J. H. Moritz Poppe. The *Essay* is mentioned in 'The History of Clock and Watch-Making', a review of Poppe's revision of it (*Edinburgh Magazine*, ns 20 [August 1802]: 92–5), which also mentions the water clock (95).

152 'massacre of St. Bartholomew': The massacre of French Protestants on St. Bartholomew's Day 1572, organized by Catherine de Medici, mother of the King of France.

153 'fair Austria... to the Swede': The first quotation comes from Johnson's *Vanity of Human Wishes* (1749), ll. 245–6; the second from Pope's *Essay on Man*, iv: 220.

154 'Dutch tiles': Delft tiles, popular in the seventeenth and eighteenth centuries to decorate fireplaces, often depicted biblical scenes.

155 'some esteem it... Epic': '[P]oets', Barbauld's contemporary Robert Anderson remarked, 'have looked upon mythology as a thing of great use in their compositions, and almost essential to the art' (Anderson, 4).

156 'You are not... as we now have them': Barbauld was up-to-date in her account of Homer. 'Since the end of the eighteenth century Homeric scholarship has

been dominated by the problem of defining the authorship, the so-called "Homeric question".... It was... suggested that each poem was created out of a compilation of shorter ballad-type poems, "lays", and brought to its present length by... collective effort, or... by the editorial activity of one man' (Howatson, 283).

157 'Thaliessin': Supposed to be one of the most ancient British bards (fl. 520–70), who recorded stories of King Arthur. Mentioned in William King, *The Art of Cookery, A Poem, in Imitation of Horace's Art of Poetry* (1708, p.19): 'Then Thaliessen rose, and sweetly strung / His *British* Harp, instructing while he sung.'

158 'Alexander... edition': According to Plutarch, 'Among the treasures and other booty that was taken from [vanquished Persian King] Darius, there was a very precious casket, which being brought to Alexander for a great rarity, he asked those about him what they thought fittest to be laid up in it; and when they had delivered their various opinions, he told them he should keep Homer's Iliad in it' (*Plutarch's Lives*, 4:30).

159 'Hither... draw light': *Paradise Lost*, 7:364. An example of Homer-reverence is William Hayley's *Essay on Epic Poetry; in Five Epistles* (1782), which mentions Homer no less than fifty-six times, beginning with 'Bright Homer bursts, magnificently clear, / The solar Lord of that poetic sphere; / Before whose blaze, in wide luxuriance spread, / Each Grecian Star hides his diminish'd head' (Hayley, I:181–4).

160 'The battle of the Frogs & Mice': Modern scholars attribute 'Batrachomyomachia, or the Battle of the Frogs and Mice', either to an anonymous poet from the time of Alexander the Great or to Lucian.

161 'Father of verse... by years': Pope, 'The Temple of Fame', ll. 184–7 (Pope, 179).

162 'Spectacle de la Nature': *Le Spectacle de la nature, ou Entretiens sur les particularités de l'histoire naturelle, qui ont parus les plus propres à rendre les jeunes gens curieux, & à leur former l'esprit*, 9 vols (1732–42) by Noël-Antoine Pluche (1688–1761), a French priest, headmaster, and teacher of rhetoric. This work was popular throughout Europe.

163 'Vertot[s]': René-Aubert Vertot (1655–1735), French clergyman and historian, author of *Histoire des révolutions de Portugal* (1690) and *Histoire des révolutions de Suède* (1695). Barbauld, like Hester Chapone, recommended reading, after Rollin's history, Vertot's *Histoire des révolutions arrivées dans le gouvernement de la république romaine* (1719). Mindful as usual of a young woman's presumed weak memory, Chapone minimizes the task: 'When you have got through Rollin, if you add *Vertot's Revolutions Romaines*... you may be said to have read as much as is *absolutely necessary* of ancient history' [1773 edn, 2:190].

164 'Rollin's Histoire Ancienne': Charles Rollin (1661–1741), whose six-volume *Histoire ancienne des Egyptiens, des Carthaginois, des Assyiens, des Babyloniens, des Mèdes et des Perses, des Macedoniens, des Grecs* (12 vols, 1730–8) became, in English as well as French, a standard text for ancient history. Hester Chapone recommended it to her niece in *Letters on the Improvement of the Mind*.

452   EXPLANATORY NOTES

165 'Rousseau's lettres botaniques': Jean-Jacques Rousseau, *Lettres élémentaires sur la botanique* (1785), written to instruct the daughter of a friend in Botany and published after Rousseau's death.
166 'for a Library': Georges-Louis Leclerc, comte de Buffon (1707–88), whose *Histoire Naturelle* (1749) was highly regarded for its style as well as for its content.
167 'M[adam]e Sévigne's lettres': Marie de Rabutin-Chantal, marquise de Sévigné (1626–96), whose letters were published in several volumes between 1734 and 1754.
168 '*Lettres Peruviennes*': Romance (1747) by Françoise d'Issembourg d'Happoncourt, Madame de Graffigny (1695–1758). The space left blank in the manuscript suggests that Barbauld did not immediately recall the author's name.
169 'M[onsieu]r de la Pierre': J.-H. Bernardin de Saint-Pierre (1737–1814), author of the novel *Paul et Virginie* (1788) and *La Chaumière Indienne* (1791). On 17 June 1798 Barbauld wrote to Lydia: 'I do not wonder you are charmed with Paul & Virginie, which I suppose by this time you have finished. It is very rich in the description of tropical productions, & also of those awful Phaenomena of nature which are met with in such climates, No painting can exceed the author's description of the fatal hurricane.... But above all he has ha[d] skill to excite by [a s]imple story, [the] sensations of love & pity, & if you have the sensibility which I believe you to have, you will not have finished the Volume without being almost heart-broken' (MS Misc. 4338, NYPL Pforzheimer Collection).
170 'La Galatée of Florian': Jean-Pierre Claris de Florian (1755–94), author of fables and fugitive verses, translator of Cervantes. His *Galatie*, imitated from the Galatea of, Cervantes, was first published in 1783.
171 'Gresset': Jean-Baptiste-Louis Gresset (1709–77). *Ver-Vert ou les voyages du perroquet de la visitation de Nevers* is a comic narrative poem first published in 1734. It tells the story of a parrot living in a convent that is sent to visit nuns elsewhere. On the way, it falls into bad company, learns to swear, and is sent back in disgrace. Joseph Johnson sold a later English translation.
172 'the best French Authors': Cadell published a six-volume collection entitled *Pièces Choisies* in 1767.

From *A Legacy for Young Ladies*

173 'he would have disdained... language': Barbauld met Samuel Johnson once in the 1770s and liked him but was angered by slighting remarks about her reported in Boswell's *Life of Johnson* (1791).
174 'the state of Germany': The 'Half-Yearly Retrospect of German Literature' in the issue of the *Monthly Magazine* dated 20 July 1802 (13:699–709), gave an account of historical, philological, and scientific work in Germany.
175 '*beau ideal*': According to the *OED*, this phrase first appeared in English in Maria Edgeworth's *Belinda* (1801). 'From poetry or romance, young people usually form their early ideas of love, before they have actually felt the

passion; and the image which they have in their own minds of the *beau ideal* is cast upon the first objects they afterward behold' (*Belinda*, 314). Barbauld and Edgeworth had met for the first time in 1799. Barbauld chose the novel for her British Novelists series (1810), volumes 49–50.

176 'this great end of your existence': A standard phrase in tracts on morality. Barbauld might be alluding to Hester Chapone: 'Equally vain and absurd is every scheme of life that...does not terminate in, that great end of our being—the attainment of real excellence, and of the favour of God' (Chapone, 64).

177 'command over your appetites': Advice typically urged on young women, as G. J. Barker-Benfield notices, quoting John Gregory against 'the luxury of eating' (Barker-Benfield, 289–90; Gregory, 28).

178 'Mrs. Betty...Mrs. Susan': Generic names for female servants.

179 'half virtue...essential to your sex and station': *Spectator* No. 631 (10 Dec. 1714, reprinted by Barbauld in her *Selections from the Spectator, Tatler, Guardian, and Freeholder*) offers 'a few hints upon "cleanliness," which I shall consider as one of the half-virtues, as Aristotle calls them' (Barbauld, *Selections*, 3:41). 'Cleanliness was another sign of the tendency toward "civilization" with which women were particularly identified' (Barker-Benfield, 290; he quotes James Fordyce, *Sermons to Young Women* [1766]: 'A dirty woman—I turn from the shocking idea').

180 'Locke...association': John Locke, *Some Thoughts Concerning Education* (1693), a foundational text for eighteenth-century education theory; Maria and Richard Lovell Edgeworth, *Practical Education* (1798), an innovative and controversial text; and Elizabeth Hamilton, *Letters on the Elementary Principles of Education* (1802), a moderately conservative work which Barbauld had reviewed. (For her review, see this volume.) 'The laws of association' refers to David Hume's theory of the association of ideas, which informed Barbauld's thinking about psychological function as well as the thinking of other writers and intellectuals, such as the Edgeworths and Samuel Taylor Coleridge.

181 'Irish howl': 'The present Irish cry, or howl, cannot boast of much melody, nor is the funeral procession conducted with much dignity. The crowd of people...at these funerals sometimes amounts to a thousand....They gather as the bearers of the hearse proceed on their way, and when they pass through any village...they begin to cry—Oh! Oh! Oh! Oh! Oh! Agh! Agh! raising their notes...in a kind of mournful howl' (Edgeworth, *Castle Rackrent* [1800], 125).

182 'your sister': The sister is likely to have been Frances Rebecca (b. 1796), who would have been 7 or 8 years old.

183 'I did so...to the south': From Epsom, Barbauld's vision takes in two of her favourite spots in Surrey: Dorking and Box Hill, where she had stayed with her brother during his convalescence in 1798. Norbury Park was the estate of the William Lock family. The extraordinary geographical expansiveness of the speaker's vision, ranging far beyond the bounds of realism, bears some resemblance to that of Charlotte Smith's speaker in *Beachy Head*, a work published posthumously in 1807 but probably composed at around the same time.

184 'The vine-covered... France': From the first line of a popular song by William Roscoe on the anniversary of the fall of the Bastille. It begins: 'O'er the vine-covered hills and gay regions of France, / See the day-star of liberty rise; / Through the clouds of detraction unsullied advance, / And hold its new course through the skies' (Roscoe, 76).

185 'girdle about the earth': *A Midsummer Night's Dream* (*NOS*, 2.1.173–6). Oberon demands that Robin 'Fetch me this herb, and be thou here again / Ere the leviathan can swim a league', and Robin replies, 'I'll put a girdle round the earth / In forty minutes'.

186 'The youth of Macedon': Alexander the Great, who was believed to be crook-necked; Bucephalus was his horse. For his conduct in the tent of Darius see the note above. Barbauld's fiction of summoning the dead recalls Lemuel Gulliver's visit to Glubbdubdrib, 'the Island of Sorcerers or Magicians' (Swift, 169); but where Swift uses the episode to debunk most history-writing, Barbauld uses it to illustrate the power of history to bring back the past.

187 'Banquo in Macbeth': In *Macbeth*, 4.1, the Witches show Macbeth a vision of eight kings who will descend from Banquo.

188 '"Guess!"...tell me': Homer's birthplace was a topic of much speculation but remained unknown, as Barbauld herself had told Lydia Rickards ('On Homer'). 'The man in the iron mask' imprisoned in the reign of Louis XIV was suspected to be Louis' half-brother; Barbauld would have read of him in Voltaire's *Siècle de Louis Quatorze* (1751).

189 'I measured...Bacon': 'Measuring' the Russian empress Catherine (d. 1797) against the ancient queen Semiramis, and Aristotle against Francis Bacon, was an instance of a literary game—comparing ancients with moderns—that Barbauld had learned in youth from Fontenelle's *Nouvelles Dialogues des Morts* (1683). She plays it at length in 'A Dialogue of the Dead, between Helen and Madame Maintenon'.

190 '*Abracadabra*': Barbauld uses it here to signify the alphabet.

191 '*Rura mihi... amnes*': Virgil, *Georgics*, 2:485: 'Dear to me then be the fields, be the streams, through the valleys that flow.' The metaphorical 'whispering gallery' of Fame is based on the real 'Whispering Gallery' in St. Paul's Cathedral in London.

192 'headless man...sword': Grotesque images such as this one appear in 'collections of alchemical emblems' and represent chemical reactions (private communication from Prof. Alexander S. Gourlay). Barbauld's immediate source is not known. The next vision, of men flying over towns without wings, presumably refers to hot-air balloons; in the summer of 1783, brothers, Joseph Michel and Jacques-Étienne Montgolfier, launched the first hot-air balloon in Annonay, France. (See Barbauld's reference to this event in 'Washing-Day' ll. 82–4.) During the short Peace of Amiens, on the evening of 21 September 1802, another French balloonist, André Jacques Garnerin, flew over London, from North Audley Street, Grosvenor Square, to a field near St. Pancras, fascinating Barbauld and other watchers on the ground.

193 'It is, to be...family': Cf. Wollstonecraft: '[S]peaking of women at large, their first duty is to themselves as rational creatures, and the next, in point of

EXPLANATORY NOTES 455

importance, as citizens, is that, which includes so many, of a mother. The rank in life which dispenses with their fulfilling this duty, necessarily degrades them by making them mere dolls' (Wollstonecraft, 257–8).

194 'As to the French...English itself': Recall Barbauld's letter in the guise of 'Miss Susan Slipslop' (in this volume), who cannot understand the French spoken by a Frenchman.

195 'Frenche...unknowe': *Canterbury Tales*: Prologue, ll. 124–6.

196 'It belongs to a Newton...the result': Cf. 'I believe there are few heads capable of making Sir Isaac Newton's calculations, but the result of them is not difficult to be understood by a moderate capacity' (Lady Mary Wortley Montagu to her daughter, 28 Jan. 1753; Montagu, 4:186).

197 '*la belle Nature*': In his essay 'Of Simplicity and Refinement in Writing' (1742), David Hume observes, 'Sentiments, which are merely natural, affect not the mind with any pleasure, and seem not worthy of our attention. The pleasantries of a waterman, the observations of a peasant, the ribaldry of a porter or hackney coachman, all of these are natural and disagreeable.... Nothing can please persons of taste, but nature drawn with all her graces and ornaments, *la belle nature*...' (Hume, *Essays*, 188).

198 'automatons...struck you?': Automata—mechanical devices that imitated human actions such as chess-playing—had been shown in London since at least the 1770s: from 1798 to 1817 one was on display at the Great Room in Spring Gardens. Panoramas were huge paintings that represented historical events; a 200-foot-long panorama of 'The Taking of Seringapatam' amazed spectators in 1800 (Altick, 350, 135).

199 'Dollond's...history': Telescopes built by the firm of Peter and John Dollond (founded 1750) enjoyed a high reputation but were very costly (*ODNB*). Expensive natural history volumes such as William Curtis's *Flora Londinensis* (two folio volumes, 1777–8), included 432 finely detailed, hand-coloured copper plate engravings.

200 'drinks...insensible': The offensive stereotype of the 'drunken Indian' lacking self-control reflects late eighteenth-century attitudes towards Indigenous peoples, which Barbauld adopts in an uncritical manner. Her stereotypical view of native Americans may have been influenced by her former Palgrave pupil, Thomas Douglas, earl of Selkirk, who wrote in defence of colonies he had founded in Canada that 'it is well known, that the propensity of the natives to intoxication is one of the most serious bars to their civilization' (*A Sketch of the British Fur Trade in North America*, 52). Barbauld could also have heard this aspersion of Native Americans from Douglas in person, for he was a close friend of her nephew Arthur Aikin.

201 'too dear': "The Regent or Pitt Diamond, is so called from its having been purchased by Mr. Pitt, governor of Bencoolen, in the Island of Sumatra, and sold by him to the Regent Duke of Orleans, by whom it was placed among the Crown jewels of France, where it now remains. Its value, as estimated by a commission of jewelers, in the year 1792, is about $2,222,400. The value given by Mrs. Barbauld, is about $4,875,000' (according to a note to this passage,

signed 'J. W. I.' in an American Barbauld anthology (Mrs. S. J. Hale, *Things by Their Right Names*. Boston: Marsh, Capen, Lyon, and Webb, 1840, 102).

202 'The dress...large kingdom': Jacques Necker (1732–1804), Minister of Finance (1771–81, 1788–9, 1789–90) to Louis XVI, tried unsuccessfully to retrench government expenses. The queen, Marie Antoinette, was notorious for extravagance.

203 'sterlet soup...half a crown a piece': Sterlet soup is made from a species of small sturgeon found in Russia (*OED*, s.v. *sterlet*). Barbauld read about Prince Potemkin's self-indulgence either in J.-H. Castéra's *Histoire de Catherine II* (1798) or in William Tooke's translation of it (*The Life of Catharine II. Empress of Russia*, 1798). In Tooke, the cherry anecdote is given in 3:219, and the soup in 3:240–1 (5th edn, Dublin, 1800). Barbauld's authority for translating Tooke's 300 rubles into 30 pounds sterling and 2,000 versts into 700 miles is not known.

204 'Vitellius...expense': According to Suetonius (*The Lives of the Twelve Caesars*), the emperor Vitellius was notorious for gluttony and once dined on a huge dish composed of 'pike-livers, pheasant-brains, peacock-brains, flamingo-tongues, and lamprey-milt' (Suetonius, 269; the Warrington Academy library held a copy among 'Greek and Roman Classics'). '[T]he confused multitude of women, of wines, and of dishes, and the studied variety of attitudes and sauces, served to revive his languid appetites' (Gibbon on the emperor Elagabalus [*Decline and Fall*, p. 179]).

205 'The belly...ears': A proverb dating at least to Plutarch and found also in Rabelais and La Fontaine.

206 'Pope Adrian...sausages': '[N]ever was there a Pope, whose table was so delicate, as that of Leo X. Men got into his favour by the invention of ragoos.... [T]hey invented a sort of sausages stuffed with the delicatest parts of peacocks, which astonished his successor Hadrian...when he looked into the expences of Leo's table' (Bayle, 2:327 and n).

207 'the lamp of Aladdin...wished for': Antoine Galland's eighteenth-century French translation of *The Book of One Thousand and One Nights* adds the story of 'Aladdin, or the Wonderful Lamp'. In 1788 John O'Keefe made the story of Aladdin into a play for the Theatre Royal, Covent Garden. The tale of Fortunatus, whose purse magically refills with money, was well-known in Europe from medieval times. Wordsworth refers to it in *The Prelude* (1805): 'Oh! Give us once again the wishing cap of Fortunatus' (V:341–2).

208 'inkle': A woven linen tape (*OED*). According to an 1845 *Statistical Account of Scotland* (6:157), its first British manufacture was in Glasgow in 1732, but the manufacture soon migrated to Manchester. The 'couple' the father describes may be historical, but remain unidentified. Their progress from frugality to elegance represents many an eighteenth-century English success story.

209 'magic-lantern': '[A]n instrument, by means of which small pictures are represented as magnified to a great size' ('J. W. I.', note in *Things by Their Right Names*, 108).

EXPLANATORY NOTES 457

210 'a riddle': In a famous tale, the ancient Greek mathematician, Archimedes (c.287–c.282 BCE), discovers the solution to a problem while in the public bath by noticing that the more his body was submerged, the more water was displaced—a measure of volume. He shouts 'Eureka!' Greek for 'I've found it!' as he runs out into the street. Modern historians believe that the tale is probably at least partly apocryphal, for Vitruvius, a Roman writer, recorded it nearly two hundred years after the supposed event. See David Biello, 'Fact or Fiction?: Archimedes Coined the Term "Eureka!" in the Bath', *Scientific American*, 8 Dec. 2006.

211 'his wife...told them': See Judges 14:12–20 for the story of Samson and his riddle.

212 'According to the fable...foot': Barbauld may well have known the riddle of the Sphinx in Greek mythology from Sophocles' tragedy *Oedipus Rex*, although she would not have read it in the original Greek. She may have seen or read John Dryden's and Nathaniel Lee's 1678 adaptation.

213 'The tree...day and night': On the 'Eastern' tree riddle, see Hasan M. El-Shamy, *Folk Traditions of the Arab World: A Guide to Motif Classification*, Vol. 1 (Bloomington, IN: Indiana University Press, 1995), 164.

214 'ancient manuscript': Anglo-Saxon riddles are preserved in a tenth-century manuscript donated to Exeter Cathedral (and hence called the 'Exeter MS'). Barbauld could have seen it on a visit to Exeter in 1799.

215 'all sorts of puzzles': Addison defines 'true wit', 'false wit', and 'mixed wit' in a series of *Spectator* papers; Barbauld included them in her 1805 anthology of Addison and Steele. Addison does not mention riddles by name, but he does list 'conundrums' among types of 'false wit'.

216 'of late he had been gloomy...comfort': The winter of 1813–14 in England was one of the coldest and snowiest on record. According to Martin Rowley, in London 'the greatest frost of the 19th century commenced on the 27th December 1813; the onset of the frost was accompanied by thick fog' ('Weather in History: 1800 to 1849', https://premium.weatherweb.net/weather-in-history-1800-to-1849-ad/).

217 'The curate...apple': In the Church of England a curate was a poorly paid substitute for an absentee priest who enjoyed the income from a parish (a 'living') without performing the duties. Sophron hopes to secure a living himself, but will instead be further burdened with an increase of family.

218 'pretty stepmother to the young gentleman': And who will long outlive Dorimant, and keep the son out of his estate. See note below.

219 'Codrus': The name occurs in Pope's 'Epistle to Dr. Arbuthnot', l. 85, but figures here simply as a satirical name.

220 'Strephon...all his life after': Hardwicke's Marriage Act (1753) required parental consent to marriages of under-age parties in England. To elude that requirement, young persons eloped to the Scottish village Gretna Green, just across the border. In 1776 Rochemont Barbauld's Warrington friend and fellow minister James Pilkington had eloped to Gretna Green with a member of his congregation; the

couple, Barbauld reported from gossip, 'had a very weeping wedding' and suffered remorse afterwards (quoted in Winterbotham, p. 68).
221 'play at taw': In taw (or ringer) players shoot marbles out of a 6- to 10-foot diameter ring.
222 'Pyrrhonists': Pyrrhonism was a school of extreme scepticism which suspended judgement on every proposition. It was founded in the fourth century BCE by Pyrrho.
223 'monstrous... little': We have not traced this joke, but *monstrous* as a cant intensifier occurs in Burney's *Cecilia*: see *OED*, 'monstrous', 8.
224 'precious metal of Potosi': Silver from the mines of Potosi in what was then Peru, now Bolivia.
225 'whether friendship... the vicious': 'That intimacy from which tenderness should flow, will not, cannot subsist between the vicious' (Wollstonecraft, *Rights of Woman*, 342). 'Friendship, in the highest sense of the word, can only subsist between persons of strict integrity...' (Chapone, 81). Barbauld agrees with both, but also, in her next sentences, qualifies both.
226 'Friends... indissoluble': Barbauld's memory of her friendship with Sarah and Elizabeth Rigby at Warrington perhaps informs this paragraph. The Rigby daughters became legendary for flirtatiousness and practical jokes, and on at least one occasion they were exiled by the Warrington Academy authorities for allegedly seducing a student. They are subjects of Barbauld poems that became famous: 'To Miss R——, on her Attendance upon her Mother at Buxton' and 'Verses Written in an Alcove'. Barbauld lost touch with the Rigbys after her marriage.
227 'the friend of our early years': In this paragraph Barbauld might have been thinking of her second cousin, Elizabeth Belsham (afterwards Mrs. Timothy Kenrick), a friend from Warrington years whose friendship endured. Elizabeth came from Exeter to comfort Barbauld after Rochemont's death.
228 'deal Floor': A floor made of pine, rather than hardwood, implying a poor person's house. The square brackets belong to the original text here.
229 'out of my estate': The mother 'keeps [him] out of his estate'—i.e. his inheritance—by his father's will, which gives her a life maintenance out of the father's assets; these will pass to the son only after her death. The squire resents his mother's longevity.
230 'memoirs of a court': Louis de Rouvroy, duc de Saint-Simon (1675–1755), wrote of Mme. de Maintenon in his *Memoirs of Louis XIV. His Court and the Regency*, first published in 1788.
231 'fine woman... of the two': 'A massy Tripod for the victor lies, / Of twice six oxen its reputed price; / And next, the loser's spirits to restore, / A female captive, valu'd but at four' (Pope, *Iliad*, p. 116).
232 'Clelia... Cassandra... Princess of Cleves': The first two women are celebrated in legend and in seventeenth-century French romances: Cloelia (said to have escaped her Etruscan captor, Porsena, and to have won his admiration by her bravery) in *Clélie* (1656–60) by Madame de Scudéry; and Cassandra

EXPLANATORY NOTES   459

(the blind seer who was doomed to have her prophecies disbelieved) in *Cassandre* (1642–5) by Gauthier de Costes de la Calprenède. *La Princess de Clèves* (1678) is a classic French novel by Madame de La Fayette, whose fictional heroine is beloved by two men.

233 'handed down to posterity': Maintenon's letters were published in French in 1753, and in English as *The Letters of Madam de Maintenon; and other eminent persons in the age of Lewis XIV* (1753).

234 'Scarron': The burlesque dramatist Paul Scarron (1610–60), Madame de Maintenon's first husband, who suffered from physical deformity.

235 'St. Cyr': The Maison Royale de Saint-Louis at Saint-Cyr, a school for poor girls founded by Maintenon, where she taught and where she sought refuge from the restraints of the court. She retired there around the time of Louis XIV's death in 1715 and died at Saint-Cyr four years later.

Reviews of Educational Books

236 'Elizabeth Hamilton': Essayist and novelist (1756?–1816), author of *Letters of a Hindoo Rajah* (1796), *Memoirs of Modern Philosophers* (1800), *Letters on the Elementary Principles of Education* (1801–2), *The Life of Agrippina, wife of Germanicus* (1804), and *Letters Addressed to the Daughter of a Nobleman* (1806). Her best-known work today is *The Cottagers of Glenburnie* (1808).

Reasons for attribution to Barbauld: The review agrees with Barbauld's opinion in her essay 'On Education' that no system of education is likely to produce perfect human beings, and with her memoir of Hester Chapone in commending moderation. It approves of Hamilton's religious position as 'rational and liberal'. Its criticisms of Hamilton's views in detail, including her views that religion should teach restraint principally and that 'the gratifications of the palate' should be deprecated, are typical of Barbauld (cf. *Lessons for Children*, with its numerous gratifications of the palate). The general outlook of this review is more favourable than Hamilton to the senses and imagination, and that is consistent with the tenor of Barbauld's work. Finally, Barbauld was the obvious choice to review a book on education, and, as a woman, might be thought best suited to review a book by another woman. That she had read Hamilton's *Letters* is implied by her making 'Grimalkin' say she has read Hamilton ('Letter from Grimalkin to Selima'). Barbauld knew Hamilton well enough in person for Hamilton to be named in 1798 as one who could introduce visiting United Irishman William Drennan to her (*Drennan-McTier Letters*, 2:397, '31' April 1798). Copy text: *Annual Review*, 1 (1803): 568–76.

237 'two treatises... all mention of them': The first treatise is probably Hannah More's *Strictures on the Modern System of Female Education* (1799); the second is *Practical Education* (1798) by Maria Edgeworth and her father, Richard Lovell Edgeworth.

238 'the law of association... discussed by philosophical writers': As Richard Lovell Edgeworth was to observe a few years later, 'this doctrine of association... is

not a new, but an old theory revived and extended. It is as old as the time of Aristotle' and had been revived and extended by David Hume, David Hartley, Priestley, and others (Edgeworth, *Professional Education*, 18).
239 'Volunteer associations': Such associations were formed for political action; e.g., the Loyal Associators active in the early 1790s.
240 'sweetmeats': 'sweatmeats' in the text; not a recorded variant spelling in the *OED*, so we have corrected this printer's error here and later in the essay.
241 'a doctrine...exceptionable': 'Miss Edgeworth's plan of an institution for having servants educated to the care of children, is certainly excellent; but would it not be an improvement upon it, if young ladies, who are all brought up in the expectation of being wives and mothers, were to receive a few instructions concerning the nature of the duties they ought in these characters to fulfill? A few plain and rational notions concerning the proper management of children from the first stage of infancy would, in all probability, be little less useful than any of the accomplishments on which they are taught to pique themselves. Were young women of all ranks to be a little instructed in the nature of the human mind, and the development of its faculties; were they to be informed of the great importance of observing the early tendencies of the disposition, and made sensible how much these early tendencies depended on the judicious or injudicious management of infancy, we should not behold young mothers treating their children as animated dolls, who were merely intended to gratify their vanity, and give variety to their amusements' (Hamilton, 1:298–9).
242 'Whatever tends...in her mind': Hamilton, 1:88–94.
243 'rejoice in the Lord': Psalms 34:14 and 97:12.
244 'With a contempt...virtues': Hamilton, 1:249–52.
245 'It is they alone...self': Hamilton, 1:301–4.
246 'critique...teaching': Hamilton's one reference to Barbauld's work for children is actually a rebuttal of Edgeworth's critique of a passage in *Lessons for Children*.
247 'If in analysing...God': Hamilton, 2:21–2.
248 'Eve was...change': *Paradise Lost*, ix.1017–18 and v.336. Evidence of Barbauld's appreciation of the sense of taste can be seen in 'A School Eclogue' (Poem XX): 'For him the matron spreads her candy'd hoard, / And early strawberries crown the smiling board; / For him crush'd gooseberries with rich cream combine, / And bending boughs their fragrant fruit resign: / Custards and sillabubs his taste invite; / Sports fill the day, and feasts prolong the night' (ll. 13–18).
249 'Mothers, I apprehend...useful': Hamilton, 2:120–3.
250 'Let us suppose...lea': Hamilton, 2:187. She quotes ll. 1–2 of the poem.
251 'What does she make...equally so': Hamilton, 2:188.
252 'Thomson's beautiful description': From Thomson, *The Seasons*: 'Summer', l. 721. The description of the elephant continues: 'O truly wise! with gentle might endow'd, / Tho' powerful, not destructive! Here he sees / Revolving

ages sweep the changeful earth, / And empires rise and fall; regardless he / Of what the never-resting race of Men / Project' (Thomson, 1:72).
253 'Miss Hamilton...*bell*': 'I well remember how eagerly I caught the information, that bells were worn by the leaders of the flock, in most parts of England. The custom was unknown in the part of the country where I passed my childhood, and consequently the first lines of a poetical description which I ardently admired, were to me unintelligible.' Hamilton then quotes in a footnote the admired passage, from John Gay's 'The Shepherd's Week: Friday; Or, The Dirge', beginning, 'When Blouselind expir'd, the wether's bell / Before the drooping flock pour'd forth her knell' (Hamilton, 2:190).
254 'If the higher powers...': Hamilton, 2:259–60.
255 'her rank and her misfortunes': Lady Jane Grey was briefly Queen of England, until executed by Henry VIII's daughter, Mary.
256 'The mother who is superior...feast': Hamilton, 2:329–31.
257 'Before your pupils...animosity': Hamilton, 2:402.
258 '*An Essay on Education*...333': William Barrow (1754–1832), Churchman. His *Essay on Education* originated as an English Essay Prize winner at Queens College, Oxford, in 1778 (*ODNB*).
 Reasons for our attribution of the essay to Barbauld: This review remarks that few books on Education have been written by people 'who have actually engaged in it as a business', as Barbauld of course had, and it responds sympathetically to Barrow's remarks about the pains of managing a school. The review defends sending children of Anglican parents to Dissenting schools, a practice Barbauld knew from Warrington Academy and Palgrave School; deploys urbane irony to censure Barrow's argument for strict and detailed training in Latin and Greek (at Palgrave, they were taught without 'that nice attention to quantities and accents which constitutes so prominent a feature in the routine grammar-school exercises of the present day', wrote William Taylor [Robberds, 1:7]); and it disapproves, tacitly, of Barrow's High-Church politics. Copy text: *Annual Review*, 1 (1803): 576–8.
259 'glasses of Herschel': William Herschel (1738–1822), musician and astronomer, famed for using a telescope of his own devising to discover the planet Uranus and many previously unknown stars.
260 'They (these grievances)...in vain': Barrow, 1:224–8.
261 'Our public schools...plan': Barrow, 1:115–17.
262 'valuable hints': As a conservative Church-of-England writer, Barrow does not mention Barbauld's books. He considers grammar books and classical writers (Demosthenes, Cicero, Lucian, Anacreon, Tacitus, and Livy) and, among the moderns, Pope, Spenser, Milton, Chaucer, and Dryden.
263 '*dissenting schools*': 'He...who sends his son to a dissenter for instruction, sends him at the hazard of being educated in doctrines, which the son will soon find to be at variance with those generally received; in a dislike to that system of political government, under which he is to live; and a disapprobation

of that form of religious worship, with which he will afterwards be constantly tempted by his interest to comply' (Barrow, 1:146).
264 *'Port Royal'*: Barrow, 2:129. The *Logique de Port-Royal* (1662) was a popular logic textbook by two Jansenists, Antoine Arnauld and Pierre Nicole, used at a monastery in Port-Royal-des-Champs, France. The Jesuits considered the Port-Royal Logic heretical, but John Locke drew inspiration from it.
265 'Italian grammar': Vincenzo Peretti, *Grammaire Italienne* (London, 1795), one of several guides to the Italian language composed by this author.
266 'an English lady': Mary Pilkington (1761–1839), children's and educational writer; author of *Tales of the Hermitage* (1798).
267 'Priscilla Wakefield': Wakefield (1751–1832), a Quaker philanthropist, published fiction for children as well as feminist economics and natural science for adults. Her *Introduction to Botany* (1796) reached eleven editions by 1841. She also founded a maternity hospital, a savings bank for children, and a female benefit society. Barbauld was acquainted with her.
268 'Mrs. Cockle': Mary Cockle, children's writer who also published poems, including, among others: 'Lines on the Lamented Death of Sir John Moore' (1810), 'Lines Addressed to Lady Byron' (1817), 'Reply to Lord Byron's Fare Thee Well' (1817), and 'Elegy on the Death of his late Majesty George the Third' (1820). Although *Important Studies for the Female Sex* may have been complimentary to other women who wrote on education, it does not mention Barbauld.
269 'simplicity and godly sincerity': 2 Corinthians 1:12.
270 *'Soirées d'Automne'*: The title page reads 'Soirées d'automne; ou, le vice puni, et la vertu récompensée; à l'instruction de la jeunesse, et pour l'usage des écoles par Mademoiselle G. Bertholet'; despite the heading here, the volume contains no English and is entirely in French, although published in London. The 5-page subscription list is headed up by the Duke of Cumberland, the Duke of Sussex, and the Duchess of York, who ordered three copies, as did the Duchess of Devonshire. G. Bertholet was also the author of *Leçons choisies, dans la morale, l'histoire, et la biographie, à l'usage des écoles et de la jeunesse* (London, 1808).
271 *'Veillées du Chateau'*: See Introduction to 'From *Evenings at Home*'.
272 'like...tears': *Hamlet* (NOS, 1.2.149).
273 'Gesner': Salomon Gessner (1730–88), Swiss poet, whose best-known work was translated (1763) as *The Death of Abel*.
274 'Edward Baldwin': A pseudonym of William Godwin (1756–1836), author of *An Enquiry Concerning Political Justice*, husband and memoirist of Mary Wollstonecraft, and publisher, under the name 'M. J. Godwin and Co.', of books for children. (William St. Clair first made this identification in *The Godwins and the Shelleys*.) Barbauld knew Godwin socially and was aware of his pseudonym.
275 'John Greig': Greig (1758?–1819) taught geography, mathematics, and writing in London and wrote six books on astronomy and arithmetic, including

EXPLANATORY NOTES 463

The Young Lady's Guide to Arithmetic (1798, sixteen editions by 1864) and *Astrography, or the Heavens Displayed* (1810).

276 'William Frederick Mylius': Mylius, of Bomheim-House Academy, Carshalton, was also Master of the academy in Red Lion Square, London, and the author or editor of several other school books, including *The First Book of Poetry. For the Use of Schools* (1811), which Barbauld reviewed, *Mylius's School Dictionary of the English Language* (1809), and *An Abridged History of England for Use at Catholic Seminaries* (1817).

277 'amusing compilation': It includes an extract from Barbauld's 'Address to the Deity' (1824 edn, p. 119).

278 'Darton and Co.': Darton (p. 279) attributes this publication to Daniel Wakefield (1776–1846), barrister, writer on politics and economics, and son of Priscilla Wakefield.

279 'Joseph Guy': Guy wrote many textbooks, including *Guy's New Latin Primer* (1815), *Guy's Exercises in Orthography* (1824), *Elements of Modern History* (1836), *Elements of Ancient History* (1836), *Elements of British History* (1836), and *The Illustrated London Geography* (1852).

280 'Mrs. Fenwick': Eliza Fenwick (1766?–1840), author of the epistolary novel *Secresy; or the Ruin on the Rock* (1795), was an early feminist and friend of Mary Wollstonecraft, William Godwin, Thomas Holcroft, Mary Hays, Charlotte Smith, and Charles and Mary Lamb. Her *Lessons for Children* was advertised as 'a sequel to Mrs. Barbauld's Lessons'.

281 'Priscilla Wakefield': See note above.

282 'Mrs Cockle': See note above.

283 'Darwin, Paley': Erasmus Darwin (1731–1802), botanist and poet; William Paley (1743–1805), liberal Churchman and author of *Natural Theology* (1802), a work Barbauld especially respected.

284 '*Guy's New British Spelling Book*': See note above.

285 '*Il vero modo...*': In English, the title is 'The True Method of Pleasing in Company'. The Italian and French appeared on facing pages to help students in both languages. The book was favourably noticed by the *Gentleman's Magazine* and *the British Critic*, but Carlo Monteggia remains obscure.

286 'antient saws...': *As You Like It* (NOS, 2.7.155).

287 'chooses to be called': Barbauld seems to have known the identity of this writer, who used the pseudonym 'Arabella Argus'. She also published with Darton a children's novel, *Adventures of a Donkey* (1815), as well as *Ostentation and Liberality* (1821) and *The Further Adventures of Jemmy Donkey* [1832].

288 'Isaac Bickerstaff': Bickerstaff was a nom de plume used by Jonathan Swift and Sir Richard Steele. 'Adam Fitz-Adam' was the nom de plume of Edward Moore (1712–57), poet and dramatist, who, with the assistance of Chesterfield, Lyttelton, and Horace Walpole, conducted a weekly periodical, *The World* (1753–7).

289 'Baldwin': See above for Mylius and for 'Edward Baldwin'.

290 'J. N. Bouilly': Jean-Nicholas Bouilly (1763–1842), French politician, playwright, and author of children's books. One of his libretti formed the basis for Beethoven's opera *Fidelio*.

291 'M. de Malesherbe's': Guillaume-Chrétien de Lamoignon de Malesherbes (1721–94), French statesman and naturalist. It was said that at his Chateau de Verneuil he had a rose garden which was secretly tended by village maidens. After he learned their secret, he made it customary for all brides in the village to carry a bouquet of roses from this garden.

292 'Emilius': Barbauld refers to Rousseau's *Emile, or On Education* (1762; English translation as *Emilius*, 1768). Rousseau's narrator describes how he curbed the wilfulness of a boy who insisted on going out by letting him go and, when outside, suffer the mocking remarks of neighbours whose cooperation had been pre-arranged. Rousseau admits that the stratagem smacks of Molière's *Monsieur de Pourceaugnac*, a comedy in which elaborate deceptions are practised in order to unite young lovers (Rousseau, *Emilius*, 1:177–8). However, neither butchers nor bakers play a part in Rousseau's stratagem.

293 'By the Author of...': Elizabeth Frank, of York, compiler of the *Memoirs of Lindley Murray* (1826) and author of *The Classical English Letter-Writer: or, Epistolary Selections* (1814). Her *Lessons for Young Persons in Humble Life* reached ten editions by 1836.

294 'perished in early life': Edward VI (reigned 1547–53), sickly heir to Henry VIII; Lady Jane Grey, titular queen of England for nine days until executed by Mary Tudor in 1553; Henry, Prince of Wales, popular elder son of James I, predeceased his father in 1612; Susanna Howard, Countess of Suffolk, noted for piety, supported her father before his execution for treason in 1649 and died of a brain disorder later that year, age 22 (*ODNB*).

295 'painted windows...': 'Il Penseroso', l. 159, slightly misquoted.

296 'By the Author of...': Mary Anne Lamb (1764–1847) and her brother Charles Lamb (1775–1834) jointly wrote both of these works. *Mrs. Leicester's School, or, The History of Several Young Ladies, Related by Themselves* (1809) was a popular collection of short stories. The Lambs also authored *Tales from Shakespeare*, which recounts in prose for children the plots of Shakespeare's plays.

297 'Mrs. Trimmer': Sarah Trimmer (1741–1810), prolific evangelical author and conservative educationalist, founded a Sunday school that by 1788 enrolled more than 300 pupils; in 1787 she opened a weekday school of industry to teach trades to working-class girls (*ODNB*). She also wrote *The Guardian of Education* (from 1802), a periodical that evaluated books for children from a conservative viewpoint. Trimmer died unexpectedly on 15 December 1810. *The Family Magazine* was an evangelical publication addressed to working-class people.

298 'The language...&c.': This paragraph is marked by Griffiths 'G.2.', i.e., as his own addition.

299 'William Frederick Mylius': For Mylius see note above. The 1820 edition of this book contains Barbauld's 'Address to the Deity' and 'The Mouse's Petition'. Her 'Ode to Content' appears in the 6th edn, 1825.

300 'By the Author of...': The author of *Lessons for Young Persons in Humble Life* is Elizabeth Frank, of York; see note above.

301 'Isaac Payne': Payne (1781–1845), a Quaker, published anonymously *Outlines of a Plan of Education* (1805), *An Introduction to Geography* (1806), and *An Atlas, for the use of schools, designed for the younger students in Geography* (1808) (Smith, *Descriptive Bibliography*, 2: 273).

302 'Vol. lii': Vol. 52 was published before Barbauld began writing for the *Monthly Review*; hence this sentence may be by Griffiths.

303 'thrones of those countries': Gustavus Vasa (1496–1560) became king of Sweden after escaping from captivity in Denmark (1519); Charlemagne was crowned emperor by the Pope in 800; Louis XVI was executed in January 1793; Louis Bonaparte was made king of Holland in 1806, Joseph Bonaparte king of Spain in 1808.

304 'John Carey, LL.D.': John Carey (1756–1826), Irish classical scholar, poet, translator, and contributor to the *Gentleman's Magazine* and the *Monthly Magazine*. Among his textbooks for children were *Latin Prosody Made Easy* (1800), *Introduction to English Composition and Elocution* (1817), and *Greek and Latin Terminations* (both 1821). His brother was the publisher and author Matthew Carey (*ODNB*).

305 'English Grammar': Lindley Murray (1746–1826) published *English Grammar* in 1795.

306 'splay-foot verse': An allusion to Samuel Butler, *Hudibras*, I.iii.192: 'In small Poets splay-foot Rhimes'.

307 'J. Carey': For Carey, see note above.

308 'excellent selection': *The Poetical Monitor: consisting of Pieces select and original... intended to succeed Dr. Watts' Divine and Moral Songs* (1805; Darton, 134). Barbauld was not the reviewer. A second edition of *A Sequel* appeared in 1815.

309 'in the present volume': This collection includes Barbauld's 'Washing-Day' (as 'The Washing Day', unattributed).

310 'her work': 'Her' suggests that Barbauld knew the writer of this unsigned work, Elizabeth Heyrick (1767–1831), an ardent abolitionist and social reformer, born to the Coltman family of Leicester (Darton, 132). The Coltmans were well known to Barbauld's father; a Coltman son had attended his school in Kibworth.

311 'Professor Carlyle': Joseph Dacre Carlyle (1758–1804), Professor of Arabic at Cambridge (*ODNB*).

312 'Miss Venning': Mary Anne Venning (1775–1830+?), author of science books for children, including *A Geographical Present* (1817), *A Botanical Catechism* (1825), *Rudiments of Mineralogy* (1830), and *Rudiments of Conchology* (1837).

313 '*qu'il n'aimoit... innocens*': 'He did not care for innocent pleasures'. Philippe-Charles d' Orléans (1674–1723), Regent during the minority of Louis XV, was notorious for sophisticated debauchery. His 'pleasures' are described in the memoirs of the Duc de Saint-Simon and Voltaire's *Histoire de Louis XV*.

314 'plans and hints in..."Practical Education"': The principal 'plans and hints' concerning women in *Practical Education* occur in a chapter that deprecates 'Accomplishments' in drawing, dancing, and music. Women are to be well educated so that they may be rational parents.

315 'Davies, A.M.': The Rev. G. J. Davies was master of Campton Academy, Bedfordshire, and master of the grammar school at Hull, according to publisher's advertisements.

316 'Thomas Tegg': Tegg (1776–1846) was chiefly a London publisher, known for his inexpensive editions.

317 'Mr. Dix': Thomas Dix, a surveyor and schoolmaster from North Walsham, also produced maps of Bedfordshire (1818), Northumberland (1818), Derby (1818), Durham (1818), York (1820, 1835), and Chester (1830). His first major work was *A Treatise on Land Surveying* (1799).

318 'By Joseph Guy': For Guy, see note above.

319 'duties of youth': 'On the Duties of the Young' (Sermon XI in Hugh Blair, Sermons, 5 vols, 1777–1801), reprinted independently in 1793 and 1799.

320 'Fenwick': Perhaps John Fenwick, the husband of Eliza Fenwick, although by 1811 he was in decline. (Thanks to Lissa Paul for this information.)

321 'G. B. Depping': Probably Georges Bernard Depping (1784–1853), a teacher of German and author of many works of history: *History of Spain* (1811), *History of the Maritime Expeditions of the Normans* (1826), *History of the Commerce between the Levant and Europe* (1830), a sympathetic *History of the Jews during the Middle Ages* (1834), and other titles (Obituary, *GM*, [January 1854]: 103).

322 'Gros': C. Gros was a compiler of school books, among them *Elements of French Conversation* (twenty-three editions by 1825) and *New Elements of Conversation*, a sequel to the present title.

This review was annotated by Griffiths 'G.2 & D°', but his portion is not distinguished from Barbauld's. Perhaps he wrote the second paragraph.

323 'C.P. Landon': Charles Paul Landon (1760–1826) was a well-regarded French painter and popular writer on art and artists. He penned *Précis historique des productions des arts, peinture, sculpture, architecture et gravure* (1801–4), a multi-volume *Annales du Musée et de l'école modern des beaux-arts* (1801–), and other works of art history (Obituary, *Annual Register of World Events for 1827*, 68:231).

324 '*ben trovati*': From the Italian saying, 'Se non è vero, è molto ben trovato' ([even] 'if it is not true, it is very well invented').

325 'Author of...': William Keegan, Master of Manor-House Academy, Kennington Lane, and author of other textbooks, including *Instructeur François* (1808). 'The Comet' was the 'Great' comet of 1811, visible for most of the year and at its brightest in October.

326 'Chesterfieldian documents': 'Chesterfieldian' refers to Philip Dormer Stanhope, 4th Earl of Chesterfield, whose *Letters...to his Son* (1774) gave advice which many regarded as cynical.

327 'Blair, Raleigh, and Mme. de Lambert': Probably Hugh Blair's sermon on the duties of youth (see note above), Sir Walter Raleigh's 'Advice to His Son', and the 'Treatise on Friendship' by the writer and salonnière Madame de Lambert (1647–1743).

328 'Priscilla Wakefield': See note above.

329 'Abbé Fenelon': Barbauld admired the works of François de Salignac de la Mothe Fénelon (1651–1715), especially his educational romance *Télémaque* (1699).

330 'John Rippingham': Rippingham also published *The Art of Extempore Public Speaking* (1813).

331 'Addison, Johnson, and Blair': Besides excerpts from Joseph Addison, Samuel Johnson, and Hugh Blair, David Hume, and Sir William Jones, Rippingham reprints one of Barbauld's *Hymns in Prose* and one of her *Remarks on Mr. Gilbert Wakefield's Enquiry into the Expediency and Propriety of Public or Social Worship*.

332 'Jillard Hort': The Rev. Willliam Jillard Hort was a prolific textbook author whose works included *The Picture of Nature, or a general Survey of the principal Objects of the Creation* (1814), *The New Geography, or an Introduction to Modern Geography, in Question and Answer* (1815), *An Introduction to Modern History* (1820), *The New Pantheon; or, an introduction to the Mythology of the Ancients* (1820), *A First Spelling Book* (1822), *An Introduction to Natural History* (1822), and *An English Dictionary of Select Words* (1822).

333 'faults... his own mistakes': Barbauld's letter to Lydia Rickards in the guise of 'Miss Fanny Flippant', like the book here reviewed, is composed of faults which Lydia is invited to correct.

334 'First French Master': Lewis Catty (d. 1824). This title was first published in 1802, by Joseph Johnson.

335 'made to sell': In 'Ode III' Peter Pindar (nom de plume of John Wolcot) gives 'sage advice to mercenary artists' in the form of verses about a razor-seller whose razors are made, not to shave but 'to sell' (Wolcot, 1:102–4).

336 '*Tous les plus...*': Racine, *Les Plaideurs*, I.i.9–10.

337 'clear these ambiguities': *Romeo and Juliet* (NOS 5.3.216).

338 'This fair writer': R. C. Dallaway, author of *The Servant's Monitor* (1815). Barbauld (or Griffiths) knew that the author of this unsigned book was a woman and may have known her identity.

339 'Mrs. H. More... subject': Hannah More, *Strictures on the Modern System of Female Education* (1799).

340 'Adlerjung': This is probably a mistake for 'Adelung': Johann Christoph Adelung (1732–1806), preacher and author of dictionaries and books on grammar (*Neue Deutsche Biographie*). William Wennington also translated Plutarch (1815).

341 'But for my mother's...': John Gay, 'The Old Hen and the Cock' (Fable XX in *Fables*, 1727); the lines are reversed.

342 'Daughter of...': Agnes Sophia Hunter Semple published under her unmarried name a volume of *Miscellanies, Designed Chiefly for the Benefit of Female Readers* (1810; 2nd edn, 1811).

343 'authors...read': In the original, 'Authors before they write should read' (Matthew Prior, 'Protogenes and Apelles', reprinted in *The Works of the English Poets*, 1779, xxxi: 10).
344 'stale and unprofitable': *Hamlet* (NOS 1.2.133).
345 'Rousseau's opinion...year': 'I forsee how much my readers will be surprised to find I have attended my pupil throughout the whole first age of life without once speaking to him of religion. He hardly knows at fifteen years of age whether he hath a soul.... [F]or, if he learns it too soon, he runs a risk of never knowing it at all' (Rousseau, *Emilius*, 2:84).
346 'Fordyce's...foundation': James Fordyce, *Sermons to Young Women* (1766). In her youth Barbauld had resented its remarks on women's friendships, and in later years she wrote scornfully of Fordyce's 'affected prettinesses and constant glitter' (quoted in *ALBVE*, 501).
347 'Abbé Bossuet's Grammar': 'Bossuet' would ordinarily signify Jacques Bénigne Bossuet (1627–1704), French bishop, theologian, and orator. But he was never an abbé, and we have not found a grammar attributed to him. Barbauld may refer to *The French Phrase Book, or Key to French Conversation*, by 'M. l'Abbé Bossut', said to be a pseudonym of Sir Richard Phillips.
348 'Father's Legacy.': John Gregory, *A Father's Legacy to His Daughters* (1774).
349 'first appeared': The first English-language edition of the work now commonly known as *One Thousand and One Nights* was published in 1706 as *The Arabian Nights' Entertainments* (*ESTC*).
350 'Caroline Barnard': Although Emily Sunstein speculates that at least some of the tales published under the pseudonym 'Mrs. Caroline Barnard' might have been written by Mary Godwin Shelley (Emily W. Sunstein, *Mary Shelley: Romance and Reality* [Baltimore, 1989], 415, 422), this identification has not been accepted by other scholars.
351 '*N'enseignons que*...': Quoted from *La Rosière de Salency* (1769) by Charles-Simon Favart (1710–92); La Rosière was reprinted in a Favart anthology, *Le Théatre Choisi* (3 vols, 1809).
352 '*The Deserted Village School*': The author of this anonymous publication, a satire on the current educational reform movement in forty-two Spenserian stanzas, was the Rev. Richard Polwhele (1760–1838). In *The Unsex'd Females* (1798), Polwhele had attacked Barbauld, Mary Wollstonecraft, Charlotte Smith, Mary Robinson, Helen Maria Williams, Mary Hays, Ann Yearsley, and Angelica Kauffman.
353 'Dr. Bell's': Dr Andrew Bell (1753–1832) encountered in India older children teaching younger by writing lessons in the sand. Back in England he promoted what came to be called the 'Madras System' in which senior pupils taught their juniors (*ODNB*). *The Deserted Village School* disparages Bell's method as new-fangled and yearns for the days of village schools and schoolmistresses.
354 'Davis': Mary Anne Davis also wrote *Helps to Devotion* (1822), *The Divine Economy of Human Life* (1823), and *A Selection from the Parables of the New Testament*, paraphrased in familiar verse for the use of children (1836).

EXPLANATORY NOTES

355 'M. Bouilly': See note above.

356 'By Arabella Argus': See note above.

357 '*Queen Mab*': Marie-Catharine le Jumel de Berneville, Countess D'Aulnoy, *The Court of Queen Mab: containing A Select Collection of Only the Best, most Instructive, and Entertaining Tales of the Fairies... To which are Added, A Fairy Tale in the Ancient English Style, by Dr. Parnell: And Queen Mab's Song* (London, 1752). These fairy tales were popular throughout the latter part of the eighteenth century.

358 'Joshua Collins': The complicated history of *A Guide to Tutors* was detailed in 1872 ('The Choice of Books', *Notes & Queries*, s.4, x: 365–6). 'Joshua Collins' may have been the pseudonym of a now-unidentified author who died before 1816.

359 'Dr. Buchanan and Dr. Clarke': Probably Dr Claudius Buchanan (1766–1815), advocate of 'Christianizing' the people of India, and Adam Clarke (1762–1832), Methodist minister and bibliographer of ancient books (*ODNB*).

360 'erroneously stated': Louis Marie Prud'homme (1752–1830), French historian and journalist, published *Revolutions de Paris* between 1789 and 1794; Barbauld refers here to his *Histoire... des erreurs, des fautes, et des crimes... commis pendant la Révolution Française* (1797). The account of an impalement was taken from J. J. Stockdale's *Sketches, Civil and Military, of the Island of Java and its Immediate Dependencies* (1811). Barbauld correctly identifies the source of the description of the burning of Hindu women as Robert Southey's *The Curse of Kehama* (1810), and Southey's poem indeed reads 'Nealliny', not 'Nealing' as in *Diurnal Readings*.

361 'A. Picquot': Picquot also wrote *Tables of Comparative Chronology, exhibiting the dates of the principal events which took place from the flood to the fall of the Roman Empire; designed to give young persons correct information respecting the progress of human society* (1818) and *Elements of Astronomy* (1828).

362 'Joseph Guy': See note above.

363 'J. H. Wiffen': Jeremiah Holmes Wiffen (1792–1836) was a Quaker poet, Liberal reformer, and translator, who ran a school at Woburn. His best-known literary work is a translation of Tasso's *Jerusalem Delivered* (1824) (*ODNB*).

364 'John Hornsey': Hornsey published *A Short English Grammar* (1793), *The Child's Monitor; or Parental Instruction... Containing a Great Variety of Progressive Lessons, Adapted to the Comprehension of Children* (1806), *The Book of Monosyllables; or, An Introduction to the Child's Monitor* (1807), *The Pronouncing Expositor; or, a New Spelling-Book* (1816), and *English Exercises* (1818).

365 'Thomas Carpenter': Carpenter, Master of the Academy at Barking, Essex, published *The Scholar's Spelling Assistant* (1796), *An English Vocabulary* (1827), *The Christian's Manual* (1828), *Devotional Reflections on the Psalms of David* (1834), *The School Speaker* (1837), *Contemplations and Devotional Reflections on the Prayers of the Church of England* (1837), and *The Young Scholar's Manual of Elementary Arithmetic* (1842).

366 'variety of extracts': Among selections from Johnson, Hume, Chapone, Blair, Thomson, and others are five excerpts by or attributed to Barbauld: 'Envy and Emulation' and 'The Masque of Nature' (renamed 'The Seasons') from *Evenings at Home*, 'Hymn V' from *Hymns in Prose for Children*, and two long excerpts from *Remarks on Mr. Gilbert Wakefield's Enquiry* (renamed 'On Social Worship' and 'Advantages of Social Worship: A Sunday Lesson'). 'Martin Smart' may be a pseudonym.

367 'By the Author': The anonymous author of *The Decoy*—and hence of the work here reviewed—is Louisa Allan.

368 'this writer's': Anne Taylor, afterwards Gilbert (1782–1866) was a member of the famous literary family, known as 'the Taylors of Ongar'. She collaborated with her sister Jane and others on *Original Poems for Infant Minds* (1804–5) and published many works in prose and poetry, including *Original Hymns for Sunday Schools* (1812). Her most famous poem is 'My Mother', so well known it was widely parodied (Darton, 250–1). Anne Taylor's sister Jane also contributed to *The Mother's Fables*, which some sources erroneously attribute to E. L. Aveline.

369 'see page 3': Page 17 in the 1861 edn: 'There's not a note in all the wood, / But she is sure to hit; / A Raven's croak, in murky mood; / A Cuckoo or Tom-tit.'

370 '*The Decoy*': The anonymous author was Louisa Allan (Gorlach, item 29).

371 'Mrs. Taylor': Ann Taylor (née Martin) (1757–1830). This title sold well. The second and third editions both appeared in 1814. By 1824, the eleventh edition was advertised (Harris, *Contributions towards a Bibliography of the Taylors of Ongar and Stanford Rivers*, 15–16).

372 'knowledge of trees and plants': 1 Kings 4:33 recounts Solomon's knowledge of plants, from the cedar tree to the hyssop. Taylor writes: 'The lofty and majestic cedar was an appropriate subject for the contemplation of king Solomon, . . . yet he . . . condescended to notice also the "hyssop that groweth on the wall. . . ." There are many cases, my dear child, wherein you may follow the example of Solomon. . . . You will do well, for instance, to consider the years of your life that are past, and those which . . . are yet in prospect. . . . With your mind thus occupied, you are comparatively contemplating the cedar of Lebanon: but would your thoughts descend to the hyssop that groweth on the wall? Then reflect on the months, the weeks, the days, the hours, the moments of which such protracted periods are composed. O, my child! Despise not even the hyssop; undervalue not your precious moments; suffer not one to be wasted; it is too precious a portion of your small span of time. They who think moments of no value, squander their years in vanity and trifles.' (117).

373 '*rushes* forth': 'Ushers' remained the reading as late as the 9th edn (1820), so it may have been intended.

374 'country gentleman': Probably a common phrase denoting readers' ignorance. A 1783 political cartoon, 'North Whitewashing Fox', carries a Latin motto 'Translated for the Country Gentlemen'.

EXPLANATORY NOTES 471

375 'James Hews Bransby': Bransby (1783–1847), Unitarian minister and schoolmaster at Moreton Hampstead, Devonshire, where the future Sir John Bowring was his student. Bowring remembered him as 'not a very wise, nor a very honest man'. However, he had 'some knowledge, more taste, and was full of pleasant anecdote' (Bowring, 46). Bransby was a frequent contributor to the *Christian Reformer* (*ODNB*).

376 'S. Rousseau': Samuel Rousseau (1764–1821) printer and linguist, taught Persian and published various works under pseudonyms. His obituary appeared in the *New Monthly Magazine* for April 1821. The *Critical Review* gave this volume a long and witheringly negative notice, concluding with the observation 'We are extremely sorry to see such a prevalent taste for increasing the number of works that fail of being useful.' It comes from the March 1814 issue (series 4, vol. V, No. 3, p. 333).

377 'he says': The quotations come, respectively, from Gray, 'Elegy in a Country Churchyard' (l. 88) and Pope, *The Odyssey*, 5:335.

378 'considerably interested': Between 1 Dec. 1811 and late January 1812 newspapers in London, Edinburgh, Salisbury, Hull, and other towns reported the kidnapping of 3- or 4-year-old Thomas Dellow by Charlotte Magnay, who took him to satisfy her navy husband's yearning for a child.

379 '*Sir Hornbook*': By Thomas Love Peacock (1785–1866), satirical novelist and poet. In spite of Barbauld's judgement, the work had five editions over five years (*ODNB*).

380 'E. Ward': The British Library Catalogue describes E. Ward as a 'Teacher of Navigation' and gives the place of publication as Liverpool. The author is probably the same E. Ward who published, also in Liverpool, *The Lunarian, or Seaman's Guide: Being a Practical Introduction to the Method of Ascertaining the Longitude at Sea, by Celestial Observations, and Marine Chronometers… Designed for the Benefit of Private Learners, as Well as for the Use of Schools* (1817).

381 'this fair writer': Elizabeth Isabella Spence (1768–1832), Scottish novelist and travel writer. Among her other early works are *Helen Sinclair* (1799), *Nobility of the Heart* (1804), *The Wedding Day* (1807), *Summer Excursions through Part of England and Wales* (1809), and *Sketches of the Present Manners, Customs, and Scenery of Scotland* (1811) (*ODNB*). See Barbauld's review of her novel, *The Curate and his Daughter: A Cornish Tale* (1813).

382 '*vally de sham*': In *The New Bath Guide* (1766), Letter V: 'I don't care a damn / For you nor your valee de sham' (1807 edn, p. 26).

383 'Mrs. Rundell': Maria Eliza Ketelby Rundell (1745–1828), author of the best seller, *A New System of Domestic Cookery* (1808). She also published *Domestic Happiness* (1806) (*ODNB*).

384 'Mr. Kirwan': Richard Kirwan (1733–1812), chemist and admirer of Joseph Priestley, known to Barbauld.

385 'observance of civility': *The Merchant of Venice* (NOS, 2:2.176).

386 'the Decoy': This book went into a second edition in 1824. The author of *The Decoy*—and hence of the book under review—was Louisa Allan.

387 'John Rippingham': See note above.
388 'esteemed English writers': Including Barbauld: extracts from *Hymns in Prose* and *Remarks on... Public Worship* (1st American edn, 1816, 95–6 and 157–8).
389 'Siret': Louis-Pierre Siret (1745–97), philologist and author of *Éléments de la langue angloise, ou méthode pratique pour apprendre facilement cette langue* (Paris, 1773).
390 'Thomas West': Unidentified but not the Thomas West who authored the famous *Guide to the Lakes* (1778), which helped to popularize the Lake District. That Thomas West died in 1779.
391 '*That I deny*': In *Tristram Shandy*, Vol. II, ch. 17, after a sermon by Yorick (Sterne himself) is read, Walter Shandy praises Church of England homiletics: 'their compositions are fine.' 'I deny it,' retorts Dr. Slop, a Roman Catholic.
392 'Mant': Alicia Catherine Mant (1788–1869) was a novelist, religious writer, and children's author. Her other works include *Montague Newburgh; or, The Mother and Son* (1814), *Caroline Lismore; or, The Errors of Fashion* (1814), *Margaret Melville*, and *The Soldier's Daughter; or, Juvenile Memoirs* (1818), *The Young Naturalist* (1824), and *The Chalk Pit* (1825). See Barbauld's reviews of Mant's books for adults.
393 'little pieces': In addition to excerpts from works by Scott, Gray, Pope, Addison, Thomson, Williams, Watts, Gay, Blair, Robinson, Bloomfield, Thrale, Moore, Cowper, de Genlis, Chatterton, Crabbe, Dryden, Rowe, and others, Haigh includes from Barbauld's *Hymns in Prose for Children* the whole of Hymns VIII, IX, X, XI, and XII, retitled and slightly altered.
394 '*An Introduction...*': This volume also came out with the same publisher under a French title in 1814: *Introduction au style epistolaire des français*. *Theory and Practice* went into a third edition by 1817 and a fourth by 1823. In 1817 Saulez brought out an abridged French grammar book: *Abrégé de la Grammaire Française*.
395 '*New Orthographical Exercises*': The *British Critic* opined, 'We deprecate many innovations introduced of late into the English language, by a pedantic and false method of pronunciation, of which there are too many instances in these "Orthographical Exercises"' (May 1816), V: 558.
396 'Anna Brownell Murphy': Anna Brownell Jameson née Murphy (1794–1860), writer and art historian, began her career as a governess. She was the author of *A Lady's Diary* (1826), republished as *Diary of an Ennuyée, Winter Studies and Summer Rambles in Canada* (1838), and many other volumes of travel writing and fiction. The *Dictionary* was expanded and updated until 1830 (*ODNB*, Anna Brownell Jameson in Benjamin Colbert, *Women's Travel Writing, 1780–1840: A Bio-Bibliographical Database*, designer Movable Type Ltd. https://btw.wlv.ac.uk. [20 May 2023]: BTW1077).
397 'Miss Edgeworth... stories': In Maria Edgeworth's *Early Lessons* (1801), the story 'Harry and Lucy' is followed by a glossary. The aim, Edgeworth wrote,

EXPLANATORY NOTES 473

was to 'give a popular meaning of the words... selected, and... to point out the necessity of accuracy... but, above all, to excite in children an appetite for knowledge' (Edgeworth, *Early Lessons*, 2:210).

398 'a late Teacher': The author may be William Singleton (*c.* 1770–1832), who taught at Ackworth School from 1807 to 1812. By 1823, when he published *The Result of a Seven Years' Mission, among Friends... with a serious address to professors in general, especially to those who pray for the conversion of the heathen*, he had left the Society of Friends (*Journal of the Friends' Historical Society*, 14 [1917]: 119).

399 'Rev. Israel Worsley': Worsley (1768–1836), a Unitarian minister who served at Lincoln and Plymouth as well as Paris and Dunkirk, also published an *Account of the State of France... and the Treatment of the English* (1806), a *Memoir of Jacob Brettell* (1810), *Observations on... Changes in the Presbyterian Societies of England* (1816), *Lectures on... Nonconformity* (1823), and *View of the American Indians... the Descendants of the Ten Tribes of Israel* (1828) (*ODNB*).

400 'By the Author': Mary Weightman, a member of the Society of Friends, was the author of *The Polite Reasoner: in letters addressed to a young lady, at a boarding school in Hoddesdon, Hartfordshire* (1787). She also published *The Juvenile Speaker: or dialogues, and miscellaneous pieces in prose and verse; for the instruction of youth, in the art of reading* (1787) and *The Friendly Monitor; or Dialogues for youth against the fear of ghosts, and other irrational apprehensions: With reflections on the power of the imagination, and the folly of superstition* (1791).

401 'that book': The Old Testament, a copy of which every family could be presumed to own. 'Book-making' signifies a mere compilation from obvious sources.

402 '*Zadig and the Basilisk*': *Zadig* (1747), by Voltaire; chapter 15 concerns itself with the search for a basilisk. The *OED* describes it as "a fabulous reptile, also called a cockatrice, alleged to be hatched by a serpent from a cock's egg" and notes that Pliny wrote about it.

403 'so *ill* expressed': A twist on 'ne'er so well expressed' (Pope, *Essay on Criticism*, l. 298).

404 'Chambaud's... P. F. Merlet': Louis Chambaud wrote *Fables Choisies* (1751) for beginners in French; see Barbauld's 'Letter to recommend French Authors'. Pierre François Merlet (1785–1866) was Professor of French at University College, London; he also published *Le traducteur; or, Historical, dramatic, and miscellaneous selections, from the best French writers* (1818).

405 '*Le Manuel Epistolaire*': *The Young Ladies' Assistant in Writing French Letters: or, Manuel épistolaire à l'usage des demoiselles anglaises* (1806) was attributed on its title page to 'N. Lambert'.

406 'C. Laisné': C. Laisné was a 'teacher of languages, formerly private tutor in the university of Paris, and author of Latin, Spanish, Portuguese, Italian and French Grammars.' *The Critical Review*, series IV, vol. VI, no. 1, July 1814, p. 96.

407 'Gil Blas': *Gil Blas* (1715), a picaresque fiction by Alain-René Lesage, popular in England; Barbauld alludes to it in her poem 'Inventory of the Contents of Dr. Priestley's Study'.

408 'Buffon and Fenelon': Georges-Louis Leclerc, Comte de Buffon (1707–88), French naturalist, director of the Jardin du Roi, and author of the thirty-six-volume *Histoire Naturelle*. François de Salignac de la Mothe-Fénelon (1651–1715) wrote *Les Aventures de Télémaque* (1693–4, in English, *The Adventures of Telemachus, Son of Ulysses*), a favourite of Barbauld's.
409 'Maternal Solicitude': See above, for Barbauld's review of *Maternal Solicitude*.

APPENDIX
'Letter to Recommend French Authors'

Barbauld's 'Letter to Recommend French Authors' provides insight into works used at Palgrave School as well as her knowledge of French writing. Works mentioned in her or Rochemont's correspondence from the school[1] include *Fables Choisies* (the collection by Louis Chambaud [1751] rather than Jean de la Fontaine's—although she highly esteemed La Fontaine), Arnaud Berquin's *L'Ami des Enfans*, Bernard le Bovier de Fontenelle's *Entretiens sur la Pluralité des Mondes* (1686), and *Le Magazin des Enfans* (1756) by Jeanne-Marie Leprince de Beaumont. Fontenelle's *Entretiens* was a favourite of hers—the copy given her at age 7 survives today—and was in general use as a teaching text for young people.[2] Berquin's *L'Ami des Enfans* began monthly publication in French in London on 1 January 1783. Barbauld subscribed, along with the Burneys, Elizabeth Carter, Hannah More, and other Establishment figures. Joseph Johnson proposed to Barbauld and John Aikin that they translate *L'Ami*, an idea they were pondering in the spring of 1783.[3] Her copies of Numbers II, IX, and XII survive today;[4] their margins bear marks perhaps designating the portions she and John Aikin thought most worth translating. In the end they did not translate *L'Ami*; an English version, *The Children's Friend*, by Mark Anthony Meilan came out in November.[5] However, she and Rochemont continued to use *L'Ami* at Palgrave: on 4 November Rochemont ordered five copies each of Numbers IV, V, and VI. Also at Palgrave Rochemont ordered three copies of Voltaire's *Histoire de Charles XII* (4 Nov. 1783), and Barbauld assigned an extract from Molière's *L'Avare* for recitation by one of the boys (26 May 1780). Molière was an early favourite, both for teaching (Charles at 13 'struggled through' the comedies) and for herself: she and Rochemont attended a recitation of *Tartuffe* in June 1802.[6]

About the works of Stéphanie Félicité Ducrest, Countess de Genlis (1746–1830), Barbauld commented often, with mingled admiration and scepticism. *Adèle et Théodore* (translated as *Adelaide and Theodore; or, Letters on Education*, 1788) drew extended comment in 'On the Origin and Progress of Novel-writing', Barbauld's preface to *The British Novelists* (1810): '[T]he stories of *Cécile* and the *Duchesse de*

---

[1] See McCarthy, '"Celebrated Academy"'.
[2] See *ALBVE*, 44–6 for Barbauld's early reading of Fontenelle.
[3] ALB to JJ, 3 June 1783 (GC, 207-08), and JA to JJ, 20 June 1783 (Laing II: 647, Edinburgh University Library).
[4] MS the Estate of Lady Rodgers.
[5] ESTC No. T126089; also *MC*, 2 January 1787.
[6] ALB to JA, 9 Sept. 1788; RB, Diary.

C. are...well told, while the sublime benevolence of M. and Mme. Lagaraye presents a cure for sorrow worthy of a Howard', but also de Genlis 'much exaggerated...filial affection' and her 'system of education...[is] too much founded on deception'.[7] In her essay 'What Is Education?' (1798) Barbauld criticized de Genlis along with Rousseau for making unreasonable demands on parents: 'it is not necessary with Rousseau or Madame Genlis to devote to the education of one child the talents and time of...grown men'.[8] But she admired *Les Veillées du Chateau* (translated in 1788 as *Evenings at the Castle*)—as did John Aikin, who imitated it in *Evenings at Home*.

Barbauld's admiration of *Télémaque* (1699) by François de Salignic de la Mothe de Fénelon was unmixed: She praised it warmly in the 'Preliminary Essay' to her *Spectator* anthology (1804) and in 'On the Origin and Progress of Novel-Writing' (1810). She reviewed an English translation of his *Education d'une Fille*. She preferred the plays of Jean Racine (1639–99) to those of Pierre Corneille (1606–84), in part, probably, because Racine was a religious dissident (a Port-Royal Catholic) and his works were traditionally read by English Dissenters. At her grandfather Jennings's academy Philip Doddridge had read Racine, and Rochemont himself at age 12 had been presented a set of Racine's *Oeuvres*.[9]

Another favourite was the historical romance, *Bélisaire* (1766), based on the life and misfortunes of the Byzantine general, Belisarius, by Jean-François Marmontel (1723–99). Barbauld cited it in her essay, 'An Enquiry into those Kinds of Distress which Excite Agreeable Sensations' (1773), and instanced it in 'On the Origin and Progress of Novel-Writing' (1810) among works in which fiction is 'allied with a great moral end' (2). The work was received, in the words of an English translator, as a fable in favour of 'civil and religious liberty',[10] and that is probably how Barbauld read it. She enjoyed Marmontel's romance *Les Incas; ou, la destruction de l'empire de Pérou* (1776) also, probably for its admiring treatment of the Incas. The 'exceptionable' chapter may be Chapter 3, which describes a ritual dance by young men and women dressed in garments which 'laissent à la beauté toute la gloire des ses charmes'.

Along with his *Histoire de Charles XII, Roi de Suède* (1731), Barbauld knew Voltaire's *Le Siècle de Louis Quatorze* (1751); she quoted from or alluded to it in 'Origin and Progress' (*British Novelists*, 1810) and 'Dialogue in the Shades' (1813, but not published until 1825). Voltaire, she wrote to her brother in May 1791 after reading Boswell's *Life of Samuel Johnson*, exerted influence in the world, unlike Johnson.[11] The satirist Nicholas Boileau (1636–1711) was another favourite: she quoted 'Satire III' in 'Origin and Progress' (16) and read one of his works (not named) with her pupil Sarah Taylor in 1807.[12]

Clearly, Barbauld's knowledge of resources in French for students was extensive and is a testament to her own love of French literature.

---

[7] 'Origin and Progress', 26–8.   [8] 'What Is Education?', 317.
[9] *ALBVE*, 46–7, 136, 589 n. 35.   [10] *Belisarius*, London, 1767, p. v.
[11] *Works*, 2:158.
[12] Susannah Taylor to her daughter Sarah, 5 March 1807; Ross, 34.

PRINCIPAL SOURCES OF THE TEXTS

Printed

The / ANNUAL REVIEW; / and / History of Literature; / for 1802. / ARTHUR AIKIN, EDITOR. / VOL. I. / LONDON: / PRINTED FOR T. N. LONGMAN AND O. REES, PATERNOSTER-ROW. / BY T. GILLET, SALISBURY-SQUARE. / 1803.

First publication of reviews of Elizabeth Hamilton and William Barrow.

EVENINGS AT HOME; / or, / THE JUVENILE BUDGET / OPENED. / Consisting of / a Variety of Miscellaneous Pieces, / for / the Instruction and Amusement of / Young Persons. / VOL. I. / LONDON: / PRINTED FOR J. JOHNSON, NO. 72, ST. PAUL'S / CHURCH-YARD. / 1792. / [PRICE ONE SHILLING AND SIXPENCE.]

Copy text: BL 1031.d.15. First publication of 'The Young Mouse', 'The Wasp and Bee', 'Alfred, a Drama', 'Canute's Reproof', 'The Masque of Nature', and 'Things by their Right Names'. 12mo.

Vol. 2, copy text BL 1031.d.15, titled as above, except VOL. II. and 1793. 12mo. First publication of 'The Goose and Horse', 'On Manufactures', 'The Flying Fish', 'A Lesson in the Art of Distinguishing', 'The Phenix and Dove', and 'The Manufacture of Paper'.

Vol, 6, copy text BL 1031.d.17, titled as above, except VOL. VI. and 1796. 12mo. First publication of 'The Four Sisters'.

THE / FEMALE SPEAKER; / OR, / MISCELLANEOUS PIECES, / IN / PROSE AND VERSE, / SELECTED FROM THE BEST WRITERS, / AND / ADAPTED TO THE USE OF YOUNG WOMEN, / BY / ANNA LÆTITIA BARBAULD. / LONDON: / PRINTED FOR J. JOHNSON AND CO., / ST. PAUL'S CHURCHYARD. / 1811.

12mo. Copy text: Collection of Paula R. Feldman; another copy in the Osborne Collection of Early Children's Books, Toronto Public Library.

HYMNS / in / PROSE / for / CHILDREN. / BY THE AUTHOR OF / LESSONS FOR CHILDREN. / LONDON: / PRINTED FOR J. JOHNSON, NO. 72, ST. PAUL'S / CHURCH-YARD. / MDCCLXXXI.

Copy text: 1781 first edition BL 1018.d.28(3). 12mo. Barbauld intervened in the 1784 third edition text.

HYMNS / in / PROSE / for / CHILDREN. / BY THE AUTHOR OF / LESSONS FOR CHILDREN. / THE SIXTEENTH EDITION, / MUCH ENLARGED. / LONDON: / PRINTED FOR J. JOHNSON AND CO. NO. 72, ST. PAUL'S / CHURCH-YARD [1814].

Copy text: BL 11632.aa.2. 12mo. First publication of three hymns (numbered X–XII).

A LEGACY / FOR / YOUNG LADIES, / CONSISTING OF / MISCELLANEOUS PIECES, / IN PROSE AND VERSE, / BY THE LATE / MRS. BARBAULD. / LONDON: / PRINTED FOR / LONGMAN, HURST, REES, ORME, BROWN, AND GREEN, / PATERNOSTER ROW. / 1826.

Supplies copy texts for: 'Pic-nic', 'Letter from Grimalkin to Selima', 'True Magicians', 'On Female Studies', 'Expense: A Dialogue', 'On Riddles', 'Letter of a Young King', 'Knowledge and Her Daughter: A Fable', 'A Lecture on the Use of Words', 'The Morning Repast', 'On Friendship', 'The Death-bed', and 'A Dialogue of the Dead, between Helen, and Madame Maintenon'. 12mo.

LESSONS / FOR / CHILDREN, / FROM / TWO TO THREE YEARS OLD. / LONDON: / PRINTED FOR J. JOHNSON, NO. 72, ST. PAUL'S / CHURCH-YARD. / MDCCLXXVIII.

Copy text: Glasgow University Sp Coll RB 4587, 16mo. Later editions title *Two to Three* as 'Part I' of what became a four-volume set. See the Introduction to *Lessons* for differences between copies dated 1778.

LESSONS / FOR / CHILDREN, / OF / THREE YEARS OLD. / LONDON: / PRINTED FOR J. JOHNSON, NO. 72, ST. PAUL'S / CHURCH-YARD. / MDCCLXXVIII.

Copy text: Glasgow University Sp Coll RB 4587, 16mo. Subsequent editions title this volume as 'Part I' of *Three Years Old* and as 'the Second [Volume]' of the four-volume set.

LESSONS / FOR / CHILDREN, / OF / THREE YEARS OLD. / PART II. / LONDON: / PRINTED FOR J. JOHNSON, / NO. 72, ST. PAUL'S CHURCH-YARD. / 1781. [PRICE SIX-PENCE.]

Copy text: Collection of Paula R. Feldman. No copies of the Joseph Johnson 1778 first edition have been located. This previously unrecorded volume is presumed to be the second edition. 16mo.

LESSONS / FOR / CHILDREN, / FROM / THREE TO FOUR YEARS OLD. / LONDON: / PRINTED FOR J. JOHNSON, NO. 72, ST. PAUL'S / CHURCH-YARD. / MDCCLXXIX.

Copy text: Glasgow University Sp Coll RB 4587. 16mo.

LESSONS / FOR / CHILDREN. / IN FOUR PARTS. / PART I. / FOR CHILDREN / FROM / TWO TO THREE YEARS OLD. / LONDON: / PRINTED FOR J. JOHNSON, NO. 72, ST. PAUL'S / CHURCH-YARD. / 1808. / [PRICE SIX PENCE.]

Copy text for 1808 additions: BL 12807.a.14.

LESSONS / FOR / CHILDREN. / IN FOUR PARTS. / PART II. / BEING THE FIRST FOR CHILDREN / OF / THREE YEARS OLD. / LONDON: / PRINTED FOR J. JOHNSON, NO. 72, ST. PAUL'S / CHURCH-YARD. / 1808. / [PRICE SIX PENCE.]

Copy text for 1808 additions: BL 12807.a.14.

LESSONS / FOR / CHILDREN. / In Four Parts. / Part III. / being the second for children / of / three years old. / London: / Printed for J. Johnson, No. 72, St. Paul's / Church-Yard. / 1808. / [Price six pence.]

Copy text for 1808 additions: BL 12807.a.14.

LESSONS / FOR / CHILDREN. / In Four Parts. / Part IV. / for children / from / three to four years old. / London: /Printed for J. Johnson, No. 72, St. Paul's / Church-Yard. / 1808. / [Price six pence.]

Copy text for 1808 additions: BL 12807.a.14.

THE / MONTHLY REVIEW; / OR / LITERARY JOURNAL, / ENLARGED: / LONDON / Volume *LXIII (1810)* to Volume *LXXVI (1815)*.

THE WORKS / OF / ANNA LÆTITIA BARBAULD. / With a Memoir / By Lucy Aikin. / In Two Volumes. / Volumes II. / London: / printed for / Longman, Hurst, Rees, Orme, Brown, and Green, / Paternoster-Row. / 1825.

8vo. First publication of 'Zephyrus and Flora' and 'Knowledge and Her Daughter'.

Barbauld, Anna Letitia. 'The Misses', *The Juvenile Forget Me Not*. Ed. Mrs. S. C. Hall, London, 1830, pp. 1–8.

Rickards, E.[dith] C.[ordelia]. 'Unpublished Letters of Mrs. Barbauld'. *Monthly Packet*. (London), ns 1 (1891): 276–85 (March), and 514–23 (May) 10:706–26.

First publication of '[Dressing Table Ornaments]'. and 'Letter from Miss Susan Slipslop to Miss Fanny Flippant'.

Manuscripts

Carl H. Pforzheimer Collection of Shelley and His Circle, New York Public Library, Astor, Lenox, and Tilden Foundations.

Holograph letters (five of them on Grammar, History, and Homer) from Barbauld to Lydia Rickards (Misc. MSS 4337, 4338, 4343-47). The letter on Grammar is dated 6 November 1800; the letters on History and Homer are undated, but the paper of one of the letters on History is watermark-dated 1799, and that letter perhaps draws from books published in 1800 and 1802. Hence the letters on Grammar, History, and Homer may be dated to 1800–2 or soon after. All holographs belong to a collection of thirty-nine Barbauld letters to Lydia Rickards, 1798–1815, with a copy in an unidentified hand of an undated Barbauld letter to Mr. Douce, recommending French books for young readers (Misc. MS 4379). The collection remained in the keeping of Rickards's collateral descendants until 2011, when it was privately purchased at auction; in 2016 it was sold to the New York Public Library Pforzheimer Collection.

GENERAL BIBLIOGRAPHY

Aikin, Charles Rochemont. Letter to Anna Letitia Barbauld, 9 Sept. 1788. MS. the Estate of Lady Rodgers.
Aikin, Charles Rochemont. Letter to Lydia Rickards, 4 Feb. 1808. MS Misc. 4381. Carl H. Pforzheimer Collection of Shelley and His Circle, New York Public Library.
Aikin, John. *The Calendar of Nature*. 2nd edn. London: J. Johnson, 1785.
Aikin, John. Letter to Anna Letitia Barbauld, 18 Feb. 1780. MS 15/21, fol. 6b. The Hornel Library, The National Trust for Scotland, Broughton House.
Aikin, John. 'On the Inequality of Conditions'. In Aikin, *Letters from a Father to his Son*. London: J. Johnson, 1794. I: 207–19.
Aikin, Lucy. Letter to William Roscoe, 29 June 1825. MS 920 ROS 70. Liverpool Record Office.
Aikin, Lucy. 'Memoir'. In Barbauld, *Works*, ed. Lucy Aikin. I: v–lxxii.
Aikin, Lucy. *Memoir of John Aikin, M.D. with a Selection of His Miscellaneous Pieces*. 2 vols. London: Baldwin et al., 1823.
Aikin, Lucy. *Memoirs, Miscellanies, and Letters*, ed. Philip Hemery Le Breton. London: Longman, 1864.
Aikin, Lucy. 'Mrs. Barbauld's MSS'. *Monthly Repository*, ns 2 (1828): 55.
Aikin, Lucy. 'Preface'. In John Aikin, *Evenings at Home*. London: Baldwin, Cradock and Joy, 1826. I: v–viii.
Altick, Richard. *The Shows of London*. Cambridge, MA: The Belknap Press of Harvard University Press, 1978.
Anderson, Robert. 'Preface to the Works of William Wilkie'. In *A Complete Edition of the Poets of Great Britain*. London: Arch, 1795. 11: 1–8.
Anstey, Christopher. *The New Bath Guide. A New Edition*. London: 1807.
Austen, Jane. *Northanger Abbey*, ed. Barbara M. Benedict and Deidre Le Faye. *Cambridge Edition of the Works of Jane Austen*, Ed. Janet Todd. Cambridge: Cambridge University Press, 2006.
Barbauld, Anna Letitia. *Lessons for Children, by Mrs. Barbauld, with Engravings and Woodcuts, Nine Original Tales; and some Lessons in Poetry*. London, [nd; c.1830].
Barbauld, Anna Letitia. Letters to John Aikin, 19 Jan. and 15 April 1780; 6 June, 16 Aug., and 5 Sept. 1787; and 19 July [1788]. MS 15/21, fols. 31, 28, 14, 15, 16, and 27. The Hornel Library, The National Trust for Scotland, Broughton House.
Barbauld, Anna Letitia. Letter to Joanna Baillie, 20 March [1822]. In Rodgers, *Georgian Chronicle*, pp. 242–3.
Barbauld, Anna Letitia. Letter to Joseph Johnson, n.d. M3725, Hackney Archives.
Barbauld, Anna Letitia. *Anna Letitia Barbauld Letters to Lydia Rickards, 1798–1815*, ed. William McCarthy. Romantic Circles Electronic Editions. www.romanticcircles.org/editions/barbauldletters/editions.2021.barbauldletters.l18.html.

Barbauld, Anna Letitia. 'The Origin and Progress of Novel-Writing'. In *The British Novelists*, ed. Barbauld. London: Longmans et al., 1810. 1: 1–62.

Barbauld, Anna Letitia. *Selections from the Spectator, Tatler, Guardian, and Freeholder: with a Preliminary Essay*, Vol. 3. London: J. Johnson, 1804.

Barbauld, Anna Letitia. *Things by their Right Names, and Other Stories, Fables, and Moral Pieces, in Verse and Prose*, ed. Mrs S.[arah] J.[osepha] Hale. Boston, 1840.

Barbauld, Anna Letitia. 'Thoughts on the Devotional Taste'. In Barbauld, *Devotional Pieces, Compiled from the Psalms and the Book of Job*. London: J. Johnson, 1775. Pp. 1–50.

Barbauld, Anna Letitia. 'What is Education?' *Monthly Magazine*, 5 (1798): 167–71.

Barbauld, Rochemont. Diary, 1–30 June 1802. MS. The Estate of Lady Rodgers.

Barker-Benfield, G. J. *The Culture of Sensibility: Sex and Society in Eighteenth-Century England*. Chicago: University of Chicago Press, 1992.

Barrow, William. *An Essay on Education*. 2 vols. London: F. and C. Rivington, 1802.

Bayle, Pierre. *The Dictionary Historical and Critical of Mr. Peter Bayle*. 2nd edn. London: Knapton et al., 1734.

Bentley, Thomas. Review of *Lessons for Children*. *Monthly Review*, 59 (1778): 25–8.

Bentley, Thomas. Review of *Lessons for Children*. *Monthly Review*, 60 (1779): 487–8.

Biello, David, 'Fact or Fiction?: Archimedes Coined the Term "Eureka!" in the Bath', *Scientific American*, 8 Dec. 2006. https://www.scientificamerican.com/article/fact-or-fiction-archimede/.

Blair, Hugh. 'Sermon XI' in *Sermons*, 17th ed., vol. 2, London: T. Cadell and W. Davies.

Boswell, James. *Life of Johnson*. London: Oxford University Press, 1953.

Bourguignon d'Anville, Jean-Baptiste. *Notice des Ouvrages de M. d'Anville*. Paris: Delance, Fuchs. 1802.

Bowring, John. *Autobiographical Recollections*. London: King, 1877.

Brewer, James Norris. *The Beauties of England and Wales; or, Original Delineations, Topographical, Historical, and Descriptive, of Each County*. London: J. Harris et al., 1813. Vol. 12 pt. II.

British Critic, 5 (May 1816): 558. Review of *New Orthographical Exercises*.

Broadie, Alexander, ed. *The Scottish Enlightenment: An Anthology*. Edinburgh: Canongate, 1997.

Brodribb, C. W. 'Mrs. Barbauld's School'. *Contemporary Review*, 148 (Dec. 1935): 731–6.

Buffon, Georges-Louis Leclerc, comte de. *Histoire Naturelle, générale et particulière*. 6 vols. Paris, 1749–56.

Burke, Edmund. *Reflections on the Revolution in France and on the Proceedings in Certain Societies in London Relative to that Event*, ed. William B. Todd. New York: Holt, Rinehart, and Winston, 1959.

Burnet, James. *Of the Origin and Progress of Language*. Vol. 1, London: T. Cadell, 1773.

Burney, Frances. *The Journals and Letters of Fanny Burney (Madame d'Arblay)*, ed. Joyce Hemlow et al. 12 vols. Oxford: Clarendon Press, 1972–84.

Caesar, C. Julius. *Libri VII de Bello Gallico*. Ed. Rene L. A. Du Pontet. Vol. 1. Oxford Classical Texts. Oxford: Oxford UP, 1900. Book IV: 22–31.

The Cambridge History of English Literature: The Period of the French Revolution, ed. A. W. Ward and A. R. Waller. Vol. 11. New York: Macmillan, 1933.

Cappe, Catharine. *An Account of Two Charity Schools for the Education of Girls: and of a Female Friendly Society in York*. York: William Blanchard, 1800.

Cappe, Catharine. 'Letter on Charity-Schools'. *Monthly Magazine*, 5 (1798): 319–20.

Carter, Elizabeth, trans. *All the Works of Epictetus*. London: Millar et al., 1758.

Carter, Elizabeth. *A Series of Letters between Mrs. Elizabeth Carter and Miss Catherine Talbot*, ed. Montagu Pennington. 4 vols. London: Rivington, 1809.

Castéra, Jean-Henri. *The Life of Catharine II. Empress of Russia*. Trans. W. Tooke. 3 vols., 2nd ed. London: T. N. Longman, 1798.

Chapone, Hester. *Letters on the Improvement of the Mind, Addressed to a Young Lady*. New edn. 2 vols. London: Walter and Dilly, 1790.

Chesterfield, Philip Dormer Stanhope, Lord. *Letters to his Son*. 8th edn. London: Dodsley, 1777.

Colbert, Benjamin. *Women's Travel Writing, 1780–1840: A Bio-Bibliographical Database*. https://btw.wlv.ac.uk.

Coleridge, Samuel Taylor. *The Watchman*, No. 9. Bristol: privately printed: 5 May 1796.

Condillac, Étienne-Bonnot de. *Essai sur l'Origine des Connoissances Humaines*. 2 vols. Amsterdam: Mortier, 1746.

Condillac, Etienne Bonnot de. *Essay on the Origin of Human Knowledge*, tr. and ed. Hans Aarsleff. Cambridge: Cambridge University Press, 2001.

'C. P. Landon'. In *The Annual Register*, or a View of the History, Politics, and Literature of the Year 1826. London: Baldwin, Cradock and Joy, 1827, p. 231.

The Critical Review, 46 (August 1778): 160. Review of *Lessons for Children*.

The Critical Review, ns 17 (August 1796): 442–6. Review of *Evenings at Home*.

The Critical Review, series IV, vol. VI, no. 1 (July 1814): 96. Review of *A Key to the re-translation of the English Examples in the French Grammar* by C. Laisne.

The Critical Review, series IV, V, no. 3 (March 1814): 333. Review of *Punctuation* by S. Rousseau.

Crosfield, John Dymond. 'Richard Smith and his Journal'. VI. *Journal of the Friends' Historical Society*, 14 (1917): 108–21.

Darton, Lawrence. *The Dartons: An Annotated Check-List of Children's Books Issued by Two Publishing Houses*, London: British Library, 2004.

De Quincey, Thomas. *Collected Writings*, ed. David Masson. Vol. 11. London: Black, 1897.

Douglas, Thomas. *A Sketch of the British Fur Trade in North America*. 2nd edn. London: Ridgway, 1816.

The Drennan-McTier Letters, ed. Jean Agnew. 2 vols. Dublin: Irish Manuscripts Commission, 1998–9.

Dryden, John. *Poems: The Works of Virgil in English, 1697*. Ed. William Frost and Vinton A. Dearing. *The Works of John Dryden*, Vols. 5–6. Berkeley: University of California Press, 1987–88.

Eclectic Review. NS 25 (1826): 79–88. Review of *A Legacy for Young Ladies*.

Edgeworth, Maria. *Belinda. The British Novelists; with an Essay, and Prefaces Biographical and Critical, by Mrs. Barbauld*, Vol. XLIX. London: Rivington, 1810.

Edgeworth, Maria. *Castle Rackrent* and *Ennui*, ed. Marilyn Butler. London: Penguin, 1992.

Edgeworth, Maria. *Harry and Lucy Concluded; being the Last Part of Early Lessons*. Vol. 3. London: Hunter et al., 1825.

Edgeworth, Maria and Richard Lovell. *Practical Education*. 2 vols. London: J. Johnson, 1798.

Edgeworth, Richard Lovell. *Essays on Professional Education*. London: J. Johnson, 1809.

Edgeworth, Richard Lovell. Letter to Mrs. Barbauld. MS Eng. Misc. c. 895. Bodleian Library, University of Oxford.

Edinburgh Magazine, ns 20 (August 1802): 92–5. Review of Poppe's revision of 'The History of Clock and Watch-Making'.

El-Shamy, Hasan M. *Folk Traditions of the Arab World: A Guide to Motif Classification*, Vol. 1. Bloomington, IN: Indiana University Press, 1995.

Enfield, William. Review of *The Parent's Assistant* by Maria Edgeworth. *Monthly Review*, ser. 2, 21 (September 1796): 89.

Feldman, Paula R. *British Women Poets of the Romantic Era: An Anthology*. Baltimore: Johns Hopkins University Press, 1997.

Feldman, Paula R. 'The Poet and the Profits: Felicia Hemans and the Literary Marketplace', *Keats-Shelley Journal*, 46 (1997): 148–76.

Ferguson, Moira. *Subject to Others: British Women Writers and Colonial Slavery, 1670–1834*. New York: Routledge, 1992.

Fletcher, Eliza. *Autobiography of Mrs. Fletcher*. Carlisle, UK: privately printed, 1874.

[Frere, Eleanor, Lady Fenn.]. *The Infant's Friend. Part II. Reading Lessons. By Mrs. Lovechild*. London: Newbery, 1797.

Genlis, Caroline Stéphanie Félicité du Crest, comtesse de. *Theatre of Education, Translated from the French of the Countess de Genlis*. 4 vols. London: Cadell and Elmsly, 1781.

Gentleman's Magazine. Ser. 2 vol. 41 (January 1854):103. 'Obituary of M. George Bernard Depping'.

George, M. Dorothy. *London Life in the Eighteenth Century*. Harmondsworth, UK: Penguin, 1966.

Gibbon, Edward. *The History of the Decline and Fall of the Roman Empire*. 3rd edn. Vol. 1. London: Strahan and Cadell, 1777.

Goffart, Walter. *Historical Atlases: The First Three Hundred Years, 1570–1870*. Chicago: University of Chicago Press, 2003.

Gorlach, Manfred. *An Annotated Bibliography of Nineteenth-Century Grammars of English*. Philadelphia: John Benjamins, 1998.

Gregory, John. *A Father's Legacy to His Daughters*. 1774. Rpt. Boston: Dow, 1834.
Grundy, Isobel. '"Slip-shod Measure" and "Language of Gods": Barbauld's Stylistic Range'. In *Anna Letitia Barbauld: New Perspectives*, ed. McCarthy and Murphy, pp. 23–36.
Hale, Sarah J. 'Preface'. In Barbauld, *Things by their Right Names*. Boston: Marsh, Capen, Lyon, and Webb, 1840, pp. 3–4.
Hamilton, Elizabeth. *Letters on the Elementary Principles of Education*. 3rd English edn. 2 vols. London: C. and J. Robinson, 1803.
Hamst, Olphar. 'The Choice of Books', *Notes and Queries*, vol. 10, no. 254 (9 Nov. 1872): 365–66.
Harris, G. Edward. *Contributions Towards a Bibliography of the Taylors of Ongar and Stanford Rivers*. Hamden, CT: Archon Books, 1965.
Harris, James. *Three Treatises: The First Concerning Art; the Second Concerning Music, Painting, and Poetry; the Third Concerning Happiness*. 4th edn. London: Nourse and Vaillant, 1783.
Holland, Thomas and John. *Exercises for the Memory and Understanding, Consisting of Select pieces in prose and verse*. 3rd edn. Manchester, 1798.
Hone, William. *The Every-Day Book; or, Everlasting Calendar of Popular Amusements, Sports, Pastimes, Ceremonies, Manners, Customs, and Events, incident to each of the three hundred and sixty-five days…forming a complete History of the Year, Months, & Seasons*. Vol. 1. London: William Tegg, 1826.
Howatson, M. C. *The Oxford Companion to Classical Literature*. 2nd edn. Oxford: Oxford University Press, 1989.
Hume, David. 'Of Simplicity and Refinement in Writing'. In Hume, *Essays and Treatises on Several Subjects*. Vol. 1. Edinburgh: Bell & Bradfute et al., 1817.
Hume, David. *The History of England, from the Invasion of Julius Caesar to the Revolution in 1688*. Vol. 2. London: Cadell, 1770.
Hutcheson, Francis. *Philosophiae Moralis Institutio Compendiaria, with a Short Introduction to Moral Philosophy*, ed. Luigi Turco. Indianapolis, IN: Liberty Fund, 2007. https://oll.libertyfund.org/title/hutcheson-philosophiae-moralis-institutio-compendiaria-1747-2007.
James, Charles. *Audi Alteram Partem; or, an Extenuation of the Conduct of the French Revolutionists from the 14th of July, 1789, until the 17th of January, 1793*. London: H. D. Symonds, 1793.
James, Felicity. 'Lucy Aikin and the Legacies of Dissent'. In *Religious Dissent and the Aikin-Barbauld Circle, 1740–1860*, ed. Felicity James and Ian Inkster. Cambridge, Cambridge University Press, 2012. Pp. 183–204.
Johnson, Joseph. *The Joseph Johnson Letterbook*, ed. John W. Bugg. Oxford: Oxford University Press, 2016.
Johnson, Samuel. *The Vanity of Human Wishes (1749): And Two Rambler Papers (1750)*. Augustan Reprint Society, No. 22. Los Angeles: William Andrews Clark Memorial Library, U of California, 1950.
Juvenile Magazine; or, an Instructive and Entertaining Miscellany for Youth of Both Sexes, 1 (1788): 135n.

Kenrick, John. *Biographical Memoir of the Late Rev. Charles Wellbeloved*. London: Whitfield, 1860.

King, William. *The Art of Cookery: A Poem, in Imitation of Horace's Art of Poetry*. London: 1708.

Knox, Vicesimus. *Liberal Education: or, a Practical Treatise on the Methods of Acquiring Useful and Polite Learning*. 3rd edn. London: Dilly, 1781.

The Lady's Monthly Museum. 'Mrs. Anna-Letitia Barbauld'. 1 (1798): 169–79.

Laertius, Diogenes. *Lives of Eminent Philosophers*, ed. R. D. Hicks. Cambridge, MA: Harvard University Press, 2014.

Le Breton, Anna Letitia. *Memoir of Mrs. Barbauld*. London: Bell, 1874.

Lim, Jessica W. H. "Unsettled Accounts: Anna Letitia Barbauld's Letters to Lydia Rickards." *Tulsa Studies in Women's Literature*, 38.1 (2019): 153–200.

'Longman's Joint Commission and Divide Ledger for 1803–07'. MS 1393 1/A. Longman Archive, University of Reading.

The London Daily Advertiser, London (25 Oct. 1796): 1. 'Eye-Water'. 'Advertisements and Notices'.

Mackinnon, Sir Frank. 'Notes on the History of English Copyright'. In *The Oxford Companion to English Literature*, ed. Paul Harvey. 2nd edn. New York: Oxford University Press, 1944.

Major, Emma. 'The Politics of Sociability: Public Dimensions of the Bluestocking Millenium'. *Huntington Library Quarterly*, 65 (2002): 175–92.

Marmontel, Jean-François. *Belisarius*. London: Vaillant, 1767.

Martineau, Harriet. *Autobiography*. Vol. 1. 1877. Rpt. London: Virago, 1983.

Martineau, Harriet. 'What Women are Educated For'. *Once a Week*, 10 August 1861, pp. 175–9.

Matthew Prior, 'Protogenes and Apelles'. *Poems on Several Occasions*. 6th edn. London: H. Lintot, 1768. Pp. 234–37.

McCarthy, William. *Anna Letitia Barbauld, Voice of the Enlightenment*. Baltimore: Johns Hopkins University Press, 2008.

McCarthy, William. '"The Celebrated Academy at Palgrave": A Documentary History of Anna Letitia Barbauld's School'. *The Age of Johnson*, 8 (1997): 279–392.

McCarthy, William. 'How Dissent Made Anna Letitia Barbauld, and What She Made of Dissent'. In *Religious Dissent and the Aikin-Barbauld Circle, 1740–1860*, ed. Felicity James and Ian Inkster. Cambridge: Cambridge University Press, 2012. Pp. 52–69.

McCarthy, William. 'Mother of All Discourses: Anna Barbauld's *Lessons for Children*'. In *Culturing the Child, 1690–1914: Essays in Memory of Mitzi Myers*, ed. Donelle Ruwe. Lanham, MD: Scarecrow Press, 2005. Pp. 85–111.

McCarthy, William. 'Uncollected Periodical Prose by Anna Letitia Barbauld'. *Studies in Bibliography*, 59 (2015): 225–48.

McCarthy, William. 'What Did Anna Barbauld Do to Richardson's Correspondence?' *Studies in Bibliography*, 54 (2001): 191–223.

McCarthy, William, and Olivia Murphy, eds. *Anna Letitia Barbauld: New Perspectives*. Lewisburg, PA: Bucknell University Press, 2014.

Milton, John. *The Complete Poetry of John Milton*, ed. John T. Shawcross. Rev. edn. New York: Doubleday Anchor, 1971.

Montagu, Lady Mary Wortley. *The Works of the Right Honourable Lady Mary Wortley Montagu*. 5 vols. London: Phillips, 1803.

Monthly Magazine. 'Half-Yearly Retrospect of German Literature'. 13 (20 July 1802): 699–709.

Monthly Review. Review of the Rev. William Jillard Hort's *Miscellaneous English Exercises*. NS 68 (May 1812): 107–8.

Montluzin, Emily Lorraine de. 'Attributions of Authorship in the *Gentleman's Magazine*, 1731–1868: An Electronic Union List'. https://bsuva.org/bsuva/gm2/.

Morning Post. 'To the Ladies'. 4 April, 1793 (No. 6225):1.

Nangle, Benjamin. 'Preface'. In *The Monthly Review, Second Series, 1790–1815: Indexes of Contributors and Articles*, ed. Benjamin Christie Nangle. Oxford: Clarendon Press, 1955. Pp. iii–xiii.

The New Oxford Shakespeare. The Complete Works. Modern Critical Edition, ed. Gary Taylor et al. Oxford: Oxford University Press, 2016.

The New Statistical Account of Scotland. Vol. 6 LANARK. Edinburgh and London: William Blackwood and Sons, 1845.

Opie, Iona, and Peter Opie, eds. *The Oxford Nursery Rhyme Book*. Rpt. Oxford: Clarendon Press, 1967.

Palgrave Enclosure Survey 1812. Suffolk Records Office. B150/1/312.

Peabody, William B. O. Review of *The Works of Anna Letitia Barbauld*. In *Christian Examiner* (Boston), 3 (1826): 299–315.

Plutarch's Lives. In *The Translation called Dryden's*, Corrected from the Greek and Revised by A. H. Clough. Vol. 4. New York: A. L. Burt, n.d.

Polwhele, Richard. *The Unsex'd Females: a Poem, Addressed to the Author of the Pursuits of Literature*. Cadell and Davies, 1798.

Pope, Alexander. *The Iliad of Homer*. Vol. 6. London: Osborne et al., 1760.

Pope, Alexander. *The Poems of Alexander Pope*, ed. John Butt. New Haven: Yale University Press, 1963.

Porter, Roy. *English Society in the Eighteenth Century*. Rev. edn. London: Penguin, 1991.

Price, Richard. *The Correspondence of Richard Price*. Vol. 3. Ed. W. Bernard Peach. Durham, NC: Duke University Press, 1994.

Priestley, Joseph. *A Description of a New Chart of History, Containing a View of the Principal Revolutions of Empire that have Taken Place in the World*. 6th edn. London: Johnson, 1786.

Priestley, Joseph. 'On Habitual Devotion'. In *The Theological and Miscellaneous Works of Joseph Priestley*. Ed. John Towill Rutt. Vol. 15. Rpt. New York: Kraus, 1972.

Priestley, Joseph. *The Rudiments of English Grammar, Adapted to the Use of Schools*. London: Rivington et al., 1771.
Review of *Hymns in Prose*. *Christian Reformer*, ns 8 (1841): 38–43.
Rapin de Thoyras, Paul. *The History of England, as well Ecclesiastical as Civil*, trans. N. Tindal. Vols. I and II, pt. 1. London: Knapton, 1726.
Records of the Worshipful Company of Stationers, 1554–1920, ed. Robin Myers. Microfilm. Cambridge: Chadwyck-Healey, 1985.
Reid, Andrew. *An Abstract of Sir Isaac Newton's Chronology of Ancient Kingdoms*. Dublin: Academic Press, 1732.
Rennell, James. *A Bengal Atlas*. [n. p.], 1781.
Rennell, James. *Memoir of a Map of the Peninsula of India*. London: Bulmer, 1793.
Rennell, James. *The Geographical System of Herodotus, examined*. London: Bulmer, 1800.
Rickards, E. C. 'Mrs. Barbauld and Her Pupil'. *Murray's Magazine*, November 1891, pp. 706–26.
Rix, Wilton Palmer. 'Early Homes. Vol. II'. MS 206.27. Rix Papers. Dr. Williams's Library, London.
Robberds, J. W. *Memoir of the Life and Writings of the Late William Taylor of Norwich*. London: Murray, 1843.
Robertson, William. *The History of America*. 3rd edn. Vol. 3. London: Strahan and Cadell, 1780.
Rodgers, Betsy. *Georgian Chronicle: Mrs Barbauld and her Family*. London: Methuen, 1958.
Rollin, Charles. *Histoire Ancienne des Égyptiens, des Carthaginois, des Assyriens, des Babyloniens, des Mèdes et des Perses, des Macédoniens, des Grecs* (12 vols., 1730–8).
Roper, Derek. *Reviewing Before the 'Edinburgh', 1788–1802*. Newark: University of Delaware Press, 1978.
Roscoe, William. *The Poetical Works of William Roscoe*. Liverpool: Henry Young, 1853.
Ross, Janet. *Three Generations of Englishwomen*. Rev. and enlarged edn. London: Unwin, 1893.
Rousseau, Jean-Jacques. *Emilius, or, a Treatise of Education*. 3 vols. Edinburgh: Donaldson, 1768.
S.A.A. 'Notable North Londoners, No. 6: Anna Letitia Barbauld', *North Londoner*, 13 March 1869, p. 13.
S.S.S. *Thornton Hall; or, Six Months at School*. London: Whittaker, 1823.
A Select Catalogue of Books in the Library Belonging to the Warrington Academy, MDCCLXXV. [Warrington: printed by William Eyres, n.d.]
Sermoneta, Vittoria Colonna Caetani, Duchess of. *The Locks of Norbury: The Story of a Remarkable Family in the XVIIIth and XIXth Centuries*. London, 1940.
Sharpe, Catherine. Letter, 25 December 1808. MS. Sharpe Papers 62, University College, London.
Smith, Adam. *An Inquiry into the Nature and Causes of the Wealth of Nations*, ed. R. H. Campbell and A. S. Skinner. 1976. Rpt, Indianapolis: Liberty Fund, 1981. http://files.libertyfund.org/files/220/0141-02_Bk.pdf.

Smith, Joseph. *A Descriptive Catalogue of Friends' Books*. 2 vols. London, 1867.
St. Clair, William. 'The Impact of Byron's Writings', in *Byron: Augustan and Romantic*, ed. Andrew J. Rutherford. New York: St. Martin's, 1990, pp. 1–25.
St. Clair, William. *The Godwins and the Shelleys*. Baltimore: Johns Hopkins University Press, 1991.
Sterne, Laurence. *The Life and Opinions of Tristram Shandy, Gentleman*. 4th ed., 2 vols. London: R. and J. Dodsley, 1760.
Stillingfleet, Benjamin. *Miscellaneous Tracts Relating to Natural History, Husbandry, and Physick. To which is added the Calendar of Flora*. 3rd edn. London: Dodsley et al., 1775.
Suetonius, Gaius Tranquillus. *The Twelve Caesars*, trans. Robert Graves. Harmondsworth, UK: Penguin, 1957.
Summerfield, Geoffrey. *Fantasy and Reason: Children's Literature in the Eighteenth Century*. Athens: University of Georgia Press, 1985.
Sunstein, Emily W. *Mary Shelley: Romance and Reality*. Baltimore: Little, Brown, 1989.
Swift, Jonathan. *The Writings of Jonathan Swift*, ed. Robert A. Greenberg and William B. Piper. New York: Norton, 1973.
Thomson, James. *The Works of James Thomson, with his Last Corrections and Improvements*. 2 vols. London: Millar, 1762.
Thompson, E. P. *The Making of the English Working Class*. New York: Vintage Books, 1966.
Thompson, Josiah. 'A Collection of Papers Containing an Account of the Original Formation of some Hundred Protestant Dissenting Congregations'. 5 vols. MS 38.7–11. Dr. Williams's Library, London.
Tortora, Phyllis G., and Ingrid Johnson. *The Fairchild Books Dictionary of Textiles*. 8th edn. New York: Bloomsbury, 2013.
Trimmer, Sarah, ed. *The Guardian of Education*. Vols. 1–2, London: J. Hatchard and F. C. and J. Rivington, 1802–3.
Vertot, René-Aubert. *Histoire des révolutions de Suède: où l'on voit les changements qui sont arrivés dans ce royaume, au sujet de la religion et du gouvernement*. 2 vols. Paris: François Barois, 1722.
Vertot, René-Aubert. *Histoire des révolutions arrivées dans le gouvernement de la république romaine*, 3 vols. Paris: François Barois, 1727.
Watts, Isaac. *Divine Songs Attempted in Easy Language for the Use of Children*. 1715. Rpt. Intro. J. H. P. Pafford. London: Oxford University Press, 1971.
Welch, d'Alté A. *A Bibliography of American Children's Books Printed Prior to 1821*. Worcester, MA: American Antiquarian Society, 1972.
Wharton, Joanna. '"The Things Themselves": Sensory Images in *Lessons for Children* and *Hymns in Prose*'. In *Anna Letitia Barbauld: New Perspectives*, ed. McCarthy and Murphy, pp. 107–26.
Winterbotham, Melanie. 'My Gretna Green Elopers'. *Family Tree*, April 2017, pp. 68–71.

Withering Family Letters. MS 263547-8. Birmingham Public Library, Birmingham, UK.

Wolcot, John. *The Works of Peter Pindar, Esq.* 3 vols. London: Walker, 1797.

Wollstonecraft, Mary. *The Vindications: The Rights of Men. The Rights of Woman*, ed. D. L. Macdonald and Kathleen Scherf. Peterborough, ONT: Broadview Press, 1997.

Wollstonecraft, Mary. *Works*, ed. Janet Todd and Marilyn Butler. Vol. 4. *Thoughts on the Education of Daughters. The Female Reader. Original Stories. Letters on the Management of Infants. Lessons.* New York: New York University Press, 1989.

Zall, P. M. 'Wordsworth's "Ode" and Mrs. Barbauld's *Hymns*'. *Wordsworth Circle*, 1 (1970): 177–9.

INDEX OF TITLES, AUTHORS, AND PROPER NAMES

Abraham (biblical patriarch), 316
Academus, 226
Academy at Barking, 469n365
Academy in Red Lion Square, 463n276
Academy in Soho-Square, 374, 389.
  See also: Barrow, Rev. William
Acanthis, Richard, 289
The Accomplished Youth: containing a Familiar View of the True Principles of Morality and Politeness. By Anon., (review by ALB), 375, 408
Ackworth School, 425, 473n398
Actium, battle of, 334
Aeschylus, *Seven Against Thebes*, [261], 440n43
Addison, Joseph, 409, 467n331, 472n393;
  See also: Steele, Richard;
  Spectator papers on wit, [350], 369–70, 457n215
Adelung, Johann Christoph, [411], 467n340
Aesop, 375, 414, 418, 433n5.1–2, 'The Flying Fish and the Dolphin', [228], 437n3
Aikin, Arthur, 72, 160, 432n74.6–8, 434n61.9;
  1821 edition of *Lessons*, 6;
  1823 (thirteenth) edition of *Evenings*, 239n1;
  editor of *A Rev*, xl, 373;
  friendship with Thomas Douglas, 455n200;
  'Henry' in 'On Manufactures', 'The Manufacture of Paper', and '[Chronology] Letter IV', 244–51, 251–3, 314;
  M Rev, 373;
  The Natural History of the Year, 431n9.3
Aikin, Charles Rochemont, xxxv, xxxvi, 1, 5, 10, 186, 217, 218, 220, 429n10.2, 430n23.1, 430n34.5, 430n43.1;
  quoted, 239, 241;

fictional dialogue with RB, 'Things...', 243;
fictional dialogue with RB, 'A Lesson...', 254, 440n34
Aikin, George, 72, 225, 432n74.6–8
Aikin, John, xxxv, 186, 217, 268, 475
  1793 first edition of *Evenings at Home*, 239–41, 259;
  Calendar of Nature, 4, 441n48;
  on influence of *Lessons*, quoted, 431n9.3
  editor, *Evenings at Home*:
    among ALB's last published educational works, xl;
    appearance in *The Female Speaker*, 370;
    bibliographical history, 239n1, 239–41;
    Contribution of short pieces and fables by ALB, xxxvii, xxxix, xli, 6, 10, 220, 226, 232, 239–41, 278;
    enjoyment of 'The Four Sisters', 259;
    first recipient of 'The Four Sisters', 278;
    influence of ALB and JA's translation of Berquin's *Ami*, 220;
    influence of de Genlis, 239, 394, 462n271, 476;
    regroupings in this volume by date of composition, xl–li;
    'The Leguminous Plants', 221–2
  editor, *MM*, 284, 327;
  letters from ALB, 270, 363;
  Miscellaneous Pieces in Prose (with Anna Letitia Aikin Barbauld), xxii;
  M Rev, 373;
  'On the Inequality of Conditions', 284;
  role in William Eyres's 1777 printing of *Lessons*, 1;
  role in 1778 printing of *Three Years Old*, 2;
  translation of prefatory essay to Pennant's *Indian Zoology*, 446n107

Aikin, Lucy:
  1826 changes to *Evenings* (fourteenth
    edition), 239n1, 241, 264;
  addition of 'Live Dolls' 281
  editor, *A Legacy for Young Ladies*, 218,
    220–2, 226, 338;
  addressee of 'The King in his
    Castle', 278;
  admiration of Sarah and Elizabeth
    Rigby ('beauties' in 'Description
    of Two Sisters'), 264;
  contribution of short pieces and fables
    by ALB, xxxvii, xxxix, xli, 218,
    220–2, 226, 263–4;
  changes to Letters I–III of Letters on
    Grammar, History, and
    Homer, 300;
  frontispiece, 335 (Fig. 13);
  Letter IV of Letters on Grammar,
    History, and Homer, 300, 313n17;
  omission of 'Live Dolls', 281;
  publication details of 'On the
    Classics', 270;
  inclusion of previously published
    pieces, 289, 313n17;
  qualities of ALB's contributions,
    quoted, 263;
  regroupings in this volume by date of
    composition, xl–li, 264;
  'The Morning Repast' in first
    edition, 359;
  title 'Allegory on Sleep' provisionally
    attributed to, 265, 441n53
  editor, *Works*:
    appearance of ALB's 'Knowledge and
      Her Daughter', 356;
    appearance of ALB's 'Zephyrus and
      Flora', 264, 268;
    Hidallan, shepherd character in tale
      written with JA, 241;
    on ALB reading Lucian, quoted, 364;
    on 'Live Dolls' in 'Memoir', quoted,
      281
  Epistles on Women, 370;
  enjoyment of 'The Four Sisters', 259;
  friendship with Catherine Sharpe,
    433n52.7;
  in 'A Letter from Miss Susan Slipslop to
    Miss Fanny Flippant', 296;
  Juvenile Correspondence, 405;
  MML, quoted, 373;
  on *Evenings*, quoted, 241
Aikin, Rev. John, xxxv, [465n310];
  addressee of *Evenings*, 260;
  M Rev, 373

Akenside, Mark, 369
'Aladdin's palace', 249, 438n20
'Alcair' (Altair, star), 277
Alcibiades, 311, 448n130
Alexander III of Macedon (the Great), 267,
  [311], 312, 315, 316, 321, [334],
  448n128, 451n158, 451n160,
  454n186
Alfred the Great, 233, 306, 437n9, 446n113
Allan, Louisa, *The Decoy*, [418], [422],
  470n367, 470n370, 471n386
Alps, 222, 311, 333
al-Rashid, Harun, [317], 450n151
Amiens, Peace of, 454n192
Anacreon, 461n262
Analytical Review, 373
Anaximander, 311, 448n131
Anderson, Robert, 'Preface to the *Works of
  William Wilkie*', 450n155
Andes, 222
Angus, William, 413
Annonay, France, 454n192.
  See Montgolfier, ...
Annual Register of World Events for 1827,
  466n323
Annual Review, xl–li, 373–4, 459n236,
  461n258
Antoinette, Marie, [345], 456n202
Antony, Mark (Marcus Antonius), 334
Arabia, 229
The Arabian Nights' Entertainment, 413,
  468n349
Archimedes, 350, 457n210
Argus, Arabella (pseudonym), 398, 414,
  463n287
Ariosto, Ludovico, *Orlando Furioso*, quoted,
  437–8n11
Aristagoras, 312, 448n132
Aristotle, 274, 321, 335, 429n9.2
Arkwright, Sir Richard, 239, 248, 438n18
Arnauld, Antoine and Pierre Nicole, *Logique
  de Port-Royal*, 392, 462n264
Arria (Arria Major), 395
Arrowsmith, Aaron, 313, 449n140
Askew, Lady Anne, 386
Aspasia, 298, 444n98
Athelney, Somersetshire, 232–3
Augustus, Gaius Julius Caesar, 312
Augustus, Philip (Philip II of France), 318
Austen, Jane, *Northanger Abbey*, quoted, 357
Aveline, E. L., 470n368

Bacon, Francis, 335, 454n189
Baldwin, Cradock, and Joy (publisher),
  369n1, 395, 396, 397, 405, 416

INDEX OF TITLES, AUTHORS, AND PROPER NAMES 493

Baldwin, Edward (pseudonym), 395, 398, 462n274. *See* Godwin, William
Bampton Lectures, 374, 389. *See* Barrow, Rev. William
Bantam Sultinate, 279, 443n78
Barbary Coast, 333
Barbauld, Anna Letitia (née Aikin):
   1805 anthology of Addison and Steele, 369, 457n215
   ambivalence towards the classics, 270
   anonymous publication of educational works, xlii
   contributions to *A Rev* and *M Rev*, 373–4
   development of social relations from pedagogic ones, 263–5, 444n94
   dramatics, 231, 263
   fables, 225
   Hebrew literature as higher authority than 'Classics', 274
   'pedagogic intent' in ALB's letters, xxxix, 263–4, 444n94
   pieces in *Evenings at Home*, xxxvii, xxxix, xli, 6, 10, 220, 226, 232, 239–41, 259–60, 263, 270, 281, 470n366
   pieces in *A Legacy for Young Ladies*, xxxvii, xxxix, xli, 218, 220–2, 226, 263–4, 278, 284, 289, 300, 313n17, 327, 329, 332, 338, 343, 348, 353, 357, 359–60, 363, 364
   professional teaching through epistolary writing, xxxviii–ix, 218, 263–4, 299–300, 444n94
   recovery of holographs of:
      letters to Lydia Rickards, xli–lii, 295, 300, 302, 306, 310, 319, 452n169;
      one riddle from 'On Riddles', to Mrs. Smith, of Tetbury, xli–lii, 348-9;
      return of letters to Lydia Rickards, 300
   science as spirituality, 221
   secular nature of *Lessons*, 2n3
   translation of *Adresse aux Anglois* by Rabaut St. Etienne, 447n118
   views on women's education, xxxviii, xxxviiin9
   Individual works:
      17 October [1810] letter to 'J. Douse' (*GC*), 322
      'An Address to the Deity', 187, 369, 435nVI.1, 463n277, 464n299

An Address to the Opposers of the Repeal of the Corporation and Test Acts, 442n70
'Allegory on Sleep', 264, 265
'Alfred, a Drama', 220, 231–3
'Animals, and their Countries', 241
'Arion', 264, 276n71
British Novelists series, volumes 49–50, 452–3n175, 475
'Canute's Reproof to his Courtiers', 220, 231–2
'The Caterpillar', 433n38.3–4
[Chronology] Letter IV, 313
'Confidence and Modesty: A Fable', 226, 230
'[Dated 6 June 1787] ALB, Letter to JA', 445n106
'[Dated 6 June 1798] Miss Rickards at Mrs. Hunt's Crescent near Birmingham', 297n9, 445n104, 446n108
'[Dated 17 June 1798] ALB to Lydia, MS Misc. 4338, Pforzheimer Collection, NYPL', 445n102
'Description of a Curious Animal lately found in the Wilds of Derbyshire', xxxviiin8, 220
'Description of Two Sisters', 264
'Dialogue in the Shades', 300n13, 476
'[Dressing Table Ornaments]', 296
'Earth', xxxvii, 218, 221–2
'Enigma', 348n3, 348n5
'An Enquiry into those Kinds of Distress which Excite Agreeable Sensations', 476
   allusion to *Lessons for Children*, [255], 440n34
'Envy and Emulation', 470n366
'Epitaph on a Goldfinch', 263, 289, 432n73.6–9
'Fashion, a Vision', 284
The Fashionable Puzzler; or, Book of Riddles…Selected by an American Lady. With Remarks on Riddles, By the late Mrs. Barbauld (New York, 1835), 348n4
The Female Speaker (1811), xl–li, 369
'Preface of the Editor', 369–70
'Book I. Select Sentences', 369
'Book II. Moral and Didactic Pieces', 369
'Book III. Narrative Pieces', 370
'Book IV. Descriptive and Pathetic', 370
'Book V. Dialogues', 370

Barbauld, Anna Letitia
   (née Aikin): (*continued*)
   'The Four Sisters', 239, 241, 259–60, 278
      inferred date range of composition; appearance in Volume 6 of *Evenings*, 259–60
      two extant manuscript copies, one unidentified, 259–60, 441n48.
      See Nicholson, Matthew *and* Warrington Academy
      history of discrepancies in presswork, 260
   'The Flying Fish', 226, 228
   [Geography, Letter III], 310
   'The Goose and Horse', 226, 228
   Hymns in Prose for Children, xxxvi, xxxvii, xl, 185–9
      1781 first edition, 186, 188–9
      1814 additions by ALB, 188–9, 212
      Christian orthodoxy in 1840 edition, xxxviin6; anonymous editor, quoted, 188
      'Hymn V', 470n366
      India, 1816 English-language edition of *Hymns* in Calcutta, 188
      in Haigh's *Introduction to the Diurnal Readings*, 472n393
      in Rippingham's *Rules*, 467n331, 472n388
      John Murray's edition (1864), xxxviin6
      Preface, quoted, 187
      transatlantic influence, 188
      translations, xxxvii, 188
   'Inventory of the Contents of Dr. Priestley's Study', 473n407
   'The Invitation', 432n12.3–4
   'The King in his Castle', 259–60, 264, 278
   A Legacy for Young Ladies:
      'A Dialogue of the Dead, between Helen and Madame Maintenon', 364, 454n189
      'A Lecture on the Use of Words', 357
      'An unfortunate maid', addendum to second edition, 348, 359
      'pic-nic', 327
      'Knowledge and Her Daughter', 356
      'Letter from Grimalkin to Selima', 329, 459n236
         reprint and review in *Eclectic Review* (1826), quoted, 329n2; 338
      'Letter of a Young King', 353
         reprint in *Eclectic Review* (1826), 353n7
      'On Expense', 263, 284, 343
      'On Female Studies', 221
      'Letter I', 338
      'Letter II', 340
      'On Friendship', 338, 359–60
      'On Riddles', xxxix, xli, 263, 348
         publication, attribution, and archival history of Riddles I–IV, 348–9nn5, 6
      'The Death-Bed', 363
         reprint and review in *Eclectic Review* (1826), 363
      'The Morning Repast', 359
      'True Magicians' (for Sarah Grace Carr), xxxix, 332, 335 (Fig. 13)
   'A Lesson in the Art of Distinguishing', 241, 254
   Lessons for Children, xxxv, xl, 1–10, 186, 459n236, 460n246
      1778–9 London first editions, 7, 10
      1808 edition, ALB's additions to all four volumes, 10–11
      basis for repackaged versions throughout 19th c., 11
      ALB's authorial and editorial control on first publications, xlii, 7, 10
      c. 1830 edition, 432n74.8–78.7
   Lessons for Children, of Three Years Old, 2, 5, 6, 7, 10, 40
      additions for 1808 edition, 6
      Dublin editions (1779), 6–7, 10
      London editions, two-volume set (1781–2), 6, 10
   Lessons for Children, of Three Years Old, part I, 433n52.7
   Lessons for Children, of Three Years Old, part II, 82
   Lessons for Children of Three Years Old, part II (1781), 6
   Lessons for Children, of Three to Four Years Old, xxxvi, 4, 6n20, 10
   Lessons for Children, of Two to Three Years Old, xxxvi, 2, 7, 10, 12
      market success and deterioration in presswork, 10
      teacher of History, English Composition, and Science at Palgrave, 218, 221, 299
      translation with JA of Berquin's *Ami*, 220
      updates to and adaptability of *Lessons*, 6n18
      letter to *GM*, in defence of Maria Edgeworth's *Tales of Fashionable Life*, 374

INDEX OF TITLES, AUTHORS, AND PROPER NAMES 495

'A Letter from Miss Susan Slipslop to Miss Fanny Flippant', 296, 444n94, 455n194, 467n333
'A Letter Recommending French Books', 295n3, 322
letters to Lydia Rickards:
  'Letter to Lydia Rickards 17 October 1803', 332
  on Homer and history, xxxix, xli, 295, 297, 299–300n13, 302, 306, 310, 313, 319, 322–3, 338, 454n188
  on other literature, quoted, 452n169
'Letter to Recommend French Authors', 220n4, 225, 473n404, 475
'Live Dolls', 264, 280
'The Manufacture of Paper', 241, 251
  English vs. French paper, 252
  origins and spread of paper, 253, 440n33
  rag-collecting and anti-Semitism, 251, 439n29
'The Masque of Nature', 241, 242; renamed 'The Seasons', 470n366
Miscellaneous Pieces in Prose (with John Aikin), 6
'The Misses', 290
MM, volume 13 [Feb. 1802], on influence of Chapone, quoted, 299n10, 359–60
'The Mouse's Petition', 464n299
'On the Classics', 264, 270
'Ode to Content', 464n299
'On Education', 459n236
'On Fashion', 263
'[On Grammar]', 300, 434n107.2
'[On Homer]', 300, 319, 454n188
'On Manufactures', xxxix, 239, 241, 244
'On the Origin and Progress of Novel-writing', quoted, 475–6
'On Plants', xxxvii, 218, 221, 223
'On the Uses of History' (1st letter), 302
'On the Uses of History' (2nd letter), 306
'Petition of a Schoolboy', 433n13.1
'The Phenix and Dove', 226, 229
'The Pine and the Olive', (Stoicism in), 225–6
Poems (1773), 441n51
Remarks on...Public Worship, 467n331, 470n366, 472n388; renamed 'On Social Worship' and 'Advantages of Social Worship: A Sunday Lesson', 470n366
'Remarks on the Inequality of Conditions', 284
'The Rich and the Poor: A Dialogue', 284
'The River and the Brook', 226, 227
'A School Eclogue' (Poem XX), 432n38.6; quoted, 460n248
Selections from the Spectator, Tatler, Guardian, and Freeholder, 453n179, 476
'Things by their Right Names', 239, 241, 243, 438n12, 455–6n201
'Thoughts on the Devotional Taste' (1775), xxxvi; quoted, 187
'To Miss R——', 458n226
'Trees', 433n75.5–7
'Venus and Adonis', 264, 277n72
'Verses Written in an Alcove', 458n226
'Washing-Day', 430n43.1, 465n309
'The Wasp and Bee', 226, 227
'What Is Education?', quoted, 475
from *Works*:
  letter to JA, envy of Hannah More as dramatist, 363
  letter to JA on modern sciences over classics, quoted, 270
  original publication of 'Knowledge and Her Daughter', 356
'The Young Mouse', 241
'Zephyrus and Flora', 264, 268
Barbauld, Rochemont, xxxv, xxxvi, 162, 217–18, 220–1, 225, 322 (Diary), 332, 434n66.5–6, 457n220, 475;
  fictional dialogue with CRA, 'Things...', 243;
  fictional dialogue with CRA, 'A Lesson...', 254
Barker-Benfield, G. J., *The Culture of Sensibility*, 453n177; quoted, 453n179
Barrow, Rev. William, *An Essay on Education*, 373, 461n260, 461n261; *Bampton Lecture* (1799), 374; quoted, 389–92, 461–2n263
Barnard, Caroline, 413, 468n350.
  See Sunstein, Emily
Bastille, 454n184
'Batrachomyomachia, or the Battle of the Frogs and Mice', [322], 451n160
Baxter, Rev. Richard, [306], 446n114
Bayle, Pierre, *Encyclopédie*, 343; quoted, 456n206

Beaumont, Jeanne-Marie Leprince de,
  Le Magazin des Enfans,
  323, 475
Bedfordshire, 466n317
  Campton Academy, 466n315
Beethoven, Ludwig van, *Fidelio*, 464n290
Beinecke Rare Book and Manuscript
  Library (Yale):
    Osborn Files, copies in unidentified hand
      of 'The Four Sisters' and 'The
      King in his Castle', 259–60, 278;
      copy in unidentified hand of
      'The Misses' in 'letters of advice
      to young ladies', 291n11; copy of
      'Riddle II', 348n5
Bell, Dr. Andrew, 414, 468n353
Belsham, Elizabeth (afterwards Kenrick):
  addressee of 'Description of Two
    Sisters', 264;
  ALB's second cousin and possible
    inspiration for 'On Friendship',
    458n227;
  comfort to ALB after Rochemont's
    death, 458n227
Bencoolen, Sumatra, 455–6n201. *See* Pitt,
  Thomas
Bennett, Rev. John, *Letters to a Young Lady*,
  329
Bentley, Thomas:
  British jasperware, [250], 439n26;
  partnership with Josiah Wedgwood, 2;
  review of *Three Years Old* in *M Rev* 59
    (1778), 2–3;
  review of *Three Years Old* in *M Rev* 60
    (1779), quoted, 434n71.1
Benyon, Mrs. (possible addressee of 'The
  Misses'), 290
Berneville, Marie-Catharine le Jumel de,
  Countess D'Aulnoy, [415],
  469n357
Berquin, Arnaud:
  L'Ami des adolescents, 323
  L'Ami des Enfans, 220, 323, 475
Bertholet, G., *Leçon choisies*, 462n270.
  See also: *Soirées…*
Bertholett, Claud-Louis, [247], 438n17
Bible:
  1 Corinthians, [200–1], 436nVII.28
  1 John, [202], 436nVII.62
  2 Corinthians, [394], 462n269; quoted,
    [394]
  2 Peter, [261]; quoted, 440n41
  Acts of the Apostles, [281]; quoted,
    443n81

Book of Daniel, quoted, [191], 435nI.16
Book of Ezekiel, quoted, [206],
  436nIX.67
Book of Genesis, [247], 435nI.3–4,
  438n15, 448n127
Book of Isaiah, 426
Book of Judges, 457n211
Book of Nahum, [199]; quoted, 436nVI.37
Book of Proverbs, 369
Book of Psalms, [380], 419, 435nIII.1,
  435nV.65, 437nXII.47, 460n243;
  quoted, [193–5], 435nIII.45–6,
  435nV.29
Books of Kings, 449n141, 470n372;
  loosely quoted, [314]
Book of Revelation, quoted, [194],
  435nV.19–20; 435nIII.43, [209],
  436nXI.28–38
Books of Samuel, [200–1], 436nVII.28
Gospel of John, quoted, [199],
  436nVI.11–12
Gospel of Mark, [209], 436nXI.28–38
Gospel of Matthew, [209], [267],
  436nXI.28–38; quoted, [216],
  437nXII.15–16, 441n56
King James Bible, 435nI.3–4
New Testament, 378–9, [394], [462n269],
  468n354
Old Testament, [369], [380], [419], [426],
  [457n211], [460n243], [470n372],
  473n401
Bickerstaff, Isaac (nom de plume), 398,
  463n288. *See* Swift, Jonathan
  and Steele, Richard
Biello, David, 'Fact or Fiction?:
  Archimedes Coined the Term
  "Eureka!" in the Bath', *Scientific
  American*, 8 Dec. 2006, 457n210
Birmingham:
  cutlery and hardware, 250
  Rickards, Lydia (ALB's pupil through
    correspondence), xxxviii–ix, xli,
    263–4, 295n1, 296, 299–300n13,
    302, 306, 310, 313, 319, 322–3,
    452n169, 467n333
Birmingham Public Library, Crowder, Lee
  (manuscript), 295n1
Blair, Dr. Hugh, 'On the Duties of the
  Young', [406], [408], [409],
  466n319, 467n327, [467n331],
  [470n366], [472n393]
Blake, William, *Songs of Innocence*, 188;
  'The Tyger', *Songs of Experience*,
  433n85.6

INDEX OF TITLES, AUTHORS, AND PROPER NAMES 497

Bloomfield, Robert, 472n393
Bluestocking Circle, 327
Bodleian Library:
  George Edward Griffiths' set of *M Rev*, 373;
  The Opie Collection, 1784 copy of *Three to Four*, 6n20
Boileau-Despréaux, Nicolas, *Satires*, 325, 371, 476
Bomheim-House Academy, Carshalton, 463n276
Bonaparte, Joseph, [402], 465n303
Bonaparte, Louis, [402], 465n303
Bonaparte, Napoleon, 402
Book of Common Prayer, 435nV.29.
  See Wallace, John Aikman
Boosey (publisher), 407, 422
Bosphorus Strait, 333
Bossuet, Jacques Bénigne, [412], 468n347
Bossut, M. l'Abbé, [412], 468n347.
  See also: Phillips, Sir Richard
Boswell, James, *Life of Johnson*, 2n5, 452n173, 476
Bouilly, Jean-Nicholas, 399, 414, 464n290
Box Hill, 298, 333, 444n99, 453n183
Bowring, Sir James, quoted, 471n375
Bransby, James Hews, 419, 471n375
Brewer, James Norris, *The Beauties of England and Wales*, 439n24
Bristol:
  Estlin family, 353
  Mrs. Estlin (addressee of 'Letter of a Young King'), 353
Bristol Channel, 333
British Channel, 333
British Critic, 463n285;
  quoted, 472n395
British Dissenters, xxxv, xxxvi, xxxvii, 187, [306], 392, 434nPreface.17, 442n70, 446n114, 461n258, 461–2n263, 476
British Library Catalogue, 471n380
British Library, four-volume set of *Lessons* (1787–8), 6–7
Brodribb, Charles William, 'Mrs. Barbauld's School', 217, 220
Bucephalus (Alexander the Great's horse), 334, 454n186
Buchanan, Dr. Claudius, 415, 469n359
Buffon, Georges-Louis Leclerc, Comte de, *Histoire Naturelle*, 324, 370, 427, 434n74.8–75.2, 446n107, 452n166, 474n408

Burke's Landed Gentry of Great Britain, 295n1
Burnet, James, Lord Monboddo, *Of the Origin and Progress of Language*, 445–6n106
Burnet, Thomas, *The Theory of the Earth*, [261], 441n44
Burney, Frances, 3, 475; *Cecilia*, 458n223; quoted, 357
Burslem, Staffordshire, 250
Butler, Samuel, *Hudibras*, quoted, [403], 465n306
Byron, Lord, George Gordon, 443n83

The Cabinet of Entertainment, a New and Select Collection of Ænigmas, Charades, Rebuses, &c., with Solutions. By Anon., (review by ALB), 375, 410
Cadell, Thomas (publisher, independent pre-1793 and post-1819), 452n172
Caesar, Gaius Julius 267, 306, 447n116, 312, 334, 449n134
Calprenède, Gauthier de Costes de la, *Cassandre*, [366], 458–9n232
Cambridge History of English Literature, 188
Camillus (Marcus Furius Camillus), 395
Canary Islands, 269
Cappe, Catharine, 'Letter', *MM* in May 1798, quoted, 280
Carey, John, 402, 403, 465n304
Carey, Matthew, [313], 449n140, 465n304
Carlyle, Joseph Dacre, 403, 465n311
Carpenter, Thomas, 417, 469n365
Carr, Frances, 332
Carr, Frances Rebecca, [332], 453n182
Carr, Sarah Grace, (addressee of 'True Magicians'), 332, (possible recipient of 'On Riddles') 348
Carr, Thomas William, 332
Carter, Elizabeth, quoted, 187; on 'Hymn XI', quoted, 436nXI.28–38; 475 translation of Epictetus, quoted, 226, 430n47.3–4; 432n27.9–31.9
The Case of Mr. Richard Arkwright and Co., 438n18
Castéra, J.-H., *Histoire de Catherine II*, 456n203. *See also*: Tooke, William
Catherine II (empress of Russia), 250–1, [313], 335, 439n26, 449n139
Catlow, Rev. Samuel, 415
Catty, Lewis, 409, 467n334

498 INDEX OF TITLES, AUTHORS, AND PROPER NAMES

Cervantes, Miguel de, *Don Quixote*, 325, 452n170, 427
Chambaud, Louis, *Fables Choisies*, 225, 323, 426, 473n404, 475
Chapone, Hester Mulso, *Letters on the Improvement of the Mind*, 299, 338, 451n164, [470n366]; quoted, 359, 446n127, 449n144, 450n146, 451n163, 453n176, 458n225; appearance in *The Female Speaker*, 370
Chapple (publisher), 411, 412, 413, 420
Charlemagne, 317–18, 402
Charles I (French king), [317], 450n149
Charles II, 446nn113–14
Château of Marly, 346
Chatterton, Thomas, 472n393
Chaucer, Geoffrey, 461n262; *Canterbury Tales*, 455n195; quoted, 341
Chester, 466n317
Chesterfield, Philip Dormer Stanhope, 4th Earl of, 463n288; *Letters... to his Son*, [310], [408], 424, 466n326; quoted, 448n125
China, 81, 250n26; silk paper, 253
Choix de Biographie. By Charles Paul Landon, (review by ALB), 375, 407
Christian Reformer, 471n375
Chronology, or the Historian's Companion. By Thomas Tegg, (review by ALB), 375, 404
Church of England, 6, [306], 392, 419, 442n70, 446n114, 461n258, 461n262, 472n391
  curates, 457n217
Cicero (Marcus Tullius Cicero), 271–2, 301, 390, 442n64, 461n262
  Catilinarian orations, 334, 335 (Fig. 13)
Clarke, Adam, 415, 469n359
Clarke, H. *Fabulæ Æsopi selectæ... With an English Translation...*, 225
  'Fable CXXIX. Of the River provoking his Spring with Reproaches', 226
Classical education (Greek and Latin language), xxxv, 270
Claudius (Tiberius Claudius Caesar Augustus Germanicus), 395
Cleomenes I (king of Sparta), 312
Cleopatra, 334

Cockle, Mary, 393, 397; poems, 462n268
Cock Street Bridge (today Denmark Bridge), 433n37.1–38.1
Colbert, Benjamin, *Women's Travel Writing: 1780–1840*, 472n396
Colburn (publisher), 397, 399, 406, 410, 414
Coleridge, Samuel Taylor, 453n180; *The Rime of the Ancient Mariner*, quoted, 434n55.2–4; *The Watchman*, quoted, 434n82.6
Collins, Rev. Joshua (possible pseudonym), 415, 469n358
Columbian Star and Christian Index (Boston) (23 January 1830), 290
Condillac, Étienne Bonnot de, *Essai sur l'origine des connoissances humaines*, 429n9.2, 445n106
Confucius, 407
Conseils à ma fille; ou nouveaux contes; i.e. Advice to My Daughter, or More Tales. By J. N. Bouilly, (review by ALB), 375, 414
Constantinople, Ottoman Empire, 333
Contes à ma fille; &c. i.e. Tales for my Daughter. By J. N. Bouilly, (review by ALB), 375, 399
A Copious Collection of Instructive and Entertaining Exercises on the French Language. By C. Laisné, (review by ALB), 375, 427
Corneille, Pierre, *Le Cid*, 325, 476
Cosmetic Warehouse (the Strand, London), 444n93
Cotsen Children's Library, PUL, 429nAdvertisement.6
Cotswolds ('Cotteswold Hills'), 382
Cowie and Co. (publisher), 413
Cowper, William, 270, 271, 329n2, 369–71, 442n62, 472n393
Crabbe, George, 472n393
Cresswick, M. (pseudonym), 369.
  See Wollstonecraft, Mary
Critical Review, 186
  46 (August 1776), review of *Lessons*, 3
  March 1814 review of *Punctuation* by S. Rousseau, 471n376
  July 1814, on C. Laisné, 473n406
Crœsus, 318
Crosby and Co. (publisher), 408, 410, 418

INDEX OF TITLES, AUTHORS, AND PROPER NAMES 499

Croxall, Samuel, 'The Fighting Cocks', *Fables of Aesop and Others*, [134–8], 433n5.1–2
The Curate and his Daughter: A Cornish Tale. By Elizabeth Isabella Spence, (review by ALB), 420, 471n381
Curtis, William, *Flora Londinensis*, [344], 455n199
'the Cuz's Chorus', 429nAdvertisement.6
Cyrus II, 314

Dallaway, R. C., *The Servant's Monitor*, [411], 467n338. See also: *Observations on the most...*
Damascus, 218
Darius III, 311, 316, 321, 334, 448n128, 451n158, 454n186
Darton and Co. (publisher), 396, 408, 414, 416, 418, 423, 424, 425, 463n278, 463n287
Darton and Harvey (publisher), 402, 405, 408, 411, 412, 422
Darton, Harvey, and Darton (publisher), 420
Darton, Lawrence, *The Dartons*, 465n308, 465n310, 470n368
Darwin, Erasmus, 270, 271, 397, 442n62, 463n283; *The Botanic Garden*, 370
D'Anville, Jean-Baptiste Bourguignon, 313, 449n137
David, King of Israel, 437nXII.47
Davies, Rev. G. J., 404, 466n315
da Vinci, Leonardo, 318
Davis, Mary Anne, 414, 468n354
Deconchy (publisher), 403
The Decoy; or an Agreeable Method of Teaching Children the Elementary Parts of English Grammar. By [Louisa Allan], (review by ALB), 375, 418
Delft tiles, [319], 450n154
Delisle, Guillaume, *Theatrum Historicum ad annum Christi quadringentesimu*, 448n126
Dellow, Thomas, 420, 471n378
Demosthenes, 390, 461n262
Denman, Thomas:
  pupil at Palgrave, 220
  Reform Bill of 1832, xix
Depping, [Georges Bernard], 406, 466n321
De Quincey, Thomas, quoted, 187

Derby, Derbyshire, 466n317
The Deserted Village School, a Poem. By [Rev. Richard Polwhele] Anon., (review by ALB), 375, 413
Dibdin, Charles, *The Islanders*, 431n19.2–4
A Dictionary of the Idioms of the French and English Languages. By a Society of Masters [Anon.], (review by ALB), 375, 410
Difficult Pronunciation, with Explanations of the Rules. Second Edition, with Additions. By Anon., (review by ALB), 375, 421
Diss (Norfolk), 217
Diurnal Readings; being Lessons for Every Day in the Year. By Anon., (review by ALB), 375, 415
Dix's Juvenile Atlas; containing 44 Maps, with Plain Directions for Copying Them. By Thomas Dix, (review by ALB), 375, 405
Dix, Thomas, 375, 405, 466n317
Dodd, Rev. William, *The Beauties of History*, [308], 447n120
Dodsley, Robert, 369
Dollond, Peter and John (telescope makers), 344, 455n199
Dorking, 297, 333, 453n183
Douce, Mr. [J.] (addressee of 'A Letter Recommending French Books'), 295n3, 322–3
Douglas, Thomas, Earl of Selkirk, *A Sketch of the British Fur Trade in North America*, quoted, 455n200
Drennan, William (United Irishman), 459n236
[Drouet, Jean-Baptiste] (post master at Varennes'), 305n111, 446n111
Dryden, John, 369, 461n262, 472n393; *Aeneid*, quoted, 437n1, 442n73; and Nathaniel Lee's 1678 adaptation of *Oedipus Rex*, 457n212
Dulau and Co. (publisher), 406, 407, 426, 427
Durham, 466n317

East Anglia, [235], 437n6
'East India possessions'/'East Indies', 274, 336
East Midlands, [235], 437n6
Eastern Tales; or Moral Allegories. By Anon., (review by ALB), 375, 413

500   INDEX OF TITLES, AUTHORS, AND PROPER NAMES

Edgeworth, Maria, 3;
  admiration of *Evenings*, 239;
  Belinda, quoted, 452n175;
  Castle Rackrent, quoted, 453n181;
  editor of ALB's 'Riddle IV', *Harry and Lucy Concluded; being the Last Part of Early Lessons*, 349;
  'Harry and Lucy' and glossary, *Early Lessons*, [424]; quoted, 472–3n397;
  Practical Education, [331], 369–70, [404], 453n180, 459n237, 460n242, 460n244, 460n245, 460n247, 460n249, 461n254, 461n256, 461n257, 466n314; quoted, 369, 377–89, 429n10.2, 430n56.4–5, 431n8.3, 431n11.5–12.1, 432n74.8–78.7, 434n68.2–3, 434n82.6, 460n241, 460n250, 460n251, 461n253.
  See also: Gray, Thomas, *Elegy*; *Tales of Fashionable Life*, 374;
  The Parent's Assistant, 4
Edgeworth, Richard Lovell, 3;
  admiration of *Evenings*, 239;
  correspondence from JJ on economics of children's books, 3n6;
  influence of *Lessons* on *Practical Education*, 3–4;
  Practical Education, [331], [377], 404, 431n11.5–12.1, 453n180, 459n237, 459–60n238, 466n314; quoted, 369, 429n8.4–5, 429n10.2, 430n23.1, 430n43.1, 430n56.4–5, 431n8.3, 434n68.2–3, 434n71.1, 434n82.6, 453n180, 459n237, 459–60n238, 466n314
Edward III, 250n25
Edward VI, 400, 464n294
Egbert, King of Wessex, 318
Elagabalus (Heliogabalus) (Marcus Aurelius Antoninus), 346, 456n204
The Elements of Arithmetic. By E. Ward, (review by ALB), 375, 420
The Elements of Conversation, French and English. By C. Gros, (review by ALB), 375, 406
Elements of French Grammar, More Especially Designed for the Use of the Gentlemen Cadets of the Royal Military Academy at Woolwich. By Lewis Catty, (review by ALB), 375, 409
Elements of Universal Geography, Ancient and Modern. By A. Picquot, (review by ALB), 375, 415
Eliot, T. S.:
  'The Love Song of J. Alfred Prufrock', 188;
  The Waste Land, 188
Ellen; or, The Young Godmother, a Tale for Youth. By Alicia Catherine Mant, (review by ALB), 375, 423
Ellis, Grace, *Memoir of Mrs. Barbauld*, 290–1n11
Eliza Cook's Journal, 290, 291n11
Elizabeth I, 318
El-Shamy, Hasan M., *Folk Traditions of the Arab World*, Vol. I, 457n213
Emerson, Ralph Waldo, xxxvii
Enfield, William:
  M Rev ns 27: 465–6, on Maria Edgeworth's *The Parent's Assistant*, 4;
  The Speaker, 369, 371
English Exercises, for Teaching Grammatical Composition on a New Principle. By John Fenwick, (review by ALB), 375, 406
An English Vocabulary. By Thomas Carpenter, (review by ALB), 375, 417
The English Pronouncing Spelling-Book. By Thomas West, (review by ALB), 375, 423
Epaminondas, 305, 446n112
'Epitaph on a Green-Finch', *Moral Philosophy*, 289
Epsom, 332
An Essay on Education. By William Barrow, (review by ALB), 374, 389, 461n258
Eton College, 391
Evening Entertainments; or Delineations of the Manners and Customs of Various Nations. By [Georges Bernard] Depping, (review by ALB), 375, 406
Exeter, 458n227
Exeter Manuscript (Anglo-Saxon riddles), [350], 457n214
Eyres, William, 1–2

Fables in Verse; from Aesop, La Fontaine, and Others. By Mary Anne Davis, (review by ALB), 375, 414
Fabricius (Gaius Fabricius Luscinus), 395

Fales Library, NYU, letter from ALB to Mrs. Estlin, MS, 353
Familiar Letters, Addressed to Children and Young Persons of the Middle Ranks. By [Elizabeth Heyrick], (review by ALB), 375, 403
The Family Magazine, 401, 464n297
A Father's Bequest to his Son, Containing Rules for Conduct through Life. By Anon., (review by ALB), 375, 412
Favart, Charles-Simon, *La Rosière de Salency*, [413], 468n351
Felix, Antonius, 381
Feldman, Paula R, iii, 7, 10, 'The Poet and the Profits', 443n83
The Female Class-Book; or, Three Hundred and Sixty-Five Reading Lessons. By Martin Smart, (review by ALB), 375, 417
Fénelon, François, 427;
  Les aventures de Télémaque, fils d'Ulysse, [324], 467n329, 474n408, 476
  Traité de l'education des filles, [325], 408–9, 476
  Traité de l'existence et des attributs de Dieu, [325]
Fenn, Ellenor, *The Infant's Friend*, 280
Fenwick, Eliza, 396; *Secresy; or the Ruin on the Rock*, 463n280; 466n320
Fenwick, John, 406, 466n320
Ferdinand VII ('King of Spain'), possible commission for Wedgwood jasperware, [251], 439n27
Ferguson, Moira, *Subject to Others*, 436nVIII.54–9
Finch, Ann (possible addressee of 'The Misses'), 290
The First Book of Poetry. By William Frederick Mylius, (review by ALB), 375, 401
First Lessons in English Grammar, Adapted to the Capacities of Children from Six to Ten Years Old. By Anon., (review by ALB), 375, 412
A First or Mother's Dictionary for Children. Jameson, Anna Brownell (née Murphy), 375, 424
Fitz-Adam, Adam (nom de plume), 398, 463n288. *See* Moore, Edward
Five-Mile Act (1662), 446n114
Fleet-Street, 281, 443n80

Flemish, 250n25
Florian, Jean-Pierra Claris de, *Galatie*, 324, 452n170
Fontenelle, Bernard Le Bouyer de:
  Entretiens sur la pluralité des mondes, 323, 364, 437nXI.11–14, 475
  Nouvelles Dialogues des Morts (Dialogues of the Dead, Ancient and Modern), 364, 454n189
Foote, Samuel, *Taste*, 219
Fordyce, James:
  Sermons to Young Women, 329, 411, 468n346; quoted, 453n179;
  appearance in *The Female Speaker*, 369
Fortunatus (folktale), 346, 456n207
A French Dictionary, on a Plan Entirely New. By William Smith, (review by ALB), 375, 425
French Phraseology. 2d Edition. By Anon., (review by ALB), 375, 419
French plays as pedagogical tools, 220
The French Scholar's Depository. By Anne Lindley, (review by ALB), 375, 412
The French Student's Vade Mecum. By the Rev. P. C. Le Vasseur, (review by ALB), 375, 399
Francis I, 318
Francis II, 318
Frank, Elizabeth, [400], [402], 464n293, 465n300
Franklin, Benjamin, 370, 407

Gagnier, John, 218
Galland, Antoine, 'Aladdin, or the Wonderful Lamp', *The Book of One Thousand and One Nights*, [249], 438n20
  French translation, 456n207
galvanism, 327–8
Garrick, David, 407
Garnerin, André Jacques, 454n192
Gay, John, *The Shepherd's Week*, 370, [386], 442n63; quoted, 271, 461n253; *Fables*, [411], 472n393; [mis-]quoted, 467n341
Gells of Derbyshire, 220, 438n18
Gell, Philip, 220
Gell, William, 220
General Advertiser, 16 November 1778 notices of *Two to Three* and *Three Years Old*, 2

Genlis, Stéphanie Félicité Ducrest, Comtesse de, 472n393, 475;
    Adèle et Théodore, [308], 323, 447n120, 475;
    Le Théatre de l'Education, 323; quoted, 220;
    Les Veillées du Chateau, 239, 323, 394, 476
gens Decia, 395
Gentleman's Magazine:
    ALB's defence of Maria Edgeworth's Tales of Fashionable Life, 374;
    John Carey, contributor, 465n304;
    notice of Monteggia's Il vero modo, 463n285;
    The Geographical Primer. By Jeremiah Holmes Wiffen, (review by ALB), 375, 416, 469n363
George II, 345
Gessner, Salomon, The Death of Abel (trans.), [395], 462n273
Gibbon, Edward, The History of the Decline and Fall of the Roman Empire, [303], 370, 446n108, 450n145; quoted, 456n204
Gillet (publisher), 403
Gilpin, William, 387
Gisborne, Thomas, Enquiry into the Duties of the Female Sex, 329
Glasgow, first British manufacture of 'inkle', 456n208
Gloucester, 353, 382
Godwin, William, [395], [398], [400], [401], [413], 463n280; An Enquiry Concerning Political Justice, 462n174
Goffart, Walter, Historical Atlases, 448n126
Golconda, 249, 438n21
Goldsmith, Oliver, 369, Animated Nature, 370
Gourlay, Alexander S., 454n192
A Grammar of the French Language. By C. Laisné, (review by ALB), 375–6, 426
Grammatical Questions on the English Grammar. By Rev. Christopher Muston, (review by ALB), 375, 417
Greig, John, 395, 462–3n275. See The World Displayed
Grey, Lady Jane, 387, 400, 461n255, 464n294
Graffigny, Françoise de (née d'Issembourg du Buisson d'Happoncourt), Les Lettres Peruviennes, 324, 452n168

Gray, Thomas, 370, 472n393;
    Elegy Written in a Country Churchyard, quoted, 385, [mis-]quoted, 471n377; 460n250;
    'Ode to Adversity', [294], 444n92
'Great' Comet of 1811, 466n325
Great Room at Spring Gardens, 455n198. See also: Porter, Robert Ker
'Greek and Estruscan artists' [standard met by artisans in Burslem], 250. See also: Burslem, Staffordshire
Gregory, John, A Father's Legacy to his Daughters, 329, [330], 412, 440n38, 468n348; quoted, 450n177
Gresset, Jean-Baptiste-Louis, Ver-Vert ou les voyages du perroquet de la visitation de Nevers, 325, 452n171
Gretna Green, 457–8n220. See Winterbotham, Melanie
Griffiths, George Edward, editor of M Rev, 373, 465n302, 467n338; editorial practices, quoted, 374, 464n298, 466n322
Griffiths, Ralph, founder of M Rev, 373
Gros, C., 406–7, 466n322
Grosvenor Square, 454n192. See also: Garnerin, André
The Guardian of Education, 188
A Guide to Tutors, Parents, and Private Students, in the Selection of Elementary School Books... by the Late Rev. Joshua Collins... A New Edition, revised and enlarged. By the Rev. Samuel Catlow, (review by ALB), 375, 415
Guy, Joseph, 396, 405, 416, 463n279
Guy's New British Reader, or Sequel to his New British Spelling Book. By Joseph Guy, (review by ALB), 375, 405
Guy's New British Spelling Book. By Joseph Guy, (review by ALB), 375, 397
Guy's School Geography. By Joseph Guy, (review by ALB), 375, 396

Hadrian (Publius Aelius Hadrianus), [312]
Haigh, Thomas, 423, 472n393
Hale, Mrs. S. J., ed., Things by Their Right Names (Boston:... 1839 & 1840 Edition), 'Preface' (1839), quoted, 438n12;
    note signed 'J. W. I.', quoted, 455–6n201, 456n209

Hall, Anna Maria, ed. *The Juvenile Forget Me Not. A Christmas and New Year's Gift, or Birthday Present for the Year 1830*, 290n10
Hamilton, Elizabeth, 459n236,
  Letters on the Elementary Principles of Education, 329, [332], 373, 374, 376, 453n180, 459n236; quoted, 430n56.4–5;
  on ALB's *Lessons* (contra Edgeworth), 460n246;
  Memoirs of Modern Philosophers, 374, 376, 459n236
Hampden, John, 305, 306, 446n113
Hampstead:
  Barbaulds and Rickards, residents of, 295n4;
  Carr family, xxxviii–ix, 263, [299], 332, 348n3, 445n105;
  'environs' in 'Zephyrus and Flora', 269;
  Galton, Mary Anne (ALB's pupil), xxxviii;
  Wynch family, 268;
  Wynch, Flora (ALB's pupil and addressee of 'On Fashion'), xxxviii, 263, 268, 270
Hampstead Heath, [269], 442n57
Hannibal (Hannibal Barca), 311, 449n133
Hardwicke's Marriage Act (1753), 457–8n220
Harris, G. Edward, 470n371
Harris, James:
  'Concerning Happiness', *Three Treatises*, 432n27.9–31.9;
  Hermes, 445n106
Harris (publisher), 404, 414
Hartley, David, 187;
  Observations on Man, 429n11.8
Harvard, 'Riddle II' holograph, Hyde Collection, Houghton Library, 348
Harry Ransom Research Center, U of Texas, 'Riddle IV' holograph, 348
Hastings, Selina, Countess of Huntingdon, 284;
  'Lady Selina' as synecdoche for Methodism, 284, 287;
  patronage of the Wesleys, 284
Hatchard (publisher), 401
Hayley, William, *Essay on Epic Poetry; in Five Epistles*, quoted, 451n159
Hays, Mary, 463n280, 468n352

Hegira, 299, 315
Hemans, Felicia, 188, 443n83
Henry IV, [306], 446n113
Henry V, [306], 446n113
Henry VII, 250n25
Henry VIII, 464n294
Henry Frederick, Prince of Wales, 400, 464n294
Heptarchy, 316, 450n147
Herculaneum, 250
Herodotus, [276], 311–12, 442n71, 448n129, 448n132
Herschel, William, 391, 461n259
Heyrick, Elizabeth, 465n310.
  See also: Kibworth, Leicester; Coltman family
Hezekiah, 314
Hill, Elizabeth, 403
  The Poetical Monitor: Consisting of Pieces Select and Original... Intended to Succeed Dr. Watts' Divine and Moral Songs, [403], 465n308
Hipparchus, 312
Hippocrates, 318
A History of France, from the Commencement of the Reign of Clovis, in 481, to the Peace of Campo Formio in 1797. By [Daniel Wakefield], (review by ALB), 375, 396
History of Rome, from the Building of the City to the Ruin of the Republic. By Edward Baldwin, Esq. [William Godwin], (review by ALB), 375, 395
The History of the Distressing Loss and Happy Recovery of Little Thomas Dellow. By Anon., (review by ALB), 375, 420
Hodgkins, George, 422
Holcroft, Thomas, 463n280
Holland, Thomas and John, eds., 'Epitaph on a Green-Finch', *Exercises for the Memory and Understanding*, 289, 432n73.6–9
Homer, 271, 300, 319–22, 335, 450–1n156, 451n159, 454n188;
  Iliad, 247, 319, 321, 364–7, 438n14, 451n158;
  Odyssey, 129, 321, 433n75.4–76.1
Hone, William, 432n29.5
Horace (Quintus Horatius Flaccus), 273, 371
Hornsey, John, 416, 469n364

504 INDEX OF TITLES, AUTHORS, AND PROPER NAMES

Hort, Rev. William Jillard, 409, 444n94, 467n332
Howard, Thomas, Earl of Arundel, [315], 449n143
Howard, Susanna, Countess of Suffolk, 400, 464n294
Howitt, Mary, 188
Howitt, William, *The Book of the Seasons*, 431n9.3
Hubba [Ubba, Viking invader], 236, 437n9
Hudson, Thomas, 438n13
Hull:
  grammar school, 466n315;
  newspapers, 471n378
Hume, David, [332], 453n180, 467n331, 470n366;
  History of England, [250]; quoted, 439n25;
  'Of Simplicity and Refinement in Writing', quoted, [342], 455n197
Humber, 235. *See also*: East Midlands
Hunt, Leigh, *The Months*, 431n9.3, 432n29.5
Hunter, R. (publisher, successor to JJ), 369n1
Hutcheson, Francis, 'Our Duties Toward Mankind', *Short Introduction to Moral Philosophy*, 187, [202], 436nVIII

Il vero modo di piacere in compagnia, &c. By Carlo Monteggia, (review by ALB), 375, 397
Immel, Andrea, xiv, 1n2, 280n7
Important Studies for the Female Sex, in Reference to Modern Manners. By [Mary] Cockle, (review by ALB), 374, 393, 462n268
Instinct Displayed, in a Collection of Well-Authenticated Facts, Exemplifying the Extraordinary Sagacity of Various Species of the Animal Creation. By Priscilla Wakefield, (review by ALB), 375, 408
Instructive Tales. By [Sarah] Trimmer, (review by ALB), 375, 401
Introduction to the Diurnal Readings. By Thomas Haigh, (review by ALB), 375, 423
An Introduction to the Epistolary Style of the French. By George Saulez, (review by ALB), 375, 423, 472n394

An Introduction to Geography. 2nd Edition. By Isaac Payne, (review by ALB), 375, 402
Ireland:
  peculiar quality of Irish spinning, 246;
  Irish greyhound, 256;
  'Irish howl', 453n181. *See* Edgeworth, Maria, *Castle Rackrent*
'*Ismael Abulfeda*' (Abulfeda, 'Prince of Hamah'), 218

James, Charles, *Audi Alteram Partem*, 447n118
James I, 464n294
Jameson, Anna Brownell (née Murphy), 424, 472n396
Jardin du Roi, 474n408. *See* Buffon, Georges-Louis Leclerc, Comte de
'J.B.' as 'John Black,' review in *GM* of *Lessons* and *Hymns*, 3n11
'J. Douse':
  11 June 1802 visitor to Barbaulds, 322;
  See Barbauld, Rochemont (Diary)
  addressee of 17 October [1810] letter from ALB (*GC*), 322. *See* Douce, Mr. [J.]
John Rylands Library at Manchester University, 7, 10
Johnson and Co. (publisher), 419
Johnson, Joseph, 186, 239, 239n1, 369, 369n1, 452n170, 475;
  advertisements for *Evenings*, 239–41;
  advertisements for *Two to Three* in *LEP* and *LC*, 2;
  advertisements for four-volume set of *Lessons*, 2–3;
  Analytical Review, 373;
  first publication of Catty's *Elements*, 467n334;
  London publisher of *Lessons*, 2, 10
Johnson, Samuel, 409, 467n331, 470n366, 476;
  A Dictionary of the English Language, 327
  appearance in *The Female Speaker*, 370;
  disparagement of *Lessons*, 2n5;
  verbal slights toward ALB, 452n173.
  See Boswell, James;
  Vanity of Human Wishes, 450n153;
  quoted, [318]
Jones, Sir William, 270, 274, 442n69, 467n331

INDEX OF TITLES, AUTHORS, AND PROPER NAMES 505

The Junior Class Book; or Reading Lessons for Every Day in the Year. By William Frederick Mylius, (review by ALB), 375, 396
The Juvenile Arithmetic, or Child's Guide to Figures. By a Lady [Anon.], (review by ALB), 375, 424
Juvenile Correspondence. By Lucy Aikin, (review by ALB), 375, 405
Juvenile Magazine, fashionable audience for *Lessons,* 5
The Juvenile Spectator. Being Observations on the Tempers, Manners, and Foibles of Various Young Persons. By Arabella Argus, (review by ALB), 375, 398
The Juvenile Spectator. Part II. Containing Some Account of Old Friends, and an Introduction to a Few Strangers. By Arabella Argus, (review by ALB), 375, 414

Kauffman, Angelica, 468n352
Keegan, William, 407–8, 466n325;
  Le Négociant Universel, 407
Kenrick, John, quoted, 373
Kenrick, Timothy, 458n227
Kent (publisher), 421
Key to Practical English Prosody and Versification. By John Carey, (review by ALB), 375, 403
A Key to the Copious Collection of Instructive and Entertaining Exercises on the French Language. By C. Laisné, (review by ALB), 375, 427
A Key to the Re-translation of the English Examples in the French Grammar. By C. Laisné, (review by ALB), 375, 427
Khaldun, Ibn ('Bohaddin'), 218
Kibworth, Leicestershire, xxxv;
  Coltman family, 465n310
King, William, *The Art of Cookery, A Poem, in Imitation of Horace's Art of Poetry,* quoted, 451n157
Kinworth Castle, 236, 437n9
Kirwan, Richard, 422, 471n384
Kitts End, Barnet, 423
Knox, Vicesimus, 3, *Elegant Extracts,* [80], 432n65.2–3
Kosciuszko, Tadeusz, [304], 446n110

Lackington and Co., 404, 416, 417
Laisné, C., 426–7, 473n406

The Lady-Birds' Lottery; or the Fly's Alphabet. By Queen Mab [Marie-Catharine le Jumel de Berneville, Countess D'Aulnoy], (review by ALB), 375, 415
Lady's Magazine (for 30 November), 290
Laertius, Diogenes, *Lives of Eminent Philosophers,* 255, 440n35
La Fayette, Madame de, *The Princess of Cleves,* [308], 447n120, 366, 458–9n232
La Fontaine, Jean de, 456n205, 475;
  Fables, 325
Lake Geneva, 333
Lamb, Charles and Mary, 463n280, 464n296
[Lambert, N.], *Le Manuel Epistolaire,* 426, 473n405
Lambert, Madame de, 'Treatise on Friendship', [408], 467n327
Landon, Charles Paul, 407, 466n323
Lapland (Scandinavia), 333
Law and Whittaker (publisher), 369n1, 419, 423, 424, 425
Laws of the Twelve Tables, 318
Lead, Lucy (Archivist at Wedgwood Museum), 439n27
Le Breton, Anna, *Memoir of Mrs Barbauld: Including Letters and Notices of Her Family and Friends*:
  appearance of 'Riddle IV' as 'Enigma', 348n5
  copy of 'Riddle IV', from ALB to Maria Edgeworth, 349
Lee, Nathaniel, 457n212
Leeds Intelligencer, advertisements for *Two to Three* and *Three Years Old* (listed in two parts), 2, 7
Leeuwenhoek, [Antonie] van, 431n19.6
Leith Hill Tower, 333
Leonidas I, 311
Lesage, Alain-René, *Gil Blas,* 427, 473n407
Lessons for Children in Three Parts. By Eliza Fenwick, (review by ALB), 375, 396
Letters Addressed to Two Absent Daughters. By Maria Eliza Ketelby Rundell, (review by ALB), 375, 421
Letters on the Elementary Principles of Education. By Elizabeth Hamilton, (review by ALB), 374, 376, 430n56.4–5
Le Vasseur, Rev. P. C., 399

Lim, Jessica W. H., 'Unsettled Accounts: Anna Letitia Barbauld's Letters to Lydia Rickards', 295n2
Lincoln Cathedral, 333
Lindley, Anne, 412
Linnaeus, Carl, 221
Lisbon, Portugal, 269
Liverpool RO:
  extant copy of 'The Four Sisters', 259. *See also*: Nicholson, Matthew
Livy (Titus Livius), 461n262
Locke, John, 306, 429n11.8;
  Some Thoughts Concerning Education, [331], [392], 453n180, [462n264];
Lock, William, [298], 444n100, 453n183
Loire Valley, 333
Lombards, 250n25
London:
  Hailes, N., Fred Westley, and A. H. Davis (publisher of *The Juvenile Forget Me Not for 1830* [1829]), 290n10;
  origin of students at Palgrave, xxxv;
  original publication of ALB's epistolary tutorials, xl;
  losses of ALB family papers and archives of the Palgrave School during German bombing in 1940, xxxvii, xxxviin7, xl, 217;
  more conveniences relative to Spain, 246;
  newspapers, 471n378;
  thirteen editions of *Evenings* in ALB's lifetime, 239;
  West-end, 269n57
London Chronicle, JJ's advertisement for *Evenings* 18–20 June 1793, 241
London Magazine, 186
London Packet, 186
London Warehouse, 251. *See* Wedgwood warehouses.
Longhope (village), 353
Longmans (publisher), 335 (Fig. 13), 369n1, 373, 399, 400, 402, 403, 409, 412, 413, 415, 416, 417, 419, 422, 425, 426, 427
Louis XIV, 318, 335, 346, 364–7
Louis XV, 465n313
Louis XVI, 402, 456n202
Louisville Public Advertiser, 19 Feb. 1830, 291n11
Loyal Associators, 460n239
Lucian of Samosata, 364, 451n160, 461n262
Lun, Cai, 440n33

Lycurgus (lawgiver of Sparta), 321
Lyttelton, George, 1st Baron, 463n288

Macaulay, Catharine, *History of England*, xxxix
Maclaurin, Colin, 'A General View of Sir Isaac Newton's Method', quoted, 221
'Madras System', 468n353. *See* Bell, Dr. Andrew
Maeterlinck, Maurice, 188
Magnay, Charlotte, 471n378. See *The History of… Little Thomas Dellow*
Mahon, Peggy, ' "Things by Their Right Names": Peace Education in *Evenings at Home*', 438n12
Maintenon, Madame de (Françoise d'Aubigné, Marquise de Maintenon), 364–7, 459n233–5;
  The Letters of Madam de Maintenon; and Other Eminent Persons in the Age of Lewis XIV, 364, [366], 459n233
Maison Royale de Saint-Louis at Saint-Cyr, 366, 459n235
Major, Emma, *The Politics of Sociability*, 327n1
Malesherbes, Guillaume-Chrétien de Lamoignon de, 399, 464n291
Manchester:
  cotton and muslin goods, 250;
  migration of manufacture of 'inkle', 456n208. *See* Glasgow
Manor-House Academy, Kennington Lane, 466n325
Mant, Alicia Catherine, 423, 472n392
Manuel Epistolaire, or, the Young Lady's Assistant in Writing French Letters. 2nd Edition. By Anon., (review by ALB), 375, 403
'Manufacture of Great Britain' [global raw materials], 246
Marmontel, Jean-François:
  Bélisaire, 324, 476;
  Les Incas, 324, quoted, 476
Martineau, Harriet, quoted, 187;
  'What Women Are Educated For', quoted, 443–4n89
Mary I of England, 318, 461n255, 464n294
Mary, Queen of Scots, 318
Mason, William:
  Caractacus, 218–19;
  The English Garden, 325

INDEX OF TITLES, AUTHORS, AND PROPER NAMES 507

Maternal Sollicitude for a Daughter's Best Interest. By [Ann] Taylor [née Martin], (review by ALB), 375, 418, 428, 474n409

Maturin, Charles Robert, 443n83

Maxims, Reflections, and Biographical Anecdotes. Selected for the Use of Young Persons. By James Hews Bransby, (review by ALB), 375, 419

May Hill, 353

McCarthy, William, 439n27
'Anna Letitia Barbauld Letters to Lydia Rickards', 1798–1815, 295n2;
Anna Letitia Barbauld, Voice of the Enlightenment (ALBVE) 217n1, 239, 268, 369n2, 432.65.9, 432n27.9–31.9, 433n88.8, 447n122, 468n346, 475, 476n9;
'"Celebrated Academy"' 217n1, 218n3, 225n7, 444n94, 475n1

Medici, Catherine de, 450n152

Mehmed II, Sultan, [317], 450n149

Meilan, Mark Anthony, *The Children's Friend*, 475. *See* Berquin, Arnaud, *L'Ami des Enfans*

Melville, Herman, xxxvii

Memnon of Rhodes, 448n128

Mentor and Amander; or, a Visit to Ackworth School. By [William Singleton?], (review by ALB), 375, 425

Merlet, Pierre François, 426, 473n404

Méthode Pratique, &c.; *i.e. A Practical Method of Learning Easily the English Language*. By George Hodgkins, (review by ALB), 375, 422

'Mexicans' (pre-colonial), 278–9n74

Michaelis, Johann David, 218

Milberger, Kurt, 441n54

Milton, John, 265n49, 301, 305, 306, 371, 461n262;
Comus, 370;
'Il Penseroso', 464n295; [mis-]quoted, 400
Paradise Lost, 441n49, 451n159, 460n248; quoted, 265, 322, 383

The Mirror of the Graces; or the English Lady's Costume. 2nd Edition. By a Lady of Distinction [Anon.], (review by ALB), 375, 410

Miscellaneous English Exercises. By Rev. William Jillard Hort, (review by ALB), 375, 409, quoted, 444n94

Mitylene (Lesbos), 276

M. J. Godwin and Co. (publisher), 395, 396, 398, 400, 401, 413, 462n274. *See* William Godwin

Mohammed, 299, 315, 407, 449n144

Molière (Jean-Baptiste Poquelin):
L'Avare, 325;
Le Bourgeois gentilhomme, 325;
Le Malade imaginaire, 325;
Le Misanthrope, 325;
Les Femmes savantes, 325

Monomatapa (southeast Africa), 125, 433n33.1–2

Montgolfier, Joseph Michel and Jacques-Étienne, 454n192

Monthly Magazine, 263n3;
John Carey, contributor, 465n304;
volume 13 [1802], 327;
'Half-Yearly Retrospect of German Literature', 20 July 1802, 452n174;
volume 13 [Feb. 1802], 299n10, 359–60, 459n236; ALB memoir of Chapone, quoted, 299;
volume 15 [1803], interest in galvanism, quoted, 327

Monthly Review, xl–li, 373–4

Monthly Repository, letter from LA on Works vs. other copies for annuals and gift books, xln13

Monthly Visitor, 14 (July 1801), 'Riddle I', published within 'Enigmas &c. for Solution', 348n5

Montagu, Elizabeth, 327

Montagu, Lady Mary Wortley, 'letter to her daughter, 28 Jan. 1753', [338], 370, quoted, 455n196

Moore, Edward, 463n288, 472n393

Moral Truths, and Studies from Natural History. Intended as a Sequel to the Juvenile Journal, or Tales of Truth. By [Mary] Cockle, (review by ALB), 375, 397

More, Hannah, 387, 475;
ALB's envy of success on the stage, 363;
appearance in *The Female Speaker*, 370;
quoted, on Elizabeth Montagu, 327;
Strictures on the Modern System of Female Education, [377], [411], 459n237, 467n339

Moreton Hampstead (school), Devonshire, 471n375

The Mother's Fables, in Verse. By [Anne Taylor], (review by ALB), 375, 418
Motte, Antoine Houdart de la, *One Hundred New Court Fables*, 'The Peach Tree and the Mulberry Tree' 226
Mount Hymettus, 309, 447n123
Mount Jura, 333
Mount Vesuvius, 38, 333
'Mrs. Dorcas', 281, 443n81
Muhammad, Al-Nasir ('sultan of Egypt'), 218
Murray (publisher), 411
Murray, Lindley, *English Grammar*, 402, 465n305
Murray's Magazine, 295
Muston, Rev. Christopher, 417
Mylius's School Dictionary of the English Language. 2nd Edition. By William Frederick Mylius, (review by ALB), 375, 398
Mylius, William Frederick, 396, 398, 401, 463n276

Nabonassar, 316
Nangle, Benjamin, 374, 374n1
Natural History of Quadrupeds, for Children. By [Louisa Allan], (review by ALB), 375, 422
Necho II (pharoah), 311, 448n129
Necker, Jacques, 345, 456n202
'Negroes', 38. *See also*: Dibdin, Charles, *The Islanders*
Nero (Nero Claudius Caesar Augustus Germanicus), 395
Netherlands:
 'Dutch' (adj.), 280, 443n79;
 Gueux, Dutch guerillas, 446–7n115;
 more conveniences (in Amsterdam) relative to Spain, 246
The New Bath Guide, Letter V, quoted, [421], 471n382
New Dialogues, in French and English. By William Keegan, (review by ALB), 375, 407
A New Introduction to Reading; Containing Many Useful Exercises, or Lessons, Adapted to the Capacities of Children of Either Sex, from Six to Twelve Years of Age. By Rev. G. J. Davies, (review by ALB), 375, 404
New Monthly Magazine, April 1821 obituary for Samuel Rousseau, 471n376

New Orthographical Exercises. By Alexander Power, (review by ALB), 375, 424, 472n395
A New System of English Grammar. By William Angus, (review by ALB), 375, 413
The New Young Man's Companion. By John Hornsey, (review by ALB), 375, 416
Newton, Sir Isaac, 221, 301, 316–17, 338, 342, 407, 450n148, 455n196
Nicholson, Matthew, 259. *See also*: Warrington Academy
Nile River Delta, 333
Norbury Park, 333, 453n183
North America, 38;
 'drunken Indian' stereotype, 345, 455n200. *See* Douglas, Thomas;
 'The Indians', 38
North Carolina Observer, 13 May 1830, 291n11
Northumberland, 466n317
'North Whitewashing Fox' (1783 political cartoon), 470n374
Norway, 256
Norwich:
 Beecroft, Judith Dixon (ALB's pupil through correspondence), xxxviii, (addressee of 'Allegory on Sleep'), 265;
 Taylor, Sarah (correspondence pupil), 476, 476n12;
 Taylor, Susannah (mother of ALB's correspondence pupils), xxxviii, 476n12
Notre Dame, 333
The Nursery Companion; or, Rules of English Grammar, in Verse. By a Lady, [Anon.], (review by ALB), 375, 418

Observations on the Most Important Subjects of Education: Containing Many Useful Hints to Mothers, but Chiefly Intended for Private Governesses. By Anon., (review by ALB), 375, 411
O'Keefe, John, *Aladdin and His Wonderful Lamp*, 456n207
On the Education of Daughters; translated from the French of the Abbé Fenelon, afterward Archbishop of Cambray. By [François de Salignac de la Mothe Fénelon], (review by ALB), 375, 408, 476

Opie, Iona and Peter Opie, eds. 'Father Francis', 430n14.3–4
'Oriental literature', including Persian and Arabic, 274
Original Letters of Advice to a Young Lady. By [Mary Weightman], (review by ALB), 375, 426
Ossian (James Macpherson), 321
Otway, Thomas, *Venice Preserv'd*, 370
Ovid (Publius Ovidius Naso):
  Fasti, 268, 431n9.3;
  Metamorphoses, [249], [260], [264], [265], [269–70], [275], [277], 370, 439n22, 441n53, 442nn60–1, 442n70, 442n72; quoted (Loeb translation), 440n37
Oxford, 333;
  Queens College, Oxford University, 461n258

Palace of Versailles, 346
Paley, William, 397;
  Natural Theology, 463n283
Palgrave Enclosure survey 1812, [146], 433n31.5
Palgrave School in Suffolk, xxxv, xxxvii, xl, 186, 217, 219, 221, 225, 231, 239, 263, 430n34.5, 461n258, 475;
  age range of pupils, 217;
  course of study, 218, 444n94;
  food gifts from home, [138–9], 433n13.1;
  forecourt/Barbauld residence, [120], [143], 433n88.8;
  male pupils, [68], 432n12.3–4, 432n65.9;
  republican structure, 217;
  social class of pupils, 226, 455n200;
  'The Death-Bed', fragment, showing ALB's interest in writing plays, 363
The Parent's Offering, or Tales for Children. By Caroline Barnard, (review by ALB), 375, 413
Paul, Lissa, 466n320
Payne, Isaac, 402, 465n301
Peabody, William, quoted, 188
Peacock, Thomas Love, [420], 471n379
Pennant, Thomas:
  British Zoology, 220;
  Indian Zoology, 446n107
Perambulations in London and its Environs. By Priscilla Wakefield, (review by ALB), 375, 397
Peretti, Vincenzo, *Grammaire Italienne*, 462n265
Periander (Corinth), 276

Pforzheimer Collection of Shelley and His Circle, NYPL, 290n9, 295n2, 297n9, 300, 302n14, 306n15, 310n16, 319n18, 320 (Fig. 12), 323n19, 452n169
Philadelphus, Ptolemy II, 316
Philip II of Spain, 318
Philistines, 350
Phillips, Sir Richard, [412], 468n347.
  See Bossut, M. l'Abbé
Philotechnic Society, 399
Picquot, A., 415–16, 469n361
Pièces Choisies des Meilleurs Auteurs François, 325, 452n172
Pilkington, James, 457–8n220
Pilkington, Mary, [393], 462n266. See *Tales of the Hermitage*
Pindar, Peter (nom de plume, John Wolcot), 'Ode III', quoted, 409, 467n335
Pisistratus (tyrant of Athens), 321
Pitt, Thomas, [345], 455–6n201
Pitt, William (the Younger), [309], 447n122
Pius, Antonius (Titus Aelius Hadrianus Antoninus Pius), 309, 447–8n124, 312
Plato, 255, 440n35, 448n130
Pliny the Elder (Gaius Plinius Secundus), 434n95.7–9, 473n402; quoted, 431n9.3;
  Naturalis Historia, [184], 434n104.4
Pluche, Noël-Antoine, *Le Spectacle de la nature*, 324, 451n162
Plutarch, *Plutarch's Lives*, 448n130, 456n205, 467n340; quoted, 451n158
The Poetical Class Book. By William Frederick Mylius, (review by ALB), 375, 401
Poetry for Children. By [Mary Anne Lamb], (review by ALB), 375, 400
Polwhele, Rev. Richard:
  'The Deserted Village School' and *The Unsex'd Females*, 468nn352–3
Polybius, 312, 448n133
Pomponius Mela, 312, 449n134
Pope, Alexander, 369, 371, 461n262, 472n393; quoted, 249n22;
  'Epistle to Dr. Arbuthnot', 457n219;
  Essay on Criticism, quoted, 272, [426], 442n65; quoted, 473n403;
  Essay on Man, 439n22, 450n153; quoted, [249], [318], 432n45.3–9;

Pope, Alexander (*continued*)
  Homer, [366], 440n36; quoted, 259, 458n231; [mis-]quoted, 471n377;
  Imitation of Horace, 273, 442n66
  The Rape of the Lock, [269], 447n58
  'The Temple of Fame', 451n161; quoted, 322
Pope Adrian VI (Adriaan Florensz Boeyens), 456n206
Pope Leo III, [402], [465n303]
Pope Leo X (Giovanni di Lorenzo de' Medici), 343, 346, 456n206
Poppe, J. H. Moritz, *An Essay Toward a History of the Origin and Progress of Clock and Watch-making*, 450n151
Porter, Robert Ker, 'The Taking of Seringapatam' (panorama), 343, [344], 455n198
Possidonius, 312
Potemkin, Prince Grigory, 346, 456n203
Potosi (formerly Peru, now Bolivia), 359, 458n224
Power, Alexander, 424
Practical English Prosody and Versification. By John Carey, (review by ALB), 402, 403
Practical Hints to Young Females, on the Duties of a Wife, a Mother, and a Mistress of a Family. By [Ann] Taylor [née Martin], (review by ALB), 375, 428
A Pretty Play-Thing for Children of All Denominations, 429n
  Advertisement, 6
Priestley, Joseph 221, 429n11.8, 471n384, 473n407;
  and Josiah Wedgwood, 439n26;
  A Description of a New Chart of History, Containing a View of the Principal Revolutions of Empire that have Taken Place in the World, 299n11, 448n127; quoted, 447n119, 447n121, 449n142, 450n150;
  Chart of Biography, 318, 450n148;
  'On Habitual Devotion', 435nVI.1; quoted, 187;
  published history lectures from Warrington, 299n11;
  lectures on History and General Policy, 299n11;
  The Rudiments of English Grammar, quoted, 429n7.4;
Priestley, Sarah (Joseph's daughter, afterwards Finch), 290
Princess (later Queen) Carolina of Brunswick, 220
Prior, Matthew, 'Protogenes and Apelles', *The Works of the English Poets*, quoted, 468n343
Prud'homme, Louis Marie, 415, 469n360
Ptolemy, Claudius, 312–13, 449n135
Punctuation; or an Attempt to Facilitate the Art of Pointing, on the Principles of Grammar and Reason. By Samuel Rousseau, (review by ALB), 375, 419
Pyrenees, 222
Pyrrho (Pyrrhonists), 356, 458n222

Quintilian (Marcus Fabius Quintilianus), 390

Rabelais, François, 456n205
Rabutin-Chantal, Marie de, Marquise de Sévigné, 324, 427, 452n167
Racine, Jean-Baptiste, 476;
  Athalie, 325;
  Bajazet, 325;
  Bérénice, [mis-]quoted, [262], 441n47;
  Brittanicus, 325;
  Esther, 325;
  Iphigénie, 325;
  Phèdre, 325;
  Les Plaideurs, quoted, 410, 467n336
Raleigh, Sir Walter, 'Advice to His Son', [408], 467n327
Rees (publisher), 421
Regent (or Pitt) Diamond, 345, 455–6n201. *See* Regent, Philippe II, *and* Pitt, Thomas
Regent, Philippe II, Duke of Orléans, quoted, 404, 465n313; 455–6n201
Rehoboam, 314
Reid, Andrew, *Abstract of Sir Isaac Newton's Chronology of Ancient Kingdoms*, 449n143, 450n148
Rennell, Major James, [313], 448n129, 449n138; quoted, 448n132
Reynolds, Sir Joshua, 245, 438n13
Richard I, 318
Richardson, Samuel, *Sir Charles Grandison*, [308], 447n120

INDEX OF TITLES, AUTHORS, AND PROPER NAMES 511

Richmond, 297
Rickards, Edith Cordelia, 290n9; quoted, 295n4;
   Monthly Packet articles, sources of ALB's letters to Lydia Rickards, 295n4,6, 296n8, 300, 444n94;
   Murray's Magazine, extracts from whole series of ALB's letters to Lydia Rickards, 295n7
Rickards, Lydia (afterwards Withering), 290, 290n9, 295, 296, 299–300n13, 302, 306, 310, 313, 319, 322–3, 332, 338, 434n107.2, 452n169, 467n333;
Rickards, Lydia (the elder), 299
Riegate, 333
Rigby, Sarah and Elizabeth:
   'beauties' in 'Description of Two Sisters', 264;
   social exile, 458n226. *See* Warrington Academy;
   subjects of 'To Miss R———' and 'Verses Written in an Alcove', 458n226
Rippingham, John, 409, 422, 467nn330–1
Rix, S. W., 432n12.3–4
Rix, W. P., 'Early Homes. Vol. II', [148-9], 434n37.1–38.1
Robins and Son (publisher), 417
Robinson, Mary, 468n352, 472n393
Robertson, William, *History of America*, quoted, 442–3n74
Rollin, Charles, *Histoire ancienne*, 324, 451nn163–4
Roscoe, William, [333], quoted, 454n184;
   History of the Life and Pontificate of Leo X, 343
Ross, Louise, 6n19
Ross-on-Wye, 353
Roth, George, 438n13
Rousseau, Jean-Jacques, 301, 476;
   Émile, or On Education, 400, [411], 464n292, quoted, 468n345;
   Lettres élémentaires sur la botanique, 324, 452n165
Rousseau, Samuel, [419], 471n376
Rowe, Nicholas, 472n393
Rowley, Martin, 'Weather in History: 1800 to 1849', 457n216
Royal Academy of Arts, 327
Royal Asiatic Society, 442n69. *See* Jones, Sir William

Royal Military Academy at Woolwich, 409
'Royal Proclamation against Seditious Writings and Publications' (May 1792), [309], 447n122
Rules for English Composition. By John Rippingham, (review by ALB), 375, 409
Rules for English Composition, 2nd Edition. By John Rippingham, (review by ALB), 375, 422
Rules for Pronouncing and Reading the French Language. By Rev. Israel Worsley, (review by ALB), 375, 425
Rundell, Maria Eliza Ketelby, 421, 471n383
Ryan (publisher), 408

Saint-Fond, Barthélemy Faujas de, 387
Saint Peter, 267n56
Saint-Pierre, J.-H. Bernardin de, 427;
   La Chaumière Indienne, 324, 452n169;
   Paul et Virginie, 324, 452n169
Saint-Simon, Duc de (Louis de Rouvroy), *Memoirs of Louis XIV. His Court and the Regency*. Book II, 364, 458n230, 465n313
Saladin, founder of Ayyubid dynasty, 218
Salisbury, newspapers, 471n378
Salisbury Plain, 333
Samson ('Sampson'), 350, 457n211.
   See Book of Judges
Saulez, George, 423–4, 472n394
'savannahs of America', 334
Scaliger, Julius Caesar, 316
Scarron, Paul, 366, 459n234
The School Cyphering Book, for Beginners. By Joseph Guy, (review by ALB), 375, 416
School of Instruction: a Present, or Reward, to Those Girls Who have Left their Sunday-School with Improvement and a Good Character. By a Lady [Anon.], (review by ALB), 375, 408
Schultens, Albert, 218
Scipio Aemilianus (Publius Cornelius Scipio Africanus Aemilianus), 312, 448n133
Scipio Africanus (Publius Cornelius Scipio Africanus), 395

Scotland:
  Edinburgh, newspapers, 471n378;
  Fletcher, Grace (ALB's pupil through correspondence), xxxviiin11;
  origin of students at Palgrave, xxxv, 455n200. *See also*: Douglas, Thomas;
Scott, Walter, 472n393
Scriptural Stories, for Very Young Children. By [Louisa Allan], (review by ALB), 375, 418
Scudéry, Madame de, *Clélie*, [366], 458n232
'Seleucidae of Syria', 316
Semiramis (legendary), 298, [325], 335, 444n98
Semple, Agnes Sophia, 411, 467n342
Seneca (Lucius Annaeus Seneca the Younger), 395
Septuagint, 316, 448n127
A Sequel to the Poetical Monitor. By Elizabeth Hill, (review by ALB), 375, 403;
  2nd edition, 465n308
A Series of Tales from a Preceptor to his Pupils. By William Wennington, (review by ALB), 375, 411
Sermon sur les devoirs de la jeunesse, &c. By M. Lenoir, (review by ALB), 375, 406
Sesotris (legendary king of ancient Egypt), 311
Shakespeare, William, 220, 318-9, 369-70, 400, 464n296;
  A Midsummer Night's Dream, [334], 454n185;
  As You Like It, quoted, [398], 463n286;
  Hamlet, quoted, [395], [411]; 407, 462n272, 468n344
  Henry IV, 407;
  Julius Caesar, 407;
  Love's Labours Lost, quoted, [39]; 431n27.3-4;
  Macbeth, 335, 407, 454n187;
  Merry Wives of Windsor, 407;
  Much Ado about Nothing, quoted, 436nX.39;
  Othello, 407;
  Richard III, 407;
  Romeo and Juliet, quoted, 410; 467n337;
  The Merchant of Venice, quoted, 422; 471n385;
Sharpe, Catherine, quoted, 433n52.7
Sharpe and Hailes (publisher), 420
Shelley, Percy Bysshe, 295n2

Shelley, Mary Wollstonecraft Godwin, 468n350
Sheridan, Richard B., *The Rivals*, 370
Sherwood and Co. (publisher), 406, 410, 415, 423
Shetland horse, 256
Siberia, 256, 333
Sidney, Algernon, 305, 306, 446n113
Simple Pleasures. Designed for Young Persons above Twelve Years of Age. By Mary Anne Venning, (review by ALB), 375, 404
Singleton, William, [425], 473n398
Sir Hornbook; or Childe Launcelot's Expedition; a Grammatico-Allegorical Ballad. By [Thomas Love Peacock], (review by ALB), 375, 420, 471n379
Siret, Louis-Pierre, *Éléments de la langue Angloise*, 422, 472n389
Smart, Martin (possible pseudonym), 417, 470n366
Smith, Adam, *Wealth of Nations*, [249], [251], 439n23, 439n28
Smith, Charlotte, 463n280, 468n352;
  Beachy Head, 453n183;
  'To the Moon', *Elegiac Sonnets*, quoted, 437nXI.15-16
Smith, William, 425
Society of Friends (Quakers), 425, 473n398, 473n400
Socrates, 309, 311, 448n130
Soirées d'Automne, &c. i.e. Autumnal Evenings, or Vice Punished and Virtue Rewarded. For the Instruction of Youth and the Use of Schools. By G. Bertholet, (review by ALB), 374-5, 394;
  subscriptions among nobility, 462n270
Sophocles, *Oedipus Rex*, 457n212
Solomon, 310, 314, 419, 470n372
Solon, 318
Souter (publisher), 424, 426
Southern Times (Columbia, SC), 19 April 1830, 291n11
Southey, Robert, 415, 469n360
Spain:
  want of conveniences relative to people in London and Amsterdam, 246;
  'Spaniards' (Conquistadors), 279
The Spanish Guitar; a Tale, for the Use of Young Persons. By Elizabeth Isabella Spence, (review by ALB), 375, 420

INDEX OF TITLES, AUTHORS, AND PROPER NAMES 513

Spectator, [350], 369, 414, 453n179, 457n215
Spence, Elizabeth Isabella, 420, 471n381
Spenser, Edmund, 405, 461n262, [468n352];
 Faerie Queene, 370
S. S. S. (author and ALB's pupil):
 A Visit to Edinburgh, xxxviiin12;
 Thornton Hall; or, Six Months at School (1823), xxxviii, xxxviiin12
Stamford, Countess of (Lady Mary Booth), [265], 441n51
Stationers' Register, 186, 239
Statistical Account of Scotland, 456n208
Stillingfleet, Benjamin:
 'Introduction' to *The Calendar of Flora*, quoted, 436nIX.48–9;
 Miscellaneous Tracts, quoted, 221, 431n9.3
Stoke Newington:
 Rivaz family, recipients of an 'Enigma' from ALB, 348n3
 Estlin family, visit on 6 January 1814, 353
Steele, Richard, 369, 457n215.
 See also: Addison, Joseph
Sterne, Laurence, *Tristram Shandy*, quoted, [423], 472n391
St. Clair, William:
 The Godwins and the Shelleys, 462n274;
 'The Impact of Byron's Writings', 443n83
St. Etienne, Rabaut, *Adresse aux Anglois*, 447n118
Stockdale, J. J., 415, 469n360
St. Pancras, 454n192. *See* Garnerin, André
St. Paul's Cathedral, 344, 405–6
 Whispering Gallery, 454n191
St. Paul's Churchyard, (JJ's shop), 6
St. Peter's Basilica, 333
St. James's Palace, 279, 443n77
Strabo, 312, 449n134
Suetonius, *The Lives of the Twelve Caesars*, quoted, 456n204
Sunstein, Emily, *Mary Shelley: Romance and Reality*, 468n350
Surry Hills, 333
Sussex Downs, 333
'Swan' (Cygnus, constellation), 277
Swift, Jonathan, 369–70;
 affinity for 'puzzles'/riddles, 350;
 Gulliver's Travels, [454n186]
A Synopsis of French Grammar. By Pierre François Merlet, (review by ALB), 375, 426

Tables of the Different Parts of Speech in French. By C. Laisné, (review by ALB), 375, 427
Tacitus (Publius Cornelius Tacitus), 461n262
Talbot, Catharine, 370
Tales of the Hermitage. 2nd Edition. Trans. by V. Peretti, (review by ALB), 374, 393
Tartary (Central Eurasia), 334
Tasso, Torquato, [*Gerusalemme liberata*], 469n363
Taylor and Hessey (publisher), 418, 428
Taylor, Ann (née Martin), 418, 428, 470n371; quoted, 470n369, 470n372
Taylor, Anne (afterwards Gilbert), 418, 470n368
Taylor, Emily, *Memories of Some Contemporary Poets*, 15–16;
 appearance of 'Riddle II', 348n5
Taylor, Jane, 329n2, 470n368
Taylor, Sarah (daughter of Susannah), 476, 476n12. *See also*: Norwich
Taylor, Susannah (mother of Sarah), 476, 476n12. *See also*: Norwich
Taylor, William, 374, 444n94; quoted, 461n258
Te Deum (hymn), 419
Tegg, Thomas, 404, 466n316
Tell, William (legendary), 306, 446n115
Tenaera (Kaap Taenarum), 276
Thales of Miletus, 311, 448n131
'Thaliessin', 321, 451n157
Thames, 235, 333, 337. *See* East Anglia
The Theatre of Education (English translation of de Genlis's play), 220
'Theban pair', 261. *See* Aeschylus, *Seven Against Thebes*
Thompson, E. P., *The Making of the English Working Class*, ch. 11, 284
Thomson, James, 470n366, 472n393;
 The Seasons, 431n9.3, 438n16; quoted, 247, 386, 460–1n252;
 The Works, 437nn9–10
Thomson, James and David Mallet, *Alfred: A Masque*, 23; quoted, 437n9–10
Thompson, Josiah, quoted in *M Rev*, I
Thoughts on Education, in Two Parts. By Agnes Sophia Semple, (review by ALB), 375, 411
Thoyras, Paul Rapin de, *History of England*, quoted, 231–3, 437n9, 439n25

Thrale, Hester (afterwards Piozzi), 472n393
Thucydides, 315
Tiber, 309
Titus (Titus Caesar Vespasianus), 395; quoted (in French), 262n47
Toledo, Fernando Alvarez de, 3rd Duke of Alba, 306, 446–7n115
Toms, Peter, 438n13
Tooke, William, *The Life of Catharine II. Empress of Russia*, (trans.), 456n203. *See also:* Castéra, J.-H.
Trafalgar, Battle of, 332
Trajan (Marcus Ulpius Traianus), 311, 395, 448n127
A Treatise on Politeness, Intended for the Use of the Youth of Both Sexes. Translated from the French. By a Lady [Anon.], (review by ALB), 375, 422
Trimmer, Sarah, 3;
  imitation of *Lessons* in *Easy Introduction to the Knowledge of Nature* (1802), 3;
  appraisal of *Evenings* in *The Guardian of Education*, 239, 241; quoted, 438n12;
  appraisal of *Hymns* in *The Guardian of Education*, 188, 435nII.33; quoted, 435nII.43, 435nIV.23–4;
  appraisal of *Lessons* in *The Guardian of Education*, 434n89.5–6;
  The Guardian of Education, 464n297
True Stories; or Interesting Anecdotes of Young Persons. By [Elizabeth Frank], (review by ALB), 375, 400
True Stories; or Interesting Anecdotes of Young Persons. By Elizabeth Frank, (2nd review by ALB), 375, 402
Tubal Cain, 247, 438n15
Tuileries, 333
'Turks', 38
Turner, William (Barbauld collector), 289
Tyrians, 278n73

University of Edinburgh Library, 7
University of Glasgow Library, 7
United States:
  circulation of ALB's epistolary tutorials, xl;
  circulation of *Evenings at Home*, 239;
  circulation of *Hymns in Prose*, xxxvii, xxxviin5;

New York, origin of students at Palgrave, xxxv

Valenciennes (French Flanders), 249
Variety, or Selections and Essays. By Priscilla Wakefield, (review by ALB), 374, 393
Vasa, Gustavus (Gustav I), 402, 465n303
Venning, Mary Anne, 404, 465n312
Vertot, René-Aubert:
  Histoire des révolutions arrivées dans le gouvernement de la république romaine, 324, 451n163;
  Histoire des révolutions de Portugal, 324, 451n163;
  Histoire des révolutions de Suède, 324, 451n163;
Vespasian (Titus Flavius Vespasianus), 395
Virgil (Publius Vergilius Maro), 273, 371;
  Aeneid, [278], 442n73;
  Georgics, 2:485, quoted, 336, 454n191
Vitellius, Aulus, 346, 456n204
Vitruvius (Marcus Vitruvius Pollio), 457n210
Voltaire (François-Marie Arouet):
  Alzire, 325;
  Histoire de Charles XII, 323, 475;
  Histoire de Louis XV, 465n313;
  La Henriade, 325;
  Lazare, 325;
  Mahomet, 325;
  Mérope, 325;
  Sémiramis, 325;
  Siècle de Louis Quatorze, 324, 454n188, 476;
  Zadig, 426, 473n402;

Wallace, John Aikman, 'There is an eye that never sleeps', *Scottish Christian Herald*, 435nV.29
Walpole, Horace, 463n288
Wakefield, Daniel, 463n278
Wakefield, Priscilla, 393, 397, 408, 463n278;
  Introduction to Botany, 462n267
Ward, E., *The Lunarian*, 471n380
Warrington Academy, xxxv, 461n258;
  and Wedgwood family, 439n26;
  copy of Suetonius's *Lives*, 456n204;
  exile of Rigby sisters, 458n226;
  JP, history instructor, 299n11;
  Matthew Nicholson, graduate and maker of copy of 'The Four Sisters', 259, 441n48

Warrington, Lancashire, xxxv, 264, 457n220, 458n227;
  glass-making industry, [114], [249], 433n75.1–4, 438n19
Washington, George, 305
Watt, Mrs. James to William Withering, 18 Nov. 1815, 295n5
Watts, Isaac:
  Divine Songs...for the Use of Children, 187, 190, [472n393]
  'Meditation in a Grove', *Horae Lyricae*, 441n54; quoted, 266
Waveney, 434n37.1–38.1, 434n42.2
Wedgwood and Bentley (British jasperware), 439n26
Wedgwood family, 438n18
Wedgwood, Josiah:
  British jasperware, [250], 439n26;
  partnership with Thomas Bentley, 2
Wedgwood Museum, 439n27
Wedgwood warehouses (locations), 439n26
Weightman, Mary, [426], 473n400
Wennington, William, 411;
  translations of Plutarch, 467n340
Wesley, John and Charles, 284
West End (village), [269], 442n57
West, Lady Mary (dedicatee of *Poems*), 441n51
West, Thomas (unidentified), 423, 472n390
Westminster Abbey, 400, 407
Westminster School, 391
Wharton, Joanna, '"The Things Themselves"', xxxvi, 5; quoted, 430n11.8
Wheatley, Phillis, 436nVIII54–9
Whichcote, Benjamin, 435nVI.1
Wiffen, Jeremiah Holmes, 416, 469n363
Wilkie and Robinson (publisher), 420
Williams, Helen Maria, 468n352, 472n393
Willis, James, 268
Wilton carpet, 293, 444n90
Winterbotham, Melanie, 'My Gretna Green Elopers', 457–8n220

Withering Family Letters, 295n5
Withering, William (*père et fils*), 295
Woburn, 469n363
Woodstock, Oxfordshire, 250, 439n24
Wollstonecraft, Mary, 462n274, 463n280, 468n352;
  fragment of ALB's lost response to *Vindication of the Rights of Woman*, xl, xln14;
  recommendation of *Hymns* in *Thoughts on the Education of Daughters*, quoted, 187;
  A Vindication of the Rights of Woman, 338, 454–5n193; quoted, 458n225;
  The Female Reader (pseudonym 'M. Cresswick'), 369, 436nVIII.54–9
Wordsworth, William:
  'Ode: Intimations of Immortality' 188;
  The Prelude, 456n207
The World, 463n288
The World Displayed: or the Characteristic Features of Nature and Art Exhibited. By John Greig, (review by ALB), 375, 395
Worsley, Rev. Israel, 425–6, 473n399
Wynch, Flora (ALB's pupil and addressee of 'On Fashion'), xxxviii, 263, 268, 270
Wynch, Rhoda Crocket (addressee of 'Zephyrus and Flora'), 268
Wynch, William, 268

Xerxes I, 316

Yazdegerd III, [316]
Yearsley, Ann, 468n352
Yeoman of the Guard, [279], 443n76
Yonge, Charlotte, 5–6
York, 466n317
York Minster Cathedral, 333
Young, Edward, [265], 369, 441n52